Tactus, Mensuration, and Rhythm in Renaissance Music

Ruth DeFord's book explores how *tactus*, mensuration, and rhythm were employed to articulate form and shape in the period from *c.* 1420 to *c.* 1600. Divided into two parts, the book examines the theory and practice of rhythm in relation to each other to offer new interpretations of the writings of Renaissance music theorists. In the first part, DeFord presents the theoretical evidence, introduces the sources and explains the contradictions and ambiguities in *tactus* theory. The second part uses theory to analyze some of the best-known repertoires of Renaissance music, including works by Du Fay, Ockeghem, Busnoys, Josquin, Isaac, Palestrina, and Rore, and to shed light on composers' formal and expressive uses of rhythm. DeFord's conclusions have important implications for our understanding of rhythm and for the analysis, editing, and performance of music during the Renaissance period.

RUTH DEFORD is Professor Emerita of Hunter College and the Graduate Center, City University of New York. Her principal areas of research are the Italian madrigal and canzonetta and music theory of the Renaissance. She has edited the canzoni of Giovanni Ferretti and the canzonettas of Orazio Vecchi. Her articles have appeared in numerous scholarly journals.

Tactus, Mensuration, and Rhythm in Renaissance Music

RUTH I. DEFORD

CAMBRIDGE
UNIVERSITY PRESS

University Printing House, Cambridge CB2 8BS, United Kingdom

Cambridge University Press is part of the University of Cambridge.

It furthers the University's mission by disseminating knowledge in the pursuit of education, learning and research at the highest international levels of excellence.

www.cambridge.org
Information on this title: www.cambridge.org/9781107064720

© Ruth DeFord 2015

This publication is in copyright. Subject to statutory exception and to the provisions of relevant collective licensing agreements, no reproduction of any part may take place without the written permission of Cambridge University Press.

First published 2015

Printed in the United Kingdom by TJ International Ltd., Padstow, Cornwall

A catalogue record for this publication is available from the British Library

Library of Congress Cataloguing in Publication data
DeFord, Ruth I.
Tactus, mensuration and rhythm in Renaissance music / Ruth I. DeFord.
 pages cm
Includes bibliographical references and index.
ISBN 978-1-107-06472-0
1. Musical meter and rhythm – History – 15th century. 2. Musical meter and rhythm – History – 16th century. 3. Mensural notation. I. Title.
ML174.D37 2014
781.2'209031–dc23
                                                                    2014026681

ISBN 978-1-107-06472-0 Hardback

Cambridge University Press has no responsibility for the persistence or accuracy of URLs for external or third-party internet websites referred to in this publication, and does not guarantee that any content on such websites is, or will remain, accurate or appropriate.

In memory of my parents, Donald D. DeFord and Leora Adams DeFord

Contents

List of figures   [*page* ix]
Acknowledgments   [xi]

Introduction   [1]

PART I   THEORY   [7]

1 Sources of information   [9]

2 Principles of mensural notation   [33]

3 Definitions and descriptions of *tactus*   [51]

4 *Tactus* and rhythm   [82]

5 *Tactus* and signs in fifteenth-century music theory   [114]

6 *Tactus* and signs in sixteenth-century music theory   [144]

7 *Tactus* and tempo   [180]

PART II   PRACTICE   [215]

8 The songs of Du Fay   [217]

9 The *L'homme armé* masses of Ockeghem, Busnoys, and Josquin   [258]

10 The five- and six-voice motets of Josquin   [301]

11 The *Choralis Constantinus* of Isaac   [339]

12 The masses of Palestrina   [375]

13 The madrigals of Rore   [408]

14 Popular songs and dances   [447]

Conclusion   [468]

Bibliography   [475]
Index of signs   [494]
General index   [496]

Figures

The author and publishers acknowledge the following sources of copyright material and are grateful for the permissions granted. While every effort has been made, it has not always been possible to identify the sources of all material used, or to trace all copyright holders. If any omissions are brought to our notice, we will be happy to include the appropriate acknowledgments on reprinting.

2.1 Mensural structure of perfect minor *modus*, imperfect *tempus*, and imperfect prolation. [*page* 38]

2.2 Mensural structure of combined perfect and imperfect *tempus*. [39]

3.1 Luca della Robbia, *Cantoria*. Florence, Museo dell'Opera del Duomo. Photo credit: Scala / Art Resource, NY. [54]

3.2 Recueil de chants royaux. Paris, Bibliothèque Nationale, Ms. fr. 1537, fol. 58^v. © BnF, Dist. RMN-Grand Palais / Art Resource, NY. [54]

3.3 Illustration from Gaffurio, *Practica musice* (Milan: Ioannes Petrus de Lomatio, 1496), fol. A1^r. [55]

3.4 Jörg Breu the Elder, small organ shutters for the Fugger Chapel in the Church of Santa Anna in Augsburg. Reproduced by permission of the Fuggersche Stiftungen. [61]

3.5 Illustration from Gregor Reisch, *Margarita philosophica* (Basel: Michael Futerius, 1517), fol. mvij^r. [62]

3.6 Subdivisions of a binary *tactus*. [70]

3.7 Subdivisions of a ternary *tactus*. [72]

5.1 Mensural categories according to Anonymous 11. [124]

6.1 Form of the whole *tactus* and half-*tactus*. After Martin Agricola, *Musica figuralis deudsch* (Wittenberg: Georg Rhau, 1532), ch. 6, fol. Giiij^r. [156]

9.1 Josquin, *Missa L'homme armé super voces musicales*, Kyrie 1, cantus and tenor (beginning). Vatican City, Biblioteca Apostolica Vaticana, Cappella Sistina, Ms. 197, fol. 1^v. © 2015 Biblioteca Apostolica Vaticana. [284]

x   List of figures

9.2   Josquin, *Missa L'homme armé super voces musicales*, Kyrie, tenor. Josquin des Prez, *Liber primus missarum Josquin* (Venice: Ottaviano Petrucci, 1502). © ÖNB Vienna.   [287]

9.3   Josquin, *Missa L'homme armé super voces musicales*, Agnus Dei 2. Vatican City, Biblioteca Apostolica Vaticana, Cappella Sistina, Ms. 197, fol. 9^v. © 2015 Biblioteca Apostolica Vaticana.   [291]

10.1 Josquin, *Illibata Dei virgo nutrix*, tenor. *Motetti a cinque, libro primo* (Venice: Ottaviano Petrucci, 1508). © ÖNB Vienna.   [309]

10.2 Josquin, *Illibata Dei virgo nutrix*: mensural structure.   [310]

10.3 Josquin, *Inviolata*, tenor. Florence, Biblioteca Medicea-Laurenziana, Ms. acq. e Doni 666 ("Medici Codex"), fol. 89^v. On concession of the MiBACT. Any further reproduction by any means is prohibited.   [320]

11.1 Isaac, *De radice Jesse*. Sebald Heyden, *De arte canendi* (Nuremberg: Johann Petreius, 1540), 114–15.   [371]

11.2 Isaac, *De radice Jesse*, with the notation "resolved" into ₵. Sebald Heyden, *De arte canendi* (Nuremberg: Johann Petreius, 1540), 116–17.   [373]

12.1 Palestrina, *Missa L'homme armé a 5*, (a) Christe and (b) Et in terra, tenor, in original notation and transcribed into C and ₵. Ludovico Zacconi, *Prattica di musica* (Venice: Girolamo Polo, 1592), fols. 116^v, 117^r, 119^r, and 119^v.   [400]

12.2 Palestrina, *Missa L'homme armé a 5*, Kyrie 2, tenor, in original notation and "resolution" in C. Pietro Cerone, *El melopeo y maestro* (Naples: Juan Bautista Gargano & Lucrecio Nucci, 1613), 1030.   [403]

12.3 Palestrina, *Missa L'homme armé a 5*, Et in terra, tenor (called "quintus"). Palestrina, *Missarum liber tertius* (Venice: Angelo Gardano, 1599). © ÖNB Vienna.   [403]

12.4 Palestrina, *Missa L'homme armé a 5*, Kyrie 2. Palestrina, *Werke*, vol. XII, ed. Franz Xaver Haberl (Leipzig: Breitkopf & Härtel, [1881]). Music Division, The New York Public Library for the Performing Arts, Astor, Lenox and Tilden Foundations.   [404]

12.5 Palestrina, *Missa L'homme armé a 5*, Kyrie 2. Palestrina, *Le opere complete*, vol. VI, ed. Raffaele Casimiri (Rome: Fratelli Scalera, [1939]).   [405]

12.6 Palestrina, *Missa L'homme armé a 5*, Kyrie 2. Anna Maria Monterosso Vacchelli, *La Messa L'homme armé di Palestrina: Studio paleografico ed edizione critica* (Cremona: Fondazione Claudio Monteverdi, 1979), 85.   [406]

Acknowledgments

This book is the product of an interest in various aspects of rhythm in Renaissance music that dates back to my undergraduate days. Many people have contributed to the formation of my ideas over the years with encouragement, guidance, and helpful criticism. When I was a first-year graduate student, I learned from Anthony Newcomb that no one knows how ternary proportions relate to binary mensurations in sixteenth-century music. That piece of information set me on a quest for an answer that led to a broadening of my research in many related directions (though admittedly not to a definitive answer to the original question). I am fortunate to have been a participant in National Endowment for the Humanities summer seminars led by Howard Mayer Brown, Leeman Perkins, and Benito Rivera, and a Mannes Institute for Advanced Studies in Music History seminar on rhythm led by David Cohen and Christopher Hasty, that gave me opportunities to further my work under the expert guidance of those scholars. I am deeply grateful to Anne Stone, with whom I had the opportunity to team-teach two seminars on medieval and Renaissance rhythm at the CUNY Graduate Center, for her penetrating questions and challenges to my ideas. The varied perspectives of the students in those seminars have also enriched my ideas. Other scholars whose advice has been helpful to me include Margaret Bent, Anna Maria Busse Berger, Alexander Blachly, Bonnie Blackburn, Sarah Davies, Theodor Dumitrescu, David Fallows, Sean Gallagher, James Haar, Jane Hatter, Cristle Collins Judd, Jessie Ann Owens, Alejandro Planchart, Ève Poudrier, and Jesse Rodin. I am especially grateful to the people who read and commented on parts of the book manuscript, including Marjorie Naughton, Anthony Newcomb, and Susan Forscher Weiss. My Hunter College colleague Richard Burke most generously read the entire manuscript and supported my efforts directly and indirectly in many ways during the years when I served as Chair of the Hunter Music Department. I thank Jonathan Gnoza and Leofranc Holford-Strevens for advice on some of the Latin texts and Raül Benavides for advice on the Spanish texts. I also thank Jeffrey Dean for graciously allowing me to use his font of musical symbols in the book. I have used that font in many of the figures, but it unfortunately proved impossible for technical reasons to include it in the main text. I am grateful to my friend Adele Siegal, who read the page proofs of the complete book, and caught a number of errors that had escaped the notice of everyone who had checked the book previously.

One of the premises of this book is my belief that the experience of live music-making is indispensable to the understanding of rhythm. I do not imagine, of course, that it is possible to reconstruct the experiences of people who lived many centuries ago, but I do believe that the process of singing the music from copies of original sources sheds invaluable light on musical notation and theoretical statements about rhythm. I am deeply indebted to Dennis Slavin, who established a group devoted to singing Renaissance music from copies of original sources at the CUNY Graduate Center many years ago and has continued to play a leading role in it since then. I have been privileged to be a member of that group from the beginning. I am grateful to all of the members of the group, especially the regular participants, including Sarah Davies, Marjorie Naughton, Stephen O'Leary, Wendy Powers, and Alan Richtmyer, for their willingness to try out pieces that I have brought to them and experiment with different ways of measuring them. Their reactions to those experiments have contributed much to the formation of my ideas.

I am grateful to the editorial staff of Cambridge University Press, in particular Victoria Cooper, Fleur Jones, and Christina Sarigiannidou, and to my copy-editor, Martin Thacker, for their expert work on the book. Their job was exceptionally challenging owing to the large number of specialized signs in the book, and I appreciate their patience in dealing with that issue.

My family has provided indispensable support for my work. My husband, Mahesh Kotecha, has shown inexhaustible patience with the demands of my work and always encouraged me to persist when the going was tough. My sons, Vicram and Vijay Kotecha, challenged me to explain the nature and importance of my work from the perspective of amateur musicians. They reminded me of the importance of making my work relevant to people beyond the narrow group of specialists who take the significance of my questions for granted. My late parents, Donald D. DeFord and Leora Adams DeFord, laid the foundation for everything that I have done. My mother was a musician who taught me the love of music and gave me my first instruction in it, and my father was a professor who modeled the pleasures of an academic career for me. This book is dedicated to their memory.

Introduction

The goal of this book is to shed light on the theory and practice of rhythm in the fifteenth and sixteenth centuries by examining them in relation to each other. The term "Renaissance" in the title is simply a label for the period from *c.* 1420 to *c.* 1600; it is not meant to imply anything about the character of the period. Part I of the book deals with theory and Part II with practice, but neither is complete without the other. Theoretical writings provide valuable information on the subject, but they are not easy to interpret. They often contain a complex mix of description, prescription, tradition, and speculation. These strands must be disentangled before the significance of any theoretical statement can be judged. Many fundamental terms and concepts, such as note value, *tactus*, diminution, proportion, etc., have different meanings in different contexts, and statements including these terms cannot be interpreted without making judgments about their meanings in each instance. It is not possible to resolve all of the ambiguities in theorists' statements, but I propose interpretations of them that seem plausible to me in light of both the traditions in which the theorists worked and the musical practices that were known to them.

Rhythmic styles and notational practices in real music are much more diverse than those described by theorists. It would be impossible to cover all of them in a single book. I have chosen a few sample repertoires to illustrate some of the possibilities and to serve as models for an approach to the issues involved. For each repertoire, I examine both the regular and the irregular aspects of rhythm and the ways in which they relate to each other and to the notated mensuration signs. The relation between signs and rhythmic styles is complex. Since there are many more styles than signs, any given sign may be associated with more than one style. Conversely, a given style may be associated with more than one sign, because the principles governing the uses of signs were never fully standardized.

Each of the repertoires that I have chosen illustrates a different issue. The songs of Du Fay include examples of all of the basic fifteenth-century mensurations, as well as some types of diminution that went out of use later on. The *L'homme armé* masses of Ockeghem, Busnoys, and Josquin display some of the most complex mensural structures of the period. The five- and six-voice motets of Josquin extend the principles of mensural organization to relatively large temporal levels, sometimes explicitly notated and sometimes not. The verses of Isaac's *Choralis Constantinus* make use of unusual rhythmic groupings that test the limits of the meanings of the signs governing them. Some of them display bizarrely complex notation that has had a major impact on modern concepts of mensural notation, although it was probably devised by a theorist, and not by the composer. The masses of Palestrina represent the classic style of sixteenth-century sacred music, which modern scholars have often regarded as the prototype for "Renaissance rhythm" in general. The madrigals of Rore illustrate another type of sixteenth-century rhythm, one that expands the limits of traditional practice for the sake of vivid expression of poetic texts. Popular songs and dances are often based on different principles of rhythm and notation from the more serious genres considered in the preceding chapters. They extend the range of rhythmic and notational possibilities beyond what is found in more prestigious music.

The term "mensural music" (*musica mensurabilis*) means simply "measured music." In the period under consideration, it was the opposite of "plainchant" (*musica plana*). Modern scholars sometimes treat it as the opposite of "metrical music." This is a false dichotomy based on an oversimplified view of the difference between "Renaissance rhythm," in which the system of measurement is sometimes alleged to have no relation to rhythmic structure, and later styles, in which time signatures and barlines are sometimes assumed to prescribe rhythmic structures in a straightforward manner. This reductive opposition does not do justice to the music of either era.

Time measurement in music is of two types: abstract and concrete. Abstract time measurement is represented by the note symbols that prescribe durations in musical notation. These values occupy positions in relation to a hierarchical grid in which smaller values function as subdivisions of larger ones. In the fifteenth and sixteenth centuries, larger levels of measurement consist of either two or three of the next smaller level. (The same is true of most modern meters, in which a bar may consist of two or three beats and a beat may consist of two or three subdivisions.) The term "mensuration" refers to the theoretical grid that serves as the system of reference for the note symbols. It is associated with a set of principles for interpreting durations on the basis of their position on the grid. Mensural notation differs from modern notation in that the same symbol may represent different durations when it falls in different places in relation to the mensural grid.

Abstract durational signs are translated into concrete units of time in musical performance by setting one notated value equal to some quantity of time and marking the recurrences of that unit in some way. This marker of time is usually a physical motion, such as the tap of a finger or foot or a movement of the hand in the air, but it may exist only in the mind. The term "tactus" refers principally to the concrete measure of time in performance, but by extension it took on several additional meanings in music theory. Since "tactus" is a fourth-declension Latin noun, its plural form is "tactus."

Rhythm in the modern sense, in which I use it in this book, is a more complex concept than mensuration or *tactus*. It includes all aspects of the perceptible organization of musical time, especially on the relatively small scales in which durations can be directly compared in memory. Since all musical events take place in time, all of them contribute to rhythm. Note durations, melody, harmony, counterpoint, texture, and text setting all play a role in the creation of rhythm. Performance nuances, such as the emphasis on certain notes by means of dynamic accent or subtle durational inequalities, also influence the way rhythm is perceived. The concept of rhythm may, but need not, include patterns of regular and/or irregular accents generated by any of the above elements of music. Renaissance theorists wrote about many of these aspects of music and the ways in which they relate to mensuration and *tactus*, but they did not have a comprehensive term for the temporal dimension of music in general.

Mensuration and *tactus* as such are not part of rhythm, because they are inaudible, but if composers or performers do anything to bring out the temporal units corresponding to them, they become part of the rhythm. If certain types of musical events, such as dissonances and cadences, are regularly correlated with certain positions in the mensuration, they make the mensural grid audible as a component of the rhythmic structure. Regular, perceptible time units exercise a powerful hold on the human psyche, probably because of their affinity with such things as heartbeat, breathing, walking, etc. Their effect may last for some time even if it is not continuously reinforced. The interest of most measured rhythms, including those of the fifteenth and sixteenth centuries, lies in the dynamic interaction between regular and irregular elements. Ignoring either of them robs rhythm of its complexity and vitality.

Mensural notation was not a single, unified system, but a collection of diverse practices that varied with time, place, genre, and composer. It was often inconsistent even within a narrowly defined repertoire. Theorists disagreed about important aspects of it, and they often objected to the notational practices of composers even when they agreed with each other.

The principal subjects of disagreement among theorists were the proper ways of notating certain mensurations and proportions and the relationships of different mensurations to each other. Some sixteenth-century theorists also adopted dogmatic attitudes about *tactus* that were at odds with the practices of most performers.

The issues that have occupied modern scholars are those that relate to analysis and performance, rather than notational propriety. A long-standing debate concerns the question of whether or not notated mensurations correspond to meaningful rhythmic structures in a manner analogous to that of modern time signatures. A related question is whether or not *tactus* is associated with accent. The other issue that has provoked disagreement among modern scholars is the relation between mensuration signs and tempo. Little attention has been paid to the musical significance of *tactus* beyond its putative role in setting tempos and governing tempo relationships among different mensurations.

The conclusions of this study are not simple, but they affirm the importance of *tactus* and mensuration as meaningful elements of rhythm in the fifteenth and sixteenth centuries. Although the roles of measuring systems, both abstract and concrete, in rhythmic structures and the ways in which they interact with irregular elements of rhythm vary greatly from one repertoire to another, the claim that they have no relation to rhythm cannot be sustained. Mensural theory and the notational system that it describes provide valuable information about rhythm that goes well beyond the mechanics of how note symbols represent temporal durations. Analysis of music in light of that theory reveals a boundless wealth of rhythmic ideas that equal those of any other period in complexity and expressive power.

Citations and translations of primary sources

Many of the theoretical texts cited in this book are available in a large number of sources of different types: multiple early editions, facsimile reprints, editions in the original language, translations into modern languages, and online texts. It would be unwieldy to cite all of them. To assist the reader in locating passages in any version of a text, I have identified the sources as follows: for manuscripts, the best available edition in the original language; for prints, the first published edition (unless otherwise specified) and one facsimile reprint, if any. For specific passages of text, I cite the book and chapter number and the name of the chapter, as well as the page or folio number, in the source. This information should enable readers to locate the passages in other versions of the texts.

Translations of quoted theoretical texts are my own unless otherwise indicated. Published translations exist for many of them, but I have used my own translations in order to clarify my interpretations of the meanings of the passages.

Musical examples

I have transcribed the musical examples in this book from copies of the original sources. The caption identifies the source of each example. Variants found in other sources are noted only when they have significant bearing on the points under discussion. Minor errors in the sources are corrected without comment.

The mensuration signs, symbols for notes and rests, and ancillary symbols such as dots, are the same as those in the sources. Readers unfamiliar with the principles of mensural notation should read Chapter 2 for an explanation of it. My reason for retaining the original symbols is that they are often essential to the points that I observe about the music. Even the notation of rests can reveal ways in which composers or scribes perceived meaningful time units. Since the voices are aligned in score, notational devices that differ from modern practice, such as perfection (equating an undotted note with three of the next smaller value) and alteration (doubling the length of a note on the basis of its position), should not cause confusion.

Regular units of the notated mensuration (usually breves) are separated with barlines through the staves in the examples. When a note continues from one bar to the next, the barline is replaced by a short line at the top of the staff. An advantage of this style is that it allows for independent barring of different voices, which is often necessary to show the relationships among simultaneous contrasting mensurations. Although the barlines do not appear in the sources, they mark units of time that are prescribed by the notated mensuration. They do not imply any a priori assumptions about the musical significance of those time units.

Text underlay is problematic in much of this repertoire. Scribes are not usually meticulous about where they place the syllables, and there is little theoretical information on the subject before the mid sixteenth century. My text underlay is editorial, and unless otherwise indicated, it is not based on systematic theoretical principles.

Specialized terminology

The technical terms in this book are explained in Chapters 2 and 3. I have relied on standard terminology as much as possible, but I have invented my own terms for two concepts for which there are no standard terms. They are:

(1) Different meanings of "tactus": I distinguish the three fundamental meanings of the term "tactus" as "performance *tactus*" (the time unit by which music is measured in performance), "compositional *tactus*" (the time unit governing compositional principles such as dissonance treatment), and "theoretical *tactus*" (the time unit traditionally associated with a mensuration sign in music theory). These terms are explained in Chapter 3.
(2) Positions within a mensural structure: I identify the beginnings of time units within a mensural structure as "initia" (a term invented by Graeme Boone). To designate the largest level of mensuration to which an *initium* applies, I qualify it as "-max" (e.g., "semibreve-max," "minim-max," etc.). This terminology is explained in Chapter 2.[1]

---

[1] The term is explained and discussed in Graeme M. Boone, "Marking Mensural Time," *Music Theory Spectrum* 22 (2000), 1–43. The suffix "-max" is my own.

PART I

Theory

1 | Sources of information

The theoretical sources that discuss time measurement in fifteenth- and sixteenth-century music are extremely diverse (see Table 1.1). They range from simple instructional manuals for beginners to sophisticated philosophical works aimed more at humanistic scholars than at practicing musicians. Some are loosely organized manuscripts intended only for the use of the authors; others are tightly structured, formal treatises. Some transmit only conventional information, while others aim to reform common practices. The significance of the views they express must be evaluated in light of the training and professional identity of the authors (to the extent that this information is known) and the nature, purpose, and intended audience of the works.

Mensural notation was not a static system, but a set of practices that developed and changed continuously throughout the fifteenth and sixteenth centuries. Changing practices led to frequent tensions between inherited theories and current realities. Composers stopped using the more complex aspects of the system around 1520 except in occasional demonstrations of theoretical erudition, but theorists continued to discuss and debate them for several more decades, in part because the music of earlier generations remained in the active performance repertoire in some places until quite late in the sixteenth century. The relation between theory and practice is quite different when theorists focus on a historical repertoire than it is when they discuss the music of their own time.

Fifteenth-century sources present different interpretive problems from sixteenth-century sources. All writings on mensuration before the 1480s are manuscripts. Many are anonymous and difficult to date. Even when the surviving copies can be dated, the dates of the contents are often unknown. Manuscript writings on music are often informal and unsystematic. Printed books that address issues of mensuration began to appear in small numbers in the 1480s and 1490s, and after *c.* 1500, nearly all significant writings on the subject were printed. Prints are almost always attributed to named authors. Their places and dates of publication are generally known, and their contents are systematically organized in ways that the print medium naturally requires. As a result, fifteenth-century writings are typically more

Table 1.1 Principal sources of theoretical information about mensuration and *tactus*

Author	Title	Date
Johannes de Muris	*Ars practica mensurabilis cantus*	Mid–late 14th century
Anonymous 5	*Ars cantus mensurabilis mensurata per modos iuris*	Late 14th century
Anonymous 10	*De minimis notulis*	Late 14th century
Prosdocimo de' Beldomandi	*Expositiones tractatus practice cantus mensurabilis magistri Johannis de Muris*	1404
Prosdocimo de' Beldomandi	*Tractatus pratice de musica mensurabili*	1408
Prosdocimo de' Beldomandi	*Tractatus practice cantus mensurabilis ad modum ytalicorum*	1412
Ugolino of Orvieto	*Declaratio musicae disciplinae*	1430s
Giorgio Anselmi	*De musica*	1434
Antonius de Luca	*Ars cantus figurati*	Mid 15th century
Anonymous	*Capitulum de quattuor mensuris, Tractatulus mensurationum, Compendium breve de proportionibus*, and *Tractatulus prolationum cum tabulis*	Mid 15th century
Anonymous 11	*Tractatus de musica plana et mensurabili*	Mid 15th century
Anonymous	*Compendium breve artis musicae*	Mid 15th century
Anonymous	*Exposition of the Proportions, According to the Teaching of "Mestre Joan Violant"* [Vaillant]	Mid 15th century
Anonymous	*Sequuntur proportiones*	Mid 15th century; copied 1460
John Hothby	Various titles	Late 15th century
Anonymous 12	*Tractatus et compendium cantus figurati*	1460–71
Johannes Tinctoris	*Proportionale musices*	1472–75
Johannes Tinctoris	*Liber de arte contrapuncti*	1476
Johannes Tinctoris	*Terminorum musicae diffinitorium*	1470s; printed c. 1495
Franchino Gaffurio	*Musices practicabilis libellum*	1480
Bartolomeo Ramis de Pareja	*Musica practica*	1482
Guilielmus Monachus	*De preceptis artis musice*	Late 15th century
Adam von Fulda	*Musica*	1490

Author	Title	Year
Anonymous	Compendium secundum famosiores musicos	1490
Anonymous (attr. B. G. Frank)	Ein tütsche musica	1491
Francesco Caza	Tractato vulgare de canto figurato	1492
Franchino Gaffurio	Practica musice	1496
Nicolaus Wollick and Melchior Schanppecher	Opus aureum	1501
Diego del Puerto	Portus musice	1504
Domingo Marcos Durán	Sumula de canto órgano, contrapunto y composicion	c. 1504
Johannes Cochlaeus	Musica (3rd edn.)	1507
Franchino Gaffurio	Angelicum ac divinum opus musice	1508
Nicolaus Wollick	Enchiridion musices	1509
Simon de Quercu	Opusculum musices	1509
Francisco Tovar	Libro de musica practica	1510
Johannes Cochlaeus	Tetrachordum musices	1511
Venceslaus Philomathes	Musicorum libri quattuor	1512
Joannes Volckmar	Collectanea quedam musice discipline	1513
Anonymous	Institutio in musicen mensuralem	1513
Bernhard Bogentantz	Collectanea utriusque cantus	1515
Stephan Monetarius	Epitoma utriusque musices practice	1515
Pietro Aaron	Libri tres de institutione harmonica	1516
Michael Koswick	Compendiaria musice artis aeditio	1516
Andreas Ornithoparchus	Musice active micrologus	1517
Sebastian of Felsztyn	Opusculum musicae mensuralis	c. 1518
Georg Rhau	Enchiridion utriusque musicae practicae, 3rd edn.	1520
Pietro Aaron	Thoscanello de la musica	1523
Giovanni Spataro	Tractato di musica	1531
Martin Agricola	Musica figuralis deudsch	1532
Sebald Heyden	Musica stoicheiosis	1532
Giovanni Maria Lanfranco	Scintille di musica	1533
Stephano Vanneo	Recanetum de musica aurea	1533
Matheo de Aranda	Tractado de canto mensurable	1535

Table 1.1 (cont.)

Author	Title	Date
Johann Frosch	*Rerum musicarum*	1535
Othmar Luscinius	*Musurgia seu praxis musicae*	1536
Nicolaus Listenius	*Musica*	1537
Auctor Lampadius	*Compendium musices*	1537
Sebald Heyden	*Musicae, id est artis canendi libri duo*	1537
Sebald Heyden	*De arte canendi*	1540
John Dygon	*Proportiones practicabiles secundum Gaffurium*	c. 1540
Pietro Aaron	*Lucidario in musica*	1545
Angelo da Picitono	*Fior angelico di musica*	1547
Heinrich Glarean	*Dodecachordon*	1547
Heinrich Faber	*Compendiolum musicae pro incipientibus*	1548
Giovanthomaso Cimello	Untitled manuscript	1540s
Claude Martin	*Elementorum musices practicae*	1550
Loys Bourgeois	*Le droict chemin de musique*	1550
Heinrich Faber	*Ad musicam practicam introductio*	1550
Adrian Petit Coclico	*Compendium musices*	1552
Vicente Lusitano	*Introdutione facilissima, et novissima di canto fermo, figurato, contraponto semplice, et inconcerto*	1553
Gregor Faber	*Musices practicae erotematum libri II*	1553
Maximilian Guilliaud	*Rudiments de musique practique*	1554
Johann Zanger	*Practicae musicae praecepta*	1554
Nicola Vicentino	*L'antica musica ridotta alla moderna prattica*	1555
Juan Bermudo	*Declaración de instrumentos musicales*	1555
Philibert Jambe de Fer	*Epitome musical*	1556
Hermann Finck	*Practica musica*	1556
Johannes Oridryus	*Practicae musicae utriusque praecepta brevia*	1557
Heinrich Glarean	*Musicae epitome*	1557

Gioseffo Zarlino	*Le istitutioni harmoniche*	1558
Ambrosius Wilphlingseder	*Erotemata musices practicae*	1563
Tomás de Sancta Maria	*Arte de tañer fantasia*	1565
Gallus Dressler	*Musicae practicae elementa*	1571
Eucharius Hofmann	*Musicae practicae praecepta*	1572
Corneille de Montfort (Blockland)	*Instruction fort facile pour apprendre la musique practique*	1573
Friedrich Beurhaus	*Musicae erotematum libri duo*	1573
Christoph Praetorius	*Erotemata musices*	1574
Jean Yssandon	*Traité de la musique pratique*	1582
Giovanni Maria Artusi	*L'arte del contraponto*	1586
Orazio Tigrini	*Il compendio della musica*	1588
Andreas Raselius	*Hexachordum*	1589
Cyriacus Schneegass	*Isagoges musicae*	1591
Ludovico Zacconi	*Prattica di musica*	1592
William Bathe	*A Briefe Introduction to the Skill of Song*	1590s
Anonymous	*The Pathway to Musicke*	1596
Thomas Morley	*A Plaine and Easie Introduction to Practicall Musicke*	1597
Seth Calvisius	*Exercitationes musicae duae*	1600
Agostino Pisa	*Breve dichiaratione della battuta musicale*	1611
Agostino Pisa	*Battuta della musica*	1611
Pietro Cerone	*El melopeo y maestro*	1613
Michael Praetorius	*Syntagma musicum III*	1618–19

difficult to interpret than sixteenth-century writings. Nevertheless, ambiguities of wording and conflicts within and between sources make the interpretation of sixteenth-century sources challenging as well.

For most of the fifteenth century, there were no differences among theories of mensuration that originated in different parts of Europe. German and Italian traditions began to diverge in the last three or four decades of the century. In the sixteenth century, theoretical writings varied distinctly by nationality. The largest number of music theory treatises appeared in Germany and Italy. Spanish and French theorists produced smaller numbers of books, but contributed some valuable information that is not found in German and Italian sources. Only four books that touch on mensural issues were printed in England in the sixteenth century, all of them in the last two decades of the century.

Fifteenth-century sources

The foundation of nearly all fifteenth-century writings on mensuration was the fourteenth-century *Ars practica mensurabilis cantus*, known as *Libellus cantus mensurabilis* in modern scholarly literature, attributed to Johannes de Muris (*c.* 1290–after 1344).[1] Surviving copies call the work "secundum Johannem de Muris," possibly implying that it is a compilation of Muris's teachings, rather than a work written by him. For convenience, I shall refer to Muris as the author. The earliest known copy of the work is found in the so-called "Berkeley Manuscript,"[2] which was copied in Paris in 1375, but most of the surviving sources (more than fifty in all) date from the fifteenth century. Muris lays out the basic principles of mensural notation, which had been developed in his own earlier writings and those of Franco of Cologne and Philippe de Vitry, clearly and concisely.[3] The systematic format of his

---

[1] Johannes de Muris, *Ars practica mensurabilis cantus secundum Iohannem de Muris: Die Recensio maior des sogenannten Libellus practice cantus mensurabilis*, ed. Christian Berktold, Veröffentlichungen der Musikhistorischen Kommission 14 (Munich: Bayerische Akademie der Wissenschaften, 1999).

[2] *The Berkeley Manuscript: University of California Music Library, Ms. 744 (olim Phillipps 4450)*, ed. and trans. Oliver B. Ellsworth, Greek and Latin Music Theory (Lincoln: University of Nebraska Press, c1984), 148–83.

[3] The most important earlier writings on mensural theory are: Franco of Cologne, *Ars cantus mensurabilis*, ed. Gilbert Reaney and André Gilles, Corpus scriptorum de musica 18 ([Rome]: American Institute of Musicology, 1974); Philippe de Vitry, *Ars nova*, ed. Gilbert Reaney, André Gilles, and Jean Maillard, Corpus scriptorum de musica 8 ([Rome]: American Institute of Musicology, 1964); and Johannes de Muris, *Notitia artis musicae*, ed. Ulrich Michels, Corpus scriptorum de musica 17 ([Rome]: American Institute of Musicology, 1972), 47–107.

work served as a model for writings on the subject throughout the fifteenth and sixteenth centuries.

Several early fifteenth-century writings on mensuration are commentaries on Muris's *Libellus*. The most extensive are the *Expositiones tractatus practice cantus mensurabilis magistri Johannis de Muris* of Prosdocimo de' Beldomandi (1404)[4] and Book 3 of the *Declaratio musicae disciplinae* of Ugolino of Orvieto (1430s),[5] which builds on the writings of Prosdocimo. Prosdocimo wrote two other works on mensuration: *Tractatus practice de musica mensurabili* (1408),[6] which is heavily dependent on Muris, though not formally a commentary on his work, and *Tractatus practice cantus mensurabilis ad modum ytalicorum* (1412),[7] which deals with fourteenth-century Italian mensural practices. Shorter commentaries that shed light on the reception of Muris's theory are found in the late fourteenth-century treatises by Coussemaker's Anonymous 5[8] and Anonymous 10[9] and a mid-fifteenth-century treatise by an otherwise unknown Antonius de Luca.[10] Giorgio Anselmi describes both Muris's system and the fourteenth-century Italian notational system in his *De musica* of 1434,[11] then proposes an alternative system of his own invention. Although his original style of

---

[4] Prosdocimo de' Beldomandi, *Expositiones tractatus practice cantus mensurabilis magistri Johannis de Muris*, in Prosdocimi de Beldemandis, *Opera*, ed. F. Alberto Gallo, vol. I, Antiquae Musicae Italicae Scriptores 3 (Bologna: Università degli Studi di Bologna, Istituto di Studi Musicali e Teatrali, 1966). The 1404 original is lost; the work survives in a revised version of 1412.

[5] Ugolino of Orvieto, *Declaratio musicae disciplinae*, ed. Albert Seay, 3 vols., Corpus scriptorum de musica 7 ([Rome]: American Institute of Musicology, 1959–62), II: 167–266.

[6] Prosdocimo de' Beldomandi, *Tractatus practice de musica mensurabili*, ed. Edmond de Coussemaker, *Scriptorum de musica medii aevi*, 4 vols. (Paris: Durand, 1864–76; repr. Hildesheim: Olms, 1963), III: 200–28.

[7] Prosdocimo de' Beldomandi, *Tractatus practice cantus mensurabilis ad modum ytalicorum*, ed. Claudio Sartori, in *La notazione italiana del Trecento in una redazione inedita del "Tractatus practice cantus mensurabilis ad modum ytalicorum" di Prosdocimo de Beldemandis* (Florence: Leo S. Olschki, 1938), 35–71.

[8] *Ars cantus mensurabilis mensurata per modos iuris*, ed. and trans. C. Matthew Balensuela, Greek and Latin Music Theory 10 (Lincoln, NE: University of Nebraska Press, 1994). Anonymous music treatises edited by Edmond de Coussemaker in *Scriptorum de musica medii aevi*, 4 vols. (Paris: Durand, 1864–76; repr. Hildesheim: Olms, 1963) are identified in modern scholarship by Coussemaker's numbers even when more recent editions of them are available.

[9] *De minimis notulis*, ed. Edmond de Coussemaker, *Scriptorum de musica medii aevi*, 4 vols. (Paris: Durand, 1864–76; repr. Hildesheim: Olms, 1963), III: 413–15.

[10] Antonius de Luca, *Ars cantus figurati*, in *Ars cantus figurati, Antonius de Luca; Capitulum de quattuor mensuris, anonymus; Tractatulus mensurationum, anonymus; Compendium breve de proportionibus, anonymus; Tractatulus prolationum cum tabulis, anonymus*, ed. Heinz Ristory, Corpus scriptorum de musica 38 (Neuhausen-Stuttgart: American Institute of Musicology; Hänssler-Verlag, 1997), 24–59.

[11] Giorgio Anselmi, *De musica*, ed. Giuseppe Massera, Historia musicae cultores, Bibliotheca 14 (Florence: Leo S. Olschki, 1961).

notation had no effect on musical practice, his treatise is noteworthy in that it contains the earliest surviving description of time beating as a means of measuring note values.

The extant writings on mensuration from the middle decades of the fifteenth century (*c.* 1440–60) are all short and relatively informal. The only one associated with a named author is the above-mentioned treatise of Antonius de Luca, which is preserved in a late fifteenth-century manuscript along with other works on a variety of theoretical topics.[12] One of the most important mid-fifteenth-century sources is the *Tractatus de musica plana et mensurabili* of Coussemaker's Anonymous 11,[13] a compilation of miscellaneous, probably unrelated, writings by several unidentified authors. Modest as they are, works like these are of great importance, because they contain the earliest information on the subject of cut mensuration signs, which soon became the most contentious and problematic issue in mensural theory. The anonymous *Compendium breve artis musicae*,[14] which probably dates from the third quarter of the century, is notable as the first source to use the term "tactus" in the sense of a unit of time measurement in music.

Three distinct strands of mensural theory emerged in the period from *c.* 1460 to *c.* 1490. The first includes the writings of the Englishman John Hothby, the Italian Guilielmus Monachus, and the Spaniard Bartolomeo Ramis de Pareja, all of whom were active in Italy. The second is a distinctive German school that includes Coussemaker's Anonymous 12 (whose treatise is well organized and systematic despite its anonymity), Adam von Fulda, and their anonymous followers. The third is a new approach pioneered by Johannes Tinctoris, the first theorist to attempt a thoroughgoing reform of the existing mensural system, and further developed by Franchino Gaffurio. The ideas espoused by all of these schools of thought shaped later mensural theories until at least the middle of the sixteenth century.

Hothby was the first theorist to describe a system for notating different levels of mensuration with combinations of circles or semicircles, numbers,

---

[12] See Jan W. Herlinger, "A Fifteenth-Century Italian Compilation of Music Theory," *Acta musicologica* 53 (1981), 90–105, for information on this source.

[13] Anonymous 11, [*Tractatus de musica plana et mensurabili*], in Richard J. Wingell, "Anonymous XI (CS III): An Edition, Translation, and Commentary," 3 vols. (Ph.D. diss., University of Southern California, 1973), I: 1–173.

[14] Anonymous, [*Compendium breve artis musicae*], in Bernhold Schmid, "Ein Mensuralkompendium aus der Handschrift Clm 24809," in *Quellen und Studien zur Musiktheorie des Mittelalters*, ed. Michael Bernhard, Veröffentlichungen der musikhistorischen Kommission 8 (Munich: Bayerische Akademie der Wissenschaften; C. H. Beck, 1990), 71–75.

and dots.[15] His writings are preserved in several manuscripts with overlapping content.[16] Guilielmus Monachus (of whom nothing is known but his name) follows Hothby's system in his *De preceptis artis musice* (*c.* 1480–90)[17] and combines it with earlier theories of cut mensuration signs. Ramis, whose *Musica practica*[18] is the first printed book to deal with issues of mensuration, adopts Hothby's system in part and provides unusually clear information on practices of time measurement in performance. His influence was transmitted to the sixteenth century through his student Giovanni Spataro.

Anonymous 12, whose *Tractatus et compendium cantus figurati*[19] dates from between 1460 and 1471, introduced a new terminology for reduced note values that remained in use in Germany throughout the sixteenth century. He also postulated for the first time a distinction between the meanings of cut signs in different mensurations. Adam von Fulda's *Musica*[20] of 1490 accepts Anonymous 12's interpretation of signs, but does not make use of his novel terminology. Adam was the first theorist to define the term *tactus* in the way that became standard in later German theory. (The isolated appearance of the term in the manuscript mentioned above had no direct followers.) Two anonymous treatises of the late fifteenth century follow Anonymous 12 closely: *Ein tütsche musica*,[21] one of the earliest writings on music in the German language, and *Compendium secundum famosiores musicos* (1490),[22] in which Adam's *tactus* table is added in a marginal note. Although these sources present no new information, they provide useful clarification of the way in which

---

[15] Earlier theorists used a variety of systems for notating mensurations. See Anna Maria Busse Berger, *Mensuration and Proportion Signs: Origins and Evolution* (Oxford: Clarendon Press, 1993), 13–28.

[16] Hothby's writings on mensuration are edited in John Hothby, *Opera omnia de musica mensurabili*, ed. Gilbert Reaney, Corpus scriptorum de musica 31 (Neuhausen-Stuttgart: American Institute of Musicology; Hänssler-Verlag, 1983).

[17] Guilielmus Monachus, *De preceptis artis musice*, ed. Albert Seay, Corpus scriptorum de musica 11 ([Rome]: American Institute of Musicology, 1965).

[18] Bartolomeo Ramis de Pareja, *Musica practica* (Bologna: [Enrico de Colonia?], 1482; repr. Bologna: Forni, 1969).

[19] Anonymous 12, *Tractatus et compendium cantus figurati*, ed. Jill M. Palmer, Corpus scriptorum de musica 35 (Neuhausen-Stuttgart: American Institute of Musicology; Hänssler-Verlag, 1990).

[20] Adam von Fulda, *Musica*, ed. Martin Gerbert, *Scriptores ecclesiastici de musica sacra potissimum*, 3 vols. (St. Blaise: Typis San-Blasianis, 1784; repr. Hildesheim: Olms, 1963), III: 359–66.

[21] Anonymous (attr. B. G. Frank), *Ein tütsche musica*, ed. Arnold Geering, 2 vols., Schriften der literarischen Gesellschaft Bern 9 (Bern: Herbert Lang, 1964).

[22] Anonymous, [*Compendium secundum famosiores musicos*], in Jill Palmer, "A Late Fifteenth-Century Anonymous Mensuration Treatise: (Ssp) Salzburg, Erzabtei St. Peter, a VI 44, 1490; cod pap. 206 × 149 mm. 75ff," *Musica disciplina* 39 (1985), 89–103.

some ambiguous statements of Anonymous 12 were understood by his immediate followers.

Tinctoris, who was of Franco-Flemish origin and worked in Naples during the 1470s and 1480s, was the greatest and most original thinker to address issues of mensuration in the first three-quarters of the fifteenth century. His writings on the subject, which date from *c.* 1472–77, include a series of short treatises on elementary notational principles, substantial books on proportions (*Proportionale musices*) and counterpoint (*Liber de arte contrapuncti*), and a dictionary of musical terms (*Terminorum musicae diffinitorium*).[23] The dictionary is the only work of his that was printed. Tinctoris's approach to the notation of musical rhythms is rigorously logical. He objects to many common conventions, including the notational system of Hothby, that do not meet his strict standard of rationality. His views had little effect on the practices of composers, but they were extremely influential on later theorists who shared his desire to impose systematic logic on musical notation. Tinctoris was the first theorist to recognize and describe in detail the relation between mensuration and dissonance treatment in composition.[24] His groundbreaking insights on that subject laid the foundation for counterpoint theory for centuries to come.

The most important mensural theorist after Tinctoris was Franchino Gaffurio. He was both a successful practicing musician, who held the prestigious post of *maestro di cappella* at the cathedral of Milan for most of his life and produced a large body of musical compositions, and an erudite scholar who wrote extensively on speculative and practical aspects of music theory. His *Practica musice* (1496)[25] was regarded as the most authoritative source of information on mensural theory throughout the sixteenth century. Gaffurio spent the years 1478–80 in Naples, where he discussed music theory at length with Tinctoris and wrote a manuscript treatise (*Musices practicabilis libellum*[26]) that was later revised as Book 2 of *Practica musice*. This treatise appeared in an Italian version by Gaffurio's

---

[23] All of his writings except *Terminorum musicae diffinitorium* ([Treviso, *c.* 1495]; repr. New York: Broude Bros., 1966) are in Johannes Tinctoris, *Opera theoretica*, ed. Albert Seay, 3 vols. in 2, Corpus scriptorum de musica 22 ([Rome]: American Institute of Musicology, 1975–78). The *Terminorum musicae diffinitorium* was written about twenty years before it was published. A new, online critical edition of Tinctoris's complete theoretical works, with translations and related studies, is in progress at http://earlymusictheory.org/Tinctoris/#.

[24] Johannes Tinctoris, *Liber de arte contrapuncti*, book 2, chs. 23–29, in Tinctoris, *Opera theoretica*, II: 121–39.

[25] Franchino Gaffurio, *Practica musice* (Milan: Ioannes Petrus de Lomatio, 1496; repr. New York: Broude Bros., 1979).

[26] Franchino Gaffurio, *Musices practicabilis libellum* (Harvard University, Houghton Library, Ms. Mus 142).

student Francesco Caza.[27] Gaffurio's views on mensuration agree for the most part with Tinctoris's, but they are less rigid and make allowance for some traditional practices that Tinctoris rejected.

Twelve years after the publication of *Practica musice* (and nearly thirty years after the composition of the *Musices practicabilis libellum*), Gaffurio published a summary of his theories in Italian under the title *Angelicum ac divinum opus musice*.[28] In this work he advocates a theory of cut signs that differs in some important respects from the theory in *Practica musice*. Sixteenth-century theorists therefore inherited two incompatible interpretations of cut signs from the theorist who was commonly regarded as the most authoritative writer on the subject. The conflict between these views became a central issue in mensural theory after Gaffurio.

An important feature of fifteenth-century mensural theories is the clear distinction between writings on mensuration and writings on proportions. Some sources treat only one of these topics; others treat both, but assign them to separate chapters or books. Theories of mensuration are practical, but theories of proportion occupy an ambiguous middle ground between speculation and practice. Proportions as applied to musical intervals had been part of *musica speculativa* since ancient times. The subject of proportions took on practical importance when theorists began to apply it to rhythm in the fifteenth century, but much of the speculative baggage traditionally associated with it remained in place. Many treatises on musical proportions, such as Prosdocimo's *Brevis summula proportionum quantum ad musicam pertinet* (1409),[29] are indistinguishable from writings on pure mathematics even if the word "music" appears in their titles. The earliest discussion of practical mensural proportions appears not in Prosdocimo's treatise on musical proportions, but in his *Tractatus practice de musica mensurabili*.[30] Despite the conceptual distinction between mensuration (which includes diminution and augmentation) and proportion, there are overlaps between the subjects, and useful information about each of them is found in treatises devoted primarily to the other. Treatises on musical proportions that address practical issues, such as the mid-fifteenth-century *Exposition of the Proportions, According to the Teaching of "Mestre Joan*

---

[27] Francesco Caza, *Tractato vulgare de canto figurato* (Milan: G. P. de Lomazzo, 1492; repr. Berlin: M. Breslauer, 1922).

[28] Franchino Gaffurio, *Angelicum ac divinum opus musice* (Milan: Gotardus de Ponte, 1508; repr. Bologna: Antiquae musicae italicae studiosi, 1971).

[29] Prosdocimo de' Beldomandi, *Brevis summula proportionum quantum ad musicam pertinet*, ed. and trans. Jan Herlinger, Greek and Latin Music Theory 4 (Lincoln: University of Nebraska Press, 1987).

[30] Prosdocimo, *Tractatus practice de musica mensurabili*, "De signis mensure," 218–19.

20 Theory

Violant" [Vaillant][31] and *Sequuntur proportiones*,[32] will be considered in this book, but treatises that have no relation to practice will not.[33]

Sixteenth-century German sources

Music played a central role in the German educational system in the sixteenth century. Many music textbooks were written in German-speaking areas to support this system.[34] A few similar books published in eastern Europe belong to the same tradition. Almost all of the authors of these books were music teachers, usually at the elementary or secondary level, but sometimes at the university level. Some would probably have regarded themselves as pedagogues, rather than theorists in the rigorous sense of the term, but they often express concern for theoretical tradition and abstract logic even in elementary books. Most music theory books published in Germany are in Latin, but a few are in German. Their style varies from extremely simple to moderately sophisticated, depending on the level of the students they address, but it is usually straightforward and without literary pretensions. Some books take the form of question-and-answer dialogues between teacher and student.

Discussions of mensural issues in these books almost always consist of compilations of information from earlier sources, often transmitted with little or no change, though subtle variations of wording may reveal important points about an author's interpretation of his sources. The authors often draw on sources that disagree both with each other and with common practice. Some writers attempt to resolve the resulting conflicts in ingenious

---

[31] *Exposition of the Proportions, According to the Teaching of "Mestre Joan Violant" [Vaillant], the teacher of Paris* (Florence, Biblioteca Nazionale, Magl. III, 70), in Israel Adler, *Hebrew Writings Concerning Music*, RISM B IX 2 (Munich and Duisberg: G. Henle, 1975), 55–77.

[32] Anonymous, *Sequuntur proportiones* (Innsbruck, Universitätsbibliothek, Cod. 962, fols. 142^r–144^r), facsimile and ed. in Renate Federhofer-Königs, "Ein Beitrag zur Proportionenlehre in der zweiten Hälfte des 15. Jahrhunderts," in *Bence Szabolcsi Septuagenario*, ed. Dénes Bartha, Studia musicologica Academiae Scientiarum Hungaricae 11 (Budapest: Akadémiai Kiadó, 1969), 148–57.

[33] For a survey of fifteenth- and early sixteenth-century writings on musical proportions, see Berger, *Mensuration and Proportion Signs*, 164–226.

[34] For overviews of this material see Klaus Wolfgang Niemöller, "Deutsche Musiktheorie im 16. Jahrhundert: Geistes- und institutionsgeschichtliche Grundlagen," in *Deutsche Musiktheorie des 15. bis 17. Jahrhunderts* I: *Von Paumann bis Calvisius*, Geschichte der Musiktheorie 8/1 (Darmstadt: Wissenschaftliche Buchgesellschaft, 2003), 69–98, and Klaus Wolfgang Niemöller, *Untersuchungen zur Musikpflege und Musikunterricht an den deutschen Lateinschulen vom ausgehenden Mittelalter bis um 1600*, Kölner Beiträge zur Musikforschung 54 (Regensburg: Gustav Bosse, 1969).

ways; others allow them to stand without comment, perhaps in the expectation that the resolution would be clear to their readers on the basis of common knowledge. As the tradition grew, successful textbooks became additional sources for later books. The number of diverse views that might appear in a single book therefore increased over time. To complicate matters further, a few theorists attempted to reform common practices, adding still more options for their successors to incorporate into their synthetic summaries. Many scholars have commented on the inconsistency of the views on *tactus* and mensuration in sixteenth-century German writings.[35] Although the inconsistency is real, it is easy to explain if the books involved are read not as isolated entities, but as part of a larger tradition in which each author built upon a heritage that accumulated over a period of more than a century.

The first printed music textbooks were written by a group of theorists associated with the University of Cologne, sometimes known as the "Cologne school": Melchior Schanppecher, Nicolaus Wollick, Johannes Cochlaeus, and Bernhard Bogentantz. The major contribution of this group to mensural theory was a reconciliation of the older German theories of Anonymous 12 and Adam von Fulda with Gaffurio's *Practica musice* and with contemporaneous performance practices. The earliest work of the Cologne school (and the first printed textbook on music) was the 1501 *Opus aureum* by Wollick and Schanppecher, in which the section on mensural music was written by Schanppecher.[36] This book went through four further editions and served as the foundation for Wollick's more extensive *Enchiridion musices*, which also includes material derived from other sources.[37] Cochlaeus wrote a short treatise called *Musica*, which appeared in three editions during his student years in Cologne, and a more extensive book entitled *Tetrachordum musices* for the Nuremberg schools.[38] Bogentantz's *Collectanea utriusque cantus*[39] draws on all of

---

[35] See for example Arthur Mendel, "Some Ambiguities of the Mensural System," in *Studies in Music History: Essays for Oliver Strunk*, ed. Harold S. Powers (Princeton University Press, 1968), 137–60.

[36] Nicolaus Wollick and Melchior Schanppecher, *Opus aureum* (Cologne: Heinrich Quentell, 1501).

[37] Nicolaus Wollick, *Enchiridion musices* (Paris: Jehan Petit et François Regnault, 1509; repr. in *Renaissance française*, ed. Olivier Trachier [Courlay, France: J. M. Fuzeau, 2005], I: 125–38).

[38] Johannes Cochlaeus, *Musica*, 3rd edn. (Cologne: Johann Landen, 1507), and *Tetrachordum musices* (Nuremberg: Johann Weyssenburger, 1511; repr. Hildesheim: Olms, 1971). Cochlaeus also wrote a short work entitled *Compendium in praxim atque exercitium cantus figurabilis* ([Cologne: Johann Landen, 1507]) that contains some practical information not in his other treatises. An edition of Cochlaeus's early writings is in preparation by Klaus-Jürgen Sachs.

[39] Bernhard Bogentantz, *Collectanea utriusque cantus* (Cologne, 1515).

these works. The writings of the Cologne school were profoundly influential on later theorists, especially in Germany, for decades to come. Theorists of the second decade of the sixteenth century who depend primarily on them include Joannes Volckmar,[40] the anonymous author of *Institutio in musicen mensuralem*,[41] Michael Koswick,[42] Stephan Monetarius,[43] and Sebastian of Felsztyn.[44] Heinrich Glarean studied with Cochlaeus in Cologne and was deeply influenced by him, though his writing on mensuration appears in his much later *Dodecachordon*[45] and takes account of other points of view as well.

A few writers active in German-speaking areas (in particular Vienna) in the first two decades of the century, including Simon de Quercu,[46] Venceslaus Philomathes,[47] and Othmar Luscinius,[48] based their theories of mensuration on Anonymous 12 and Adam von Fulda with little or no influence from Gaffurio. Philomathes, who studied and taught at the University of Vienna, composed his *Musicorum libri quattuor* in hexameters to facilitate memorization of the material. His verses proved popular with later textbook authors, including Georg Rhau and Martin Agricola, who quoted attractive excerpts from his work even when the content of those passages did not agree with the views in the authors' main texts.[49]

Andreas Ornithoparchus's *Musice active micrologus*[50] of 1517 disrupted the widespread consensus on mensural issues achieved by the Cologne school and its followers. Ornithoparchus was not a professional musician,

---

[40] Joannes Volckmar, *Collectanea quedam musice discipline* (Frankfurt an der Oder, 1513).

[41] Anonymous, *Institutio in musicen mensuralem* (Erfurt: Johann Knapp, 1513).

[42] Michael Koswick, *Compendiaria musice artis aeditio* (Leipzig: Wolffgang Stöckel, 1516).

[43] Stephan Monetarius, *Epitoma utriusque musices practice* (Cracow: Florian Ungler, 1515; repr. Cracow: Polskie Wydawnictwo Muzyczne, 1975).

[44] Sebastian of Felsztyn. *Opusculum musicae mensuralis* (Cracow: J. Haller, [*c*. 1518]; repr. Cracow: Polskie Wydawnictwo Muzyczne, 1979).

[45] Heinrich Glarean, *Dodecachordon* (Basel: Heinrich Petri, 1547; repr. New York: Broude Bros., 1967). An extract of this work, which includes a few new observations relating to mensuration, is *Musicae epitome, sive Compendium ex Glareani Dodecachordo* (Basel: [Heinrich Petri, 1557]).

[46] Simon de Quercu, *Opusculum musices* (Vienna: Johann Winterburg, 1509).

[47] Venceslaus Philomathes, *Musicorum libri quattuor* (Vienna: Hieronymus Vietor & Johannes Singrenius, 1512).

[48] Othmar Luscinius, *Musurgia seu praxis musicae* (Strassburg: Johann Schott, 1536). Luscinius's work was written about twenty years before it was published.

[49] Rhau quotes some of Philomathes's verses in his *Enchiridion utriusque musicae practicae* (see note 53). He also reprinted Philomathes's book twice (Leipzig, 1518 [part IV only], and Wittenberg, 1534). Agricola quotes Philomathes in several of his writings and wrote a commentary on Philomathes's work: *Scholia in musicam planam Venceslai Philomatis* (n.p., 1538).

[50] Andreas Ornithoparchus, *Musice active micrologus* (Leipzig: Valentin Schumann, 1517); trans. John Dowland (London: T. Adams, 1609); repr. of both in *A Compendium of Musical Practice*, ed. Gustave Reese and Steven Ledbetter (New York: Dover, [1973]).

but a humanist scholar who lectured on music at the universities of Tübingen, Heidelberg, and Mainz. He received advice for the section of his book on mensuration from Georg Brack, the former Kapellmeister of the Duke of Württemberg.

Ornithoparchus drew heavily on Anonymous 12, Wollick, Cochlaeus, and Gaffurio, but was dissatisfied with the ways in which his predecessors glossed over the inconsistencies among their sources and the discrepancies between theory and practice. His approach was to adopt Gaffurio's theory of signs in the Italian (with Latin title) *Angelicum ac divinum opus musice*, which he must surely have read, although he acknowledges only Latin works as his sources, and to interpret the *Practica musice* in a new way that brought it into line with Gaffurio's later work. He took a dogmatic stand on the issue of *tactus* and condemned musicians who did not observe his theories as ignoramuses, calling them (in John Dowland's colorful translation) "not compounders of Harmonies, but rather corruptors, children of the furies, rather than of the Muses."[51] He even went so far as to suggest that the prayer of Christ on the cross, "Father pardon them, they know not what they doe," might be applied to them.[52]

Despite Ornithoparchus's humanistically inspired disdain for practitioners who were ignorant of theory (or interpreted it differently than he did), many teachers of practical music who came after him felt obliged to integrate his views into their textbooks. They could not, however, sacrifice instruction in real practices in the interest of abstract theory, nor did they wish to reject wholesale the earlier theories that Ornithoparchus condemned. The challenge they faced was monumental, and their success in meeting it, though necessarily incomplete, is admirable. The first theorist to face the challenge was Georg Rhau, who served as Kantor of the Thomasschule and Thomaskirche in Leipzig and taught at the University of Leipzig from 1518 to 1520. Two editions of his *Enchiridion utriusque musicae practicae* were published during those years by Valentin Schumann, who had issued Ornithoparchus's *Musice active micrologus* the year before Rhau's arrival in the city.[53] In 1523 Rhau settled in Wittenberg, where he took over a publishing business that issued eleven

---

[51] Ornithoparchus, *Musice active micrologus*, trans. John Dowland, book 2, ch. 8, 49.
[52] Ibid., 49–50.
[53] The first edition of Rhau's *Enchiridion utriusque musicae practicae* was published in Wittenberg by Johann Rhau-Grunenberg (probably his uncle) in 1517. Valentin Schumann issued two more editions of the work in Leipzig (1518 and 1520). The 1520 edition is the first to contain the book on mensural music.

more editions of his book, along with books by Martin Agricola[54] and Nicolaus Listenius[55] that adopt similar points of view on mensural issues. Listenius's *Musica* was one of the most popular textbooks of the century. It appeared in forty-six editions in the five decades following its initial publication. Other books that adopt Rhau's approach to reconciling Ornithoparchus's views with practice include Johann Frosch's *Rerum musicarum*[56] and Auctor Lampadius's *Compendium musices*.[57]

The reasonably comfortable accommodation between theory and practice that was achieved by Rhau and his followers was once again undermined by the writings of Sebald Heyden, a former student of Cochlaeus whose views departed radically from those of his teacher. Although Heyden had professional obligations as a music teacher in his role as rector of the school of St. Sebald in Nuremberg, he was also a humanist scholar and rigorous intellectual who, like Ornithoparchus, was troubled by mismatches between theory and practice. He believed as a matter of faith that the mensural practice of composers of the Josquin generation, unlike the practices of his own time, had been strictly rational and consistent, and he aimed to recover what he believed to be the original, authentic mensural system and to persuade his contemporaries to adopt it. He based his ideas primarily on a study of musical compositions, rather than earlier theorists, whom he found to be hopelessly confused and uninformative about the issues that concerned him. This approach might have led him to meaningful insights if his interpretations had not been warped from the outset by the assumption that there was a single formula underlying all fifteenth-century uses of mensuration signs – a simplistic view that was possible only after the people with first-hand knowledge of the practices in question were no longer living. Heyden's first work on music, *Musica stoicheiosis* (1532),[58] is largely conventional, though it contains hints of the future direction of his thoughts. His *Musicae, id est artis canendi libri duo* (1537)[59] and *De arte canendi* (1540),[60] which he regarded as later editions of *Musica stoicheiosis*,

---

[54] Martin Agricola, *Musica figuralis deudsch* (Wittenberg: Georg Rhau, 1532; repr. Hildesheim and New York: Georg Olms, 1969).
[55] Nicolaus Listenius, *Musica* (Wittenberg: Georg Rhau, 1537; repr. [of 1549 edn.] Berlin: M. Breslauer, 1927).
[56] Johann Frosch, *Rerum musicarum* (Strassburg: Peter Schöffer & Mathias Apiarius, 1535; repr. New York: Broude, 1967).
[57] Auctor Lampadius, *Compendium musices* (Bern: Mathias Apiarius, 1537).
[58] Sebald Heyden, *Musica stoicheiosis* (Nuremberg: Friedrich Peypus, 1532).
[59] Sebald Heyden, *Musicae, id est artis canendi libri duo* (Nuremberg: Johann Petreius, 1537).
[60] Sebald Heyden, *De arte canendi* (Nuremberg: Johann Petreius, 1540; repr. New York: Broude, 1969).

present increasingly dogmatic versions of his novel ideas. Most of the lengthy dedication of *De arte canendi* is devoted to an attack on current musical practices that rivals that of Ornithoparchus in its vehemence.

Heyden was widely admired as a learned man, and the rigorous logic of his theory appealed to many of his contemporaries, but only two later theorists (Gregor Faber[61] and Johannes Oridryus[62]), both writing in the 1550s, accepted his views without qualification. Others, including Heinrich Faber,[63] Johann Zanger,[64] and Hermann Finck,[65] attempted to reconcile his theories with real practices, just as the Cologne school had reconciled earlier German theories with Gaffurio and Rhau had reconciled the Cologne theories with Ornithoparchus. Still others borrow text and examples from Heyden where it suits their purposes, but ignore or reject the dogmatic elements of his theory. Even Ambrosius Wilphlingseder, who worked as cantor under Heyden at the school of St. Sebald, bases the explanation of *tactus* in his *Erotemata musices practicae* on Listenius, rather than Heyden.[66] Eucharius Hofmann characterizes Heyden's theory as intellectually sophisticated, but impractical.[67] Glarean refers to Heyden as a distinguished musician ("insignis musicus"),[68] yet seems to express annoyance with his pedantry.[69] Adrian Petit Coclico is even less charitable, alleging that mensural complications like those that occupied Heyden "contribute nothing to singing clearly, but more to debating and quarreling."[70] Elementary textbooks, such as Heinrich Faber's *Compendiolum*

---

[61] Gregor Faber, *Musices practicae erotematum libri II* (Basel: Heinrich Petri, 1553).

[62] Johannes Oridryus, *Practicae musicae utriusque praecepta brevia* (Düsseldorf: Jacob Baethen, 1557), ed. in Renate Federhofer-Königs, *Johannes Oridryus und sein Musiktraktat* (Cologne: Arno Volk, 1957), 65–157.

[63] Heinrich Faber, *Ad musicam practicam introductio* (Nuremberg: Johann Berg and Ulrich Neuber, 1550).

[64] Johann Zanger, *Practicae musicae praecepta* (Leipzig: Georg Hantzsch, 1554).

[65] Hermann Finck, *Practica musica* (Wittenberg: Georg Rhaus Erben, 1556; repr. Bologna: Forni, 1969).

[66] Ambrosius Wilphlingseder, *Erotemata musices practicae* (Nuremberg: Heussler, 1563), book 2, ch. 14 ("De Cantus mensura seu Tactu"), 320–21.

[67] Eucharius Hofmann, *Musicae practicae praecepta* (Wittenberg: Johann Schwertel, 1572), part II, ch. 6 ("De diminutione"), fol. Ivi^r.

[68] Glarean, *Dodecachordon*, book 1, ch. 4 ("De clavibus et vocum per easdem deductionibus, item de notularum figuris"), 6.

[69] Ibid., book 3, ch. 7 ("De tactu sive cantandi mensura"), 205. Glarean does not criticize Heyden by name, but is probably referring to him when he says, "although I hate the pedantry of some men, I would certainly also like to use [the signs] in the way in which they were first received" ("ego certe, ut quorundam morositatem odi, ita hac quoque parte receptis semel, uti velim").

[70] "... haec ad perspicue canendum nihil conducunt, verum magis ad disceptandum et rixandum." Adrian Petit Coclico, *Compendium musices* (Nuremberg: Johann Berg and Ulrich Neuber, 1552; repr. Kassel: Bärenreiter, 1954), part II, "De tactu et mensura," fol. Hii^v. Coclico, like Glarean, does not mention Heyden by name, but Heyden's book is clearly one that provoked his scorn.

musicae pro incipientibus[71] – the most popular text of its time, with some fifty editions over a period of seventy years – often dispense altogether with the theoretical complexities that intrigued Heyden and explain in the simplest possible terms how musicians interpreted mensural notation in practice.

The most important point about Heyden's theory is neither the substance of his ideas nor their short-lived vogue in mid-century Germany, but their reception by scholars of the nineteenth and twentieth centuries.[72] Heinrich Bellermann, the first modern scholar to attempt to recover the principles of mensural notation, based his interpretation of mensuration signs almost exclusively on Heyden. His book, first published in 1858, went through four editions, the latest of which appeared as recently as 1963.[73] It laid the foundation for interpretations of the system by later scholars such as Johannes Wolf,[74] Curt Sachs,[75] and Willi Apel.[76] Although numerous scholars of the past fifty years have challenged Heyden's rigid views, few have escaped the tendency to revise or broaden his point of view, rather than rejecting it outright as a valid interpretation of the earlier mensural system. Even Carl Dahlhaus, who concludes a brilliant study of sixteenth-century *tactus* theory with the statement that Heyden's theory "does not clarify the older mensural system, but contradicts it," replaces Heyden's single, inflexible *tactus* with three equally rigid, proportionally interrelated *tactus*.[77] To interpret earlier theorists fairly, it is essential to read them without any of the preconceptions that modern scholars have inherited from Heyden.

---

[71] Heinrich Faber, *Compendiolum musicae pro incipientibus* ([Brunswick, 1548]; repr. [of 1594 edn.] Bologna: Forni, 1980).

[72] See Ruth I. DeFord, "Sebald Heyden (1499–1561): The First Historical Musicologist?" in *Music's Intellectual History*, ed. Zdravko Blažeković and Barbara Dobbs Mackenzie (New York: Répertoire International de la Littérature Musicale, 2009), 3–15.

[73] Heinrich Bellermann, *Die Mensuralnoten und Taktzeichen des XV. und XVI. Jahrhunderts* (Berlin: G. Reimer, 1858; 4th expanded edn., ed. Heinrich Husmann, Berlin: W. de Gruyter, 1963).

[74] Johannes Wolf, *Geschichte der Mensural-Notation* (Leipzig: Breitkopf & Härtel, 1904; repr. Hildesheim: Olms, 1965).

[75] Curt Sachs, *Rhythm and Tempo: A Study in Music History* (New York: Norton, 1953; repr. New York: Columbia University Press, 1988).

[76] Willi Apel, *The Notation of Polyphonic Music, 900–1600*, 5th edn. (Cambridge, MA: The Mediaeval Academy of America, 1953).

[77] "Sein [Heydens] Irrtum aber zeigt, daß die Tactustheorie Sebald Heydens das ältere Mensuren- und Proportionensystem nicht erklärt, sondern ihm widerspricht." Carl Dahlhaus, "Zur Theorie des Tactus im 16. Jahrhundert," *Archiv für Musikwissenschaft* 17 (1960), 39. Dahlhaus later concluded that there was no single formula (whether based on one *tactus* or three) that governs all relations among mensuration signs. See his "Die Tactus- und Proportionenlehre des 15. bis 17. Jahrhunderts," in *Hören, Messen, und Rechnen in der frühen Neuzeit*, Geschichte der Musiktheorie 6 (Darmstadt: Wissenschaftliche Buchgesellschaft, 1987), 333–61.

By c. 1570, German theorists lost interest in the traditional mensural system and the theoretical controversies surrounding it. Gallus Dressler[78] and Eucharius Hofmann[79] explain modern mensural practices in a simplified way that relates them to older theory, while later theorists, including Friedrich Beurhaus,[80] Christoph Praetorius,[81] Andreas Raselius,[82] Cyriacus Schneegass,[83] and Seth Calvisius,[84] often make no mention of obsolete concepts and signs. Michael Praetorius explains many old signs in his *Syntagma musicum* (1614–20) for the sake of completeness, but regards them as useless for notating meaningful musical ideas.[85]

Sixteenth-century Italian sources

The music-theoretical writings produced in Italy in the sixteenth century were quite different from those produced in Germany. Most of the authors were pure theorists in the sense that they were seriously interested in understanding the rational principles on which music was based. Their intended audiences were other music theorists and professional musicians, not students who were looking primarily for practical instruction. Issues relating to mensuration were among the topics that engendered lively debates among these theorists, whether or not the matters in question had any practical significance.

The most important Italian books that deal with mensural theory in the decades following Gaffurio's *Angelicum ac divinum opus musice* are Pietro Aaron's *Libri tres de institutione harmonica*,[86] *Thoscanello de la musica*,[87] and *Lucidario in musica*,[88] Giovanni Maria Lanfranco's *Scintille di*

---

[78] Gallus Dressler, *Musicae practicae elementa* (Magdeburg: Wolfgang Kirchner, 1571).
[79] Eucharius Hofmann, *Musicae practicae praecepta* (Wittenberg: Johann Schwertel, 1572).
[80] Friedrich Beurhaus, *Musicae erotematum libri duo* (Dortmund: Albert Sartorius, 1573; repr. Cologne: Arno Volk-Verlag, 1961).
[81] Christoph Praetorius, *Erotemata musices* (Wittenberg: Johann Schwertel, 1574).
[82] Andreas Raselius, *Hexachordum* (Nuremberg: Gerlach, 1589).
[83] Cyriacus Schneegass, *Isagoges musicae* (Erfurt: Georg Baumann, 1591).
[84] Seth Calvisius, *Exercitationes musicae duae* (Leipzig: Franz Schnellboltz, 1600).
[85] Michael Praetorius, *Syntagma musicum*, vol. III (Wolfenbüttel: Elias Holwein, 1618–19; repr. Kassel: Bärenreiter, 1958–59), part II, ch. 7 ("De tactu, seu notarum mensura; (italis battuta) & signis"), 48–79.
[86] Pietro Aaron, *Libri tres de institutione harmonica* (Bologna: Benedetto di Ettore, 1516; repr. New York: Broude Bros., 1978).
[87] Pietro Aaron, *Thoscanello de la musica* (Venice: Bernardino & Matheo de Vitali, 1523; repr. [of 2nd edn., *Toscanello in musica*] Bologna: Forni, 1999).
[88] Pietro Aaron, *Lucidario in musica di alcune oppenioni antiche, et moderne con le loro oppositioni, et resolutioni* (Venice: Girolamo Scotto, 1545; repr. New York: Broude, 1978).

musica,[89] and Stephano Vanneo's *Recanetum de musica aurea*.[90] Aaron's *Libri tres* and Vanneo's *Recanetum* are in Latin (though both were first written in Italian and then translated by others); the other three are in Italian, as are nearly all Italian books on music theory after the 1530s. Italian theorists follow Gaffurio's view of cut signs in the *Angelicum ac divinum opus musice*, not the view in his *Practica musice*, regardless of their differences of opinion on other mensural issues. Lanfranco lists Ornithoparchus (who likewise based his interpretation of cut signs on the *Angelicum ac divinum opus musice*) among the authorities he has consulted and seems to have been particularly influenced by his work.[91] Angelo da Picitono also depends heavily on Ornithoparchus in his *Fior angelico di musica*.[92]

The leading Italian theorists of the first half of the sixteenth century were personally acquainted and carried on discussions of music-theoretical matters through letters, as well as published writings. Giovanni Spataro, a former student of Ramis who worked as *maestro de canto* at the basilica of San Petronio in Bologna, was at the center of an extensive correspondence involving Aaron, Lanfranco, Giovanni del Lago, and others that spanned the years 1517–43.[93] His letters contain numerous comments about subtle matters that were rarely addressed in formal treatises. Spataro communicated very little with Gaffurio because of a deep-seated personal animosity, as well as profound differences of theoretical opinion, between the two men. He never wrote a comprehensive treatise on music, but his views on mensural issues can be ascertained from his letters and from two polemical works in which he launched impassioned attacks on the published views of Gaffurio.[94]

Italian music theory in the second half of the sixteenth century was dominated by Gioseffo Zarlino's *Le istitutioni harmoniche*.[95] Zarlino was one of the greatest and most influential music theorists of all times. He had

---

[89] Giovanni Maria Lanfranco, *Scintille di musica* (Brescia: Lodovico Britannico, 1533; repr. Bologna: Forni, 1988).

[90] Stephano Vanneo, *Recanetum de musica aurea* (Rome: Valerio Dorico, 1533; repr. Bologna: Forni, 1969).

[91] Lanfranco, *Scintille di musica*, "Dalla divisione dell'opera" (unnumbered page preceding table of contents).

[92] Angelo da Picitono, *Fior angelico di musica* (Venice: Agostino Bindoni, 1547).

[93] *A Correspondence of Renaissance Musicians*, ed. Bonnie J. Blackburn, Edward E. Lowinsky, and Clement A. Miller (Oxford: Clarendon Press, 1991).

[94] Giovanni Spataro, *Dilucide et probatissime demonstratione . . . contra certe frivole et vane excusatione de Franchino Gafurio* (Bologna: Hieronymus de Benedictis, 1521; repr. Berlin: M. Breslauer, 1925), and *Tractato di musica . . . nel quale si tracta de la perfectione da la sesqualtera producta in la musica mensurata exercitate* (Venice: Bernardino de Vitali, 1531; repr. Bologna: Forni, [1970]). The first of these works covers a broad range of issues; the second is concerned exclusively with mensuration.

[95] Gioseffo Zarlino, *Le istitutioni harmoniche* (Venice, 1558; repr. New York: Broude Bros., 1965).

little interest in mensuration and even allowed some uncharacteristic inconsistencies to slip into his discussions of mensural issues. The few observations that he offers on the subject, however, are of considerable value. Giovanni Maria Artusi[96] and Orazio Tigrini[97] offer simplified versions of Zarlino's theory.

A few Italian theorists pursued ideas about mensuration that were independent of the mainstream views of their time. Nicola Vicentino, who is known for his idiosyncratic ideas about the application of the ancient Greek genera to modern music, includes some novel observations about mensuration and tempo in his *L'antica musica ridotta alla moderna prattica*.[98] Vicente Lusitano, a Portuguese musician living in Rome in the 1550s, describes unusual subdivisions of the beat in his *Introdutione facilissima, et novissima di canto fermo, figurato, contraponto semplice, et inconcerto*.[99] Giovanthomaso Cimello, who did not publish his theoretical works, left two manuscript treatises that include comments about practices of time measurement that are not addressed by other theorists.[100] Ludovico Zacconi, who was trained in Italy and sang under Lassus in Munich, includes copious material on mensural issues in his *Prattica di musica*.[101] He wrote in an informal, conversational style and enriched his discussions with personal observations and anecdotes that provide unique insights into performance subtleties that other theorists never mention. Agostino Pisa, a self-styled *musico speculativo e prattico* (also a priest and doctor of canon and civil law, but probably not a professional musician), wrote the only treatise of the period devoted exclusively to the subject of *tactus*.[102] He approached the

---

[96] Giovanni Maria Artusi, *L'arte del contraponto* (Venice: Giacomo Vincenzi & Ricciardo Amadino, 1586; repr. Bologna: Forni, 1980).

[97] Orazio Tigrini, *Il compendio della musica* (Venice: Ricciardo Amadino, 1588; repr. New York: Broude, 1966).

[98] Nicola Vicentino, *L'antica musica ridotta alla moderna prattica* (Rome: Antonio Barre, 1555; repr. Kassel: Bärenreiter, 1959).

[99] Vicente Lusitano, *Introdutione facilissima, et novissima di canto fermo, figurato, contraponto semplice, et inconcerto* (Rome: Antonio Blado, 1553; repr. [of 1561 edn.] Lucca: Libreria Musicale Italiana Editrice, 1988).

[100] See James Haar, "Lessons in Theory from a Sixteenth-Century Composer," in *Essays on Italian Music in the Cinquecento*, ed. Richard Charteris, Altro Polo (Sydney: Frederick May Foundation for Italian Studies, 1990), 51–81.

[101] Ludovico Zacconi, *Prattica di musica* (Venice: Girolamo Polo, 1592; repr. Hildesheim: Olms, 1982) and *Prattica di musica, seconda parte* (Venice: Alessandro Vincenti, 1622; repr. Hildesheim: Olms, 1982). See Ruth I. DeFord, "Zacconi's Theories of *Tactus* and Mensuration," *The Journal of Musicology* 14 (1996), 151–82.

[102] Agostino Pisa, *Breve dichiaratione della battuta musicale* (Rome: Bartolomeo Zannetti, 1611; repr. Lucca: Libreria Musicale Italiana, c1996). An expanded version of this work appeared the same year under the title *Battuta della musica* (Rome: Bartolomeo Zannetti, 1611; repr. Bologna: Forni, 1969).

subject from an abstract, speculative point of view and discussed many common beliefs and practices that he found objectionable on theoretical grounds.

Sixteenth-century Spanish, French, and English sources

Although the great bulk of the original work in mensural theory appeared in Germany and Italy in the sixteenth century, other countries produced some studies that provide additional perspectives on problematic issues.[103] Music theory books that include discussions of mensuration appeared sporadically in Spain throughout the sixteenth century. They range from elementary introductions to ambitious studies directed at the most advanced readers. Four books from the last decade of the fifteenth century and first decade of the sixteenth are similar in scope and character to the German music theory books of the same period: Guillermo Molins de Podio's *Ars musicorum*,[104] Diego del Puerto's *Portus musice*,[105] Domingo Marcos Durán's *Sumula de canto órgano*,[106] and Francisco Tovar's *Libro de musica practica*.[107] Juan Bermudo's later *Declaración de instrumentos musicales*[108] is a grand synthesis of speculative and practical theory. Tomás de Sancta Maria's *Arte de tañer fantasia*[109] is a book about keyboard playing that touches on mensuration only as it pertains to that skill. Pietro Cerone's *El melopeo y maestro*[110] is a monumental compendium of sixteenth-century ideas on a broad range of musical topics. The

---

[103] For surveys of French and English music theory in this period, see Barry Cooper and Wilhelm Seidel, *Entstehung nationaler Traditionen: Frankreich, England*, Geschichte der Musiktheorie 9 (Darmstadt: Wissenschaftliche Buchgesellschaft, 1986). On Spanish theory, see Francisco José León Tello, *Estudios de historia de la teoría musical*, 2nd edn. (Madrid: Consejo Superior de Investigaciones Cientificas, 1991), 193–646.

[104] Guillermo Molins de Podio (Despuig), *Ars musicorum* (Valencia: Peter Hagenbach & Leonhard Hutz, 1495; repr. [Bologna]: Forni, 1975).

[105] Diego del Puerto, *Portus musice* (Salamanca: [J. de Porras], 1504; repr. Madrid: Joyas Bibliográficas, 1976).

[106] Domingo Marcos Durán, *Sumula de canto órgano, contrapunto y composicion* (Salamanca: [Giesser?], [c. 1504]; repr. Madrid: Joyas Bibliográficas, 1976).

[107] Francisco Tovar, *Libro de musica practica* (Barcelona: Johann Rosenbach, 1510; repr. Madrid: Joyas Bibliográficas, 1976).

[108] Juan Bermudo, *Declaración de instrumentos musicales* (Osuna: Juan de Leon, 1555; repr. Kassel: Bärenreiter, 1957).

[109] Tomás de Sancta Maria, *Libro llamado arte de tañer fantasia* (Valladolid: Francisco Fernandez de Cordova, 1565; repr. Geneva: Minkoff, 1973).

[110] Pietro Cerone, *El melopeo y maestro* (Naples: Juan Bautista Gargano & Lucrecio Nucci, 1613; repr. Bologna: Forni, 1969).

work belongs in the Spanish tradition mainly on grounds of language, since the author was Italian, though it incorporates much material from earlier Spanish sources. Matheo de Aranda's *Tractado de canto mensurable*[111] was published in Portugal, but is also written in Spanish.

The most important book dealing with mensural issues that was published in France before 1550 is Wollick's *Enchiridion musices* of 1509, the substance of which derives from the author's work with Schanppecher in Cologne combined with additional material from Gaffurio's *Practica musice*. It was probably written for students at the University of Paris, where Wollick was teaching at the time. Books of a different type, usually written in French and directed primarily at musical amateurs, began to appear in the 1550s. The earliest are Claude Martin's *Elementorum musices practicae*[112] and Loys Bourgeois's *Le droict chemin de musique*.[113] Bourgeois refers respectfully to Heyden, but adopts an independent stance on mensural issues and includes several innovative ideas on the subject. Maximilian Guilliaud's *Rudiments de musique practique*[114] draws much material from Martin, and Corneille de Montfort's *Instruction fort facile pour apprendre la musique practique*[115] is modeled closely on Bourgeois. Bourgeois's influence may account for the elements of Heyden's thought that turn up in Philibert Jambe de Fer's *Epitome musical*[116] and Jean Yssandon's *Traité de la musique pratique*[117] as well.

Sixteenth-century English writings on music that deal with mensural issues are limited to a tiny handful of manuscripts, including an interesting commentary on Gaffurio's theory of proportions by John Dygon,[118] and

---

[111] Matheo de Aranda, *Tractado de canto mensurable* (Lisbon: German Galharde, 1535).

[112] Claude Martin, *Elementorum musices practicae pars prior* (Paris: Nicolas Du Chemin, 1550; repr. in *Renaissance française*, ed. Olivier Trachier [Courlay, France: J. M. Fuzeau, 2005], II: 113–40). An abridged French translation with the title *Institution musicale* (Paris: Nicolas Du Chemin, 1556; repr. in *Renaissance française*, ed. Olivier Trachier [Courlay, France: J. M. Fuzeau, 2005], III: 237–44) appeared six years later.

[113] Loys Bourgeois, *Le droict chemin de musique* (Geneva: [Jean Gérard], 1550; repr. in *Renaissance française*, ed. Olivier Trachier [Courlay, France: J. M. Fuzeau, 2005], I: 49–112).

[114] Maximilian Guilliaud, *Rudiments de musique practique* (Paris: Nicolas Du Chemin, 1554; repr. in *Renaissance française*, ed. Olivier Trachier [Courlay, France: J. M. Fuzeau, 2005], II: 229–44).

[115] Corneille de Montfort (*dit* Blockland), *Instruction fort facile pour apprendre la musique practique* (Lyon: Jean de Tournes, 1573; repr. in *Renaissance française*, ed. Olivier Trachier [Courlay, France: J. M. Fuzeau, 2005], IV: 251–310).

[116] Philibert Jambe de Fer, *Epitome musical* (Lyon: Michel du Bois, 1556; repr. in *Renaissance française*, ed. Olivier Trachier [Courlay, France: J. M. Fuzeau, 2005], III: 197–236).

[117] Jean Yssandon, *Traité de la musique pratique* (Paris: Adrian Le Roy & Robert Ballard, 1582; repr. in *Renaissance française*, ed. Olivier Trachier [Courlay, France: J. M. Fuzeau, 2005], IV: 169–212).

[118] John Dygon, *Proportiones practicabiles secundum Gaffurium*, ed. and trans. Theodor Dumitrescu (Urbana and Chicago: University of Illinois Press, c2006).

four printed books from the last two decades of the century: William Bathe's *A Brief Introduction to the True Art of Music*,[119] which survives only in a seventeenth-century manuscript copy, Bathe's later *A Briefe Introduction to the Skill of Song*,[120] the anonymous *Pathway to Musicke*,[121] and Thomas Morley's celebrated *A Plaine and Easie Introduction to Practicall Musicke*.[122] All of them are directed at musical amateurs. They depend heavily on Continental sources for their information on mensuration, but also provide interesting details on distinctively English concepts and notational practices. Morley's book is by far the most substantial of the group. The list of authorities at the end of that book includes many of the most important Italian and German mensural theorists of the sixteenth century, but not Heyden and his followers, whose ideas had no relevance to Morley's concerns.[123] Despite Morley's wide reading, his interpretation of mensural theory is shaped more by the practices that he knew from experience than by the information that he found in his sources.

---

[119] William Bathe, *A Brief Introduction to the True Art of Music*, ed. Cecil Hill, Critical Texts 10 (Colorado Springs: Colorado College Music Press, 1979).

[120] William Bathe, *A Briefe Introduction to the Skill of Song* (London: Thomas East, [1596?]; repr. Kilkenny, Ireland: Boethius Press, c1982).

[121] Anonymous, *The Pathway to Musicke* (London: [by J. Danter] for William Barley, 1596).

[122] Thomas Morley, *A Plaine and Easie Introduction to Practicall Musicke* (London: Peter Short, 1597; repr. Westmead, Farnborough, Hants, England: Gregg International, 1971).

[123] Ibid., unnumbered final page. Morley may not actually have consulted all of the works on his list, and he certainly used some sources that he did not list, but his list is of interest in that it shows which sources he regarded as especially authoritative. Both his work and *The Pathway to Musicke* depend heavily on Lucas Lossius's *Erotemata musicae practicae* (Nuremberg: Johann Berg and Ulrich Neuber, 1563; repr. Bologna: Forni, 1980), which is in turn a summary of conventional views in earlier German textbooks, for information on mensural issues.

2 | Principles of mensural notation

Mensural notation, like modern rhythmic notation, measures notes in relation to other notes. There is no absolute standard of reference (analogous to a metronome mark) for the duration of any note. In any given performance, some time unit, called the *mensura* or *tactus*, is articulated physically or mentally for the purpose of keeping time, but it is often unclear which value should be equated with the *tactus*, and we can never be sure exactly how long that value should last. A study of mensural rhythm must therefore begin with the relative note values within a given mensuration, which are usually unambiguous.[1]

Notes and rests

Written note symbols are called "figures" in mensural theory. All figures were originally black. During the second quarter of the fifteenth century, there was a gradual shift from black to white (or "void") notation, in which the figures were outlined, but not filled in. This graphic change had no effect on the meanings of the symbols, but it altered the forms of the figures representing the shortest values. The addition of a flag to the right of a stem reduces a figure to the next smaller value. In white notation, the minim is usually reduced to the semiminim by filling in the notehead, rather than adding a flag; further levels of reduction are shown with flags.

Every figure has a corresponding rest. The breve rest, which occupies the space from one line to the next on a staff, is the source of all other rest signs. Longer rests are multiples of the breve rest, and shorter ones are divisions of it. Rests may be written anywhere on the staff.

The notes and rests used in the period under consideration are shown in Table 2.1.

---

[1] The standard English-language textbook on mensural notation is Apel, *The Notation of Polyphonic Music*. A briefer treatment of the subject is found in Richard Rastall, *The Notation of Western Music: An Introduction*, 2nd edn. (Leeds University Press, 1998), 61–117. The present chapter is not a comprehensive survey of the topic, but a summary of the concepts needed for understanding the discussions in this book.

Table 2.1 Notes and rests

	Notes Black	Notes White	Rests
Maxima	▐┐	▐┐	
Long	▐	▐	≣
Breve	■	◫	=
Semibreve	♦	◊	—
Minim	♩	↓	⌐
Semiminim	♪	♩	⌐
Fusa (chroma)	♬	♪	⌐
Semifusa		♬	⌐

Ligatures

In addition to figures representing individual notes, there are symbols called "ligatures" that represent two or more notes with a single sign. The values of notes in a ligature depend on the shape of the sign. Ligatures are descendants of chant neumes that represent more than one pitch. The rules for interpreting them appear arbitrary out of context, but they make sense in historical perspective. They are as follows (see Example 2.1):

(1) If the first note is higher in pitch than the second, it is a breve if it has a stem descending to the left and a long if it has no stem.
(2) If the first note is lower in pitch than the second, it is a breve if it has no stem and a long if it has a descending stem on the right.
(3) If the last note is higher in pitch than the penultimate, it is a long if it has a descending stem on the right and a breve if it has no stem.
(4) If the last note is lower in pitch than the penultimate, it is a long if it is square and a breve if it is oblong.
(5) If there is an ascending stem to the left of the first note, the first two notes of the ligature are semibreves. This rule overrides the four preceding ones.
(6) All other notes are breves unless they are modified in one of the following ways: (a) a descending stem on the right makes a note into a long; (b) a rectangular (rather than square) shape makes a note into a maxima. Some theorists disapproved of these modifications, but they were common in practice.

Example 2.1 Ligatures. B = breve; L = long; S = semibreve; M = maxima.

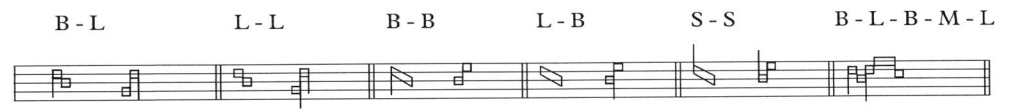

Ligatures are a notational convenience in that they save space and may be quicker to write than individual figures. They also clarify text setting, because notes in a ligature are in principle sung to a single syllable, though exceptions are possible in practice. They are of limited use for suggesting rhythmic groupings beyond those implied by the text setting, however, because they are seldom applied systematically and they often vary from one source to another.

It is customary to represent ligatures in modern editions with square brackets above the notes. That convention is observed in the musical examples in this book.

Levels of measurement

Note values are measured in relation to a set of hierarchically ordered levels of measurement. The relation of each value to the next smaller one forms one level of mensuration. The four largest levels are classified as primary in fifteenth- and sixteenth-century mensural theory. They are called major *modus* (maxima/long), minor *modus* (long/breve), *tempus* (breve/semibreve), and prolation (semibreve/minim). Smaller levels have no names.

On each of the primary levels, the larger value may be worth either two or three of the next smaller one. A level is called "perfect" if the larger value is worth three of the next smaller one and "imperfect" if it is worth two. The terms "major" and "minor" are synonymous with "perfect" and "imperfect," respectively, in reference to prolation. For example, the breve is worth three semibreves in perfect *tempus* and two semibreves in imperfect *tempus*; the semibreve is worth three minims in perfect (or major) prolation and two minims in imperfect (or minor) prolation; etc. Minims and smaller values are always imperfect.

The number of mensural levels varies from one piece to another. Most pieces have regular *tempus* and prolation, but minor *modus* is limited to relatively complex works and major *modus* is extremely rare. Both levels of *modus* went out of use after the early sixteenth century.

The four primary levels of mensuration are independent. Any combination of perfect and imperfect mensurations on different levels is possible. If only *tempus* and prolation are involved, there are four possible combinations:

(1) Perfect *tempus* with perfect prolation
(2) Perfect *tempus* with imperfect prolation
(3) Imperfect *tempus* with perfect prolation
(4) Imperfect *tempus* with imperfect prolation

Each of these mensurations may be combined with perfect or imperfect minor *modus* for a total of eight combinations of minor *modus*, *tempus*, and prolation. If major *modus* is included, the number of possible combinations is sixteen.[2]

Mensuration signs

Theorists describe many signs for different levels of mensuration, only a few of which were common in practice.[3] The standard signs for *tempus* and prolation were circles and dots. A complete circle represents perfect *tempus*, and a semicircle represents imperfect *tempus*. In fourteenth-century theory, three dots inside the circle or semicircle represent perfect prolation and two dots represent imperfect prolation. By the fifteenth century, the usual symbols were a single dot for perfect prolation and no dot for imperfect prolation. The standard fifteenth- and sixteenth-century signs for the four possible combinations of *tempus* and prolation are as follows:

---

[2] Some theorists propose systems that do not allow for all combinations of major and minor *modus*, but the complete system (as described, for example, by Tinctoris) does not limit the ways in which perfect and imperfect measurement on different levels may be combined. See Johannes Tinctoris, *Tractatus de regolari valore notarum*, in Johannes Tinctoris, *Opera theoretica*, ed. Albert Seay, 3 vols. in 2, Corpus scriptorum de musica 22 ([Rome]: American Institute of Musicology, 1975–78), I: 125–38. Apel, *The Notation of Polyphonic Music*, uses the term "maximodus" for what Renaissance theorists called "major *modus*." His term is a modern invention.

[3] See Berger, *Mensuration and Proportion Signs*, 12–32, for a historical survey of these signs.

Perfect *tempus* with perfect prolation	⊙
Perfect *tempus* with imperfect prolation	O
Imperfect *tempus* with perfect prolation	⊆
Imperfect *tempus* with imperfect prolation	C

Signs representing *modus* were never standardized, and *modus* was often unsigned even when it was present. Tinctoris recommends sets of rests preceding the sign of *tempus* and prolation: perfect or imperfect long rests for minor *modus*, and groups of three or two such rests for major *modus*.[4] This system was rare in practice. John Hothby and his followers describe a set of signs that modern scholars call *modus cum tempore* signs.[5] These signs, some of which were common in practice, represent perfect or imperfect minor *modus* with a circle or semicircle and perfect or imperfect *tempus* with a figure 3 or 2 following the circle. In theory, prolation may be shown by the presence or absence of a dot in the circle, but *modus cum tempore* signs were rarely applied to mensurations with perfect prolation in practice. Hothby extends the system to include signs with two numbers following the circle or semicircle to represent both levels of *modus*, but those signs almost never appear in practical sources. The commonly used *modus cum tempore* signs are:

Perfect *modus* with perfect *tempus*	O3
Perfect *modus* with imperfect *tempus*	O2
Imperfect *modus* with perfect *tempus*	C3
Imperfect *modus* with imperfect *tempus*	C2

These signs are ambiguous, because they could denote diminution or proportions in addition to, or instead of, *modus* and *tempus*. They are discussed in Chapters 5 and 6 below.

Mensural structure

I shall call the underlying mensural organization of a piece the *mensural structure* and the time span corresponding to a given value in that structure a *time unit* of the mensuration. Early theorists call the time unit

---

[4] Tinctoris, *Tractatus de regolari valore notarum*, chs. 7–10, 129–30.
[5] John Hothby, *De cantu figurato*, ch. 2 ("De signis et mensuris"), 28, *Sequuntur regulae cantus mensurati*, ch. 2 ("De signis et mensuris"), 21, and *Regulae cantus mensurati*, ch. 2 ("De signis et eius proportionibus"), 53–54, all in Hothby, *Opera omnia de musica mensurabili*, ed. Gilbert Reaney, Corpus scriptorum de musica 31 (Neuhausen-Stuttgart: American Institute of Musicology; Hänssler-Verlag, 1983).

38   Theory

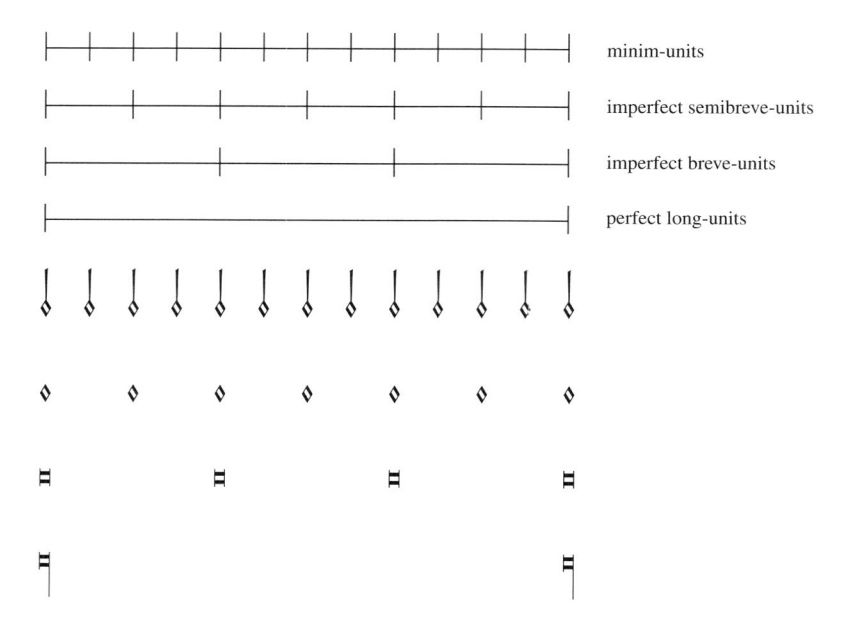

Figure 2.1 Mensural structure of perfect minor *modus*, imperfect *tempus*, and imperfect prolation.

corresponding to the breve a *tempus*, but they have no standard terms for analogous units on other mensural levels. Time units may be distinguished by the note value to which they correspond: minim-unit, semibreve-unit, etc. For example, a mensuration with perfect minor *modus*, imperfect *tempus*, and imperfect prolation has three breve-units in each long-unit, two semibreve-units in each breve-unit, and two minim-units in each semibreve-unit (see Figure 2.1). This terminology makes it possible to refer to the time units defined by the notation without specifying which unit corresponds to the *tactus* or imposing terms such as "beat" and "bar" on music for which they may not be appropriate.

I shall call the point at which a time unit begins an *initium*.[6] *Initia* correspond to the vertical strokes in Figure 2.1. Because mensural structure is hierarchical, every *initium* on one level is also an *initium* on all smaller levels. An *initium* that applies to a given level, but not to larger levels, will be qualified with the suffix "-max." For example, the beginnings of both of the first two semibreve-units in Figure 2.1 (row 2) are semibreve *initia*, but the

---

[6] This term was coined by Graeme M. Boone in "Marking Mensural Time," *Music Theory Spectrum* 22 (2000), 1–43. Boone uses the term "pulse" for what I call "time unit" and "pulse framework" for what I call "mensural structure."

Principles of mensural notation 39

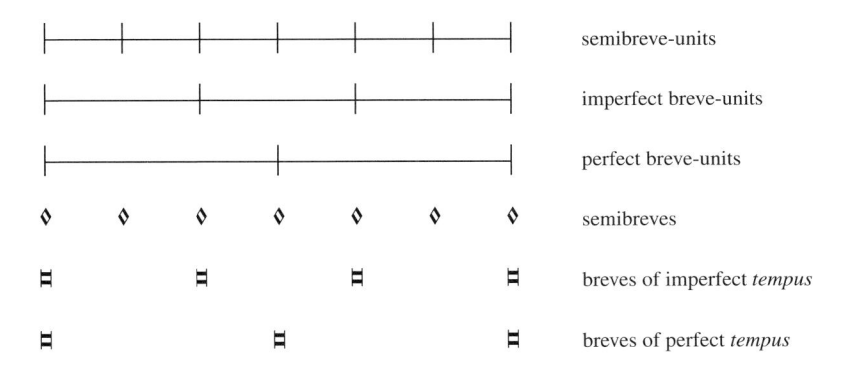

Figure 2.2 Mensural structure of combined perfect and imperfect *tempus*.

second one is a "semibreve-max *initium*," because it is not an *initium* on the level of the breve (row 3) or the long (row 4).

In complex compositions, different mensurations may be superimposed in simultaneous combinations. The *initia* of simultaneous mensurations must coincide at regular points in order for the parts to fit together, but they may be independent between these points. Figure 2.2 illustrates the structure of superimposed perfect and imperfect *tempus*. The semibreve *initia* coincide in the two mensurations, but the breve *initia* coincide only after groups of six semibreves. By implication, therefore, groups of six semibreves emerge as another level of the composite mensural structure.

Imperfection and alteration

On imperfect levels of mensuration, the note values are fixed and unalterable, but on perfect levels, they may be changed by procedures that keep notes that are normally perfect within the bounds of their own time units. *Imperfection* is the removal of a third of the value of a perfect note and the replacement of that value with one or more shorter notes. *Alteration* is the doubling of a smaller note for the purpose of aligning the following perfect (or imperfected) note with the beginning of a new time unit.

Imperfection is required in two situations unless some feature of the notation overrides it: (1) A note that is normally perfect is preceded by the next smaller note (or its equivalent in shorter values) within its time unit. (2) A note that is normally perfect begins on its own *initium* and is followed by a single note of the next smaller value or by four or more such notes (or the equivalent in shorter values). The former type of imperfection is

Example 2.2 Imperfection (a) *a parte ante* and (b) *a parte post*. Numbers represent semibreve counts.

Example 2.3 Alteration. Numbers represent semibreve counts.

Example 2.4 Imperfection (a) *ad partem* and (b) *ad partes*. Numbers represent semibreve counts.

called *a parte ante* and the latter is called *a parte post*. Example 2.2 illustrates both types of imperfection of a perfect breve in perfect *tempus*. Barlines separate the breve-units, and numbers above the notes show the lengths of the notes as measured in semibreves. Analogous principles apply to perfect prolation and perfect *modus*. No imperfection occurs if a perfect note falls on its own *initium* and is followed by another note of the same value or by two or three notes of the next smaller value or their equivalent. The prohibition of imperfection of a note that is followed by another of the same value also applies to notes that are displaced with respect to the mensural structure.

If a perfect or imperfected note is written at a point that would otherwise be the last third of a perfect time unit, the preceding note is altered (i.e., doubled in value), so that the perfect note begins on its own *initium*. For example, if a pair of semibreves followed by a breve begins on a breve *initium* in perfect *tempus*, the second semibreve is altered and the breve begins on the following breve *initium* (see Example 2.3). The altered semibreve has the same duration as an imperfected breve. It is used because of the rule that prohibits imperfection of a note before another of the same type.

If a note has the value of two or more perfect notes on smaller mensural levels, its component parts may be imperfected *a parte ante*, *a parte post*, or both. For example, a long in imperfect *modus* and perfect *tempus*, which is equivalent to two perfect breves, may be imperfected by semibreves preceding or following it, or both (see Example 2.4). This type of imperfection is

Example 2.5 Rests (a) in perfect *tempus* and (b) in imperfect *tempus*.

called *ad partem* or *ad partes*. Other complications, such as the imperfection of altered notes, are also possible, but rare.

Rests may not be imperfected or altered, but they may cause imperfection or alteration of the surrounding notes. They are notated in ways that conform to the mensural structure. For example, consecutive semibreve rests in perfect *tempus* are notated on the same line if they belong to the same breve-unit and on different lines if they belong to different breve-units. A rest equal to two semibreves in imperfect *tempus* is notated as a breve rest if both semibreves belong to the same breve-unit, but as two semibreve rests if it occupies parts of two different breve-units (see Example 2.5). Similarly, a rest equal to three breves in perfect *modus* is notated as a perfect long rest if it occupies a single long-unit, but as two rests (one equal to one breve and the other equal to two breves) if it occupies parts of two different long-units. These principles are not always strictly observed in practice, especially on mensural levels that are weakly articulated in the music, but theorists regard them as obligatory.

Dots

Dots have two functions in mensural notation: to mark regular or displaced mensural *initia* on perfect levels and to add half the value to imperfect notes. Theorists classify and name different types of dots in various ways, depending on the context in which they appear and the effect that they produce. The simplest terminology is the one in which the former type is called a *dot of division* and the latter is called a *dot of addition*.

In the vast majority of cases, dots of division mark regular mensural *initia*. Their function is to override the usual rules for imperfection and alteration. For example, if a note that is normally perfect is followed by a dot of division, it cannot be imperfected by the preceding or following notes. Conversely, if a note that is normally perfect is followed by the next smaller value and then by a dot of division, the smaller note must imperfect the perfect one regardless of what follows it (see Example 2.6). Dots of division

Example 2.6 Dots of division. Numbers represent semibreve counts.

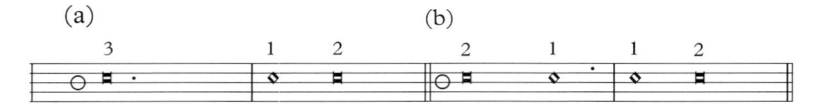

that cause imperfection are sometimes written above or below the notes, rather than next to them. That convention will be used in the examples in this book.

Dots of addition apply only to imperfect notes. They function the same way as dots in modern notation.

Syncopation

Syncopation is a technique by which notes that belong theoretically to the same time unit are separated by intervening notes. Johannes de Muris defines it as the separation of notes that belong to the same perfection. (His term "perfection" refers to what I call "time units" in both perfect and imperfect mensurations.) The technique may apply to any level of the mensuration:

Sincopa est divisio circumquaque figure per partes separatas, que numerando perfectiones ad invicem reducuntur; et potest fieri in modo, tempore et prolatione.[7]	Syncopation is the division of a figure into separate parts that are brought together in counting perfections. It may be made in *modus*, *tempus*, and prolation.

Tinctoris gives a more compact version of the same definition of syncopation in his *Diffinitorium*:

Sincopa est alicujus notae interposita majore per partes divisio.[8]	Syncopation is the division of any note into parts by an interposed larger [note].

Syncopation in these definitions applies not to individual notes, but to complete time units that are interrupted by other complete time units on the same mensural level. Sixteenth-century theorists sometimes use the term in

---

[7] Johannes de Muris, *Ars practica mensurabilis cantus*, ch. 9 ("De sincopa"), 65.
[8] Tinctoris, *Terminorum musicae diffinitorium*, s.v. "Sincopa."

Example 2.7 Syncopation in imperfect and perfect *tempus*. Numbers represent semibreve counts. Notes in boxes connected by curved lines are counted together to make complete mensural units. Each example begins on a breve *initium*.

the modern sense in which only the displaced notes are called "syncopated." Zarlino, for example, defines syncopation in the same way as Muris and Tinctoris, then applies the term to the notes that are displaced by the technique as well:

| La Sincopa adunque si fa da una figura, o nota, che le vadi avanti, la qual sia di valore della metà della figura sincopata ... [9] | Syncopation is therefore made by a figure, or note, that precedes it, which has the value of half of the syncopated note ... |

Syncopation may occur on both perfect and imperfect mensural levels, though it is much more common on imperfect levels (see Example 2.7). When it occurs on perfect levels, the isolated notes that form part of an incomplete time unit imperfect the nearest possible note, so that the *initia* realign with the mensural structure as soon as possible. In Example 2.7a, the semibreves are syncopated by the intervening breve. In Examples 2.7b and c, the first semibreve would normally imperfect the first breve *a parte ante*, but it cannot do so because that breve is followed by another breve or by a dot that prevents imperfection. It therefore imperfects the second breve in Example 2.7b, thereby realigning the notes with the mensural structure. In Example 2.7c, no imperfection occurs, because the perfect breve-unit initiated by the first note is completed by the two semibreves following the breve. The dot of division in Example 2.7c marks a displaced *initium*, rather than a regular one.

Syncopations may be nested, such that an entire syncopation on one mensural level separates notes on the next higher level. In Example 2.8, the second note of bar 27 (a minim) is counted with the second and third notes of bar 28 (two semiminims) to form a syncopation on the semibreve level. Since there is no note on the second breve *initium* (which falls on the dot after the fourth note), there is also a syncopation on the breve level: the first

---

[9] Zarlino, *Le istitutioni harmoniche*, book 3, ch. 49 ("Della sincopa"), 210.

Example 2.8 Nested syncopation. Du Fay, *Donnés l'assault*, bars 27–28: cantus. After New Haven, Yale University Library, Beinecke Rare Book and Manuscript Library, Ms. 91 ("Mellon Chansonnier"), fols. 71^v–73^r.

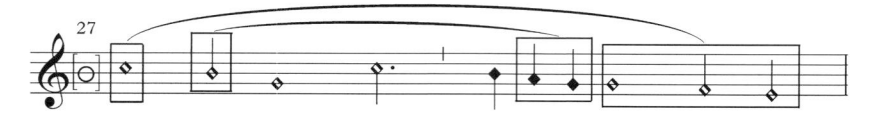

note of bar 27 (a semibreve) is counted with the last three notes of bar 28 (a semibreve and two minims) to complete the perfect breve-unit that starts with the first note of the example.

The rules of notation prohibit the syncopation of rests. Rests may fall in syncopated positions, but when they do, they must be notated as pairs of shorter rests conforming to the mensural structure, not as single long rests, as shown in Example 2.5. Zarlino explains this rule in relation to the integrity of the time units of the mensuration and warns that improperly notated rests may confuse singers and cause them to lose track of the *tactus*:

Non è però lecito, ne sta bene il sincopare le Pause ... Conciosia che si rompe la Misura, & il Tempo, che naturalmente casca sopra il principio di ciascuna, sotto i lor segni propij ... & genera anco incommodo alli Cantori, i quali confidandosi spesse volte nella loro integrità, non pensando che'l Tempo sia in loro variato, senza tenerne memoria, & conto alcuno, pongono la Battuta nel loro principio, & per tal maniera ingannati, vengono necessariamente ad errare cantando.[10]	But it is not allowed and does not work well to syncopate rests ... because this breaks the measure and time that fall naturally on the beginning of each [mensural unit] under their proper signs ... and it also creates inconvenience to the singers who, often trusting the integrity [of the rests], not thinking that the mensuration has changed without their having remembered or noticed, place the *tactus* at the beginning [of the rests], and misled in this way, come necessarily to err in singing.

Scribes and printers do not always follow this rule, but it is the norm in practical, as well as theoretical, sources.

---

[10] Ibid.

Coloration

Coloration is a technique for changing the values of notes by writing them in a different color from the surrounding notes (red or void in black notation; black in void notation). In any given context, it applies principally to one value and secondarily to other values. It usually reduces the principal value to which it applies by a third and makes all notes imperfect.[11] Its effect on other values depends on whether the principal value is perfect or imperfect. Coloration occasionally applies only to the second half of a breve or long. In that case, the note is understood to be equivalent to two of the next smaller value tied together, the first one normal and the second colored.

When coloration applies principally to a perfect note, it imperfects that note. Three colored notes or their equivalent fill the time unit that would normally be filled by two perfect notes or their equivalent. The values of shorter notes that were already imperfect in the mensuration, such as semibreves in perfect *tempus*, are unchanged in this type of coloration. The rhythms created by this coloration are called "hemiola" in modern terminology. They are illustrated in Example 2.9. A variant form of hemiola coloration appeared in the sixteenth century in response to the disappearance of the principle of alteration in practice. To avoid imperfecting a note before another note of the same written form, composers would color only the note to be imperfected and the preceding note(s) within the same perfect time unit, as in Example 2.10. From a traditional theoretical point of view, this coloration is incomplete, because the note to which the coloration principally applies (in this case the breve) should come in groups of three.

Example 2.9 Hemiola coloration. Numbers represent semibreve counts.

Example 2.10 Incomplete coloration. Numbers represent semibreve counts.

---

[11] Other interpretations of coloration that developed in the sixteenth century are discussed in Chapter 6.

Example 2.11 Syncopation caused by the separation of colored notes. Du Fay, *Quel fronte signorille*, bars 13–16: cantus. After Oxford, Bodleian Library, Ms. Canon. Misc. 213, fol. 73ʳ.

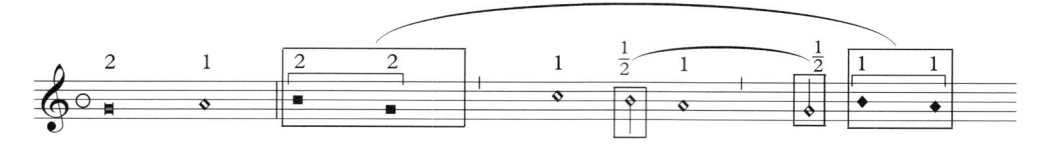

Example 2.12 Triplet coloration. Numbers represent semibreve counts.

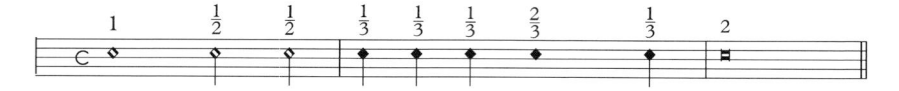

Although hemiola coloration involves a grouping of notes that conflicts with the mensural structure, it is not syncopation, because it does not involve the separation of notes that belong together in a mensural sense. It may, however, be associated with syncopation. If the notes forming a colored unit are separated, they create both syncopation and hemiola, as in Example 2.11. This example also includes a syncopation on the semibreve level that is nested within the syncopated colored unit.

When coloration applies principally to an imperfect note, as in Example 2.12, it creates triplets, rather than hemiola rhythms. When it applies to an isolated pair of unequal notes, such as a breve and semibreve or a semibreve and minim, it may be interpreted as a dotted rhythm instead of a triplet. In other words, the unequal notes may be in 3:1, rather than 2:1, relation to each other, as in Example 2.13. The total value of the colored group of notes remains the same.

This interpretation was first advocated unequivocally by Pietro Aaron in 1516[12] and was standard from then on, but it existed as an alternative to the triplet interpretation in the later fifteenth century as well. Tinctoris mentions the practice for the purpose of condemning it,[13] and Florentius de

---

[12] Aaron, *Libri tres de institutione harmonica*, book 2, ch. 18 ("De triplici brevium ac semibrevium differentia"), fol. 27ʳ.

[13] Tinctoris, *Proportionale musices*, book 1, ch. 6 ("De genere superparticulari"), 23. See Ronald Woodley, "Minor Coloration Revisited: Okeghem's *Ma bouche rit* and Beyond," in *Théorie et analyse musicales (1450–1650)*, ed. Bonnie J. Blackburn and Anne-Emmanuelle Ceulemans (Louvain-la-Neuve, Belgium: Université Catholique de Louvain, 2001), 39–63, for a discussion of this issue. Woodley quotes and discusses the passage in which Tinctoris objects to interpreting coloration as a dotted rhythm, ibid., 45–49.

Example 2.13 Coloration representing dotted rhythms. Numbers represent semibreve counts.

Faxolis, whose treatise dates from between 1485 and 1492, describes it without taking a stand on its propriety.[14] Practical sources provide further evidence for its existence in the fifteenth century. In the second half of the sixteenth century, the principle of "squaring off" ternary rhythms in this way was sometimes extended in ways that require rhythms notated as triplets to be read as duple rhythms in other contexts as well. This issue is discussed in Chapter 6.

Internal indicators of mensuration

In the early fifteenth century, many pieces lacked mensuration signs, especially in their opening sections. Signs became more common in later sources, but singers were always expected to know how to determine the mensuration of a piece on the basis of internal features of the music when signs were lacking. The internal signs that identify mensurations are rests, dots, and coloration. They are interpreted as follows:

Rests: Two rests (such as semibreve or minim rests) on the same line imply that the next larger value is perfect. If the next larger value were imperfect, a rest of that duration would be written as a single rest of the next larger value or as two rests on different lines, depending on whether its halves belonged to the same time unit or to two different time units. A perfect long rest implies perfect minor *modus*, because a rest of that length would be divided into two rests in imperfect minor *modus*.

Dots: If a dot appears after a note, but no note (or pair of notes) equal to half the value of the note follows immediately or after a few intervening notes, the dot must be a dot of division. For example, a semibreve followed by a dot of addition requires a minim (or its equivalent) to complete the semibreve-unit that begins with the dot. If no minims or an even number of minims follow a dotted semibreve, the dot must be a dot of division, and at

---

[14] Florentius de Faxolis, *Liber musices* (= *Book on Music*), ed. and trans. Bonnie J. Blackburn and Leofranc Holford-Strevens (Cambridge, MA, and London: The I Tatti Renaissance Library/Harvard University Press, 2010), book 3, ch. 11, 186.

least one level of the mensuration must be perfect. In rare cases, the note that completes the time unit corresponding to a dot of addition appears before, rather than after, the dotted note, such that, for example, a minim followed by a dotted semibreve might fill two semibreve-units.

Coloration: Groups of three colored notes of a particular value or their equivalent often imply that the colored notes belong to a perfect mensural level. This clue is not infallible, because coloration may also apply to imperfect notes, but it is often a useful guideline.

Modifications of note values

The mensural system includes a variety of signs that indicate not only mensuration, but also various modifications of note values. These modifications may affect the tempo, the durations of notes relative to other notes in the same piece, the value that is to be equated with the *tactus*, or any combination of these factors. The procedures that modify note values in these senses are called diminution, augmentation, proportions, *acceleratio mensurae*, etc. The meanings of these terms and the interpretation of the signs that represent them are problematic. They are discussed in the following chapters.

Note values may also be modified by verbal instructions called "canons." Tinctoris defines canon as "a rule that shows the wish of the composer in some obscure way."[15] Canons may prescribe systematic increases or decreases in note values, as well as notational transformations such as reading a part backward, reversing the direction of the melodic intervals, omitting the rests, etc. Although they are often cryptic, the contrapuntal relations among the voices make their solutions unambiguous once they are deciphered.

Relationships among mensurations

When different mensurations are combined, either simultaneously or successively, the issue of which note, if any, has the same duration in all of them becomes critical. In simultaneous relations, the question can always be answered empirically, because the voices fit together in only

---

[15] "Canon est regula voluntatem compositoris sub obscuritate quadam ostendens." Tinctoris, *Terminorum musicae diffinitorium*, s.v. "Canon."

Example 2.14 Minim equivalence among simultaneous mensurations. Ockeghem, *Missa prolationum*, Kyrie, bars 1–4. After Vatican City, Biblioteca Apostolica Vaticana, Ms. Chigi C VIII 234 ("Chigi Codex"), fol. lxxxxviii[v]–lxxxxviiii[r]. Numbers represent minim counts. The third note in the bass is altered because it is followed by a breve.

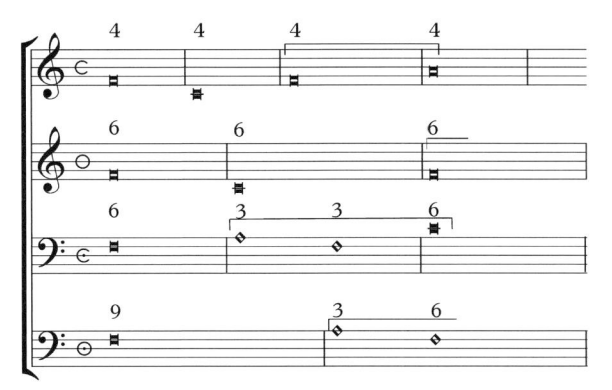

one way. In such cases, it is nearly always the minim that is identical in all simultaneous mensurations.[16] This principle is illustrated in Example 2.14. The breves are worth four minims (two imperfect semibreves) in C, six minims (three imperfect semibreves) in O, six minims (two perfect semibreves) in ₵, and nine minims (three perfect semibreves) in ☉. The semibreves in ₵ and ☉ are normally worth three minims, but the second semibreve in ☉ in the example is altered, because it is followed by a breve (not shown, but the same as the fourth note of the voice in ₵). The minims of all mensurations are equal. The breve *initia* align in all mensurations only every 36 minims (nine breves of C, six of O and ₵, and four of ☉). The example is a type of piece called a "mensuration canon," in which two or more voices are derived by reading the same written notes in two or more different mensurations simultaneously. In this case, the upper and lower pairs of voices are both mensuration canons.

When different mensurations appear successively, rather than simultaneously, it is usually impossible to be sure how they relate to each other. Any of the most common values (breves, semibreves, or minims) might keep the same duration from one mensuration to the next, or consecutive mensurations might be independent and have no common standard of measure. This issue is discussed in Chapter 7.

---

[16] Berger, *Mensuration and Proportion Signs*, 168–78, discusses exceptions to this principle in pieces from the early fifteenth century.

Mensuration and rhythm

The principles of mensural notation require those who write and read it to be aware of the mensural structure. The rules for writing and reading notes on perfect levels depend directly on the positions of notes with respect to the time units of the mensuration. Although rests cannot be altered or imperfected, their notation also depends on their location within the mensural structure. Theories of syncopation make sense only on the premise that the mensural structure is an essential component of the rhythmic design of a composition. Nevertheless, the notated mensuration is not always a reliable guide to the audible mensural structure of a piece. Although binary or ternary groupings that are regular throughout a piece rarely contradict the notation, the number of levels implied by the notation does not always match the number articulated in the music. Breves or longs may be grouped regularly with no notational indication of *modus*. Conversely, semibreves or minims may be grouped irregularly even if the notation specifies perfect or imperfect *tempus* or prolation. The number of mensural levels articulated in music may vary within a piece. The functional mensural structure of a piece depends on regularities in the audible rhythmic structure, not on the notated mensuration. The factors that determine this audible structure are discussed in Chapter 4.

Small-scale contradictions between rhythmic groupings and mensural structure, in contrast to wholesale mismatches, are ubiquitous. They give rise to two basic interpretive questions about mensural rhythm: (1) Does mensural structure imply a hierarchy of *ictus* (implicit accent) on different levels? (2) Do conflicts between rhythm and mensuration override the mensural structure, or do they create audible tension against it? Both questions have been subject to long-standing scholarly controversies and will be discussed in the following chapters.

Relations between rhythm and mensuration are complex and variable. Nevertheless, the notational system and the theoretical principles underlying it imply that mensural structure is an integral component of rhythm and that it cannot be ignored in the analysis of rhythms written in mensural notation.

3 | Definitions and descriptions of *tactus*

In order to translate the abstract values of mensural notation into actual time values in performance, one of the notes must be equated with a unit of real time and used as a standard of measure for the others. The most common terms for that value were "mensura" in the fifteenth century and "tactus" in the sixteenth century. "Mensura" is a more general term than "tactus." It sometimes has other meanings in the fifteenth century, and it often means "mensuration" (the perfect or imperfect quality of the notes), rather than "tactus," in the sixteenth century.[1] Both terms have equivalents in vernacular languages (*tatto, tacte, Takt*, tact; *mensura, mesure, Mensur*, measure). Other synonyms include *battuta* (*batue, Schlag*, beat), *compas*, and, less often, *tempus, morula, ictus, praescriptus, dimentio*, and stroke. Modern scholars generally use the term "tactus."

These terms could refer to as many as six distinct, but closely related, aspects of musical time measurement.[2] The first three are independent; the second three may be defined in relation to any of the first three:

(1) The physical motion, such as a series of taps or movements of the hand in the air, that measures time in performance. I shall call this action and the unit of time to which it corresponds the "performance *tactus*."
(2) The time unit that serves as a standard of reference for various aspects of rhythm, such as the rate of contrapuntal motion, dissonance treatment, and syncopation, in a composition. I shall call this unit the "compositional *tactus*."
(3) The time unit that functions as the theoretical standard of measure under a given sign. I shall call this unit the "theoretical *tactus*."
(4) A time unit of the mensural structure corresponding to any of the above definitions. I shall call this time unit the "*tactus*-unit."

---

[1] See Eunice M. Schroeder, "*Mensura* According to Tinctoris, in the Context of Musical Writings of the Fifteenth and Early Sixteenth Centuries" (Ph.D. diss., Stanford University, 1985), for a study of this term.
[2] Wolf Frobenius, "Tactus," in *Handwörterbuch der musikalischen Terminologie*, ed. Hans Heinrich Eggebrecht (Wiesbaden: F. Steiner, [1972–]), discusses various meanings of the term "tactus," including its application to the formulaic figures used in organ playing in the fifteenth century.

(5) The abstract quantity of time corresponding to any of the above definitions. I shall call this quantity the "value of the *tactus*."

(6) The concrete quantity of time corresponding to any of the above definitions. I shall call this quantity the "duration of the *tactus*." It is analogous to a modern metronome mark.

These different meanings of "tactus" do not always apply to the same value in a given piece. For example, a piece may have a breve theoretical *tactus* and a semibreve compositional *tactus*. In that case, the performance *tactus* might be either the breve or the semibreve, depending on the choice of the performers, and the definitions of "tactus" in relation to mensural structure, abstract note durations, and concrete note durations may be based on either value. Example 3.1 illustrates the various meanings of the term *tactus* in relation to an excerpt from the Benedictus of Josquin's *Missa L'homme armé sexti toni*. The theoretical *tactus* (no. 3) of ¢ is the breve according to most theorists of Josquin's time, but the compositional *tactus* (no. 2) of this example is the semibreve, because the counterpoint moves mostly in semibreves and dissonances are no longer than a minim. The performance *tactus* (no. 1), shown by arrows above the staff, may be either the breve or the semibreve. If *tactus*-units (no. 4) are defined on the basis of the breve *tactus*, they are the time units separated by barlines in the example. Using the same standard of reference, the value of the *tactus* (no. 5) is a breve; the value of every semibreve is therefore a half-*tactus* regardless of where it falls in relation to the *tactus*-units. The duration of the *tactus* (no. 6), indicated by arbitrary metronome marks for purposes of illustration, is MM 40 in relation to the breve *tactus* or MM 80 in relation to the semibreve *tactus*; it may vary from one performance to another without affecting the other definitions of the *tactus*.

Example 3.1 Josquin, *Missa L'homme armé sexti toni*, Benedictus, bars 11–19. After *Missae Josquin*, book 1 (Venice: Petrucci, 1502).

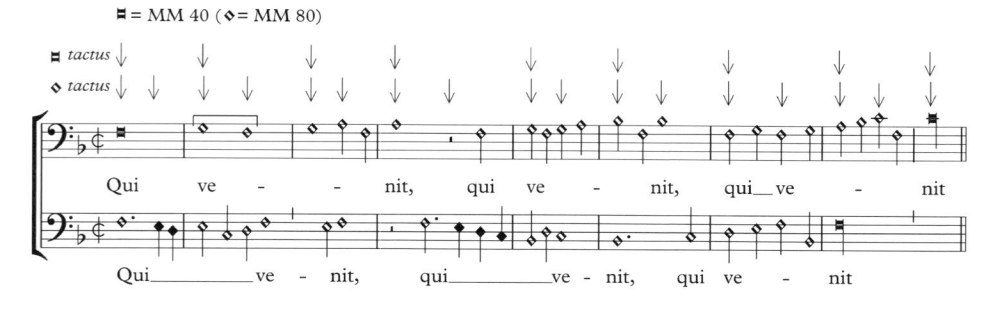

Tactus as physical motion

Information about the physical measurement of musical time is scarce before *c.* 1470, but abundant thereafter. Different descriptions of the performance *tactus* provide different types of information about the forms it could take.[3] Some fifteenth-century theorists describe it as an act of touching something with the hand or foot. Others describe it more abstractly, without specifying the physical nature of the measurement. Sixteenth-century theorists usually characterize it as a motion of the hand in the air, though some mention other options as well. This change coincides with a change in common performance practice. Groups of fifteenth-century singers most often kept time by touching each other's backs, so that the *tactus* was communicated by feel, rather than sight. Iconographic sources testify to the widespread use of this practice (see Figures 3.1–3.3).[4] Figure 3.1, which dates from the 1430s, is a detail from Luca della Robbia's *Cantoria* for the Florence Cathedral. Figure 3.2 is a detail from a sixteenth-century miniature depicting Ockeghem and other musicians singing from music on a lectern in the *Recueil de chants royaux* (Paris, Bibliothèque Nationale, fr. 1537). Figure 3.3, from the opening page of Gaffurio's *Practica musice* of 1496, shows a similar scene with a teacher and a group of boys. Singers tapping each others' shoulders are visible in all of them. Around 1500, it became common for one person to lead a group with a visible beat. The nature of the

---

[3] The most important surveys of fifteenth- and sixteenth-century writings on *tactus* are: Frobenius, "Tactus"; Georg Schünemann, "Zur Frage des Taktschlagens und der Textbehandlung in der Mensuralmusik," *Sammelbände der Internationalen Musikgesellschaft* 10 (1908–09), 73–114; Georg Schünemann, *Geschichte des Dirigierens*, Kleine Handbücher der Musikgeschichte nach Gattungen 10 (Leipzig: Breitkopf & Härtel, 1913; repr. Hildesheim: Olms, 1965), 36–68; and J[oannes] A[ntonius] Bank, *Tactus, Tempo and Notation in Mensural Music from the 13th to the 17th Century* (Amsterdam: Annie Bank, 1972), 94–257.

[4] See Schünemann, *Geschichte des Dirigierens*, 36–68, Joseph Smits van Waesberghe, "Singen und Dirigieren der mehrstimmigen Musik im Mittelalter: Was Miniaturen uns hierüber lehren," in *Mélanges offerts à René Crozet*, ed. Pierre Gallais and Yves-Jean Rion (Poitiers: Société d'études médiévales, 1966), 1345–54, and Jane Hatter, "Col tempo: Musical Time, Aging and Sexuality in 16th-Century Venetian Paintings," *Early Music* 39 (2011), 3–14. Schünemann (p. 40) interprets the raised hand of the boy in the front in Figure 3.3 as a depiction of conducting with the hand, but it seems more likely that the boy is just turning the page. The older man, clearly the master of the boys, is tapping the shoulders of the two boys in front of him. I thank Jane Hatter for suggesting this interpretation of the illustration to me.

Figure 3.1 Luca della Robbia, *Cantoria*. Florence, Museo dell'Opera del Duomo.

Figure 3.2 Recueil de chants royaux. Paris, Bibliothèque Nationale, Ms. fr. 1537, fol. 58^v.

sixteenth-century performance *tactus* was variable, however, and was undoubtedly influenced by the size of the group, the performance context, and the preference of the performers.

Three fifteenth-century sources contain descriptions of musical time measurement by means of touch. The earliest is Giorgio Anselmi's *De musica* of 1434:

Definitions and descriptions of tactus 55

Figure 3.3 Illustration from Gaffurio, *Practica musice* (Milan: Ioannes Petrus de Lomatio, 1496), fol. A1r.

Cantor neque admodum accelerans cantum vel in longam vocem protrahens pedis anteriora quatit immota calce, vel manum admovet manui aut dorso discipuli quantum potest equaliter.[5]	The singer, neither speeding up the song too much nor drawing the notes out too long, taps the front of his foot, keeping the heel still, or touches his hand to the hand or the back of the student, as equally as possible.

Anselmi calls the time unit to which this motion corresponds the *mensura*. The earliest known use of the term *tactus* for the same phenomenon appears in an anonymous manuscript dated *c.* 1450–75. The author uses the term "fingers" as a short-hand for the act of touching with the fingers: "three fingers" implies a group of three touches, and "two fingers" implies a group of two touches, each equal to a semibreve:

Duplex est tempus, scilicet perfectum et imperfectum. Perfectum est, quod continet numerum ternarium in semibrevibus et illud debet tangi tribus digitis, id est tactibus. Sed tempus imperfectum est, quod continet numerum binarium in semibrevibus et illud debet tangi duobus digitis, ut supra.[6]	*Tempus* is of two types, namely, perfect and imperfect. Perfect is that which contains the number three in semibreves, and it must be touched with three fingers, that is *tactus*. But imperfect *tempus* is that which contains the number two in semibreves, and it must be touched with two fingers, as above.

Bartolomeo Ramis de Pareja compares the measure of musical time, which he calls *mensura* or *morula*, to the pulse in his *Musica practica* of 1482 and explains how it is realized in performance:

---

[5] Anselmi, *De musica*, 171.   [6] Anonymous, [*Compendium breve artis musicae*], 74.

| Cum igitur cantor recte et commensurate cantare desiderat, instar pulsus istius pedem aut manum sive digitum tangens in aliquem locum canendo moveat.[7] | Thus when the singer wishes to sing correctly and with good measure, he should move his foot or hand or finger, touching in some place, like this pulse. |

Other theorists describe time measurement in more abstract terms. Johannes Tinctoris gives the following definition in his *Terminorum musicae diffinitorium*:

| Mensura est adaequatio vocum quantum ad pronunciationem.[8] | *Mensura* is a standard of measurement for the notes with respect to performance. |

The term "adaequatio" in this definition has no obvious English equivalent. I have translated it as "a standard of measurement," in conformity with its function, but it also implies a sense of equalizing or normalizing the measurement. Tinctoris does not explain the means by which this measurement is to be accomplished in practice, though he makes it clear that the definition applies to live music-making, and not simply to measurement in the abstract. He was more concerned with the compositional *tactus*, which he also calls "mensura," than with the performance *tactus*, which he seems to have regarded simply as a means to an end.

Adam von Fulda (1490) likewise describes *tactus* in relatively abstract terms. He associates the concept with both motion and touch, but does not describe these phenomena explicitly as physical acts:

| Tactus est continua motio in mensura contenta rationis. Tactus autem per figuras et signa in singulis musicae gradibus fieri habet; nihil enim aliud est, nisi debita et conveniens mensura, modi, temporis et prolationis, secundumque horum diminutionem et | *Tactus* is a continuous motion contained in the measure of one level of the mensuration. *Tactus* is to be made through figures and signs in the individual levels of music; for it is nothing other than a proper and suitable measure of *modus*, *tempus*, and prolation. According to the |

---

[7] Ramis de Pareja, *Musica practica*, pt. III, tr. 1, ch. 2 ("In quo signa per quae numeri distinguuntur"), 67.

[8] Tinctoris, *Terminorum musicae diffinitorium*, s.v. "Mensura."

| augmentationem figurae notarum tanguntur, cuius priorem agnitionem signa indicare habent.⁹ | diminution and augmentation of these [levels], the written notes, of which the signs are meant to give prior knowledge, are touched. |

Adam's subsequent explanation of which note is equated with the *tactus* under each sign clarifies the meaning of this quotation. The *tactus* may apply to the breve, the semibreve, or the minim, depending on the sign. The levels of *modus*, *tempus*, and prolation are defined as diminished or augmented in the sense that the number of *tactus* by which a given figure is measured varies with the sign.

Adam also gives two definitions of *tempus:* one closely related to his definition of *tactus* and the other based on the perfect or imperfect quality of the breve. The former, apart from the reference to continuous motion, is a paraphrase of the definition of *tempus* in the thirteenth-century *Ars cantus mensurabilis* of Franco of Cologne.[10]

| Tempus est mensura prolata vel omissa sub uno motu continuo; vel sic: tempus est duarum vel trium semibrevium aut valoris earum contra brevem positio ... Sed planae musicae tempus est tempus durationis eiusdem, tempus enim mensurae musicae per tactum moveri habet. De hoc Naso ait: Ipsa quoque assiduo volvuntur tempora motu.¹¹ | *Tempus* is the measure of a sounding [note] or a rest under one continuous motion, or *tempus* is the placement of two or three semibreves or their equivalent value in the time of a breve ... But the *tempus* of plainchant is the time of the same duration, for the time of the measure of music must be moved through the *tactus*. Of this Ovid says: Times themselves also revolve by continuous motion. |

In both of these quotations, Adam associates the measure of musical time with motion, though he implies that this motion is somehow contained in the music, rather than imposed on it by an external measurement. This concept of time is based on Aristotle's *Physics*. For Aristotle, time is a continuous quantity that can be known only through continuous change. Change measures time, but time also measures change. Aristotle's

---

[9] Adam von Fulda, *Musica*, pt. III, ch. 7, III: 362.
[10] Franco of Cologne, *Ars cantus mensurabilis*, ch. 1, 25.
[11] Adam von Fulda, *Musica*, pt. III, ch. 4, III: 360–61. Adam's quotation from Ovid is from *Metamorphoses*, book 15, line 27.

preferred model for the change that measures time is a change of place – i.e., a physical motion – but other types of change may serve the same function.[12] As an action that takes place in time, sounding music may be regarded as a kind of change that both measures time and is measured by time. Adam prefers this conceptual model to one that defines musical time in relation to an external physical motion. His statement that the notes "make" the *tactus*, rather than simply being measured by it, suggests this perspective. His point of view does not preclude the possibility of regulating musical time by means of an external motion, but it avoids the philosophical problem of making musical time dependent on a measure that is not part of the music itself. As a musician, Adam probably took the practice of physical time measurement for granted, but as a theorist, he preferred to approach the issue more abstractly. The quotation from Ovid with which the second passage concludes confirms the philosophical orientation of his thought.

Adam's definition of *tactus* incorporates the idea of touch, as well as continuous motion. This aspect of his explanation relates to Aristotle's concept of measuring time, as opposed to simply recognizing its existence. Although time is continuous, it can be measured only by dividing it into discrete units that are separated by points, or "nows." These points articulate time, but do not occupy time. Adam equates the process of measuring with the act of touching, both in the final sentence of the first passage above and, by implication, in the term "tactus" itself. For him, as for the anonymous author quoted previously, "touching" notes is synonymous with measuring them. The touches mark points in time, and thus make time measurable. Touch, like motion, may be understood metaphorically, rather than physically, in Adam's definition, but it is nevertheless an essential component of his concept.[13]

Later definitions often describe *tactus* as a visible motion of the hand or other object. Definitions of this type sometimes point out the reversal of direction that is an unavoidable component of this motion. One of the earliest descriptions of this type is found in Gaffurio's *Angelicum ac divinum opus musice* (1508):

Li Curiosi posteri hano ascripto la mensura de uno tempo sonoro a	Later investigators ascribed the measure of one unit of sounding

---

[12] Aristotle, *Physics*, book 4, chs. 10–13.
[13] Adam's definition of *tactus* is discussed in Boone, "Marking Mensural Time," 28–32. Boone interprets Adam's definition in purely durational terms and does not take account of the punctual aspect of time measurement that it implies.

la semibreve ... distincto in duy moti aequali de tempo ... [14]	time to the semibreve ... divided into two motions, equal in time ...

The definition of *tactus* in Andreas Ornithoparchus's *Musice active micrologus* (1517), translated by John Dowland (1609), implies this principle through the term "successive motion":

Unde Tactus est motio successiva in cantu, mensure equalitatem dirigens. Vel est quidam motus, manu praecentoris signorum indicio formatus, cantum dirigens mensuraliter.[15]	Wherefore *Tact* is a successive motion in singing, directing the equalitie of the measure: Or it is a certaine motion, made by the hand of the chiefe singer, according to the nature of the marks, which directs a Song according to Measure.

Many German theorists combine elements of Adam's and Ornithoparchus's definitions of *tactus*, interpreting Adam's "continuous motion" not as Aristotelian time, but as a motion of the conductor's hand. The first to do so was Georg Rhau, whose *Enchiridion utriusque musices practicae*, part II, appeared three years after Ornithoparchus's book:

Tactus est continua motio praecentoris manu signorum indicio, facta, Cantum dirigens mensuraliter. Habet autem fieri in singulis Musicae Gradibus, per figuras et signa, variaturque secundum signorum diversitatem, Quare nihil aliud est, quam debita et conveniens mensura, Modi, Temporis & Prolationis.[16]	*Tactus* is a continuous motion of the conductor's hand, given the indication of the signs, directing the song mensurally. It is to be made in the individual levels of music by means of figures and signs and is varied according to the variety of the signs; for it is nothing other than a proper and suitable measure of *modus*, *tempus*, and prolation.

Similar formulations appear in German school books throughout the sixteenth century.

Several sixteenth-century theorists mention the possibility of conducting with a baton, which may either touch something or simply be waved in the air. Jan Blahoslav, who studied in Wittenberg in 1544–45 when Rhau was town councillor there, describes time-keeping by touching a book, pulpit, or

---

[14] Gaffurio, *Angelicum ac divinum opus musice*, book 3, ch. 1 ("De la consyderatione et descriptione de le figure del canto mensurato"), fol. Fi^v.
[15] Ornithoparchus, *Musice active micrologus*, book 2, ch. 6 ("De tactu"), fol. Fiij^v.
[16] Rhau, *Enchiridion utriusque musicae practicae*, book 2, ch. 7 ("De tactibus"), fol. Giii^v.

other object with a baton as the normal practice for singers who are not experienced enough to do without a visual aid of that type.[17] Juan Bermudo (1555) describes the use of a baton, which he dislikes, both for touching a book and for marking time in the air. He says that he has seen choirs that were not in time with the *tactus* that was marked by the tip of the baton, but does not explain the reason for the problem clearly.[18] The baton functioned as a symbol of authority, and might also be used to guide singers, in the hands of people who led choirs singing plainchant in the Middle Ages.[19] Figure 3.4 shows a conductor leading a small choir with a baton. He stands behind the singers, like the teacher tapping the boys on the shoulder in Figure 3.3, and on a higher level. If the placement of the musicians is realistic, the baton may have tapped something audibly, since it would be difficult for the singers to see its tip. Although the conductor is clearly the leader of the group, the man in the foreground still taps the *tactus* on the shoulder of the boy next to him.[20] The painting, by Jörg Breu the Elder, is found on the small organ shutters in the Fugger chapel in the church of Santa Anna in Augsburg. It dates from the second decade of the sixteenth century. Figure 3.5 shows a man with a baton along with other symbolic representations of the art of music surrounding an image of Lady Musica in Gregor Reisch's *Margarita philosophica*.[21]

Some theorists mention that the *tactus* may be represented not only by the movement of various parts of the body (with the optional aid of a baton), but also in the mind. Stephano Vanneo explains as follows in his *Recanetum de musica aurea* of 1533:

| Haec igitur mensura … est ictus seu percussio quaedam levis, quae a musicis manu vel pede, vel quovis alio instrumento manu tento fieri solet, Et haec eadem tacite fieri | Therefore this *mensura* is a beat or a kind of light tap, which is usually made by musicians with the hand or foot or any other instrument held in the hand. And it may also |

---

[17] Jan Blahoslav, *Musica: to gest knjžka zpěwákům náležité zprávy v sobě zavírající*, 2nd edn. (Ivančice, 1569), in Thomas Paul Sovik, "Music Theorists of the Bohemian Reformation: Translation and Critique of the Treatises of Jan Blahoslav and Jan Josquin" (Ph.D. diss., Ohio State University, 1985), ch. 8 ("O taktu"), 172–73.
[18] Bermudo, *Declaración de instrumentos musicales*, book 1, ch. 19 ("De algunos avisos para los que rigen el choro"), fol. Ci^r. I thank Raül Benavides for his assistance with the translation of the passage in which Bermudo discusses conducting with a baton and for confirming my impression that Bermudo's comments on the practice are ambiguous.
[19] Elliott W. Galkin, *A History of Orchestral Conducting: In Theory and Practice* (Stuyvesant, New York: Pendragon Press, 1988), 487–89.
[20] I thank Sarah Davies for calling my attention to this image and sharing her ideas about it with me.
[21] See Manfred Hermann Schmid, "Die Darstellung der Musica im spätmittelalterlichen Bildprogram der 'Margarita philosophica' von Gregor Reisch 1503," *Hamburger Jahrbuch für Musikwissenschaft* 12 (1994), 247–61.

Figure 3.4 Jörg Breu the Elder, small organ shutters for the Fugger Chapel in the Church of Santa Anna in Augsburg.

potest id est sine ulla evidenti expressaque alicuius instrumenti percussione ... sed animo atque mente ea observanda erit.[22]

be made silently, that is, without any overt or audible striking of any instrument ... but observed in the mind.

Subdivisions and groupings of *tactus*

Theorists often describe the opposite motions that constitute the visible *tactus* as measured subdivisions. The extent to which they emphasize the two-part nature of the motion varies. Some characterize the *tactus* as a

---

[22] Vanneo, *Recanetum de musica aurea*, book 2, ch. 8 ("De tribus mensuris quibus cantum metimur"), fol. 54[r].

Figure 3.5 Illustration from Gregor Reisch, *Margarita philosophica* (Basel: Michael Futerius, 1517), fol. mvij^r.

single motion divided into two parts, while others explain it as a pair of separate motions in opposite directions. The difference between these concepts is subtle, since the relative degree of emphasis on the first and second parts of the motion may vary along a continuum, but the different ways in which theorists explain the division of the *tactus* suggest a range of possibilities for the character of its division.

No comparable information exists about methods of marking regular groups of *tactus* in performance, although singers were expected to be aware of those groups when they were part of the mensural structure. In the case of ternary groups (such as perfect breves when the *tactus* is the semibreve), that awareness is indispensable for simply reading the note values. There is no evidence that musicians marked groups of *tactus* by means of visual distinctions in the form of the *tactus*. They may have counted groups of *tactus* mentally or on their fingers, or they may have grouped the *tactus* in visible ways that theorists do not mention.

The earliest reference to a subdivision of the *tactus* appears in the context of a discussion of the analogy between *tactus* and pulse in Gaffurio's *Practica musice* (1496):

Rectam autem brevis temporis mensuram Physici aequis pulsuum motibus accomodandam esse consentiunt: Arsim & thesim quas Diastolen & Sistolen vocant in uniuscuiusque pulsus mensura aequaliter comprobantes . . . [23]	Physicians agree that an accurate measure of a short unit of time should be accommodated to the equal motions of the pulse, establishing arsis and thesis, which they call diastole and systole, equally in each measure of the pulse . . .
Neoterici postremo rectae semibrevi temporis unius mensuram ascripserunt: diastolen & sistolen uniuscuiusque semibrevis sono concludentes. Cumque Diastole & Sistole seu Arsis & Thesis quae contrariae sunt ac minimae quidem in pulsu: solius temporis mensura consyderentur: semibrevem ipsam integra temporis mensura dispositam: duas in partes aequas distinxere: quasi altera Diastoles in mensura pulsus tanquam in sono: altera Sistoles quantitatem contineat.[24]	Recent theorists finally assigned the measure of one unit of time to the regular semibreve, including diastole and systole in the sound of each semibreve. Since diastole and systole, or arsis and thesis, which are opposites and the shortest units of pulse, are contained in a single measure of time, they divided the semibreve itself, corresponding to a complete measure of time, into two equal parts, as if one contained the diastole in the measure of the pulse, as in sound, and the other the value of the systole.

Here Gaffurio does not explain how, or even whether, the *tactus* and its subdivisions relate to physical motion, but in the passage from his *Angelicum ac divinum opus musice* quoted above (pp. 58–59), he equates the halves of the *tactus* (which he calls "mensura") with up and down motions, presumably of the hand. The larger context of that passage is as follows:

Nam secundo che la mensura del pulso humano se consydera in uno tempo diviso in duy moti: cioe in uno ascendente & l'altro descendente: quali son dicti da Physici	For just as the measure of the human pulse is considered as a unit of time divided into two motions, that is, into one ascending and the other descending, which

---

[23] Gaffurio, *Practica musice*, book 2, ch. 1 ("Mensuram temporis in voce Poetae et Musici brevem et longam posuere"), fol. aai^v.
[24] Ibid., book 2, ch. 3 ("De consyderatione quinque essentialium figurarum"), fol. aaiij^r.

sistole & diastole: da Musici Arsis & thesis: cosi li Curiosi posteri hano ascripto la mensura de uno tempo sonoro a la semibreve aequale al tempo del pulso: & e distincto in duy moti aequali de tempo quali son dicati & applicati a doe minime.[25]	are called by physicians systole and diastole, by musicians arsis and thesis, in the same way later investigators ascribed the measure of one unit of sounding time to the semibreve equal to the time of the pulse and divided into two motions, equal in time, which are called and applied to two minims.

It is unclear which half of the *tactus* (downstroke or upstroke) comes first, because Gaffurio's analogies among diastole/systole, arsis/thesis, and up/down are inconsistent. In *Practica musice*, the parts of the pulse are characterized as diastole/arsis and systole/thesis, but in *Angelicum ac divinum opus musice*, they are systole/arsis/up and diastole/thesis/down. The significance, if any, of this reversal is unclear. Perhaps it demonstrates that Gaffurio was concerned only with the concept of a motion divided into two parts, not with a more specific analogy between the parts of the pulse and the parts of the *tactus*. The order in which the motions are mentioned does not necessarily mean that arsis is the first half of the *tactus*. Gioseffo Zarlino develops similar analogies between *tactus* and pulse in *Le istitutioni harmoniche* and likewise mentions systole/rising before diastole/falling, but he states explicitly that the falling motion is the first part of the *tactus*.[26] No theorist describes the upward motion unambiguously as the first part of the *tactus*, and the majority make it clear that the downward motion comes first.[27] Since a *tactus* marked in the air is a representation of the act of

---

[25] Gaffurio, *Angelicum ac divinum opus musice*, book 3, ch. 1 ("De la consyderatione et descriptione de le figure del canto mensurato"), fol. Fi^v.

[26] Zarlino, *Le istitutioni harmoniche*, book 3, ch. 48 ("Della battuta"), 207. The relevant passage is quoted on p. 79 below.

[27] Bank, *Tactus, Tempo and Notation*, 231, claims that Lanfranco, Vanneo, Angelo da Picitono, Zarlino, Salinas, Aiguino Illuminato, Zacconi, Cerretto, and Cerone place the upstroke before the downstroke of the *tactus*, but none of them does so unambiguously and some clearly place the downstroke first. Bank takes the traditional linguistic habit of mentioning arsis before thesis as evidence that theorists regarded the upstroke as the first part of the *tactus*, but this evidence is weak. Zarlino, for example, states explicitly that the downstroke is first in the passage quoted on p. 79 below. Zacconi, *Prattica di musica, seconda parte*, book 1, ch. 13 ("Della misura, & battuta, con la quale si sogliano misurare, & agiustar le figure Musicali quanto al valore"), 14, says that the note on a *tactus* begins when the motion reaches its lowest point, but this does not mean that the downstroke precedes the upstroke, as Durán makes clear in his detailed description of *tactus* quoted on pp. 65–66 below. The correspondence of the low point with the beginning of the note is a corollary of the function of the *tactus* as a symbolic tap; it applies to a modern downbeat, as well as to the sixteenth-century *tactus*.

tapping, and since touching a physical object was a common means of marking the *tactus* throughout the sixteenth century, it would be logical for the downward motion to come first even when no object was touched.

In Gaffurio's descriptions, the subdivisions of the *tactus* are subordinate to the overall unity of the motion, but some theorists reverse the priorities, defining the complete *tactus* as a pair of distinct motions. Martin Agricola (1532), for example, first defines *tactus* in terms derived from Adam and Ornithoparchus, then defines the whole *tactus* as a pair of half-*tactus*:

Das nidderschlagen und das auffheben zu hauff / macht allzeit einen Tact ... [28]	The downstroke and the upstroke together always make one *tactus* ...

Some theorists state or imply that the degree of emphasis on the subdivision of the *tactus* is related to the speed of the *tactus* or the number of notes that it measures: a slower *tactus*, or one that measures a larger number of notes, may be more distinctly divided than a faster one or one that measures fewer notes. The most detailed explanation of this principle is found in Domingo Marcos Durán's *Sumula de canto órgano* of *c.* 1504:

Compas ... Dividese en compas llano o entero. E en partido o compasejo ...	*Compas* is of two types: plain or whole [breve] *compas*, and *compasejo* or split [semibreve] *compas* ...
Item es dividido el compas llano en quatro quartas partes. La primera comiença en principio cayendo el golpe. Y simul tempore en cayendo començamos a cantar. La segunda es la meytad del tempo que ay de que da el golpe fasta el levantar dela mano y en dando el golpe: successive sine mora: començamos a cantar. La tercera comiença en levantando la mano precise: dura fasta que la tenemos alta: y començamos a cantar: simul tempore en començando a alçar la mano. La quarta es de que comiença a abaxar la mano hasta	The plain *compas* is divided into four quarters. The first begins at the beginning, with the stroke falling, and at the same time in falling we begin to sing. The second is half the time from giving the stroke to the raising of the hand and giving the [next] stroke; without delay we begin to sing. The third begins precisely with the raising of the hand; it lasts until we get to the top, and we begin to sing at the same time that we begin to raise the hand. The fourth is from when we begin to lower the hand until it falls and falls [i.e., reaches the low point]

---

[28] Agricola, *Musica figuralis deudsch*, ch. 6 ("Vom Schlag odder Tact"), fol. Giiij^r.

que cae y cae y suena el golpe. E en llegando la mano arriba simul tempore començamos a cantar y en dando el golpe precise, comiença otro compas.

Item parte se el compas [compasejo] en dos partes yguales: porque no tardamos mas de una a otra que de otra a otra.

La primera comiença en dando el golpe simul tempore y dura hasta ya que queremos alçar la mano. La segunda comiença en començando a alçar la mano: simul tempore, y dura hasta que da el golpe. Y en dando simul tempore, comiença otro compas. Y assi successivamente procede el canto por sus compasses hasta el cabo.[29]

and the downstroke sounds. And we begin to sing at the same time that the hand starts falling. And precisely when giving the stroke another *compas* begins.

The *compas* [*compasejo*] is divided into two equal parts, because we do not take more time from one [part] to the next than from the next to the next.

The first begins at the same time as giving the stroke and lasts until we are to raise the hand. The second begins at the same time that we begin to raise the hand and lasts until the [next] stroke. And at the same time that the stroke is given, another *compas* begins, and the song proceeds thus successively through its *compasses* until the end.

Durán describes two types of motion corresponding to the *compas*: one divided into four parts (each equal to a minim) and the other into two. Although he does not explicitly equate the second type with the *compasejo*, which measures half as many notes as the whole *compas*, that association is implied by the structure of his discussion. Both resemble a modern conductor's duple-time beat in that the beat begins at the low point, the hand is still on the first half of the *compas*, and the upstroke also begins at the low point. This type of motion creates a distinct articulation on each half of the unit.[30]

---

[29] Durán, *Sumula de canto órgano*, ch. 19 ("Del compas que es: y de su division"), fols. aviii^v–b^r. Durán defines the whole *compas* as four minims and the *compasejo* as two minims. He says that performers may use whichever they choose as long as the *compasejo* is twice as fast as the whole *compas*; the durations of the notes are therefore the same under both of them.

[30] Carl Dahlhaus maintains that stops between motions give the beat an accentual quality and that stopped beats were standard in the seventeenth century, but not earlier. He cites Francesco Piovesana's *Misure harmoniche regolate* (Venice: Gardano, 1627) in "Die Tactus- und Proportionenlehre des 15. bis 17. Jahrhunderts," 360–61, to support that position. This type of beat was not new in the seventeenth century, however. Durán's four-part beat is essentially the same as Piovesana's. Zarlino's also describes a four-part beat consisting of two motions and two stops (see below).

Ornithoparchus likewise implies that a *tactus* that measures more notes is more distinctly divided than one that measures fewer notes. He describes the larger *tactus* (Durán's whole *compas*) as a measure that is made by "a slow, and in a sense reciprocal [i.e., divided], motion" ("mensura, tardo ac motu quasi reciproco facta"), but says nothing about the division of the smaller *tactus* (Durán's *compasejo*).[31] This may imply that the smaller *tactus* does not have pronounced subdivisions.

Agostino Pisa describes a performance *tactus* that is in effect an upside-down version of the standard *tactus* in his *Battuta della musica* (1611): the high point of the motion is the beginning of the *tactus* and the low point is the middle. This form of *tactus* is speculative, rather than practical. Pisa's intention was to reform, not describe, the common understanding of *tactus*, though he cites earlier sources that he believes offer support for his point of view.[32] Ludovico Zacconi was impressed with the erudition of Pisa's arguments, but not with his conclusions. He distinguishes the practical musician, for whom the *tactus* begins at the low point, from the speculative musician, for whom it begins at the high point, and refers his readers to Pisa's treatise for a learned discussion of the latter point of view.[33]

Theorists from *c.* 1500 onward distinguish a "proportionate" *tactus*, which usually applies to a note with ternary subdivision, from the other forms of *tactus*.[34] The first source to describe a distinct type of subdivision for the proportionate *tactus* is Agricola's *Musica figuralis deudsch* (1532). Agricola and many later theorists divide the *tactus* unequally when it applies to a ternary note, placing ⅔ of the time on the downstroke and ⅓ on the upstroke:

Der Proporcien Tact. Ist / welcher drey Semibre. als in Tripla / odder drey Minimas als inn Prolatione	The proportionate *tactus* is that which comprises three semibreves, as in *tripla*, or three minims, as in

---

[31] Ornithoparchus, *Musice active micrologus*, book 2, ch. 6 ("De tactu"), fol. Fiij^v.

[32] Pisa, *Battuta della musica*, ch. 2 ("Che cosa significhi questa parola POSITIONE nella battuta"), 50–63, and *passim*. Pisa, who was not a professional musician, lists fifty-two common conceptions about the subject that he regards as incorrect, ibid., ch. 11 ("Catalogo dell'errori reprobati in questa dichiaratione"), 132–36.

[33] Zacconi, *Prattica di musica, seconda parte*, book 1, ch. 13 ("Della misura, & battuta, con la quale si sogliano misurare, & agiustar le figure Musicali quanto al valore"), 14.

[34] The earliest reference to the proportionate *tactus* is in Wollick, *Enchiridion musices*, book 5, ch. 6 ("De notularum partibus tractu et valore"), fol. Gv^v. Wollick applies it to triple and *sesquialtera* proportions when they are combined with other mensurations, as well as when they appear in all voices. He says nothing about the subdivision of any of the types of *tactus* that he discusses. Some theorists, such as Listenius, *Musica*, part II, ch. 10 ("De tactu"), fols. e5^r–e5^v (in the 1549 edn.), apply the concept of proportionate *tactus* to all proportions, not only those with ternary subdivisions.

perfecta / begreiftt. Von diesem Tact sihe an ... volgends Exempel.[35]	perfect prolation. Regarding this *tactus*, see ... the following example.

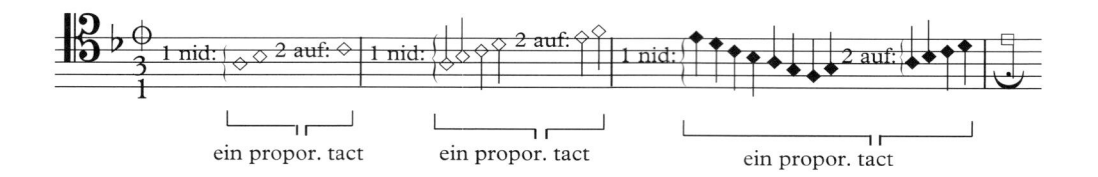

[musical notation example with "1 nid:", "2 auf:" markings and "ein propor. tact" brackets]

Sebald Heyden and his followers object to the unequally divided *tactus*, but confirm through their complaints that it was universally practiced.[36]

There is a logical correlation between marking the *tactus* with the hand and conceiving it as a divided motion.[37] A tap is in principle a unitary marker of time, but a motion of the hand must return to its initial position in order to be repeated. There are, however, exceptions to this correlation. Tomás de Sancta Maria devotes much attention to the subdivision of the *tactus*, but advises keyboard players to mark it with their feet, since their hands are not available for that purpose while they are playing:

Damos por consejo a los nuevos tañedores, que la principal cuenta tengan con el medio compas ... porque por experiencia vemos que todos los que no tañen a compas, peccan en el medio compas ... y especialmente para los nuevos tañedores es muy importante y necessario llevar el compas y el medio	We advise new players to give the main attention to the half-*tactus*, because we see from experience that all of those who do not play with good measure make mistakes on the half-*tactus* ... and especially for new players it is very important and necessary to mark the *tactus* and the half-*tactus* with the foot,

---

[35] Agricola, *Musica figuralis deudsch*, ch. 6 ("Vom Schlag odder Tact"), fol. Giiij[v].
[36] Heyden, *De arte canendi*, book 1, ch. 5 ("De tactu"), 41, and book 2, ch. 7 ("De unica Tactuum aequabilitate, in quantumlibet diversis cantuum speciebus servanda: Deque mutua variorum Signorum resolutione"), 110.
[37] This point is discussed in Alexander Blachly, "*Mensura* versus *Tactus*," in *Quellen und Studien zur Musiktheorie des Mittelalters* 3, ed. Michael Bernhard, Veröffentlichungen der Musikhistorischen Kommission 15 (Munich: Bayerische Akademie der Wissenschaften, 2001), 445.

| compas con el pie, pues que tañendo no se puede llevar la mano.[38] | because one cannot raise the hand while playing.. |

Conversely, many theorists describe the *tactus* as a motion of the hand, but say nothing about its subdivision. Zacconi describes a *tactus* made by the hand that has the form of an undivided, tap-like motion in his *Prattica di musica* of 1592. Although he disapproves of such a *tactus*, his complaint demonstrates that it existed in practice:

| Hò veduto anco questo di più nel batter cosi presto: che gl'atti d'uno intervallo e l'altro ... non essendo equali, sono alterati di brutta, e mostruosa alteratione, essendo sempre più tempo nella levata, che nella caduta, e pare apunto che quel tale che batte, nel calar della mano, tocchi sempre cose, che lo punghino, ò scottino.[39] | I have also seen this in such fast beating: the motions from one interval to the next, ... not being equal, are altered in an ugly and monstrous way, there being always more time on the upstroke than on the downstroke, and it seems that in lowering his hand, the person who is beating always touches things that sting or shock him. |

It is noteworthy that Zacconi associates this beat that lacks measured subdivisions with a fast tempo. His observation agrees with hints in the writings of other theorists that the degree of emphasis on the subdivision of the *tactus* is related to the speed of its motion.

The picture that emerges from these descriptions is that the subdivisions of the *tactus* could range from non-existent to equal in weight with the whole *tactus*. Thus, for example, a semibreve *tactus* could articulate semibreves without marked subdivision, divided semibreves with the semibreve *initia* are more strongly marked than the minim-max *initia*, or minims of equal weight. In the same way, a breve *tactus* could articulate breves without marked subdivision, divided breves with the breve *initia* more strongly marked than the semibreve-max *initia*, or semibreves of equal weight. These possibilities are represented schematically for imperfect *tempus* in Figure 3.6. The direction of the arrowheads represents the direction of motion of the hand. Arrowheads with stems represent motions with greater emphasis than arrowheads without stems. Motions

---

[38] Sancta Maria, *Arte de tañer fantasia*, "Del compas" (unnumbered chapter between ch. 5 and ch. 6), fol. 8ᵛ.
[39] Zacconi, *Prattica di musica, seconda parte*, book 1, ch. 65 ("Della concertatione della Musica, e sua soministratione"), 56.

(a) semibreve *tactus*

↓ ↑ ↓ ↑ ↓ ↑ ↓ ↑								Divided; subdivisions of equal weight
↓ ˆ ↓ ˆ ↓ ˆ ↓ ˆ								Divided; subdivisions of unequal weight
↓ ↓ ↓ ↓								Undivided

(b) breve *tactus*

↓ ↑ ↓ ↑				Divided; subdivisions of equal weight
↓ ˆ ↓ ˆ				Divided; subdivisions of unequal weight
↓ ↓				Undivided

𝄎   ◊   ◊

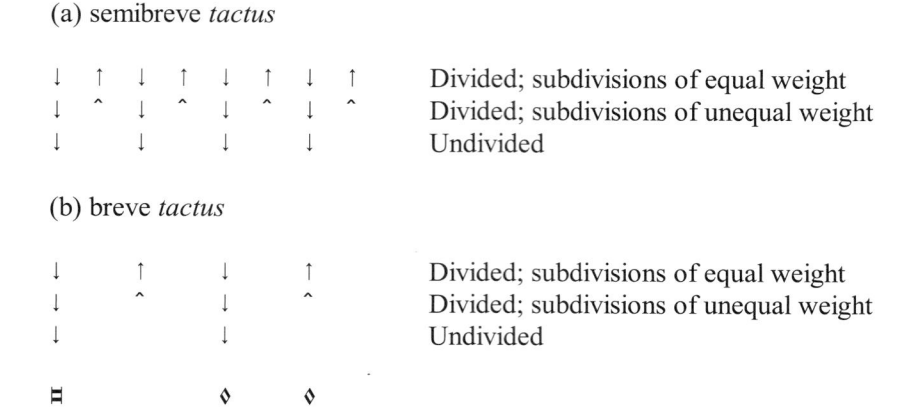

Figure 3.6 Subdivisions of a binary *tactus*.

that return the hand to the starting position without emphasis are unmarked.

Each of the basic categories of *tactus* in Figure 3.6 (semibreve and breve) may represent a wide range of temporal structures. The differences between the two categories may be less pronounced than the differences among subtypes within each category. For example, the undivided semibreve *tactus* is similar in effect to the divided breve *tactus* with subdivisions of equal weight; both articulate semibreves, the former with a series of downstrokes and the latter with alternating down- and upstrokes. The main difference between them is that the reversal of the direction on the second semibreve of the breve *tactus* facilitates singers' awareness of the mensural pairing of semibreves.

There is no evidence that singers changed the level of the *tactus* within a piece or section under a single sign, though they may have done so on occasion. It is more likely that they varied the articulation of the subdivisions of the *tactus* to adapt the physical motion to changing musical rhythms. Theorists do not discuss such performance subtleties, but the fact that both the physical *tactus* and the time unit to which it corresponds in a composition may be subdivided to various degrees suggests the possibility of matching the division of the *tactus* to the musical rhythms to facilitate performance. The opening of Orazio Vecchi's *Il bianco e dolce cigno* (Example 3.2) provides an extreme example, in which the music switches suddenly from undivided semibreves to equally stressed minims for humorous effect. The two rhythms represent old-fashioned and modern musical styles, the former associated with Arcadelt's classic madrigal that

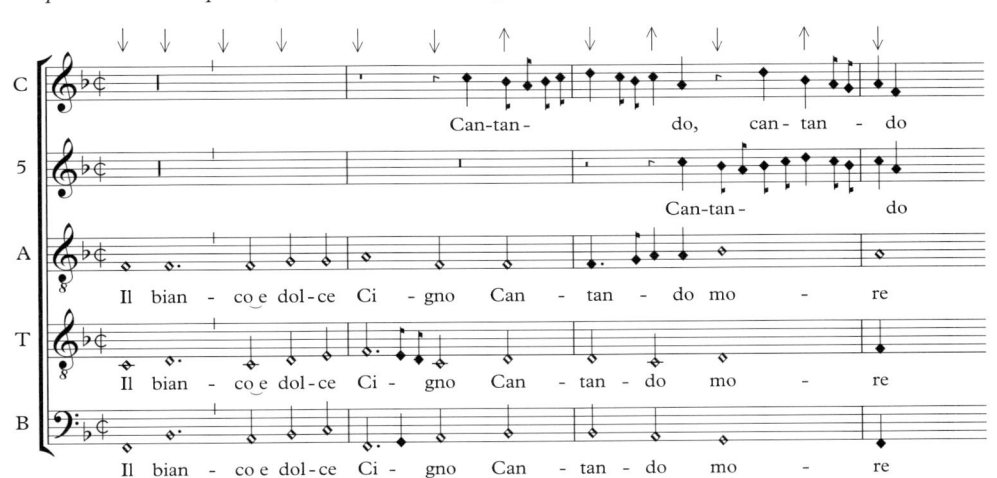

Example 3.2 Orazio Vecchi, *Il bianco e dolce cigno*, bars 1–5. After Vecchi, *Madrigali a cinque voci . . . libro primo* (Venice: Gardano, 1589).

Vecchi quotes in the opening bars (an octave lower than the original, for added absurdity) and the latter with Vecchi's amusing musical commentary on it. The rhythm is tricky, but it can be managed with a steady semibreve *tactus* if the singers begin marking the subdivision at the point where the upper voices enter. Pronounced subdivision of the *tactus* in the preceding bars would destroy the elegance of the opening rhythmic gesture. If singers mark the *tactus* in the mind, rather than with a physical gesture shared by all voices, the lower voices would continue with the undivided semibreve *tactus* while the upper pair marks the minim subdivisions.

There is less overlap between the types of temporal marking represented by the semibreve and breve *tactus* in perfect *tempus* than in imperfect *tempus*, because the divided perfect breve *tactus* does not mark all semibreves equally. In an unequally divided breve *tactus*, only two of the three semibreves are articulated at all, and the downstroke is inevitably emphasized more strongly than the upstroke because of its greater length. Some theorists advocate an equally divided, imperfect breve *tactus* for perfect *tempus* under certain circumstances. It articulates all semibreves equally, to the point that alternate breve *initia* correspond to upstrokes, rather than downstrokes. It is an awkward measure, because singers must count the ternary groups of semibreves in conflict with the *tactus* in order to apply the rules of perfection, imperfection, and alteration that perfect *tempus* requires, but it is sometimes necessary when perfect *tempus* in one voice is combined with a different

(a) semibreve *tactus*

↓ ↑ ↓ ↑ ↓ ↑ ↓ ↑ ↓ ↑ ↓ ↑   Divided; subdivisions of equal weight
↓ ˆ ↓ ˆ ↓ ˆ ↓ ˆ ↓ ˆ ↓ ˆ   Divided; subdivisions of unequal weight
↓   ↓   ↓   ↓   ↓   ↓   Undivided

(b) perfect breve *tactus*

↓   ˆ   ↓   ˆ   Divided; subdivisions of unequal weight
↓   ↓   Undivided

(c) imperfect breve *tactus*

↓   ↑   ↓   ↑   ↓   ↑   Divided; subdivisions of equal weight

▬   ◊   ◊   ◊

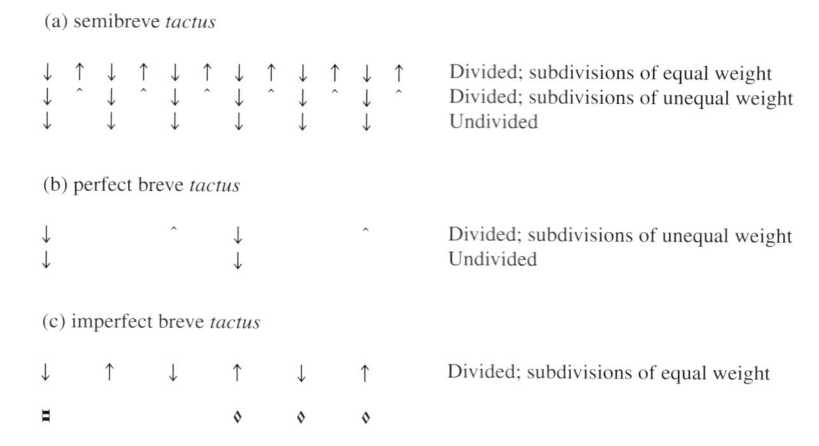

Figure 3.7 Subdivisions of a ternary *tactus*.

mensuration in another voice.[40] It was probably never common when all voices are in perfect *tempus*. Different forms of semibreve and breve *tactus* in perfect *tempus* are represented schematically in Figure 3.7.

The quality of the *tactus*

Two aspects of the quality of the *tactus* have been subject to long-standing scholarly debates: whether the *tactus* is a punctual or a durational marker and whether or not it is associated with an accent, or *ictus*, not in the sense of dynamic stress, but in the more general sense of metric emphasis.[41] These questions are often regarded as synonymous in that punctual marking is equated with *ictus* and durational marking with the absence of *ictus*, but this equation is an oversimplification. The time associated with *ictus* always has real duration; a moment that occupies no time cannot carry *ictus*, though we might imagine a punctual marker, such as a drum beat, as occupying no time. It is also possible for a complete, measured duration to carry *ictus* in relation to another measured duration; we might feel, for example, that the

---

[40] Tinctoris, for example, requires this *tactus* for duple proportion of perfect *tempus* in *Liber de arte contrapuncti*, book 2, ch. 25 ("Quomodo discordantiae circa partes notarum cantus mensuram dirigentium in proportione binaria constitutarum et per naturam quantitatis cui subiiciuntur perfectarum admittendae sint"), 128.

[41] Both of these issues are discussed in Boone, "Marking Mensural Time."

ictus associated with a suspension applies to the full duration of the dissonance, not only to its beginning.

Another issue is whether the quality of *ictus*, if it exists, applies to the performance *tactus* or the compositional *tactus* – i.e., whether it is inherent in the music or represented by the nature of the motion that measures the music. Although these questions are logically related, they are distinct and not necessarily identical. It is possible that *ictus* in the performance *tactus* might serve only to help performers place the notes in the correct places, but not imply any audible emphasis on the notes to which it corresponds. Conversely, the performance *tactus* might lack an *ictic* quality, but the music might generate its own sense of *ictus* through the placement of dissonances, cadences, etc.

The distinction between punctual and durational concepts of time is a matter of degree, not absolute opposition. Aristotle's view that time is a continuous quantity that can be measured only in discrete units separated by punctual markers is not simply an abstract concept, but a description of the way time is experienced in reality. Theoretical descriptions of *tactus* vary in the extent to which they emphasize one or the other of these perspectives, but both must be present, at least implicitly, for the concept of time measurement to make any sense. Definitions that equate *tactus* with touching or tapping emphasize the punctual aspect of measurement. Adam von Fulda's popular definition of *tactus* as continuous motion emphasizes the durational aspect, but also incorporates punctual divisions of continuous time, as discussed above.

Theorists who discuss the *ictic* character of the *tactus* favor a distinct, but light, articulation. Vanneo, for example characterizes the *tactus* as "a kind of light tap" ("percussio quaedam levis") in the passage quoted above. Sancta Maria insists on the necessity of a tap-like articulation for both the downstroke and the upstroke of the *tactus*, whether or not the motion involves tapping an object physically:

Y aunque el golpe que hiere en alto, no tenga en que topar, como el que hiere en baxo, pero con todo esso se ha de herir como si en alguna cosa topasse, como muchas vezes vemos llevarse el compas en vago sin topar la mano en baxo nì en alto, y con todo esso herir con la	And although the stroke that is beaten upward has nothing to touch, as the one that is beaten downward does, nevertheless with all of them one must beat as if something were touched; we often see the *compas* given abstractly, without touching the hand against

mano como si topasse en baxo y en alto.[42]

anything at the bottom or the top, and all of these beats with the hand are as if there were a touch at the bottom and the top.

He characterizes this articulation as a light emphasis, which is to be made equally on the downstroke and the upstroke:

Cada golpe assì baxo como alto, se hiera un poco rezio con impetu, y de mas desto, ambos a dos se hieran con ygualdad, esto es que no se hiera mas rezio el golpe baxo que el alto, nì el alto que el baxo.[43]

Every *tactus*, both the downstroke and the upstroke, is beaten with a slight force; and furthermore, both must be beaten equally, that is, one should not beat the downstroke with more force than the upstroke or the upstroke with more than the downstroke.

Sancta Maria's insistence on the equal weight of the two parts of the *tactus* does not invalidate the points made previously about the range of possible degrees of emphasis on the upstroke. His *tactus* is one type, but not the only one, that was practiced.

Zacconi discusses the relation between the quality of the *tactus* and the various terms by which it is known. His discussion points out all of the essential concepts associated with *tactus:* duration, measurement, and physical articulation. He prefers the term "tatto" to "battuta" because it captures the appropriate lightness of the articulation:

Però si ha da sapere che l'attione, ò l'atto che si fa, à far che le dette figure s'informino di suono & prendino il lor dovere, alle volte si chiama tempo, alle volte misura, alle volte battuta et alle volte tatto ... Quelli che lo chiamano tempo, lo chiamano per cagione ch'egli ha convenienza & similitudine col tempo dell'Orologgio; che

It should be known that the action that is made so that the said figures may be realized in sound & take their due [time] is sometimes called *tempo*, sometimes *misura*, sometimes *battuta*, and sometimes *tatto* ... Those who call it *tempo* do so because it has a relation and similarity to clock time; just as that time, as it moves, gives us distinct

---

[42] Sancta Maria, *Arte de tañer fantasia*, "Del compas" (unnumbered chapter between ch. 5 and ch. 6), fol. 8^r.
[43] Ibid., fol. 8^v.

si come quel tempo mentre che si muove, ci da distinta & chiara cognitione delle hore: cosi ancora considerano che per quel atto veniamo à godere & a fruire le harmoniose modulatione & concenti ... Quelli che lo chiamano misura fondano le raggioni nel valor delle figure che per quella attione vengano misurate. Gli altri similmente che lo chiamano battuta pigliano occasione di chiamarlo cosi dalla percussione ò atto percossibile che battendo si suol mostrare; che ciò sia il vero vediamo chiaramente che quest'atto non è altro che moto che contiene in se una levata & una cadduta: & perche nel levare & cadere par che ci entri un atto di battere per questo lo chiamano battuta. Quelli ultimamente che lo chiamano tatto, considerano che con altro meglio nome il non si può chiamare; per rispetto che il battere ricerca un atto forzato & vehemente, & questa attione non essendo ne vehemente ne forzata gli pare che meglio sia di chiamarlo tatto da quel moto che in se ritiene simile a un tatto gentile.[44]

and clear knowledge of the hours, in the same way they consider that through that action we come to enjoy and realize the harmonious changes and musical sounds ... Those who call it *misura* base their reasoning on the value of the figures that are measured by that action. Similarly, the others who call it *battuta* take the opportunity to name it in this way from the beating or beat-like act that is shown in beating. That this is true we see clearly, because this action is nothing other than a motion that contains in itself a rise and a fall; and since in rising and falling it appears that one undertakes an act of beating, for this reason they call it *battuta*. Finally, those who call it *tatto* consider that it cannot be called better by any other name, in the sense that beating calls for a forceful and vehement act, and this action, being neither vehement nor forceful, they feel it is better to call *tatto*, since the motion has a character similar to a gentle touch.

Some theorists, including Joachim Burmeister, point out the importance of making the physical motions that mark the *tactus* small and discreet:

In vitium cadit quando Cantor inter mensurandum vel manus vel brachij gesticulationem vel

The singer does badly in measuring when he displays a gesticulation or position of either his hand or his

---

[44] Zacconi, *Prattica di musica*, book 1, ch. 32 ("Che cosa sia misura, tatto, & battuta"), fol. 20^v.

compositionem ad athletarum vices exhibet. Quò modestior fuerit motus, eo ornatior & gratiorem aspectum merebitur.⁴⁵

arm like that of athletes. The more modest the motion is, the more elegant it is, and the more pleasing an appearance the singer will achieve.

Judging by the observations of some writers, however, performers did not always follow the advice of theorists to make the *tactus* light and modest. Bermudo complains about conductors who beat the book with a baton or clap their hands audibly in church.⁴⁶ Venceslaus Philomathes provides an amusing litany of undesirable conducting practices: beating forcefully with both hands, stamping the feet, and bobbing the head like a swan:

Sunt quibus est usus moderari turpibus odas
Gestibus, egregios mores se scire putantes,
Atque exquisitam cantorum conditionem
Mensuram quidam palmis moderantur utrisque
Eminus expaßis, veluti cum in lite duorum
Alter in alterius nequit insultare capillos
Unguibus, extensa loetale minatur inermi
Certamen duplici palma. Multos quoque vidi
Mensuram pede signantes calcante, caballus
Ut satur in viridi ludendo cespitat herba
Luxuriatque salax. Plerique imitantur holorem

There are those whose habit it is to lead songs with unsightly gestures, thinking that they know distinguished customs and a special manner of the singers. Some mark the *tactus* with both palms widely spaced, as if in the quarrel of the two of them one could not attack the other's hair with his nails, and the extended palm threatens lethal battle to its unarmed double. I have also seen many marking the *tactus* with a stamping foot, like a sated pack-horse who, playing in the green, stumbles in the grass and lustfully runs riot. Some imitate a swan when leading music; just as he sings with a bent neck, they stoop over while singing.

---

⁴⁵ Joachim Burmeister, *Musica autoschediastike* (Rostock: Christoph Reusner, 1601), Accessio III, section II, "De antiphonis," fol. Aa4ʳ.
⁴⁶ Bermudo, *Declaración de instrumentos musicales*, book 1, ch. 19 ("De algunos avisos para los que rigen el choro"), fol. Cijʳ.

Neuma gubernantes, velut hic cervice reflexa
Drensat, ita soliti conquiniscunt modulando.[47]

Theorists sometimes draw analogies between *tactus* and other repetitive motions or sounds. These analogies may shed light on the quality that they associated with *tactus*, though they must be interpreted cautiously. One common analogy was with the striking of the hours on mechanical clocks. Several theorists advise beginning students to practice measuring notes of different values in relation to the steady striking of a clock. The first to do so was Hans Gerle, in a 1532 book about lute playing.[48] Hermann Finck explains this pedagogical method in detail. He advises the student to practice counting in time with the clock in order to learn how to place one, two, three, or four syllables on each stroke. A single syllable (such as "eins") is spoken like a semibreve, two syllables (such as "viere") like two minims, three syllables (such as "sechzehen") like a minim plus two semiminims, and four syllables (such as "siebenzehen") like four minims.[49] Instructions like this, which apply only to the training of beginners, tell us little about the understanding of *tactus* on a more sophisticated level, but they demonstrate that the punctual aspect of time measurement was important on a basic, practical level. Some theorists, including Othmar Luscinius (1536)[50] and Claude Martin (1550),[51] compare the *tactus* to the striking of a clock in the context of a general explanation of the concept, rather than for specific training purposes like Gerle's and Finck's.

Theorists with a humanistic orientation often compare the *tactus* to the human pulse. The earliest such analogy, which appears in Ramis de Pareja's *Musica practica*, is brief and undeveloped. Ramis equates the *tactus* with the time from the diastole to the systole of the pulse:

---

[47] Philomathes, *Musicorum libri quattuor*, book 3, ch. 1 ("De regimine plani cantus"), fol. Eiiij[r]. The translation of the sentence on foot stamping is based on Boone, "Marking Mensural Time," 43, n. 92.

[48] Hans Gerle, *Musica teusch auf die Instrument* (Nuremberg: Jeronimus Formschneider, 1532), "Ein Prob wie du die Mensur solt lernen," fols. Biii[v]–Biiij[r].

[49] Finck, *Practica musica*, book 2, "De tactu," fols. Fij[v]–Fiij[r]. Finck's claim to have invented this method is not convincing, since Gerle makes the same point more than twenty years earlier.

[50] Luscinius, *Musurgia seu praxis musicae*, Comm. I, ch. 9 ("De his, quae potissimum ad praxim conducere videntur"), 83.

[51] Martin, *Elementorum musices practicae*, book 2, ch. 5 ("De tactu sive cantandi mensura"), 27.

| Mensura enim, ut diximus, est illud tempus sive intervallum inter diastolen et systolen corporis eucraton comprehensum. De cuius inaequali alteratione insurgunt inaequales musicae proportiones.[52] | Mensura therefore, as we said, is that time or interval contained between the diastole and the systole of a healthy body. From its unequal alternations arise the unequal proportions of music. |

Gaffurio develops the analogy between *tactus* (or *mensura*) and pulse more fully in the passages from his *Practica musice* and *Angelicum ac divinum opus musice* quoted above. For him, the *tactus* corresponds to the complete pulse and its halves to the diastole and systole. Later theorists follow his approach.[53]

Analogies between *tactus* and pulse may suggest something about the character of the *tactus*, though their interpretation is not straightforward. Pulse, like *tactus*, may be understood in both a punctual and a durational sense. The analogy between them does not privilege either perspective. Pulse has some degree of *ictic* quality, but the importance of that quality to theorists is unclear. Gaffurio does not mention *ictus* as such, though his equation of diastole with downstroke and systole with upstroke in the *Angelicum ac divinum opus musice* may imply some sense of greater stress on the former, especially considering that he was forced to reverse the parallels between diastole/systole and arsis/thesis proposed in the *Practica musice* to make this equation work in relation to upward and downward motions of the hand. Zarlino's parallels between the parts of the pulse and the parts of the *tactus* are the same as Gaffurio's. His translation of systole as "tightening" ("ristrengimento") and diastole as "broadening" ("allargamento") may convey a stronger sense of differentiation between the parts of the *tactus* than Gaffurio's description. His addition of still parts between the motions of both the pulse and the *tactus* also suggests a stronger articulation than a simple alternation of direction of motion might imply:

---

[52] Ramis de Pareja, *Musica practica*, pt. III, tr. 1, ch. 2 ("In quo signa per quae numeri distinguuntur"), 67.

[53] On analogies between music and pulse, see Dale Bonge, "Gaffurius on Pulse and Tempo: A Reinterpretation," *Musica disciplina* 36 (1982), 167–74; Bonnie J. Blackburn, "Leonardo and Gaffurio on Harmony and the Pulse of Music," in *Essays on Music and Culture in Honor of Herbert Kellman*, ed. Barbara Haggh, "Épitome musical" 8 (Paris: Minerve, 2001), 128–49; and Nancy C. Siraisi, "The Music of Pulse in the Writings of Italian Academic Physicians (Fourteenth and Fifteenth Centuries)," *Speculum* 50 (1975), 689–710.

Percioche se noi consideraremo le qualità, che si ritrovano in l'uno et l'altro; cioè nella Battuta; et nel Polso, che da i Greci è detto σφυγμός, ritrovaremo tra loro molte convenienze: conciosiache essendo il Polso ... un certo allargamento et ristrengimento; o pur vogliamo dire alzamento, et abbassamento del cuore, et delle arterie, viene ad esser composto ... di due movimenti, et di due quiete, delle quali cose similmente la Battuta viene ad esser composta; et prima di due movimenti, che sono la Positione et la Levatione, che si fa con la mano, ne i quali si trova lo allargamento, et il ristrengimento, overo lo alzamento, et abbassamento nominato, che sono due movimenti contrarij; et dipoi due quiete ... Et si come la Medicina chiama il primo movimento συϛολή, et il secondo διαϛολή; cosi la Musica nomina la Positione, overo il Battere θέσις, et la Levatione ἄρσις.[54]	If we consider the qualities that are found in the one and the other, that is, in the *battuta* and the pulse, which is called *sphugmos* by the Greeks, we will find many similarities between them. The pulse is ... a certain broadening and tightening, or we could say raising and lowering, of the heart and the arteries. It is composed ... of two movements and two still parts. Similarly, the *battuta* is composed of the same things: first of two movements, which are the lowering and raising that are made by the hand, in which are found the broadening and tightening, also called raising and lowering, which are two opposite movements, and then of two still parts ... And just as medicine calls the first movement systole and the second diastole, music similarly calls the lowering, or beating, thesis and the raising arsis.

Both Gaffurio and Zarlino discuss analogies of the *tactus* to poetic feet, as well as to the pulse. Since the parts of poetic feet may be distinguished by length, accent, or both, this analogy does not contribute much toward clarifying their understanding of the character of the *tactus* in music.

Zacconi describes many potential problems in the administration of the *tactus* that will strike a familiar chord with anyone who has ever performed music with a group:

Egli deve essere si equale, saldo, stabile, e fermo, che nella divisione	[The equal *tactus*] should be so equal, solid, stable, and firm that

---

[54] Zarlino, *Le istitutioni harmoniche*, book 3, ch. 48 ("Della battuta"), 207.

non se li possi conoscere pur una minima parte d'inequalità ... se vogliano riuscirne con honore non hanno da cantare: perche l'uso che hanno di cantare fa che nelle sincope e ne i passi difficili ancor essi s'alterino sentendo gli altri sincopare ... Il debito de quelli che lo reggano è di reggerlo chiaro, sicuro, senza paura, & senza veruna titubatione ... & se bene per vaghezza del cantare, i cantori alle volte ritardano alquanto, egli non deve riguardar a quella ritardanza: ma attendere al officio suo ... che s'egli vuole ritardar col tatto fin che il cantore habbia perfettamente informato le figure di suono, in ogni tatto converà ritardare; perche il cantore si piglia auttorità sempre di pronuntiar la figura dopò il tatto: per farla sentire con maggior vaghezza ... Similmente ancora quel che ho detto della titubatione, l'ho detto per haver veduto alcuni a empir il tatto pieno de tremoli; di modo che chi l'havesse volute dividere nella divisione non haveria potuto cavar altro che una quantità de detti tremoli ... Oltra di questo nasce alle volte occasione di summinstrar quest'atto col'intervento de gli instrumenti: & perche nel sonar delle Viole, ò de Tromboni essi sonatori fanno attione simile alle attioni del tatto: per questo bisogna esser avertito di non	in its division one cannot discern the least bit of inequality ... [Inexperienced conductors], if they wish to succeed in this with honor, should not sing, because the practice of singing makes them alter [the *tactus*] in syncopations and difficult passages when they hear others syncopate ... The duty of those who control the *tactus* is to make it clear, secure, without fear, and without any trembling ... And even if for the beauty of the song the singers sometimes slow down somewhat, he [the leader] must not pay attention to that slowing, but attend to his duty ... because if he waits with the *tactus* until the singer has finished the sound, he will slow down in every *tactus*, since singers always take the license to produce the note after the beat, to make it sound more attractive ... Similarly, what I said about trembling I said because I have seen some fill the *tactus* with *tremoli*, so that anyone who wanted to divide it at its division would not have been able to get anything but a quantity of these *tremoli* ... Besides this, the occasion sometimes arises to administer [the *tactus*] with the participation of instruments, and since in playing viols, or trombones, the players make a motion similar to the motion of the *tactus*, it is necessary to warn [the

| lasciarsi co gl'atti loro cavar di tempo, & uscir di misura.[55] | conductor] not to let himself lose time or depart from the measure because of their motions. |

As the above sample of theoretical comments demonstrates, the concept of *tactus* from the late fifteenth century to the end of the sixteenth was rich and multivalent. *Tactus* could be anything from a musical analogue of Aristotelian time or the human pulse to a simple series of taps used to keep time in performance. It was both an internal component of the music and an external measure that regulated the process of transforming the abstract time values of musical notation into the concrete time units of a live performance. It could be a unitary measure or one that was divided into equal or unequal parts. It served both to mark points in time and to measure the durations of time between those points. Performers interpreted it in a variety of ways, not all of which were to the liking of theorists. To appreciate the significance of *tactus* in music, we must look beyond categorical questions, such as which value corresponds to the *tactus*, how fast it moves, and whether or not it is associated with accent, and explore the deeper ways in which *tactus* in all of its senses relates to the structuring of time in music.

---

[55] Zacconi, *Prattica di musica*, book 1, ch. 33 ("Della division del tatto & sua sumministratione"), fol. 21ᵛ.

4 | *Tactus* and rhythm

Mensural structure is a meaningful aspect of musical rhythm only if it is articulated by different types of musical events on different temporal levels. Levels that are present in the notation, but not marked in audible ways, are irrelevant to the compositional structure of a work. The most important types of rhythmic events that differentiate levels of mensuration are contrapuntal structure, surface rhythm (including syncopation and hemiola), cadences, and text setting. All of them are potentially hierarchical in that they can generate articulations that vary in strength, from subtle to pronounced. They interact in complex ways that may reinforce or conflict with one another.

Different levels of mensuration have different functions in the structure of a composition. In principle, one level, which may be defined as the compositional *tactus*, plays a central role in regulating all aspects of rhythm. Theorists call attention to the special importance of that level. Tinctoris calls the value corresponding to it "the note directing the measure," or "the note by which the song is measured."[1] Adam von Fulda's description of *tactus* as a unit that is inherent in the music, rather than imposed on it from the outside, implies a similar concept.[2] Smaller levels of mensuration function as subdivisions of the *tactus* in a compositional sense, and larger levels function as groups of *tactus*. The first level of subdivision or grouping sometimes performs musical functions analogous to those normally associated with the *tactus* itself. Although it is usually clear which value is the principal compositional *tactus* of a given piece, there are cases in which two adjacent levels of mensuration share *tactus*-like functions to a degree that makes it difficult or impossible to determine which is the *tactus* and which is the subdivision or grouping. The compositional *tactus* may also shift between adjacent levels within a piece.

Theorists take the imperfect semibreve as the principal model for the note corresponding to a binary compositional *tactus*, though they sometimes illustrate other possibilities as well. The theoretical model for the note

---

[1] "Nota mensuram dirigens" or "nota secundum quam cantus mensuratur" (in various grammatical forms), in Tinctoris, *Liber de arte contrapuncti*, book 2, chs. 24–34, 124–45.
[2] Adam von Fulda, *Musica*, pt. III, ch. 7, III: 362. See Chapter 3, pp. 56–58, above.

corresponding to a ternary compositional *tactus* may be either the perfect semibreve or the perfect breve. When the compositional *tactus* falls on other values, the principles associated with these *tactus* may be extended to rhythmic relationships on other levels.

The performance *tactus* corresponds in principle to the same value as the compositional *tactus*, but the relation between the two types of *tactus* is not always straightforward. A divided performance *tactus* might correspond to two compositional *tactus*. When the compositional *tactus* is ambiguous or changes within a piece, the performance *tactus* might correspond to either of the levels that function as *tactus* in a compositional sense.

Contrapuntal structure on the level of a binary *tactus*

The compositional *tactus* is closely related to the structure of the counterpoint underlying a piece. Theorists explain the contrapuntal foundation of music as a succession of note-against-note intervals between pairs of voices. One of these voices (called the "tenor") is primary and the other is secondary. The principles governing two-voice counterpoint may be extended to accommodate larger numbers of voices, but two voices are sufficient for most theoretical demonstrations. The intervals constituting the contrapuntal framework must be consonant, and they are subject to familiar voice-leading constraints, such as the prohibition of parallel perfect consonances. In real compositions, this framework is decorated with non-structural pitches that may be either consonant or dissonant.

The distinction between structural and ornamental intervals is not a categorical opposition, but a classification that may vary along a continuum. Dissonant intervals are clearly excluded from the structural framework, but consonant intervals may have different structural weights depending on the context. Example 4.1 shows a series of progressions in which the intervals on minim-max *initia* range from purely ornamental to relatively prominent from a structural point of view. In Example 4.1a, the second minim is dissonant and therefore cannot be part of the underlying structure. In Example 4.1b, the analogous note is consonant, but the contrapuntal progressions on the minim level are weak, because only one voice moves and the motion is stepwise. In Examples 4.1c and d, both voices move, but the parallel, stepwise motion in Example 4.1c creates weaker contrapuntal progressions than the contrary motion and melodic skip in one voice in Example 4.1d. In Example 4.1e, the motion of the two voices is staggered by means of syncopation, producing a series of

Example 4.1 Hypothetical contrapuntal progressions.

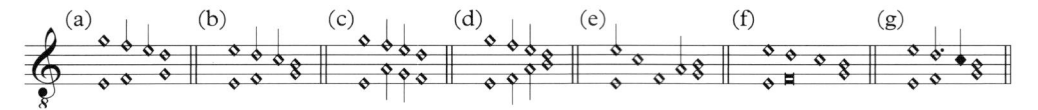

five different intervals. Because of the tenor rhythm, the progression may be heard as a series of three structural intervals on the semibreve level, though it is unclear which of the intervals are structural and which are ornamental. On the minim level, however, the intervals that divide the first and second semibreve-units also have some degree of structural weight. Ambiguities of this type are not analytical weaknesses, but powerful compositional resources. They make it possible for contrapuntal structures to proceed on two or more hierarchical levels with a wide range of relationships among the levels.

Contrapuntal structure is inseparable from rhythm. I shall use the term "contrapuntal rhythm," by analogy with "harmonic rhythm" in later music, for the rhythm of the structural contrapuntal progressions on which a piece is based. Rhythm influences the ways in which counterpoint is perceived. For example, if the third interval of the progression in Example 4.1b is a semibreve, as in Example 4.1f, it has more structural weight than it has if it is a minim. If it is reduced to a semiminim, as in Example 4.1g, it becomes so light that it can only be heard as ornamental. Conversely, counterpoint influences the perception of rhythm. If strong contrapuntal progressions appear on short rhythmic values, those values have more mensural weight than they would if the contrapuntal rhythm moved only in larger values. Contrapuntal rhythm tends to be perceived as a series of equal values, while the rhythms that include all consonant intervals are more varied. The tension between the forces of regularity and irregularity in the contrapuntal rhythm generates much of the rhythmic energy of a piece.

The compositional *tactus* of a piece corresponds to the principal value in which the contrapuntal rhythm proceeds. When there are two levels of contrapuntal structure, the larger one is normally the *tactus* and the smaller one its first subdivision. Theorists make this point clear through the way in which they explain contrapuntal structures. The standard approach is to illustrate first note-against-note counterpoint in semibreves, then diminished (ornamented) counterpoint against a tenor that moves in semibreves, and finally two voices in which both voices have varied rhythms. The openings of Tinctoris's examples of the first two categories are shown in

Example 4.2 Johannes Tinctoris, Example of simple counterpoint (beginning). *Liber de arte contrapuncti*, book 2, ch. 19.

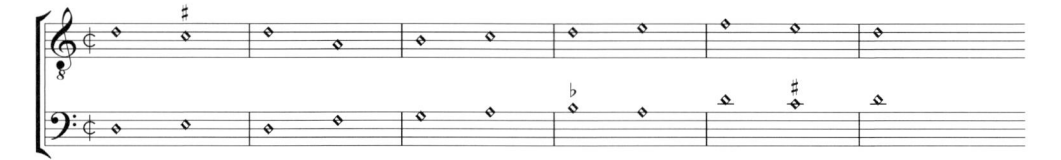

Example 4.3 Johannes Tinctoris, Example of diminished counterpoint over a tenor in semibreves (beginning). *Liber de arte contrapuncti*, book 2, ch. 19.

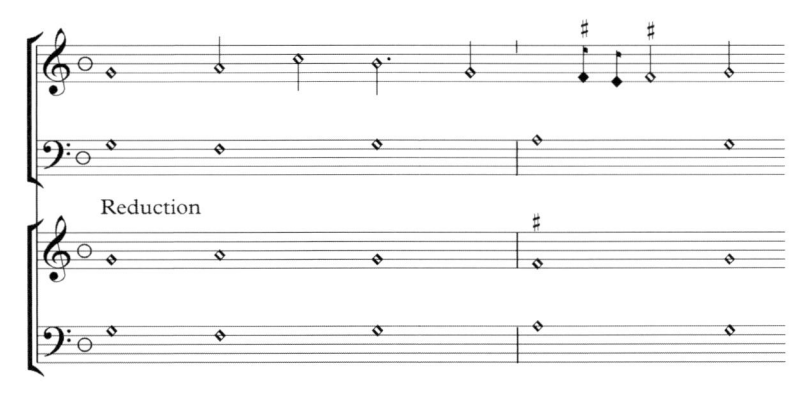

Reduction

Examples 4.2 and 4.3; Example 4.3 also includes a hypothetical reduction showing the underlying contrapuntal structure. In Example 4.2, the contrapuntal rhythm consists only of semibreves. In Example 4.3, the contrapuntal rhythm moves in semibreves on a fundamental level, because the tenor moves only in semibreves, but weaker contrapuntal progressions also appear on the minim level in the second and third semibreve-units. I have identified the A and G in the upper voice in bar 1 as more structural than the C and B because they make a smoother progression, but either of the upper-voice notes in the second and third semibreve-units would create correct counterpoint and could be judged to be part of the deeper contrapuntal structure.

The rules for handling dissonance, which theorists from Tinctoris on explain in relation to the *tactus*, are a corollary of the principles of contrapuntal rhythm. Because the contrapuntal rhythm moves at a rate corresponding to the *tactus*, dissonances may not be longer than a half-*tactus*; a longer dissonance would displace the required structural consonance on the *tactus* on which it occurred. Dissonances other than suspensions may not appear at the beginning of the *tactus*, because they might obscure the

Example 4.4 Johannes Tinctoris, Example of dissonance treatment in relation to an imperfect semibreve *tactus* (tenor and discantus). *Liber de arte contrapuncti*, book 2, ch. 23.

Example 4.4 (cont.)

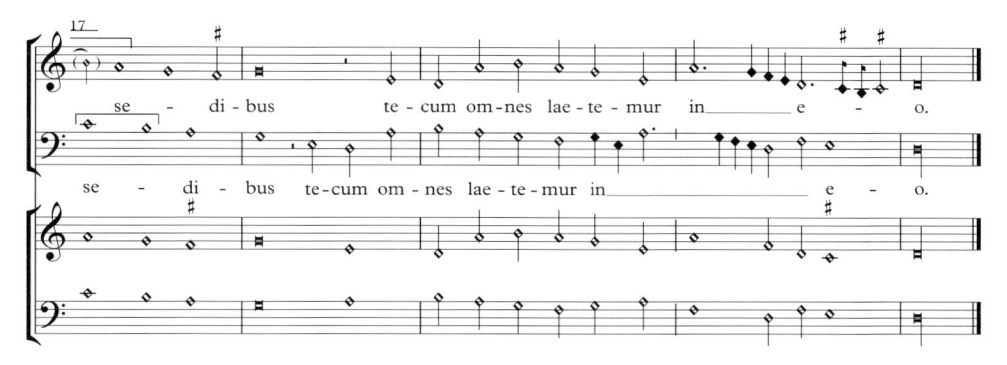

structural interval corresponding to the *tactus*. Tinctoris explains the prohibition of non-suspension dissonances at the beginning of the *tactus* on grounds that the first part of the *tactus* is heard more strongly than the subsequent parts.[3] Suspensions may fall on the *tactus* because their function is simply to delay a structural consonance. Since they are held over from the previous structural consonance, the underlying contrapuntal progression is easily perceived.[4] Nevertheless, suspensions have special force in marking the *tactus* aurally, because they call attention to the temporal points at which the expected consonances are temporarily denied.

Example 4.4 shows the tenor and discantus of one of Tinctoris's examples of dissonance treatment in relation to the imperfect semibreve *mensura* in perfect *tempus*. The example illustrates the ways in which variations in the contrapuntal rhythm may shape the temporal structure of a piece. The structural intervals are mostly semibreves and minims; the stronger progressions are on the semibreve level, because only one voice moves on most minim-max *initia*. Tinctoris subordinates the semibreve progressions to the breve in bar 1 to establish both levels of mensuration at the outset. He slows the contrapuntal rhythm by repeating structural intervals on consecutive semibreves to mark the penultimate notes of major cadences in bars 9 and 11 and to mark the separation between phrases in bar 15. Conversely, he places strong contrapuntal progressions on minims to increase the drive to

---

[3] Tinctoris, *Liber de arte contrapuncti*, book 2, ch. 31 ("Quibus ex causis parvae discordantiae a musicis assumi permittantur"), 140.

[4] An anonymous theorist of the fifteenth century explains syncopation, which he associates with dissonant suspensions, explicitly as a displacement of structural consonances. *De vera et compendiosa seu regulari constructione contrapuncti*, in *Anonymi Tractatus de cantu figurativo et de contrapuncto (c. 1430–1520)*, ed. Christian Meyer, Corpus scriptorum de musica 41 (n.p.: American Institute of Musicology; Hänssler-Verlag, 1997), 62.

the cadences in bars 2, 13–14, and 19–20. The progression of parallel sixths on consecutive semiminims in bar 2 is the only potentially structural progression in the piece that occurs in values shorter than minims. It is rather jarring rhythmically. In real music, such progressions normally appear only where contrapuntal motion in minims has been established as a norm for some time.

Theorists acknowledge the special role of the minim subdivision of the *tactus*, as well as the semibreve *tactus* itself, in relation to counterpoint. Tinctoris says that dissonances may be regulated in relation to either the semibreve or the minim when the *tactus* is the imperfect semibreve, implying that the structural motion of the counterpoint may likewise proceed either in semibreves or in minims.[5] Although he allows dissonances to last as long as a half-*tactus*, he prefers dissonances that are limited to a quarter-*tactus*, probably because of the potentially *tactus*-like role of the minim in the counterpoint.[6] In Example 4.4, dissonances are limited to a quarter-*tactus* when the contrapuntal rhythm moves in minims, but sometimes last as long as a half-*tactus* (despite Tinctoris's stated preference) when it moves in semibreves.

Zarlino gives more theoretical weight to the half-*tactus* than Tinctoris does, but still makes it clear that the minims are contrapuntally subordinate to the semibreves. Minims have a strong structural role in that at least one voice is required to move on every minim except at the beginning of a piece. In his discussion of diminished counterpoint over a tenor in semibreves, Zarlino initially requires every minim to be consonant because of the aural prominence of the points corresponding to the downstroke and upstroke of the *tactus*:

Onde sopra ogni Semibreve contenuta nel Soggetto, potremo porre due Minime … con questo ordine però, che … ciascuna di loro siano consonanti: percioche queste due parti della Semibreve sono considerate grandemente dal senso; per rispetto della Battuta, la quale si considera in due modi, cioè nel battere, & nel levare.[7]	Thus over every semibreve of the subject we may place two minims … but with this consideration, that … each of them be consonant, because these two parts of the semibreve are recognized strongly by the sense with respect to the *tactus*, which is considered in two ways, namely, in the downstroke and in the upstroke.

---

[5] *Liber de arte contrapuncti*, book 2, ch. 23 ("Quod in simplici contrapuncto discordantiae non sunt admittendae, sed in diminuto, et primo qualiter circa partes minimae in utraque prolatione et circa partes semibrevis in minori"), 121.

[6] Ibid., book 2, ch. 29 ("Quomodo multi numquam supra integram partem dimidiam notae secundum quam mensura cantus dirigitur, immo supra minorem tantum assumunt"), 139.

[7] Zarlino, *Le istitutioni harmoniche*, book 3, ch. 42 ("Delle contrapunti diminuiti a due voci, & in qual modo si possino usar le dissonanze"), 195.

Example 4.5 Gioseffo Zarlino, Example of dissonance treatment in relation to a semibreve *tactus* (beginning). *Le istitutioni harmoniche* (Venice, 1558), book 3, ch. 42.

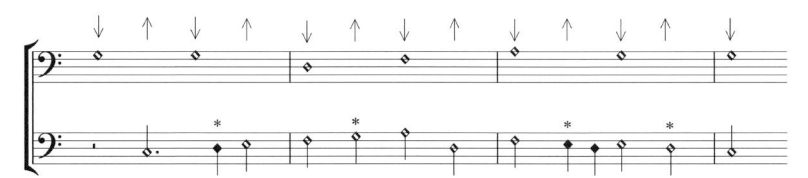

Similarly, semiminims that fall on the downstroke or the upstroke of the *tactus* must normally be consonant. Nevertheless, the semibreve trumps the minim on a higher structural level. Minims that fall on the upstroke may be dissonant if they move in stepwise motion, and semiminims that fall on the upstroke may be dissonant in stepwise descending motion, as shown in Example 4.5. For Zarlino, suspensions always fall on the downstroke of the *tactus* and are resolved on the upstroke, reinforcing the contrapuntal priority of the whole *tactus* over the half-*tactus*. The more uniform rhythmic style that he favors does not allow for suspensions on the half-*tactus*, like the one that Tinctoris wrote in bar 2 of Example 4.4. The rules prohibiting parallel perfect consonances apply in some cases to the intervals on consecutive semibreves even if there is another consonance on the second half of the first semibreve, because an intervening minim may not have enough structural weight to counteract the sense of progression from one semibreve to the next. Zarlino justifies this rule in the case where one voice has a stepwise descending minim followed by two semiminims with the explanation that "passages of two semiminims preceded by a minim … are nothing but a diminution of the conjunct movement made by two semibreves."[8]

Theoretical rules of counterpoint are addressed to composers and singers of improvised counterpoint, not to analysts, but they may be applied in reverse to yield information about the compositional *tactus* in relation to which a piece was conceived. When most of the strong contrapuntal progressions in a piece fall on one mensural level, that level may be identified as the compositional *tactus*. Weaker progressions, or strong progressions that appear only in short passages, may fall on the subdivision of the *tactus*. Dissonances provide confirming evidence, but they are insufficient to

---

[8] "Li passaggi, che fanno le due Semiminime non sono altro, che la Diminutione del movimento congiunto, che fanno insieme due Semibrevi." Ibid., book 3, ch. 47 ("Che 'l porre una dissonanza, overo una pausa di minima tra due consonanze perfette di una istessa specie, che insieme ascendino, o discendino, non fa, che tali consonanze siano replicate"), 206.

establish the *tactus* on their own. They may be limited to the level of the subdivision of the *tactus*, as Tinctoris recommends, or they may occasionally last for a whole *tactus*, as Tinctoris confirms even though he disapproves of the practice.[9] Contrapuntal considerations do not always identify the *tactus* unambiguously, but they provide vital information about the mensural character of a piece. The number of mensural levels that participate in the contrapuntal structure, their relative prominence, and the fixed or changing relations among them are essential aspects of every piece, whether or not one level emerges as the central unit of measure for all of the rhythms of a piece.

Contrapuntal structure on the level of a ternary *tactus*

When contrapuntal progressions relate primarily to a ternary level of the mensuration, the relation between contrapuntal structure and *tactus* is more complex. (Ternary levels are usually perfect, but in coloration, the mensural groups are ternary even though the notes are notationally imperfect.) A ternary unit of the mensuration may contain one, two, or three structural intervals. When it contains only one, the *tactus* falls on the ternary unit and dissonances may appear on the second or the third part of the *tactus*. When it contains three, each of them corresponds to one binary *tactus*, as in Example 4.4. When it contains two, the situation is more complex, because one of the intervals must be twice as long as the other. This asymmetry complicates the issue of equating the *tactus* and its subdivisions with levels of the mensuration.

When two structural intervals appear on one ternary unit of the mensuration, either the shorter or the longer one may be first. Scholars sometimes call the former rhythms "iambic" and the latter "trochaic," but this terminology can be misleading. Since short notes tend to be grouped with the longer ones to which they are closest in time, the short notes in long-short-long-short patterns are more likely to be heard as upbeats, while the long notes in short-long-short-long patterns are more likely to be heard as afterbeats. Poetic texts with iambic meter may be set to either rhythm, but they fit more naturally with long-short patterns with upbeats, while poetic texts with trochaic rhythms fit more naturally with short-long patterns.

---

[9] Tinctoris, *Liber de arte contrapuncti*, book 2, ch. 29 ("Quomodo multi numquam supra integram partem dimidiam notae secundum quam mensura cantus dirigitur, immo supra minorem tantum assumunt"), 139.

I shall therefore avoid the terms "iambic" and "trochaic" and call the two types of divisions simply short-long and long-short.

Tinctoris is the only theorist to discuss the relation between contrapuntal structure and a ternary *tactus*. He limits dissonances to a third of the *tactus* and allows them only on the second of the three parts, because he believes the third part is "expressed more strongly" than the second.[10] In practice, however, dissonances are common on both the second and the third parts of a ternary *tactus*. Tinctoris also points out that suspensions may occur only over the second of the three parts.

Given the paucity of information about the ternary *tactus* in theoretical writings, the principles governing it must be deduced empirically. Du Fay's Sequence *Iste sunt due olive* (Example 4.6) provides an example. It includes sections in ternary mensurations with one, two, and three cantus-firmus notes (marked with asterisks in the example) in each ternary unit. The cantus-firmus notes are not strictly correlated with the structural intervals of the counterpoint – some are dissonant, and thus cannot have structural function, and some contrapuntally significant points are not associated with a cantus-firmus note – but the correlation is close enough to demonstrate the differences among the three types. Example 4.6a is in imperfect *tempus*/perfect prolation. It has one structural interval in each perfect semibreve-unit except before cadences, where there are sometimes two. Dissonances are infrequent, but there are suspensions lasting for a minim (a third of the ternary unit) on the second third of the semibreve-unit in bars 7 and 11. The compositional *tactus* is clearly the perfect semibreve. Example 4.6b is in perfect *tempus*/imperfect prolation. It has three structural intervals in most breve-units and more than three in some places, especially where the contrapuntal motion shifts to the minim before cadences in bars 3 and 7. Dissonances are limited to minims, which in this case are a sixth of the ternary unit. The example conforms to Tinctoris's illustration of the semibreve *tactus* in perfect *tempus* (Example 4.4); the compositional *tactus* is clearly the semibreve. Example 4.6c is also in perfect *tempus*/imperfect prolation, but it has only two structural intervals per breve-unit. Dissonances are limited to minims and shorter values, but the suspension in bar 5 falls on the second semibreve of a perfect breve-unit (a position analogous to that of the suspension in Example 4.6a, bar 7), and the third note of the discantus in the penultimate bar is a dissonance that falls on a

---

[10] Ibid., book 2, ch. 26 ("De admissione discordantiarum circa partes notarum secundum quas totaliter aut principaliter mensura cantus dirigitur et quae in proportione ternaria constitutae vel perfectae vel augmentatae vel imperfectae quovismodo sint"), 130.

Example 4.6 Du Fay, *Iste sunt due olive*, discantus and tenor: (a) verse 6; (b) verse 1; (c) verse 4. After Trent, Castello del Buonconsiglio, Monumenti e Collezioni Provinciale, 1374 (formerly 87), fols. 61ʳ–63ʳ.

semibreve *initium*. Du Fay distinguishes the types of ternary mensuration in this piece with different signs: ₵ for perfect prolation with one structural interval per perfect semibreve, O for perfect *tempus* with three structural intervals per perfect breve, and ɸ for perfect *tempus* with two structural intervals per perfect breve.[11]

The compositional *tactus* of Example 4.6c differs in character from that of both Example 4.6a and Example 4.6b. It falls logically on the breve, with the structural intervals functioning as subdivisions of unequal length, but the emphasis on the subdivisions is greater than in any mensural type

---

[11] In the sole source of this piece (the manuscript Trent 87), the upper-voice sign looks like ₵, rather than ɸ. ɸ was clearly intended, as the coloration in bars 12–14 confirms. The tenor and contratenor have the sign ɸ. The G in the discantus in bar 13 is white, but must be black to be notationally correct. It has been corrected in the example.

Example 4.6 (cont.)

considered so far. A semibreve *tactus* would impede the flow of the contrapuntal rhythm, because half of the structural intervals would last for two *tactus*, rather than one. Dissonances as long as a semibreve could in principle appear where a structural interval lasts for two semibreves. Du Fay does not take advantage of that possibility in this example, although the dissonance on the third semibreve *initium* in the penultimate bar falls on the second half of a structural interval that lasts for two semibreves. The mensural type represented by this example occupies an uneasy middle ground between mensurations with one and three structural intervals per breve-unit, or with perfect breve and imperfect semibreve compositional *tactus*. It may shade in either direction, sometimes to the extent that it is difficult or impossible to distinguish it from one of the other types.

Example 4.6 (cont.)

Surface rhythm

Mensural structure is articulated by surface rhythms as well as contrapuntal rhythms. The presence of a note at any point provides some degree of articulation at that point. By extension, the larger the number of notes in different voices that fall at a particular point, the stronger the articulation will be at that point. Relative durations also create differing degrees of emphasis. Longer notes are by nature more prominent than shorter ones. This principle is known as *agogic accent*. The greater the difference in length between two notes, the stronger the agogic accent on the longer one.

Different patterns of agogic accents bring out different levels of the mensural structure. Example 4.7 illustrates this principle with divisions of the breve in order of decreasing emphasis on the breve level and increasing emphasis on the semibreve level. The breve level predominates in Examples

Example 4.7 Rhythms with binary divisions of the breve on two levels.

4.7a and b, especially the former because of its strong agogic accent and the absence of articulation on the second semibreve-unit. Example 4.7c is mensurally neutral. Example 4.7d has an agogic accent on the second semibreve-unit that undermines the primacy of the breve over the semibreve. Example 4.7e treats both semibreves equally; it emphasizes the semibreve level more strongly than Example 4.7c because of the strong agogic accents on the semibreves. Dotted rhythms in which the shorter notes precede the longer ones, and the agogic accents therefore contradict the mensural hierarchy, are theoretically possible, but rare. They are normally limited to mensural levels larger than the compositional *tactus*. Zacconi forbids them explicitly on the *tactus* and smaller levels.[12]

Because there is a limit to the number of levels that can be meaningfully differentiated, rhythmic activity on smaller levels tends to equalize the emphasis on larger values and thereby counteract patterns of grouping on larger levels. Conversely, an absence of rhythmic activity on smaller levels encourages the perception of larger groups. The shortest note values in a piece are usually two or three levels below the compositional *tactus* (semiminims or *fusae* if the *tactus* is the semibreve). Values three levels below the *tactus* are limited to rhythmically ornamental functions. For example, *fusae* may be limited to pairs that begin on semiminim-max *initia*, as in Example 4.4 above.

Syncopation

Syncopation is closely related to *tactus*. Zarlino places his chapter on syncopation immediately after the chapter on *tactus* and explains the reason for doing so as follows:

La sincopa veramente non si può conoscere dal Musico senza la cognitione della Battuta, onde era conveniente,	Syncopation truly cannot be known by the musician without an understanding of the *tactus;* therefore it

---

[12] Zacconi, *Prattica di musica*, book 1, ch. 46 ("Se le figure minori possano essere anteposte alle maggiori & come le si antepongano"), fols. 33^v–34^r.

che primieramente si ragionasse di lei, come di quella, che è molto necessaria alla sua cognitione.[13]	was appropriate to discuss [the *tactus*] first, as that which is very necessary to the understanding [of syncopation].

One of the functions of syncopation is to enliven the rhythmic surface by staggering the pitches that form the contrapuntal structure. It stands to reason, therefore, that syncopation applies primarily to the principal level of the contrapuntal rhythm, which is the level of the compositional *tactus*. Zarlino defines syncopation not only in the traditional way, as the separation of notes that are counted together, but also as a note that begins on the upstroke of the *tactus* and continues through the following downstroke:

Onde quella figura, o nota si chiama Sincopata … quando incomincia nella levatione della battuta, & è sotto posta anco alla positione; ne mai può cascare, come porta la sua natura, sotto la positione, fino a tanto, che non ritrovi una figura minor, overo altre figure, che siano equale a questa di valore, con le quali si accompagni, & ritorni, ove la battuta hebbe principio.[14]	Thus this figure, or note, is called syncopated when it begins on the upstroke of the *tactus* and is also placed on [i.e., continues through] the downstroke; nor can it fall, as its nature demands, on the downstroke until another shorter figure is found, or other figures that are equal to it in value, with which it goes together and returns to the place where the *tactus* begins.

Zarlino follows this statement with the observation that the note corresponding to the *tactus* normally begins on the *initium* of the *tactus*-unit. Syncopation is a disruption of this norm.[15]

Syncopation may also apply to the level of the subdivision or grouping of the *tactus*. On the level of the subdivision, it may relate to the contrapuntal structure in either of two ways: it may stagger the notes of structural progressions, as in Example 4.4, bars 2 and 13, or it may perform a purely ornamental rhythmic function over a single structural interval, as in Example 4.6b, bar 7. The former rhythm articulates the level of the subdivision of the *tactus* more strongly than the latter does. Zarlino is concerned mainly with syncopation on the level of the compositional *tactus*, though he mentions the possibility of syncopated semibreves when the *tactus* is the breve.[16] Zacconi distinguishes true syncopations, which for him fall entirely within the *tactus*-unit (and thus apply to the level of the

---

[13] Zarlino, *Le istitutioni harmoniche*, book 3, ch. 49 ("Della sincopa"), 209.   [14] Ibid.
[15] Ibid.   [16] Ibid.

Example 4.8 Types of syncopation in relation to a semibreve *tactus*: (a) Displaced note = two *tactus* (Balbi's syncopation *in nota et non in mensura*); (b) Displaced note = one *tactus* (Balbi's syncopation *in nota et in mensura*; Zacconi's *contra tatto*; Anonymous 12's *duplicatio maior*); (c) Displaced note = a half-*tactus* (Zacconi's true syncopation; Anonymous 12's *duplicatio brevior* in half-values).

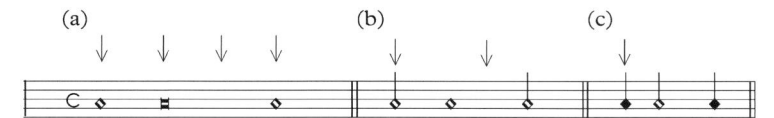

subdivision), from *contra tatto* rhythms in which the displaced note has the same value as the *tactus*. For him, displaced semibreves are syncopated when the performance *tactus* is the breve, but *contra tatto* when the performance *tactus* is the semibreve.[17] Anonymous 12 makes a similar distinction. He uses the idiosyncratic term "duplicatio" for syncopation on grounds that syncopated notes are split between two mensural units and thus belong to both of them. He classifies rhythms consisting of two minims separated by one or more semibreves as "duplicatio maior" (equivalent to Zacconi's "contra tatto") when the *tactus* is the semibreve, as in O or C, and as "duplicatio brevior" (equivalent to Zacconi's true syncopation) when the *tactus* is the breve, as in ₵ or C2.[18]

Marco Antonio Balbi discusses syncopation on the level of groupings of *tactus*, as well as on the level of the *tactus* itself. He identifies two categories of syncopations: "against the note and not against the *mensura*" ("in nota et non in mensura") and "against the note and against the *mensura*" (in nota et in mensura"). The former are rhythms in which the note preceding the displacement equals a whole *tactus* (e.g., two semibreves separated by a breve when the *tactus* is the semibreve), and the latter are rhythms in which the note preceding the displacement equals a half-*tactus* (e.g., two minims separated by a semibreve when the *tactus* is the semibreve). He says that musicians pay little attention to the former type, because it does not divide the *tactus*, but that the latter produces many marvelous effects.[19] Example 4.8 illustrates different types of syncopation in relation to a semibreve *tactus*.

The definition of syncopation as the separation of notes that belong together mensurally does not call attention to the tension between the

---

[17] Zacconi, *Prattica di musica*, [part I], book 1, ch. 52 ("Delle Sincope; con le sue vere, & reale distintioni a perfetta dimostratione che cosa sieno"), fols. 40ᵛ–41ᵛ.
[18] Anonymous 12, *Tractatus et compendium cantus figurati*, ch. 13 ("De duplicatione"), 70–71.
[19] Marco Antonio Balbi, *Regula brevis musice practicabilis* (n.p., n.d.), "De Sincopa," fol. Aᵛʳ.

syncopation and the mensural structure in the way that modern definitions of syncopation do. Nevertheless, the fact that the technique is understood as a deviation from an expected norm implies that some such tension must exist. Sebald Heyden characterizes this tension as an active conflict:

Syncopatio vulgo dicitur, quoties Semibrevium Notularum quantitas, aequabilitati Tactuum, aliquandiu quasi obstrepit, et contra venit. De eo dissidio nos ita hic breviter praecipimus: Ut canens, Tactuum aequabilitati, de Notularum quantitate nihil concedat, sed fortiter in discrepando pergat, donec ipsae Notulae sese cum Tactu reconcilient.[20]	It is colloquially called syncopation whenever the value of semibreve notes disturbs, as it were, the equality of the *tactus* and goes against it for some time. Concerning this conflict we briefly teach the following here: in singing, one should yield nothing from the quantity of the notes to the equality of the *tactus*, but strongly persist in the discrepancy until these notes are reconciled with the *tactus*.

Banchieri calls the conflict a kind of tugging or straining of the parts against each other:

Averta il prudente Cantore nel dire queste sincope far sì che si oda quel stiracchiamento con gratia pronuntiato & baldanzosamente sin tanto che s'unisse.[21]	The prudent singer should be careful to sing these syncopations in such a way that one hears the tugging expressed gracefully and boldly until [the voices] unite.

This tension may be subtle. It need not be strongly emphasized in performance, but syncopation is meaningless as a rhythmic technique unless performers and listeners perceive the distinction between rhythms that conform to the mensural structure and rhythms that conflict with it. All of the above quotations demonstrate that performers were very much aware of this issue.

Syncopation serves not only to enliven the surface rhythms and generate rhythmic tension, but also to bind together time units on the level of the complete syncopated pattern. Because the notes that are separated by the syncopation belong together mensurally, the time unit in which the pattern

---

[20] Heyden, *De arte canendi*, book 2, ch. 6 ("De augmentatione et diminutione"), 109.
[21] Adriano Banchieri, *Cartella musicale nel canto figurato, fermo, et contrapunto*, 3rd edn. (Venice: Giacomo Vincenti, 1614; repr. Bologna: Forni, 1968), [part II], doc. 17 ("Delle sincope maggiori et minori"), 43. Banchieri defines syncopation as a displacement in one voice combined with a rhythm that conforms to the *tactus* in another voice. His "contra battuta" (unlike Zacconi's) is a rhythm in which the displacement appears in all voices simultaneously.

Example 4.9 Syncopated semibreves that fall only within breve-units. Du Fay, *Donnés l'assault*, bars 13–17. After New Haven, Yale University Library, Beinecke Rare Book and Manuscript Library, Ms. 91 ("Mellon Chansonnier"), fols. 71^v–73^r.

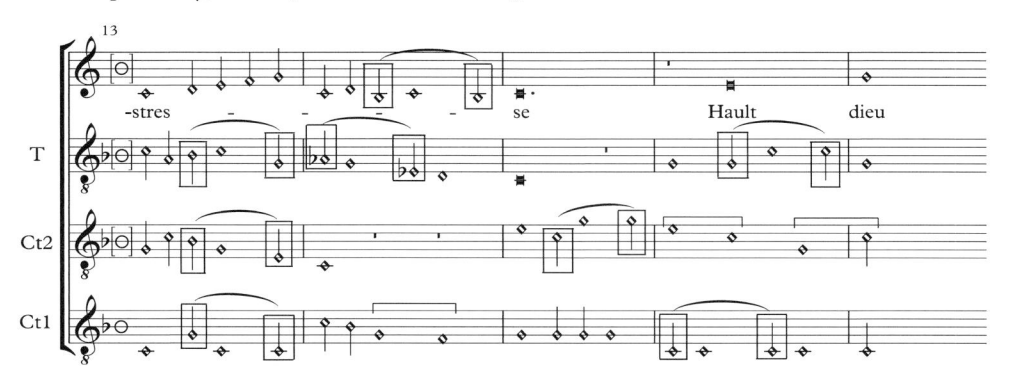

Example 4.10 Syncopated semibreves that continue for an extended period and cross breve *initia*. Du Fay, *Donnés l'assault*, bars 34–37. After New Haven, Yale University Library, Beinecke Rare Book and Manuscript Library, Ms. 91 ("Mellon Chansonnier"), fols. 71^v–73^r.

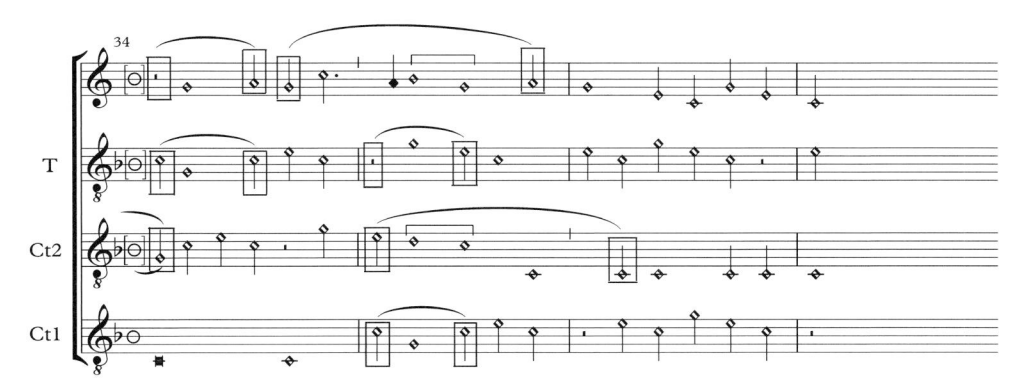

begins is not complete until the entire pattern ends. Syncopation can therefore create regular groupings of *tactus*. If, for example, syncopated semibreves fall only within breve-units, but do not cross breve *initia*, as in Example 4.9, the breves will stand out as audible units of the mensuration. If syncopations do not occur at regular points in relation to the next larger mensural level, or if they continue for a long time, they weaken the mensural groupings on higher levels. In Example 4.10, the presence of syncopation over three consecutive breve *initia* in at least one voice obscures the ternary

Example 4.11 Ludovico Zacconi, Example of hemiola in relation to a ternary *tactus* (end of example). *Prattica di musica*, book 3, ch. 76.

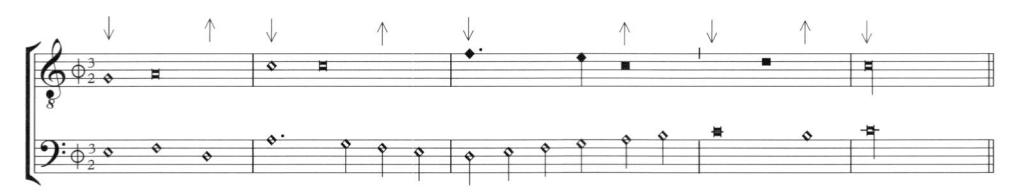

grouping of the semibreves and enhances the larger continuity of the passage. Both of these examples come from the same song. Du Fay uses the change from regular breve-units to continuity over a longer span to build a sense of climax toward the end of the piece.

Hemiola

Hemiola resembles syncopation in several ways. It entails rhythms that conflict with the mensural structure, and it creates rhythmic tension and binds time units of the mensuration together. Its effect, like that of syncopation, depends on its relation to the *tactus*. It may consist either of three time units on two ternary *tactus*, as in the passage in black notes in Example 4.11, or of three groups of two *tactus* in place of two groups of three *tactus*, as in the passages in black notes in Example 4.12. (There is no doubt about the intended *tactus* in these examples, since that information is given in the treatises in which they are found.)

Although syncopation and hemiola are normally distinct, the difference between them is sometimes blurred in complex rhythms. Hemiola usually involves an imperfected note that crosses a mensural *initium* and therefore requires coloration for its notation, but if the value that crosses the *initium* is broken into smaller values, coloration is not necessary, and it may be unclear whether the rhythm should be understood as hemiola or syncopation. In Example 4.13, the six semibreves of the contratenor could be interpreted either as hemiola or as syncopation. The former interpretation is shown in Example 4.13a, with the beginnings of the hemiola units marked with wedges. The latter is shown in Example 4.13b, with the notes that are counted together in the syncopation placed in boxes and connected by a curved line. Although the choice might go either way, the difference is significant from a theoretical point of view, because the conceptual basis

Example 4.12 Franchino Gaffurio, Example of hemiola in relation to a binary *tactus* in ternary groups (excerpts): (a) black long + breve; (b) three black breves. *Practica musice*, book 2, ch. 11.

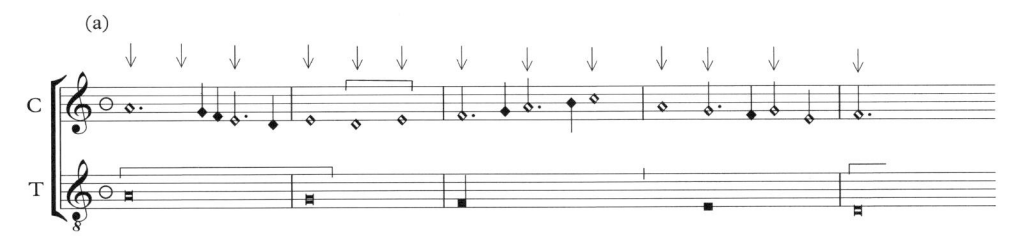

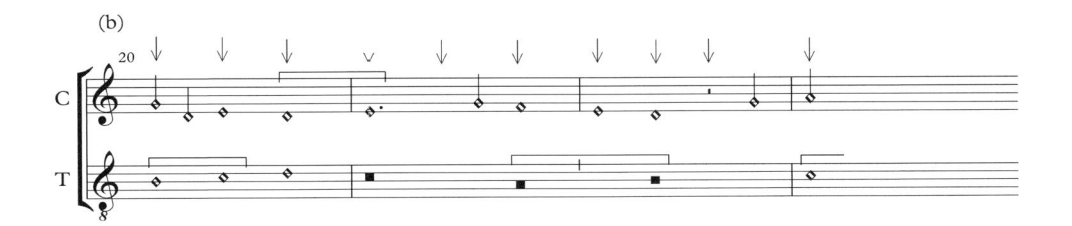

of the mensural structure depends on which notes are counted together. The decision will have an impact on the performance of the passage as well. The low G in bar 27 is more prominent mensurally if it functions as an *initium* on the level of the imperfect breve in hemiola than if it is the third of a displaced group of three semibreves. The prominence of the note in performance should reflect the way the performers understand the mensural structure of the passage.

Cadences

Cadences are syntactic articulations that mark the ends of temporal units of music, from phrases and subphrases to sections and entire compositions. Technically, a cadence consists of a contrapuntal progression from an imperfect consonance to a perfect consonance with motion by half step in one voice. If the half step does not appear in the scale on which the piece is based, it is normally supplied by the performers. More than two voices may be involved in a cadence, but two are sufficient to define the technique. Cadences are often ornamented with suspensions. Suspensions were so closely associated with cadence that Zarlino goes so far as to

Example 4.13 Du Fay, *Craindre vous vueil*, bars 26–28: (a) with the contratenor rhythm interpreted as hemiola; (b) with the same rhythm interpreted as syncopation. After Oxford, Bodleian Library, Ms. Canon. Misc. 213, fol. 5^r.

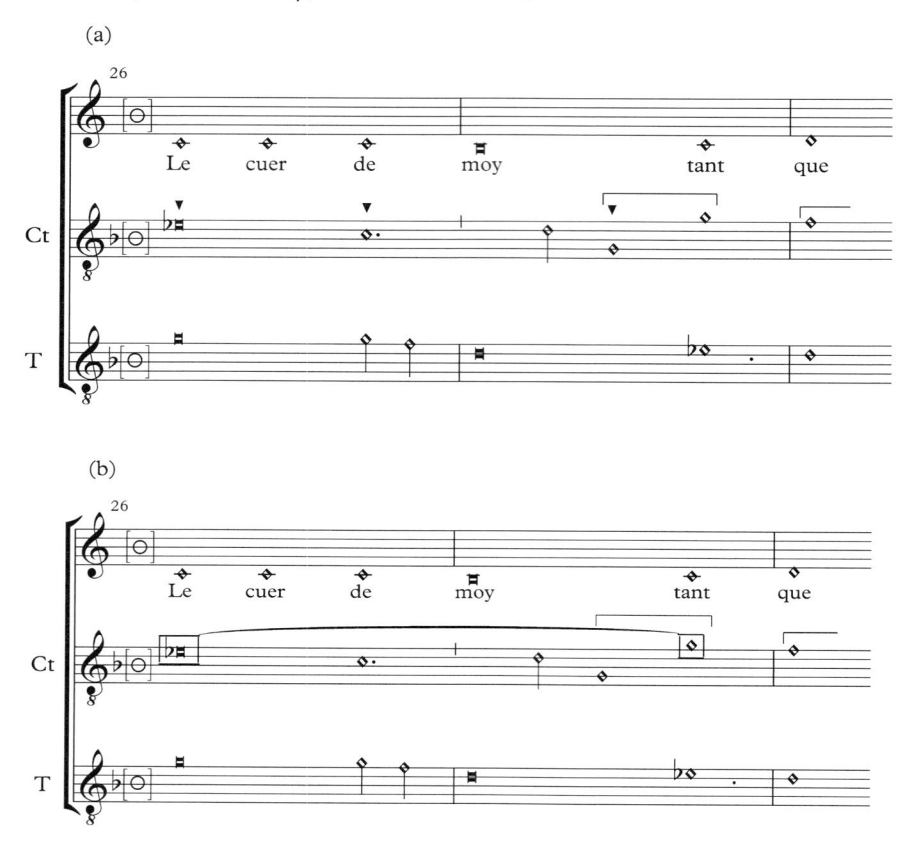

define every suspension as part of a cadence; if the progression set up by the suspension does not continue as expected, he classifies the cadence as "evaded."[22]

Cadences are the most prominent contrapuntal progressions in a piece. They vary in strength, but even the weaker ones have greater structural weight than non-cadential progressions. They therefore play a central role in projecting the mensural structure of a piece. In principle, the contrapuntal rhythm of cadences conforms to the prevailing contrapuntal

---

[22] Zarlino, *Le istitutioni harmoniche*, book 3, ch. 54 ("Il modo di fuggir le cadenze; & quello, che si hà da osservare, quando il soggetto farà il movimento di due, o più gradi"), 226.

Example 4.14 Cadences: (a) unornamented; (b) with simple suspension; (c) with ornamented suspension.

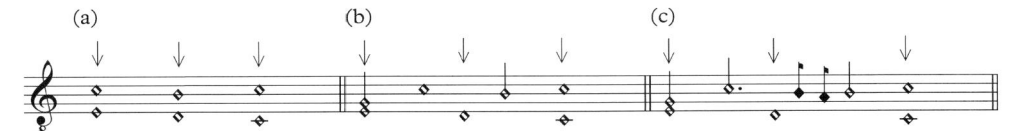

rhythm of the piece. Cadences are never syncopated with respect to the compositional *tactus*; when they are syncopated with respect to larger mensural levels, their placement undermines the listener's perception of those levels. The penultimate interval of a cadence normally lasts for one compositional *tactus*, so that the final interval falls on the *initium* of the *tactus*-unit. If there is a suspension, its resolution marks the first level of subdivision of the *tactus*. If the resolution is ornamented, the ornament marks the second level of subdivision. These possibilities are illustrated in relation to a semibreve *tactus* in Example 4.14. In Example 4.14a, the subdivision of the *tactus* is unmarked. In Example 4.14b, it is marked lightly by the suspension, and in Example 4.14c, it is marked more strongly by the ornamentation of the suspension. (The ornament may have various forms, all of which have similar rhythmic effects if the resolution falls in the same place.)

Zarlino illustrates cadences only in these rhythmic forms, but Tinctoris also includes cadences in which the penultimate has a length of two *tactus* or a half-*tactus* in Example 4.4, bars 2–3, 9–10, 11–12, and 13–14. Some theorists assign cadences with different rhythmic forms to different categories: *maggiore* when the penultimate is a breve, *minore* when it is a semibreve, and *minima* when it is a minim.[23] These possibilities complicate the mensural implications of cadences. Cadences with breve or minim penultimates might imply a temporary compositional *tactus* on the breve or the minim, or they might be interpreted as having penultimates of two *tactus* or a half-*tactus* in relation to a semibreve compositional *tactus*. The choice depends on the structure of the cadences and the musical context in which

---

[23] Vicentino, *L'antica musica ridotta alla moderna prattica*, book 3, ch. 24 ("Dichiaratione delle tre sorti di Cadentie da noi dette, maggiori, minori, e minime; che s'usano nelle compositioni, de i canti fermi, & figurati, con punto & senza, con i loro essempi, et di sua natura"), fols. 51^r–51^v, and book 3, ch. 34 ("Dimostratione delle tre sorti di Cadentie à quattro voci composte, della maggiore, et della minore, & della minima tutte della Musica participata & mista"), book 3, ch. 34, fols. 57^v–58^r.

Example 4.15 Cadences with breve and minim penultimates. Arrows represent possible interpretations of the cadences in relation to the compositional *tactus*.

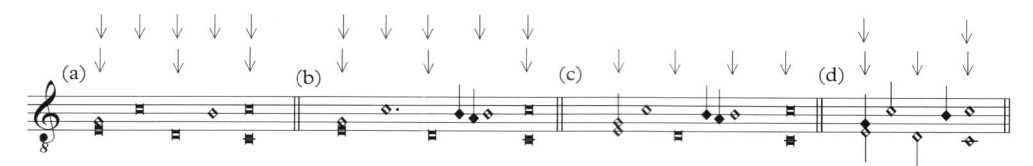

they occur. Example 4.15 illustrates various possibilities. Examples 4.15a and 4.15b are the same as Examples 4.14d and 4.14c in double values. Since the cadential progressions move in breves, they suggest a compositional *tactus* on the breve, but they may also be understood as cadences with penultimates lasting for two compositional *tactus*, each equal to a semibreve. The latter interpretation is possible even for Example 4.15a, which has a semibreve dissonance. Tinctoris chastises composers who write suspensions that last for a whole *tactus*, thereby confirming that they exist,[24] and Gaffurio comments that suspensions may last for a full semibreve (the only value he acknowledges as a compositional *tactus*) without elaborating the point.[25] Example 4.15c implies a semibreve compositional *tactus* and a cadential penultimate of two *tactus* because the preparation of the suspension is a minim, leading the listener to expect that the suspension will also be a minim. The ornament delays the resolution and will normally be mistaken for the resolution when it first appears. Example 4.15d implies a minim compositional *tactus*. When it appears in a context in which the prevailing compositional *tactus* is the semibreve, it generates strong mensural emphasis on the level of the subdivision.

Ternary mensurations add further complications to the mensural functions of cadences. Their *tactus* may correspond either to a binary note that comes in ternary groups (such as a semibreve in perfect *tempus*) or to the ternary note itself. In the former case, the cadential possibilities are analogous to those illustrated above. Penultimates of two *tactus* in a ternary mensuration begin on the second of a group of three *tactus*, as in bar 9 of Example 4.4. If the *tactus* is a ternary note, the penultimate may last for

---

[24] Tinctoris, *Liber de arte contrapuncti*, book 2, ch. 29 ("Quomodo multi numquam supra integram partem dimidiam notae secundum quam mensura cantus dirigitur, immo supra minorem tantum assumunt"), 139.

[25] Gaffurio, *Practica musice*, book 3, ch. 4 ("Quae & ubi in contrapuncto admittendae sint discordantiae"), fol. ddiij^v.

Example 4.16 Cadences in relation to a ternary *tactus*: (a) whole *tactus*, no suspension; (b) ⅔ *tactus*, no suspension; (c) ⅔ *tactus* with suspension; (d) ⅔ *tactus* with ornamented suspension.

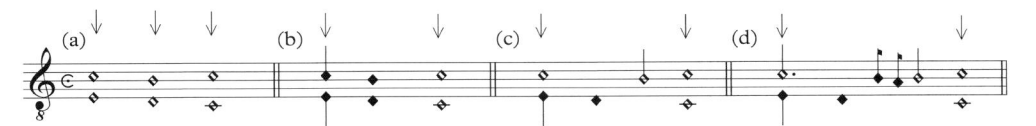

either a whole *tactus* or two-thirds of a *tactus*, as shown in Example 4.16. If there is a suspension, the penultimate must be two thirds of the *tactus*.

Text setting

Differential levels of emphasis are implicit not only in the rhythms that articulate mensural structures, but also in the verbal texts that are an essential component of vocal music. Emphasis, or accent, in verbal texts may result from a variety of factors, including the pronunciation of individual words, the relative importance of different words, and, in the case of poetic texts, the position of words and syllables in relation to the metrical structure of the poem. These different types of accents may coincide or conflict within the text itself. In a musical setting, verbal accents interact in complex ways with musical accents. From one point of view, musical accents create emphases that contribute to the interpretation of the verbal text. From the opposite point of view, verbal accents are an independent form of emphasis that influences the perception of musical rhythms. The presence of any new syllable on a note gives that note a stronger articulation than it would have within a melisma. The stronger the verbal emphasis on the syllable, the greater the emphasis that accrues to the note through the text.

The interaction between musical and verbal accents in fifteenth- and sixteenth-century music varies from one genre and style to another. In general, however, the rate of declamation does not exceed the first level of subdivision of the *tactus*. A binary compositional *tactus* therefore accommodates two syllables. A ternary compositional *tactus* can accommodate three syllables, but it more often has only two syllables, one twice as long as the other. These principles relate to the general tendency for the first level of accent in verbal texts to fall on alternate syllables. When this is the case, accented syllables generally fall on the *tactus* and unaccented syllables on the subdivision.[26] There are of course countless exceptions to this principle, but as an initial approximation it creates a foundation for matching the rhythmic structures of music and text.

Regular groups of *tactus*

Regular rhythmic articulation of the compositional *tactus* is obligatory in mensural music. Regular groups of *tactus* are optional, but common. Several techniques may articulate levels of the mensuration above that of the *tactus*. Phenomena that create mensural emphasis, such as final notes of cadences or accented syllables of text, may appear regularly on a level of *initium* above that of the *tactus*. For example, if the *tactus* is the semibreve and the cadential finals and text accents fall only on breve *initia*, the *tactus* will be heard in regular groups corresponding to the breve level of the mensuration. Similar groupings can be produced by long notes that begin on higher-level *initia* and by syncopation and hemiola that fall exclusively within mensural units on a higher level.

Groups of compositional *tactus* are treated much more flexibly in practice than the *tactus* itself. If they are present, they are usually established audibly at the beginning of a piece. After that, they may disappear temporarily or permanently, or they may remain audible, but be subject to occasional irregularities that never appear on the level of the *tactus*. They may be prominent or subtle. In some cases, they are implied by the notation, but have no effect on the audible structure of the music. The variable role of groups of *tactus* is an important criterion for distinguishing different mensural types in music.

Compositional *tactus* and performance *tactus*

Compositional *tactus* and performance *tactus* differ in fundamental ways. The compositional *tactus* is a structural component of music. Although it is not always possible to equate it unequivocally with one mensural level, the factors that define it can be identified and evaluated on the basis of the written score. The performance *tactus*, in contrast, is an external

---

[26] Graeme M. Boone, *Patterns in Play: A Model for Text Setting in the Early French Songs of Guillaume Dufay* (Lincoln: University of Nebraska Press, 1999), uses this principle as the foundation for a theory of text setting in the early songs of Du Fay.

time-keeping device that enables performers to measure and interpret rhythms. It is a means to an end, not an end in itself. We cannot observe the performance *tactus* of earlier periods directly, though we can obtain information about it from theoretical writings.

Despite these differences, theorists assume that *tactus* in these two senses is so closely related that they rarely distinguish the two meanings of the term explicitly. This is because the performance *tactus* both reflects and influences the way performers feel and project the compositional *tactus*. The relation between the two is not as simple as a one-to-one correspondence, however. As discussed in Chapter 3, the performance *tactus* is subject to a range of shadings in its groupings and subdivisions that parallel the variable relations among the compositional *tactus* and its subdivisions and groupings. If the compositional *tactus* falls clearly on one level of the mensuration and is not strongly subdivided or grouped, the performance *tactus* will normally fall on the same level. Alternatively, a strongly divided performance *tactus* may articulate one compositional *tactus* on the downstroke and another on the upstroke, such that the performance *tactus* corresponds to two compositional *tactus*.

The choice of which value to use as the performance *tactus* is important, because it affects the way performers feel the mensural structure on a deep, physical level. Several sixteenth-century theorists make this point. Zacconi, for example, argues passionately for the importance of choosing the correct subdivision of a *tactus* that measures ternary notes; in his view, the wrong choice ruins the effect of the music entirely.[27] He is more flexible in allowing a choice of *tactus* in imperfect *tempus*, though he points out that performers who choose a semibreve *tactus* in ₵ will be unaware of syncopated breves.[28] If syncopated breves are a significant part of a compositional design, it is important for singers to be aware of them. Spataro complains that composers fail to recognize errors of counterpoint because they use the semibreve as a performance *tactus* when they should use the breve, and this practice makes them unaware of contrapuntal relationships on the breve level.[29] Some theorists regard the breve performance *tactus* as more elegant than the semibreve, because it brings out rhythmic relations on larger levels and prevents excessive emphasis on smaller levels at the expense of longer time

---

[27] Zacconi, *Prattica di musica*, book 3, chs. 6, 8, 9, 23, 25, 26, 29, 31–34, 36, and 72. See DeFord, "Zacconi's Theories of *Tactus* and Mensuration," 165–69, for a discussion of Zacconi's views on this issue.
[28] Zacconi, *Prattica di musica*, book 1, ch. 52 ("Delle Sincope; con le sue vere, & reale distintioni a perfetta dimostratione che cosa sieno"), fol. 40ᵛ.
[29] Spataro, Letter of 30 January 1531 to Aaron, in *A Correspondence of Renaissance Musicians*, 416.

spans. Auctor Lampadius, for example, comments as follows in his *Compendium musices* of 1537:

Qua ratione cantores eruditi tactum Maiorem praeferunt? Ob eius suavitatem, hoc est, quod notae sub eo prolatae argutius ac lepidius resonant, atque sub minore; sed illa differentia perraro observatur.[30]	Why do sophisticated singers prefer the major [breve] *tactus*? For its suavity, that is, because notes measured by it sound more melodious and pleasing than under the minor [semibreve *tactus*]; but this distinction is very rarely observed.

Some theorists insist on rigid associations between performance *tactus* and mensuration signs for reasons that are more pedantic than musical, but musical considerations surely played a role in musicians' judgments about performance *tactus*.

These principles may be illustrated in relation to the Benedictus of Josquin's *Missa Pange lingua*. The section is a duo in imperfect *tempus*, notated with the sign ₵. The first ten breves consist of five statements of a single, two-breve motive performed in alternation on different pitch levels. The motive is shown in Example 4.17. The rhythm of the motive works in three simultaneous ways, as shown by markings above the example. First, the minim-units are grouped in an unmistakable 3+3+2 pattern (Example 4.17a) created by the pitches, surface rhythms, and declamation. The most prominent pitches are the first one (by virtue of its position) and the highest one (by virtue of its pitch and length). The placement of the latter on the fourth minim-unit sets off the first three minim-units as a group and may lead the listener to expect the beginning of a new group after three more minim-units. The declamation reinforces this pattern, since the accented syllable falls on the highest note. Second, there is a syncopation on the

Example 4.17 Josquin, *Missa Pange lingua*, Benedictus, bars 1–2. After Vatican City, Biblioteca Apostolica Vaticana, Cappella Sistina, Ms. 16, fols. xliii[r]–xliv[v].

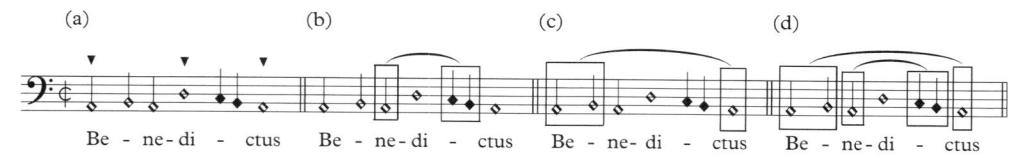

---

[30] Lampadius, *Compendium musices*, "De dimensione vel tactibus," fol. Dviij[r].

semibreve level, since the fourth note separates the preceding minim from the following pair of semiminims with which it is counted (Example 4.17b). Third, there is a syncopation on the breve level, since the entire semibreve syncopation, from the minim preceding the displaced semibreve through the semiminims following it, separates the first two minims from the last semibreve with which they are counted (Example 4.17c). The syncopation binds together the entire two-breve unit, because the mensural unit that begins with the first note is not complete until the end of the second breve-unit. Example 4.17d shows both of the nested syncopations.

Contemporaneous theory offers several alternatives for the performance *tactus* of pieces in ¢. The *tactus* may fall on either the semibreve or the breve; in either case, it may be strongly divided, weakly divided, or undivided. Example 4.18 shows six possible performance *tactus* by which the rhythm could be measured: the semibreve without marked subdivision or with subdivisions of equal or unequal weight, and the breve without marked subdivision or with subdivisions of equal or unequal weight. In the example, points that are emphasized equally are shown with arrows and points that are marked less strongly are shown with arrowheads without stems. The semibreve *tactus* with subdivisions of equal weight emphasizes the rhythms on the minim level, and thus brings out the 3+3+2 pattern most strongly. The other *tactus* bring out the syncopations, but do not reinforce the grouping of minims. The undivided semibreve and the breve with subdivisions of equal weight bring out the syncopation on the semibreve level at the

Example 4.18 Josquin, *Missa Pange lingua*, Benedictus, bars 1–2: (a) semibreve *tactus*; (b) breve *tactus*.

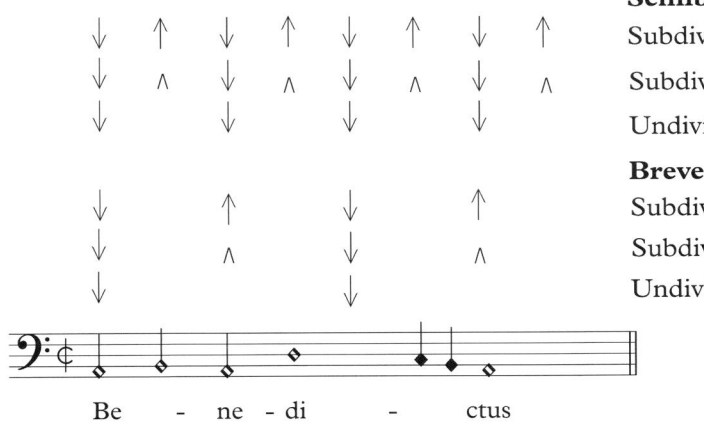

Example 4.19 Hypothetical variants of the rhythm of Example 4.18.

expense of the syncopation on the breve level. The undivided breve *tactus* does the opposite; it encourages a flowing rhythm with little articulation of any mensural groupings. The breve *tactus* with subdivisions of unequal weight brings out the syncopations on both the breve and the semibreve levels.

Which performance *tactus* does the most justice to the multiple relationships in this rhythm? My preference is for the breve with subdivisions of unequal weight, not because I believe the grouping of minims is unimportant, but because I believe it is strong enough to come across on its own, whereas the syncopations will not be clear without some reinforcement from the performers. The performance *tactus*, which is inaudible, will of course not accomplish this by itself, but a semibreve or divided breve performance *tactus* will encourage a slight emphasis on the third note, enabling it to be recognized as a semibreve *initium*, rather than simply as the last member of a group of three minims. A performance *tactus* in which all semibreves are equally emphasized might encourage too much emphasis at that point. That interpretation not only obscures the natural grouping of the minims, but obstructs the continuity of the two-breve unit. These distinctions are subtle, but vital. The rhythm works because of the tension among all three of the ways in which the notes are grouped. If one grouping overshadows the others, the rhythm loses its subtlety. The crude variants shown in Example 4.19 illustrate the importance of the delicate balance among these conflicting groupings. In Example 4.19a, the rhythm is purely ternary, and in Example 4.19b it is purely binary. Neither of these variants begins to approximate the complexity and subtlety of Josquin's rhythm.

A brief look at the complete Benedictus (Example 4.20) demonstrates the application of other concepts in this chapter to a piece of real music. The semibreve functions as the compositional *tactus* throughout the section, as the semibreve syncopation in the opening motive suggests. Once the two voices begin to sing simultaneously, there are one or two structural intervals on every semibreve. The contrapuntal rhythm slows to the level of the breve only after the principal cadences, in bars 21, 33, and 38. Contrapuntal progressions on the minim level are often weaker when they end on

Example 4.20 Josquin, *Missa Pange lingua*, Benedictus (complete). After Vatican City, Biblioteca Apostolica Vaticana, Cappella Sistina, Ms. 16, fols. xliii^v–xliv^r.

minim-max *initia* than when they end on semibreve *initia*, but strong contrapuntal progressions appear on all minims before cadences, as in Tinctoris's example (Example 4.4). Non-suspension dissonances are limited to semiminims (a quarter of the compositional *tactus*) and fall on weak semiminim *initia* except in stepwise descending figures, as Zarlino recommends. Suspensions are minims. Syncopations occur on both the semibreve and the breve levels; the latter may take the form of either nested syncopations, as illustrated above, or dotted semibreve + two semiminim figures in syncopated positions, as in bars 29–31. The shortest notes with separate syllables of text are minims (half of the compositional *tactus*).

The surface rhythm is relatively uniform throughout the section, but Josquin builds a sense of acceleration by reducing the size of the largest prominent mensural level from the long to the breve, and then from the breve to the semibreve, as the music develops. Breves are never entirely out of the picture; cadential finals fall only on breve *initia*, but within phrases, the breve level is at times overshadowed by the semibreve level. The level of the long (i.e., the pairing of breves) is prominent in bars 1–10. It continues through the cadence in bar 15, though the voice entries on semibreve-max *initia* in bars 11 and 13 weaken it somewhat. It is overshadowed in bar 16 by a voice entry on a minim-max *initium* that shifts the melodic subject with respect to the semibreve *initium*. This gesture calls attention away from mensural relationships on the level of the long and breve and focuses it on the level of the semibreve. The cadence in bar 21 lines up with the long-units of the initial mensural structure and reinforces that level with a note that lasts for a full long in the tenor. It is unclear whether or not the listener should perceive it as a return to and reconfirmation of the long-unit, or whether the long-unit has been erased from memory for too long to be meaningful at that point. In any case, long-units play no further role after bar 23. Imitation moves to the interval of the breve at that point, but there is little, if any, differentiation of the semibreve *initia* in the passage that follows. The equality of semibreves is great enough that the subject that begins in bars 22–23 can be displaced by a semibreve upon repetition in bars 29ff (plus upbeat). The cadence in bars 32–33 restores the breve-units to audible prominence. Subsequent cadences, in bars 37–38, 42–43, and 47–48, are perhaps frequent enough to keep the breve-units alive as an audible level of mensural structure from bar 32 to the end. The four phrases from bar 29 to the end are all five breves long. The five-breve unit thus plays a role in the temporal design at this point, though it is not part of the notated mensural structure.

What do the rhythms of the complete section imply about the performance *tactus*? Given the regularity of the semibreve compositional *tactus*, the divided breve and the semibreve (with or without marked subdivision) are the only reasonable possibilities. These *tactus* have different effects on the articulation and perception of rhythms on all levels. By keeping performers aware of the breve-unit, the breve *tactus* encourages a sense of suspense when the breve level goes underground and resolution when it resurfaces. A semibreve *tactus*, in contrast, encourages freer grouping of semibreves where the breve-unit is not functional and projects the return of the regular breve-unit as a more relaxed event. On a smaller scale, a breve *tactus* encourages a more flowing performance of the contrapuntal progressions in minims, since it does not articulate subdivisions of semibreves, while a semibreve *tactus* encourages the option of bringing out minim contrapuntal progressions through marked articulation of the subdivisions. Either *tactus* is possible, and the differences between them are subtle, but the choice nevertheless deserves serious consideration.

The compositional *tactus*, which was normally mirrored by the performance *tactus*, is an essential component of mensural rhythms. Surface rhythms might reinforce it or work against it, but in either case, the relation of the surface rhythms to the *tactus* is a crucial component of any rhythmic idea. Syncopated rhythms are defined differently in theory, and produce different effects in practice, from rhythms that align with the *tactus*. A long-standing scholarly myth alleges that *tactus* is a purely external time-keeping device that has nothing to do with rhythm.[31] Although several scholars have attempted to refute that idea,[32] it still persists in some studies.[33] The rhythmic significance of the *tactus* varies from one repertoire to another, but regular, audible measurement on the level of the compositional *tactus* was the foundation of all measured rhythms in the fifteenth and sixteenth centuries.

[31] This myth originated with Schünemann, "Zur Frage des Taktschlagens und der Textbehandlung in der Mensuralmusik," and Schünemann, *Geschichte des Dirigierens*, 36–68. Schünemann characterizes the *tactus* as "only an external means of orientation" ("nur ein äußerliches Orientierungsmittel") in the former study (p. 95) and insists that it has no accentual implications.

[32] See for example Edward E. Lowinsky, "Early Scores in Manuscript," *Journal of the American Musicological Society* 13 (1960), 126–73; Edward Houghton, "Rhythm and Meter in 15th-Century Polyphony," *Journal of Music Theory* 18 (1974), 190–212; and Boone, "Marking Mensural Time," 1–43.

[33] For example, Rebecca Herissone, *Music Theory in Seventeenth-Century England* (Oxford University Press, 2000), 54, claims that early theorists did not say "that the downbeat should be equated with a strong pulse and the upbeat with a weak one." She uses Bank's questionable interpretation of some sixteenth-century descriptions of the *tactus* as an up-down, instead of a down-up, motion, to support the point (see Chapter 3, p. 64 n. 27). But what could theorists like Tinctoris and Zarlino mean when they say that the first part of the *tactus* is expressed more forcefully, or strikes the hearing more strongly, than the second part, if not that the first part carries an accent by virtue of its position? Ignoring the *ictic* character of the *tactus* leads to a one-dimensional understanding of mensural rhythms that does not do justice to the complex and subtle rhythmic interactions like those in the Josquin Benedictus discussed above.

5 | *Tactus* and signs in fifteenth-century music theory

Fifteenth-century writings on musical time measurement are difficult to interpret. They assume the reader's understanding of terms, concepts, and practices that are no longer familiar, and they often exhibit ways of thinking that seem foreign to us. Few theorists discuss the value or duration of the *tactus* explicitly until the last three or four decades of the fifteenth century. Earlier theorists provide indirect information on those subjects by relating them to concepts of standard and modified methods of time measurement. They normally describe only the modified methods and take the standard method for granted as a basis for comparison. Modified measurements are applied to "note values," which may be understood as numbers of *tactus*, absolute durations, or relative durations, depending on the context. The *tactus* units in which "note values" are measured may be understood as performance *tactus*, compositional *tactus*, or theoretical *tactus*. Because of these ambiguities, modern scholars have often interpreted theoretical statements on the subject in radically different ways.[1]

Modified methods of measuring are often associated with specialized signs in both theory and practice, but the meanings of these signs are not consistent. Most signs could represent more than one method of measurement, and most methods of measurement could be represented by more than one sign. The meanings of signs in practice, and the applicability of modified methods of measurement in the absence of signs, must therefore be judged on the basis of context. The goal of a study of the theoretical meanings of signs should not be to establish a formula for interpreting them, but to investigate the range of possible meanings of each sign and to postulate criteria for making informed choices among them.

Concepts of time measurement

The standard method of measuring musical time, called *ut iacet* ("as it lies") in the fifteenth century, was to apply the performance *tactus* to a semibreve

---

[1] These issues are discussed in Ruth I. DeFord, "On Diminution and Proportion in Fifteenth-Century Music Theory," *Journal of the American Musicological Society* 58 (2005), 1–67.

of moderate duration. The methods of modifying it were called "diminution," "augmentation," and "proportions."

Diminution reduces the "values" of the notes in one of two ways: either the performance *tactus* is shifted to the breve, so that the number of *tactus* on each figure is reduced to half or a third of what it would be with *ut iacet* measurement, or the duration of the *tactus* is reduced (i.e., the *tactus* is made faster), so that the number of *tactus* on each figure is unchanged, but the amount of absolute time that each note takes is reduced. Diminution measured in breves may apply to one or more voices in simultaneous relation to other voices that are measured in semibreves, in which case the two methods of measuring must be proportional. It may also apply to all voices in a piece or section of a piece, in which case it need not be proportional to anything. Fifteenth-century theorists describe all of these possibilities, but their terms for them are not consistent. I shall distinguish them as follows: "proportional diminution" has a breve performance *tactus* and appears simultaneously with *ut iacet* or augmented measurement in other voices; "mensural diminution" has a breve performance *tactus* in all voices; "acceleratio mensurae" has a semibreve performance *tactus* that is faster than usual by an unspecified amount. The breve *tactus* of mensural diminution was usually slower than the standard *ut iacet tactus*, but not twice as slow. Mensural diminution and *acceleratio mensurae* could therefore lead to equivalent reductions in the absolute durations of the written notes (or "metronome speed"); in other words, performance with a fast semibreve *tactus* was an alternative to performance with a slow breve *tactus*.

Examples 5.1 and 5.2 illustrate all types of diminution in imperfect and perfect *tempus*. In imperfect *tempus*, proportional and mensural diminution are measured in imperfect breves. In perfect *tempus*, the same types of diminution may be measured in either perfect or imperfect breves, though the latter option was purely theoretical in the case of mensural diminution. When proportional diminution of perfect *tempus* is measured in perfect breves, the *ut iacet* equivalent is perfect prolation, because a perfect breve in diminution is equivalent to a perfect semibreve *ut iacet*. When it is measured in imperfect breves, the *ut iacet* equivalent is perfect *tempus* (cf. Examples 5.2b and 5.2c). The metronome marks in the examples illustrate approximate relations among signs and are not meant to be prescriptive. In principle, minims have the same duration in all *ut iacet* mensurations, so that a perfect breve is 50 percent longer than an imperfect breve, though this relation applies literally only in complex, proportionally organized compositions. For purposes of illustration,

Example 5.1 Types of measurement in imperfect *tempus*: (a) *ut iacet*; (b) proportional diminution; (c) mensural diminution; (d) *acceleratio mensurae*. C represents *ut iacet* measurement and ¢ represents proportional diminution, mensural diminution, and *acceleratio mensurae* in this example.

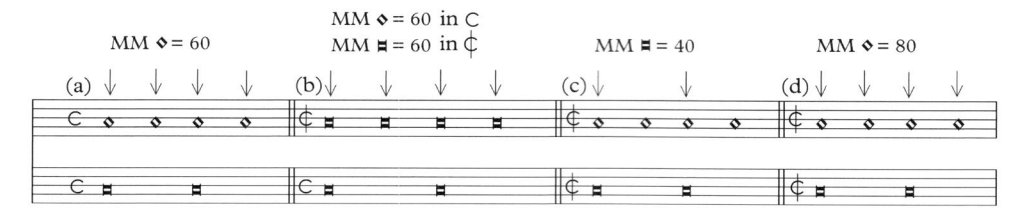

Example 5.2 Types of measurement in perfect *tempus*: (a) *ut iacet*; (b) proportional diminution (2:1) measured in perfect breves; (c) proportional diminution (2:1) measured in imperfect breves; (d) mensural diminution measured in perfect breves; (e) mensural diminution measured in imperfect breves; (f) *acceleratio mensurae*. O represents *ut iacet* measurement and Φ represents proportional diminution, mensural diminution, and *acceleratio mensurae* in this example.

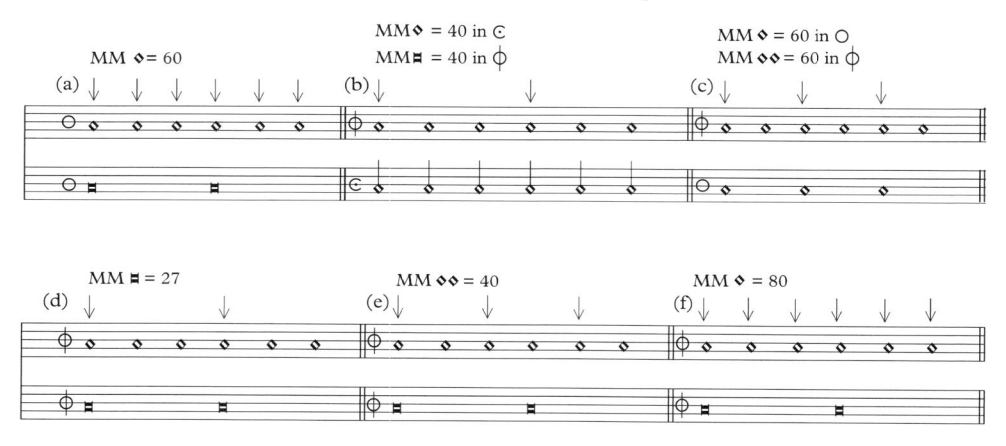

I have chosen metronome marks that give the semibreves of mensural diminution and *acceleratio mensurae* the same duration in both imperfect and perfect *tempus*, but none of these techniques implies a fixed metronome speed.

The earliest theoretical discussion of diminution applies only to proportionally reduced repetitions of motet tenors. It appears in Muris's *Ars practica mensurabilis cantus*, which dates from the mid–late fourteenth century and served as the standard text on mensural theory for most of the fifteenth century. Muris defines diminution as the replacement of each note by the next smaller value:

... pro maxima in diminutione ponitur longa, pro longa brevis, pro brevi semibrevis, pro semibrevi minima.[2]	... for a maxima in diminution a long is placed, for a long a breve, for a breve a semibreve, and for a semibreve a minim.

This definition originally applied to written-out repeats in which each note of the original statement of a musical idea is replaced by the next smaller value in the repeat. Diminution in this sense does not change the perfect or imperfect quality of the written notes, except that, as Muris's detailed rules specify, perfect longs are replaced by perfect breves when the original mensuration is perfect *modus* with imperfect *tempus*. Muris explains that diminution reduces the values of notes in 2:1 ratio when either the *modus* or the *tempus* is imperfect and in 3:1 ratio when both the *modus* and the *tempus* are perfect. Fifteenth-century theorists continued to copy and paraphrase Muris's text even after diminution came to be practiced in new ways to which these ratios do not apply.

The concept of mensural diminution arose as a result of a change in the usual method of notating tenor repeats in diminution around 1400. Instead of writing out repeats in the next smaller values, composers or scribes would notate the tenor only once and leave it to the performers to read each note like the next smaller value in diminution. The easiest way to accomplish this was to read the original statement with a semibreve performance *tactus* and the diminution with a breve performance *tactus*. By extension, the concept of diminution came to apply to any music that was measured with a breve performance *tactus*, whether or not it had any relation to music that was measured with a semibreve performance *tactus*.[3] The earliest theoretical description of what is probably mensural diminution is found in Prosdocimo's 1404 commentary on Muris's *Ars practica mensurabilis cantus*. Prosdocimo notes with disapproval that diminution is no longer limited to tenors of motets, as Muris maintains, but appears also in other genres, such as ballades, and in voices in which it is not a proportionally reduced repeat of a previously stated idea.[4] These contexts are likely to be mensural, rather than proportional, since proportional notation is not common in them.

Mensural diminution can be described in proportional terms if "note values" are defined by *tactus* counts, rather than durations. If the value of a

---

[2] Muris, *Ars practica mensurabilis cantus*, ch. 11 ("De diminutione"), 76.

[3] The concept of diminution in a mensural, but not proportional, sense resulted from a series of changes in notational practices in the early fifteenth century. I will discuss these changes, which are too complex to summarize in detail here, in a forthcoming study of Muris's theory of diminution and its reception by later theorists.

[4] Prosdocimo, *Expositiones tractatus practice cantus mensurabilis magistri Johannis de Muris*, 207.

semibreve in imperfect *tempus* is one *tactus ut iacet*, it is a half-*tactus* in mensural diminution. The semibreve (along with all other notes) thus loses half of its "value" in diminution even if the durations of the semibreve *tactus* and the breve *tactus* are unrelated. This is the same as saying that a quarter note in modern $\frac{2}{2}$ time has half the "value" of a quarter note in $\frac{4}{4}$ time on grounds that it is worth half a beat in the former and a whole beat in the latter, regardless of the metronome speed. If the *tempus* is perfect, shifting the performance *tactus* from the semibreve to the breve reduces the number of *tactus* on each note to a third, rather than half. Nevertheless, the terms "per medium," "per semi," and "semiditas," which imply 2:1 diminution, were commonly applied to mensural diminution of both imperfect and perfect *tempus* throughout the fifteenth century.

Acceleratio mensurae is a later concept that first appears in theoretical writings in the later fifteenth century. It functions as an alternative to mensural diminution when rhythms can be measured more conveniently in semibreves than in breves. It may have existed in practice before it is documented in theory, but pieces with signs calling unambiguously for diminution in which a semibreve performance *tactus* seems desirable on musical grounds appeared around the same time that *acceleratio mensurae* was first described by theorists. It therefore seems likely that the concept and practice arose after the mid fifteenth century as a result of the increased use of short notes and small-scale rhythmic complications in music that was considered to be in diminution.

Augmentation is the opposite of diminution. It means placing the performance *tactus* on the minim. In practice, it was always proportional. Prosdocimo provides the earliest definition, which is modeled on Muris's definition of diminution, in his *Tractatus practice de musica mensurabili* (1408):

Augmentatio est pronuntiatio note minoris in valore note sibi immediate majoris ... In tali augmentatione semper ponitur nota major pro nota sibi immediate minori, verbi gratia ... semper pro semiminima ponitur minima, et pro minima semibrevis, et pro semibrevi brevis et pro brevi longa et pro longa maxima.[5]	Augmentation is the performance of a smaller note with the value of the next larger note ... In this type of augmentation, a larger note is always placed for the next smaller note; for example ... for a semiminim a minim is always placed, and for a minim a semibreve, and for a semibreve a breve and for a breve a long and for a long a maxima.

---

[5] Prosdocimo, *Tractatus practice de musica mensurabili*, "De augmentatione," III: 225.

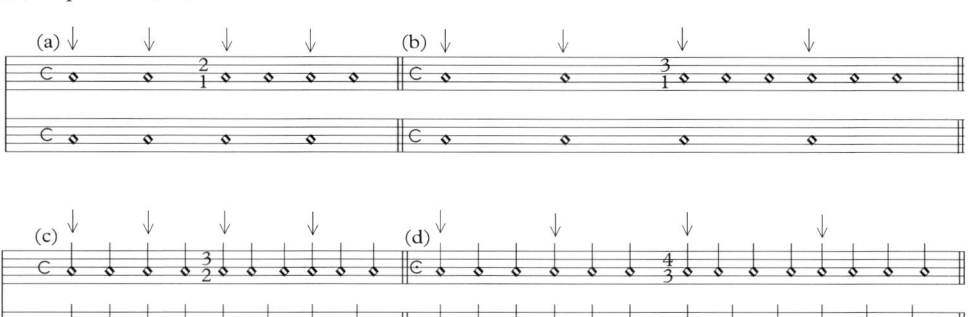

Example 5.3 Proportions: (a) duple; (b) triple; (c) *sesquialtera* (3:2); (d) *sesquitertia* (4:3).

Proportions, in contrast to diminution and augmentation, are defined not by the level or the duration of the *tactus*, but by the number of notes that occupy a given unit of time. They are classified on the basis of the ratio of the new to the old number of notes in the time unit: a proportion is duple if two notes take the place of one, triple if three notes take the place of one, etc. The number of categories of proportion that theorists apply to music varies. Many discuss proportions that are of little or no practical importance, and some invent musical examples to illustrate these hypothetical entities. The categories of proportions commonly found in real music are duple (2:1), triple (3:1), *sesquialtera* (3:2), and *sesquitertia* (4:3). They are illustrated in Example 5.3.

Proportions as understood by most theorists differ from diminution and augmentation in two essential respects. First, they may alter the grouping of the written notes. If a proportion calls for three notes in the time of one or two, the notes in the proportion will come in groups of three; if it calls for four notes in the time of three, the notes in the proportion will come in groups of four. These new groupings may alter the perfect or imperfect quality of the notes. If notes of a particular type come in groups of three, the next larger value is normally perfect; if they come in groups of two or four, it is normally imperfect. Prosdocimo explains this principle as follows:

Item scire debes, quod iste figure sic diminute habent reduci ad mensuras superius in primo capitulo nominatas, quod videre poteris si bene considerabis, nam figure	You must know that the notes diminished in this way are to be assimilated to the mensurations named above in the first chapter, as you will be able to see if you consider well. Diminished

diminute que in proportione sexquialtera cantantur, sicut tres pro duabus, habent reduci ad perfectiones mensurarum, et possunt perfici, imperfici, evacuari, alterari, et breviter omnes passiones pati quas pati possunt figure recte perfectiones mensurarum habentes. De figuris vero in aliis proportionibus diminutis considera tu, et invenies mensuras ad quas reducuntur si subtiliter speculaberis.[6]	notes that are sung in *sesquialtera* proportion, as three for two, are to be assimilated to notes that are perfect in mensuration. They can be perfected, imperfected, notated in void, [and] altered; briefly, they may be subjected to all of the effects to which figures that are properly perfect in mensuration may be subjected. Consider the figures that are diminished in other proportions, and you will discover the mensurations to which they are assimilated if you think critically.

Second, proportions apply principally to one level of the mensuration and only secondarily to other levels. If a proportion changes the quality of the notes, the proportional ratios may apply differently to different values. For example, in a triple proportion that applies primarily to semibreves in imperfect *tempus*, as in Example 5.3b, the semibreves are in 3:1 ratio to the *ut iacet* semibreves of the imperfect *tempus*, but the breves are in 2:1 ratio, because breves are perfect in the proportion and imperfect in the mensuration to which it refers.

Despite the fundamental differences between diminution and proportions, there are overlaps between them that led to overlaps between the terminology and signs that were applied to them. The effect of proportional diminution is often indistinguishable from that of a proportion. The simultaneous combination of diminished and *ut iacet* voices in Example 5.1b results in a 2:1 proportion between the figures. This relationship may therefore be called "duple proportion," rather than "proportional diminution." Conversely, the triple proportion in Example 5.3b could be classified as perfect *tempus* in diminution combined with imperfect *tempus ut iacet*, rather than as triple proportion. Because of these similarities, the term "proportion" may apply loosely to the technique that I call "mensural diminution." The mensural diminution in Example 5.1c might be called "duple proportion" on grounds that it is measured like duple proportion, even though it is not proportional to anything in a durational sense, and the mensural diminution in Example 5.2d might be called "triple proportion"

---

[6] Ibid., "De signis mensure," III: 219.

because three semibreves are measured with one *tactus*, as in Example 5.3b. I shall use the term "proportion" in quotation marks to distinguish the purely mensural sense of the term from the literal meaning that applies to durational relationships.

Unmodified signs of *tempus* and prolation

Unmodified signs of *tempus* and prolation (O, C, ☉, and ₵) were associated in theory with a *tactus* on the imperfect or perfect semibreve throughout the fifteenth and sixteenth centuries. In practice, however, O and C could also be used generically to indicate mensuration, but not *tactus*. In other words, the presence or absence of diminution was not always specified by the sign. The generic use of O and C was standard in English practice and sometimes applies to the music of Continental composers as well.[7]

☉ and ₵ are more problematic. They disappeared almost entirely as *ut iacet* signs around 1430, then resurfaced as signs of augmentation in proportional relation to *ut iacet* or diminished mensurations in Continental music, in imitation of English practice, around the 1450s. Some theorists associate them with a perfect semibreve *tactus*.[8] Others regard the minim as their usual *tactus*, although the theorists who express this view are all too late to have any authority for the practices of the early decades of the century. Tinctoris implies that their *tactus* depends on the context. He alludes in passing to the possibility of a perfect semibreve *tactus* in perfect prolation, but says that the *tactus* should be the imperfect semibreve when perfect prolation is compared directly (in simultaneous or successive relation) to imperfect prolation.[9] His example of dissonance treatment in perfect

---

[7] See Margaret Bent, Introduction to *Fifteenth-Century Liturgical Music II: Four Anonymous Masses*, Early English Church Music 22 (London: Stainer and Bell, 1979), x and xiv, and Rob C. Wegman, "Concerning Tempo in the English Polyphonic Mass, c. 1420–70," *Acta musicologica* 61 (1989), 48.

[8] For example, the treatment of diminution by Anonymous 11 discussed below implies a perfect semibreve *tactus* in perfect prolation *ut iacet*. Guilielmus Monachus, *De preceptis artis musice*, 25, implies that the usual *tactus* of perfect prolation is the perfect semibreve when he explains *sesquitertia* (4:3) proportion of ₵ as singing two semibreves (= four minims) on one *tactus*. Since four minims take the place of three in this proportion, ₵ must be presumed to have three minims, or one perfect semibreve, per *tactus*. Like many fifteenth-century theorists, Guilielmus takes that basic method of measuring for granted and explains only the modified one.

[9] "Since music in major prolation is sometimes measured not according to the whole semibreve or according to the single minim, but according to the imperfect semibreve, that is, two minims..." ("Subinde quoniam cantus maioris prolationis aliquando non secundum integram semibrevem

prolation is based on a minim compositional *tactus*,[10] yet he objects to the use of perfect prolation to represent augmentation in relation to other signs unless that meaning is confirmed by a proportion or canon.[11] Ramis upbraids him harshly for this view on grounds that the acceptance of a practice by great composers is sufficient to justify it theoretically.[12] Adam von Fulda associates all signs of perfect prolation (C, O, and even O2) with a minim *tactus*.[13] His inclusion of O2 in this category is puzzling. The sign is extremely rare in practice, and Adam may have included it only in the interest of symmetry. Since he has three signs for a breve *tactus* (O2, C2, and ₵) and three for a semibreve *tactus* (O, C, and Φ), he may have felt a need to have three for the minim *tactus* as well.

Cut signs

Fifteenth-century theorists associate cut mensuration signs, which begin to appear in practical sources around the 1420s, with diminution in all of its senses.[14] They often define signs followed by a number 2 as synonyms of cut signs, especially before the 1460s, when circles and semicircles followed by numbers came to be interpreted as *modus cum tempore* signs in some instances. Most theorists apply these modifications only to signs with imperfect prolation (Φ, ₵, O2, C2), but some use a stroke through signs of perfect prolation (Φ, ₵) as well. Both the stroke, which symbolically cuts the sign in half, and the number 2 following a sign imply that the values of the notes are reduced by half. In the later fifteenth century, cut signs could represent *acceleratio mensurae*, as well as mensural and proportional diminution. The sign Φ could also have a variety of non-mensural meanings.[15]

---

vel secundum minimam solam, sed secundum semibrevem imperfectam, hoc est duas minimas, mensuratur . . . "). Tinctoris, *Liber de arte contrapuncti*, book 2, ch. 28 ("De admissione discordantiarum circa partes semibrevis in prolatione maiori consistentis quando secundum duas partes eius mensura cantus dirigitur"), 136–37.

[10] Ibid., book 2, ch. 23 ("Quod in simplici contrapuncto discordantiae non sunt admittendae, sed in diminuto, et primo qualiter circa partes minimae in utraque prolatione et circa partes semibrevis in minori"), 122.

[11] *Proportionale musices*, book 3, ch. 3 ("Quando proportiones signandae sint"), 48–49.

[12] *Musica practica*, part III, tract. 1, ch. 2 ("In quo signa per quae numeri distinguuntur"), 68.

[13] *Musica*, part III, ch. 7, III: 362.

[14] See Alexander Blachly, "Mensuration and Tempo in Fifteenth-Century Music: Cut Signatures in Theory and Practice" (Ph.D. diss., Columbia University, 1995), for an extensive study of fifteenth-century cut signs in both theory and practice.

[15] Most of the evidence for non-mensural meanings of Φ is found in practical sources, but Φ is defined as a sign of repetition in the anonymous *Tractatulus de cantu mensurali seu figurativo*

Several sources of the mid fifteenth century explain cut signs and signs followed by a number 2 in a way that makes sense only if the diminution to which they refer is mensural. The most comprehensive is the *Tractatus de musica plana et mensurabili* of Anonymous 11, which pertains to practices of the second quarter of the century, although its date of copying was somewhat later. The author defines diminution in terms derived directly from Muris:

Sed diminucio sic habet fieri: maxima posita, longa cantatur; qua posita, brevis proferetur; ea posita, semibrevis cantatur. Talis autem si ponitur, minima profertur; qua posita, semiminima habet cantari, ut patet in exemplo illo:[16]	But diminution is to be made thus: if a maxima is placed, a long is sung; if [a long] is placed, a breve will be uttered; if [a breve] is placed, a semibreve is sung; but if [a semibreve] is placed, a minim is uttered; if [a minim] is placed, a semiminim is to be sung, as may be seen in this example:

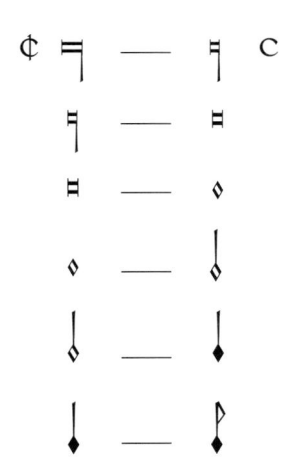

This example appears in one of the spaces surrounding a circular diagram illustrating relative note values in all combinations of perfect and imperfect

---

musice artis, ed. F. Alberto Gallo, Corpus scriptorum de musica 16 ([Dallas, Texas]: American Institute of Musicology, 1971), 37. Non-mensural meanings of the sign are not discussed here, because this chapter is devoted to theoretical definitions of signs. On that issue, see Margaret Bent, "The Early Use of the Sign ϕ," *Early Music* 24 (1996), 199–225.

[16] Anonymous 11, *Tractatus de musica plana et mensurabili*, I: 152–53.

124   Theory

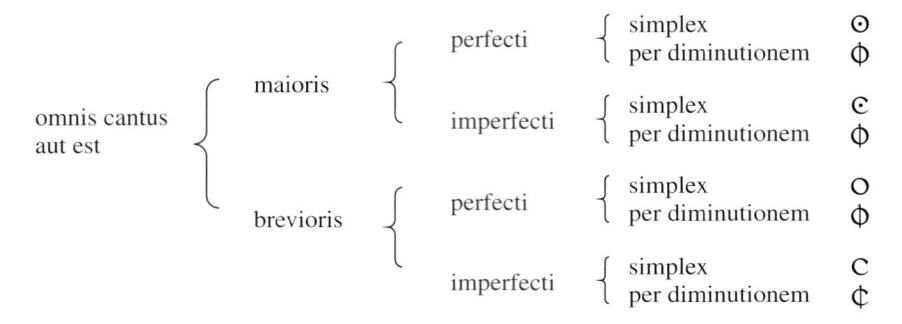

```
                    ┌                ┌ perfecti   ┌ simplex            ⊙
                    │   maioris     ┤            └ per diminutionem   ⦶
                    │               │
                    │                └ imperfecti ┌ simplex            ₵
omnis cantus       ┤                             └ per diminutionem   ⦶
aut est             │
                    │                ┌ perfecti   ┌ simplex            O
                    │   brevioris   ┤            └ per diminutionem   ⦶
                    │               │
                    └                └ imperfecti ┌ simplex            C
                                                  └ per diminutionem   ₵
```

Figure 5.1 Mensural categories according to Anonymous 11.

modus, *tempus*, and prolation. Additional diagrams and comments pertaining to mensuration and diminution appear in the remaining spaces. They include two lists of signs. The first represents diminution of each mensuration with a cut version of its *ut iacet* sign:

Signum maioris prolacionis temporis perfecti:	⊙
Signum maioris prolacionis temporis imperfecti:	₵
Signum maioris prolacionis [temporis perfecti] per semi	⦶
Signum prolacionis maioris temporis imperfecti per semi	₵
Signum brevioris prolacionis temporis perfecti	O
Signum brevioris prolacionis temporis perfecti per semi	⦶
Signum minoris prolacionis temporis imperfecti	C
Signum brevioris prolacionis temporis imperfecti per semi	₵

The second represents diminution of ⊙ and ₵, as well as O, with the sign ⦶ (see Figure 5.1). The reason for the discrepancy between the two lists is that diminution of perfect *tempus* and diminution of perfect prolation are functionally equivalent.[17] For this author, C2 and O2 are synonymous with ₵ and ⦶, respectively:

Eciam illud signum diminucionis [C2] equivalet huic ₵; similiter illud ⦶ huic O2 secundum modernissimos cantores.[18]	Also this sign of diminution [C2] is equivalent to this ₵; similarly, this ⦶ to this O2 according to the most modern singers.

---

[17] This is because a perfect breve in diminution may be thought of as equivalent to either a perfect semibreve *ut iacet* or half of a perfect breve *ut iacet*, as shown in Examples 5.2b and c. The diagram in Figure 5.1 also appears in the appendix to one of the sources of the *Tractatus et compendium cantus figurati* of Anonymous 12.

[18] Anonymous 11, *Tractatus de musica plana et mensurabili*, I: 155.

The reason for interpreting the above descriptions as mensural diminution is that diminution signs have a quantitative effect on note "values" even though they do not depend on a direct comparison to *ut iacet* signs for their meaning. They produce a quantitative reduction in *tactus* counts, but not necessarily in durations. They may represent proportional diminution if they are combined with *ut iacet* signs in simultaneous relation, but that is not their primary meaning. The author does not say whether the breve *tactus* of Φ is perfect or imperfect, but his general definition of diminution as applying the *tactus* to the next larger written value implies that it is perfect. The common practice of equating Φ in 2:1 proportion with ₵ in the early fifteenth century supports that interpretation.

Later theorists interpret Φ, and sometimes also ₵, not as proportional or mensural diminution, but as *acceleratio mensurae*. The first theorist to do so was Anonymous 12, whose treatise dates from *c.* 1460–71. He defines ₵ as a sign of mensural diminution, which he calls *semiditas*, and Φ as a sign of *acceleratio mensurae*, which he calls *diminutio*. *Semiditas* reduces the number of *tactus* by which each note is measured, but *diminutio* makes the *tactus* itself faster. His term *sincopatio* includes both techniques. (This definition of "syncopation" is unique to Anonymous 12 and his followers and unrelated to the standard definition of the term discussed previously.[19]) The author explains "syncopation" as follows:

Sincopatio ... est valoris notarum ablatio cuius duae sunt species, scilicet semiditas et diminutio. Semiditas est alicuius cantus medietatis ablatio, et habet fieri in tempore imperfecto minoris prolationis imperfectae, et eius est tale signum quum paragraphum, id est unus simplex tractus, ponitur in medio semicirculi, ut hic: ₵, ₵ ... Secunda species est diminutio, et est alicuius cantus tertiae eius partis ablatio. Et habet fieri in tempore perfecto, tam prolationis perfectae quam imperfectae ... et eius est	Syncopation ... is the removal of value from notes, of which there are two types, namely *semiditas* and diminution. *Semiditas* is the removal of half of a song [i.e., that which is sung], and it is to be made in imperfect *tempus* with imperfect minor prolation, and its sign is thus, when a stroke, that is one simple line, is placed in the middle of a semicircle, like this: ₵, ₵ ... The second type is diminution, and it is the removal of a third part of any song. And it is to be made in perfect *tempus*, with both

---

[19] This use of the term is modeled on the definition of syncopation as the excision of a syllable from the middle of a word (which results in the shortening of the word) in rhetoric.

signum non unum sed plura quia in pluribus fieri habet. Primo quum paragraphum ponitur in medio unius circuli integri non habentis in medio punctum, ut hic: ϕ; huius modi cantus medietas non tollitur sed solum tertia pars, hoc tantum est dicere quod velocius canitur quam si paragraphum non poneretur in medio.[20]

perfect and imperfect prolation ... and it has not one sign, but many, because it is to be made in many [contexts]. First, when a stroke is placed in the middle of a whole circle without a dot in the middle, like this: ϕ. From this type of song half is not removed, but only a third; that is to say only that it is sung faster than if the stroke were not placed in the middle.

The author goes on to include cut signs of perfect prolation among the signs that mean *diminutio*, rather than *semiditas*. The removal of half of the value of the notes implies shifting the *tactus* to the breve in ¢, as in the writings of Anonymous 11 and others, but the removal of a third in ϕ must refer to a reduction of the duration of the *tactus*, not the number of *tactus* by which notes are measured, since reducing the number of *tactus* on each note by a third is not practical. The author's concluding statement, which equates *diminutio* simply with faster performance, supports this interpretation. It is unclear how literally the reduction by a third is to be taken. It certainly cannot be an exact ratio when ϕ is not compared to an *ut iacet* sign in the same piece, and it is probably meant only as an approximation in any case. The anonymous author of *Ein tütsche musica* (1491), whose work is heavily dependent on Anonymous 12, describes ϕ as "perhaps a third or a half faster" than O,[21] implying that the degree of speeding of the *tactus* is not precisely defined. Adam von Fulda agrees with Anonymous 12 in classifying ¢ as a sign of a breve *tactus* and ϕ as a sign of a semibreve *tactus*, but says nothing about the duration of either *tactus*.[22]

Tinctoris, whose writings date from the 1470s, is the first theorist to define both ϕ and ¢ as signs of *acceleratio mensurae*, but his explanation of ¢ makes it clear that it is not the performance *tactus*, but the compositional *tactus*, that is faster in ¢ than in C. He accepts ¢ as a sign of duple proportion – albeit one that is only marginally tolerable – on grounds that both duple proportion and ¢ as a "prolation" (an independent sign that applies to all voices) are sung *ad medium*. This implies that ¢ means mensural diminution when it appears in all voices even though it means

---

[20] Anonymous 12, *Tractatus et compendium cantus figurati*, ch. 11 ("De sincopatione"), 64–65.
[21] Anonymous, *Ein tütsche musica*, II: 52.   [22] Adam von Fulda, *Musica*, part III, ch. 7, III: 362.

acceleratio mensurae from the point of view of the compostional *tactus*; in other words, the compositional *tactus* is a semibreve that is faster than usual, but two compositional *tactus* are combined in one performance *tactus*:

Alii vero pro signo duplae signum temporis imperfecti minorisque prolationis cum tractulo traducto [₵] accelerationem mensurae ut praemissum est denotante, quo cantus vulgariter ad medium dicitur, tantummodo ponunt ... Quod ... tolerabile censeo propter quandam aequipollentiam illius proportionis [2:1] ac istius prolationis [₵]. Dum enim aliquid ad medium canitur, duae notae sicut per proportionem duplam uni commensurantur.[23]	Some use as a sign of duple proportion only the sign of imperfect *tempus* and minor prolation with a stroke [₵], which represents acceleration of the *mensura*, as explained previously, by which the song is popularly called *ad medium* ... This ... I consider tolerable because of a certain equivalence between the former proportion [2:1] and the latter prolation [₵]. For when something is sung *ad medium*, two notes are measured together to one, as in duple proportion.

Tinctoris was the first theorist to make an implicit distinction between the compositional *tactus*, which he discusses in detail from the point of view of dissonance treatment, and the performance *tactus*, in which he seems to have had little interest. He insists on the fundamental distinction between ₵ in all voices, which is an independent mensuration (or "prolation") with a semibreve compositional *tactus*, and duple proportion of imperfect *tempus*, which is dependent on C and has a breve compositional *tactus*. Although he accepts the common practice of using the same sign for both mensural types on grounds that they share the same performance *tactus*, he is reluctant to do so because of the very different compositional principles that they require. His example of ₵ as a sign of duple proportion, with which he illustrates the above quotation, is shown in Example 5.4.

The first theorist to identify the semibreve as the performance *tactus*, as well as the compositional *tactus*, of both Φ and ₵ was Gaffurio. Like most fifteenth-century theorists, he makes his points about *tactus* in ways that are difficult to interpret in light of more familiar ways of conceiving the issue, but close analysis of his text leaves little doubt that he understood both Φ and ₵ as signs of *acceleratio mensurae* in his writings up to and including the

---

[23] Tinctoris, *Proportionale musices*, book 3, ch. 2 ("Qualiter proportiones signandae sint"), 45–46. See DeFord, "On Diminution and Proportion," 41–44, for a more detailed discussion of this passage.

Example 5.4 Petrus de Domarto, *Missa Spiritus almus* (excerpt), after Tinctoris, *Proportionale musices*, book 3, ch. 2.

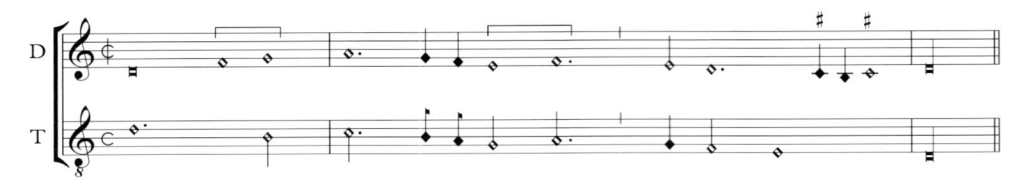

Practica musice of 1496. Gaffurio defines diminution in general as "the removal of a certain quantitative value from the figures themselves" ("abstractio certi valoris quantitativi ab ipsis figuris").[24] He distinguishes three types of diminution: diminution by canon, diminution by proportion, and diminution by stroke (i.e., by cut signs). His definition of diminution by canon is nearly identical to Muris's definition of diminution in general. It entails reading each figure like another written figure in accordance with a verbal canon, although Gaffurio allows for the possibility of substitutions other than reading each figure like the next smaller one. He characterizes this type of diminution as a variation of the quantity of the figures in relation to their original, or essential, meanings. Diminution by canon is therefore mensural diminution:

Canonice consyderatur diminutio quum figurarum quantitates declinant et variantur in mensura secundum canonis ac regulae inscriptam sententiam. Puta hac descriptione Maxima sit longa: Longa brevis & huiusmodi. tunc maxima ipsa ponitur pro longa: Longa pro brevi: Brevis pro semibrevi. Semibrevis pro minima.[25]	Diminution is considered canonically when the quantities of the figures are reduced and varied in measure according to a written canonic instruction or rule. For example, through this instruction, "Let a maxima be a long, a long a breve, etc." a maxima itself is placed [in writing] for a long, a long for a breve, a breve for a semibreve, a semibreve for a minim.

Diminution by proportion is in effect the same procedure, but it is notated with numbers, rather than canons. It is conceived as a reduction of note values in a numerical ratio, rather than as a process of reading each note like a different written value. This terminology confirms the conceptual distinction between reading notes like the next smaller value (the traditional

[24] Gaffurio, *Practica musice*, book 2, ch. 14 ("De diminutione"), fol. cciiij^r.   [25] Ibid.

Example 5.5 Example of "duple proportion" in all voices, after Gaffurio, *Practica musice*, book 4, ch. 3, fol. ffi^r.

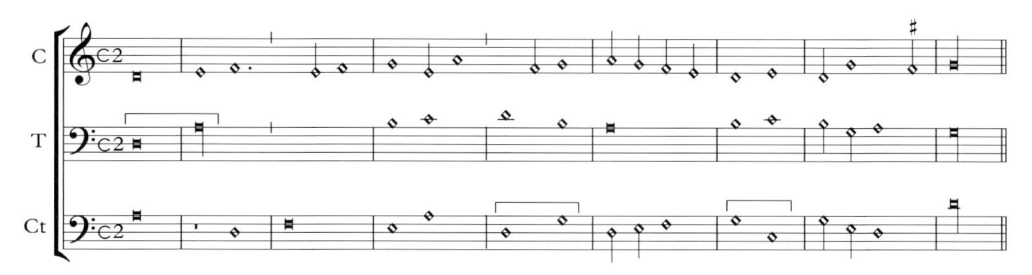

definition of diminution) and placing two notes in the time of one (the traditional definition of duple proportion) even when the results of the two procedures are identical:

Proportionabiliter sumpta diminutio est quae proprijs numerorum characteribus certam proportionem probantibus constituitur. Haec enim figuras ipsas minuit secundum dispositae proportionis consyderationem.[26]	Diminution understood proportionally is that which is based on the proper characters of the numbers specifying a certain proportion. It diminishes the figures themselves according to the ratio of the indicated proportion.

Although Gaffurio uses the term "proportion" in this definition, the procedure that he describes is not a proportion in the strict sense of the term, but a reduction of the number of *tactus* by which the notes are measured. "Proportion" must therefore be understood in its informal sense, as a synonym for mensural diminution, in this context. Gaffurio gives an example of the technique (Example 5.5), with the sign C2 in all voices, in the chapter on duple proportion in book 4 of the treatise.[27] It conforms to Tinctoris's definition of ¢ as a "prolation" in that the compositional *tactus* is the semibreve, but the performance *tactus* is the breve.

Diminution by stroke, in contrast, is almost certainly *acceleratio mensurae*. It is a procedure that affects the *mensura* itself, not the "values" of the notes, which are implicitly defined as numbers of *mensurae*, or *tactus*, rather than as durations. The term "semibreve" functions here as a synonym for "mensura" or "tactus":

---

[26] Ibid.
[27] Ibid., book 4, ch. 3 ("De genere multiplici & eius speciebus"), fol. Ffi^r. See DeFord, "On Diminution and Proportion," 51–56, for a more detailed discussion of Gaffurio's definition of "diminution by proportion."

| Virgulariter disposita diminutio est quae in hac mensurabili figurarum descriptione per virgulam signum temporis scindentem declaratur: haec propriae temporali competit mensurae: non ipsis figuris: namque tali signo ipsa minuitur mensura: non notularum numerus. Brevis enim temporis perfecti sive diminute sive integre deducatur tres semper continet semibreves integra perfectione servata. Eodem quoque modo duas semper semibreves possidere pernoscitur brevis temporis imperfecti: etiam ipsi diminutioni subiecta ... [28] | Diminution notated by stroke is that which is indicated in the notation of measurable figures by a stroke cutting the sign of *tempus*. It applies to the measure of time itself, not to the figures, for under this sign the *mensura* itself is diminished, not the number of the notes. For the breve of perfect *tempus*, whether interpreted in a diminished or integral manner, always contains three semibreves, preserving its whole perfection. Also in the same way the breve of imperfect *tempus* is always understood to contain two semibreves, even when subject to this diminution ... |

Gaffurio illustrates "diminution by stroke" with Example 5.6. He comments that the [semibreve] *tactus* in this diminution is generally twice as fast as the [breve] *tactus* of "diminution by proportion," implying that mensural diminution and *acceleratio mensurae* are alternative ways of achieving the same unspecified degree of reduction of the duration of the written values. The amount of speeding of the notes is at the discretion of the singers:

| Verum cum dupla proportio caeteris & divisione & pronuntiatione sit proportionibus notior atque facillima: mensurae huiusmodi virgulariter consyderata diminutio: in duplo velocior: duplae scilicet aequipolens proportioni: solet a cantoribus frequentius observari.[29] | But since duple proportion [in a mensural sense] is more familiar than other proportions and easiest in division and performance, this type of diminution of the *mensura* by stroke, twice as fast, and equivalent to duple proportion, is most often observed by singers. |

---

[28] Gaffurio, *Practica musice*, book 2, ch. 14 ("De diminutione"), fol. cciiij^r.
[29] Ibid., fol. cciiij^v.

Example 5.6 Example of "diminution by stroke," after Gaffurio, *Practica musice*, book 2, ch. 14, fol. cciiij[v].

Several sources support the conclusion that "diminution by stroke" means *acceleratio mensurae* in Gaffurio's *Practica musice*. In an earlier, unpublished version of Book 2 of the treatise, Gaffurio cites the authority of Tinctoris, who defines cut signs explicitly as *acceleratio mensurae*, to support his interpretation of diminution by stroke.[30] Some sixteenth-century theorists adopt this interpretation unequivocally. Stephan Monetarius, for example, glosses his paraphrase of Gaffurio's explanation of diminution by stroke with the words "faster motion":

In huiusmodi signis non figurarum numerus, sed mensuralis (velociori motu) adimitur quantitas.[31]	In this type of signs [those cut by a stroke] not the number of the figures, but the duration of the *mensura* is reduced (through faster motion).

Glarean paraphrases Gaffurio's explanation of cut signs with a statement that the *tactus* moves faster and illustrates it with Gaffurio's example (Example 5.6):

Quoties autem volunt Musici tactu festinandum esse … lineam per circulum vel semicirculum deorsum ducunt sic ⌽, ¢ atque hoc	Whenever musicians want the *tactus* to move faster … they draw a line downward through the circle or semicircle thus ⌽, ¢ and they call

---

[30] Gaffurio, *Musices practicabilis libellum*, ch. 14 ("De diminutione"), quoted in DeFord, "On Diminution and Proportion," 49–50.

[31] Monetarius, *Epitoma utriusque musices practice*, book 2, ch. 10 ("De augmentatione et diminutione"), fol. Fi[r].

quidem Pathos diminutionem vocant, non quod notularum aut valor, aut numerus diminuatur, sed quod tactus fiat velocior.[32]

this effect diminution, not because either the value or the number of the notes is reduced, but because the *tactus* is made faster.

For reasons that are not entirely clear, Gaffurio changed his interpretation of cut signs in his *Angelicum ac divinum opus musice* of 1508. In that treatise, he advocates an imperfect breve *tactus* for both ¢ and ¢. For the first time in the history of *tactus* theory, Gaffurio complains about a discrepancy between the theoretically correct *tactus* of signs and the *tactus* commonly used by performers:

Quando se ritrova el signo del tempo cioe el circulo & el Semicirculo traversato con una virgula Ciascuna figura se diminuira in mensura: & non in numero suarum partium de meza la sua ordinaria quantita: ut exempli gratia: per el circulo traversato Una nota breve perfecta contiene trey semibreve: quale se cantarano in mensura de una semibreve & meza. Ma traversato el semicirculo Una nota breve quale contiene doe semibreve se cantara in mensura de una semibreve ... et questa è dicta proprie diminutione ... Molte altre consyderatione per corruptella son usurpate da cantori quali procedeno non con ratione alcuna: ma con proprio arbitrio.[33]

When the sign of *tempus*, that is the circle or semicircle, is cut with a stroke, each note is diminished in measure, and not in the number of its parts, by half of its normal quantity. For example, through the cut circle a perfect breve contains three semibreves that are sung in the *mensura* of one and a half semibreves. But if the semicircle is cut, a breve that contains two semibreves is sung in the *mensura* of one semibreve ... This is properly called diminution ... Many other interpretations are taken through corrupt practice by singers who proceed not with any reason, but according to their own will.

To sing three semibreves of ¢ "in the *mensura* of one and a half semibreves" and two semibreves of ¢ "in the *mensura* of one semibreve" can only mean that the *tactus* of both signs is the imperfect breve. In the case of ¢, this view is simply a return to the traditional interpretation of the sign

---

[32] Glarean, *Dodecachordon*, book 3, ch. 8 ("De augmentatione diminutione ac semiditate"), 205–06.
[33] Gaffurio, *Angelicum ac divinum opus musice*, book 3, ch. 10 ("In trey modi se diminuiscano le figure"), fol. Fvi^v.

as mensural (or incidentally proportional) diminution. For ϕ, however, the interpretation is largely new. The only earlier theorists to interpret ϕ in this way are Guilielmus Monachus and Diego del Puerto.[34] Guilielmus includes ϕ in an exhaustive list of signs (most of them purely theoretical) in which a stroke or a number 2 invariably reduces the number of *tactus* on each note by half. He was clearly aware of the discrepancy between the imperfect breve *tactus* and the perfect breves of the mensuration in his interpretation of ϕ, because he takes the trouble to point out that the perfect quality (or "number") of the breves is not changed, even though their measure is reduced by half. Like Gaffurio, he uses the term "semibreve" as a synonym for "tactus"; he states that ϕ reduces the value of the maxima from twelve "semibreves" to six, although it is not the number of written semibreves, but the number of *tactus*, in a maxima that is reduced in this way:

ϕ Hoc signum est medium precedentis [O] quod tenet parem numerum, sed de media parte diminuitur, quoniam maxima quae valebit 12 semibreves non valet nisi sex, et longa quae valebit sex semibreves non valet nisi tres, et sic diminuendo alias figuras de dimidia parte secundum tempus, non autem secundum numerum, ut dictum est supra.[35]	ϕ This sign is half of the preceding [O] in that it contains the same number [i.e., the same perfect or imperfect quality], but diminished by half, since a maxima that will be worth 12 semibreves is worth only six, and a long that will be worth six semibreves is worth only three, and similarly diminishing the other figures by half in terms of time, but not in terms of number, as stated above.

One possible explanation for Gaffurio's change of opinion, which he never acknowledged as such, is that he decided that the theoretical classification of cut signs as *per medium* should be taken literally, as it is in Guilielmus's theory. If the term *per medium* is taken to mean reducing the number of *tactus* on every written note by half, it follows that the *tactus* of ϕ must be the imperfect breve. This interpretation of the sign appears to have been speculative in origin, and later theorists who advocate it often echo Gaffurio's complaint that singers do not observe it in practice.

Gaffurio's new theory of cut signs in the *Angelicum ac divinum opus musice* may be related to his new characterization of *tactus* as a motion of

---

[34] Guilielmus Monachus, *De preceptis artis musice*, 45, and Diego del Puerto, *Portus musice*, "De tempore," fols. avi^v–avii^r.

[35] Guilielmus Monachus, *De preceptis artis musice*, 45.

the hand, rather than a more abstract form of measure, in that treatise. Perhaps he felt that a single up or down motion of the hand (technically half of a *tactus*) was musically more appropriate to the semibreve of ¢ and ϕ than a pair of motions in both directions on each semibreve. That method of measuring ϕ, however, entails a mismatch between the pairs of semibreves implied by the motion and the groups of three semibreves that are part of the structure of the mensuration. Performers who measure in this way must count groups of three semibreves against the binary groups implied by the *tactus* in order to apply the rules of imperfection and alteration that perfect *tempus* requires.

Proportion signs

Theorists advocate a variety of signs for the proportions commonly used in fifteenth-century music. Prosdocimo and Ugolino prefer fractions in which the numerator represents the new number of figures that fill a time unit and the denominator represents the number of the same figure that fill the same unit outside of the proportion.[36] For example, $\frac{2}{1}$ means that two figures take the time otherwise occupied by one of the same figure, $\frac{3}{2}$ means that three figures take the time otherwise occupied by two, etc. Later fifteenth-century theorists usually prefer single numerals for proportions in which a whole number of figures replaces one: 2 for duple proportion, 3 for triple, and 4 for quadruple. These numbers can be ambiguous. The number 2 could represent either duple proportion or mensural diminution *per medium*, though theorists often distinguish those meanings by using a mensuration sign plus a 2 for diminution and a 2 alone for duple proportion. Most theorists associate the number 3 with triple proportion, though some define it as *sesquialtera*.[37] In practice, it usually represents *sesquialtera* in proportional contexts. *Sesquialtera* could also be notated with coloration.

---

[36] Prosdocimo, *Tractatus practice de musica mensurabili*, "De signis mensure," 218; Ugolino, *Declaratio musicae disciplinae*, book 3, ch. 5 ("De signis modum, tempus et prolationem distinguentibus"), 210.

[37] Treatises that define 3 as a sign of triple proportion include Anonymous 11, *Tractatus de musica plana et mensurabili*, I: 164–65; Anonymous 12, *Tractatus et compendium cantus figurati*, ch. 15 ("De proportionibus"), 75; and Adam von Fulda, *Musica*, part IV, ch. 8, III: 379. Guilielmus Monachus, *De preceptis artis musice*, 21, is one of the few fifteenth-century theorists to use 3 to represent *sesquialtera*. The sign appears in a musical example, not in the verbal description of the proportion.

Some theorists propose mensuration signs, usually modified in some way, as symbols for proportions.[38] The only symbol of this type that was commonly used after *c.* 1420 was a reversed semicircle (ↄ) for *sesquitertia* (4:3) proportion. This proportion usually calls for four minims in the time of three minims of perfect prolation or four semibreves in the time of three semibreves of perfect *tempus* or a preceding *sesquialtera* proportion. In exceptional cases, it represents 4:3 proportion in imperfect *tempus* and prolation, where the three notes that are replaced by four are not a complete mensural unit.[39] Because the notes in the proportion come in binary groups, all values in the proportion are imperfect. Guilielmus Monachus says that signs with reversed semicircles (ↄ, ↄ, and ↄ) are *per medium* of the same signs with regular semicircles. The rationale for his interpretation of ↄ is that 4:3 proportion of ₵ places four minims on a *tactus* that previously had three, and four minims is twice the number on the theoretical *tactus* of C. In his examples, however, he uses ↄ only to represent *sesquitertia* proportion of ₵.[40]

Tinctoris argues vigorously against the use of single numbers or modified mensuration signs as signs of proportion and allows only fractions to serve that function.[41] He also maintains, contrary to the position of Prodocimo quoted above and the usual practice of composers, that proportions cannot change the mensuration without a change of mensuration sign. For example, if a triple proportion places three semibreves in the time of one semibreve of C, the breves of the proportion should not be perfect unless the proportion sign is accompanied by a sign of perfect *tempus*. The logic of his position is unassailable. A proportion is by definition a relation between two numbers, and such a relation cannot be represented by a single number. Mensuration and proportion are distinct entities that should not be conflated with a single sign. Logic notwithstanding, however, many composers continued to notate proportions with single numbers and to treat notes in proportions as perfect when the next smaller value comes in ternary groups throughout the following century and beyond.

Although diminution and proportion are conceptually distinct, proportional relations between simultaneous voices could be, and often were, notated by combining signs of diminution or augmentation with *ut iacet*

---

[38] See Anna Maria Busse Berger, "The Origin and Early History of Proportion Signs," *Journal of the American Musicological Society* 41 (1988), 403–33, and *Mensuration and Proportion Signs*, 168–78, for surveys of these symbols.

[39] An example of this proportion in imperfect *tempus* and prolation is found in the Benedictus of Ockeghem's *Missa prolationum*.

[40] *De preceptis artis musice*, 15–16, 25, 45–53.

[41] Tinctoris, *Proportionale musices*, book 3, ch. 2 ("Qualiter proportiones signandae sint"), 45.

signs or with each other. Signs of diminution or augmentation generate 2:1 or 1:2 relations with *ut iacet* signs and 4:1 relations with each other when they appear simultaneously. For example, ₵ is in 2:1 ratio with C and O, ℭ and ☉ are often in 1:2 ratio with O, and ₵ is often in 4:1 ratio with ℭ and ☉ in simultaneous relations. (The latter two relations are not universal, because perfect prolation does not always represent augmentation in simultaneous relations.) Proportion signs usually appear within voices in the middle of pieces, while signs of diminution or augmentation more often specify relations between different voices at the beginning of a piece.

Proportions in simultaneous relations are never ambiguous in practice even if their signs may have more than one meaning in theory, because the context makes their interpretation clear. Proportion signs that appear in all voices, however, are problematic. They were often conflated with the *modus cum tempore* signs discussed below.

Circles and semicircles followed by numbers

Toward the middle of the fifteenth century, theorists began to define circles or semicircles followed by numbers as signs of *modus cum tempore*. In these signs, a circle or semicircle represents perfect or imperfect minor *modus* and a 3 or 2 following it represents perfect or imperfect *tempus*. The four common signs of this type are O3 (perfect *modus*/perfect *tempus*), O2 (perfect *modus*/imperfect *tempus*), C3 (imperfect *modus*/perfect *tempus*), and C2 (imperfect *modus*/imperfect *tempus*). They may have been invented by Du Fay, who used them in a large collection of Mass Propers that he composed for Cambrai in the 1440s.[42] The first theorist to discuss them was John Hothby. Hothby expands the principle underlying them to generate signs with three elements (circles or semicircles and numbers) that represent major *modus*, minor *modus*, and *tempus* and adds dots inside the circles or semicircles to indicate perfect prolation. He also proposes an alternative system in which the levels of mensuration are represented by concentric circles, rather than circles plus numbers.[43] The only signs in this large family that have any practical significance are the four listed above.

[42] See Alejandro Enrique Planchart, "Guillaume Du Fay's Benefices and His Relationship to the Court of Burgundy," *Early Music History* 8 (1988), 167. For an overview of the uses of O2 in the fifteenth century, see Sean Gallagher, *Johannes Regis*, "Épitome musical" (Turnhout: Brepols, 2010), 104–14.

[43] John Hothby, *Opera omnia de musica mensurabili*, 21, 53–57. An earlier interpretation of O2 as diminution of perfect *tempus*, mentioned in one of the passages from Anonymous 11 quoted

Hothby says nothing about how these signs are measured in performance, but later theorists usually interpret them as signs of diminution, as well as perfect or imperfect *modus*. Adam von Fulda classifies O2 and C2 as signs that call for a breve *tactus*.[44] Guilielmus Monachus says that C2 requires a breve *tactus* and that many people interpret O2 the same way.[45] Ramis explains the measurement of all four signs and their relation to the measurement of *ut iacet* signs of *tempus* and prolation as follows:

Et cum per primum cecinerit signum quadripartitum [O3, C3, O2, C2], mensuram istam ponat in brevi; tunc enim longa in istis O3 O2 tribus temporis morulis mensurabitur, in istis vero C3 C2 duabus ... Ipsa vero mensura in istis duobus O2 C2 per medium in duo tantum semibreves secatur quatuorque minimas. In istis vero O3 C3 aequaliter in tres dividitur semibreves sex quoque minimas ...	And when [the singer] sings [music in] the first group of four signs [O3, C3, O2, C2], he should place this *mensura* on the breve; for then the long in these O3 O2 will be measured with three *morulae* [*mensurae*] of time, but in these C3 C2 with two ... This *mensura* in these two O2 C2 is cut in half into only two semibreves and four minims. But in these O3 C3, it is divided equally into three semibreves and six minims ...
Sin vero per secundum cecinerit signum quadripartitum [Ö, ¢, O, C] morulam ponet in semibrevi et tunc brevis tres mensuras valebit in istis Ö O, duas vero tantum in his ¢ C; et sicut in aliis divisa fuit aequaliter in duas aut in tres semibreves, ita in istis [in] duas minimas aut in tres, prout signum perfectionem aut imperfectionem denotat, dividetur.[46]	But if he sings [music in] the second group of four signs [Ö, ¢, O, C], he will place the *morula* on the semibreve, and then the breve will be worth three *mensurae* in these Ö O, but only two in these ¢ C; and just as in the others [the first four signs] it [the *mensura*] was divided equally into two or three semibreves, so in these, it will be divided into two or three minims, as the sign indicates perfection or imperfection.

Ramis observes that singers sometimes shift the *mensura*, or *tactus*, to the next smaller value when there are too many notes. This license, which is more likely to apply to signs with a breve *tactus* (since they generally have

---

above (p. 124), was obsolete in practice by c. 1420. See Berger, *Mensuration and Proportion Signs*, 148–63, for a detailed discussion of *modus cum tempore* signs.

[44] *Musica*, part III, ch. 7, III: 362.   [45] *De preceptis artis musice*, 49.
[46] *Musica practica*, part III, tract. 1, ch. 2 ("In quo signa per quae numeri distinguuntur"), 67–68.

more notes on the theoretical *tactus*), confirms that *acceleratio mensurae* was an alternative to mensural diminution in *modus cum tempore* signs, just as it was in cut signs:

Aliquando autem propter cantus nimiam diminutionem cantores mensuram, quae in brevi erat observanda, ponunt in semibrevi, et si erat in semibrevi tenenda, transferunt illam in minima ...[47]	Sometimes, however, singers place the *tactus* that should have been on the breve on the semibreve, and if it should have been on the semibreve, they transfer it to the minim, on account of the excessive diminution of the song.

Signs that combine circles and numbers are the most ambiguous signs in the mensural system. Some theorists explain C2 in the older sense in which it does not specify *modus*, while others include imperfect *modus* as part of its definition. The difference between the two meanings is slight. Since imperfect *modus* in the broadest sense means only that longs are imperfect, which they are by default in any case, it does not necessarily imply regular mensural pairing of breves. O2 is more likely than C2 to represent real mensural grouping on the *modus* level, because there is little point in notating longs as perfect if the perfect long-unit has no role in the structure of a piece.

O3 and C3 are more problematic. As *modus cum tempore* signs, they ought to represent perfect *tempus* with perfect or imperfect *modus* and a perfect breve *tactus*, as Ramis recommends, but since the number 3 had a long-standing association with both triple and *sesquialtera* proportion, it usually functions as a proportion (in either the formal or the informal sense), rather than as a sign of *tempus*, in practice. Regular *modus* is rare in music with these signs. Another complication is that 3 may be taken to represent *sesquialtera* proportion of minims, rather than triple or *sesquialtera* proportion of semi-breves. This interpretation is the usual one for C3 in practice, despite the common theoretical definition of the sign as imperfect *modus* with perfect *tempus*.[48] To ensure that the number 3 specifies perfect breves, rather than perfect semibreves, the signs may be written in cut form: ϕ3 and ¢3.

When a sign including a 3 (O3, C3, ϕ3, or ¢3) is used in a purely mensural sense, without reference to an *ut iacet* sign, it may be conceived informally as either triple or *sesquialtera* "proportion." If three semibreves are measured with one performance *tactus*, the mensuration may be compared to

---

[47] Ibid., 68.
[48] Guilielmus Monachus, *De preceptis artis musice*, 47–48, says that 3 may represent either perfect breves or perfect semibreves, but in the sign C3 it always represents perfect semibreves. This statement is true in most cases.

triple proportion of C or O with a semibreve *tactus* (three semibreves instead of one per *tactus*) or to *sesquialtera* proportion of ₵ with a breve *tactus* (three semibreves instead of two per *tactus*). Tinctoris was horrified by the theoretical sloppiness of the common understanding of these signs. He comments as follows on Ockeghem's use of the sign O3 in the song *L'autre d'antan*, in which the *tactus* (both compositional and performance) is the perfect breve:

Ex quo confunditur inexcusabilis error Okeghem, qui suum carmen bucolicum L'autre dantan ab omni parte numeris aequalibus compositum nedum signo proportionis, sed illo qui a quibusdam triplae, ab aliis sesquialterae per se et male attribuitur signavit … Dum vero carmen praemissum, scilicet L'autre dantan aut aliud similiter signatum habent imperiti dicunt repente canamus sesquialtera est. O puerilis ignorantia aequalitatis proportionem inaequalitatis asserere! Nec existimo compositorem, quamvis ita secundum aliquos signaverit, ita dici voluisse, sed ut carmen suum concitae instar sesquialterae cantaretur. Ad quod efficiendum virgula per medium circuli cuiusque partis traducta sufficiebat. Nam proprium est ei mensurae accelerationem significare sive tempus perfectum sive imperfectum sit, ut in infinitis etiam suis compositionibus apparet, cuius in utroque forma talis est: ɸ ₵.[49]

Thus is refuted the inexcusable error of Ockeghem, who signed his bucolic song *L'autre d'antan*, which is composed in equal numbers in all parts, not only with a sign of proportion, but one that is interpreted on its own, and badly, as triple by some and as *sesquialtera* by others … When the unskilled have the preceding song, that is *L'autre d'antan*, or another that is similarly signed, they say immediately, "let us sing – it is *sesquialtera*." O childish ignorance to attribute a proportion of inequality to equality! Nor do I believe the composer wished to say that, although according to some he signed in this way, but that his song should be sung like an excited *sesquialtera*. To accomplish this, a stroke drawn through the middle of the circle of each part would have sufficed. For it is proper to it [the stroke] to signify acceleration of the *mensura*, whether the *tempus* is perfect or imperfect, as appears in innumerable compositions of his, of which the form in both [types of *tempus*] is: ɸ ₵.

---

[49] *Proportionale musices*, book 1, ch. 3 ("Divisio proportionum"), 14–15. Bonnie J. Blackburn discusses this passage from Tinctoris in "Did Ockeghem Listen to Tinctoris?" in *Johannes Ockeghem: Actes du XLe Colloque international d'études humanistes, Tours, 3–8 février 1997*, ed. Philippe Vendrix, "Épitome musical" 1 (Paris: Klincksieck, 1998), 603–12.

For Tinctoris, a proportion must be a quantitative relationship between different signs in the same piece. The only proportion that can exist in a piece with a single sign is a "proportion of equality" among the voices; calling the mensuration of such a piece "sesquialtera" makes no logical sense. Furthermore, a proportion cannot be represented by a single number, such as the single number 3 in the sign O3, because it is by definition a relation between two terms. Tinctoris of course understood perfectly well that Ockeghem's sign represented what I call mensural diminution with a perfect breve *tactus*, but he refused to accept the use of terms and signs referring to proportions in this informal sense.

Despite the impeccable logic of his argument, Tinctoris's view entails a problem that he did not confront. In his theory, the sign ϕ requires a semibreve *tactus*, but triple and *sesquialtera* proportions require a *tactus* on the perfect breve or perfect semibreve. Ockeghem's song, which appears in different sources with all four of the common signs followed by a 3 (O3, C3, ϕ3, and ₵3), has a perfect breve compositional *tactus*. The sign ϕ that Tinctoris recommends for it is therefore not appropriate in relation to the deeper aspects of his own theory, even if that sign implies a tempo similar to that of a *sesquialtera* proportion. The song includes semibreve dissonances, which Tinctoris would find unacceptable in ϕ, but not in *sesquialtera* or triple proportion with a perfect breve *tactus*. There is, however, no sign in Tinctoris's system for a perfect breve or perfect semibreve *tactus* that applies to an entire piece.

Gaffurio defends Ockeghem's sign and others of a similar type, perhaps because he recognizes this deficiency. He gets around the theoretical difficulty of a proportion without a standard of reference by suggesting that the "proportions" in such pieces relate to an imaginary sign preceding them:

Quandoque autem per aequalia signa in singulis partibus cantilenae disposita inaequalis describitur proportio: ut exempli gratia si notavero omnes cantilenae partes ... uno eodemque proportionis signo puta sub semicirculo ... solo binarii numeri charactere pro dupla proportione disposito ... sic enim sumenda est huiusmodi concentus	But when an unequal proportion is described with the same signs in each of the parts, as for example if I were to write all parts of a song ... with one and the same sign of proportion, for example, a semicircle ... with only the sign of the number 2 placed for duple proportion ... this type of song is to be understood in the following way ... I think that the

consyderatio … cuiuscunque partis notulas in duplo velociores consimilibus imperfecti temporis signo praesuppositis: tamquam praecedentibus in proportione censeo computandas. quod & Ockeghem in cantilena Lautredantan disposuit … Nectamen solius numeri dispositionem in proportionis demonstratione non egre fero: namque praetactum est proportionem minus quam in duobus terminis non posse constitui.[50]	notes of each part are to be counted twice as fast as similar [notes] of a presumed sign of imperfect *tempus*, as if in proportion to the preceding [notes], as Ockeghem also did in the song *L'autre d'antan* … Nevertheless, I can hardly tolerate the use of a single number to represent a proportion, because, as explained previously, a proportion cannot consist of fewer than two terms.

Gaffurio's examples of this principle have the signs C2 (Example 5.5 above) and Φ3 (the sign in his version of the Ockeghem example). After his rigorous explanation of the logical justification for these signs, his disapproval of "proportions" notated with single numbers (a respectful nod to Tinctoris) has a decidedly halfhearted ring.

These principles leave open the question of how the metronome speed of these signs relates to that of other signs. Since the number 3 could mean triple proportion, *sesquialtera* proportion, or mensural diminution with no proportional relation to another sign, its tempo implication is unclear when it applies to all voices of a piece or section. This issue is discussed in Chapter 7.

Signs and performance practice

Theoretical explanations of fifteenth-century signs confirm that while signs convey information about both the level of the *tactus* in all of its senses and the duration of the notes, they do not prescribe them in a formulaic way. Theorists often allow a choice of performance *tactus*, and when they recommend a faster *tactus* for one sign than another, they never ground their advice on a well-defined speed for the basic *tactus* and rarely specify the degree of difference between one *tactus* and another. Some explicitly relegate the choice of *tactus* to the domain of performance practice. Nicolo

---

[50] *Practica musice*, book 4, ch. 3 ("De genere multiplici & eius speciebus"), fols. eeviii[v]–ffi[r].

Burzio, for example, says that diminution is very popular among modern singers, but does not suggest any correlation between the practice and notational signs.[51]

Even if there were no such uncertainties in theoretical writings, inconsistencies in the uses of signs in practice would preclude the possibility of determining *tactus* and tempo solely on the basis of signs. Many fifteenth-century pieces have no signs, and a significant number have different signs in different sources. The correlation between signs and compositional *tactus*, which (unlike performance *tactus*) can be observed in the written music, is not always consistent. Compositional styles often support the theoretical implications of signs, in that music with diminution signs places more emphasis on the breve level and less on the semibreve level than contemporaneous music with *ut iacet* signs. In such cases, the signs merely confirm what could be inferred on the basis of the music itself. The issue becomes problematic when signs appear to contradict, rather than confirm, an interpretation that would result from an analysis of the music. Such cases might be explained in any of three possible ways: (1) the sign in the source(s) is incorrect; (2) the sign has a different meaning from the one assigned to it by theorists; (3) the sign overrides the implications of the musical style and calls for a *tactus* with a value and/or duration that could not be guessed without it.[52] The choice among these alternatives involves interpretive judgments that rarely lead to unequivocal conclusions.

The many varieties of signs in fifteenth-century music and the inconsistencies in their definitions in theory and practice may give the impression that the mensural system was unnecessarily complex and redundant. If the sole purpose of notation were to convey literal, quantitative information about the durations of notes, that impression would surely be valid, but notation conveys a wealth of qualitative, as well as quantitative, information about musical time measurement. Signs have different connotations with respect to the number of levels of mensuration in a piece, their relative prominence, the kinds of rhythms that may be expected on each level, and more subjective qualities such as stylistic level, affective character, and tempo in a sense that goes beyond "metronome mark."

---

[51] *Musices opusculum* [= *Florum libellus*] (Bologna: Ugo Ruggeri, 1487; repr. Bologna: Forni, 1969), tract. 3, ch. 8 ("De diminutione"), fols. fv^v–fvi^r.

[52] This issue is the root of the disagreement between Margaret Bent and Rob C. Wegman over the interpretation of ϕ in pieces where music under that sign is indistinguishable in style from music in O. See Chapter 7, p. 199 n. 55.

Some ambiguities in the definitions of signs are an inevitable consequence of the complexity and subtlety of the meanings they may convey. Those ambiguities are not simply obstacles to deciphering symbols, but sources of insight into the numerous ways in which the temporal dimension of music may be understood.

6 | *Tactus* and signs in sixteenth-century music theory

The relation between mensural theory and practice in the sixteenth century was quite different from what it was in the fifteenth century. The principles of notation were fully developed by the end of the fifteenth century, but changes in musical style led to changes in the relation between theory and practice throughout the sixteenth century. By *c.* 1520 the only signs in common use were ₵ and signs of *sesquialtera* or triple proportion.[1] The sign C was revived with a new meaning in the madrigal around 1540, but other fifteenth-century signs remained permanently obsolete. Nevertheless, theorists continued to discuss the older signs throughout the sixteenth century, both because they were a traditional component of music pedagogy and because music of the Josquin generation remained in the active performance repertoire in some places until the end of the century. The resulting discrepancies between theory and practice are a consistent theme in sixteenth-century mensural theory.

Most theorists draw on three types of sources for their ideas about mensuration: earlier theoretical writings, abstract reasoning, and direct knowledge of the practices of their own times. Some also derive ideas through the analysis of older music that they knew only from written sources. Theorists aimed both to uphold traditional theories and to describe practices that they knew from experience. Some also aimed to construct comprehensive, logically consistent systems that were intellectually satisfying whether or not they conformed to practice. For this purpose they invented signs that were never used in real music and defined existing signs in ways that did not agree with their generally understood meanings. This practice was motivated by a desire to explain the structure of musical time in an abstract, theoretical sense. It is analogous to Glarean's invention of a Lydian mode with B-naturals that did not exist in practice on grounds that it was necessary for the symmetry and completeness of his modal system.[2]

---

[1] Spataro observed and lamented this development in a letter of 4 January 1529 to Giovanni del Lago, in *A Correspondence of Renaissance Musicians*, 336.

[2] On Glarean's Lydian mode, see Harold S. Powers, "Music as Text and Text as Music," in *Musik als Text: Bericht über den Internationalen Kongress der Gesellschaft für Musikforschung Freiburg im Breisgau 1993*, ed. Hermann Danuser and Tobias Plebuch, 2 vols. (Kassel: Bärenreiter, 1998), I: 21–26.

Conflicts among theoretical views arose because of discrepancies among different authorities, rational inconsistencies within theoretical systems, and differences between older theories and contemporaneous practices. Theorists dealt with these conflicts in a variety of ways, depending on their personal inclinations and the purposes of their writings. Some describe only theory or practice without mentioning any discrepancy between them; some acknowledge the conflict and castigate musicians who do not observe the rules of strict theory in practice; and some find ways to accommodate conflicting views without denying the validity of any of them. The numerous ways in which they approach this challenge provide fascinating insights into the process of reasoning about music in the sixteenth century, even if they contribute little to our knowledge of compositional or performance practice.

Simple and cut signs of perfect and imperfect *tempus*: O, C, Φ, ₵

The simple and cut forms of the signs of perfect and imperfect *tempus* (O, C, Φ, and ₵) are by far the most important signs in the mensural system. Even in the heyday of complex mensural designs, the overwhelming majority of compositions used only signs from this group. All theorists of the fifteenth and sixteenth centuries agree that the *tactus* of O and C is the semibreve in both theory and practice.

Sixteenth-century theorists inherited three different theoretical models for the interpretation of cut signs:

(1) Anonymous 12, Adam von Fulda, and their followers call for a breve *tactus* in ₵ (called *semiditas*) and a semibreve *tactus* in Φ (called "diminution"). Anonymous 12 says that Φ is a third faster than O, but implies that this quantity is only an approximation.
(2) Tinctoris and Gaffurio (in *Practica musice*) call for a semibreve *tactus* in both ₵ and Φ that is faster by an unspecified amount than the semibreve *tactus* of C and O. Both imply, however, that a breve performance *tactus* is also possible in ₵. Tinctoris defines the compositional *tactus* of ₵ as the semibreve, but implies that its usual performance *tactus* is the breve. Gaffurio states that the semibreve *tactus* of ₵ is twice as fast as the breve *tactus* of C2, which he characterizes as nearly synonymous with ₵, since both belong to the general category of diminution. This suggests that, in reality, both signs could be measured with either a semibreve *tactus* that is faster than the semibreve *tactus* of C or a breve *tactus* equal to two such semibreve *tactus*.

(3) Guilielmus Monachus and Gaffurio (in *Angelicum ac divinum opus musice*) call for an imperfect breve *tactus* in both ¢ and ⊘. Guilielmus gives the impression of defining cut signs on the basis of a mechanical formula, rather than a nuanced analysis, but his view may be one that had some currency in southern Europe in the last decades of the fifteenth century. Gaffurio is the first theorist to advocate an imperfect breve *tactus* in ⊘ as a matter of principle and the first to complain that common practices of time measurement in performance do not agree with theoretical rules.

Whatever their theoretical persuasions, nearly all sixteenth-century theorists give the same information about how their contemporaries measured time in practice. The standard performance *tactus* of O, C, ⊘, and ¢ was the semibreve, and it was somewhat faster in cut signs than in uncut signs. A slow breve *tactus* was also an option in ¢, but it was rarely used. Johannes Cochlaeus called it old-fashioned as early as the first decade of the century.[3] The only exceptions to these principles are simultaneous proportional relationships, in which signs must be governed by their theoretical *tactus*, or else all of them must use a *tactus* on the next smaller value, in order to fit together properly. A few theorists claim that the breve *tactus* had some currency in practice, but they associate it idealistically with some distant time or place. Glarean claims in his *Dodecachordon* (1547) that it was used in earlier times and is still common in much of Germany,[4] but in his *Musicae epitome*, written only ten years later, he says that it had been customary in Germany some sixty years earlier.[5] Michael Praetorius says in his *Syntagma musicum* (1614–20) that it was common in the time of Lassus (late sixteenth century) and is still used in some distinguished chapels and schools,[6] but this claim conflicts with all other evidence on the subject.

Northern European theories of cut signs

Northern European theorists before Sebald Heyden drew primarily on earlier German traditions (Anonymous 12 and Adam von Fulda) and

---

[3] Cochlaeus, *Compendium in praxim atque exercitium cantus figurabilis* ([Cologne: Johann Landen, 1507]), ch. 11 ("De tactu in communi"), fol. [4]ʳ. This small treatise, which is not described accurately in any modern source, consists of four unnumbered folios. It was probably published in Cologne by Johann Landen in or shortly after 1507.

[4] Glarean, *Dodecachordon*, book 3, ch. 7 ("De tactu sive cantandi mensura"), 203.

[5] Glarean, *Musicae epitome*, book 2, ch. 7 ("De tactu sive cantandi mensura"), 117.

[6] Praetorius, *Syntagma musicum*, vol. III, book 2, ch. 7 ("De tactu, seu notarum mensura; (italis batttuta) & signis"), 49.

Gaffurio's *Practica musice* as authorities on mensural issues. Andreas Ornithoparchus complicated matters by basing his views on Gaffurio's *Angelicum ac divinum opus musice* (though he claimed to have found those views in the *Practica musice*), and Heyden added a large dose of speculative reasoning to the mix. Other theorists synthesized all of these views, replacing outright conflicts with more or less consistent positions that took account of different opinions on problematic issues. The notorious conflicts among sixteenth-century *tactus* theories can be understood in this context as sincere attempts to reconcile conflicting theories with each other and with common practice. The arguments involved may strike a modern reader as strained, but we can appreciate their ingenuity if we accept the importance of the intellectual integrity of the mensural system to sixteenth-century theorists.

A few theorists of the first two decades of the century transmit the views of Anonymous 12 and Adam von Fulda without comment. The most influential of them was Venceslaus Philomathes, whose *Musicorum libri quattuor* was written in a verse form that lends itself to rote memorization, not to weighing alternative possibilities. Philomathes explains cut signs as follows:

Cifra rotae dextro lateri binaria iuncta Innuit, ut tactu nota prendatur brevis uno. Si quoque semirotam cifra quacunque vacantem Linea pertransit, mensuram signat eandem, Quod vulgo signum vocitatur semiditatis ... Linea perfectum per signum ducitur unquam Ocius harmoniae causa ut tactus moveatur. Diminuensque huiuscemodi signum vocitatur.[7]	A number two joined to the right side of a circle [O2] indicates that a breve is to be taken as one *tactus*. If a line cuts a semicircle without any number [¢], it indicates the same *mensura*. This sign is popularly called [a sign] of *semiditas* ... A line is drawn through a perfect sign [Φ, etc.] at any time so that the *tactus* will move faster for the sake of the harmony. And this type of sign is called diminishing [i.e., a sign of diminution].

---

[7] Philomathes, *Musicorum libri quattuor*, book 2, ch. 7 ("De tactu"), fol. dij^v. Other sources that transmit the same view are Simon de Quercu, *Opusculum musices*, [part II], De Sincopa, fols. fiv^v–G^r, and Luscinius, *Musurgia*, Commentarius primus, ch. 9 ("De his, quae potissimum ad praxim conducere videntur"), 84–85. The authors of all of these books were active in Vienna in the first decade of the sixteenth century. Luscinius (whose book was finished in 1518, although it was not published until 1536) allows students to use a semibreve *tactus* in O2 and ¢ until they develop enough skill to use the breve *tactus*.

The Cologne school (Melchior Schanppecher, Nicolaus Wollick, Johannes Cochlaeus, and Bernhard Bogentantz) undertook the task of reconciling this theory with the view that both ¢ and ⌽ call for a fast semibreve *tactus*, a position that agreed both with Gaffurio's *Practica musice* and with common practice. Their strategy was to distinguish the theoretical *tactus* from the performance *tactus* in ¢, so that they could acknowledge the breve as the theoretical *tactus* without requiring the same *tactus* to be used in performance. The essence of the argument is already present in Schanppecher's section of the *Opus aureum* of 1501, which makes little direct reference to Gaffurio:

Semiditas fit in tempore imperfecto, quando semicirculus per tractum dividitur ut hic ¢; ibi enim dumtaxat medietas omnium notarum canitur. Diminutio autem fit in tempore perfecto, quando circulus dividitur per tractum ut hic ⌽, ibi enim solummodo tertia pars notarum aufertur. Vult enim cantum in tali signo modicum velocius tangi debere quam in illo O. Sunt enim unum et idem in esse et valore.[8]	*Semiditas* is made in imperfect *tempus*, when a semicircle is divided by a stroke, like this ¢; for here exactly half of each note is sung. Diminution, however, is made in perfect *tempus*, when a circle is divided by a stroke, like this ⌽; for here only a third of the notes is removed. That means that in this sign [⌽] one should touch a little faster than in this one O, for they are one and the same in essence and value.
Una semibrevis in singulis signis unum valet tactum, altera tamen pars, ut dictum est, in signorum diminutione sola canitur. Hinc est, quod in huiusmodi signis vel notulae velocius tangi debent vel semper duo tactus simul accipi pro uno ita videlicet, ut tunc una brevis tangetur tactu. Nos tamen primum modum observemus tangendo semper semibrevem tactu in singulis musicae gradibus proportionibus demptis.[9]	One semibreve is worth one *tactus* in individual signs, but, as stated above, only half is sung in signs of diminution. That is, in signs of that type [¢ and ⌽] either the notes must be touched a little faster or two *tactus* must always be taken as one, so that a breve is touched with a *tactus*. We will observe the first method, always touching a semibreve as the *tactus* in the individual levels of music, with the exception of proportions.

---

[8] Schanppecher, *Opus aureum*, pt. III, ch. 3 ("De signis et syncopatione"), 60. (Parts I and II of this book were written by Nicolaus Wollick.)

[9] Ibid., ch. 4 ("De tactu et notarum valore"), 61.

Table 6.1 Note values in *tactus* counts, from Wollick and Schanppecher, *Opus aureum*[1]

O2	18 maxima	6 longa	2 brevis	1 Semibreve	½ minima
C2	8 maxima	4 longa	2 brevis	1 Semibreve	½ minima
O	12 maxima	6 longa	3 brevis	1 Semibreve	½ minima
C	8 maxima	4 longa	2 brevis	1 Semibreve	½ minima
ɸ	12 maxima	6 longa	3 brevis	1 Semibreve	½ minima
¢	8 maxima	4 longa	2 brevis	1 Semibreve	½ minima
⊙	12 maxima	6 longa	3 brevis	1 Semibreve	minima
ℭ	8 maxima	4 longa	2 brevis	1 Semibreve	minima

[1] The table shows that the semibreve (whether perfect or imperfect) is the *tactus* of O2, C2, O, C, ɸ, ¢, ⊙, and ℭ. The signs are handwritten in the first edition (Nicolaus Wollick and Melchior Schanppecher, *Opus aureum* [Cologne: Heinrich Quentell, 1501], part III, ch. 4, fol. B1ᵛ), because the printer evidently did not have the symbols for them. This example is based on the copy of the 1504 edition in Paris, Bibliothèque Nationale, fol. Giᵛ, in which the signs are printed. There is no sign for ⅓ of a *tactus* for the minim in perfect prolation, presumably because the printer did not have it.

Schanppecher supports this explanation with a table (Table 6.1) that shows the (imperfect or perfect) semibreve as the *tactus* of all mensurations. Like many of his German followers, he assumes that if minor *modus* is perfect, major *modus* is perfect as well, though there is no basis for this view in practice.

Schanppecher's arguments appear to be contradictory, but they are not. Since the theoretical *tactus* is the breve of ¢ and the semibreve of C, the stroke removes exactly half the value of the notes in relation to the theoretical *tactus*, even though the performance *tactus* of ¢ may be a semibreve that is only a little faster than the semibreve *tactus* of C. Similarly, the statement that the notes lose a third of their value in ɸ is not incompatible with the statement that ɸ is simply a little faster than O, since Anonymous 12 himself implies that diminution by a third is to be understood as an approximation. O and ɸ are one and the same in "essence and value" even though ɸ is faster than O, because both "essence" and "value" refer to the number of *tactus* by which each figure is measured, not to the duration of the *tactus*.

Wollick and Cochlaeus draw heavily on Schanppecher's explanation of *tactus*, but integrate Gaffurio's chapter on diminution more fully into their texts. Wollick includes the above passages from Schanppecher almost verbatim in his *Enchiridion musices* of 1509. To clarify the relations among the different types of *tactus*, he invents the terms "tactus maior" for the breve *tactus*, "tactus minor" for the semibreve *tactus*, and "tactus proportionatus" for a *tactus* that measures three semibreves. The category of "tactus minor" includes both the moderate semibreve *tactus* of uncut signs and the faster semibreve *tactus* of cut signs:

[Tactus] Maior is est qui tempus: hoc est: brevem unico motu tangit. Minor qui et facillimus est solam semibrevem suo motu complet ... Proportionatus tactus est quando simul tres semibreves tanguntur.[10]	The major [*tactus*] is that which measures one *tempus*, that is, a breve, with one motion. The minor [*tactus*], which is the easiest, includes only a semibreve in its motion ... The proportionate *tactus* is when three semibreves are touched together [in one *tactus*].

In a later chapter, Wollick paraphrases Gaffurio's chapter on diminution in its entirety, but glosses it with an explanation of diminution and *semiditas* that follows Schanppecher (and thus, indirectly, Anonymous 12).[11]

Like Wollick, Cochlaeus includes close paraphrases of both Schanppecher and Gaffurio in separate chapters of his *Musica* of 1507.[12] He includes a *tactus* table in his *Compendium ... cantus figurabilis* that gives the same information as Schanppecher's with the sign O3 added and the *tactus* counts shown for the semiminim, *fusa*, and *semifusa*.[13] Here again the semibreve (whether perfect or imperfect) is the *tactus* of all signs, both integral and diminished. Cochlaeus confirms Schanppecher's implication that the breve *tactus* of ₵ is slow, since it is equal to two semibreve *tactus* that are only a little faster than the semibreve *tactus* of integral mensurations. After illustrating how to calculate the number of *tactus* on any note by explaining why a maxima in imperfect *tempus* with perfect major and minor *modus* has eighteen semibreve *tactus*, Cochlaeus explains the slow breve *tactus* as follows:

---

[10] Wollick, *Enchiridion musices*, book 5, ch. 6 ("De notularum partibus, tractu et valore"), fols. Gv^r–Gv^v.

[11] Ibid., book 5, ch. 11 ("De diminutio et semiditate"), fols. Hiiii^r–Hiiii^v. Wollick credits Gaffurio explicitly with the information in this chapter.

[12] Cochlaeus, *Musica*, 3rd edn., "De diminutione" and "De tactu," fols. C4^r–C4^v and D^r–D^v.

[13] Cochlaeus, *Compendium ... cantus figurabilis*, ch. 6 ("De notarum valore"), fol. [2]^v.

| Si brevis in semiditatis signo aut consimili mensuretur tactu: quod idem est tangendo tardius. tunc maxima in eo novem continet tactus ac longa tres et sic deinceps.[14] | If the breve in a sign of *semiditas* or the equivalent is measured with the *tactus*, which is the same thing measuring slowly, then a maxima in it contains nine *tactus*, a long three, etc. |

In other words, measuring with a slow breve *tactus* is equivalent to measuring with a fast semibreve *tactus*. The breve *tactus* must be twice as slow as the semibreve *tactus* of ¢ in any given piece at a given metronome speed, and the latter is a little faster than the semibreve *tactus* of uncut signs.

In his *Tetrachordum musices* of 1511, Cochlaeus integrates the material that he takes from Schanppecher and Gaffurio more fully. To avoid the logical awkwardness of saying that notes lose half their value when they are measured with a semibreve *tactus* in ¢, he limits the definition of *semiditas* to simultaneous relations between diminished and undiminished signs:

| Quid est semiditas? Est alterius partis temporalis mensurae imminutio: fit solum in tempore imperfecto, per hoc signum ¢ vel per haec signa O2 C2. Duae nanque semibreves sic unicum complent tactum, in una cantus parte, quando unica tactum perficit in altera parte signo non diminuto per virgulam scindentem, aut numerum appositum.[15] | What is *semiditas*? It is the removal of half of the measure of time. It is made only in imperfect *tempus*, through this sign ¢ or these signs O2 C2. In this way two semibreves fill a *tactus* in one part [voice] of the song while a single [semibreve] fills a *tactus* in another part [voice] with a sign that is not diminished by a stroke cutting it or a number next to it. |

Several other theorists of the second decade of the century follow the basic teachings of the Cologne school, but modify them subtly in an attempt to tighten the logic of their arguments. Joannes Volckmar reduces Wollick's three *tactus* types to two: *generalis* and *specialis*. The former is the semibreve and the latter is everything else, including the breve *tactus* of *semiditas*. Although Volckmar acknowledges in his text that all signs except augmentation and proportions may use the *tactus generalis*, he includes a diagram based on Adam von Fulda (with the sign ⊙2 omitted)

---

[14] Cochlaeus, *Musica*, 3rd edn., "De tactu," fol. D^r.
[15] Cochlaeus, *Tetrachordum musices*, tract. IV, ch. 7 ("De augmentatione et diminutione"), fol. Eiii^v.

that shows only the theoretical *tactus* of each sign.[16] The anonymous author of the *Institutio in musicen mensuralem* acknowledges that some people make a distinction between *tactus generalis* and *tactus specialis*, but shows only the semibreve *tactus* in his table.[17] Michael Koswick accepts Volckmar's two categories of *tactus*, but classifies the fast semibreve *tactus* of diminution as *specialis*, rather than *generalis*.[18]

Ornithoparchus manipulates Wollick's *tactus* types by moving the semibreve *tactus* of uncut signs from the category of *tactus minor* to that of *tactus maior*. The *tactus maior*, which he regards as the correct theoretical and performance *tactus* of all signs, is now the semibreve of O and C and the imperfect breve of Ø and ₵:

Tactus tripartitus est: maior scilicet, minor et proportionatus. Maior, est mensura, tardo ac motu quasi reciproco facta. Hunc tactum et integrum et totalem nominant auctores. Et quoniam verus est omnium cantilenarum tactus: Semibrevem non diminutam suo motu comprehendit: vel brevem, in duplo diminutam. Minor, est maioris medium: quem Semitactum dicunt. Quoniam semibrevem in duplo diminutam suo motu mensurat, indoctis tantum probatus.[19]	There are three types of *tactus*: major, minor, and proportionate. The major [*tactus*] is a measure made by a slow and quasi-reciprocal motion. Writers call this *tactus* both integral and total. And since it is the true *tactus* of all signs, it includes the undiminished semibreve or the breve diminished in duple in its motion. The minor [*tactus*] is half of the major; it is called half-*tactus*, since it measures a semibreve diminished in duple with its motion. It is approved only by the unlearned.

Two *tactus* tables (Tables 6.2 and 6.3), one for integral signs and one for diminished signs, illustrate these points.[20] Unlike Schanppecher and Cochlaeus, Ornithoparchus includes many signs in his tables that are extremely rare in practice. For no apparent reason, he treats the sign ⊙2 as a *modus cum tempore* sign, but other signs with a 2 as diminution. His theory is based heavily on speculation and does not agree with common practice, as he readily admits.

---

[16] Volckmar, *Collectanea quedam musice discipline*, [part II], ch. 9 ("De tactibus"), fols. D^r–D^v.
[17] Anonymous, *Institutio in musicen mensuralem*, tract. III, "De tactu," fol. Ciij^r.
[18] Koswick, *Compendiaria musice artis aeditio*, [book 2], ch. 5 ("De tactu: semiditate: augmentatione et diminutione"), fols. Lij^r–Lij^v.
[19] Ornithoparchus, *Musice active micrologus*, book 2, ch. 6 ("De tactu"), fol. Fiij^v.
[20] Ibid., book 2, ch. 6 ("De tactu"), fol. Fiv^r, and 8 ("De diminutione"), fol. Fvi^r.

Table 6.2 Note values in *tactus* counts *ut iacet*, from Ornithoparchus, *Musice active micrologus*[1]

⊙3	27	9	3	1				
O3	27	9	3	1	½			
C3	12	6	3	1	½			
⊙2	12	6	2	1				
⊙	12	6	3	1		4ᵒʳ tactum unum	8 tactum unum	16 tactum unum
₵	8	4	2	1				
O	12	6	3	1	½			
C	8	4	2	1	½			
𝅗	𝅗	𝅝	♩	♪	♪	♪	♪	♪

[1] The table shows that the *tactus* is the perfect or imperfect semibreve of ⊙3, O3, C3, ⊙2, ⊙, ₵, O and C. After Andreas Ornithoparchus, *Musice active micrologus* (Leipzig: Valentin Schumann, 1517), book 2, ch. 6, fol. Fiv^r.

Table 6.3 Note values in *tactus* counts in diminution, from Ornithoparchus, *Musice active micrologus*[1]

⌽	6	3	1 ½	½				
⌽	6	3	1 ½	½				
O2	6	3	1	½				
₵	4	2	1	½	4ᵒʳ unum tactum	8 unum tactum	16 unum tactum	32 unum tactum
₵	4	2	1	½				
C2	4	2	1	½				

[1] The table shows that the *tactus* is the imperfect breve of ⌽, ⌽, O2, ₵, ₵, and C2. After Andreas Ornithoparchus, *Musice active micrologus* (Leipzig: Valentin Schumann, 1517), book 2, ch. 8, fol. Fvi^r.

Since the semibreve *tactus* of undiminished signs had always been understood to be slower than the semibreve *tactus* of diminished signs, including it in the category of *tactus maior*, rather than *tactus minor*, is not in itself a drastic move, but including ⌽, as well as ₵, among signs in which the theoretical *tactus* is the imperfect breve is a radical departure from the views of Ornithoparchus's German predecessors. Although Ornithoparchus attributes this idea to Gaffurio's *Practica musice*,[21] he must surely have derived it from the *Angelicum ac divinum opus musice* and interpreted the

[21] Ibid., book 2, ch. 8 ("De diminutione"), fol. Fv^r.

Practica musice in light of the later source, because all earlier theorists (and most later ones) understood Gaffurio's description of diminution by stroke in *Practica musice* to mean *acceleratio mensurae*, not mensural diminution. This view is quite radical, but Ornithoparchus makes it appear to be only a minor modification of the views of the Cologne school by affirming that the semibreve is the *tactus* of all signs, then excluding diminution, as well as proportions and augmentation, from this general rule:

Semibrevis in omnibus signis (diminutionis, augmentationis, ac proportionum demptis) tactu mensuratur integro.[22]	A semibreve in all signs (with the exception of diminution, augmentation, and proportions) is measured with a whole *tactus*.

Placing the *tactus* on the imperfect breve in ¢ creates a mismatch between the *tactus* and the perfect breves of the mensuration. Recognizing this problem, Ornithoparchus invents a new rule requiring pieces in ¢ to have an even number of breves, so that they will end on the downbeat of the *tactus*. He admits, however, that this rule is not observed in practice.[23]

The most radical feature of Ornithoparchus's theory is his insistence that the performance *tactus* must always be the same value as the theoretical *tactus*. Earlier theorists struggled to find justifications for the contradiction between the breve theoretical *tactus* and the semibreve performance *tactus* of ¢, but Ornithoparchus – who was not a practicing musician – castigated composers and performers mercilessly for their failure to measure cut signs in breves.[24] Later theorists who respected Ornithoparchus's learning, but disagreed with his view that practice must always conform to theory, had the unenviable task of attempting to reconcile his theory with the views of more open-minded theorists and with their own practical experience. Georg Rhau established the model for such a reconciliation in his *Enchiridion*. His strategy was to adopt Cochlaeus's limitation of the term *semiditas* to diminished signs in simultaneous proportional relation to integral signs, and then to apply Ornithoparchus's theory of *tactus* in diminution only to those relationships. Rhau includes both of Ornithoparchus's *tactus* tables in the 1520 edition of his book, but he applies the table of diminished values only to *semiditas* in this restricted (proportional) sense.[25] The tables are omitted from later editions of the book.

---

[22] Ibid., book 2, ch. 6 ("De tactu"), fol. Fiv^r.
[23] Ibid., book 2, ch. 8 ("De diminutione"), fols. Fv^r–Fvi^r.   [24] Ibid.
[25] Rhau, *Enchiridion*, [part II], ch. 4 ("De augmentatione & diminutione"), fol. Diiij^r and 7 ("De tactibus"), fol. Giiij^v. The section of the book dealing with mensuration, which appears for the

Martin Agricola, whose rigorous attempt to reconcile Ornithoparchus with both earlier theorists and common practice has been unjustly maligned, adopts logical techniques from both the Cologne school and Rhau.[26] He accepts Ornithoparchus's definition of *tactus* types, in which both the semibreve of uncut signs and the imperfect breve of cut signs are classified as *tactus maior*, and supports the point with Ornithoparchus's tables. He then expands the category of *tactus minor*, or half-*tactus*, so that it includes the minim of uncut signs, as well as the semibreve of cut signs. This strategy creates a satisfying symmetry between the two categories of signs, since both cut and uncut signs now have a *tactus maior* and a *tactus minor*:

Der gantze Tact. Ist / welcher eine ungeringerte Semibrevem odder eine Brevem in der helfft geringert / mit seiner bewegung / begreifft.	The whole *tactus* is that which contains an undiminished semibreve or a breve diminished by half in its motion.
Der halbe Tact. Ist das halbe teil vom gantzen / Und wird auch darumb also genant / das er halb soviel / als der gantze Tact / das ist / eine Semibrevem inn der helfft geringert / odder eine ungeringerte Minimam mit seiner bewegung / das ist / mit dem nidderschlagen und auffheben begreifft.[27]	The half *tactus* is half of the whole, and it is called this because it contains half of the whole *tactus*, namely, a semibreve diminished by half or an undiminished minim, in its motion, that is, in the downstroke and upstroke.

Both the whole *tactus* and the half-*tactus* (a complete *tactus minor*, not half of a *tactus maior*) consist of a downstroke and an upstroke. The difference between them is in their classification, not their form. A figure illustrating both categories of *tactus* (Figure 6.1) shows the semibreve as the *tactus* of all signs. The semibreve is classified as a whole *tactus* in O, C3, and C, and as a half-*tactus* in Φ, O2, ₵, and C2. The figure implies that the

---

first time in this edition, is not called part II, but it is usually bound with the section of the book on plainchant.

[26] Arthur Mendel, "Some Ambiguities of the Mensural System," singled out Agricola as a theorist whose statements about mensuration and *tactus* were particularly ambiguous and inconsistent. Agricola's inconsistencies are a result of his attempt to reconcile the conflicting views of his predecessors. His allegedly conflicting claims usually apply to different contexts or different definitions of terms.

[27] Agricola, *Musica figuralis deudsch*, ch. 6 ("Vom schlag odder Tact"), fols. Giii[v]–Giiij[r]. Agricola adds a discussion of the minim whole *tactus* in augmentation (fol. H[r]) and illustrates it with a table that parallels the tables of integral mensuration (fol. Gvi[r]) and diminution (fol. Hv[v]) that he based on Ornithoparchus.

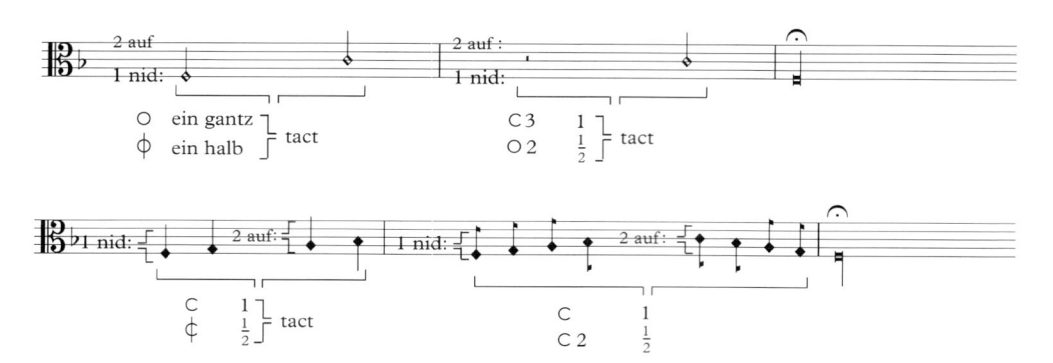

Figure 6.1 Form of the whole *tactus* and half-*tactus*. After Martin Agricola, *Musica figuralis deudsch* (Wittenberg: Georg Rhau, 1532), ch. 6, fol. Giiijʳ.

semibreve is the normal performance *tactus* of every sign, regardless of the theoretical category to which it belongs. Agricola's explanation is a cumbersome way to make this simple point, but his purpose was to justify common practice in relation to inherited theory, not to explain what everyone knew from experience. Although the use of the *tactus maior* (breve) in cut signs and the *tactus minor* (minim) in uncut signs might be theoretically possible, Agricola illustrates these options only in the context of simultaneous proportions. Their function in other contexts is to satisfy the demands of theory, not to explain performance practice.

Sebald Heyden created a spectacular, though short-lived, sensation in German mensural theory with the novel idea that there was only one correct *tactus* for all signs, and that the notes must always adapt to the *tactus*, not the *tactus* to the notes. This *tactus* was a pair of equal down and up motions that applied to different notes under different signs. Each sign specified the note corresponding to the *tactus*, and that note was always the same regardless of the context in which the sign appeared. Integral signs placed the *tactus* on the semibreve; signs of diminution placed it on the imperfect breve, and signs of augmentation placed it on the minim. Signs of proportion placed it on the note that was equivalent to the integral semibreve, even if they appeared in all voices and were "proportions" only in the informal sense. By advocating fixed relations among signs regardless of context, Heyden eliminated the distinction between diminution or augmentation and proportion, and between the formal and informal meanings of the term "proportion."

Heyden developed this theory over the course of the three editions of his treatise: *Musica stoicheiosis* (1532), *Musicae, id est artis canendi libri duo* (1537), and *De arte canendi* (1540). It appears in a mild form in the first edition and becomes increasingly rigid and dogmatic in successive editions of the book. Heyden never claimed that his theory conformed to the practices of his contemporaries, but he believed it was a faithful reconstruction of the lost practices of earlier generations. The most unusual feature of *Musica stoicheiosis* is that the topics of augmentation and diminution are discussed in the section on proportions, rather than in separate chapters, as they had been in all earlier writings on the subject.[28] Heyden seems to have conceived the idea of measuring note values in all signs on the basis of a simple formula not as a theoretical dogma, but as a way of helping students understand the principle of placing the *tactus* on different notes. By associating every sign with a single *tactus*, he avoids both the complications of different *tactus* types and the condition that a sign might require one *tactus* in proportional relations and another when it applies to all voices. He explains the principle as follows:

| Tactu hoc modo percepto, nihil plane scrupuli reliquum sit, quin & Augmentationem & Diminutionem, tum facilime pueri intelligant. Quod utraque ex huius Tactus dimensione tota pendeat. Necque aliud sibi velit illa, quam ut plures: haec ut pauciores Notule eidem Tactui adaptentur. Sciant ergo pueri & Augmentationem & Diminutionem relative dici, ad Semibrevis Notulae essentialem quantitatem, qua ipsa integro tactu sub his signis O C valet.[29] | When *tactus* is understood in this way, clearly no obstacle remains for boys to understand both augmentation and diminution very easily, because both depend on the whole measure of this *tactus*. The latter means nothing other than that more notes, and the former that fewer notes, must be adapted to this same *tactus*. Boys should know that both augmentation and diminution are defined in relation to the essential quantity of the semibreve, by which the semibreve itself is worth a whole *tactus* in these signs O C. |

By 1537, the principle of measuring ₵ and Φ with an imperfect breve *tactus* had evolved in Heyden's thought from a rule of thumb to an inflexible dogma. The *tactus* was increasingly associated not only with fixed note values, but also with a fixed duration, in successive editions of his book, such that all signs were governed by a comprehensive system of invariable proportional relationships. In the dedication of the 1540 edition, Heyden launched a bitter attack on the interpretation of *tactus* by his contemporaries that rivals Ornithoparchus's diatribe in rhetorical force.[30]

---

[28] Heyden, *Musica stoicheiosis*, "De mensura proportionum," fols. C4r–C6v.
[29] Ibid., fol. C5r.   [30] Heyden, *De arte canendi*, letter of dedication, fols. A1v–A6v.

Example 6.1 Example of major *tactus* in perfect *tempus*, bars 1–4. After Hermann Finck, *Practica musica* (Wittenberg: Georg Rhaus Erben, 1556), fols. Fiij^v–Fiiij^r. The first six notes of the discantus, bar 3, are apparently printed a third too high in the source. They are corrected in the example.

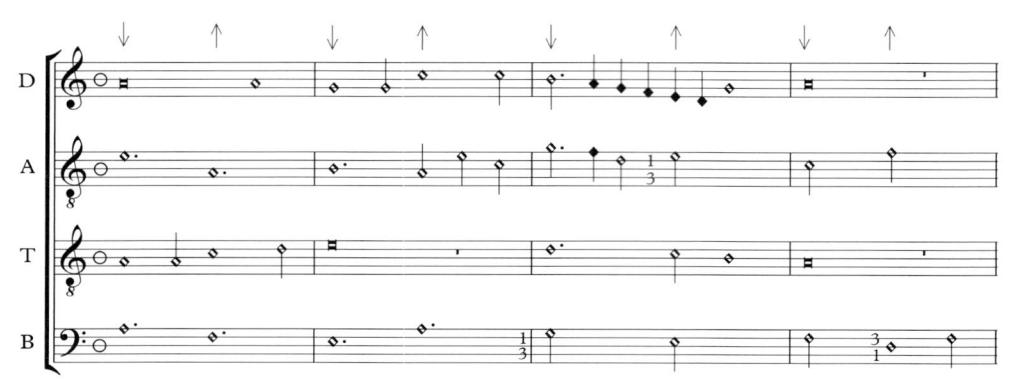

Heyden's theory evoked no immediate response, but it created something of a crisis for German theorists of the 1550s. Gregor Faber and Johannes Oridryus adopted Heyden's views fully and uncritically,[31] but other theorists struggled to reconcile them with the practices they knew from experience. Heinrich Faber claimed that Heyden was right in theory, but allowed students to use a semibreve *tactus* in cut signs for greater ease.[32] Hermann Finck took a similar position, but with less conviction. After a lengthy discussion and illustration of the three types of *tactus*, he comments without explanation that older musicians had only two types of *tactus*: perfect and imperfect.[33] In a later chapter, he paraphrases a sentence from Heyden claiming that there is only one correct type of *tactus* as if it were simply an afterthought, but he allows various types of *tactus* for teaching purposes.[34] He seems to have misinterpreted the concept of *tactus maior* in perfect *tempus* in light of Heyden's theory, such that an equally divided breve *tactus* in that mensuration corresponds to a perfect breve, rather than an imperfect breve. To illustrate the point, he composed an example (Example 6.1) in which the rhythms consist mostly of groups of three minims that are easy to perform with this *tactus*, but bear no resemblance to the rhythms of real

---

[31] Faber, *Musices practicae erotematum libri II*, book 1, ch. 9 ("De tactu"), 45–47; Oridryus, *Practicae musicae utriusque praecepta brevia*, part II, ch. 4 ("De tactu et mensura"), 107–10.

[32] Faber, *Ad musicam practicam introductio*, part II, ch. 5, fols. S4^r–S4^v. Faber paraphrases Ornithoparchus's definitions of *tactus* types, but observes that the minor *tactus* is the only one currently used by singers.

[33] Finck, *Practica musica*, book 2, "De tactu," fol. Gij^r.   [34] Ibid., "De prolatione," fol. Ki^v.

pieces in perfect *tempus*, with or without the stroke of diminution that some theorists associate with the choice of the *tactus maior*.[35] The example is of interest in that it reveals an unspoken assumption that the *tactus* should articulate real rhythmic groups, even though it is a speculative demonstration that reveals nothing about actual performance practices. Johann Zanger follows Heyden in proposing a strict correlation between signs and *tactus* and borrows many examples from Heyden, but he seems not to have understood Heyden's definitions. He reverses the view of all of his predecessors by associating the breve *tactus* with integral signs and the semibreve *tactus* with diminished signs, but he uses the term breve *tactus* to mean the type of measurement that other theorists call a minim *tactus*.[36] The result is a garbled attempt to reconcile Heyden's theory with the fact that the semibreve was the standard *tactus* of diminished signs in practice. Since Zanger's theory measures integral signs in minims, it produces the correct relations among signs in proportional relations, though it does so by measuring all signs with a *tactus* on the next smaller value from the one advocated by Heyden.

By *c*. 1560 the furor over Heyden's reformist ideas had largely passed. German theorists from then to the end of the century contribute no new ideas on the subject of *tactus*. Some continue to advocate one of the traditional three-*tactus* systems, sometimes with a respectful nod toward Heyden's view, while others abandon the complications of *tactus* theory altogether and simply state that the semibreve is the *tactus* of both integral and diminished signs. Even the traditional tempo distinction between the two types of signs is not always mentioned, especially in books directed at elementary students. As early as 1548, Heinrich Faber illustrated note values in ₵ on the basis of a semibreve *tactus* without comment in his elementary *Compendiolum musicae*.[37] Christoph Praetorius distinguishes essential, augmented, and diminished mensurations, but includes only simultaneous proportions in the latter two groups, in his *Erotemata musices* of 1574.[38] Joachim Burmeister defines only two types of *tactus* – equally and unequally divided – in his *Musica autoschediastike* of 1601 and says that there is no point in distinguishing between major and minor *tactus*, because differences of tempo are

---

[35] Ibid., "De tactu," fols. Fiij^r–Fiiij^r.
[36] Zanger, *Practicae musicae praecepta*, [part II], ch. 2 ("De gradibus"), fols. Hij^v–Hiij^v. Zanger's bizarre misunderstanding of the term breve *tactus* is clear from his examples.
[37] Faber, *Compendiolum musicae*, ch. 5 ("De figuris"), fol. A6^v.
[38] Praetorius, *Erotemata musices*, book 3, ch. 4 ("De cantus notularumque mensura"), fol. I^v.

subject to the judgment of the conductor and have nothing to do with the essence of music.[39]

Heyden's theory had some impact in France, as well as in Germany, although most French theorists were more interested in practice than in speculative theories of *tactus*. Loys Bourgeois claims on Heyden's authority that the ancients had only one type of *tactus*, which was applied to the semibreve in integral signs and the breve in diminution.[40] He does not mention the possibility of a semibreve *tactus* in diminution, although his association of the breve *tactus* with the ancients seems to imply that it is no longer in use. Other French theorists of the 1550s, including Claude Martin, Maximilian Guilliaud, and Philibert Jambe de Fer, state without qualification that the *tactus* of cut signs is the semibreve.[41] Guilliaud distinguishes between standard tempo and diminution and says that the ancients represented diminution with cut signs, but that the moderns make no distinction between cut and uncut signs.[42] Jean Yssandon departs from his French predecessors by espousing Heyden's single-*tactus* theory as late as 1582, but does not make a major point of the issue.[43]

Southern European theories of cut signs

The attitude of Italian and Spanish theorists toward cut signs was quite different from that of their northern European colleagues. Those who discuss the matter between the time of Gaffurio's *Angelicum ac divinum opus musice* (1508) and Zarlino's *Le istitutioni harmoniche* (1558) are nearly unanimous in their view that the *tactus* of both ₡ and Φ is the imperfect breve. Many note that performers do not observe this principle in practice, but they do not always object seriously to the discrepancy between theory and practice. The most likely reason for the difference between northern and southern views of cut signs is that the *Angelicum ac divinum opus musice* was widely read in Italy and Spain, and readers naturally assumed that it was a legitimate summary of Gaffurio's views in *Practica musice*.

---

[39] Burmeister, *Musica autoschediastike*, Accessio III, section II, "De antiphonis," fol. Aa^v.
[40] Bourgeois, *Le droict chemin de musique*, ch. 6 ("Du tacte"), fols. C3^r–C3^v.
[41] Martin, *Elementorum musices practicae*, book 2, ch. 6 ("De vulgatissima graduum musicalium commixtione, in qua imperfecta esse omnia depraehendes"), 28; Guilliaud, *Rudiments de musique practique*, part II, ch. 8 ("Du touchement, ou mesure du chant"), fol. Cij^r; Jambe de Fer, *Epitome musical*, ch. 7 ("Les noms & valeur des notes ... "), 31.
[42] Guilliaud, *Rudiments de musique practique*, part II, ch. 8 ("Du touchement, ou mesure du chant"), fol. Cij^r.
[43] Yssandon, *Traité de la musique pratique* (Paris, 1582), part II, "De la batue, ou tact, & à scavoir-mon si elle a des especes"), 17–18.

Southern theorists before Zarlino who advocate an imperfect breve *tactus* in ₵ and Φ include Francisco Tovar, Pietro Aaron, Giovanni Spataro, Giovanni Maria Lanfranco, Stephano Vanneo, Matheo de Aranda, Angelo da Picitono, Vicente Lusitano, and Juan Bermudo.[44]

Nicola Vicentino gives a confusing account in which both C and ₵ call for a breve *tactus*.[45] In a later chapter, C is a sign of a semibreve *tactus* when many black notes (semiminims and smaller values) are present:

Altri segnano i canti tutti neri con il segno imperfetto non tagliato; & quella compositione da Cantanti è detta cantare à misura di breve.[46]	Others sign completely black songs with the uncut imperfect sign, and such compositions are called by singers singing to the short measure.

This passage is one of the few theoretical references to the notation of the so-called *note nere* madrigals that became popular in the 1540s and were characterized by rhythms with numerous semiminims under the sign C. The term *misura di breve* must mean short measure, not breve *tactus*, in this context, since pieces of this type have the compositional *tactus* on the minim and need a divided semibreve *tactus*, or even a minim *tactus*, in performance.

In the second half of the century, Italian and Spanish theorists lost interest in the distinction between cut and uncut signs. They generally describe only two types of *tactus* – equal and unequal – and say little or nothing about the possibility of a breve *tactus* in cut signs. Many do not even mention Φ, and none expresses strong convictions about its *tactus*. Zarlino established the precedent for this approach in Le istitutioni harmoniche. He mentions the possibility of equal *tactus* on both the breve and the semibreve in his chapter on the *battuta*, but does not associate the

---

[44] Tovar, *Libro de musica practica*, book 2, ch. 7 ("De tiempo diminutivo y de ssus figuras"), fol. XX[v]; Aaron, *Lucidario in musica*, book 3, ch. 6 ("Come il cantore dee oſſervare la misura ne segni de modulati concenti dal musico, & compositore ordinati"), fols. 20[r]–21[r]; Spataro, *Tractato di musica*, ch. 24 ("In quale figura, over nota de la sesqualtera (primamente) data: cada la perfectione"), fol. fiv[r]; Lanfranco, *Scintille di musica*, part II, "Della battuta," 67; Vanneo, *Recanetum de musica aurea*, book 2, ch. 19 ("De diminutione seu notularum variatione"), fols. 62[v]–63[r]; Matheo de Aranda, *Tractado de canto mensurable*, conclusion quarta ("De circulos y numeros: que demuestran el tiempo y la prolacion: y de las pausas y circulos que demuestran el modo mayor y menor"), fols. av[v]–avi[r]; Angelo da Picitono, *Fior angelico di musica*, book 2, ch. 3 ("Delli segni del tempo con prolatione"), fol. R[v]; Lusitano, *Introdutione facilissima*, "Del canto figurato," fol. 7; and Bermudo, *Declaración de instrumentos musicales*, book 2, chs. 20–22, fols. Di[v]–Dij[r].

[45] Vicentino, *L'antica musica ridotta alla moderna prattica*, book 4, ch. 8 ("Regola di batter la misura con tre ordini con l'essempio"), fol. 76[r].

[46] Ibid., book 4, ch. 10 ("Regola di comporre le note nere nel segno perfetto & imperfetto; & nell'emiolia maggiore & minore, & nella proportione di equalità, & nella sesqualtera"), fol. 77[r].

choice with specific signs,[47] and he treats the semibreve as the *tactus* without reference to signs in his discussion of dissonance treatment.[48] The only hint that he recognizes the breve as the theoretical *tactus* of ₡ appears in his discussion and examples of syncopation, in which he illustrates syncopated semibreves in C and syncopated breves in ₡.[49] Artusi follows him exactly in this respect.[50] Tigrini classifies *tactus* types as equal and unequal, but does not mention a distinction between breve and semibreve *tactus*.[51] Sancta Maria, Zacconi, and Banchieri acknowledge that the breve is the theoretical *tactus* of ₡, but accept the fact that it is not used in practice.[52]

The only theorists in this group who insist that the performance *tactus* must match the theoretical *tactus* as a matter of principle are Tovar and Bermudo. Bermudo derived much of his information on *tactus* from Ornithoparchus, whom he follows in condemning practitioners who perform cut signs with a semibreve *tactus*.[53] Tovar took a unique position in rejecting the sign Φ altogether on grounds of the mismatch between its imperfect breve theoretical *tactus* and the perfect breves of the mensuration. He complains that people who use that sign interpret it incorrectly as a sign of a fast semibreve *tactus* (*compaset*):

Es consuetud entre los componedores que quieren partir el circulo retundo con linea desta manera [Φ]. Y es falso porque tal señyal significa dupla y dupla en numero ternario no puede ser por que el medio de tres es uno y medio y unitas es indivisible. no que los tales pongan la tal señyal por dupla mas quieren que luego que sea tal señyal la cantoria se aya de cantar apresurada no	It is the custom among composers to divide the circle with a line in this manner [Φ]. This is false, because that sign represents *dupla*, and *dupla* cannot exist in the number three, since half of three is one and a half, and unity is indivisible. But those who use this sign do not mean *dupla*; rather they want that where this sign appears the song must be sung

---

[47] Zarlino, *Le istitutioni harmoniche*, book 3, ch. 48 ("Della battuta"), 208.
[48] Ibid., book 3, ch. 42 ("Delli contrapunti diminuiti a due voci, & in qual modo si possino usar le dissonanze"), 195–99.
[49] Ibid., book 3, ch. 49 ("Della sincopa"), 209–10.
[50] Artusi, *L'arte del contraponto*, "Della battuta" and "Della sincopa," 28–29.
[51] Tigrini, *Il compendio della musica*, book 4, ch. 16 ("Della battuta"), 123.
[52] Sancta Maria, *Arte de tañer fantasia*, ch. 6 ("De las figuras"), fol. 9^v; Zacconi, *Prattica di musica*, book 1, ch. 36 ("Quali sieno i segni del tatto"), fols. 24^r–26^r; Banchieri, *Cartella musicale*, [part II], document 3 ("De gli dui tempi perfetti maggiore et minore"), 28–29.
[53] Bermudo, *Declaración de instrumentos musicales*, book 3, ch. 36 ("Dela diminucion"), fols. Ciijv–Ciiij^v.

diminuyendo la cantidad de las figuras: por la qual voluntad y platica nacio la particion del compas el qual se dize el compaset . . .[54]	faster, not diminishing the quantity of the figures. From this opinion and practice arises the division of the *compas* that is called *compaset* . . .

Tovar also complains about the use of the *compaset* in ₵. The fact that Domingo Marcos Durán expresses no objection to the *compaset* (or *compasejo*, as he calls it) in his *Sumula de canto órgano*,[55] which was written shortly before Gaffurio's *Angelicum ac divinum opus musice*, supports the hypothesis that it was the influence of the latter book that led many theorists after 1508 to associate cut signs in general, and ₵ in particular, with an imperfect breve *tactus*.

Most southern theorists were willing to grant practice some independence from theory, though many give reasons why the theoretical *tactus* is preferable in cut signs or advise composers to write in such a way that the theoretically correct *tactus* is at least feasible. Aaron points out that measuring cut signs with a semibreve *tactus* causes performers to mistake *sesquialtera* proportion for *tripla*.[56] Spataro complains that the practice of measuring everything in semibreves causes musicians to lose sight of the differences between the compositional principles associated with different *tactus*. He maintains, for example, that certain types of dissonance are allowed on the third minim of the breve-unit when the *tactus* is the breve, but not when it is the semibreve, and he associates different types of syncopation with each *tactus*.[57] Matheo de Aranda advises students to learn note values in relation to each other, rather than as numbers of *tactus*, since different performers use different *tactus*, but he dislikes the practice of measuring all signs in semibreves because it destroys the unique character associated with each *tactus*. His comments on the subject, though vague, imply that the choice of *tactus* concerns not just theoretical propriety, but musical expression. He

---

[54] Tovar, *Libro de musica practica*, book 2, ch. 15 ("Dela perficion de los dichos generos mediante circulos y numero de arithmetica"), fol. XXIII[v]. The sign in the source in this passage is O, but the logic requires ₵.

[55] Domingo Marcos Durán, *Sumula de canto órgano*, ch. 19 ("Del compas que es y de su division"), fols. aviii[v]–b[r].

[56] Aaron, *Lucidario*, book 3, ch. 6 ("Come il cantore dee oſservare la misura ne segni de modulati concenti dal musico, & compositore ordinati"), fols. 20[r]–20[v].

[57] Spataro, letters of 30 January 1531 and 4 March 1533 to Aaron, in *A Correspondence of Renaissance Musicians*, 416 and 620–21.

characterizes different types of *tactus* as "proportions" in the informal sense:

Cada manera de compas muestra su Harmonia y diferencia y Melodia y gracia de canto: Por lo qual es bien seguir las dichas tres maneras de compas quando se demostraren: y no ir contra toda orden y composicion de proporciones.[58]	Every type of *tactus* displays its own harmony, distinctiveness, melody, and grace in singing. Therefore it is good to follow the above three types of *tactus* when they are shown, and not to go against all order and structure of proportions.

Lanfranco and Zacconi accept the semibreve *tactus* as a practical reality, but advise composers to avoid syncopated breve rests that will cause confusion for performers who choose to measure cut signs in breves. Zacconi believes that the sign ₵ should be used only for pieces in which the rhythms are suited to measuring in breves in case performers should prefer to observe the literal meaning of the sign, but admits that many composers do not observe this principle.[59] Banchieri does not regard the breve *tactus* as a realistic possibility for music in ₵, but nevertheless calls the semibreve *tactus* in that sign "an abuse that has become a custom."[60]

Southern theorists were interested in the implications of different signs with respect to the largest regular unit of measure that was applicable in a piece, as well as the unit corresponding to the performance *tactus*. In older theory, the largest regular unit was the breve of O, C, Ø, and ₵, but that convention was undermined by new theories of *tactus* and new mensural practices in the sixteenth century. In the early decades of the century, the breve was still regarded as the largest obligatory unit of measure in all of these signs. Pieces were required to consist of a whole number of breves, and breve rests were not supposed to be notated in syncopated positions. By the 1530s, however, composers began to treat the theoretical *tactus*, and sometimes even the performance *tactus*, as the largest regular unit of measure in imperfect *tempus*, and theorists accepted the idea that the theoretical *tactus* was more important than the breve as the governing unit of time measurement. Spataro admits in a 1531 letter to Aaron that he has mistakenly written an odd number of semibreves in a composition, but says that the error is not serious,

---

[58] Matheo de Aranda, *Tractado de canto mensurable*, "Declaracion de algunas cosas: que en este tractado se contienen," fols. Dii^v–Diii^r.

[59] Lanfranco, *Scintille di musica*, part II, "Delle note sincopate: & che cosa e Sincopa," 66–67; Zacconi, *Prattica di musica*, book 1, ch. 36 ("Quali sieno i segni del tatto"), fol. 25^r.

[60] Banchieri, *Cartella musicale*, [part II], document 3 ("De gli dui tempi perfetti maggiore et minore"), 29.

because the composition is in C; if the work had been in C2, the error would have been much greater.[61] Lanfranco makes a similar distinction in importance between the observance of the breve-units in C and ₵:

... molti di quelli sono, che non solamente mancono della misura del numero binario sotto la imperfettione del segno del Tempo intero [C]: ma anchora sotto la misura del segno del Tempo imperfetto traversato [₵], che e pur troppo grande errore: Perche, si offende la misura: & il Tempo: & senza misura ogni cosa si guasta.[62]	Many of these [composers] err not only in the measuring of the binary number [of semibreves] under the sign of integral imperfect *tempus* [C], but also under the sign of cut imperfect *tempus* [₵], which is a very great error, because it offends against measure and time, and without measure, everything is ruined.

Lanfranco also picked up Ornithoparchus's argument that pieces in Φ should be measured in units of six semibreves, so that their measurement would conform both to the perfect breves of the mensuration and to the imperfect breve performance *tactus*.[63] This rule was entirely speculative and never applied to real pieces (or sections of pieces) in Φ, since the imperfect breve *tactus* in that mensuration was also, at least for the most part, a theoretical fiction.

Later theorists repeat traditional rules about the proper lengths of pieces in Φ and ₵, but acknowledge increasingly that the theoretical *tactus* is the largest unit of time that really matters. Zarlino includes Lanfranco's rules in a chapter devoted to the practices of older musicians and even invents the fiction that ₵ originally required regular pairing of breves, apparently by analogy with the equally fictitious pairing of breves in Φ, but he admits that his contemporaries do not always respect the integrity of even the breve-units, let alone the long-units, whether the signs are cut or uncut.[64] Zacconi says that the semibreve is the largest theoretical unit of measure in C and that many composers observe the rule that pieces in ₵ should have a whole number of breve-units without even knowing the reason for it.[65]

---

[61] Spataro, letter of 30 January 1531 to Aaron, in *A Correspondence of Renaissance Musicians*, 415–16.
[62] Lanfranco, *Scintille di musica*, part II, "Della battuta," 68.   [63] Ibid.
[64] Zarlino, *Le istituitioni harmoniche*, book 3, ch. 67 ("Del tempo, del modo, & della prolatione; et in che quantità si debbino finire, o numerare le cantilene"), 270.
[65] Zacconi, *Prattica di musica*, book 2, ch. 18 ("Un ordine che tengano i compositori nel comporre, che molti non sanno le cause; & qual ordine si deveria tenere se si componesse una cantilena modale"), fol. 98^r.

At this point the theoretical *tactus* in imperfect *tempus* has become equivalent to the modern concept of measure or bar in the sense of the largest time unit in which a piece is regularly organized. It is normally divided into two compositional *tactus*, or "beats." The theoretical *tactus* may correspond either to a single performance *tactus* with each half distinctly articulated or to two performance *tactus*, each half as long as the theoretical *tactus*. This is the same as saying that a modern duple meter may be measured either by the down + up motions of a conductor's beat (a single performance *tactus* in sixteenth-century terms) or by undifferentiated taps, each corresponding to one beat. The fact that many terms for both beat and bar in modern languages derive from sixteenth-century terms for *tactus* is a consequence of this distinction between theoretical and performance *tactus* in the sixteenth century.[66]

Signs of perfect prolation: ⊙, ꜀, ⌽, ₵

By the beginning of the sixteenth century, perfect prolation had been obsolete as an independent mensuration for nearly seventy years. It remained in use in combination with other signs, usually (though not always) as a sign of augmentation, only until *c.* 1500. This inconvenience did not deter sixteenth-century theorists from expressing opinions about the meanings of its signs as independent mensurations throughout the century. Theorists valued the mensural system as a theoretical concept, and perfect prolation played a role in the completeness and symmetry of the system. Sixteenth-century views of perfect prolation have no authority as documents of performance practices of earlier periods, but they are of interest for the light that they shed on the thought processes of music theorists.

The majority of sixteenth-century theorists claim that perfect prolation has three minims per *tactus* when it appears in all voices and one minim per *tactus* when it is combined with imperfect prolation. Precedents for this view were established by Cochlaeus in Germany and Aaron in Italy.[67]

---

[66] Terms for bar that derive from sixteenth-century terms for *tactus* include Takt, mesure, battuta, compás, and measure. Terms for beat that derive from synonyms of these words include Schlag, battement, batido, and beat.

[67] Cochlaeus, *Musica*, 3rd edn., part II, "De augmentatione," fols. Civ^v–D^r, and *Tetrachordum musices*, tract. 4, ch. 7 ("De augmentatione et diminutione"), fol. Eiij^v; Aaron, *Toscanello in musica*, book I, ch. 38 ("Cognitione, et modo di cantar segno contra a segno necessarii"), fols. F^r–Fii^r.

Heyden takes a contrary view, insisting that the minim is the normal *tactus* of perfect prolation, because of his commitment to the principle that every sign must have the same *tactus* in every context. In his view, a stroke through a sign of perfect prolation shifts the *tactus* to the imperfect semibreve, and a stroke plus the numbers $\tfrac{3}{2}$ shifts it to the perfect semibreve. Heyden calls these three types of perfect prolation "integral" (minim *tactus*), diminished (imperfect semibreve *tactus*), and proportionate (perfect semibreve *tactus*).[68] A few other theorists, both before and after Heyden, likewise identify the minim as the normal *tactus* of perfect prolation without qualification.[69] Agricola classifies the minim as the whole *tactus* of augmented perfect prolation and says that in ordinary perfect prolation, three minims are sung to a proportionate *tactus*.[70] This view agrees with the majority opinion and calls explicitly for a proportionate *tactus* when there are three minims per *tactus*.

Signs composed of circles or semicircles with numbers: O3, C3 O2, C2 etc.

Almost all sixteenth-century theorists accept the custom of notating *modus* and *tempus* with combinations of circles and numbers despite the strenuous objection of Tinctoris and the milder objection of Gaffurio to the practice. None of them complains openly about the signs, though some, including Zarlino and his followers, do not mention them in their discussions of *modus*. The principal *modus cum tempore* signs in sixteenth-century theory were O3, C3, O2, and C2. Versions of these signs with dots (⊙3, ꞒЗ, ⊙2, Ꞓ2), strokes (ɸ3, ¢3, ɸ2, ¢2), or dots and strokes (ɸ3, ¢3, ɸ2, ¢2) also appear. In each case, the circle or semicircle represents perfect or imperfect minor *modus* and the 3 or 2 represents perfect or imperfect *tempus*. A dot added to the sign represents perfect prolation, and a stroke through the sign represents diminution. A few theorists also mention circles with two numbers for major and minor

---

[68] Heyden, *De arte canendi*, book 2, ch. 2 ("De prolatione"), 64–72.
[69] Theorists before Heyden, such as Philomathes, *Musicorum libri quattuor*, book 2, ch. 7 ("De tactu"), fol. Dii^v, probably got the idea of a minim *tactus* in perfect prolation from Adam von Fulda. Later theorists, such as Bourgeois, Gregor Faber, and Oridryus, probably took it from Heyden.
[70] Agricola, *Musica figuralis deudsch*, ch. 6 ("Der Proporcien Tact") and ch. 7 ("Von der Augmentatio odder grösserung des gesangs"), fols. Giiij^v–H^r.

modus and *tempus*, in conformity with the system of Hothby. Since those signs were of no practical importance, they will not be considered here.

The central theoretical issue with respect to *modus cum tempore* signs was whether or not they implied diminution. Many theorists either state explicitly or imply through their texts and *tactus* tables that the signs could mean either integral or diminished measurement. Some assign two different meanings to the same sign, often without comment. Cochlaeus, for example, lists O3 among the signs that normally have a semibreve *tactus*,[71] but says elsewhere that the sign means diminution with three semibreves per *tactus*.[72] Ornithoparchus says that a number 2 always represents diminution,[73] but includes ⊙2 in his table of integral signs (Table 6.2 above). These examples might appear to be contradictory, but they can be explained better as alternative meanings for the same signs. Heyden states explicitly that *modus cum tempore* signs may or may not imply diminution, though in a large table summarizing the principles of *tactus* in eighteen different signs, they always mean diminution.[74]

An interpretation of a sign as diminution has different meanings depending on whether the sign in question represents perfect or imperfect *tempus*. If O2 and C2 are taken as signs of diminution, they are theoretically equivalent to ₵ with perfect or imperfect *modus*. Since diminution of ₵ could mean either a slow breve *tactus* or a fast semibreve *tactus*, the same option applies to O2 and C2 as signs of diminution. Theorists often state that the number 2 in a *modus cum tempore* sign has (or may have) the same meaning as the stroke in ₵.[75] The diminution indicated by O3 and C3, in contrast, places the *tactus* on the perfect breve and makes the signs equivalent to triple or *sesquialtera* proportion from the point of view of *tactus*.

In practice, O2 is equivalent to ₵ with perfect *modus* and C2 to ₵ with either imperfect *modus* or no regular *modus*. O3 and C3, however, almost

---

[71] *Tetrachordum musices*, tract. 4, ch. 7 ("De augmentatione et diminutione"), fol. Eiij^v.
[72] Ibid., fol. Eiiii^r, and *Musica*, 3rd edn., part II, "De diminutione," fol. Civ^v.
[73] Ornithoparchus, *Musice active micrologus*, book 2, ch. 8 ("De diminutione"), fol. Fvi^r.
[74] Heyden, *De arte canendi*, book 2, ch. 4 ("De mensura modi"), 81, and ch. 7 ("De unica Tactuum aequabilitate, in quantumlibet diversis cantuum speciebus servanda: Deque mutua variorum Signorum resolutione"), 120.
[75] The functional equivalence between the number 2 in the signs O2 and C2 and the stroke in the sign ₵ is suggested by the similarity of diminution by proportion and diminution by stroke in Gaffurio's chapter on diminution (*Practica musice*, book 2, ch. 14). Rhau applies the traditional German option of a faster semibreve *tactus* or a slower breve *tactus* explicitly to signs followed by a 2, as well as to cut signs. Rhau, *Enchiridion*, [part II], ch. 7 ("De tactibus"), fol. Giiij^r.

always represent mensurations with three semibreves or three minims per *tactus* and no regular *modus*. Their classification as *modus cum tempore* signs is a theoretical fiction that contributes to the elegance of the mensural system as an abstract concept, but does not conform to real practice. Most of the *modus cum tempore* signs with dots, strokes, or dots and strokes are rare or non-existent in practice, but like O3 and C3 in that capacity, they make it possible for theorists to construct systems that account for all hypothetical possibilities, whether or not composers had occasion to use them.

Proportion signs

The theory of musical proportions retained much of the mix of speculative and practical elements in the sixteenth century that it had in the fifteenth century. Some theorists treat the mathematical foundations of the subject in detail and describe many more proportions than composers ever used in practice, some limit their discussion to proportions found in real music, and some dispense with the topic altogether. As in the earlier period, the term had both a formal meaning, in which it referred to ratios of simultaneous note values in different voices, and an informal meaning, in which it referred simply to the measuring of notes with a *tactus* other than the imperfect semibreve. Theorists do not always keep the two meanings distinct.

The proportions that were most often said to be useful in music are duple (2:1), triple (3:1), quadruple (4:1), *sesquialtera* (3:2), and *sesquitertia* (4:3). The symbols that theorists propose for them are most often ratios of two numbers, which leave no room for ambiguity. Some proportions could also be represented by simultaneous combinations of different mensuration signs or by special symbols. When different signs were combined, the general rule was that all of them should be measured with their theoretical *tactus*, even if that *tactus* was not the one the theorist recommends for them in non-proportional contexts. Nearly all sixteenth-century theorists agree that perfect prolation in combination with another sign implies a minim *tactus*, despite the objection of Tinctoris to that principle. Cut signs and signs followed by a number 2 imply an imperfect breve *tactus* in simultaneous relation with other signs. They are normally defined as *semiditas* (in the strict sense of the term) or duple proportion in that context, though Philibert Jambe de Fer defines C as augmentation when it is combined with ₵ or a synonymous sign, evidently implying that its *tactus* becomes the

Example 6.2 Josquin, *Missa L'homme armé sexti toni*: Credo, bars 234–39. After Vatican City, Biblioteca Apostolica Vaticana, Ms. Chigi C VIII 234 ("Chigi Codex"), fols. clxxxx^v–clxxxxi^r.

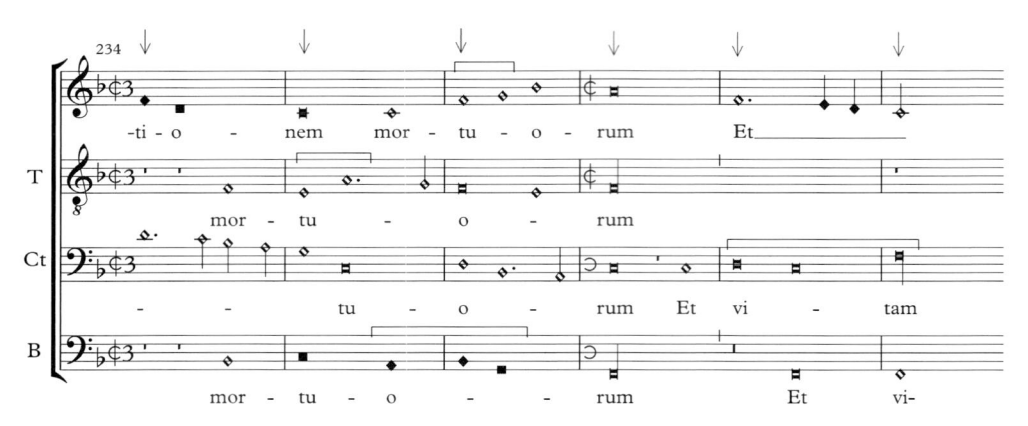

minim in that case.[76] If a sign is both cut and followed by a number 2, it represents quadruple proportion.

The sign ↄ has a curious history in sixteenth-century theory. It had been a standard sign of *sesquitertia* proportion in the fifteenth century (though Tinctoris and Gaffurio disapprove of it) and continued to be interpreted as such by many sixteenth-century theorists. In its traditional sense, its *tactus* has four minims when it follows a mensuration or proportion with three minims per *tactus* and four semibreves when it follows a proportion with three semibreves per *tactus*. Since a *tactus* with four minims can be thought of as duple proportion of C and a *tactus* with four semibreves can be thought of as duple proportion of ₵, theorists began to think of ↄ as an independent sign of duple proportion. Aaron was the first theorist after Guilielmus Monachus to define it that way. The example he gives is the end of the Credo of Josquin's *Missa L'homme armé sexti toni* (Example 6.2), in which ↄ is both *sesquitertia* proportion of the preceding ₵3 and duple proportion of the simultaneous ₵. Aaron says that the sign may mean either duple or *sesquitertia* proportion, but he interprets it as duple proportion in this example.[77] Ornithoparchus picked up the definition of ↄ as duple proportion (probably from Aaron) and glossed it with an amusing explanation: notes lose half their value under a semicircle that opens to the left because it

---

[76] Jambe de Fer, *Epitome musical*, ch. 7 ("Les noms & valeur des notes sans ligature en temps imparfaitz ainsi. ₵ C C2 ↄ autant vaut l'un que l'autre: si ce n'est, que le second se trouve en une partie seule & non aux autres, lors ladite partie augmentera du tout, de la moytie"), 30–31.

[77] Aaron, *Libri tres de institutione harmonica*, book 2, ch. 32 ("Quomodo index contra indicem idest signum contra signum ut dicitur cani debeat"), fol. 35^v.

is a female sign, and thus weaker than the male version that opens to the right.[78] Rhau took the sign from Ornithoparchus, but failed to understand that it could be duple proportion of either C or ¢ depending on the context. He assumed that the reversal of the semicircle removed half of the value of the notes in C and invented a cut version of the sign (𝄵) to represent duple proportion of ¢.[79] For subsequent theorists, reversing the semicircle in any sign (including Ɔ and 𝄵) became a way to remove half the value of the notes.[80] Heyden even creates a bizarre composite sign for quadruple proportion (¢ Ɔ) by combining the cut and reversed semicircles.[81] All of these new signs are products of theoretical speculation, not compositional practice, but composers occasionally adopted them to display their erudition after the theorists invented them.

The only proportions of real importance in sixteenth-century music are triple and *sesquialtera*. Other proportions are very rare after the second or third decade of the century despite their continued importance as a subject of theoretical speculation. *Tripla* and *sesquialtera* usually appear in all voices and rarely overlap with other mensurations in the sixteenth century. Although they are called "proportions," the term applies to them primarily in the informal sense in which they designate three semibreves or three minims per *tactus* without any necessary proportional relation to another sign. Theorists held conflicting opinions about their notation, tempo, *tactus*, and rhythmic interpretation. Problems of tempo will be considered in Chapter 7.

Sixteenth-century theorists and composers applied a daunting variety of terms and signs to these "proportions." The principal time unit in which they are measured may consist of groups of three semibreves or

---

[78] Ornithoparchus, *Musice active micrologus*, book 2, ch. 13 ("De proportione"), fol. Hij^v.

[79] Rhau, *Enchiridion*, [part II], ch. 11 ("De proporcione, in qua totum musicae consistit negocium"), fol. L^r.

[80] Guilielmus Monachus provides a precedent for this view. He states that reversing the semicircle is a general *per medium* sign and includes Ɔ and ↄ among signs to which this generalization applies (*De preceptis artis musice*, 16), but later defines and illustrates Ɔ as a sign of 4:3 proportion (ibid., 25). His writing is too disorganized and inconsistent to represent a coherent theory.

[81] Heyden does not discuss this sign, but it appears in his example of Isaac's *De radice Jesse*, in *De arte canendi*, book 2, ch. 7 ("De unica Tactuum aequabilitate, in quantumlibet diversis cantuum speciebus servanda: Deque mutua variorum Signorum resolutione"), 114–15. The symbol that looks like this sign in the *tactus* table in this chapter (p. 120) is actually two independent signs, each representing duple proportion. On the likelihood that Heyden, rather than Isaac, devised the proportion signs in this example, see Ruth I. DeFord, "Who Devised the Proportional Notation in Isaac's *Choralis Constantinus*?" in *Heinrich Isaac and Polyphony for the Proper of the Mass in the Late Middle Ages and Renaissance*, ed. David J. Burn and Stefan Gasch, "Épitome musical" (Turnhout: Brepols, 2011), 167–213.

three minims, either white or black. The symbols representing them include all of the signs of perfect and imperfect *tempus*, with and without dots or strokes, with the number 3 or the fraction $\frac{3}{2}$ or $\frac{3}{1}$ appended to them. Signs of perfect prolation may also represent *sesquialtera* without additional figures, and the number 3 or the fraction $\frac{3}{2}$ or $\frac{3}{1}$ may appear without a sign of *tempus*. Signs with a 3 (O3, C3, ☉3, ꞒC3, ΦO3, ¢3, Φ3, ¢3) double in theory as *modus cum tempore* signs. The same signs with $\frac{3}{2}$ or $\frac{3}{1}$ in place of 3 function only as signs of "proportions." Some theorists place the number 3 below the mensuration sign to distinguish "proportions" from *modus cum tempore* signs.[82] Coloration, which may be annotated with a number 3 preceding an extended passage or written before, above, or below each ternary group of notes, is yet another means of representing these proportions. The ternary groups in proportions of this type are minims in signs of perfect prolation (with or without numbers) and semibreves in signs that include ¢ or Φ, but may be either minims or semibreves under other signs. Theorists sometimes say that proportions should be notated in groups of minims when they relate to integral signs and in groups of semibreves when they relate to signs of diminution, but they rarely went much further in attempting to bring order to this chaotic system.[83] Even Heyden directed his energy at reforming the notation of binary signs and commented only in passing on the inconsistency of the notation of ternary proportions in practice.[84] Zacconi

---

[82] This custom originated with Petrucci's editor Petrus Castellanus. See Bonnie J. Blackburn, "The Sign of Petrucci's Editor," in *Venice 1501: Petrucci e la stampa musicale*, ed. Giulio Cattin and Patrizia dalla Vecchia (Venice: Fondazione Ugo e Olga Levi, 2005), 415–29. Glarean, *Dodecachordon*, book 3, ch. 6 ("De signis"), 201–02, and ch. 8 ("De augmentatione diminutione ac semiditate"), 206, says that some people regard signs consisting of circles or semicircles with numbers as *modus cum tempore* signs and comments that the number 3 is sometimes placed below the circle to show that the sign means diminution with three semibreves per *tactus*. Heyden, *De arte canendi*, book 2, ch. 6 ("De augmentatione et diminutione"), 102–03, suggests writing the number 2 or 3 somewhat below the circle or semicircle when the signs represent proportions and at the same level when they represent *modus cum tempore*. Finck, *Practica musica*, book 2, "De diminutione," fol. Oiij[r], says explicitly that a circle or semicircle with a number at the same level represents *modus cum tempore*, while a number below a circle or semicircle represents a proportion. These distinctions were rarely observed in practice.

[83] Aaron, *Toscanello in musica*, book 2, ch. 33 ("Del superparticulare genere"), fol. Lii[v], says that *sesquialtera* should be notated in semibreves in relation to cut signs and minims in relation to uncut signs and warns that *sesquialtera* notated in semibreves following an uncut sign will usually be interpreted as *tripla* (three semibreves in place of one on each *tactus*) in practice.

[84] Heyden suggests that signs such as C3 and ¢3 should represent triple proportion, the former in relation to a semibreve *tactus* and the latter in relation to a breve *tactus*, but leaves open the possibility that signs with a number 3 might represent *sesquialtera*, rather than *tripla*. *De arte canendi*, book 2, ch. 6 ("De augmentatione et diminutione"), 105.

proposed a systematic method for notating ternary proportions, but it had no impact on practice.[85]

The terminology applied to these proportions is almost as chaotic as the signs. Many theorists call them "hemiola" or "hemiolia" when they are notated in black and "tripla" or "sesquialtera" when they are notated in white; others object to this usage, since the terms "hemiola" and "sesquialtera" are synonymous in a mathematical sense.[86] Glarean prefers to limit the terms "tripla" and "sesquialtera" to true proportions and suggests the term "trochaic" or "tribrachic" for mensurations with three equal notes per *tactus* that are not proportional to another sign.[87] Hofmann uses the term "tripla vulgaris" for what Glarean calls "trochaic" or "tribrachic."[88] Some theorists call ternary proportions "major" when they are notated in groups of semibreves and "minor" when they are notated in groups of minims.[89] Some call them "tripla" when they appear in all voices and "sesquialtera" when they are in simultaneous three-against-two relation to another voice.[90] Vicentino, Banchieri, and others distinguish "proportions of equality" (ternary rhythms in all voices) from "proportions of inequality" (ternary rhythms against simultaneous binary ones).[91] Since ternary proportions of equality were the only proportions commonly used in the late sixteenth century, the term "proportion" itself became synonymous with them in popular usage. Zacconi limits the term "proportions" to proportions of equality and invents the term "opposed numbers" for all simultaneous relationships that theorists traditionally call "proportions."[92] This situation was nothing new in the sixteenth century. Tinctoris had decried the use of the terms "tripla" and "sesquialtera" (which he said were synonymous in

---

[85] Zacconi's system is discussed in DeFord, "Zacconi's Theories of *Tactus* and Mensuration," 164–66.

[86] Tinctoris makes this point in *Proportionale musices*, book 1, ch. 6 ("De genere superparticulari"), 25.

[87] Glarean, *Dodecachordon*, book 3, ch. 8 ("De augmentatione diminutione ac semiditate"), 206.

[88] Hofmann, *Musicae practicae praecepta*, part II, ch. 6 ("De diminutione"), fol. Kiiij^r.

[89] Zacconi, for example, distinguishes major and minor proportions in this way. *Prattica di musica*, book 3 ("Quante specie de Proportioni si ritrovano"), ch. 37, fols. 153^v–154^r.

[90] Bourgeois distinguishes *tripla de temps* (three semibreves per *tactus*) and *tripla de prolation* (three minims per *tactus*), both of which appear in all voices simultaneously, from *sesquialtera* or *hemiolia*, a true proportion in which three notes in one voice correspond to two in another. *Le droict chemin de musique*, chs. 4–5, fols. B5^r–C3^r.

[91] Vicentino, *L'antica musica ridotta alla moderna prattica*, book 4, ch. 31 ("Delle proportioni musicali, che à questi tempi da Prattici della musica son' usate"), fols. 87^r–88^r; Banchieri, *Cartella musicale*, part II, docs. 5–8, 29–32.

[92] Zacconi devotes the entire third book of his *Prattica di musica* to an explanation and defense of the distinction between proportions and opposed numbers in his sense of the terms.

popular usage) for mensurations that were not true proportions as early as the 1470s,[93] but to no avail.

Theorists argued about the proper way to notate rhythms in ternary proportions, as well as what to call them and what signs to use for them. Tinctoris and Gaffurio insist that note values in triple and *sesquialtera* proportions be treated as imperfect when they relate to imperfect signs (e.g., C_2^3 or C ... $\tfrac{3}{2}$) and perfect when they relate to perfect signs (e.g., O_2^3 or O ... $\tfrac{3}{2}$).[94] Most theorists, however, accept the general practice of applying the rules of perfection, imperfection, and alteration to white notes in ternary proportions on grounds that these notes come in regular groups of three. Spataro defends the perfect quality of notes in ternary proportions with great passion, because he views that principle as essential to his abstract concept of the mensural system.[95] This issue has no impact on the way in which notes are read in practice, since the context always makes it clear whether they are to be understood as perfect or imperfect, but it is important in relation to theorists' conceptual understanding of the mensural system.

An issue that did have practical importance for the realization of these proportions in performance is the choice and form of the *tactus*. Theorists are unanimous in their view that the three notes that form a ternary group in a ternary proportion, whether semibreves or minims, are sung to one *tactus* when they appear in all voices. They say nothing about the subdivision of that *tactus* before the 1530s, but from then on, many say that the *tactus* is equally divided when it measures ternary rhythms against simultaneous binary ones and unequally divided when it measures ternary rhythms in all voices. Agricola provides the earliest known description of the unequally divided *tactus* (which he equates with the term "proportionate *tactus*") and shows through examples that the first two-thirds of the *tactus* fall on the downstroke and the last third on the upstroke.[96] His discussion implies that this *tactus* is not a new invention. Many later theorists confirm the point. Heyden objects strenuously to the unequal *tactus*, since he regards all signs as proportional and believes that the measurement of proportions requires a *tactus* of unchanging duration and form, yet he and his followers confirm

---

[93] Tinctoris, *Proportionale musices*, book 1, ch. 3 ("Divisio proportionum"), 14–15.

[94] Tinctoris, *Proportionale musices*, book 3, ch. 5 ("Considerandum esse in quibus modo, tempore et prolatione proportiones fiant"), 53; Gaffurio, *Practica musice*, book 4, ch. 5 ("De genere superparticulari & eius speciebus"), fols. giiij^v–ggiiij^r.

[95] This point is so important to Spataro that he refers to it in the title of his *Tractato di musica ... nel quale si tracta de la perfectione da la sesqualtera producta in la musica mensurata exercitate*.

[96] Agricola, *Musica figuralis deudsch*, ch. 6 ("Vom Schlag odder Tact"), fols. Giiij^v–Gv^r.

that the unequal *tactus* was universally used for ternary proportions in all voices despite their objections.[97] Zacconi devotes many pages of his *Prattica di musica* to a defense of the unequal *tactus*. He claims that the character of ternary rhythms depends on their relation to the *tactus* and that performing them with the wrong *tactus* destroys their effect. He appreciates both ternary rhythms with equal *tactus*, which he calls "sesquialtere," and ternary rhythms with unequal *tactus*, which he calls "proportions," but insists that they must be kept distinct and notated in such a way that performers will not confuse them. The latter usually have what he calls the pure and natural rhythms of proportions: lilting, dance-like ternary patterns with an energetic feel and strongly metrical character.[98]

There is sporadic evidence from the 1530s on that ternary rhythms set against simultaneous binary rhythms, which were measured with an equally divided *tactus*, were sometimes altered so as to conform to the binary rhythms of the other voices. This practice is an extension of the common (though not universal) fifteenth-century practice of reading colored notes in a binary context (e.g., a black semibreve + black minim, or a black breve + black semibreve) as dotted rhythms, rather than triplets. Sixteenth-century theorists treat this interpretation of isolated pairs of colored notes as a norm.[99] Agricola and Bourgeois extend the principle much further and offer "squared-off" binary resolutions of extended passages of *sesquialtera*, as shown in Examples 6.3 and 6.4. Agricola's examples are single voices in a four-voice context.[100] Bourgeois's are single voices, but the principle that he illustrates applies only when ternary rhythms are combined with binary rhythms, since that condition is part of his definition of *sesquialtera*.[101] It is unclear how widespread this practice was. It may even be that Agricola and Bourgeois did not intend

---

[97] Heinrich Faber, for example, confirms that three types of *tactus* are standard in practice, but accepts Heyden's view that true musicians use only one type and condemns the proportionate *tactus* as contrary to the nature of art. Nevertheless, he admits that the proportionate *tactus* conforms to ternary proportions better than an equally divided *tactus* does, and he allows students to use it until they develop the skill to sing those proportions in the way that he regards as correct. *Ad musicam practicam introductio*, book 2, ch. 5, fol. T1^r.

[98] See DeFord, "Zacconi's Theories of *Tactus* and Mensuration," 161–69.

[99] For a sample of sixteenth-century texts that support this interpretation of coloration in binary mensurations, see Ronald Woodley, "Minor Coloration Revisited," appendix, 61–63.

[100] Agricola, *Musica figuralis deudsch*, ch. 12 ("Von den Proportionibus"), fols. Mvi^v–Mvii^v.

[101] Bourgeois, *Le droict chemin de musique*, ch. 5, fols. C^r–C3^r. Bourgeois gives the example twice, first under the sign ϕ_2^3 (resolved to ϕ) as shown, then in half-values under the sign C$_2^3$ (resolved to C). He then gives analogous examples for *hemiolia de temps* and *hemiolia de prolation*, which are the same proportions notated in black notes.

Example 6.3 *Sesquialtera* rhythms resolved into "squared-off" binary rhythms. After Martin Agricola, *Musica figuralis deudsch* (Wittenberg: Georg Rhau, 1532), chapter 12, fols. Mvi^v–Mvii^v: discant and bass. The O2 of the discantus is in duple proportion to the ¢ of the bass; the *sesquialtera* of O2 is therefore triple proportion ($\frac{3}{2} \times \frac{2}{1}$) in relation to the bass. According to Agricola's theory, the performance *tactus* (shown by arrows) is the breve of O2 and the imperfect semibreve of ¢ in this context.

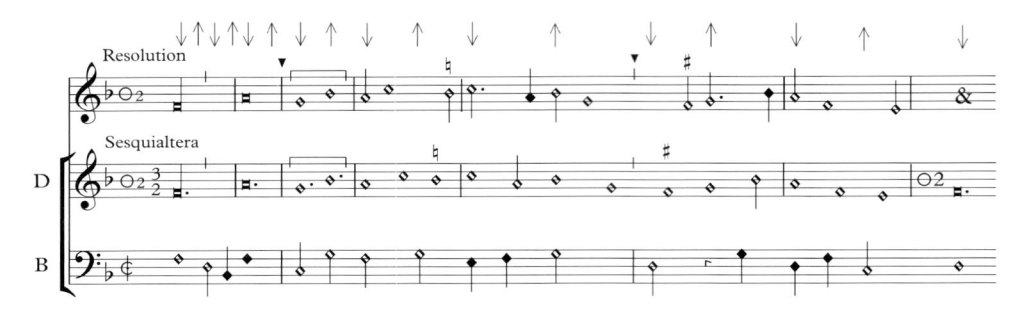

Example 6.4 *Sesquialtera* rhythms resolved into "squared-off" binary rhythms. After Loys Bourgeois, *Le droict chemin de musique* (Geneva: [Jean Gérard], 1550), chapter 5, fol. C^v. The alteration of the semibreve before a long in bar 6 is irregular.

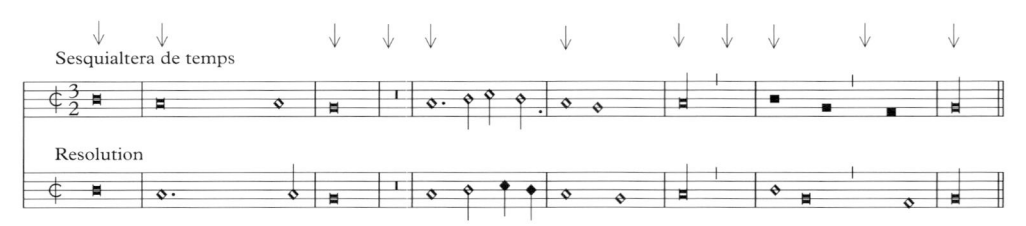

for their resolutions to be taken literally, but were simply attempting to show where notes of *sesquialtera* rhythms fall in relation to the *tactus* by approximating them as closely as possible in ¢ or O2. Agricola's example is in any case highly artificial; its notation and rhythms are extremely complex and not at all like *sesquialtera* rhythms in real music. Other theorists describe three-against-two rhythms in ways that emphasize the conflict between the groupings. Zacconi is particularly explicit; he characterizes *sesquialtera* as two contrary actions, one of the *tactus* and the other of the notes.[102] By the early seventeenth century, however, the practice of eliminating three-against-two conflicts in performance by

---

[102] "due attioni contrarie, una del tatto, & l'altra delle figure." Zacconi, *Prattica di musica*, book 3, ch. 36 ("Che aiuto diano le sesquialtere, & l'emiolie alle cantilene ordinarie"), fol. 153^v. See DeFord, "Zacconi's Theories of *Tactus* and Mensuration," 165–66.

adapting the ternary rhythms to the binary *tactus* had become the norm.[103]

Proportions other than triple and *sesquialtera* are almost never found in all voices simultaneously, but an isolated example of an unconventional proportion by the composer-theorist Giovanthomaso Cimello sheds interesting light on the concept of *tactus* and its relation to rhythm in the mid sixteenth century. Cimello never published a theoretical treatise, but two manuscripts containing his ideas survive, and his book entitled *Libro primo de canti a quatro voci* contains several pieces that experiment with unusual mensural ideas. Two of the madrigals are written in what Cimello calls "subduple proportion." Since there was no standard sign for this mensuration as Cimello conceives it, he notates the pieces in C and indicates the proportion with a canonic rubric. This proportion is to be performed with a minim *tactus*.[104] The minim is the largest regular unit of measure in a piece; one of the pieces with the proportion even contains an odd number of minims. The *tactus* must be understood as a distinctly divided, two-part unit, because the primary compositional *tactus* is the semiminim. Texted *fusae* and syncopated semiminims are common, and there is even a syncopated *fusa*, though dissonances are occasionally as long as a semiminim (see Example 6.5). The notation of the piece is a theoretical demonstration, not an instance of normal practice. As such, it is an interesting illustration of how a theoretically minded composer thought about the concepts of mensuration and *tactus*. Cimello understood the theoretical (minim) *tactus* as a unit that is composed of two compositional (semiminim) *tactus*. The performance *tactus* that he expected must have been a divided minim that articulates each semiminim distinctly. The largest obligatory unit of measure in the piece is the theoretical *tactus*.[105]

[103] Michael Collins, "The Performance of Sesquialtera and Hemiolia in the Sixteenth Century," *Journal of the American Musicological Society* 17 (1964), 5–28, claims that the practice of squaring off ternary rhythms when they are combined with binary ones was standard throughout the sixteenth century, but many of the theorists he cites, including Zacconi, cannot reasonably be interpreted as advocates of that position. Frederick Neumann, "Conflicting Binary and Ternary Rhythms: From the Theory of Mensural Notation to the Music of J. S. Bach," *Music Forum* 6 (1987), 95–107, refutes many of Collins's arguments on this subject.

[104] Giovanthomaso Cimello, *Libro primo de canti a quatro voci* (Venice: Gardano, 1548).

[105] One of the manuscripts that transmits Cimello's theory refers to the use of a minim *tactus* for situations other than augmentation, though Cimello does not approve of the practice. This is the only source I know that identifies the minim as a real (as opposed to purely theoretical) *tactus* in a context other than augmentation in one voice combined with integral or diminished measurement in another. The minim is, however, the largest regular unit of measure in some sixteenth-century pieces of light-hearted character, and so a minim *tactus* must have existed in practice, even if theorists did not consider it worthy of acknowledgment. On Cimello's theory, see James Haar, "Lessons in Theory from a Sixteenth-Century Composer," 51–81.

Example 6.5 Giovanthomaso Cimello, *Hor son qui lasso*, bars 11–15, after *Libro primo de canti a quatro voci* (Venice: Gardano, 1548), 29. The piece is labeled "Versi di sonetto del Petrarca per lo novo segno del tempo imperfetto raddoppiato, che fa la proportione subdupla, e si canta una minima per botta intera" ("Verses of a sonnet of Petrarch with the new sign of doubled imperfect *tempus*, which makes subduple proportion, and a minim is sung to a complete beat").

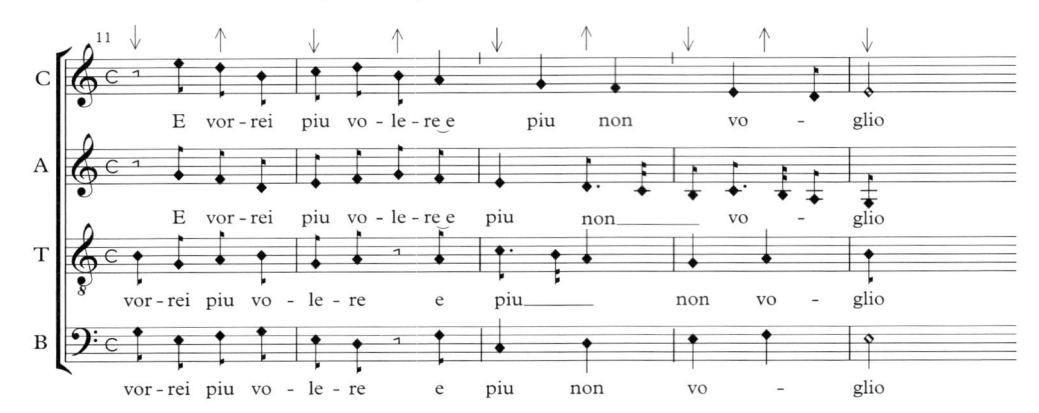

[Musical notation: four vocal parts (C, A, T, B) setting the text "E vorrei piu vo-le-re e piu non vo-glio"]

Analogous principles apply to the semibreve *tactus* of C and the breve *tactus* of ₵ in ordinary sixteenth-century practice.

By the middle of the sixteenth century, some theorists began to take the attitude that proportions other than *tripla* and *sesquialtera* had no legitimate function, since their rhythms could be written more easily under simple signs and the purpose of musical notation was to represent audible sounds, not mathematical abstractions. One of the first to express this attitude was Glarean, who believed that musical proportions often functioned more as a display of ostentation than as artistic techniques. He sums up his attitude as follows:

Ars, ut ars est, tradi debet. At res ipsa nunc clamat, superfluum esse tot proportionum observationes ... ut in quibus maior labor in addiscendo quam suavitas gratiave in cantando esse constet.[106]	Art should be transmitted as art. Moreover, the matter itself now shows that the observance of so many proportions is superfluous ... since there is more labor in learning them than sweetness or grace in singing them.

Coclico and Vicentino agree wholeheartedly.[107] Burmeister declines to discuss proportions other than ternary mensurations in all voices, because

---

[106] Glarean, *Dodecachordon*, book 3, ch. 12 ("De proportionibus musicis"), 227.
[107] Coclico, *Compendium musices*, part II, "De prolationibus usitatis," fol. Gij^r; Vicentino, *L'antica musica ridotta alla moderna prattica*, book 4, ch. 31 ("Delle proportioni musicali, che à questi tempi da Prattici della musica son' usate"), fol. 87^v.

"it is the height of insanity to complicate a song that can be written in simple notes with obscure signs."[108] Praetorius explains proportions with binary mensurations reluctantly, because some composers still use them, but complains that they are of no use, and that even experienced musicians are often "confused, obstructed, and altogether confounded" by them.[109] The reversal of attitudes since the time of Gaffurio, for whom mastery of proportions was the height of musical erudition, is complete.

---

[108] "Summa dementia est, cantionem, quae simplicibus notis scribi potest, obscuris signis perplexare." Burmeister, *Musica autoschediastike*, Accessio III, section II, "De antiphonis," fol. Aa2^v.

[109] "Nicht allein die Jugend in den Schulen, sondern auch offtmahls geübte Musici Vocales & Instrumentales in Capellen perturbirt, remorirt, auch wol gar confundirt werden." Praetorius, *Syntagma musicum*, vol. III, part II, ch. 7 ("De tactu, seu notarum mensura; (italis battuta) & signis"), 54.

7 | *Tactus* and tempo

Tempo is one of the most elusive aspects of music. Since the issue is problematic even when composers assign metronome marks to their works, it is not surprising that clues about tempo in the fifteenth and sixteenth centuries, when there were no mechanical devices for measuring time on the scale of the musical *tactus*, are very difficult to interpret. Theoretical statements that relate (or may relate) to tempo are often ambiguous and subject to more than one interpretation, and clear statements are generally too imprecise to be of much use. Many overconfident claims about tempo have been made in the scholarly literature. One of the most extreme is that of Willi Apel, who says that "there can be no doubt that throughout the history of music prior to 1600 the notational signs indicated not only relative values ... but also ... absolute temporal durations," and that "proportional signs, if used simultaneously in all the parts, represent the tempo marks, nay, the metronomic marks, of the fifteenth and sixteenth centuries."[1] Scholars often interpret theoretical statements about the number of *tactus* by which the notes are measured as statements about absolute duration even if the sources they cite make no claim that the duration of the *tactus* is fixed.[2] Analogies between *tactus* and related motions, such as the human pulse or striking clocks, have also been interpreted uncritically as statements about tempo when they may have been meant to characterize other aspects of *tactus*.[3]

---

[1] Apel, *The Notation of Polyphonic Music*, 5th edn., 189–90.

[2] Richard Sherr, for example, interprets Zacconi's view that the performance *tactus* should be the breve of O2 and the semibreve of O when the signs appear simultaneously to mean that O in this combination had its standard tempo and O2 was twice as fast, but the context of Zacconi's statement makes it clear that this is not what he meant. Richard Sherr, "The Performance of Josquin's *L'homme armé* Masses," *Early Music* 19 (1991), 264.

[3] For example, Howard Mayer Brown and Claus Bockmaier interpret Gaffurio's analogy between *tactus* and pulse as a straightforward tempo prescription in "Tactus," *Oxford Music Online*, www.oxfordmusiconline.com (accessed 7 December 2013): "Gaffurius ... wrote that one *tactus* equalled the pulse of a man breathing normally, suggesting that there was an invariable tempo then of MM = c. 60–70 for a semibreve in *integer valor*." They add that the duration of the *tactus* could vary in practice, but do not question their interpretation of Gaffurio's metaphor. Dale Bonge challenges this interpretation, claiming that Gaffurio's analogy is a humanistic attempt to relate music to medicine, not a statement about tempo, in "Gaffurius on Pulse and Tempo: A

An investigation of tempo must begin with a distinction between absolute tempo and relative tempos within pieces. This distinction is not as clear-cut as it might appear, because the extent to which different signs in a piece are heard in relation to one another is variable. At one extreme are signs that are simultaneous and must therefore be proportional. Beyond that, signs may appear in immediate succession within a continuous passage, or they may apply to different formal sections demarcated by strong cadences, different *partes* separated by complete pauses, different movements of a mass separated by intervening liturgical actions, or different works that have no relation to one another. Tempos that are heard in immediate or close juxtaposition are more likely to have been identical or proportional than tempos that apply to more independent units of music. Theorists say much more about relative tempos than absolute tempos, but they do not specify whether their comparisons among signs are meant to apply only within pieces or among all pieces in which the signs appear. Apart from simultaneous proportions, the signs they compare fall into three categories: integral mensurations, diminution, and ternary "proportions." Theoretical statements about absolute tempo are less common and less specific than statements about relations among different signs, but they provide helpful clues to the ways in which musicians of the time thought about the subject.

Relations among integral mensurations

When signs that call for different relative values (such as perfect vs. imperfect *tempus* or prolation) are compared, the question of which value is the same from one sign to another naturally arises.[4] There are two basic conceptual models for the relations among integral mensurations in fifteenth- and sixteenth-century theory: one claims that the value that remains constant from one sign to another is the minim, and the other claims that it is the breve. The theory of minim equivalence derives from French notational practices of the fourteenth century and the theory of breve equivalence from Italian practices. These models are shown in Example 7.1. If minims are equal and the breve of C (four minims) is taken as the standard of reference, the breve of O and ₵ (six minims) is ½ longer and the breve of ⊙

Reinterpretation," *Musica disciplina* 36 (1982), 167–74. Ephraim Segerman reads Gaffurio's analogy as support for a much slower tempo than other scholars have drawn from it, but still interprets it only in relation to tempo, in "A Re-examination of the Evidence on Absolute Tempo before 1700 – I," *Early Music* 24 (1996), 228–35.

[4] For general information on this topic, see Berger, *Mensuration and Proportion Signs*, 51–119.

Example 7.1 Comparison of breve equivalence and minim equivalence among basic mensurations.

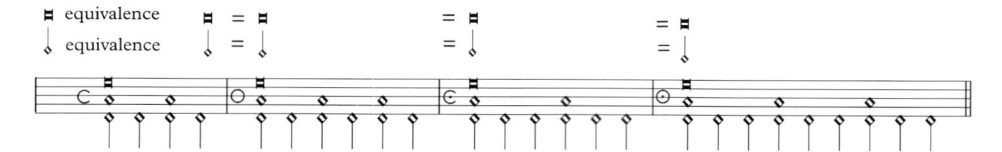

(nine minims) is ¾ longer. If breves are equal, the minim of O and ¢ is ⅔ as long as the minim of C and the minim of ⊙ is 4/9 as long. If these relationships are taken as tempo prescriptions, the differences among them are quite extreme. If, for example, C breve = MM 30, the minims of all mensurations will be MM 120 under minim equivalence, but under breve equivalence, minims of O and ¢ will be MM 180 and minims of ⊙ will be MM 270. Another possibility is that the semibreve may be the value that is constant from one mensuration to another, such that the perfect semibreve of ⊙ and ¢ equals the imperfect semibreve of O and C. Since the semibreve functioned as the usual *tactus* of all integral mensurations, semibreve equivalence among mensurations would seem to be a logical possibility.[5] Unfortunately, all theoretical statements about tempo relations between perfect and imperfect prolation date from many decades after perfect prolation went out of use as a simultaneous mensuration in all voices and therefore have no value as documents of performance practice.

The most explicit advocates of minim equivalence are Tinctoris and Gaffurio. Tinctoris was concerned above all that simultaneous proportions be defined on the basis of minim equivalence among signs. As an example of this principle, he faults Du Fay for applying a sign of *sesquialtera* to a proportion in which three perfect breves (nine semibreves) are set equal to two imperfect breves (four semibreves), claiming that the proportion should have been called 9:4, not 3:2.[6] He evidently regards minims as equivalent in successive relations within pieces as well, since he prescribes an imperfect semibreve *tactus* for perfect prolation that immediately follows imperfect prolation.[7] Gaffurio is even more explicit in upholding

---

[5] Evidence supporting this position is discussed ibid., 87–119.
[6] Tinctoris, *Proportionale musices*, book 1, ch. 3 ("Divisio proportionum"), 14.
[7] Tinctoris, *Liber de arte contrapuncti*, book 2, ch. 28 ("De admissione discordantiarum circa partes semibrevis in prolatione maiori consistentis quando secundum duas partes eius mensura cantus dirigitur"), 136–37.

the principle of semibreve (and therefore minim) equivalence between perfect and imperfect *tempus:*

Errant insuper qui semibrevem imperfecti temporis quod dimidium brevis compraehendat maiorem vocant. eam vero quae tertiam brevis perfectae continet partem: putant minorem: cum unaquaeque semibrevis eadem prolatione computata alteri semibrevi sit semper aequalis. nec obstat quod una dimidiam: altera tertiam brevis notulae possideat partem: cum breves ipsae dissimili sint quantitate dispositae.[8]	Those who call the semibreve of imperfect *tempus* greater because it contains half of a breve, and think that the semibreve that contains a third of a breve is less, are wrong, because every semibreve that is counted in the same prolation is always equal to every other. Nor does it matter that one is half and the other a third of a breve, because the breves themselves are dissimilar in quantity.

The earliest theorist to advocate equal breves explicitly was Anselmi,[9] but the one who defended the position most forcefully was Spataro. Spataro based his views on those of his teacher, Ramis, whose treatise contains only one statement that addresses the topic directly:

Semibrevis vero nomen habet ex re, cum brevis in duas semibreves secetur; cum vero in tres, appellantur minores.[10]	The semibreve takes its name from the situation in which a breve is divided into two semibreves; but when [it is divided] into three, they are called "smaller."

This sentence appears in a paragraph in which Ramis explains the derivation of note names in philosophical terms. The breve is called "tempus" (time) because it is the central unit of measure in relation to which all others are defined. It is called "brevis" (short) because time is short, "for a thousand years in thy sight are but as yesterday when it is past."[11] A long is longer than a breve; a semibreve in imperfect prolation is half of a breve; etc.

Spataro devoted an entire treatise to the defense of this position and its implications. He complains about the moderns who make no distinction between the semibreves of perfect and imperfect *tempus* or the minims of

---

[8] Gaffurio, *Practica musice*, book 2, ch. 8 ("De tempore"), fol. aaviij[v].
[9] Anselmi, *De musica*, part III, 170–72.
[10] Ramis de Pareja, *Musica practica*, part III, tract. 1, ch. 1, 80.   [11] Ibid., quoting Psalm 90:4.

perfect and imperfect prolation, thereby making a third of a note into half of it:

... per la ignorantia: & mala consuetudine de alcuni moderni scriptori tutti li segni ... se possono riducere: & cantare per uno solo segno: & questo adviene: perche non fanno alcuna differentia intra la semibreve del tempo imperfecto: & la semibreve del tempo perfecto: similmente: non fanno alcuna differentia: intra la minima de la prolatione imperfecta: & la minima de la prolatione perfecta: in modo: che (senza consideratione) fanno: che la parte media de uno tutto / e equale / a la parte terza de esso tutto.[12]	... through the ignorance and bad custom of some modern writers, all signs can be reduced to and sung under a single sign. This happens because they do not make any distinction between the semibreve of imperfect *tempus* and the semibreve of perfect *tempus*, and similarly between the minim of imperfect prolation and the minim of perfect prolation, so that (without due consideration) they make half of a whole equal to a third of that whole.

All of the above theorists were speculative thinkers who placed great stock in the rationality, consistency, and uniformity of the mensural system. It is unclear whether, or to what extent, they intended their views to be taken as prescriptions for tempo in performance. Anselmi regards breves as conceptually equal and equates the breve with the physical *tactus* (which he calls "mensura"), but states explicitly that the duration of the *tactus* may vary within moderate limits.[13] Ramis implies a similar attitude when he explains (without objection) that performers place the *mensura* on the semibreve when it should theoretically be on the breve, if a piece has too many short notes.[14] Such a shift in the level of the *mensura* surely implies a longer duration for the semibreve as well.

Spataro finds beauty and intellectual satisfaction in the symmetry of the mensural system with the breve at its center. He observes that there are two levels of measurement above the breve (minor and major *modus*) and two levels below (*tempus* and prolation) that may be perfect or imperfect.[15] The

---

[12] Spataro, *Tractato di musica*, ch. 5 ("Come primamente el tempo sia (da li musici) diviso in parte"), fol. Aviii^v.
[13] Anselmi, *De musica*, part III, 171.
[14] Ramis de Pareja, *Musica practica*, part III, tract. 1, ch. 2 ("In quo signa per quae numeri distinguuntur"), 84.
[15] Spataro, *Tractato di musica*, ch. 11 ("Come el tempo (in musica exercitato) sia inteso / essere perfecto: & imperfecto"), fols. b5^v–c^v.

breve must be an immutable quantity, since all other values are derived from it through multiplication or division:

Ma se noi vogliamo (sanamente) intendere la predicta auctorita di Aristides: el si concedera: che el tempo musico sia individuo: & minimo: non in quanto minimo: ma inquanto elemento primo: & immutabile principio: dalquale (ut diximus) dependono ciascuna de le altre consideratione del mensurato canto.[16]	But if we wish (reasonably) to understand the above authority of Aristides, we will consider that *tempus* in music is individual and minimal, not in the sense of the smallest thing, but in the sense of a first element and immutable principle, on which (as we said) all of the other considerations of mensural song depend.

Spataro admits that from the point of view of *mensura*, ʘ, ₵, O, and C measured in semibreves are analogous to the *modus cum tempore* signs O3, C3, O2, and C2 measured in breves, but he objects to this reasoning because it gives *tempus* the proper function of *modus* (a variable, rather than fixed, quantity) and makes major *modus* irrelevant. If, as Gaffurio believes, the perfect breve is longer than the imperfect breve, it is not truly "perfect" (in the sense of whole and complete), but augmented.[17] That notion contradicts Spataro's concept of the breve as *tempus*, the fundamental unit that defines all temporal relations, analogous on a metaphorical level to time in the mind of God as Ramis explains.

The application of Spataro's theory to the determination of tempo in performance depends on how the "immutable" quantity of the breve is to be understood. Spataro may have meant that the breve should have the same absolute duration in all mensurations, or he may have meant only that the value of the breve is the conceptual quantity from which all other quantities are derived. Although the former interpretation cannot be ruled out, several considerations make the latter more likely. First, Spataro characterizes his treatise as "very scholarly and mathematical" in a letter to Aaron, to whom the work is dedicated.[18] This suggests that his interest was in conceptual issues, not performance practice. Second, he claims to adhere to Ramis's precepts, and Ramis did not object to discrepancies between theory and

---

[16] Ibid., ch. 4 [incorrectly labeled "5" in the edition] ("Quale de le cinque figure / essentiale sia (comunamente) applicata al tempo"), fols. A6ᵛ–A7ʳ.

[17] Ibid., ch. 6 ("De le convenientie: lequali hanno insieme li quatro segni da li antichi inventi: & li quatro segni da li moderni usitati"), fols. bᵛ–b2ᵛ.

[18] "molto docta et in mathematica fondata." Spataro, letter of 30 January 1531 to Aaron, in *A Correspondence of Renaissance Musicians*, 421.

practice in matters of time measurement. Third, he never attempts to define the duration of the breve in relation to an external standard, as he should logically have done if performance tempo were his main concern. Fourth, he suggests the possibility in one of his letters that Aaron may have expected a certain composition in C to have a breve *tactus*, rather than a semibreve *tactus*, on grounds that one of the dissonances would be incorrect in relation to a semibreve *tactus*. Similarly, he excuses an error in counting breves in a composition of his own on grounds that the sign is C and the *tactus* is the semibreve; the same error would have been much more serious if the sign were C2, which requires a breve *tactus*. There is no implication that the choice of *tactus* has anything to do with the metronome speed of either piece.[19] In light of Spataro's lofty, philosophical speculations, the concept of *tempus* as the equivalent of "metronome mark" seems quite mundane. Even if he did mean that the breve should have the same absolute duration in all mensurations, however, he acknowledges that the principle of breve equivalence does not agree with the practice of his contemporaries.[20]

If Spataro's view makes more sense as speculative theory than as a prescription for performance tempos, the same is true to an even greater extent of the views of Aaron and Lanfranco, both of whom found Spataro's arguments for breve equivalence to be theoretically convincing. Aaron advocates minim equivalence on the authority of Gaffurio in his earlier works,[21] but switches his allegiance to Spataro in his latest work.[22] It is hard to imagine that his judgment of appropriate performance tempos would have been drastically altered by this change of theoretical position. Lanfranco follows Spataro explicitly in deriving all note values from the multiplication and division of the breve, but he says nothing about equating the value of the breve with a unit of absolute time and admits that the moderns treat the semibreve, rather than the breve, as a complete measure of time.[23]

The views of Tinctoris and Gaffurio are equally open to consideration as speculative theory, although they include practical elements as well.

---

[19] Spataro, letter of 4 March 1533 to Aaron, in *A Correspondence of Reniassance Musicians*, 620–21.

[20] *Tractato di musica*, ch. 16 ("Responsione facta a quello: che nel capitolo precedente: e stato dicto da Franchino"), fol. cvi^r.

[21] Aaron, *Libri tres de institutione harmonica*, book 2, ch. 32 ("Quomodo index contra indicem idest signum contra signum ut dicitur cani debeat"), fols. 33^v–36^r, and *Toscanello in musica*, book 1, ch. 38 ("Cognitione, et modo di cantar segno contra a segno necessarii"), fols. Eiv^v–Fii^r.

[22] Aaron, *Lucidario in musica*, Resolutione (of Openione XIII), fol. 13^r. Aaron states explicitly that he has changed his mind on this issue. See Berger, *Mensuration and Proportion Signs*, 64–65.

[23] Lanfranco, *Scintille di musica*, part I, "Delle pause," 35, and part II, "Del modo, tempo: & prolatione," 40.

Tinctoris seems to require minim equivalence between successive mensurations within a piece as a practical policy, since he determines the *tactus* of perfect prolation following imperfect prolation on that basis, but he insists that proportions can apply only to different parts of a single piece, not to relations between independent pieces.[24] By this logic, the principle of minim equivalence in a strict sense (which he would have classified as a "proportion of equality") should also be excluded from comparisons among independent works.

The theorists discussed above are the only ones who claim explicitly that either minims or breves are equivalent among different mensurations. Close reading of less rigorous theorists reveals subtle differences in thought between those who derive the mensural system from a central breve and those who construct it from the aggregation of minims. These differences are apparent in the order in which theorists define note values, the ways they explain the forms of mensuration signs, and the types of symbols they accept as signs of proportions. Although there may be a correlation between these aspects of a theorist's thought and his inclination to compare mensurations on the basis of breve or minim equivalence,[25] there is no evidence that most theorists conceived the mensural system as a rigorously consistent package in which relationships among signs were the same under all circumstances. If there were two and only two systems governing tempo relations among signs, and if those systems differed as drastically as a literal interpretation of breve and minim equivalence would imply, one would expect more theorists to have taken an explicit stand on the issue. The fact that theorists with speculative ambitions were the only ones to address the matter implies that practical options were more varied and not limited to strict equivalence of any kind.

Diminution

Most of the statements about tempo in fifteenth- and sixteenth-century theory are found in the context of discussions of diminution. Theories of diminution present two problems with respect to tempo: first, determining

---

[24] Tinctoris, *Proportionale musices*, book 1, ch. 3 ("Divisio proportionum"), 13–14.
[25] Berger, *Mensuration and Proportion Signs*, 54–79, uses these criteria as indirect evidence to distinguish theorists who favor equal breves from those who favor equal minims. The differences between these groups in the conceptual understanding of the mensural system are important, but I am not convinced that these conceptual orientations can be equated with views on relative tempos.

the amount of the increase in metronome speed that diminution implies, and second, identifying the circumstances in which it should be applied. Theorists are frustratingly vague on both issues, and practical sources sometimes seem to contradict theory even when the theorists are relatively clear.

Modern scholars sometimes claim that signs of diminution (cut signs and signs followed by a figure 2) are twice as fast as integral signs in fifteenth- and sixteenth-century theory. This claim is based on two untenable assumptions: first, that terms such as "note value" always refer to duration, rather than *tactus* counts,[26] and second, that the *tactus* had a more or less fixed duration in all pieces. Another source of confusion is the common failure to distinguish between the formal and informal meanings of the term "proportion." Theorists who define diminution as "duple proportion" in the informal sense do not necessarily mean that it is twice as fast as integral measurement, since the informal sense of the term refers only to the number of notes per *tactus*, not to the duration of the *tactus*. *Tactus* counts can be equated with duration only if the *tactus* has a fixed duration in all contexts. Although scholars often take that principle as axiomatic (Willi Apel goes so far as to define *tactus* as "a fixed, i.e., unchangeable unit of time"[27]), there is not a shred of evidence for it before the 1540 edition of Heyden's *De arte canendi*, and even Heyden is more ambivalent about it than a superficial reading of his treatise would imply. A few earlier sources *may* be interpreted to mean that diminution is twice as fast as integral measurement, but alternative interpretations are generally more plausible. In contrast, evidence that the speed of the *tactus* was variable is abundant.[28]

---

[26] Schanppecher's statement that notes have the same "essence and value" in O and Ȯ even though Ȯ is faster than O is one of many that prove that the concept of "note value" normally meant a number of *tactus*, rather than a duration, in theoretical writings. See Chapter 6, p. 148 above.

[27] Apel, *The Notation of Polyphonic Music*, 147.

[28] The issue of the tempo relationship between cut and uncut signs has been highly contentious in modern studies. Eunice Schroeder proposes a series of changing meanings for Ȯ in theoretical writings (first twice as fast, then a third faster, then again twice as fast) in "The Stroke Comes Full Circle: Ȯ and ₵ in Writings on Music, ca. 1450–1540," *Musica disciplina* 36 (1982), 119–66. Anna Maria Busse Berger argues that cut signs are always twice as fast in "The Myth of *diminutio per tertiam partem*," *The Journal of Musicology* 8 (1990), 398–426; "Cut Signs in Fifteenth-Century Musical Practice," in *Music in Renaissance Cities and Courts: Studies in Honor of Lewis Lockwood*, ed. Jessie Ann Owens and Anthony M. Cummings, Detroit Monographs in Musicology/Studies in Music 18 (Warren, MI: Harmonie Park Press, 1997), 101–12; and *Mensuration and Proportion Signs*, 120–63. Rob C. Wegman, "What Is 'acceleratio mensurae'?" *Music and Letters* 73 (1992), 515–24, and Alexander Blachly, "Reading Tinctoris for Guidance on Tempo," in *Antoine Busnoys: Method, Meaning, and Context in Late Medieval Music*, ed. Paula Higgins (New York: Oxford University Press, 1999), 399–427, present strong evidence from both theory and practice that cut signs call for an unspecified amount of speeding that is

Descriptions of diminution that do not or need not require double speed are ubiquitous in the fifteenth and sixteenth centuries. Most fifteenth-century theorists, following Muris, define diminution either as singing a note like the next smaller value or as removing half of the value of the notes. If "value" is understood as a number of *tactus* or *mensurae*, these definitions say only that the *tactus* of diminished mensurations is the breve and imply nothing specific about the relative tempos of integral and diminished measurement. Statements that the speed of the *tactus* should fall within moderate limits imply that notes of a given type (such as semibreves) will be somewhat faster in diminution than in integral mensurations, but this condition allows for a broad range of interpretations. Anonymous 12 says that Φ and other diminished perfect mensurations are a third faster than integral mensurations, but his immediately following statement implies that the fraction is not to be taken literally.[29] The author of *Ein tütsche musica* says that notes in Φ are "perhaps a third or a half" faster than notes in O.[30] Tinctoris says that a stroke through a *tempus* sign represents *acceleratio mensurae*, but does not specify the degree of acceleration that it involves.[31] Gaffurio follows him when he says that in signs cut by a stroke, the *mensura* is diminished, but not the notes – in other words, the *tactus* is faster (by an unspecified amount), but the number of *tactus* on each note of a given form (such as a semibreve) is unchanged.[32]

Countless sixteenth-century sources describe signs of diminution as "a little faster," or simply "faster" without qualification, than integral signs. Some of the statements of the Cologne theorists and of Monetarius, Glarean, and Tovar that make this point are quoted in Chapters 5 and 6. Many others could be added to this list. Rhau, for example, says that *modus cum tempore* signs imply diminution, which means slightly faster measuring:

Porro, omnis numerus additus circulo vel semicirculo, praeterque quod numeri rationem explicat ...	Every number added to a circle or semicircle, in addition to specifying the way [the notes] are numbered,

---

normally less than double. Richard Sherr accepts the orthodox interpretation of the theoretical evidence, but admits that this interpretation is often musically implausible, in "Tempo to 1500," in *Companion to Medieval and Renaissance Music*, ed. Tess Knighton and David Fallows (New York: Schirmer Books, 1992), 334: "Technically, these [O2 and Φ following O] should always require 'diminution by half' (speeding up semibreves by a factor of two while keeping the tempo/beat the same), but such an interpretation seems on occasion to create speeds that are much too fast."

[29] See Chapter 5, p. 126, above. [30] Anonymous, *Ein tütsche musica*, II: 52–53.
[31] Tinctoris, *Proportionale musices*, book 1, ch. 3 ("Divisio proportionum"), 15, and book 3, ch. 2 ("Qualiter proportiones signandae sint"), 45.
[32] Gaffurio, *Practica musice*, book 2, ch. 14 ("De diminutione"), fol. cciiij^r.

diminutionem etiam indicat, Hoc est (cantum paulo cicius emoderandum esse) declarat.[33]	also signifies diminution; that is, it means that the song is to be measured a little faster.

Statements about the slowness of the breve *tactus* in diminution make the same point in a different way.[34] Luscinius says that notes of a given type are a little faster in imperfect *tempus*, which is measured with a breve *tactus*, than in perfect *tempus*, which is measured with a semibreve *tactus*, and that the slower *tactus* tempers the faster notes in the latter:

Est autem mos ille iam ab omnibus harmonice compositionis magistris observatus, ut in alicuius magni operis contextu, primas sibi vendicet perfectio: … qui etiam principio haud inepte convenit, ob affectatam quandam moram, quae motus cuiuslibet initio a physicis tribuitur. Ternarium autem numerum proxime consequitur binarius, id est, temporis imperfectio, in qua paulo celerius notulae proferuntur. Unde & tactu utimur longiore, puta qui duas semibreves complectitur, quo mora tactus, celeritatem notularum temperemus.[35]	It is a custom now observed by all masters of harmonic composition that in the context of any large work, perfection is used first … This [type of] opening is not at all inappropriate, because of a certain pleasing slowness that is attributed to the beginning of any motion by physicists. Binary number then immediately follows ternary – that is, imperfect *tempus*, in which the notes are sung a little faster. Therefore we also use a longer *tactus* [in imperfect *tempus*], that is, one that contains two semibreves, so that we temper the fastness of the notes with the slowness of the *tactus*.

The custom to which this passage refers is that of writing opening sections of pieces in O and subsequent sections in ₵. Luscinius explains later in the same paragraph that his point applies only when a sign of diminution (a figure 2 or a stroke) is associated with the sign of imperfect *tempus*; without such a sign, the *tactus* of imperfect *tempus* is the semibreve.

Michael Praetorius makes the same point about tempering faster notes with a slower *tactus* in his comparison of C and ₵ a century later, but applies it to slower and faster versions of the semibreve *tactus*:

---

[33] Rhau, *Enchiridion*, part II, ch. 5 ("De signis"), fol. Eiii[r].
[34] Cochlaeus's explanation of that principle is quoted in Chapter 6, p. 151 above.
[35] Luscinius, *Musurgia seu praxis musicae*, Commentarius primus, ch. 9 ("De his, quae potissimum ad praxim conducere videntur"), 84.

Quia Madrigalia & aliae Cantiones, quae sub signo C, Semiminimis & Fusis abundant, celeriori progrediuntur motu; Motectae autem quae sub signo ₵ Brevibus et Semibrevibus abundant, tardiori: Ideo hîc celeriori, illic tardiori opus est Tactu, quò medium inter duo extrema servetur, ne tardior Progressus auditorum auribus pariat fastidium, aut celerior in Praecipitium ducat, veluti Solis equi Phaëtontem abripuerunt, ubi currus nullas audivit habenas.[36]	Since madrigals and other songs that are full of semiminims and *fusae* under the sign C move faster, while motets, which are full of breves and semibreves under the sign ₵ [move] more slowly, it is proper that a mean between the extremes be preserved by a faster *tactus* in the latter and a slower *tactus* in the former, so that the slower motion does not create weariness in the ears of the listeners and the faster does not lead to a precipice, as when the horses of the Sun ran away with Phaëthon when their chariot did not obey the reins.

In light of such overwhelming evidence that theorists did not define signs of diminution as twice as fast as integral signs, the few sources that might lend themselves to that interpretation deserve close examination. The principal source of the idea is the concluding sentence of Gaffurio's chapter on diminution in *Practica musice*. After describing the three categories of diminution (by canon, proportion, and stroke) and making it clear that the first two are measured in breves and the third in semibreves, Gaffurio writes:

Verum cum dupla proportio caeteris et divisione et pronuntiatione sit proportionibus notior atque facillima: mensurae huiusmodi virgulariter consyderata diminutio: in duplo velocior: duplae scilicet aequipolens proportioni: solet a cantoribus frequentius observari.[37]	But since duple proportion is more familiar than other proportions and easiest in division and performance, this type of diminution of the *mensura* by stroke, twice as fast, and equivalent to duple proportion, is most often observed by singers.

Given the context, this sentence makes sense only if "diminution by proportion" is understood to mean "proportion" in an informal sense – i.e., placing the *tactus* on a note other than the semibreve. "Duple

---

[36] Praetorius, *Syntagma musicum*, vol. III, part II, ch. 7 ("De tactu, seu notarum mensura; (italis battuta) & signis"), 50.
[37] Gaffurio, *Practica musice*, book 2, ch. 14 ("De diminutione"), fol. cciiij^v.

proportion" is measuring with an imperfect breve *tactus* that must be slower than the semibreve *tactus* of integral mensurations, as Cochlaeus and others explain. This interpretation of the sentence makes more sense than a reading that makes cut signs twice as fast as uncut signs for several reasons. First, it agrees with the views of many other theorists, including Tinctoris, whom Gaffurio cites in support of his view in an early version of this passage, and the Cologne theorists, who depend heavily on Gaffurio as an authority in mensural matters. Second, it agrees with the usual practice of Gaffurio's time, and Gaffurio says explicitly that the tempo he describes is the one practiced by singers, not one demanded by a theory that conflicts with practice. He cannot be expressing a dogmatic opinion about tempo in this sentence, because he characterizes the tempo as the one "most often observed by singers," not the one that is required by theory. Third, Gaffurio (unlike Tinctoris) defends the use of ostensibly proportional signs, such as C2, as independent mensurations, and those signs cannot have been proportional to anything, because they have no standard of reference within a piece. Fourth, Gaffurio's analogy between *tactus* and pulse applies to the semibreve in both cut and uncut signs. Whatever this analogy may mean with respect to tempo, it makes more sense as a metaphor if the two types of signs differ in tempo by a factor of less than 2:1.[38]

Later theorists, including Cochlaeus, Ornithoparchus, and Agricola, removed this sentence from its context and used it in ways that make it appear to prescribe a 2:1 tempo relation between cut and uncut signs. Cochlaeus places it after a sentence that conflates Anonymous 12's definition of diminution as removal of a third and Gaffurio's statement that notes in cut signs have the same "value" as notes in uncut signs. In this new context, the sentence implies that removal of half is an alternative to removal of a third – a comparison that has nothing to do with Gaffurio's point:

| In diminutione nanque non notularum numerus minuitur (manet enim signum perfectum) sed tertia mensurae pars adimitur. Velocior nanque sic est tactus quam si virgula circulum non intersecet, quamvis utrobique idem sit notarum valor et ternaria perfectio. At | In diminution it is not the number of notes that is diminished (for the sign remains perfect), but a third part of the measure is removed. Thus the *tactus* is faster than if a stroke did not cut the circle, although in both [signs] the value of the notes and the ternary |

---

[38] These arguments are discussed in more detail in DeFord, "On Diminution and Proportion," 51–56.

quia dupla proportio est facilior, ideo persepe in duplo fit mensurae diminutio.[39]	perfection are the same. But since duple proportion is easier, diminution of the measure is very often double.

The meaning of the last sentence in this context is not at all clear. It cannot refer to removal of half of the number of *tactus*, because Cochlaeus defines the *tactus* of diminution explicitly as the semibreve.[40] If it means that the semibreve *tactus* of diminished signs is often twice as fast as the semibreve *tactus* of integral signs, it contradicts Cochlaeus's earlier explanation of how a slow breve *tactus* works as an alternative to a fast semibreve *tactus* in diminution. This interpretation is also difficult to reconcile with his limitation of the term *semiditas* to simultaneous relations later in the same chapter. If diminution were twice as fast as integral mensuration, the term *semiditas* could logically apply to it as well. The idea that 2:1 diminution is somehow easier than 3:2 diminution seems to have arisen through the misleading interpretation of Gaffurio's "duple proportion" as an alternative to a 3:2 reduction of values in diminution. The reasoning is at best questionable if it applies to successive relations within a piece and altogether senseless if it applies to independent works with different signs. Perhaps Cochlaeus found the sentence confusing and simply worked it into his text, however awkwardly, in deference to Gaffurio's authority. Another of the Cologne theorists, Bernhard Bogentantz, omits the problematic sentence from the otherwise complete, verbatim copy of Gaffurio's chapter on diminution in his *Collectanea utriusque cantus*, presumably because he did not understand it.[41]

Ornithoparchus is even less clear about how he understands the tempo relationship between integral and diminished signs. His paraphrase of the above passage from Cochlaeus is as follows:

Diminutio, ut veteres sensere: est tertie partis ab ipsa mensura abstractio. Sed recentiorum laudabilior est opinio ac verior, qui diminutionem a semiditate non disternant. Ut Joannes Tinctoris ... et Franchinus	Diminution, as the ancients believed, is the removal of a third part of the measure. But the opinion of the moderns, which does not distinguish diminution from *semiditas*, is more praiseworthy and

---

[39] Cochlaeus, *Tetrachordum musices*, tract. IV, ch. 7 ("De augmentatione et diminutione"), fol. Eiii^v.
[40] Ibid., tract. IV, ch. 6 ("De signis et tactibus"), fol. Eiii^r.
[41] Bogentantz, *Collectanea utriusque cantus*, part II, ch. 10 ("De diminutione"), fol. Dii^r.

Gafforus ... sanxerunt. Est itaque diminutio medie partis in mensura prescisio, nil discrepans a Semiditate: nisi quod in signis perfectis, ac figuris ternario numero metiendis reperitur.[42]

truer, as Johannes Tinctoris ... and Franchino Gaffurio ... established. Diminution is therefore a cutting of the measure in half, in no way differing from *semiditas* except that it is found in perfect signs and figures measured by the number three.

Since Ornithoparchus defines the proper *tactus* of diminution as the breve, his version of this passage could be interpreted to mean that he thinks the ancients reduced the number of *tactus* on each note by a third in diminution – a procedure that would indeed be unreasonably difficult. If this is what he meant, his statement need not imply anything about the duration of the *tactus*. It is possible, however, that he meant that the duration of the notes should be reduced by half in diminution. Since he says that musicians do not perform music in the way that he believes is correct, his view cannot be taken as evidence for real performance practice in any case. His attribution of the theory of a breve *tactus* in ¢ to Tinctoris is pure fantasy. He probably based the idea on Gaffurio's acknowledged respect for his predecessor, since he could hardly have held that view if he had read Tinctoris's *Proportionale musices* himself.

The theorist who advocates double speed in diminution most clearly is Heyden. His idea that the *tactus* should have the same duration in all signs developed gradually over the three editions of his treatise and was never entirely unambiguous. In the 1532 edition, he explains how measuring every sign with its theoretically correct *tactus* can aid singers in the realization of proportions. He says that proportion signs, among which he includes signs of augmentation and diminution, change the number of notes per *tactus*, not the *tactus* itself,[43] but this condition need not imply that the *tactus* has the same duration in all signs. In the 1537 edition, he says that making the *tactus* faster or slower does not change its identity:

Ab aliis quidem tria Tactuum genera traduntur, quae et vulgus Cantorum in cantando iamdiu

Three types of *tactus*, which the common herd of singers has accepted in singing for a long time, are

---

[42] Ornithoparchus, *Musice active micrologus*, book 2, ch. 8 ("De diminutione"), fol. Fv^r.

[43] Heyden, *Musica stoicheiosis*, "De proportione dupla," fols. C4^v–C5^r. The passage in which this point is discussed is unfortunately corrupt and cannot be translated literally, though the general sense of it seems clear. Some of the text appears to have been omitted in the process of printing the book. I thank Leofranc Holford-Strevens for his advice on this matter.

recepit. Verum si quis ipsius artis ... naturam ... rectius perspiciat, utique convincetur, non nisi unicum Tactus genus esse ... Non enim, si omnino dividendus Tactus sit, ex eo alius erit, si lentius aut concitatius ipse moveatur. Sed potius, si aut plures, aut pauciores Notulas absolvat.[44]	taught by others. But if one examines the nature of this art ... more correctly, he will certainly be convinced that there is only one type of *tactus* ... For if the *tactus* is to be divided, there will not be another one resulting from it [i.e., it will not change into another type of *tactus*] if it moves slower or faster itself, but rather if it applies to more or fewer notes.

This passage seems to acknowledge that a slower or faster *tactus* is legitimate as long as it measures the correct number of notes in each sign (why else would Heyden make the point that changing the speed of the *tactus* does not change its identity?), but in 1540, Heyden adds a sentence to this passage that seems to contradict the spirit of the last sentence:

Quod vetustiores Musici, si concitatiorem aut lentiorem cantum vellent, id non per celeriorem aut tardiorem Tactum, sed per ipsarum Notularum, aut protractiorem aut contractiorem valorem praestiterunt.[45]	For if older musicians wanted a faster or slower song, they showed this not through a faster or slower *tactus*, but through longer or shorter values of the notes themselves.

Most of Heyden's discussion of the speed of the *tactus* appears in the newly written dedication of the 1540 edition, rather than in the main text. The main point of the dedication is that all signs are proportionally interrelated, whether they are used simultaneously or successively. Heyden's primary concern seems to have been to ensure strict proportionality among signs within pieces, rather than to prescribe a fixed tempo for all pieces:

Mirum ergo est, hoc non animadversum esse a paulo superioris aetatis Musicis, videlicet: Non plures Tactuum species esse posse in	It is strange, therefore, that it was not realized by musicians of a little earlier time that many species of *tactus* cannot exist in a proportional

---

[44] Heyden, *Musicae, id est artis canendi libri duo*, book 1, ch. 5 ("De tactu"), 35–36.
[45] Heyden, *De arte canendi*, book 1, ch. 5 ("De tactu"), 41.

Proportionum ratione, sed unicam, ac eandem, quae sibi perpetuo similis sit, esse oportere, cum id ex variarum Proportionum concentu, facillime potuissent discere. Nam Integrum Tactum in Integris Diminutum in Dupla: et Proportionatum in Tripla, illi concinnere nunquam potuerunt.[46]

relation, but that there must be only one, which is always the same. They could have learned this very easily from the harmonies of various proportions, for they could never harmonize the whole *tactus* in integral signs, the diminished *tactus* in *dupla*, and the proportionate *tactus* in *tripla*.

Heyden admits that his view does not conform to the practice of his own time. His argument for it is based solely on the assertion that signs must have the same meaning in all contexts, even though many theorists state explicitly that this is not the case. His account confirms in the clearest possible terms that the speed of the *tactus* was variable, even within pieces, in his day:

Cum enim tam multiplices Tactuum species ob hoc tantum excogitatas videamus, ut motum cantus subinde mutarent, nunc tardiorem, nunc concitatiorem, nunc properantissimum faciendo. Quaeso ergo, quid nam illos novatores, de Proportionibus, Augmentationibus, ac Diminutionibus intellexisse credamus? Certum utique est, ex arte ipsa, quod illi per diversas species Tactus praestare voluerunt, idem veteres per integritatem, aut diminutionem Signorum, aut Proportiones, multo et rectius, et artificiosius praestitisse.[47]

For when we see so many species of *tactus* invented only for the purpose of changing the speed of a song, making it now slower, now faster, now very fast, how, I ask, are we to think these innovators understood proportions, augmentations, and diminutions? It is certain from the art itself that they wished to show through diverse species of *tactus* the same thing that older musicians showed much more correctly and artfully through the wholeness or diminution of the signs or through proportions.

Heyden identifies the period around 1450–1500 as the time when the constant *tactus* was practiced, but surviving evidence from that period does not support his idealized view of it. His followers picked up and promoted many aspects of his theory, but none of them makes the point that the *tactus* should have a fixed duration. Perhaps they ignored that issue

---

[46] Ibid., Dedication, fol. A3^v. [47] Ibid., fol. A3^r.

because they were unable to reconcile it with convictions about tempo that they developed through musical experience.

Sixteenth-century Italian and Spanish theorists rarely say anything about tempo relations between integral and diminished signs. The issue may have seemed more pressing to the Germans, because they usually advocated a semibreve *tactus* for both types of signs and therefore needed a way to explain the difference between them. Southern theorists may have felt that the association of diminished signs with a breve *tactus* distinguished them sufficiently from integral signs, so that explicit discussion of tempo was not necessary. Spataro's miscellaneous comments about cut signs in his letters do not imply that he associated them with fixed tempos. Aaron, however, says in his *Lucidario* that cut signs are twice as fast as uncut signs:

Perche le note del segno tagliato si cantano piu velocemente per lo doppio, per laqual cosa sara meglio diffinire, che la diminutione non sia altro, che quando una nota ha vertu della metà del suo valore intero.[48]	Since notes in cut signs are sung twice as fast, it is better to define diminution as nothing other than when a note has the force of half of its complete value.

The purpose of this point is to argue that diminution should be defined as a loss of half of the value of the notes, rather than as singing notes like the next smaller value, since the latter definition does not work for ¢ as Aaron understands it (with the *tactus* on the imperfect breve). Aaron may have based the idea that cut signs are twice as fast as uncut signs on the new rhythmic style associated with the sign C in *note nere* madrigals, which he mentions in the same book.[49] Some pieces of that type resemble contemporaneous pieces in ¢ notated in half-values and might have called for a tempo in which the notes had about twice the average duration of the notes in ¢. That relationship between the two signs in Italian madrigals lasted only a few years, however, and was never universally adopted.

Modern scholars have proposed that ¢ might be understood as 2:1 proportional diminution of O in a way that does not make all of the notes twice as fast in ¢ by assuming breve equivalence between O and C. If ¢ is twice as fast as C and the breves of O and C have the same duration, four semibreves of ¢ equal three semibreves of O, as shown in Example 7.2. The relationship is 2:1 on the breve level when the imperfect breves of ¢ are

---

[48] Aaron, *Lucidario in musica*, book 3, ch. 9 ("Qual sia stato il primo, e 'l secondo segno da gli antichi, & dotti musici dimostrato"), fol. 24ᵛ.
[49] Ibid., book 3, ch. 15 ("Oppenione, & resolutione, circa i mandriali a note nere"), fols. 29ᵛ–30ʳ.

198 Theory

Example 7.2 ₵ as duple proportion of O, based on breve equivalence between C and O.

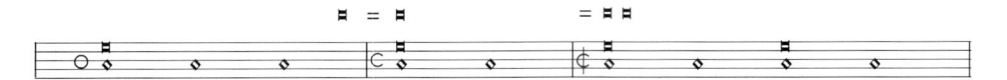

compared to the perfect breves of O, but 4:3 on the semibreve level. Since Aaron advocates breve equivalence in the *Lucidario*, this theory might be invoked to explain his puzzling statement that notes in diminution are twice as fast as notes under integral signs. The idea is elegant and attractive, but it is unlikely that fifteenth- or sixteenth-century theorists conceived the relation between O and ₵ in this way. No theorist of the time proposes this explanation – not even Spataro, who devotes an entire treatise to the principle of breve equivalence. Aaron draws no connection between his observation about the tempo of diminution and the theoretical equivalence of breves, and the theory cannot apply to ⌽, which Aaron mentions explicitly in connection with the idea of double speed. No theorist before Heyden defines the relation between integral and diminished signs as a proportion in the strict sense (i.e., as a relation that applies to note durations, rather than *tactus* counts), and many describe it in qualitative, not quantitative, terms. Proportions in the strict sense must by definition be measured with a constant *tactus*, and the *tactus* of O and ₵ in 4:3 relation on the semibreve level have different durations, regardless of whether ₵ is measured in breves or semibreves. The 4:3 relation is musically pleasing and may very well have existed in practice, but defining it as a duple proportion of breves is a modern idea.[50]

Not long after Heyden launched his revolutionary theory of constant *tactus*, other theorists began to say that there was no difference between integral and diminished signs in practice. The first to do so were French writers of the 1550s, whose intended readers were neither academics nor speculative theorists, but musical amateurs. Claude Martin describes both cut and uncut signs, but mentions no difference between them.[51] Maximilian Guilliaud says that the ancients represented diminution with strokes, but that in his day there is no difference between cut and uncut

---

[50] This interpretation is proposed by Berger in "The Relationship of Perfect and Imperfect Time in Italian Theory of the Renaissance," *Early Music History* 5 (1985), 26–28, and *Mensuration and Proportion Signs*, 84–86. Berger argues for the interpretation of ₵ as duple proportion of O with breve equivalence between C and O on grounds that ₵ and ↺ are synonymous and four semibreves of ↺ equal three semibreves of O. This reasoning is questionable, because the idea of equating ₵ with ↺ developed later than the practice of using O and ₵ for different sections of pieces.

[51] Martin, *Elementorum musices practicae*, book 2, ch. 6 ("De vulgatissima graduum musicalium commixtione, in qua imperfecta esse omnia depraehendes"), 28.

signs.[52] Philibert Jambe de Fer says that ¢ and C have distinct meanings only when they appear simultaneously.[53] Some German and Italian theorists after *c.* 1570 define signs without distinguishing between integral and diminished measurement, though others uphold the idea that cut signs represent diminution well beyond 1600.

Even if we could be sure exactly how fifteenth- and sixteenth-century theorists understood the relation between integral and diminished mensurations, uncertainties would remain about how to apply the principles to the choice of tempos in practice. Within any given musical repertoire, pieces with signs of diminution typically have a larger proportion of long notes than pieces with integral signs, and they usually have at least some rhythms that suggest a compositional *tactus* on a higher level as well, though the specific differences vary greatly from one repertoire to another. When signs correlate well with differences of musical style, it is reasonable to assume that composers intended for the theoretical definitions of the signs to apply. There are instances, however, in which integral signs are applied to music that seems to require diminution on the basis of musical style and *vice versa*. English composers rarely used signs of diminution before the late fifteenth century, yet their compositional practices suggest that they recognized a distinction between integral and diminished measurement.[54] Signs of diminution are also lacking in some Continental pieces in which diminution seems to have been intended, whether through inadvertence or in imitation of English practice. Conversely, cut signs appear in some pieces in which the musical style implies integral measurement. Scholars have debated whether the sign or the style should take precedence in determining the tempo of such pieces.[55] Theoretical evidence

---

[52] Guilliaud, *Rudiments de musique practique*, part II, ch. 8 ("Du touchement, ou mesure du chant"), fol. Cij^r.

[53] Jambe de Fer, *Epitome musical*, ch. 7 ("Les noms & valeur des notes sans ligature en temps imparfaitz ainsi. ¢ C C2 ↄ autant vaut l'un que l'autre: si ce n'est, que le second se trouve en une partie seule & non aux autres, lors ladite partie augmentera du tout, de la moytie"), 30–31.

[54] On this issue, see Rob C. Wegman, "Concerning Tempo in the English Polyphonic Mass, *c.* 1420–70," *Acta musicologica* 61 (1989), 40–65.

[55] Margaret Bent identifies a number of pieces signed ¢ for which diminution seems inappropriate on musical grounds in "The Early Use of the Sign ¢," *Early Music* 24 (1996), 199–225; "The Use of Cut Signatures in Sacred Music by Binchois," in *Binchois Studies*, ed. Andrew Kirkman and Dennis Slavin (Oxford University Press, 2000), 277–312; and "The Use of Cut Signatures in Sacred Music by Ockeghem and His Contemporaries," in *Johannes Ockeghem: Actes du XLe Colloque international d'études humanistes, Tours, 3–8 février 1997*, ed. Philippe Vendrix, "Épitome musical" 1 (Paris: Klincksieck, 1998), 641–80. She argues that in such cases, the stroke through the *tempus* sign does not mean diminution. Rob C. Wegman challenges her view, arguing on grounds of theoretical testimony that a stroke through a *tempus* sign always means diminution, in "Different Strokes for Different Folks? On Tempo and Diminution in Fifteenth-Century Music," *Journal of the American Musicological Society* 53 (2000), 461–505. Bent's

provides no basis for answering this question, and musicians may well have disagreed about the matter even when the music was new.

Johann Zanger reports a fascinating anecdote in which musicians of the chapel of the archduke of Austria disagreed about the tempo of the Pleni of Josquin's *Missa L'homme armé super voces musicales*. The example has the sign C, although imperfect *tempus* was almost always signed ¢ at the time:

Sic ratione non diminuti circuli subsequens Iosquini exemplum ex Missa Lomme arme, Arnoldus de Bruk Ro. Regiae maiestatis Archipsaltes ad tactum ◫ retulit. Verum Stephanus Mahu eodem in exemplo absentiam virgulae pariter in omnibus vocibus mensurae tarditatem indicare adservit, cuius sententiam & Erasmus Lapidicida Musicus, praeter caeteros eius aetatis acutissimus comprobavit, quorum ex iudicio octavum axioma conformavimus.[56]	Thus Arnold von Bruck, Kapellmeister of the King of the Romans [Archduke Ferdinand I], interpreted the following example in the mensuration of the undiminished [semi]circle [C], from Josquin's *Missa L'homme armé*, with a breve *tactus*. But Stephan Mahu maintained that the absence of the stroke in all voices in the same example indicated the slowness of the measure. His opinion was confirmed by Erasmus Lapicida, a very astute musician among those of their age. We agree with their opinion on the basis of the eighth axiom.

Bruck was Kapellmeister to Archduke Ferdinand I from 1527 to 1545, and Mahu was his assistant during the 1530s. Zanger, who joined the chapel in 1527, studied with both of them. If musicians of this caliber could not agree on the meaning of Josquin's sign a decade after the composer's death, it is not surprising that modern scholars are unable to resolve such dilemmas. It is unlikely that there was ever universal agreement on issues of this type.

Ternary proportions

Signs of triple and *sesquialtera* proportion are even more problematic than signs of diminution from the point of view of tempo.[57] They are ambiguous

---

response to Wegman is found ibid., 597–612. I believe that Bent's view is correct. See Ruth I. DeFord, "The *Mensura* of Φ in the Works of Du Fay," *Early Music* 34 (2006), 111–36.

[56] Zanger, *Practicae musicae praecepta*, part II, ch. 2 ("De gradibus"), fols. Kiv^r–L^v.

[57] This issue is discussed in Ruth I. DeFord, "Tempo Relationships between Duple and Triple Time in the Sixteenth Century," *Early Music History* 14 (1995), 1–51.

for two reasons. First, the ambiguity of the *tactus* of ₵ led to ambiguities in the interpretation of ternary proportions that were compared directly to it. Second, the term "proportion" had both formal and informal meanings in relation to *tripla* and *sesquialtera*. In the formal sense, the terms meant 3:1 or 3:2 ratios of note durations; in the informal sense, they meant mensurations with three semibreves or three minims on one *tactus* with no necessary proportionale relation to another mensuration. Although the same ambiguity applies to the term "duple proportion," the problem is more acute in the case of *tripla* and *sesquialtera*, because there was no alternative term, such as "diminution," that might distinguish the informal from the formal definitions of these concepts. The numerous signs that represent *tripla* and *sesquialtera* likewise make no distinction between proportional and non-proportional interpretations.

The terms and signs associated with *tripla* and *sesquialtera* were commonly used without distinction at least as early as the 1470s, as Tinctoris's complaint about musicians' applying both terms to mensurations such as the O3 of Ockeghem's *L'autre d'antan* makes clear.[58] Vanneo complains that composers often notate proportions in O or C as *sesquialtera* (in groups of three semibreves), but expect them to be performed as triple proportion:

Aliud insuper non mediocre vitium universam fere musicorum manum temere sequi animadverti, cum ante sesquialteram ex his duobus alterum praeponant signum O C ... Deinde ipsi sesquialtere proportioni breves ac semibreves dedicant notulas, inventes treis semibreves unico ictu contineri ac mensurari, quo nil ineptius est in sesquialtera proportione, id enim potius triplae congruit proportioni.[59]	I have also observed that another not insignificant error results inadvertently from the writing of nearly all musicians: when they place before *sesquialtera* one of these two signs O C ... then they write breves and semibreves in *sesquialtera* proportion, you would find that three semibreves are contained in and measured by one *tactus*. Nothing is more unsuitable in *sesquialtera* proportion, for this applies rather to triple proportion.

Aaron points out that the same confusion arises when people measure ₵ with a semibreve *tactus*:

---

[58] *Proportionale musices*, book 1, ch. 3 ("Divisio proportionum"), 14–15.
[59] Vanneo, *Recanetum de musica aurea*, book 2, ch. 30 ("De signorum ac notularum sesquialterae proportionis compositione"), fol. 68ʳ.

| Per lo qual segno [¢] eßi danno la misura sopra la semibreve, & questo inconveniente commettono per poter con piu loro facilita cantare ... conciosia cosa che dopo molte note nascera una sesqualtera habitudine ... io vorrei un poco, che mi diceßero questi tali ... che proportione sara quella? Certo non si puo dire, che eßa habbia da eßere sesqualtera, ma tripla.[60] | For that sign [¢] they place the measure on the semibreve, and they commit this impropriety in order to be able to sing with greater ease ... If after many notes there is a *sesquialtera* proportion ... I would like these people to tell me ... what proportion will it be? Certainly it cannot be said to be *sesquialtera*, but *tripla*. |

Other theorists allow coloration to represent either *sesquialtera* or triple proportion without complaining about the inconsistency. Finck, for example, explains hemiola as follows:

| Hemiola ... nihil differt in Musica a sesquialtera, nisi colore notarum. Interdum tamen a Musicis pro tripla proportione usurpatur, cum in omnibus vocibus simul accidit.[61] | Hemiola ... does not differ in music from *sesquialtera* except in the color of the notes. But sometimes it is used by musicians for triple proportion when it appears simultaneously in all voices. |

Gallus Dressler says that groups of three colored semibreves are measured with two *tactus* when they are simultaneous with binary rhythms in other voices and with one *tactus* when they are found in all voices, likewise implying that they are in triple proportion in the latter case.[62] Numerous musical sources also provide evidence for a lack of distinction between *tripla* and *sesquialtera* in practice. Ternary passages notated in groups of three semibreves in vocal works are often transcribed as groups of three minims under the same sign in intabulations,[63] and rhythms notated as groups of semibreves in *sesquialtera* are occasionally aligned with rests in other voices in a way that shows that they must be interpreted as triple proportion. In Example 7.3a, bar 19, a combination of a black breve plus semibreve

---

[60] Aaron, *Lucidario in musica*, book 3, ch. 6 ("Come il cantore dee oßervare la misura ne segni de modulati concenti dal musico, & compositore ordinati"), fols. 20ʳ–20ᵛ.
[61] Finck, *Practica musica*, "Hemiola," fol. Riᵛ.
[62] Dressler, *Musicae practicae elementa*, book 3, ch. 9 ("De proportionibus"), fol. N3ᵛ.
[63] For examples, see DeFord, "Tempo Relationships," 16–20.

Example 7.3 Coloration as triple proportion. (a) Marenzio, *Dolorosi martir*, bars 18–19. (b) Marenzio, *Perch'io non ho speranza* bars 9–10.

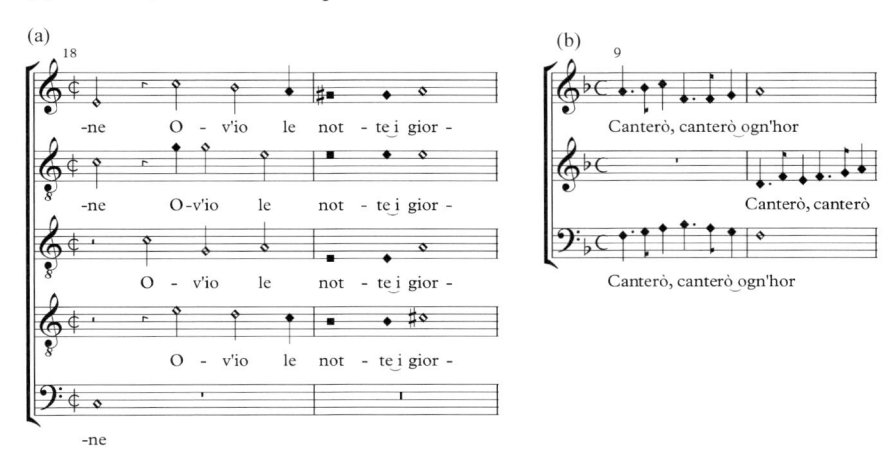

(equivalent to three semibreves) in the upper voices corresponds to half of a breve rest, equivalent to a semibreve rest, in the bass. In Example 7.3b, each group of three black minims (the first two in the form of a dotted minim + semiminim) corresponds to half of a semibreve rest or note in another voice. The black notes must be minims and semiminims, not semiminims and *fusae*, because the triplet rhythm indicates that they are to be understood as coloration.

Signs of *tripla* and *sesquialtera* that apply to whole pieces cannot be interpreted as proportions in the strict sense, as Tinctoris rightly insists. There is considerable evidence, both theoretical and musical, that they were not always interpreted as strict proportions within pieces either. Glarean recommends using a different term, such as "trochaic" or "tribrachic," to distinguish non-proportional ternary rhythms from true proportions:

Caeterum in his quoque signis O3, C3 nostra aetas tactus diminutionem nimis licenter usurpavit, ut treis semibreveis uno tactu, magnifico quidem illo, et augustiore numerentur: Vulgus cantorum nunc triplam improprie vocat, quippe quae ad nullas unas notulas comparationem habeat, ut poscit	Moreover our age has also used diminution of the *tactus* in these signs O3, C3 much too freely, such that three semibreves are counted in one *tactus*, indeed a grand and majestic *tactus*. The common herd of singers now improperly calls this *tripla*, although it is not proportional to any one note, as the

tripla Ratio, sed in quatuor vocibus aequo valore incedit. Eam ego Trochaicam dicere malim, quanquam Iambum saepe in conclusionibus habet, et Tribrachyn, ut duobus his pedibus communem ... Caeterum Triplam. Hemioliam, ac Trochaicam formam multi distinguere, imo discernere nequeunt. Cum Tripla ad Hemioliam, in celeritatis ratione sit dupla. At Trochaicae, et alia mensura, et alia canendi formula, longe a Tripla atque ab Hemiolia distincta.[64]	triple ratio requires, but moves in equal values in the four voices. I prefer to call it "trochaic," although it often has an iamb at the end, and "tribrachic," which is common to both of these feet ... Furthermore, many cannot distinguish or even recognize triple, hemiola, and the trochaic form, although *tripla* is twice as fast as hemiola, but the trochaic form differs very much from *tripla* and hemiola, both through a different *mensura* and through a different manner of singing.

Hofmann makes the same point. He calls non-proportional ternary rhythms "tripla vulgaris":

Vera Tripla haec est, quae comparat tres notas cum una. Est autem praeter hanc & alia Tripla vulgaris, quae ex aequo in omnibus vocibus incedit, tactu proportionato.[65]	True *tripla* is that which compares three notes with one. Besides this, there is also another colloquial *tripla* (*tripla vulgaris*), which moves equally in all voices to a proportionate *tactus*.

Burmeister does not even consider the possibility that such rhythms might be proportional, but he justifies the term "proportionate *tactus*" on grounds that the two strokes of that *tactus* are in 2:1 relation to each other.[66] Zacconi ironically uses the term "proportions" exclusively for ternary rhythms that are not proportional and classifies proportions in the strict sense as "opposed numbers," not "proportions."[67] Michael

---

[64] Glarean, *Dodecachordon*, book 3, ch. 8 ("De augmentatione diminutione ac semiditate"), 206, and ch. 10 ("De alteratione"), 214.

[65] Hofmann, *Musicae practicae praecepta*, part III ("De proportionibus"), fol. Kiv^r.

[66] Burmeister, *Musica autoschediastike*, Accessio 3, section 2, "De antiphonis," fols. Aa^v–Aa2^r.

[67] Zacconi, *Prattica di musica*, book 3. Zacconi uses the term "proportions of unequal figures" as a synonym for "opposed numbers." The mensurations that he calls "proportions" without qualification are "proportions of unequal figures and *tactus*" – i.e., ternary mensurations in all voices that are measured with an unequal *tactus*. Most of book 3 is devoted to an

Example 7.4 ϕ^3_2 with the semibreve equivalent to a minim of ₵.

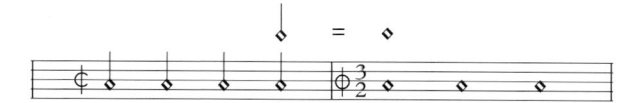

Praetorius says that groups of three semibreves on one *tactus* in ₵ should be slower than groups of three minims on one *tactus* in C.[68] Since for him the semibreve *tactus* of ₵ is faster than the semibreve *tactus* of C, the *tactus* of these proportions cannot have the same duration as that of the binary mensuration in both cases.

There is evidence that the note corresponding to a third of an unequal *tactus* (a semibreve or minim) in *sesquialtera* could sometimes equal a minim of ₵.[69] By extension, a minim of *sesquialtera* might equal a semi-minim of C (see Example 7.4). Agricola explains as follows:

Gleich wie sich die beide Ciffern 3 und 2 in Proportione sesquialtera zu hauff haben/also wird der Proporcien Tact wenn er langsam/ gegen dem gantzen/odder gegen dem halben/so er risch geschlagen wird/geachtet und abgemessen/als ein Exempel. Der halbe Tact in diesem zeichen ₵ begreifft solcher ♩♩ ii, aber der Porporcien Tact alzeit der ♩♩♩ iii. Darumb wird der Proporcien Tact/soviel als eine Minima ♩ langsamer dann die andern beide gefüret.[70]	Just as the two numbers 3 and 2 relate to each other in *sesquialtera* proportion, the proportionate *tactus* is measured in the same way when it is taken slowly in relation to the whole *tactus* or fast in relation to the half-*tactus*. For example, the half-*tactus* in this sign ₵ contains two minims, but the proportionate *tactus* always contains three minims. Therefore the proportionate *tactus* is taken as much as one minim slower than the other two.

---

explanation and defense of this distinction. See DeFord, "Zacconi's Theories of *Tactus* and Mensuration," 151–82.

[68] Praetorius, *Syntagma musicum*, vol. III, part II, ch. 7 ("De tactu, seu notarum mensura; (italis battuta) & signis"), 52–53.

[69] Franz-Jochen Machatius calls this proportion "spielmännische Reduktion" ("players' diminution"), or a type of diminution used by practical musicians, in contrast to theorists' diminution, which is always *sesquialtera* or *tripla*. See his "Über mensurale und spielmännische Reduktion," *Die Musikforschung* 8 (1955), 139–51. Walther Dürr presents additional evidence for this practice in *Zwei neue Belege für die sogenannte 'spielmännische' Reduktion*, Biblioteca di Quadrivium, Estratti (Bologna: Arti Grafiche Tamari, 1958).

[70] Agricola, *Musica figuralis deudsch*, ch. 6 ("Vom schlag odder Tact"), fol. Gv^r.

Jambe de Fer may mean the same thing when he says that *tripla de temps* and *hemyolia de temps* (which are notated in groups of three semibreves) are less than imperfect *tempus* by half.[71] This interpretation is found unambiguously in a few practical sources as well.[72] Although this proportion would be classified as duple on the basis of duration, theorists did not think of it as a duple proportion, because its salient feature is the measurement of three equal notes on one *tactus*, not the duple relation to a preceding sign.

Most of the evidence for non-literal interpretations of *tripla* and *sesquialtera* dates from the 1520s and later. Although the concept of these mensurations as "proportions" in the informal sense existed much earlier, it is unclear whether that interpretation was common when the signs appeared in successive relation to binary signs. Sections of pieces notated in *sesquialtera* usually begin simultaneously in all voices, but there are instances in which they do not. When a *sesquialtera* passage overlaps with ₵, the proportion must be interpreted literally as long as the overlap lasts, and this implies that the literal interpretation should continue throughout the passage. Such examples have been taken as evidence that a literal interpretation of *sesquialtera* was the norm even when it does not overlap with ₵.[73] That reasoning is difficult to reconcile with the evidence that ₵ was normally measured with a semibreve *tactus* and *sesquialtera* (notated in groups of three semibreves) with a perfect breve *tactus* by the late fifteenth century. A literal interpretation of *sesquialtera* requires the *tactus* to be twice as slow in the proportion as in ₵, and no theorist mentions such a practice. The musical styles of *sesquialtera* passages in ₵ did not change significantly from the late fifteenth to the late sixteenth century, and it is hard to imagine that their usual tempo would have increased to as much as twice as fast during that period. How this contradictory evidence should be interpreted is not at all clear. It is likely that practices were always more variable than a single form of evidence might suggest.

---

[71] "*Tripla* of *tempus* is less in its entirety by half than imperfect *tempus*; *hemiolia* of *tempus* similarly" ("Tripla de temps est moindre en tout, de la moytie que temps imparfait, hemyolia de temps au semblable"). Jambe de Fer, *Epitome musical*, ch. 9 (no title), 40. This statement could be taken to mean that a semibreve of *tripla de temps* or *hemiolia de temps* (i.e., one of a group of three semibreves that together constitute one *tactus*) equals a minim of imperfect *tempus*.

[72] See DeFord, "Tempo Relationships," 46–50.

[73] Martin Ham, "A Sense of Proportion: The Performance of Sesquialtera ca. 1515–ca. 1565," *Musica disciplina* 56 (2011), 79–274.

Absolute tempo

Fifteenth- and sixteenth-century evidence relating to absolute tempo is even more difficult to interpret than evidence relating to relative tempos. Theorists rarely say anything about absolute tempo except in very general terms, and they almost never explain it unambiguously in relation to an external standard. Even Heyden, who may have implied that all mensuration and proportion signs should relate to a fixed unit of time, never attempted to give his readers an estimate of the duration of that unit in absolute terms. Nevertheless, the common characterization of diminution as somewhat faster than integral mensuration implies that there must have been relatively standard tempos associated with integral and diminished measurement within any given repertoire.

In the earliest known description of physical time measurement in music, Anselmi characterizes the duration of the *tactus* (which he places on the breve) as variable, but moderate.[74] The idea that the *tactus* (whether breve or semibreve) should be moderate recurs sporadically in later writings, such as those of Cochlaeus[75] and Matheo de Aranda.[76] Ornithoparchus describes the *tactus maior* (the semibreve of integral signs or the breve of diminished signs) as slow and the *tactus minor* (the semibreve of diminished signs) as twice as fast.[77] Since he rejects the latter as improper, he may have regarded it as faster than moderate, though his reasoning is based on his interpretation of authority, not on aesthetic judgment.

Some theorists suggest analogies between *tactus* and external actions that may have implications relating to tempo. The most common is the analogy between music and pulse, which appears for the first time as a music-theoretical issue in the writings of Ramis and Gaffurio. Ramis compares the *tactus* to the interval between the diastole and the systole of the pulse and equates it with the breve in *modus cum tempore* signs and the semibreve in simple *tempus* signs. He conceives of the pulse as unequally divided and models unequal musical proportions on its division.[78] Gaffurio compares the *tactus* to the complete pulse, which he equates with the semibreve, and

---

[74] Giorgio Anselmi, *De musica*, part III, 171.
[75] Cochlaeus, *Compendium . . . cantus figurabilis*, ch. 11 ("De tactu in communi"), fol. [4]ʳ.
[76] Matheo de Aranda, *Tractado de canto mensurable*, [part I], ch. 3 ("De pausas: y de tres maneras de compas"), fol. aνᵛ.
[77] Ornithoparchus, *Musice active micrologus*, book 2, ch. 6 ("De tactu"), fol. Fiijᵛ.
[78] Ramis de Pareja, *Musica practica*, part III, tract. I, ch. 2 ("In quo signa per quae numeri distinguuntur"), 83. Bonnie J. Blackburn interprets Ramis's text to mean that the semibreve *tactus* is equated with the interval from diastole to systole and the breve *tactus* with the complete pulse, though Ramis does not make this distinction explicit. See her "Leonardo and Gaffurio on

conceives of it as equally divided.[79] Later theorists follow his view. It is unlikely that both Ramis and Gaffurio understood these comparisons as tempo prescriptions; if they did, the tempos they recommend would differ by a factor of two or three.[80] Gaffurio's analogy relates more plausibly to tempo than Ramis's on the basis of musical considerations, though whether or not he meant it in that sense is unclear. In *Practica musice*, he places the analogy between *tactus* and pulse on equal footing with the analogy between *tactus* and poetic feet and frames the comparison in terms that suggest a metaphorical relation between the concepts.[81] In *Angelicum ac divinum opus musice*, he compares the semibreve to the "time" of the pulse, perhaps implying a more concrete analogy between the two phenomena.[82] Since the semibreve is the pulse of both integral and diminished mensurations, however, Gaffurio's analogy must allow for considerable latitude if it is meant as a tempo prescription at all. Fra Mauro characterizes the analogy between *tactus* and pulse explicitly as a metaphor.[83]

Another comparison between *tactus* and pulse appears in the writings of the physician Michaele Savonarola (1384–1468), for whom the relationship is definitely based on absolute time. Savonarola regards musical tempos as sufficiently standard and memorable that physicians can use them as a standard for measuring the pulse, rather than *vice versa*. Savonarola estimates the healthy pulse as slower than *quaternaria* (C with no values shorter than minims in the French system), but faster than *senaria imperfecta* (₵ in the French system). Since both the note value that Savonarola equates with the pulse and the tempo relation between the two mensurations are open to debate, scholars have drawn widely differing conclusions about how his principles should be applied to music. One interpretation sets the perfect

Harmony and the Pulse of Music," in *Essays on Music and Culture in Honor of Herbert Kellman*, ed. Barbara Haggh, "Épitome musical" 8 (Paris: Minerve, 2001), 142.

[79] Gaffurio, *Practica musice*, book 2, ch. 1 ("Mensuram temporis in voce poetae & musici brevem & longam posuere"), fol. aai^v, and 3 ("De consyderatione quinque essentialium figurarum"), fol. aaiij^r.

[80] Gaffurio borrowed a copy of Ramis's *Musica practica* from Spataro and covered it with marginal notes criticizing many of Ramis's ideas – a disrespectful act for which Spataro never forgave him. The copy is now in the Civico Museo Bibliografico Musicale in Bologna. Since he did not comment on Ramis's statement about pulse, he must not have taken it to be incompatible with his own views on the subject.

[81] Gaffurio, *Practica musice*, book 2, ch. 1 ("Mensuram temporis in voce poetae & musici brevem & longam posuere"), fol. aai^v.

[82] Gaffurio, *Angelicum ac divinum opus musice*, book 3, ch. 1 ("De le consyderatione & descriptione de le figure del canto mensurato"), fol. Fi^v.

[83] Fra Mauro da Firenze, *Utriusque musices epitome*, ed. Frank A. D'Accone, Corpus scriptorum de musica 32 (Neuhausen-Stuttgart: Hänssler, 1984), ch. 17 ("Della misura, polso o ver battuta del canto"), 76.

semibreve of Savonarola's *senaria imperfecta* at around MM 75 and the imperfect semibreve of his *quaternaria* around MM 150. Since minims are equal in all mensurations in French theory, this places the standard French minim (⅓ of a semibreve of ₵) between MM 225 (= 3 × 75) and 300. Another interpretation sets the minims of Savonarola's *senaria imperfecta* at MM 60 and that of his *quaternaria* at MM 80.[84]

Other analogies between *tactus* and analogous temporal actions are even harder to interpret. Hans Buchner estimates the speed of the *tactus* as equivalent to two steps of a man walking moderately, but moderate walking is an even less precise measure than the human pulse.[85] Finck equates a minim of perfect prolation measured in perfect semibreves with a common weed-cutter's whack:

Perfecta prolatio est, ubi semibrevis tres minimas continet, aut semibrevis integro tactu, iuxta veterum Musicorum consuetudinem mensuratur, so wirt eine minima einen gemeinen Krauthackerischen schlag gelten.[86]	Perfect prolation is when a semibreve contains three minims, or a whole semibreve is measured with one *tactus* according to the custom of old musicians; then a minim will be worth a common weed-cutter's whack.

The lowliness of the metaphor and the switch from Latin to German at this point suggest that Finck may have meant the comment more as a touch of humor than as useful information about tempo. Hans Neusidler estimates the duration of the semibreve *tactus* as about the same as the stroke of the bells on tower clocks or the numbers that people say aloud when counting money.[87] It is possible that he simply picked up the analogy between *tactus* and bells from Gerle (see p. 77), who uses the bells to illustrate the evenness, rather than the duration, of the *tactus*. Since little is known about the

---

[84] The former interpretation is found in Werner Friedrich Kümmel, "Zum Tempo in der italienischen Mensuralmusik des 15. Jahrhunderts," *Acta musicologica* 42 (1970), 156, and the latter in Segerman, "A Re-examination of the Evidence on Absolute Tempo before 1700 – I," 228. Most scholars regard the tempos for which Segerman claims to find evidence to be impossibly slow, but the fact that he is able to defend them theoretically demonstrates the degree of uncertainty involved in all interpretations of the early evidence regarding tempo.

[85] Hans Buchner, *Fundamentbuch* (Basel, Universitätsbibliothek, Ms. F.I.8ª), in Hans Buchner, *Sämtliche Orgelwerke*, vol. I, ed. Jost Harro Schmidt, Das Erbe deutscher Musik 54, Abteilung Orgel/Klavier/Laute 5 (Frankfurt: Henry Litolff's Verlag, 1974), 8.

[86] Finck, *Practica musica*, "De prolatione," fol. Ki^v.

[87] Hans Neusidler, *Ein newgeordent künstlich Lautenbuch* (Nuremberg: Petreius, 1536), fols. biii^v–biv^r.

timing of the strokes of sixteenth-century clocks, the analogy is of limited use in any case.

There are two known instances in which writers before 1600 estimate musical time units in relation to clock time. The earliest appears in the *Liber de musica* of Johannes Vetulus de Anagnia (1351). Scholars disagree on how to interpret it, but it is in any case too early to apply to the music considered in this book.[88] Leonardo da Vinci uses the concept of *tempo armonico* to measure non-musical motions, such as the velocity of flowing water. He does not define this unit in technical musical terms, but he estimates it as $1/1080$ of an hour in one place and $1/3000$ of an hour in another. If the former value is equated with the perfect breve of O and the latter with the semibreve, the resulting tempos are ◊= MM 54 for the former and ◊= MM 50 for the latter.[89] Although these equations cannot be translated into simple formulas for determining musical tempos in practice, it is significant that Leonardo, like Savonarola, regarded musical tempos as more precise measures of time than mechanical instruments.

There is considerable evidence beginning in the 1530s for the choice of tempos on the basis of factors other than the conventional implications of mensuration signs. Heyden's complaint about the variety of tempos used by his contemporaries is clear evidence of this practice, even though he did not approve of it. Cimello, who advocates a conservative interpretation of the mensural system including a *tactus* of moderate speed, nevertheless says that some motets, madrigals, and villanellas should be sung faster in order to give greater pleasure:

| ... cantando un mottetto un madriali ò canzone villanesche si debbe stringere la battuta che con tale varie di estrettezza più piaccon e più dilettino.[90] | ... in singing a motet or madrigal or *canzone villanesca*, one should speed up the beat, since with that variety of speed they please and delight more. |

Spanish sources beginning with Luys Milán's *El maestro* (Valencia, 1536) use terms such as *espacio* (slow), *mesurado* (measured), *apresurado*

---

[88] On Vetulus, see F. Alberto Gallo, *La teoria della notazione in Italia dalla fine del XIII all'inizio del XV secolo*, Antiquae musicae italicae subsidia theorica (Bologna: Tamari Editori, 1966), 65–70; Gallo, "Die Notationslehre im 14. und 15. Jahrhundert," in *Die mittelalterliche Lehre von der Mehrstimmigkeit*, ed. Hans Heinrich Eggebrecht, Geschichte der Musiktheorie 5 (Darmstadt: Wissenschaftliche Buchgesellschaft, 1984), 322–25; and Segerman, "A Re-examination of the Evidence on Absolute Tempo before 1700 – I," 227–28.

[89] See Blackburn, "Leonardo and Gaffurio on Harmony and the Pulse of Music," 141–42.

[90] Quoted in James Haar, "Lessons in Theory from a Sixteenth-Century Composer," 81, n. 60.

(hurried), and *apriessa* (fast) to specify gradations of tempo.[91] Zacconi says that the tempo of sacred music should remain within moderate limits, but the tempo of secular music may be whatever the performers like. He complains, however, that some conductors take sacred works much faster than he feels is appropriate.[92] Praetorius, after a lengthy discussion of the different ways in which composers of the late sixteenth century distinguish the meanings of ¢ and C, concludes that tempo should be determined on the basis of the text and musical style of a piece:

Es kan aber ein jeder den Sachen selbsten nachdencken, und ex consideratione Textus & Harmoniae observiren, wo ein langsamer oder geschwinder Tact gehalten werden müße.[93]	But everyone can contemplate these things for himself and observe from a consideration of the text and the music where a slower or faster *tactus* should be taken.

Burmeister says that tempo may be determined subjectively because it has nothing to do with the essence of music:

Nihil enim impedit sive protractiorem sive velociorem geras mensuram, quo minus una eademque maneat mensura. Productio enim & velocitas nihil ad substantiam rei conferunt. quandoquidem sint arbitraria, ut quae chorudiœceta arbitrio subjecta sunt.[94]	Nothing prevents you from taking a slower or faster *tactus*, as long as the *tactus* remains one and the same. Slowness and speed contribute nothing to the substance of the matter, since, as things that are subject to the judgment of the conductor, they are arbitrary.

This freedom nevertheless has its limits, since Burmeister also says that the *tactus* should be moderate, but slower when there are many short notes than when there are not.[95]

It is not always clear whether theoretical comments about tempo variability apply only to relations among independent pieces, or whether the tempo might also vary within a piece. Given Heyden's concern for

---

[91] See Charles Jacobs, *Tempo Notation in Renaissance Spain*, Wissenschaftliche Abhandlungen 8 (Brooklyn: Institute of Medieval Music, [c1964]), and Luis Gásser, *Luis Milán on Sixteenth-Century Performance Practice* (Bloomington: Indiana University Press, 1996), 70–74.
[92] Zacconi, *Prattica di musica*, part II, book 1, ch. 65 ("Della concertatione della musica, e sua soministratione"), 56.
[93] Praetorius, *Syntagma musicum*, vol. III, part II, ch. 7 ("De tactu, seu notarum mensura; (italis battuta) & signis"), 51.
[94] Burmeister, *Musica autoschediastike*, Accessio III, section II, "De antiphonis," fol. Aaᵛ.
[95] Ibid., fol. Aa4ʳ.

proportional relations among signs, it is likely that his complaint about inconsistent tempos implies that his contemporaries changed tempo within pieces, probably at points where the mensuration changes. Other theorists advise singers to vary the tempo in order to bring out the affect of the words. Vicentino may be the earliest to do so. He recommends that singers imitate the techniques of orators by underlining changes of affect with changes of dynamics and tempo:

& la esperienza, dell'Oratore l'insegna ... che hora dice forte, & hora piano, & più tardo, & più presto, e con questo muove assai gl'oditori ... che effetto faria l'Oratore che recitasse una bella oratione senza l'ordine de i suoi accenti, & pronuntie, & moti veloci, & tardi, & con il dir piano & forte[?] ... Il simile dè essere nella Musica.[96]	And the experience of the orator teaches us that he speaks now loudly, now softly, and slower and faster, and with that he moves the listeners greatly. What effect would an orator have if he recited a beautiful speech without proper attention to the accents, the pronunciation, and fast and slow motions, and speaking softly and loudly[?]... The same must be true in music.

Cyriacus Schneegass makes a similar point:

Mensurae servanda est aequalitas, ne harmonia deformetur vel perturbetur: Sed tamen pro ratione textus, tardiore tactu interdum uti, maiorem maiestatem & gratiam habet, & cantum mirifice exornat.[97]	The equality of the measure should be preserved, so that the harmony is not deformed and disrupted; but nevertheless, using a slower *tactus* from time to time on account of the words has greater majesty and grace and adorns the song marvelously.

Frescobaldi takes the tempo variability of modern madrigal performance as axiomatic and uses it as a model for the performance of his toccatas.[98]

Time measures music, but music also measures time. Since time cannot exist without change, the patterns of change that constitute a musical composition not only measure time, but also create it, within the context

---

[96] Vicentino, *L'antica musica ridotta alla moderna prattica*, book 4, ch. 42 ("Regola da concertare cantando ogni sorte di compositione"), fol. 89ᵛ (incorrectly numbered 88 in the print).
[97] Cyriacus Schneegass, *Isagoges musicae* (Erfurt: Baumann, 1591), "De canendi elegantia," fol. Giiiᵛ.
[98] Girolamo Frescobaldi, Preface to *Toccate e partite d'intavolatura di cimbalo ... libro primo*, 2nd edn. (Rome: Nicolò Borboni, 1616), no page number.

of that work. The complex, reciprocal relations between musical time and external time cannot be reduced to categorical formulas. Writers of the fifteenth and sixteenth centuries left us with much to contemplate on this topic, but we cannot apply their recommendations to practice without filtering them through the lens of our own critical judgment.

PART II

Practice

8 The songs of Du Fay

Guillaume Du Fay (*c.* 1400–74) was the most prolific composer of surviving secular songs in the second and third quarters of the fifteenth century and by common consensus the greatest composer of his generation. Approximately eighty of his songs are found in extant manuscripts. (The exact number is uncertain, because some songs attributed to him in the sources are of questionable authenticity.) Most of them are French, but a few are Italian and two are Latin. About two-thirds date from the earlier part of his life (from the 1420s to the mid 1430s) and about one-third from the later part. The most important source of his early songs is the manuscript Oxford, Bodleian Library, Canonici Misc. 213 (hereafter Ox),[1] which contains forty-five songs attributed to him. It was copied by a single, exceptionally careful scribe in the Veneto region between *c.* 1428 and *c.* 1436. The songs in that manuscript have long been regarded as the core of Du Fay's early secular output.

Table 8.1 lists all of the French and Italian songs that David Fallows believes can be attributed to Du Fay without doubt, along with one (no. 50, *Bien veignés vous*) that I have retained in spite of Fallows's doubts because it involves interesting mensural issues.[2] They are grouped by mensuration and listed within groups in the order in which they appear in volume VI of Heinrich Besseler's complete edition of Du Fay's works.[3] The Latin songs are excluded, as are two songs in which only one voice is attributed to Du Fay in the sources. Besseler organized the songs first by language, then by poetic-musical form within each language. He subdivided the largest category (French rondeaux) further on the basis of mensuration. Within each group, he placed the songs in what he believed to be the chronological

---

[1] Introduction and facsimile, ed. David Fallows, Late Medieval and Early Renaissance Music in Facsimile 1 (Chicago and London: University of Chicago Press, 1995).
[2] David Fallows, *The Songs of Guillaume Dufay: Critical Commentary to the Revision of Corpus mensurabilis musicae, ser. I, vol. VI,* Musicological Studies and Documents 47 (Neuhausen-Stuttgart: American Institute of Musicology, 1995).
[3] Guillaume Dufay, *Opera omnia*, ed. Heinrich Besseler, 6 vols., Corpus mensurabilis musicae 1 (Rome: American Institute of Musicology, 1951–66); rev. edn. of vol. VI, ed. David Fallows (n.p.: American Institute of Musicology, 2006). The order and classification of the songs is the same in the revised edition of vol. VI as it is in the original edition.

Table 8.1 Mensurations in Du Fay songs[1]

Number and title	Form	Sign[2]	Hamm[3]	Besseler[4]	Boone[5]	Schroeder[6]	Fallows/Gallagher[7]	Compositional tactus[8]
Imperfect *tempus*/perfect prolation								
1 *L'alta belleza tua*	Ballata	–	1	¢			Early	S
4 *La dolce vista*	Ballata	–	2a	¢			Middle[9]	S
13 *J'ay mis mon cuer*	Ballade	–	1	¢	3		Early	S
14 *Je me complains*	Ballade	–	2a	¢	3		Early	S
36 *Je ne suy plus*	Rondeau	–	2a	¢	1		Early	S
37 *Je veuil chanter*	Rondeau	–	1	¢	1		Early	S
38 *Ce jour de l'an*	Rondeau	¢	1	¢	3		Early	S
39 *Ce moys de may*	Rondeau	–	2a	¢	3		Early	S
40 *Belle plaisant*	Rondeau	–	2a	¢	1		Early	S
41 *Pour ce que veoir*	Rondeau	–	1	¢	4		Early	S
42 *J'atendray tant*	Rondeau	–	2a	¢	3		Early	S
43 *Par droit je puis bien*	Rondeau	–	1	¢	4		Early	S
44 *Ma belle dame souveraine*	Rondeau	–	2a	¢	3		Early	S
45 *Helas, ma dame*	Rondeau	–	2a	¢	4		Early	S
Perfect *tempus*/imperfect prolation								
3 *Passato è il tempo*	Ballata	O	1	O-old		[2]	Early	S
5 *Vergene bella*[10]	Canzone	–O𝄵	4	𝄵O𝄵-old		[1 3 1]	Early	B S B
7 *Quel fronte signorille*	Unclear[11]	O	2b	𝄵-old[12]	3		Early	S
8 *Dona gentile*	Rondeau	O	7	O-new		[3]	Late	S
16 *C'est bien raison*	Ballade	–O𝄵	4	𝄵O𝄵-old	5 𝄵 m 𝄵	[1 3 1]	Early	B S B
18 *Ce jour le doibt*	Ballade	–	7	𝄵-old	5 – mixed	1	Early	B
19 *Se la face ay pale*	Ballade	O	7	O-old	6 – O	(3) [2]	Early	S
22 *De ma haulte*	Virelai	O	9	O-new		[3]	Late	S
27 *Adieu ces bons vins*	Rondeau	–	2b	O-old	4 – O	2	Early	(S)/B
28 *Resvelons nous*	Rondeau	–	1	O-old	1 – O	3	Early	(S)/B

32 Je requier	Rondeau	–	1	O-old	6 – mixed	(2) [3][13]	Early	B
33 Pouray je avoir	Rondeau	–	7	O-old	6 – mixed	(2) [3]	Early	B
34 Navré je sui	Rondeau	–	1	O-old	6 – O	2	Early	S/(B)
35 Helas, et quant	Rondeau	–	1	O-old		2	Early	S
47 Belle, vueilliés vostre mercy	Rondeau	ϕ	4	ϕ-old	2 – ϕ	[1]	Early	B
48 Pour l'amour	Rondeau	–	2b	ϕ-old	3 – ϕ	1	Early	B
49 Hé compaignons	Rondeau	–	2b	ϕ-old	4 – ϕ	1	Early	B
51 Je n'ay doubté	Rondeau	–	7	ϕ-old		[2]	Early	B
52 Je donne a tous	Rondeau	–	1	ϕ-old	6 – mixed	2	Early	B
53 Se ma dame je puis veir	Rondeau	–	1	ϕ-old	6 – mixed	2	Early	B
54 Mon cuer me fait	Rondeau	–	1	ϕ-old	3 – ϕ	1	Early	B
57 Je prens congié	Rondeau	–	7	ϕ-old		2	Early	B
58 Estrinés moy	Rondeau	–	2b	ϕ-old	6 – mixed	2	Early	B
59 Bon jour, bon mois	Rondeau	–	2b	ϕ-old	5 – mixed	2	Early	B
60 Or pleust a Dieu	Rondeau	–	7	ϕ-old	6 – mixed	3	Early	(S)/B
61 Craindre vous vueil	Rondeau	O	7	ϕ-new	6 – mixed	3	Early	S
63 Mille bonjours	Rondeau	O	7	ϕ-new		[3]	Middle	(S)/B
64 Puisque celle	Rondeau	–	7	ϕ-new		[3]	Early	(S)/B
65 J'ay grant [dolour]	Rondeau	O	2a	ϕ-new		[3]	Middle	S
66 Entre les plus plaines	Rondeau	O	7	ϕ-new		[3]	Late	S
67 Qu'est devenue leaulté	Rondeau	–	7	O-new		[3]	Late	S
68 Va t'en, mon cuer	Rondeau	–	7	O-new		[3]	Late	S
69 Las, que feray?	Rondeau	O	7	O-new	6 – mixed	2	Early	B
70 Donnés l'assault	Rondeau	O	7	O-new		[3]	Middle	S
71 Mon bien, m'amour	Rondeau	–	7	O-new		[3]	Middle	S
72 En triumphant[14]	Rondeau	–	9	O-new		[3]	Late	S
73 Par le regard	Rondeau	O	7	O-new		[3]	Middle	S
74 Franc cuer gentil	Rondeau	–	9	O-new		[3]	Middle	S
75 Adyeu quitte	Rondeau	–	7	O-new		[3]	Middle	S
85 Seigneur Leon	Rondeau	O	7	ϕ-new		[2]	Middle	B
92 Le serviteur	Rondeau	O	9	O-new			Middle	S

Table 8.1 (cont.)

Number and title	Form	Sign[2]	Hamm[3]	Besseler[4]	Boone[5]	Schroeder[6]	Fallows/ Gallagher[7]	Compositional tactus[8]
Perfect *tempus*/perfect prolation								
30 *Belle, vueillés moy retenir*	Rondeau	⊙	3	⊙-old	2		Early	S
31 *Ma belle dame, je vous pri*	Rondeau	⊙	1	⊙-old	5		Early	S
Imperfect *tempus*/imperfect prolation								
6 *Dona, i ardenti ray*	Unclear[15]	C	2b	₵-old			Early	S
23 *Helas mon dueil*	Virelai	C	9	₵-new			Late	S
26 *Entre vous*	Rondeau	C	1	₵-old	1		Early	S
76 *Adieu m'amour*	Rondeau	₵	8	₵-new			Late	B
77 *Ne je ne dors*	Rondeau	₵₵	8	₵-new			Late	B
80 *La plus mignonne*[16]	Rondeau	C	8a	₵-new			Late	S
81 *Puisque vous estez*	Rondeau	C	8a	₵-new			Late	S
82 *Du tout m'estoie*	Rondeau	₵	9	₵-new			Late	S
83 *Vostre bruit*	Rondeau	₵/C2/C	9	₵-new			Late	S
Multiple consecutive mensurations								
11 *Resvelliés vous*	Ballade	[c]O ₵	1	₵ O-old ₵	2	– [2] –	Early	S S S
15 *Mon chier amy*	Ballade	[c]O ₵	2	₵ O-old ₵	4	– [3] –	Early	S S S
24 *Malheureulx cuer*	Virelai	O ₵	9	O-new ₵			Late	S B
78 *Belle, vueillés moy vengier*	Rondeau	₵/C 3	8	₵-new 3			Late	S pB
79 *Dieu gard la bone*	Rondeau	₵/C2 3	8b	₵-new 3			Late	S B
Multiple simultaneous mensurations								
29 *Je ne puis plus*	Rondeau	[O]+proportions	2b	O-old+ proportions	? -mixed	[1]	Early	B+proportions
46 *Belle, que vous ay je*	Rondeau	O+C+₵	1	O+C+₵			Middle	S
50 *Bien veignés vous*	Rondeau	[O]+₵+proportion	2b	O+₵+proportion	2 – ₵	[1]	Early	S+B
84 *Les douleurs*	Rondeau	O+C	9	Both[17]			Late	S

[1] This table includes all of the songs that David Fallows attributes to Du Fay without doubt in *The Songs of Guillaume Du Fay: Critical Commentary to the Revision of Corpus mensurabilis musicae, ser. 1, vol. VI* ([Neuhausen-Stuttgart]: American Institute of Musicology/Hänssler Verlag, 1995) except for the two with Latin texts (nos. 9 and 10) and two in which only one voice is attributed to Du Fay in the sources (nos. 12 and 86). All of them except no. 92 were judged authentic by Besseler. Besseler also accepts nine songs (nos. 2, 17, 20, 21, 25, 55, 56, 62, and 67) that Fallows regards as doubtful. Fallows questions the authenticity of no. 50, but I have retained it, because it appears in the generally authoritative manuscript Oxford, Canon. Misc. 213 and because it illustrates interesting mensural issues.

[2] This column includes all signs that are found in at least one voice in one or more sources of a song. Internal signs of *sesquialtera*, duple, and triple proportion in individual voices are not shown. When different signs appear in different sources, they are separated by forward slashes. Plus signs indicate different signs in different simultaneous voices. For pieces with more than one mensuration, the mensurations of unsigned sections are shown in brackets.

[3] Hamm's mensural categories that appear in Du Fay's songs are as follows: (1) [c. 1415–23] Semibreve–minim movement in C, O, and ₵; no semiminims. (2) [1423–29] Semibreve–minim movement in O; breve–semibreve movement in ₵. (2a) [c. 1415–29] ₵ with flagged semiminims. (2b) [1423–33] O and ₵ with no semiminims or a few flagged semiminims. (3) [1426–31] ₵ and ɸ with flagged semiminims. (4) [1426–33] ɸ with flagged semiminims. (7) [1433–c. 1455] Perfect *tempus* with colored semiminims and no *fusae*. (8) [1435–c. 1460] O and ɸ (breve-semibreve movement) with colored semiminims and no *fusae*. (8a) [1435–c. 1460] O and ₵ (semibreve–minim movement) with colored semiminims and no *fusae*. (8b) [c. 1454–74] ɸ (semibreve-minim movement) with colored semiminims and no *fusae*. (9) [c. 1454–1474] Use of *fusae*.

[4] Besseler's categories of perfect *tempus* are identified explicitly for the French rondeaux. They may be inferred for other genres on the basis of his principles of transcription. O-older style is in $\frac{3}{4}$ with barlines; ɸ-older style is in $\frac{6}{4}$ or $\frac{6}{4}\frac{3}{4}$ with barlines; O-newer style is in $\frac{3}{4}$ with *Mensurstriche*; ɸ-newer style is in $\frac{6}{4}\frac{3}{4}$ with *Mensurstriche*.

[5] Boone's numbers, which correspond to chronological categories, are from "Du Fay's Early Chansons," 248–64. Boone estimates the following approximate dates for them: (1) "early" [to 1423]; (2) 1423–24; (3) 1425–26; (4) 1426–27; (5) late 1420s; (6) "late Ox style" [early-mid 1430s]. His style categories are summarized ibid., 249–64.

[6] Schroeder classifies Du Fay's early songs in perfect *tempus* in four groups based on whether the number of semibreve dissonances in them is 14 or more, 3–5, 1–2, or 0. My categories in this column are modeled on hers, but I have combined her second and third categories to form the following groups: (1) many semibreve dissonances; (2) few semibreve dissonances; (3) no semibreve dissonances. The distinction between groups (1) and (2) is not always clear-cut. I propose (in brackets) classifying some songs in group (1) if their semibreve dissonances are prominent, even if they are not numerous. For songs that Schroeder did not classify, I have provided categories based on her criteria in brackets. My counts of semibreve dissonances often disagree with hers. These discrepancies lead me to propose different classifications (in brackets) for some pieces.

[7] Fallows groups Du Fay's songs into two large categories: early (before c. 1440) and late (after c. 1450). Sean Gallagher, "Seigneur Leon's Papal Sword: Ferrara, Du Fay, and His Songs of the 1440s," *Tijdschrift van de Koninklijke Vereniging voor Nederlandse Muziekgeschiedenis* 57 (2007), 17–28, provides evidence for

Table 8.1 (cont.)

dating some songs in the 1440s. I have classified them as "Middle." The cut-off points between early and middle, and between middle and late, are not always clear.

[8] The compositional *tactus* proposed for each song is the one that I believe to be the most prominent. The values are perfect or imperfect depending on their quality in the mensuration.

[9] Gallagher, "Seigneur Leon's Papal Sword," 18–20, suggests that this song dates from the 1440s.

[10] This work is more properly classified as a song-motet with Italian text, rather than a song. I have retained it here because Besseler includes it among the songs and because it provides a useful model for the correlation of signs and rhythmic styles.

[11] Besseler classifies the form as a rondeau, but Fallows, *The Songs of Guillaume Dufay*, 42–43, rejects that classification.

[12] Although this piece and no. 61 have identical music except for an added line in no. 61, Besseler transcribed no. 7 with barlines and no. 61 (which he classified explicitly as newer style) with *Mensurstriche*. His inconsistency illustrates the subtlety of the distinction between the styles and the element of subjectivity that may play a role in distinguishing them.

[13] The unique semibreve dissonance in this piece (bar 2) is entirely atypical and must be a scribal error. The D in the contratenor should surely be E, as it is in Fallows's revised edition of Dufay, *Opera omnia*, vol. VI.

[14] Besseler's title, *Je triomphe*, is incorrect. See David Fallows, "Two More Dufay Songs Reconstructed," *Early Music* 3 (1975), 358–60. The correct text appears in Fallows's revised edition of Dufay, *Opera omnia*, vol. VI.

[15] Besseler classifies the form as a rondeau, but Fallows, *The Songs of Guillaume Dufay*, 42–43, rejects that classification.

[16] Besseler's title, *Ma plus mignonne*, is incorrect. See Fallows, *The Songs of Guillaume Dufay*, p. 216. The correct text appears in Fallows's revised edition of Dufay, *Opera omnia*, vol. VI.

[17] The two signs represent a mensuration canon in which the upper voices read the music in both mensurations simultaneously. Besseler mistook them for alternative mensurations. See Fallows, *The Songs of Guillaume Dufay*, 229. The correct version of the music appears in Fallows's revised edition of Dufay, *Opera omnia*, vol. VI.

order of composition. His chronology has been refined by later studies, but its broad outlines are still accepted.

Du Fay composed songs in all of the mensurations that were current in his day. The numbers of songs in each mensuration in Table 8.1 are as follows:

Imperfect *tempus*/perfect prolation	14
Perfect *tempus*/imperfect prolation	41
Perfect *tempus*/perfect prolation	2
Imperfect *tempus*/imperfect prolation	9
Different mensurations in different sections	5
Different mensurations in simultaneous relation	4

Perfect *tempus*/imperfect prolation is the only mensuration that Du Fay used extensively in songs from all periods of his life. All but one of his songs in perfect prolation were probably composed before *c.* 1430,[4] and seven of the nine in imperfect *tempus*/imperfect prolation date from the 1450s and 1460s.

Mensuration signs are rare in the early song manuscripts; they are more common in later sources, but they were never used consistently. The mensurations of the songs are never in doubt, however. They can be determined on the basis of internal notational features when they are not specified by signs. Table 8.1, column 3, shows all of the signs that appear in any source of each song.[5] Many of them are absent in some sources or some voices of the pieces. The songs in Ox, with few exceptions, have signs only when the mensuration or rhythm is unusual in some way. All songs with two or more mensurations in simultaneous relation have signs and/or canonic rubrics to clarify their mensural structures. Songs with different mensurations in successive relation have signs where the mensuration changes, but not at the beginning. Initial signs appear in all of the songs in the uncommon mensurations of imperfect *tempus*/imperfect prolation (C) and perfect *tempus*/perfect prolation (⊙ or ϕ), but in only four of the thirty-seven in imperfect *tempus*/perfect prolation (₵) or perfect *tempus*/imperfect prolation (O). Three of the latter four signs may have been prompted by unusual rhythms. One of the two songs

---

[4] Sean Gallagher, "Seigneur Leon's Papal Sword: Ferrara, Du Fay, and His Songs of the 1440s," *Tijdschrift van de Koninklijke Vereniging voor Nederlandse Muziekgeschiedenis* 57 (2007), 18–20, proposes a date in the 1440s for *La dolce vista*.

[5] See Fallows, *The Songs of Guillaume Dufay*, for details about the signs in all of the sources of every song.

signed ℭ has unique strings of texted semiminims.[6] The two signed O are discussed below.

Du Fay's songs have been the subject of numerous studies, many of which focus on issues of chronology and rhythm. Charles Hamm proposed a chronology for all of Du Fay's works on the basis of notational features, which are of course closely related to rhythm, in 1964.[7] His chronological categories are shown in Table 8.1, column 4. Graeme Boone refined the chronology of the French songs in Ox in his 1987 dissertation.[8] His categories are shown by the numbers in Table 8.1, column 6. David Fallows revised the chronology of the later songs in his 1982 monograph on Du Fay.[9] He argued that most of the late songs probably date from the 1450s and 1460s, not from the late 1430s and 1440s as previously believed, and that Du Fay wrote few secular songs between 1439 and 1450. This theory made it possible for him to distinguish broad categories of "early" and "late" songs. Subsequent research has revised the dates of some of the sources of Du Fay's songs and revealed the need for a "middle" category, corresponding roughly to the decade of the 1440s. Sean Gallagher has identified the pieces that should be assigned to that category on grounds of musical style and current views regarding the dates of the sources.[10] Table 8.1, column 8, shows the chronological categories proposed by Fallows as revised by Gallagher.

Besseler, Boone, and Eunice Schroeder discuss the problematic distinction between *ut iacet* and diminished versions of perfect *tempus*, represented by the signs O and ϕ in Table 8.1. Each of these scholars takes a different approach to the issue, and each of them draws slightly different conclusions. Besseler's and Boone's classifications are shown in Table 8.1, columns 5 and 6. Besseler specifies a distinct category (O or ϕ) for every song in perfect *tempus* in his edition of Du Fay's works.[11] He further subdivides songs in both perfect and imperfect *tempus* into "old" and "new" styles on the basis of chronology. Boone analyzes the rhythmic character of the songs in Ox.[12] He does not

---

[6] No. 12, *La belle se siet*, which is excluded from Table 8.1 because only cantus II is attributed to Du Fay in Ox. See Fallows, *The Songs of Guillaume Dufay*, 61–62.

[7] Charles Hamm, *A Chronology of the Works of Guillaume Dufay Based on a Study of Mensural Practice*, Princeton Studies in Music 1 (Princeton University Press, 1964; repr. New York: Da Capo, 1986).

[8] Graeme M. Boone, "Dufay's Early Chansons: Style and Chronology in the Manuscript Oxford, Bodleian Library, Canonici misc. 213" (Ph.D. diss., Harvard University, 1987).

[9] David Fallows, *Dufay*, rev. edn., Master Musicians (New York: Vintage Books, 1988), 151–64.

[10] Gallagher, "Seigneur Leon's Papal Sword," 17–28.

[11] These categories are labeled explicitly only for the French rondeaux, but they are implied by Besseler's editorial policies for the other songs. See p. 232 below.

[12] Boone, "Dufay's Early Chansons," 156–268.

classify them explicitly, but his descriptions imply general categories of O, Φ, and "mixed" for the ones in perfect *tempus*. Schroeder distinguishes mensural categories on the basis of dissonance treatment.[13] Her four groups, based on the number of semibreve dissonances in a piece, are reduced to three in Table 8.1, column 7, by combining her categories of "1–2 dissonances" and "3–5 dissonances" into a single category.

Boone has also studied the relationship between mensuration and text setting in the French songs of Ox.[14] His general conclusion, which he calls the "text-setting model," is that there is a consistent correlation between mensural *initia* and the positions of syllables in poetic lines. If a line has an even number of syllables (usually eight or ten), all even-numbered syllables beginning with the fourth fall on a mensurally significant *initium*; if it has an odd number of syllables, the same principle applies to all odd-numbered syllables beginning with the first. The *initium* in question is usually the perfect semibreve in imperfect *tempus*/perfect prolation, the perfect breve in perfect *tempus* with perfect or imperfect prolation, and the imperfect breve in imperfect *tempus*/imperfect prolation, but when syllables appear on shorter values than usual, the relevant *initium* may shift temporarily to the next lower level. There are exceptions to these norms, but they are rare enough to demand explanation. These principles, which also apply to some extent to the later songs, are of vital importance to the mensural character of Du Fay's French songs.

Imperfect *tempus*/perfect prolation

Imperfect *tempus*/perfect prolation (C) is the sole mensuration in fourteen of the songs in Table 8.1; it appears in the outer sections of two songs and in simultaneous combination with O and C in one song. The styles of these pieces are more uniform than those of any other mensural category. Nevertheless, Du Fay achieves striking rhythmic variety even with the limited means that he employs in this mensuration.

---

[13] Eunice Schroeder, "Dissonance Placement and Stylistic Change in the Fifteenth Century: Tinctoris's Rules and Dufay's Practice," *The Journal of Musicology* 7 (1989), 366–89. Schroeder discusses the mensural classifications of Du Fay's songs in Robert Davis Reynolds, Jr., "Evolution of Notational Practices in Manuscripts between 1400–1450" (Ph.D. diss., Ohio State University, 1974). Reynolds's analyses add nothing essential to those of Besseler, Boone, and Schroeder, and so I have not included them here.

[14] Graeme M. Boone, *Patterns in Play: A Model for Text Setting in the Early French Songs of Guillaume Dufay* (Lincoln: University of Nebraska Press, 1999).

Example 8.1 Du Fay, *Pour ce que veoir*, bars 1–15. After Oxford, Bodleian Library, Ms. Canon. Misc. 213, fol. 18ᵛ.

The typical features of this mensuration may be observed in *Pour ce que veoir* (Example 8.1). The (perfect) semibreve is always the compositional *tactus*, and the grouping of semibreves is always audible, though occasionally irregular. A performance *tactus* on the perfect semibreve fits the rhythms comfortably. The rhythms are constructed almost entirely from white breves, semibreves, and minims, and black breves and semibreves. Semiminims appear sporadically in about half of the pieces, but their rhythmic role is purely decorative. The tenor notes in the penultimate intervals of cadences almost always last for two or three minims. Those that last for two minims (which may be notated as imperfect semibreves or altered minims) may be decorated with suspensions in the discantus, as in Example 8.1, bars 3 and 14. On rare occasions, phrase ends are marked by cadences in which the penultimate note in the tenor is a minim.

The contrapuntal rhythm establishes the role of the semibreve as the compositional *tactus*. Almost every semibreve-unit contains one or two consonant intervals between the tenor and each of the other voices. In the exceptional cases where there are three consonances in a semibreve-unit, one of the progressions usually involves melodic motion in only one voice. Consonances lasting for a breve are normally limited to beginnings and ends of phrases. There is a mix of long-short and short-long patterns in the semibreve-units with two consonances. Minim dissonances other than suspensions, which appear mostly on the second and third minims of the semibreve-unit, are common.

Surface rhythms on the minim and semiminim levels reinforce the perfect semibreve compositional *tactus*. The rhythms within each semibreve-unit most often consist of three minims or an imperfect semibreve (or altered minim) plus a minim, the latter in either order, in each voice. At least one voice normally has a different pattern from the others, and it is common to find a distinct pattern in each voice. Semiminims are usually limited to pairs on the second or third minim of the semibreve-unit; pairs of semiminims on the semibreve *initium*, which place more emphasis on the minim level of the mensuration, appear in only two of the eighteen pieces in this mensuration (*Je me complains* and *Je ne suy plus*). Syncopated minims are equally rare; they are found (in *Je me complains* and *La dolce vista*) only in cadential ornaments within the semibreve-unit, where they do not threaten the integrity of the semibreve as the governing *tactus*. Rhythms consisting of a dotted minim plus semiminim are found only occasionally, beginning in most cases on the second minim of the semibreve-unit.

Text setting is likewise governed by the perfect semibreve *tactus*. Each *tactus* normally carries a maximum of two syllables except at the beginnings of phrases, where there may be three. Most of the exceptions to this principle occur in the non-courtly songs *La belle se siet* (not in Table 8.1) and *Je ne suy plus*. Since the text settings are largely syllabic except for melismas at ends of phrases, the conformity of the declamation to Boone's text-setting model provides strong reinforcement to the *tactus*.

Two songs with sections in ₵ make extensive use of values shorter than the minim, although their contrapuntal rhythms are the same as those of more typical pieces in that mensuration. The ballades *Resvelliés vous* and *Mon chier amy* include long, melismatic flourishes of minims in duple proportion (equivalent to semiminims), and the former also includes a flourish of minims in triple proportion. These songs are longer, more formal pieces than the others in this mensuration. The fast flourishes add to their rhythmic variety and enhance the dignity of their character.

The grouping of *tactus* in pairs to produce regular imperfect *tempus* in ₵ is accomplished by the placement of breves, hemiola rhythms, and cadences. The great majority of breves and hemiola groups (notated with coloration) appear within the breve-unit of the mensuration, and almost all cadences fall on breve *initia*. Despite the audible clarity of the breve-units, extra semibreve-units not belonging to the initial mensural structure appear occasionally. They are usually placed at strategic points for special rhythmic

Example 8.2 Du Fay, *Ce moys de may*: (a) bars 5–10; (b) bars 15–24. After Oxford, Bodleian Library, Ms. Canon. Misc. 213, fol. 17ᵛ.

effects. In *Par droit je puis bien*, an added semibreve-unit marks the end of the texted portion of the canonic voices. In *L'alta belleza*, the same technique creates a strong subdivision after the first phrase of the B section. The only piece in ₵ in which the pairing of semibreves is seriously irregular is *Je veuil chanter*. In that piece, the tenor and discantus enter a semibreve apart in imitation, and the first cadence, which would normally establish the breve *initium*, falls on a semibreve-max *initium*.

Du Fay gives each of the sixteen songs in this mensuration a unique rhythmic stamp. Examples 8.2 and 8.3 illustrate a few of the ways in which the norms of the mensuration may be manipulated for different effects. In the first texted phrase of the rondeau *Ce moys de may* (Example 8.2a), hemiola patterns generate rhythmic imitation of the opening motive on two different levels: black breve + semibreve and white imperfect semibreve + minim. The second bar of the phrase is one of the very few spots in Du Fay's songs in which hemiola appears simultaneously in all voices, implying momentarily that the hemiola corresponds to the main mensuration of the piece, although the true mensuration has been established in the textless introduction and is immediately restored in the following bars. The regular pairing of semibreves is clear throughout the A section. At the beginning of the B section (Example 8.2b, bars 15–20), the opening rhythmic motive in its faster form is imitated at the interval of the semibreve in all voices, creating syncopated coloration groups that undermine the regularity of the breve-units and enhance the continuity of the phrase. The return of the opening rhythms in the last phrase (Example 8.2b, bars 21–24) rounds off the form.

The rondeau *Par droit je puis bien* (Example 8.3) is one of the most subtle of Du Fay's songs in ₵. It has two discantus voices in canon at the unison, a contratenor (*concordans cum fuga*) that may be sung with the canon to

Example 8.2 (cont.)

[musical notation for Ct and T voices, measures 15–20+, with text: "-e Chan-tons, dan-sons, et me-nons chie-re ly -" and "-e Pour de - spi - ter ces fe - lons en - vi - eux"]

make a three-voice song, and another contratenor (*concordans cum omnibus*) that may be added to the other voices to make a four-voice song. Its special features are a result of its unusual text rhythm and musical texture. If the opening line of the poem, "Par droit je puis bien complaindre et gemir" ("By right I may well complain and moan"), followed the normal principles of French poetry, there would be a *coupe* (a caesura after the fourth syllable of a ten-syllable line) after the word "puis" ("may"). The word "bien" ("well") would then be grouped with, and therefore modify, "complaindre" ("By right I may – well complain and moan"). Du Fay, however, apparently understood the word "bien" to modify "puis" ("By right I may well – complain and moan"), shifting the secondary accent of the line from the fourth to the fifth syllable and effectively overriding the *coupe*. The textual accent on syllable seven (the second syllable of "complaindre") reinforces this rhythmic irregularity, since subtle metric accents normally fall on even-numbered syllables of ten-syllable verses. Rather than abandoning the text-setting model for this line, Du Fay sets "puis" in a regular position on a semibreve *initium* and places a strong tonic and agogic accent on the following minim *initium* to underscore the word "bien." The first syllable of "complaindre" (syllable 6 of the line) likewise falls regularly on a semibreve *initium*, but the textually more prominent second syllable is

230 Practice

Example 8.3 Du Fay, *Par droit je puis bien*: (a) bars 1–8; (b) bars 18–22. After Oxford, Bodleian Library, Ms. Canon. Misc. 213, fols. 18^v–19^r.

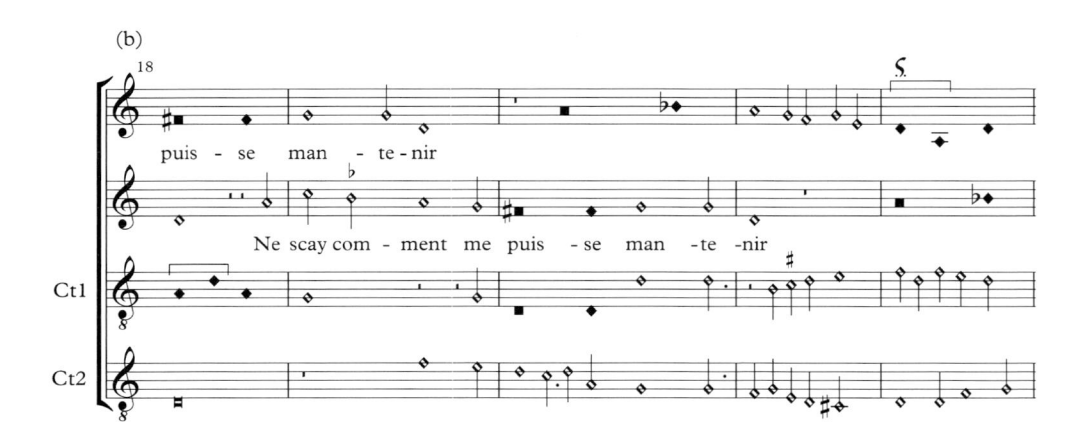

emphasized by an agogic accent. Since the word "droit" ("right') is the most important of the first four words, textual emphases fall on the second minim *initium* of each of the first three semibreve-units, so that the grouping of minim-units implied by the text accents and surface rhythms is 1–3–3–5–6. The interplay of mensural emphasis, which corresponds to the underlying meter of the text, and musical emphasis generated by other means, which brings out the text accents that conflict with the poetic meter, gives this phrase its rhythmic vitality.

The two contratenors counteract the rhythmic irregularities of the discantus voices and establish the semibreve and breve *initia* as a foundation for them. In the opening bar, the contratenor *concordans cum omnibus* brings out the semibreve *initia*, while the contratenor *concordans cum fuga* establishes the breve *initia* by means of hemiola. Yet another level of complication is added when the second canonic voice enters. The two-breve spacing of the canon articulates the long-unit, which is reinforced by the cadences on long *initia* in bars 1–7; thereafter the long disappears from the functional mensural structure. Hemiola rhythms appear frequently, but never in syncopated positions, keeping the listener aware of the breve *initia* throughout the piece.

At the end of the texted portion of the canon (Example 8.3b, bar 20), Du Fay adds a semibreve-unit to the mensural structure to strengthen the formal articulation and separate the coda from the body of the song. Because the breves have been so regular up to that point (counteracting the conflicting rhythms within the breve-unit), this added time unit stands out as an intentional deviation from the established pattern. The choice of where to insert the extra semibreve in the modern edition is of course editorial. Barring mechanically in conformity with the initial mensuration is possible, though it would cause the piece to end in the middle of a breve-unit. Because Du Fay's rhythms are regularly organized in relation to the breve-units before and after bar 20, adding the semibreve-unit in that bar reflects the mensural structure that is built into the rhythmic design of the work.

Perfect *tempus*/imperfect prolation: early songs

Du Fay's songs in perfect *tempus*/imperfect prolation (hereafter "perfect *tempus*") are much more numerous and varied than those in imperfect *tempus*/perfect prolation. Table 8.1 includes forty-one songs in perfect *tempus* throughout, five with one section in perfect *tempus* and other sections in contrasting mensurations (including two in which perfect *tempus* is notated as a proportion), and one in which a section in perfect *tempus* is followed by two sections with simultaneous proportions. Twenty-nine of these forty-seven songs are early and seventeen are late.

The central issue in Du Fay's songs in perfect *tempus* is the distinction between *ut iacet* and diminished forms of the mensuration. For convenience, I shall use the signs O and ₵ to represent those categories, although ₵ does not always imply diminution in the sources of Du Fay's works.[15] Du Fay uses two distinct rhythmic styles in his early works in perfect *tempus*, one associated with *ut iacet* measurement and the other with diminution. The distinction between the styles becomes increasingly blurred over time and eventually disappears. Although most scholars agree that the distinction is significant, they do not agree on exactly how it should be defined or which pieces belong in which category. Given the theoretical definition of diminution as a breve (compositional and/or performance) *tactus*, I shall examine the songs from the point of view of the compositional *tactus*. The performance *tactus* cannot be determined with certainty, but a performance *tactus* that agrees with the compositional *tactus* is likely to bring out the rhythms more effectively than one that does not. Where the compositional *tactus* is ambiguous or changes within a piece, either a breve or a semibreve performance *tactus* may be appropriate.

In his complete edition of Du Fay's works, Besseler classifies Du Fay's songs in perfect *tempus* in four categories: *tempus perfectum* (O) older style, *tempus perfectum diminutum* (₵) older style, *tempus perfectum* newer style, and *tempus perfectum diminutum* newer style.[16] These categories are listed as O-old, ₵-old, O-new, and ₵-new in Table 8.1. Besseler labels them only for the French rondeaux, but his classifications can be inferred for the other songs on the basis of his editorial principles. Songs in older style use barlines (through the staves), and songs in newer style, which have more syncopations across breve *initia*, use *Mensurstriche* (lines between, but not through, the staves). Songs in O are transcribed in $\frac{3}{4}$, and songs in ₵ are transcribed in $\frac{6}{4}$ or $\frac{6}{4}\frac{3}{4}$ ($\frac{6}{4}$ with occasional $\frac{3}{4}$ bars inserted).

Besseler regards the presence of imperfect *modus* (which need not be strictly regular) as the defining feature of ₵.[17] This hypothesis is

---

[15] The meanings of ₵ in Du Fay's works are discussed in DeFord, "The *Mensura* of ₵ in the Works of Du Fay."
[16] Dufay, *Opera omnia*, vol. VI.
[17] Heinrich Besseler, *Bourdon und Fauxbourdon: Studien zum Ursprung der niederländischen Musik*, rev. edn., ed. Peter Gülke (Leipzig: Breitkopf & Härtel, 1974), 120. Besseler does not explain this principle in his edition of Du Fay's works, but occasional remarks in his editorial

problematic, both theoretically and practically. Although Muris defines diminution in relation to combinations of *modus* and *tempus*, most fifteenth-century theorists define it simply as measuring in breves, whether or not the breves come in regular groups. Imperfect *modus* is a common, but not universal, feature of Du Fay's early songs with a breve compositional *tactus*. There is no clear-cut distinction between songs with and without *modus*. Occasional extra breve-units, analogous to extra semibreve-units in ₵, are always possible in imperfect *modus*, but such irregularities are so frequent in some of Du Fay's songs that it is impossible to distinguish songs with irregularities on the *modus* level from songs in which *modus* simply does not exist. Besseler's decision to transcribe some songs in $\frac{6}{4}\frac{3}{4}$, rather than $\frac{3}{4}$, appears at times to be arbitrary.

Boone uses other rhythmic criteria to distinguish between O and Φ in Du Fay's early French songs.[18] His classifications agree significantly, but not perfectly, with Besseler's. Unlike Besseler, he describes numerous songs as "transitional" or "mixed" in mensural character. He associates O with rhythms in which long-short divisions of the breve predominate and Φ with rhythms in which short-long and long-short divisions are mixed. Other features typical of Φ are the rhythmic pattern ♦♦.♪ and florid melismatic passages. There is some logical connection between short-long rhythms and a breve *tactus*. Cadences with a breve *tactus* are most effective when the penultimate note of the tenor lasts for ⅔, rather than ⅓, of the *tactus*, because that rhythm makes the penultimate interval more prominent and enables it to support a suspension. When the rhythms of cadences are predominantly of this type, short-long rhythms are normally prominent within phrases as well, and those rhythms determine the general flavor of the piece. Nevertheless, the contrast between predominantly long-short and short-long rhythms is not always correlated with the distinction between explicitly signed O and Φ in Du Fay's works, and the association of florid melismas with mensural types is not consistent enough to serve as a reliable basis for mensural classification.

Schroeder interprets Φ as mensural diminution with the *tactus* on the *imperfect* breve in the early fifteenth century and as *acceleratio mensurae*

---

prefaces confirm that *modus* was his criterion for distinguishing between O and Φ. In the preface to volume VI, p. ix, for example, he cites the presence of longs at the midpoints of nos. 64 (*Puisque celle*) and 66 (*Entre les plus plaines*) as evidence that Du Fay regarded the breves as paired in those songs and concludes on that basis that their mensuration is Φ. He finds no pairing in the group of songs beginning with no. 67 (*Qu'est devenue leauté*), and therefore concludes that the mensuration in that group is O (pp. ix–x).

[18] Boone, "Dufay's Early Chansons," 156–268.

with a *tactus* on the semibreve in the later fifteenth century.[19] She distinguishes four categories of Du Fay songs in perfect *tempus* on the basis of the number of dissonant semibreves they contain: many (14 or more), few (3–5), very few (1–2), and none. A simplified version of her system in which the second and third categories are merged is shown in Table 8.1. By comparing Du Fay's practice with Tinctoris's rules for dissonance treatment in relation to the *tactus*, Schroeder concludes that the songs with many semibreve dissonances are in ф with an imperfect breve *tactus*, those with no semibreve dissonances are in O, and those with a few semibreve dissonances may be in either ф interpreted as *acceleratio mensurae* or O. She sees a chronological development in this pattern, with the number of semibreve dissonances in ф declining over time as the meaning of the sign ф shifts from mensural diminution to *acceleratio mensurae*, but she finds no hard and fast lines between these categories. As shown in Table 8.1, the pieces with many semibreve dissonances are generally those that all scholars classify as ф, while those with few or none are those that Boone often classifies as transitional or mixed on other grounds.

Schroeder's data are significant, but I would modify her interpretation of them in several ways. First, since the *tactus* of early ф is the perfect breve, not the imperfect breve, as she assumes, the rules of Tinctoris with which it should be compared are those that apply to a *tactus* on a three-part note. Du Fay was more liberal than Tinctoris in allowing dissonances on the *initium* of the *tactus*, but the lengths of his dissonances conform for the most part to Tinctoris's rules. Second, while prominent semibreve dissonances imply a breve *tactus*, their absence does not exclude that *tactus*, because dissonance is always optional. When semibreve dissonances are infrequent or absent, the *tactus* must be judged on the basis of other factors. Third, Besseler's belief that the distinction between O and ф remains meaningful throughout Du Fay's life, which Schroeder takes as a given, is open to serious question. Du Fay did not use cut signs after *c.* 1450,[20] and there is no evidence that he regarded diminished perfect *tempus* as a distinct mensural category after that time. There is no evidence that he ever regarded cut signs as symbols of *acceleratio mensurae*, since he stopped using them before that meaning became common. Stylistic evidence suggests that the distinction between *ut iacet* and diminished forms of perfect *tempus* ceased to be meaningful in his songs by the mid 1430s.

---

[19] Schroeder, "Dissonance Placement and Stylistic Change in the Fifteenth Century."
[20] I thank Alejandro Planchart for this information.

Gallagher discusses Du Fay's rhythmic styles in perfect *tempus* on the basis of chronological developments, rather than distinctions within a single time period.[21] He notes that Du Fay's early songs in perfect *tempus* usually have two stresses in each breve-unit (which may correspond to long-short or short-long rhythms), while the later songs usually have three. Changes in Du Fay's use of dotted minims correlate with this development. Those values are absent in the earliest songs; they appear only in syncopated positions in slightly later songs, and fall on semibreve *initia* only in songs from the mid 1430s on. Dotted minims on a semibreve *initium* emphasize the following semibreve *initium* and suggest a *tactus* on the semibreve.

Several of Du Fay's early songs provide evidence for his understanding of the distinction between *ut iacet* and diminished perfect *tempus*. The ballades *Resvelliés vous* (no. 11) and *Mon chier amy* (no. 15) include contrasting sections explicitly signed ℭ and O, while the canzone *Vergene bella* (no. 5) and the ballade *C'est bien raison* (no. 16) include analogous sections signed Φ and O. Each of these pieces has three sections in the order [ℭ] O ℭ or [Φ] O Φ. They belong to a family of early fifteenth-century works in various genres (mostly song-motets) that feature the distinctive rhythmic style associated with Φ, occasionally notated in half-values in ℭ.[22] Since the functions of ℭ and Φ are analogous in these designs, Φ must imply diminution (a perfect breve *tactus* analogous to the perfect semibreve *tactus* of ℭ) in these cases; by extension, O must imply mensuration *ut iacet*. The signs by themselves do not provide sufficient evidence for a mensural contrast between O and Φ, especially considering that the opening sections of these pieces are unsigned, but the contrast between the rhythmic styles of the middle and outer sections of *Vergene bella* and *C'est bien raison* is clear-cut.

Example 8.4 shows the opening bars of *Vergene bella*. All aspects of the style conform to the norms of a perfect breve *tactus*. There are usually two structural intervals in each breve-unit of the mensuration except at beginnings and ends of phrases, where there may be only one, and in the approaches to cadences, where there may be three. Each breve-unit contains a maximum of two syllables of text except at phrase beginnings, where there may be three. When three syllables fall within a breve-unit, they correspond to only one or two structural intervals. The breves are regularly paired by means of longs and hemiola coloration, which always begin on long *initia*,

---

[21] Gallagher, "Seigneur Leon's Papal Sword," 21–28.
[22] Julie E. Cumming, *The Motet in the Age of Du Fay* (Cambridge University Press, 1999), 99–124, calls motets with this pattern of signs "cut-circle motets." She provides evidence that *Vergene bella* was regarded as a motet despite its Italian text (p. 120) and that Du Fay's ballades with similar mensural plans are closely related to cut-circle motets (pp. 119–22).

Example 8.4 Du Fay, *Vergene bella*, bars 1–21. After Oxford, Bodleian Library, Ms. Canon. Misc. 213, fols. 133ᵛ–134ʳ.

and by cadences, which fall exclusively on long *initia*. The penultimate notes of cadences in the tenor are usually perfect or imperfect breves or altered semibreves. Dissonant semibreves are common and may fall at any point within the breve-unit.

In these respects, ϕ is like ℭ notated in double values, but in other respects the two mensurations are quite different. The range of note values in ϕ is wider than in ℭ and includes everything from longs to pairs of semiminims. Minims are much more prevalent in ϕ than *fusae* in ℭ; long strings of them are often found in melismas. The semibreve has more rhythmic and contrapuntal autonomy in ϕ than the minim in ℭ, and modest numbers of syncopated semibreves are common in ϕ. Surface rhythms feature a mix of long-short and short-long patterns, as in ℭ, but the rhythm ♩♩.♪ is much more common than the equivalent in half-values in ₵. This rhythm is found only in melismas in *Vergene bella* (e.g., in bar 16 of Example 8.4) and *C'est bien raison*, but often carries two syllables in other pieces in ₵.

Five other songs of Du Fay match the style of the outer sections of *Vergene bella* and *C'est bien raison* so closely that there seems to be little doubt that they are likewise in ₵. They are *Ce jour le doibt*; *Belle, vueilliés vostre mercy*; *Pour l'amour de ma doulce amye*; *Hé compaignons*; and *Mon cuer me fait*. All of these songs have numerous semibreve dissonances and other style features similar to those of *Vergene bella*. The pairing of breve-units is regular or disturbed by no more than one unpaired unit except in *Ce jour le doibt*, in which there are enough irregularities to raise doubts about whether imperfect *modus* is intended. It may be for this reason that Boone characterizes *Ce jour le doibt* as mixed, rather than ₵, though in other respects the style is pure ₵.[23] Some of the other pieces in this group take liberties with the pairing of breves by placing occasional longs or hemiola rhythms in syncopated positions with respect to the long *initium* and placing occasional cadences on breve-max *initia*. None of these irregularities casts any doubt on the role of the breve as the compositional *tactus*, which is the defining feature of diminution in contemporaneous music theory.

Another eight early songs resemble the songs of the preceding group in all respects except that the number of dissonant semibreves is significantly reduced and the pairing of breves is often irregular or non-existent. This group includes *Je requier*; *Pouray je avoir*; *Je donne a tous*; *Se ma dame je puis veir*; *Je prens congié*; *Estrinés moy*; *Bon jour, bon mois*; and *Las, que feray*. These pieces are of slightly later date than those in the preceding group. Besseler classifies *Je requier* and *Pouray je avoir* as O, presumably because they have no regular *modus*, and perhaps also because they avoid semibreve dissonances. Boone classifies the ones in Ox as "transitional."[24] Although the reduction in the number of semibreve dissonances may imply a greater autonomy for the semibreve in this group than in the preceding one, the contrapuntal rhythm still points clearly to the perfect breve as the compositional *tactus*. Breve (or altered semibreve) cadential penultimates in the tenor outnumber semibreves by a factor of at least 2:1, and usually much more, in these works.

The middle sections of *Resvelliés vous*, *Mon chier amy*, *Vergene bella* (Example 8.5), and *C'est bien raison*, which are signed O in the sources, differ categorically from the preceding pieces. The range of note values is

---

[23] Boone, "Dufay's Early Chansons," 223–26 and 260.   [24] Ibid., 260–64.

Example 8.5 Du Fay, *Vergene bella*, bars 40–54. After Oxford, Bodleian Library, Ms. Canon. Misc. 213, fols. 133ᵛ–134ʳ.

narrower than in ϕ. Longs are excluded, and hemiola coloration is rare. Pairs of semiminims are also rare, though longer passages of minims in duple, triple, or *sesquialtera* proportion are possible. Breves never come in regular groups. The contrapuntal rhythm is variable, but normally includes some passages in which there are three or more intervals in each breve-unit. The rate of declamation drops occasionally to the level of the minim. Syncopated semibreves are more common than in ϕ. Rhythmic patterns are predominantly long-short, and the pattern ♦♦.♩ is entirely absent. Semibreve dissonances are rare and always take the form of passing tones in stepwise descending motion on the second semibreve of a breve-unit. Dissonances of this type reinforce the long-short feel of the rhythm by subdividing the longer subdivision of the breve-unit. Semibreves normally outnumber perfect or imperfect breves as penultimate notes of the tenor in cadences by a factor of at least 2:1 (Example 8.5 is exceptional in this respect), though semibreve cadential penultimates are rarely reinforced with suspensions.

This style of perfect *tempus* is much less common in Du Fay's early songs than the style associated with ϕ. Apart from the preceding works, the only songs that display it unequivocally are the ballata *Passato è il tempo*, the ballade *Se la face ay pale*, and the rondeau *Helas, et quant vous veray*. The latter two have metrically unusual texts featuring lines with odd numbers of syllables. *Helas, et quant vous veray* is also exceptional in that its declamation does not conform to Boone's text-setting model. The unusual features of the texts may be related to the unusual mensural character of the two French songs in this group.

Some features of this style are found in *Adieu ces bons vins* and *Resvelons nous*. All scholars who have discussed the mensuration of these pieces classify them as O, but a comparison of *Adieu ces bons vins* (which is dated 1426 in Ox) with Du Fay's Gloria *de quaremiaux* (Example 8.6), which dates from about the same time, casts doubt on this classification. The Gloria has a tenor that is stated seven times in explicitly signed mensurations: twice in O, once in Φ, three times in C, and once in ₵. The signs are correlated with clearly contrasting mensural types. The first section in O (Example 8.6a) has declamation on minims (with as many as six syllables on a breve), several syncopated semibreves, and only one semibreve dissonance (a passing tone, not shown in the example, like those in other pieces in O), while the section in Φ (Example 8.6b) has a maximum of two syllables per breve, three semibreve dissonances (including a passing tone in ascending motion, bar 27), and a more fluid rhythm that avoids syncopated semibreves

Example 8.6 Du Fay, Gloria *de quaremiaux*: (a) bars 1–13; (b) bars 27–39. After Bologna, Museo Internazionale e Biblioteca della Musica, Ms. Q15, fols. 169ᵛ–170ʳ. The notation in the source is black with void coloration.

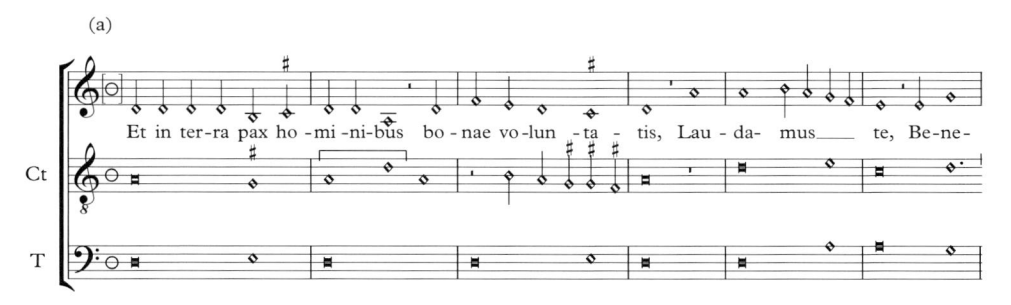

Example 8.6 (cont.)

entirely. The altered semibreve penultimate in the tenor of the final cadence is decorated with a syncopated figure in O, but with a suspension followed by three minims in ¢. A *tactus* on the semibreve in O and the perfect breve in ¢, conforming to the theoretical definition of the signs, is appropriate to the rhythms that Du Fay associates with the signs in this piece. (The original notation in this example is black with void coloration, but the meanings of the notes are the same as those of the examples in void notation with black coloration. The transcription in the example is in void notation, to facilitate comparison with the other examples in the chapter.)

Adieu ces bons vins (Example 8.7) is strikingly similar to the section of the Gloria in ¢. If the *tactus* of ¢ is the perfect breve in the Gloria, *Adieu ces bons vins* should logically have a perfect breve *tactus* as well, in which case its mensuration is ¢, not O. Its rhythmic style is clearly different from that of the songs in ¢ discussed above, but rhythm and *tactus* are not the same thing, and it is possible that a perfect breve *tactus* could accommodate both rhythmic styles. *Resvelons nous* is similar to *Adieu ces bons vins*, but lacks semibreve dissonances.

The four remaining early songs in perfect *tempus* mix features of ¢ and O to a greater extent than any of the ones discussed previously. *Navré je sui* has rhythms that resemble those of ¢, but both of its sections begin with imitation in all three voices at the interval of the semibreve – a technique

Example 8.7 Du Fay, *Adieu ces bons vins*, bars 1–13. After Oxford, Bodleian Library, Ms. Canon. Misc. 213, fol. 140ʳ.

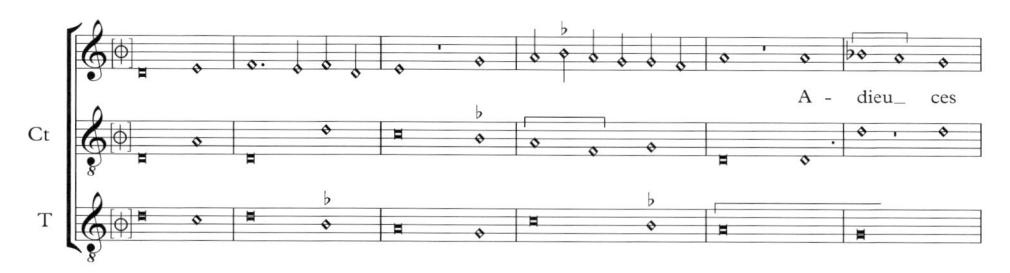

Example 8.8 Du Fay, *Navré je sui*, bars 1–5. After Oxford, Bodleian Library, Ms. Canon. Misc. 213, fol. 78ᵛ.

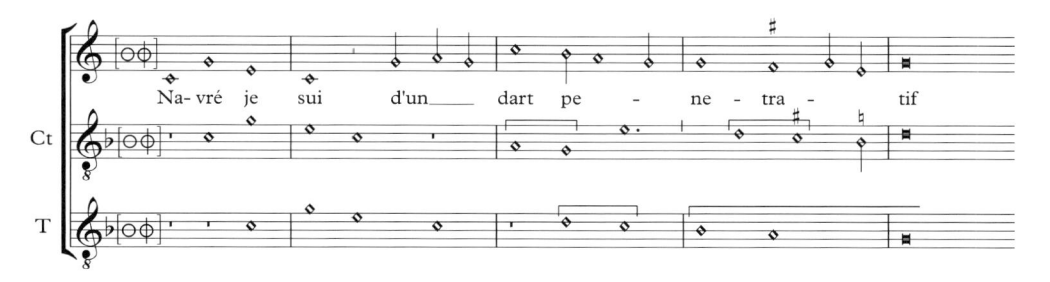

found nowhere else in Du Fay's songs. The first of these passages is shown in Example 8.8. The imitation places strong emphasis on the semibreve, counteracting the predominant short-long feel of the rhythm. The last texted phrase contrasts with the preceding phrases in its long-short declamation, which switches back to short-long only at the cadence. All scholars classify the piece as O. A semibreve performance *tactus* may be necessary to bring out the effect of the imitation at the semibreve interval, but the rhythms on the breve level are also strong, and a breve performance *tactus* is not out of the question.

Example 8.9 Du Fay, *Or pleust a Dieu*: (a) bars 1–6; (b) bars 29–35. After Oxford, Bodleian Library, Ms. Canon. Misc. 213, fol. 71ᵛ.

Or pleust a Dieu (Example 8.9) is in the conventional ϕ style until the melismatic final phrase (Example 8.9b), which features such intense semibreve syncopations that it would be difficult to perform with any *tactus* other than the semibreve. There is even a cadence on a semibreve-max *initium*, unique among Du Fay's early songs, in bar 30. Nevertheless, a breve performance *tactus* creates an exhilarating effect in the final phrase that a semibreve performance *tactus* fails to capture even if the notes move at the same speed with either *tactus*.

Quel fronte signorille and *Craindre vous vueil*, which share the same music with an added phrase at the end of the latter, display some features of ϕ, but their compositional *tactus* is the semibreve and their contrapuntal rhythms move in minims at some points. Their surface rhythms are quite complex; they include numerous syncopated semibreves and a group of four consecutive semiminims. *Craindre vous vueil* was the last song of Du Fay to be copied into Ox and is believed to be the latest song of the "early" group on grounds of both stylistic and codicological evidence.[25] Its features become common in Du Fay's later songs.

A surprising result of this investigation is that clear-cut examples of O are rare and generally associated with special functions in Du Fay's early songs. They appear in four works with sections in contrasting mensurations (three French ballades and one Italian canzone), one other Italian song (*Passato è il tempo*), and two French songs with texts in unusual poetic meters (*Se la face ay pale* and *Helas, et quant vous veray*). The standard French text-setting model, which calls for no more than two syllables per breve except at phrase beginnings, may have suggested a contrapuntal rhythm that moves predominantly at the rate of two intervals per breve, implying a *tactus* on the perfect breve, in these songs. The two songs that are signed O in Ox (*Passato è il tempo* and *Quel fronte signorille*) are the only ones in perfect *tempus*, apart from pieces with sections in contrasting mensurations, that have mensuration signs in that source. They belong to the small group of songs in perfect *tempus* with a semibreve compositional (and presumably performance) *tactus*. Since mensuration signs often signal unusual mensurations in Ox, the presence of those signs might suggest that perfect *tempus* in Du Fay's early songs was normally presumed to be performed in diminution in the absence of indications to the contrary. That pattern is not entirely consistent, but it is suggestive nevertheless.

The mixing of features associated with a breve and semibreve compositional *tactus* in the later songs of this "early" group implies a gradual breakdown of the distinction between *ut iacet* and diminished perfect *tempus* from a compositional point of view. Performers, however, must choose one *tactus* or the other for any given realization of a piece. In such cases, the distinction between *ut iacet* mensuration and diminution becomes a matter of performance practice, rather than composition. It may be impossible to say whether a song itself is in O or Ø, but it is possible to say that a given performance uses a breve or a semibreve *tactus*. We cannot know how performers made these decisions or whether composers had a single performance *tactus* in mind for a given piece, but the choice of performance *tactus* affects the experience of the rhythm and should be considered carefully by modern musicians who sing the music.

The question of the difference of tempo, if any, between diminished and *ut iacet* perfect *tempus* has no categorical answer. When the two types of mensuration are juxtaposed in the same piece, as in *Vergene bella*, the

---

[25] Fallows, *The Songs of Guillaume Dufay*, 45. Fallows explains that *Quel fronte signorille* must be the earlier version and *Craindre vous vueil* a contrafactum.

stylistic contrast between them implies that the written notes should move somewhat faster in ⌽ than in O, but since the range of values is the same in both forms of the mensuration, the difference between them cannot have been as great as 2:1.[26] Since the songs without internal changes of mensuration cannot be divided into fixed stylistic categories, it is unlikely that they were associated with fixed categories of tempo. Judgments about the tempos of individual pieces must be based on internal stylistic evidence, since we have no other sources of information that are specific enough to provide useful guidelines on this issue.

Perfect *tempus*/perfect prolation

Du Fay wrote only two songs in perfect *tempus* with perfect prolation: *Belle, vueillés moy retenir* and *Ma belle dame, je vous pri*. Both are early works found only in Ox. The former is signed ⌽ and the latter ⊙. In both cases, the signs are found only in the top voices. The reason for the distinction between the signs is unclear. *Ma belle dame* has minims in all voices, while *Belle, vueillés* has them only in the top voice. ⊙ applies to all voices in *Ma belle dame*, but ⌽ may apply only to the top voice, with the other voices understood as O, in *Belle, vueillés*. If this is the case, the stroke through the sign may mean that the perfect semibreves of the top voice are equivalent to the imperfect semibreves of the lower voices.[27] Since the sign ⌽ is very rare and appears nowhere else in Du Fay's works, the meaning of the stroke in this context cannot be determined with certainty.

Perfect prolation functions differently in these songs than it does in the songs in ₵. The contrapuntal rhythm progresses in (perfect) semibreves and (perfect or imperfect) breves, and there are never more than two structural

---

[26] Alejandro Enrique Planchart, "The Relative Speed of *Tempora* in the Period of Dufay," *Royal Musical Association Research Chronicle* 17 (1981), 36–38, postulates a 3:2 relation between the mensurations in *Vergene bella*, but the only evidence for this proportion is the considerably later theory of Anonymous 12, whose statement on the subject may be interpreted as an approximation in any case.

[27] Planchart, "The Relative Speed of *Tempora*," 38, suggests this interpretation of the stroke in the sign ⌽. He assumes that the other voices are implicitly signed O and uses the resulting 3:2 relationship of minims between the two signs as evidence for interpreting the tempo relation between ⌽ and O as 3:2. Since simultaneous and successive mensurations are routinely subject to different principles, however, I do not find this argument convincing. A 3:2 relation between the sections of *Vergene bella* is aesthetically pleasing and may have been intended, but contemporaneous theory does not provide sufficient evidence to establish an exact proportion between cut and uncut signs in successive relations.

Example 8.10 Du Fay, *Ma belle dame*, bars 1–8. After Oxford, Bodleian Library, Ms. Canon. Misc. 213, fol. 139ᵛ.

intervals on a breve except in the approaches to important cadences. Minims serve only a decorative function, analogous to that of *sesquialtera* passages in O, from a contrapuntal point of view. Subdivisions of the breve are predominantly long-short, and tenor cadential penultimates are invariably semibreves. If the semibreves were imperfect, *Ma belle dame* (Example 8.10) and *Belle, vueillés* would be very similar to *Adieu ces bons vins*. Nevertheless, the ternary division of the semibreves places greater emphasis on the semibreve level and makes a semibreve performance *tactus* more likely in these songs than in *Adieu ces bons vins*. The fact that Du Fay wrote passages of minim *sesquialtera* (which have the same mensural structure as perfect prolation) in songs in O, but not in ⊘, supports this interpretation. On the other hand, he placed nine notes on the *tactus* in a passage of triple proportion in ₵ in *Resvelliés vous*, and so he cannot have regarded that many notes on a *tactus* as impossible.

Perfect *tempus*/imperfect prolation: middle and late songs

Du Fay's middle and late songs in perfect *tempus* differ strikingly from his early songs in that mensuration. Rhythmic intricacies on the semibreve level are much more common, and the grouping of breves is correspondingly less significant. The breve-unit remains crucial to the mensural structure, but it may be temporarily obscured or suspended by complex rhythms on the semibreve level. It is more prominent in some songs than in others, but the semibreve always functions as the compositional *tactus* in at least some passages, and often throughout entire songs. Besseler maintained the classifications of O and ⊘ for this repertoire, assigning songs to the latter category when they had longs at the beginning or midpoint, but this distinction does not correlate consistently with other aspects of rhythm and seems to me to be arbitrary. Although Du Fay draws rhythmic features from his earlier works in both O and Φ in these songs, the ways in which he combines them are too varied to support a classification into two distinct types. Since all of the songs evidently require a semibreve performance *tactus* to manage their complexities on the semibreve level, it seems reasonable to classify them uniformly as O.

Several features contribute to the increased mensural articulation of semibreves in these songs. The contrapuntal rhythms include at least some passages in which structural intervals appear on consecutive minims, though passages with two intervals per breve are also common. Semibreve dissonances are excluded entirely, even in the passages with slow contrapuntal rhythms. There is much more syncopation on the semibreve level than in the early songs. Syncopated semibreves often cross breve *initia*, prompting Besseler to use *Mensurstriche*, rather than barlines through the staff, in his transcriptions. Dotted minim-semiminim rhythms often replace semibreves in syncopated positions, adding further complexity to the syncopation on that level. Semibreves that function as cadential penultimates in the tenor may be brought out with suspensions, and the resolutions of those suspensions may be ornamented, emphasizing the semibreve level still further.

The mensural autonomy of the semibreve level leads to correspondingly greater autonomy for values smaller than the semibreve. Semiminims are not limited to pairs on weak minim-units, but appear in pairs or groups of four beginning on semibreve *initia*. Three songs (*De ma haulte et bonne aventure*, *Malheureulx cuer*, and *En triumphant*) have pairs of *fusae* that function rhythmically like semiminims in the early songs, and one (*Franc cuer gentil*) has dotted semiminim-*fusa* rhythms. Syncopations appear not only on the semibreve level, but also on the minim level in *De ma haulte et bonne aventure*; *Malheureulx cuer*; *Mon bien, m'amour*; and *En triumphant*, and the minim even functions as the penultimate sonority of a cadence – complete with suspension! – in *En triumphant*.

These small-scale rhythmic intricacies do not undermine the role of the breve in the mensural structure. The principal aspects of the music that articulate the breve level are cadences, imitation, and declamation. The great majority of cadences fall on breve *initia*, though cadences on semibreve-max *initia* appear occasionally. The usual interval of imitation between voices (where it exists) is the breve. Text setting is based for the most part on the older text-setting model in which metrically stressed syllables coincide with breve *initia* and there are no more than two syllables per breve

Example 8.11 Du Fay, *En triumphant*: (a) bars 1–5; (b) bars 16–27. After Porto, Biblioteca Pública Municipal, Ms. 714, fols. 76^v–77^r. The notation in the source is black with red coloration.

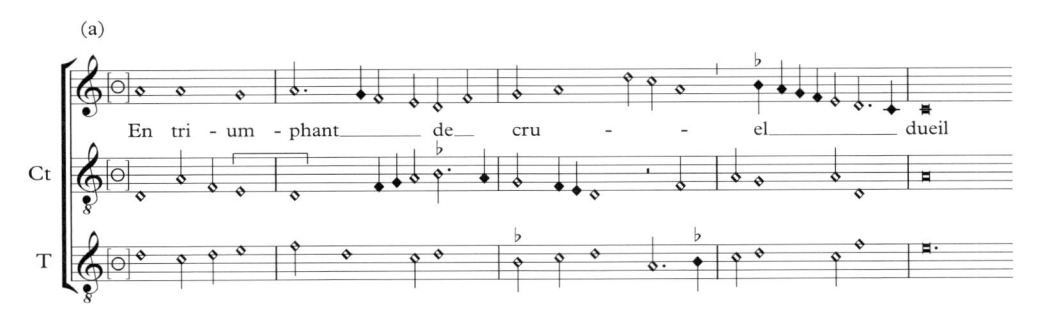

except at phrase beginnings, though rhythmic complications sometimes necessitate exceptions to this pattern.

Du Fay makes use of the full range of rhythmic techniques from both early and late styles in his late songs in perfect *tempus*. The widest range of styles in a single song is found in *En triumphant* (Example 8.11). In all phrases except the fourth, the rhythms are quite syncopated and the text setting is melismatic. It is difficult to be sure where the syllables belong, but Du Fay seems to have taken some liberties with the text-setting model. The mensural autonomy of the semibreves may allow them to function as significant *initia* in a piece like this even if minims do not carry separate syllables. The last phrase of the song (Example 8.11b, bars 23–27) articulates semibreves in extreme ways: contrapuntal progressions on minims, and even semiminims (bar 24, third semibreve-unit); pairs of *fusae*; a cadence on the third semibreve of the breve-unit (bar 23); syncopated minims; and a minim cadential penultimate decorated with a suspension (bar 23). The rhythms of bars 22–25 obscure the breve-unit entirely, and no one would be likely to notice if Du Fay had violated the rules of this mensuration by ending the piece in a place other than a breve *initium*. By contrast, the fourth phrase (Example 8.11b, bars 16–20) would be at home in one of Du Fay's earliest songs in 𝇋. It has only two structural intervals per breve and includes a hemiola rhythm, patterns of ♦ ♦ . ♪, an altered semibreve cadential penultimate, and no syncopation of any kind. The song demonstrates Du Fay's extraordinary ability to integrate drastically diverse rhythmic materials within a tiny song and make them fit together convincingly. The secret of his success is his ability to manipulate rhythms simultaneously on many levels of mensuration without sacrificing any level to the demands of another.

Example 8.11 (cont.)

(b) [musical notation with text: "Et ne sa - roie mon mal de - scri - pre Ne di - re ce dont je me dueil."]

Perfect tempus signed 3

Two of Du Fay's late songs (*Belle, vueillés moy vengier* and *Dieu garde la bone*) include sections in perfect *tempus* that are signed 3. Theorists define that sign as either triple or *sesquialtera* proportion. In either case it calls for a perfect breve *tactus*. It is unclear whether or not the sign represents an exact tempo proportion, as well as a breve *tactus*, in Du Fay's songs. If it does, the proportion should surely be *sesquialtera*, rather than triple, since the latter would be inordinately fast.

The rhythms of these proportions have some affinity with that of Du Fay's early ₵ (even to the point of including some semibreve suspensions), but they are considerably more complex. Despite Besseler's editorial barring, there is no regular pairing of breves. Hemiola rhythms include not only

Example 8.12 Du Fay, *Belle, vueillés moy vengier*, bars 40–52. After Florence, Biblioteca Nazionale Centrale, Ms. Mag. XIX.176, fols. 38^v–40^r.

black longs, breves, and pairs of semibreves, but the equivalents of black breves subdivided into dotted rhythms that are notated as dotted white semibreves plus minims. Rhythmic units consisting of groups of two semibreves may last for several breves, creating extended conflicts between duple and triple groups of semibreves. Hemiola and syncopation work together to the point that they become indistinguishable in these passages. The concluding line of *Belle, vueillés moy vengier* (Example 8.12) illustrates this point. The rhythms increase in complexity throughout the passage, providing a powerful drive to the cadence without any increase in the surface rate of motion. Although these rhythms are challenging to perform with a perfect breve *tactus*, the notation calls for that interpretation, and the tension between the *tactus* and the rhythms is essential to the effect. If performers were to take the easy way out and measure the passage in semibreves, they would rob the music of much of its excitement.

Imperfect *tempus*/imperfect prolation

Table 8.1 includes nine songs in imperfect *tempus*/imperfect prolation (hereafter "imperfect *tempus*") throughout and three in which imperfect *tempus* is found in one section only. Two of them are early and ten are late. The preponderance of late songs in this mensuration reflects a general increase in importance of imperfect *tempus* in the second half of the fifteenth century.

Imperfect *tempus* theoretically allows for a distinction between mensuration with and without diminution, just as perfect *tempus* does, but Besseler did not address the issue systematically in relation to imperfect *tempus*. He chose modern time signatures of $\frac{2}{2}, \frac{4}{4}, \frac{4}{4}$ ($\frac{8}{8}$), and even $\frac{2}{4} \frac{4}{4}$ ($\frac{4}{8}$) for these songs, depending on how he felt the rhythms. The signs in the sources are of little help in distinguishing between diminished and undiminished forms of imperfect *tempus*. Both of the early songs are signed C in Ox. About half of the late ones are signed C and half ₵ in the sources, but there is no consistent correlation between signs and musical styles, and the cut signs undoubtedly stem from the scribes, not the composer. Both signs appear in different sources of two songs, and C2 appears as an alternative for ₵ in one source of one song.

The two early songs in C (*Dona, i ardenti ray* and *Entre vous*) resemble Du Fay's early songs in O except that the semibreves are in groups of two, rather than three. Both of them appear to call for a performance *tactus* on the semibreve. Note values are limited to breves, semibreves, and minims, with the exception of a single dotted minim + semiminim pair. The contrapuntal rhythm moves mostly in semibreves with occasional breves. Dissonances are limited to minims, and minims occasionally carry separate syllables of text. Both breves and semibreves may be syncopated. Syncopations cross breve *initia* occasionally, but not often. Cadences always end on breve *initia*. The penultimate notes of cadences in the tenor are usually semibreves, but suspensions never appear over semibreves. A few cadential penultimates are breves, which may carry suspensions with ornamented resolutions, so that the dissonance does not exceed a minim, and a few are minims.

Du Fay's late songs in imperfect *tempus* parallel his late songs in perfect *tempus* in many ways, though the semibreve never has quite the same degree of autonomy in imperfect *tempus* that it sometimes achieves in perfect *tempus*. The range of note values is much greater than in the early songs in C, including everything from the long to the semiminim, and syncopations across breve *initia* are common. None of these songs has regular *modus* throughout despite Besseler's barring of them in longs. The relative degree of emphasis on the breve and semibreve levels varies, and there is no clear-cut distinction between songs with a breve compositional *tactus* and songs with a semibreve compositional *tactus*. Besseler arranged the eight rondeaux (nos. 76–83) in an order corresponding to increasing emphasis on the semibreve level. Although there are no sharp distinctions in mensural character among these songs, I have suggested a breve compositional *tactus* for *Adieu m'amour*, *Ne je ne dors*, and *Malheureulx cuer* and a semibreve compositional *tactus* for the other songs in Table 8.1 on the basis of the different relative weights of the breve and semibreve units in the two groups. The ideal performance *tactus* for all of them is the divided breve, which allows for a range of subdivision to bring out different levels of rhythmic articulation on the semibreve level. A semibreve performance *tactus* is also possible for the songs in which the semibreve functions as the principal compositional *tactus*. As in the case of songs in perfect *tempus*, the absence of categorical distinctions among songs with diminished and *ut iacet* mensuration implies that the tempos of these pieces must be judged on the basis of their styles and cannot be determined by formulas.

In the three songs for which I suggest a breve compositional *tactus*, the contrapuntal rhythm moves mostly in semibreves with occasional breves, and strong progressions on minims are rare or non-existent. Cadences always conclude on breve *initia*. Cadential penultimates in the tenor are more often breves than semibreves, and suspensions may be as long as semibreves. Notes shorter than semibreves never carry separate syllables, and the text setting conforms for the most part to the text-setting model. The sense of motion in breves gives these pieces an exceptionally flexible and fluid character, because the principal pulse is also the largest regular unit of temporal organization.

Du Fay uses this feature to particular advantage in *Adieu m'amour* (Example 8.13). The breve-units are clear and regular throughout the A section (bars 1–15), though their grouping is free and unpredictable. At the

Example 8.13 Du Fay, *Adieu m'amour*: (a) bars 1–11; (b) bars 33–42; (c) hypothetical recomposition of bars 33–42 (cantus and tenor). After Porto, Biblioteca Pública Municipal, Ms. 714, fols. 70ᵛ–72ʳ. The notation in the source is black with red coloration.

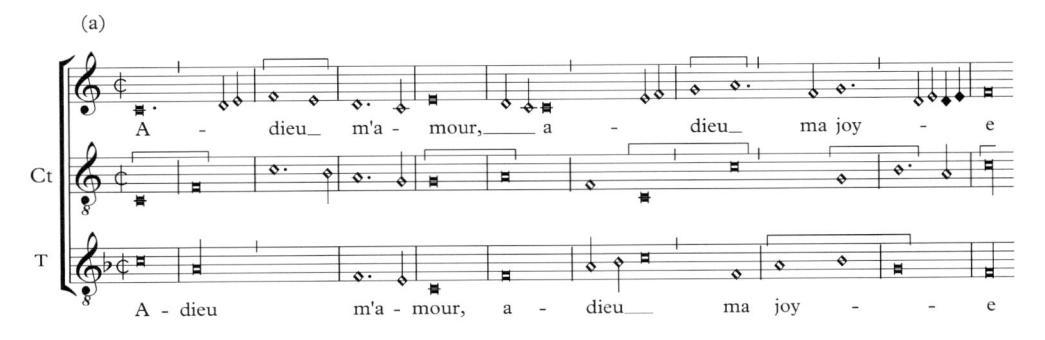

Example 8.13 (cont.)

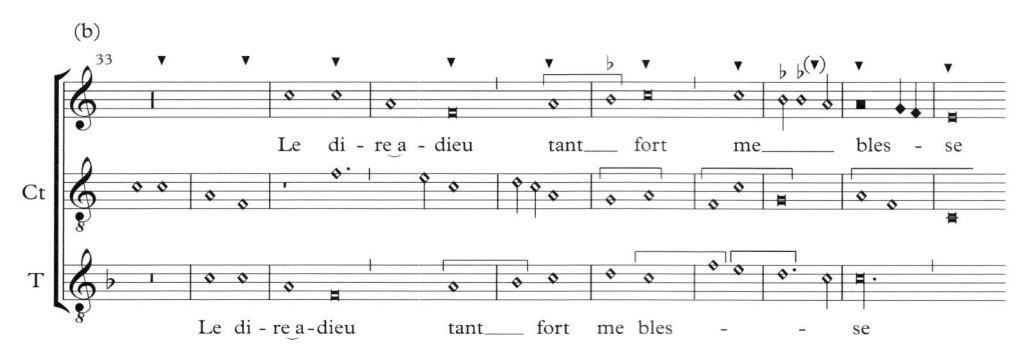

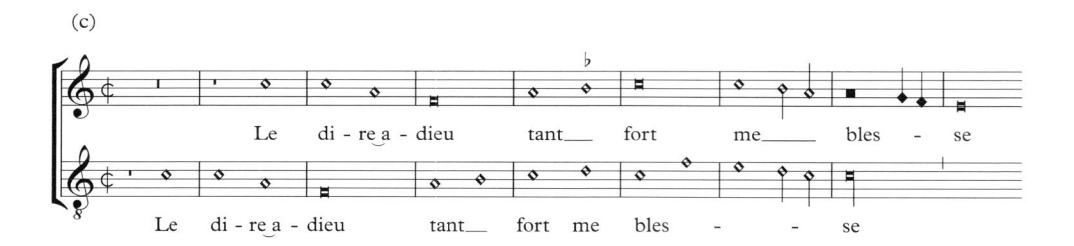

beginning of the B section (Example 8.13b), Du Fay shifts the music wholesale by a semibreve with respect to the breve *initium*, so that the rhythms sound quite regular. The listener is unlikely to be aware of the mensural displacement. Agogic accents and even-numbered syllables of text fall at places that sound like breve *initia* (marked with wedges in the example), but at the end of the phrase, on the word "blesse" ("wounds"), the rhythms are suddenly and forcibly realigned with the real breve *initium*. Rather than creating a resolution of tension, as such cadential realignments normally do, this device "wounds" the rhythm just as "saying farewell" wounds the singers of the song. At the same time, the melody of the discantus collapses and fails to complete the cadence with the tenor. It is unclear exactly where the first syllable of "blesse" should fall, but I have placed it on the unexpected breve *initium*, where it reinforces the rhythmic contortion most effectively. Example 8.13c shows a revised (and very bland) version of the discantus and tenor that conforms to the rhythmic and contrapuntal implications of the phrase. Comparing it to what Du Fay wrote illustrates the extent of his departure from standard rhythmic norms at this point. A breve performance *tactus* not only enhances the flowing quality of the song, but drives home the tension in this phrase, because the singers must struggle to make the rhythms work against the *tactus* even at the beginning of the phrase, and this struggle prepares the wrenching resolution at the end.

The special rhythmic effects in the songs in imperfect *tempus* for which I have suggested a semibreve compositional *tactus* are similar to those in the late songs in perfect *tempus* with a semibreve *tactus*, but the breve level is somewhat stronger and the semibreve level somewhat weaker in imperfect *tempus* than in perfect *tempus*. The contrapuntal rhythm progresses mostly in semibreves with occasional breves and moves to the level of the minim infrequently. Many songs include breve cadential penultimates with semibreve suspensions even when their small-scale rhythms are quite intricate. Cadences in places other than breve *initia* are rare, and there is only one syncopated minim and one pair of *fusae* in this entire set of songs. These differences may relate to the common practice of performing pieces in imperfect *tempus* with a divided breve *tactus*, rather than a semibreve *tactus*, even when the compositional *tactus* was clearly the semibreve. They may also reflect inherent differences between duple and triple mensural groupings; since groups of two semibreves are shorter than groups of three semibreves, imperfect *tempus* may lend itself more easily to a style in which the level of the *tactus* is flexible or ambiguous.

Simultaneous contrasting mensurations

Du Fay wrote four songs in simultaneous contrasting mensurations: two early (*Je ne puis plus* and *Bien veignés vous*), one middle (*Belle, que vous ay je*) and one late (*Les douleurs*).[28] In *Je ne puis plus*, the contrast affects only the level of *modus*, but in the other three, it affects mensural groupings on lower levels. These pieces raise questions about how mensural groupings that conflict notationally are to be interpreted in performance. Are the songs supposed to sound polymetric, or are the multiple mensurations simply a notational device that does not affect the sound of the rhythms? This question must be addressed separately in each instance and does not always have an unambiguous answer.

Bien veignés vous (Example 8.14) features a mensuration canon between the discantus and the tenor. Both voices are in unsigned perfect *tempus*,

---

[28] For insightful comments on the first three of these, see Ursula Günther, "Polymetric *rondeaux* from Machaut to Dufay: Some Style-Analytical Observations," in *Studies in Musical Sources and Styles: Essays in Honor of Jan LaRue*, ed. Eugene K. Wolf and Edward H. Roesner (Madison, WI: A-R Editions, 1990), 103–08.

Example 8.14 Du Fay, *Bien veignés vous*, bars 1–5. After Oxford, Bodleian Library, Ms. Canon. Misc. 213, fol. 34ᵛ.

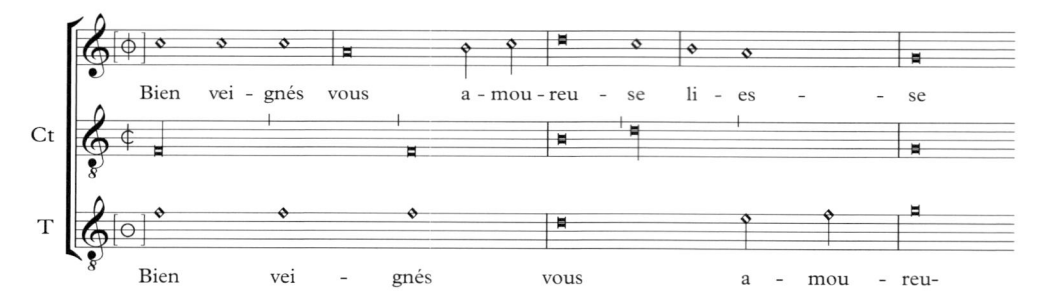

with the discantus in duple proportion to the tenor. The music of the two parts is written only once; a verbal canon instructs the tenor to derive his part from the discantus by singing the part *ut iacet* at the lower fifth. This implies that the reader of the notation would be expected to recognize the style of the discantus as ϕ, rather than O, since the *ut iacet* interpretation, not the proportion, is specified by the canon. If the tenor sings *ut iacet* (i.e., with a semibreve *tactus*), however, the discantus must sing with an *imperfect* breve *tactus*, rather than a perfect breve *tactus*, in order to make the proportion work. Although the rhythm of the contratenor is similar to that of the tenor, that voice is written in ¢ with implied perfect *modus*, rather than O, perhaps to clarify the fact that both the contratenor and the discantus must have an imperfect breve performance *tactus*.[29] The canonic melody has a strong ternary character that is clearly audible in both the discantus and the tenor. The lower voices provide a continuous hemiola against the pairs of perfect breves in the discantus, but the effect is different from that of ordinary hemiolas because the *tactus* conforms to the slower ternary groups, rather than to the faster ones. The contrapuntal rhythm of the song is governed by the tenor, and dissonances corresponding to semibreves of the discantus are numerous. Fallows questions the attribution of the song to Du Fay on grounds that the dissonances are not typical of Du Fay's style.[30] It may be, however, that Du Fay regarded the *ut iacet* mensuration of the tenor as the principal mensuration and therefore felt that the semibreves of the discantus (corresponding to minims of the tenor) could be treated more freely than they would be if the mensuration of the discantus were the principal one.

[29] Besseler bars the contratenor in imperfect longs on the assumption that ¢ implies imperfect *modus*, but the sign does not imply anything one way or the other about *modus*, and the rhythmic groupings clearly imply perfect *modus* (matching the perfect *tempus* of the tenor) in this case.

[30] Fallows, *The Songs of Guillaume Dufay*, 148.

Example 8.15 Du Fay, *Les douleurs*, bars 1–12. After Dijon, Bibliothèque Publique, Ms. 517, fols. 130ᵛ–131ʳ (new fols. 133ᵛ–134ʳ).

Belle, que vous ay je has a tenor in ₵, a discantus in O, and a contratenor in C. The only feasible *tactus* is the imperfect semibreve, divided distinctly enough to allow the singers of ₵ to count ternary groups of minims against it. A *tactus* on the minim (the common measure of all of the mensurations) is technically possible, but it would make the rhythmic groupings difficult to feel and conflict with the *sesquialtera* rhythms that appear later in the song. The placement of cadences is governed by the breves of O and ₵ and sometimes conflicts with the breves of C. It is unclear whether Du Fay expected the mensurations to conflict audibly, or whether the grouping of minims in ₵ and semibreves in C should sound like those in O despite the notated mensurations.

Les douleurs (Example 8.15) is a late song with a mensuration canon between the upper two voices, one of which is read in O and the other in C.[31] Since all but one of the breves of O are imperfected, the rhythms of the two voices are nearly identical except in the breve rests, which are perfect in O

---

[31] Besseler misinterpreted the two mensurations in the discantus to mean that the piece could be performed in either perfect or imperfect *tempus* and transcribed both versions in his edition. The correct interpretation with the mensuration canon is found in Fallows's revised edition.

and imperfect in C. The rest in the opening bar creates a spacing of a perfect breve between the canonic voices; the last note of the first phrase and the rests following it expand the spacing to two perfect breves. There are two *concordans* voices, one notated in O and the other in C. The compositional and performance *tactus* must be the semibreve. The contrapuntal rhythm moves smoothly in semibreves throughout the piece, with only occasional, weak progressions in minims, giving the piece a calm, even flow quite different from many of Du Fay's other songs. The two mensurations are united on the level of *modus*: all cadences fall on the *initia* of groups of six semibreves, which correspond to imperfect longs of O and perfect longs of C.

Continuous hemiola relations create a gentle ebb and flow within the slow-moving long-units. They are created not only by the conflicting mensurations, but also by the rhythmic patterns in both mensurations. In the first long-unit, for example, both of the canonic voices sound like perfect *tempus*, because both have the same rhythm despite the differences in their notation. Agogic, tonic, and textual accents on the fourth note make it sound like a mensural *initium* even though it is not notated as such in cantus I. Both contratenors produce hemiola against this rhythm, because the one that is notated in O begins with coloration. In the second and third long-units, the text placement (which cannot be determined unambiguously from the source) will determine whether the canonic voices are heard in groups of two or three semibreves. The word "sens" is the sixth syllable of the line, and its placement therefore marks a point that will be heard as a mensural *initium* because of the familiarity of the standard text-setting model. If that word falls on the semibreve high F, the semibreves will be grouped in pairs, but if it falls one note later, the declamation will follow the characteristic short-long pattern of perfect *tempus*. There are no objective criteria for choosing between these alternatives. I have suggested placing it in different locations in the two voices, each in conformity with its own mensuration. This detail allows the contrasting mensurations to be heard even though the musical rhythms of the two voices are identical. Whether or not that was the composer's intention is impossible to know.

It is hard to imagine a more diverse arsenal of rhythmic techniques than those illustrated in this chapter. Contrasts among different mensurations, different *tactus* within the same mensuration, and different combinations of mensurations in both successive and simultaneous relation create the foundation for Du Fay's mensural types, but the diverse interactions among mensuration, *tactus*, and rhythm within each type generate as much variety as the differences among the types themselves. Numerous scholars have attempted to organize Du Fay's mensural procedures into clear-cut categories, but the diversity of his compositional techniques defies efforts to pin them down in this way. The regularities implied by his notated mensurations are the foundation for his rhythms, but the level of the *tactus* is often ambiguous and the rhythms interact with the mensural norms in ways that create conflicting groupings of many kinds. These conflicts give the songs their rhythmic vitality and enable the composer to capture the affects, and sometimes the specific details, of his poetic texts with great sensitivity. The challenge to performers is to project both the regular and the irregular elements of the rhythms in a way that maintains the dynamic tension between them and does not allow either to overshadow the other.

9 | The *L'homme armé* masses of Ockeghem, Busnoys, and Josquin

Compositions based on the song *L'homme armé* occupy a special place in the history of fifteenth- and sixteenth-century music. They include an anonymous monophonic song, a polyphonic song of questionable authorship that survives in two different versions (a three-voice combinative chanson and a four-voice textless arrangement), and more than forty masses. Scholars have debated the origin, character, and chronology of these works for many decades. Recent research suggests that the monophonic song is the work of a trained composer associated with the court of Burgundy. The polyphonic song, which is attributed to an otherwise unknown "Borton" in one source, probably dates from the 1450s and may be by Du Fay. The earliest masses are those of Du Fay and Ockeghem, both of which were most likely composed shortly after May 1461.[1] Among the later works in the tradition, the one by Busnoys, probably composed around 1468, and two by Josquin, which probably date from the 1490s, were particularly influential.[2] The masses of Ockeghem, Busnoys, and Josquin are considered in this chapter.

Many masses in the *L'homme armé* tradition feature exceptional displays of compositional virtuosity. The cantus firmus is subjected to transposition, melodic inversion, retrograde motion, and numerous forms of modal and mensural transformation. Canons of various types, including mensuration canons, are common. Composers of *L'homme armé* masses were aware of

---

[1] See Alejandro Enrique Planchart, "The Origins and Early History of *L'homme armé*," *The Journal of Musicology* 20 (2003), 305–57, for a summary of the history and present state of research on the early history of the song and the polyphonic works based on it, along with many new findings on the subject. Planchart discusses the origin and attribution of the song and the dates of the Du Fay and Ockeghem masses ibid., 314–25 and 333–35.

[2] Planchart discusses the date of the Busnoys *Missa L'homme armé* ibid., 350–52. Jesse Rodin, "'When in Rome . . .': What Josquin Learned in the Sistine Chapel," *Journal of the American Musicological Society* 61 (2008), 313–30, places Josquin's *Missa L'homme armé super voces musicales* in the 1490s, in part on grounds of its apparent borrowings from the *L'homme armé* mass of Marbriano de Orto, which Josquin would have encountered during his tenure in the Sistine choir beginning in 1489. Bonnie J. Blackburn suggests a date in the 1480s in "Masses Based on Popular Songs and Solmization Syllables," in *The Josquin Companion*, ed. Richard Sherr (Oxford University Press, 2000), 65. She argues on stylistic grounds that the *Missa L'homme armé sexti toni* is probably later than the *Missa L'homme armé super voces musicales*.

each other's works and sought to compete with their predecessors and outdo them in technical complexity.[3] Mensural complications are an important feature of this competition. The four masses considered here make use of thirteen different mensuration signs that relate to each other in a variety of ways. Among them, they demonstrate a large number of the possible meanings of mensuration signs in the period. Although several studies have been devoted to these issues, basic problems regarding *tactus* and tempo relationships among signs remain unresolved.

One of the reasons for the popularity of the *L'homme armé* tradition was the wealth of symbolic connotations that it entailed. The tradition apparently originated at the Burgundian court, where the armed man was associated with the Order of the Golden Fleece and the idea of a crusade, but the topic lent itself readily to other associations of both spiritual and military character.[4] The technical complications in the masses are often not ends in themselves, but a means of symbolic representation of abstract ideas. This aspect of the works is beyond the scope of the present study.

The song

The only surviving source of the monophonic version of the *L'homme armé* song is a manuscript now located in Naples that contains six anonymous masses based on it. The melody is divided into eight segments separated by long rests, which are required in the polyphonic setting. Example 9.1 shows an edited version of the melody with the long rests omitted and the sections and phrases labeled for reference. The breve in bar 9 is changed to a semibreve, and the preceding note is changed to an altered minim, by analogy with bars 26–27.

The form of the song is ternary, and there is a distinct contrast of register between the A and B sections. The metrically regular rhythm is reinforced by the syllabic text setting. As a mass cantus firmus, the melody often has a B-flat, but the "major" version was probably the original. The phrase structure is asymmetrical. The A section has 11 (5+6) semibreves, the B section has 12 (4+4+4), and the A' section has 9 (5+4), making the total length 31

---

[3] See David J. Burn, "'Nam erit haec quoque laus eorum': Imitation, Competition and the *L'homme armé* Tradition," *Revue de musicologie* 87 (2001), 249–87.

[4] See William F. Prizer, "Music and Ceremonial in the Low Countries: Philip the Fair and the Order of the Golden Fleece," *Early Music History* 5 (1985), 128–29; Craig Wright, *The Maze and the Warrior: Symbols in Architecture, Theology, and Music* (Cambridge, MA: Harvard University Press, 2001), 175–205; and Planchart, "The Origins and Early History of *L'homme armé*," 352–54.

Example 9.1 *L'homme armé* song. After Naples, Biblioteca Nazionale, Ms. VI E 40, fol. 58ᵛ.

[Musical notation: Three systems showing phrases labeled A 1, 1a, 2, 2a; B 1, 2, 3; A' 1, 1a, 2, with text underlay:
"L'o-me, l'o-me, l'o-me ar -mé, l'o-me ar-mé, l'o-me ar - mé doibt on doub - ter, doibt on doub - ter.
On a fait par-tout cri - er que cha-cun se vien-gne ar - mer d'un hau-bri-gon de fer.
L'o - me, l'o - me, l'o-me ar - mé, l'o-me ar-mé, l'o-me ar - mé doibt on doub - ter."]

semibreves if the final long is not counted. These asymmetries are a result of the fanfare-like tags (phrases A-1a, A-2a, and A′-1a) that are added to phrases A-1, A-2, and A′-1 in imitation of trumpet calls that relate to the military text. The length of 31 semibreves has been interpreted as a symbol of the 31 *chevaliers* of the Order of the Golden Fleece.[5]

The song is notated in perfect semibreves under the sign 3, which in this case represents a *tactus* on the perfect semibreve and implies nothing about larger mensural groupings. In popular usage, this mensuration would have been called "sesquialtera," although it has no proportional relation to another sign. The note values are limited to semibreves (perfect and imperfect) and minims (normal and altered) – i.e., notes with a value of one *tactus*, ⅔ *tactus*, and ⅓ *tactus*. Most *tactus*-units have only one pitch except at the ends of phrases. The same rhythm could have been notated with perfect breves, rather than perfect semibreves. The anonymous composer may have chosen semibreves because a perfect breve *tactus* (under whatever sign) is often associated with more complex rhythms and may therefore suggest a slower tempo than a perfect semibreve *tactus*.

The three-voice *Il sera par vous/L'homme armé* is a humorous piece that teases the aging Burgundian singer Simon le Breton about the possibility of his going on a crusade. It features the *L'homme armé* tune in the tenor (in a variant form, with E instead of G as the sixth note of the B-1 and B-2 phrases) and combines it with a courtly rondeau in the superius; the contratenor features elaborations of the fanfare motive and other snippets of the

---

[5] Richard Taruskin, "Antoine Busnoys and the *L'Homme armé* Tradition," *Journal of the American Musicological Society* 39 (1986), 271–73.

Example 9.2 [Du Fay?], *Il sera par vous/L'homme armé*, bars 1–10. After New Haven, Yale University Library, Beinecke Rare Book and Manuscript Library, Ms. 91 ("Mellon Chansonnier"), fols. 44ᵛ–45ʳ.

[Musical notation: Three-voice score with Superius, Contratenor (Ct), and Tenor (T) parts, all in C3 mensuration. Text underlay: Superius – "Il se-ra par vous con-ba-tu Le doub-té Turcq"; Contratenor – "L'o-me, l'o-me ar-mé, l'o-me ar-mé, l'o-me ar-mé, doibt on doub-ter"; Tenor – "L'o-me, l'o-me, l'o-me ar-mé, l'o-me ar-mé, l'o-me ar-mé doibt on doub-ter"]

tune. The mensuration is C3, which has the same meaning as 3 in the monophonic song, but the mensural structure is more complex, because the superius phrases are independent of the phrases of the cantus firmus and the superius rhythms sometimes create hemiola against the other voices (see Example 9.2).[6]

Ockeghem, *Missa L'homme armé*

Ockeghem's *L'homme armé* mass is the first to notate the cantus firmus in perfect prolation, which represents augmentation in relation to imperfect prolation. It is not the first Continental work to employ this notational convention, which Tinctoris disapprovingly calls the "English error,"[7] but it was influential in popularizing the technique. Ockeghem and his contemporaries often preserved the visual appearance of a cantus firmus and

---

[6] My example adopts the version of the text and underlay in Alejandro Enrique Planchart, "Two Fifteenth-Century Songs and Their Texts in a Close Reading," *Basler Jahrbuch für historische Musikpraxis* 14 (1990), 28. I have barred the example in semibreves, rather than breves, because the semibreves are not paired mensurally.

[7] Johannes Tinctoris, *Proportionale musices*, book 3, ch. 2 ("Qualiter proportiones signandae sint"), 47.

indicated alterations of its sound (including augmentation, transposition, retrograde performance, omission of rests, etc.) by means of verbal canons or notational conventions such as the interpretation of perfect prolation as augmentation. Since the *L'homme armé* song was associated with notation in perfect semibreves, it is understandable that composers often retained that notation in masses, rather than rewriting the cantus firmus in double values in perfect *tempus*.

Ockeghem's work survives in two sources: Vat 234 (the "Chigi Codex") and Vat 35. There are numerous differences between them, but only one discrepancy in mensuration signs: the tenor of the Qui tollis has ₵ in Vat 234 and ¢ in Vat 35. It is unclear which sign Ockeghem intended, since the mensural relationship in that section is unusual.[8] Table 9.1 shows the cantus-firmus segments, mensuration signs, and compositional *tactus* in each section of the mass. There are four combinations of simultaneous signs in the work: O + ₵ (Kyrie 1, Kyrie 2, Et in terra, Et unam sanctam, Sanctus, and Agnus 1), O + ʘ (Patrem), ¢ + ₵ (Osanna, Agnus 3), and ¢ + ¢ (Qui tollis, in Vat 35). Four signs appear in all voices simultaneously: O (Pleni, Agnus 2), C (Benedictus), ₵ (Christe, Et resurrexit), and 3 (Qui tollis – concluding section).

Large-scale symmetries govern the overall mensural structure of the work. All five movements begin with O in the non-tenor voices and ₵ or ʘ in the tenor. There is no musically meaningful distinction between ₵ and ʘ in these contexts. Breve rests are imperfect in the former and perfect in the latter, but there is no audible grouping of written semibreves, and sections do not always end on breve *initia*. The second cantus-firmus section of each movement has a contrasting mensuration in which the prevailing rate of motion is probably somewhat faster: ₵ in the Kyrie and Credo, and ¢ (with varying relations to the cantus firmus) in the Gloria, Sanctus, and Agnus Dei. Sections without the cantus firmus separate those with cantus firmus in the Sanctus and Agnus Dei. Kyrie and Credo have a third cantus-firmus section with the same mensuration as the first. The internal symmetry of the Kyrie extends to the identical lengths of Kyrie 1 and Kyrie 2 – a relationship made possible by the omission of phrase 2a in Kyrie 1.[9]

---

[8] There is an extra semibreve in the Agnus Dei, b. 121, in the manuscript Vatican City, Biblioteca Apostolica Vaticana, Ms. Chigi C VIII 234 ("Chigi Codex"), that must be an error, since it causes the movement to end on a semibreve-max *initium*. The version of the movement in Vatican City, Biblioteca Apostolica Vaticana, Cappella Sistina, Ms. 35 ends correctly on a breve *initium*.

[9] Fabrice Fitch, *Johannes Ockeghem: Masses and Models*, Ricercar 2 (Paris: H. Champion, 1997), 50–51, points out this and other durational symmetries in the Kyrie. Fitch analyzes the mass in detail ibid., 50–56.

Table 9.1 *Ockeghem, Missa L'homme armé*

Section	C.f. segment	Mensurations	Compositional *tactus*
Kyrie 1	A (without 2a)	O◊◊◊ / ℂ↓↓↓	◊ / ↓
Christe	B	ℂ	◊ (perfect) or ↓
Kyrie 2	A′	O◊◊◊ / ℂ↓↓↓	◊ / ↓
Et in terra	Complete	O◊◊◊ / ℂ↓↓↓	◊ / ↓
Qui tollis	Complete	₵ ◳◳◳ → 3 ◊◊◊ / ₵ ↓↓↓↓↓↓ → 3 ↓↓↓ / (ℂ)[1]	◳ (imperfect)→◳ (perfect) / ◊ (imperfect)→◊ (perfect)
Patrem	Complete (↓5th)	O◊◊◊ / ⊙↓↓↓	◊ / ↓
Et resurrexit	Complete (↓5th)	ℂ	◊ (perfect) or ↓
Et unam sanctam	A B (↓5th)	O◊◊◊ / ℂ↓↓↓	◊ / ↓
Sanctus	A B	O◊◊◊ / ℂ↓↓↓	◊ / ↓
Pleni	—	O	◊
Osanna	A′	₵ ◳◳◳ / ℂ ↓↓↓	◳ / ↓
Benedictus	—	C	◊
Osanna	ut supra		
Agnus 1	A (↓8ve)	O◊◊◊ / ℂ↓↓↓	◊ / ↓
Agnus 2	—	O	◊
Agnus 3	B A′ (↓8ve)	₵ ◳◳◳ / ℂ ↓↓↓	◳ or ◊ / ↓ or ↓

1 The tenor sign in this section is ℂ in Vat 234 and ₵ in Vat 35.

The cantus firmus is largely independent of the other voices in melody and rhythm. The contrast between its strongly metrical rhythms and the more flexible rhythms of the other voices is an important aspect of the style of the work. Ockeghem varies the rhythm of the cantus firmus by using rests to shift phrases or parts of phrases with respect to the semibreve *initium*. Because of the rules of imperfection and alteration, these shifts sometimes alter the durations of notes even though the notated values remain unchanged. These

264 Practice

Example 9.3 Ockeghem, *Missa L'homme armé*, variants of the cantus firmus in different movements. After Vatican City, Biblioteca Apostolica Vaticana, Ms. Chigi C VIII 234 ("Chigi Codex"), fols. 33ᵛ–43ʳ.

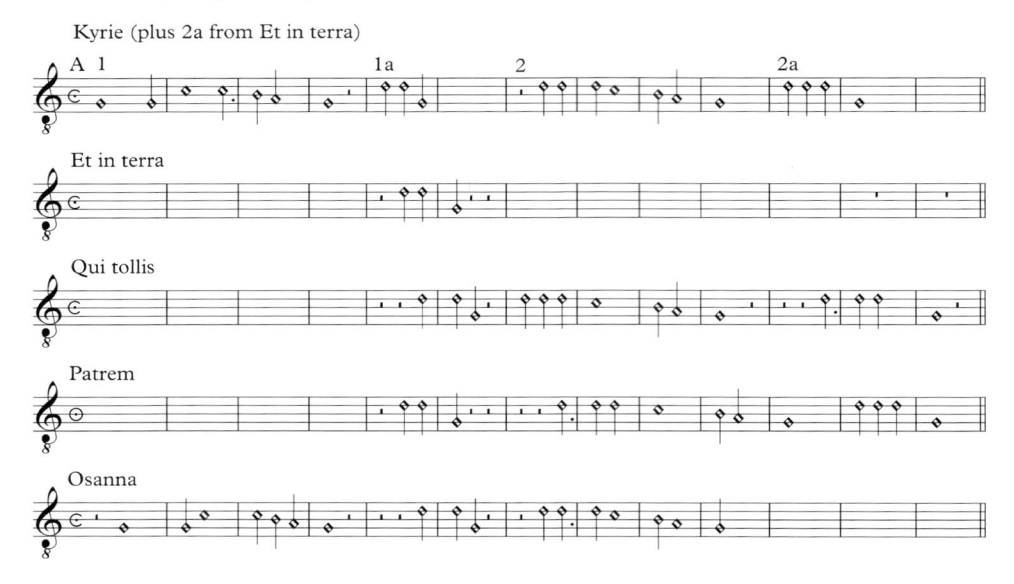

[Musical notation showing cantus firmus variants for Kyrie (plus 2a from Et in terra), Et in terra, Qui tollis, Patrem, and Osanna, labeled with phrases 1, 1a, 2, 2a]

complications increase gradually over the course of the mass and are resolved in the end. The rhythms of the cantus firmus are shown in their original written values, with barlines separating the semibreve-units, in Example 9.3.[10] The Kyrie is the standard of reference. Subsequent movements are shown only where they differ from the Kyrie, except that the return of the original rhythm in phrase 2 of the Osanna is included. When there is only one semibreve in a bar, it is perfect; when there are two minims in a bar, the second is altered.

The effect of these variations is compounded by the variety of ways in which the mensuration of the cantus firmus interacts with that of the other voices. When ₵ or ⊙ is combined with O, a minim of perfect prolation equals a semibreve of O. The rhythmic style associated with this combination of signs is the norm to which other styles in the work must be compared (see Example 9.4). Note values range mostly from breves to minims, with a few semiminims and occasional pairs of *fusae* on minim-max *initia*. The compositional *tactus* is the semibreve of O, and the performance *tactus* must be the same value. (References throughout the following discussion are to the written values of the non-tenor voices unless otherwise indicated.) Breve-units are audibly marked. Cadences fall only on breve *initia*, and

---

[10] Fitch, *Johannes Ockeghem*, 52, shows the notation of the complete cantus firmus in all movements. Example 9.3 is an abbreviated version of his example.

Example 9.4 Ockeghem, *Missa L'homme armé*, Kyrie 1, bars 1–8. After Vatican City, Biblioteca Apostolica Vaticana, Ms. Chigi C VIII 234 ("Chigi Codex"), fols. 33ᵛ–34ʳ.

the rhythm of the cantus firmus articulates breve-units between cadences. Penultimate intervals of cadences are mostly semibreves, but occasionally imperfect breves or altered semibreves. Suspensions are minims (as in bar 7) or ornamented semibreves in which the dissonance is no longer than a minim (as in bar 3). Non-suspension dissonances are mostly semiminims and *fusae*, but occasionally minims. Syncopated notes are mostly semibreves, but occasionally minims, especially in concluding passages of sections in which the tenor introduces free material in a rhythmic style like that of the other voices. Like Du Fay, Ockeghem often speeds up the note values and the contrapuntal rhythm to create a sense of climax at the end of a section.

The two sections in which C is combined with ₵ in both sources are reserved for the ends of the last two movements of the work. (Since the Osanna is repeated, the same signs appear in the middle of the Sanctus as well). In this combination, a minim of C equals a breve of ₵. A breve performance *tactus*, which is theoretically correct in ₵, is a practical

Example 9.5 Ockeghem, *Missa L'homme armé*, Sanctus (Osanna), bars 56–65. After Vatican City, Biblioteca Apostolica Vaticana, Ms. Chigi C VIII 234 ("Chigi Codex"), fols. 40ᵛ–41ʳ.

necessity in this case. A semibreve *tactus* would require a semiminim *tactus* for ℃, which would weaken the ternary grouping of minims and make the tricky rhythms that result from the displacement of rests difficult to read. The compositional *tactus* of ₵ is sometimes ambiguous. In the Osanna (Example 9.5), it is clearly the breve. All cadences fall on breve *initia*, penultimate intervals of cadences are breves (equal to tenor minims), and suspensions are semibreves, with or without ornamental resolutions. Although the cantus firmus would be expected to group the breves in sets of three, since its groups of three minims (corresponding to three breves of the other voices) are distinctly audible, Ockeghem avoids the obvious by beginning the cantus firmus on the second breve-unit of the other voices and transforming its rhythm in such a way that it implies groups of 1+3+3+2, rather than 3+3+3, breves in the opening phrase. The rests between the cantus-firmus phrases are long enough that no regular grouping of breves lasts long. In the Agnus Dei 3, there is more emphasis on the semibreve-units and less on the breve-units than in the Osanna. Penultimate intervals of cadences are sometimes semibreves, there are no semibreve dissonances, and syncopated semibreves are common. As if to compensate for the fussiness of the small-scale rhythms, Ockeghem lays out the cantus firmus in regular phrases that create a clear sense of perfect minor *modus* where it is present in this section (see Example 9.6).

In the Qui tollis, which has the signs ℃ + ₵ in Vat 234 and ₵+ ₵ in Vat 35, a minim of perfect prolation equals a semibreve, rather than a breve, of ₵. The stroke through the sign in Vat 35 is evidently meant to signal this distinction, though whether it was Ockeghem or someone else who added

Example 9.6 Ockeghem, *Missa L'homme armé*, Agnus Dei 3, bars 47–56. After Vatican City, Biblioteca Apostolica Vaticana, Ms. Chigi C VIII 234 ("Chigi Codex"), fols. 42ᵛ–43ʳ.

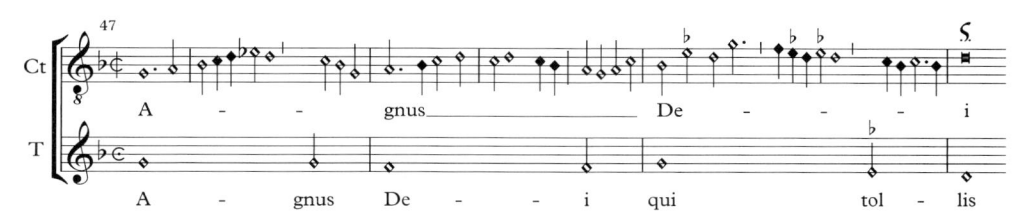

Example 9.7 Ockeghem, *Missa L'homme armé*, Gloria (Qui tollis), bars 46–55. After Vatican City, Biblioteca Apostolica Vaticana, Ms. Chigi C VIII 234 ("Chigi Codex"), fols. 35ᵛ–36ʳ.

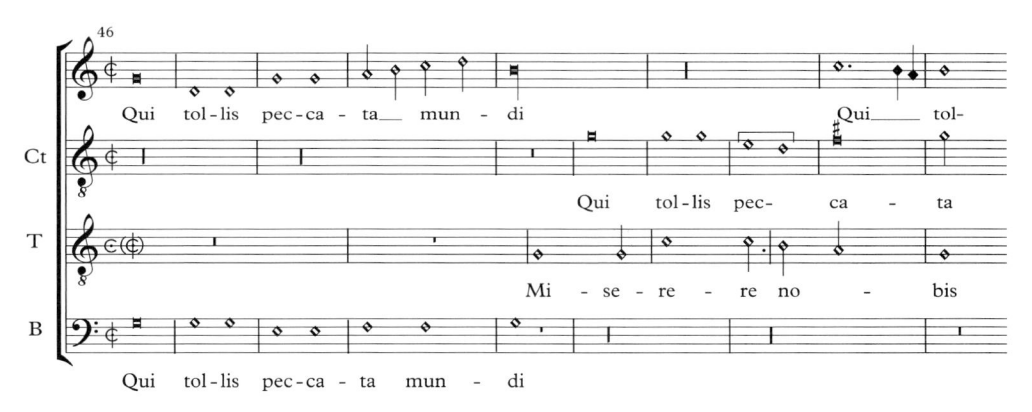

the stroke to the sign is not known. This is a more complex relationship than those discussed previously, because the ternary groups of minims in the cantus firmus conflict with the binary groups of semibreves, which are clearly articulated, in the other voices. The performance *tactus* must nevertheless be the breve of ¢, which corresponds to the *imperfect* semibreve of ¢, and the tenor must count groups of three minims against a *tactus* that marks groups of two minims. To complicate matters further, the tenor enters quite surprisingly on the upbeat of the *tactus* (see Example 9.7).

The voices are partially reconciled in the B section of the cantus firmus, where phrase beginnings coincide with mensural *initia* under both signs, and fully reconciled in the concluding section ("Tu solus"), where all voices adopt a *sesquialtera* proportion, notated with the figure 3, with the *tactus* on the perfect semibreve of the tenor and the perfect breve of the other voices (see Example 9.8). Here the cantus firmus has the same sign and *tactus* that it has in the song, and the only mensural complications are simple hemiolas. The

Example 9.8 Ockeghem, *Missa L'homme armé*, Gloria (Tu solus), bars 116–24. After Vatican City, Biblioteca Apostolica Vaticana, Ms. Chigi C VIII 234 ("Chigi Codex"), fols. 35ᵛ–36ʳ.

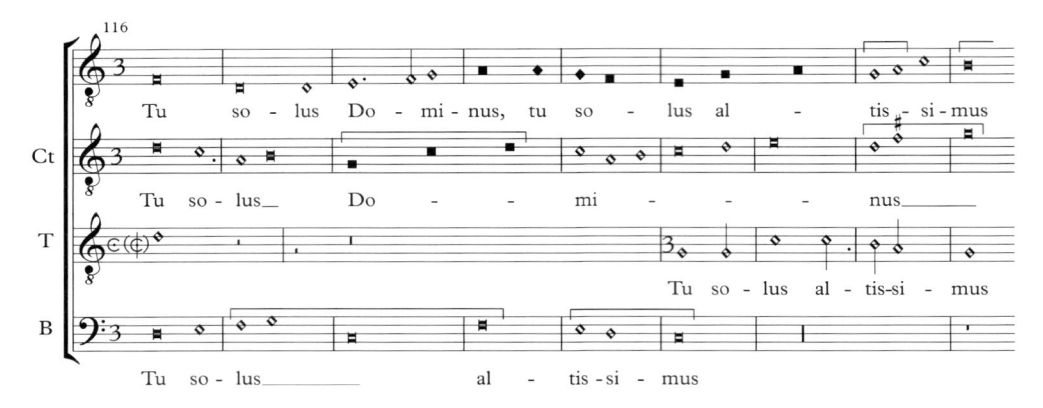

proportion sign appears at different points in different voices. The breve rest immediately preceding it in the tenor is syncopated irregularly, and the proportion begins, very unusually, at a point that does not coincide with a semibreve *initium* of the preceding mensuration. This detail confirms the necessity of a breve performance *tactus* for ¢ in this section. A semibreve *tactus* would require a doubling of the duration of the *tactus* for the *sesquialtera* passage, and the non-simultaneous arrival of the *sesquialtera* sign in different voices would lead to major confusion if that option were chosen.

The sign O behaves differently when it appears in all voices (in Pleni and Agnus Dei 2) than it does when it is combined with perfect prolation. Semibreves are more distinctly divided and less regularly grouped when the sign is independent. Breve-units are established at the beginning of each section, but thereafter play little or no role in the mensural structure. Some cadences fall on semibreve-max *initia*, and Agnus Dei 2 even ends on the second semibreve of the breve-unit. The penultimate intervals of cadences may be as short as minims, and syncopated minims are common. At the beginning of Agnus Dei 2 (Example 9.9), the breve-units are established by the entry of the second voice and the cadence on the breve *initium* in bar 26, but they are reinforced infrequently thereafter. The ending of the section in the middle of a breve-unit is irregular and may even be an error, but it is unlikely to be noticeable to a listener, since the preceding passage is made up of minims and semiminims and includes contrapuntal progressions on values as short as semiminims. The section with all voices in C (Benedictus) has similar rhythms and likewise ignores the breve-units

Example 9.9 Ockeghem, *Missa L'homme armé*, Agnus Dei 2, bars 24–30. After Vatican City, Biblioteca Apostolica Vaticana, Ms. Chigi C VIII 234 ("Chigi Codex"), fols. 41^v–42^r.

after the opening bars. Two considerations may explain the focus on the semibreve-units, rather than breve-units, in the sections in O and C: first, the cantus firmus, which articulates the breves in most movements, is absent, and second, passages scored for two or three voices typically focus on shorter rhythmic values than passages with full scoring, as if to compensate for the thinness of the texture with the greater intricacy of the rhythm.

The most problematic sign in the mass is ℭ where it appears in all voices of a section (in Christe and Et resurrexit). This mensuration was so rare by the 1460s that there is no practical tradition to which it can be compared, and the recommendations of theorists concerning its performance *tactus* are contradictory. Tinctoris recognizes the possibility of minim, imperfect semibreve, and perfect semibreve *tactus* in perfect prolation.[11] The imperfect semibreve (the only feasible *tactus* in Example 9.7) is unlikely, because it is awkward and does not match any regular value in the mensuration. Pietro Aaron claims that perfect prolation in all voices requires a perfect semibreve *tactus* and cites Ockeghem's *Missa L'homme armé* to illustrate the point,[12] but his testimony is too late to be based on direct knowledge of Ockeghem's practice. Where the cantus firmus is present, the musical style of ℭ implies a perfect semibreve *tactus* (see Example 9.10), but where it is absent, the compositional *tactus* sometimes shifts to the minim and syncopated

---

[11] See Chapter 5, pp. 121–22.
[12] Aaron, *Toscanello in musica*, book 1, ch. 38 ("Cognitione, et modo di cantar segno contra a segno necessarii"), fol. Fii^r. See Chapter 6, p. 166.

Example 9.10 Ockeghem, *Missa L'homme armé*, Kyrie (Christe), bars 14–17. After Vatican City, Biblioteca Apostolica Vaticana, Ms. Chigi C VIII 234 ("Chigi Codex"), fols. 33ᵛ–34ʳ.

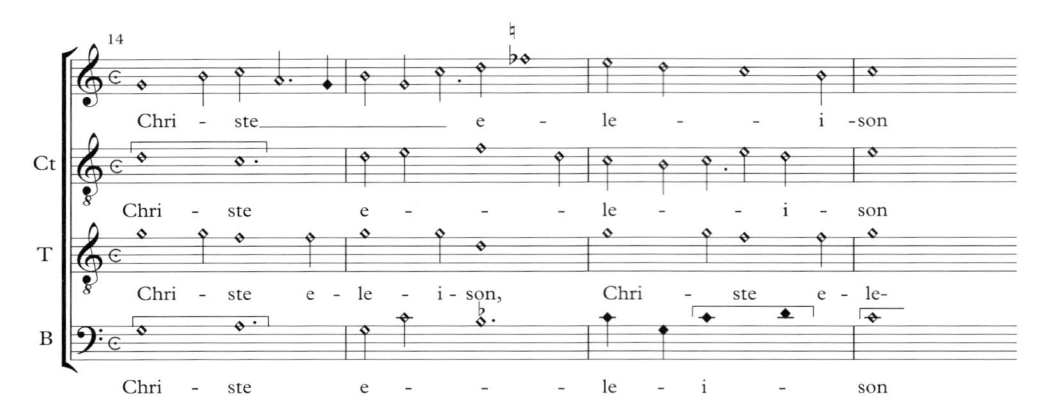

Example 9.11 Ockeghem, *Missa L'homme armé*, Credo (Et resurrexit), bars 90–93. After Vatican City, Biblioteca Apostolica Vaticana, Ms. Chigi C VIII 234 ("Chigi Codex"), fols. 37ᵛ–38ʳ.

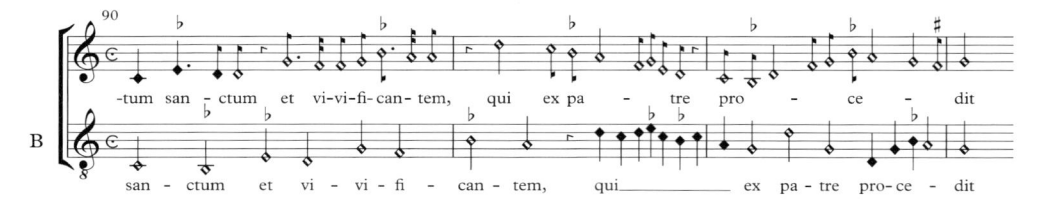

minims temporarily undermine the audibility of the semibreve-units (see Example 9.11). Although either a minim or a perfect semibreve performance *tactus* is musically possible and theoretically justifiable for these sections, I believe the perfect semibreve is preferable, both because it conforms to the feel of the rhythm most of the time and because the contrasting rhythms, including the hemiola cadences in Example 9.10 and the intricate subdivisions in Example 9.11, stand out more vividly in relation to it than they do in relation to a minim *tactus*. The difficulty of performing passages like Example 9.11 with a perfect semibreve *tactus* enhances the tension that they generate and the sense of resolution that comes with the restoration of the perfect semibreve-units when the cantus firmus re-enters.

The issue of tempo relationships among the signs in this mass is independent of the issue of the performance *tactus* associated with different signs. Theoretical evidence does not provide unequivocal support for any interpretation, but the musical evidence discussed above suggests reasonable possibilities. The duration of the semibreve may be the same in O and C throughout the work, whether or not these signs are combined with perfect prolation, though there is no evidence that tempos under a given sign must be strictly constant throughout a work. The generally accepted view that the semibreves of ¢ and O should relate in an exact or approximate 4:3 ratio makes sense here for the same reasons that apply to other works of the period. This relationship of course makes the perfect prolation slower when it is 4:1 augmentation in relation to ¢ than when it is 2:1 augmentation in relation to O.

The problem of ℭ in all voices is more acute. Some scholars believe it should have the same tempo as ℭ combined with O (a minim of ℭ equals a semibreve of O), while others advocate a tempo twice as fast (a minim of ℭ equals a minim of O) on grounds that perfect prolation does not mean augmentation when it appears in all voices.[13] Since the compositional *tactus* is mostly the perfect semibreve in ℭ, it makes sense to interpret the sign *ut iacet* (as Aaron recommends), but that interpretation means only that the performance *tactus* should be the perfect semibreve. Tempo is a separate issue. A possible alternative between the extremes of a 1:1 and a 2:1 ratio between the minims of O and the minims of ℭ *ut iacet* is a 4:3 ratio, analogous to the relation between O and ¢ in 4:3 proportion on the semibreve level. This interpretation leads to a perfect semibreve *tactus* in ℭ that is twice as slow as the semibreve *tactus* in O, but the surface motion feels faster, since the most prominent values are semibreves in O and minims in ℭ *ut iacet*. ℭ *ut iacet* appears in this mass in places where ¢ would normally be expected, and it makes sense for the two signs to produce a similar mensural contrast with the preceding O. The ratio of perfect semibreves of ℭ *ut iacet* to perfect breves of O in this interpretation is 3:2, the ratio that Anonymous 12 recommends between and ⌽ and other diminished signs with ternary mensuration. All of these possible proportions are illustrated in Example 9.12. The metronome marks are relative, not absolute; they are too slow for performance tempos, but the numbers shown are easy to compare. The exact proportion is not critical as long as the change in mensural character comes across effectively.

---

[13] Scholars who advocate interpreting ℭ in all voices as augmentation in this mass include Bent, "The Use of Cut Signatures in Sacred Music by Ockeghem and His Contemporaries," 647, and Jaap van Benthem, preface to Johannes Ockeghem, *Missa L'homme armé, Masses and Mass Sections* II, fasc. 2 (Utrecht: Koninklijke Vereniging voor Nederlandse Muziekgeschiedenis, n.d.), XII. Taruskin, "Antoine Busnoys and the *L'Homme armé* Tradition," 261, n. 15, interprets ℭ in all voices as integral.

272   Practice

Example 9.12 Possible proportional relations between O (Kyrie) and ℭ *ut iacet* (Christe) in Ockeghem's *Missa L'homme armé*: (a) O; (b) O ◊ = ℭ ↓; (c) O ↓ = ℭ ↓; (d) O ⁞⁞⁞⁞ = ℭ ⁞⁞⁞. Arrows represent the performance *tactus*. Metronome marks represent relative, not absolute, durations.

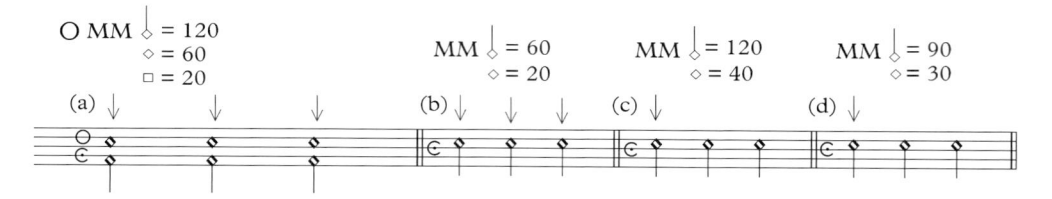

Busnoys, *Missa L'homme armé*

Busnoys's *Missa L'homme armé* was composed in obvious emulation of and competition with Ockeghem's mass. There are many analogies between the works, as well as some important features that set them apart. Busnoys's work survives in seven sources, five of which have the sign O2, while the other two have ℭ, in the Christe and Benedictus.[14] Table 9.2 lists the cantus-firmus segment, mensuration signs, and number of written breve-units in each section and the proportional lengths of the sections according to two different interpretations that have been proposed. Cantus-firmus segments are indicated by bar numbers, rather than formal sections, because Busnoys divides the cantus firmus in ways that do not correspond to its formal structure.

Busnoys's mass is very similar to Ockeghem's in its overall mensural layout. The works are analogous in the following ways: (1) Each movement begins with a section in O with the tenor in perfect prolation functioning as augmentation. (2) One later section of each movement has a sign that probably requires diminution with respect to the opening section. The Christe, Qui tollis, Et incarnatus (analogous to Ockeghem's Et resurrexit), Osanna, and Agnus 3 are signed O2 in Busnoys; that sign is combined with ℭ in 4:1 ratio in all of them except the Christe. The analogous signs in Ockeghem are ℭ (Christe, Et resurrexit) or ₵ combined with ℭ or ₵ (Qui tollis, Osanna, Agnus 3). Since O2 may be equivalent to ₵ with perfect minor *modus*, the signs in the Qui tollis, Osanna, and Agnus 3 are strictly analogous on the level of *tempus*. If my interpretation of ℭ *ut iacet* as a kind of perfect-mensuration analogue of ₵ is correct, there is also a strong analogy between the Christe and Et resurrexit/Et incarnatus sections of the two masses.

---

[14] See Antoine Busnoys, *Collected Works*, part 3, ed. Richard Taruskin, Masters and Monuments of the Renaissance 5 (New York: Broude Trust, 1990), 18, for information about the mensuration signs in the sources of this work.

Table 9.2 Busnoys, *Missa L'homme armé*

				Ratios	
Section	C.f. bars	Mensurations	Breve count (non-tenor voices)	Taruskin[1]	Brothers[2]
Kyrie	1–15	O / ⊙	18	9	3
Christe	—	O2 or C[3]	24	8	2
Kyrie	16–end	O / ₵	18	9	3
Et in terra	1–18	O / ⊙	54	9	3
Qui tollis	18–end	O2 / ₵	72	4	2
Tu solus	Complete	C3	18	3	1 or ⅔[4]
Patrem	1–15 (↓4th)	O / ⊙	54	3	3
Et incarnatus	16–end (↓4th)	O2 / ₵	93		
Confiteor	1–5, 12–27 (↓4th)	₵	36	1	1
Sanctus	1–19	O / ⊙	36	12	4
Pleni	—	O	27	9	3
Osanna	20–end	O2 / ₵	54	6	3
Benedictus	—	O2 or C	36	8	2
Osanna	ut supra				
Agnus 1	1–15 (inverted)	O / ⊙	36	4	4
Agnus 2	—	O	27	3	3
Agnus 3	16–end (inverted)	O2 / ₵	54	2	3

1 Assuming ₵ for Christe and Benedictus and 2:1 ratio between O2 and O.
2 Assuming O2 for Christe and Benedictus and 4:3 ratio between O2 and O.
3 O2 in Vat 14; C in Vat 234. (Same in Benedictus.)
4 1 if C3 ♩ = O ♩; ⅔ if C3 ♪ = O ♪.

(3) Kyrie 2 has the sign O, with ₵ functioning as augmentation in the tenor, in both works. (4) The Pleni and Agnus 2, which have reduced scoring and no cantus firmus, have the sign O. (5) The Benedictus has reduced scoring and a sign of imperfect *tempus*: ₵ in Ockeghem; O2 or C in Busnoys, depending on which sources are correct. (6) The Gloria ends with a section in *sesquialtera*. (7) The two-against-three conflict that is featured in Ockeghem's Qui tollis appears in a more complex form in Busnoys's Confiteor.

In a detailed study of Busnoys's *Missa L'homme armé*, Richard Taruskin proposed that the lengths of the sections in the entire work are governed by a set of Pythagorean proportions (see Table 9.2).[15] With only two exceptions (the 9:4 ratio between the Et in terra and Qui tollis and the non-proportional Et incarnatus), the internal proportions among the sections of every movement correspond to ratios that generate the perfect consonances and the whole tone. The series culminates in the 12:9:6:8 ratios of the Sanctus, which represent the division of the octave (12:6) into a perfect fifth (12:8, 9:6) and a perfect fourth (12:9, 8:6) separated by a whole tone (9:8). The Et incarnatus, which appears almost exactly at the midpoint of the mass, departs strikingly from the other sections in that its length (in tenor semibreves) corresponds to the symbolic number 31.

Taruskin's analysis is based on the following relations among signs:

$$O\,/\,C\,\diamond = \odot\,/\,\mathbb{C}\,\vert = O2\,\natural = \mathbb{C}\,\vert\vert = \mathfrak{D}\,2/3\,\natural = C3\,\vert\vert$$

These relations are derived through the following reasoning: (1) Semibreve equivalence between O and C was normally assumed. (2) The ratio of the minim of ⊙ and ℭ to the semibreve of O and the breve of O2 in simultaneous relations is given by the counterpoint. If the minim of ⊙ and ℭ is constant throughout the work, the breve of O2 must equal the semibreve of O. (3) If the stroke in ₵ cancels the augmentation implied by ℭ and restores minim equivalence between perfect and imperfect prolation, two minims of ₵ must equal two minims (or one semibreve) of O. (4) The relation between ₵ and 𝔇 is given by the counterpoint. (𝔇 is *sesquitertia* of ₵: four minims, or one breve, of 𝔇 equal three minims of ₵. The breve of 𝔇 is therefore ⅔ of the semibreve of O.) (5) The argument for equating C3 with ₵ is simply that it makes the proportional scheme work. A further assumption required by Taruskin's scheme is that the sign of the Christe and Benedictus, which differs in different sources, should be C, not O2.

Taruskin's analysis has been challenged on several grounds. The most serious issues involve the interpretation of the proportional relations among the signs and the choice of C as the sign for the Christe and Benedictus: (1) If the relation of O2 to O is strictly proportional, the relation between the signs may be more likely to be 4:3 than 2:1 on the semibreve level. Theorists generally regard O2 as equivalent to ₵ with perfect minor *modus*, and an exact or approximate 4:3 relation between ₵ and O in successive relation is supported by many forms of evidence.[16] Busnoys himself used that ratio between C2 (which is theoretically equivalent to ₵ on the breve level) and O in his explicitly Pythagorean motet *In hydraulis*.[17] On the other hand, the note

---

[15] Taruskin, "Antoine Busnoys and the *L'Homme armé* Tradition," 269–73.
[16] See Chapter 7, pp. 197–98.
[17] Taruskin discusses evidence for this interpretation in Busnoys, *Collected Works*, part 3, 76–79.

values that Busnoys writes in O2 in this mass do not differ from those in O, and so the semibreves of those signs may be equal in this case. This interpretation is supported by theoretical testimony that *modus cum tempore* signs do not always mean diminution. (2) ¢ may be duple proportion of C, but this interpretation cannot be verified on the basis of either theoretical evidence or the relationships among signs within the work. ¢ may simply represent C with a perfect semibreve *tactus* and not prescribe a specific tempo. (3) C3 as a proportion sign normally means *sesquialtera*, with three minims of C3 equal to two minims of O or C, not minim equivalence between C3 and O. (4) O2 is a more probable sign than C for the Christe and Benedictus, both because it makes the perfect *modus* explicit and because it is a less common sign that is unlikely to have arisen through scribal initiative.[18]

Taruskin counters some of the objections to his interpretations of signs by asserting that the proportions in Busnoys's mass are abstract, conceptual symbols that have nothing to do with performance tempos.[19] Nevertheless, he indicates these proportions in his edition of the work without warning the user that he does not mean for them to be taken literally.[20] He also reduces the values in 2:1 ratio in O and 4:1 ratio in O2, making the latter look twice as fast on the page, and he bars O in breves of the original notation and O2 in perfect longs. He defends his choice of C for the Christe and Benedictus on grounds that the Pythagorean design must be intentional and can therefore be used as evidence for the choice of sign.[21]

Thomas Brothers reconsiders the proportions in the work using O2 for the Christe and Benedictus and a 4:3 ratio between O2 and O. He takes account of both minim equivalence and *sesquialtera* proportion as possible relations between C3 and O. His result is a set of proportions that are simpler than Taruskin's but still aesthetically pleasing (see Table 9.2).[22]

There is no way to be sure whether or not Busnoys intended for some or all of the proportions among sections in this work to represent Pythagorean concepts, but it is clear that large-scale proportional design plays a central role in his mass. The foundation of the design is the consistent use of perfect minor *modus*, at least in the abstract. (The audibility of the grouping of breves is a separate matter that will be discussed below.) Duple and triple multiples of the ternary groups of breves generate proportional symmetries

---

[18] These issues are discussed in Rob C. Wegman, Letter to the editor, *Journal of the American Musicological Society* 42 (1989), 437–43.

[19] Letter to the editor, *Journal of the American Musicological Society* 42 (1989), 447–49.

[20] Busnoys, *Collected Works*, part 2.   [21] Taruskin, Letter to the editor, 450–51.

[22] Thomas Brothers, "Vestiges of the Isorhythmic Tradition in Mass and Motet, ca. 1450–1475," *Journal of the American Musicological Society* 44 (1991), 18–22.

on many levels, not only within movements, but throughout the work. The lengths of the opening sections of the five movements, all of which combine O and ⊙, are 18, 54, 54, 36, and 36 breves, respectively; they relate to each other as 1:3:3:2:2 regardless of their relation to other signs. Similarly, the three sections apart from Et incarnatus that combine O2 with ℭ (Qui tollis, Osanna, and Agnus 3) have lengths of 72, 54, and 54 breves, which relate to each other as 4:3:3. Kyrie 2 is the same length as Kyrie 1, and Christe and Benedictus (24 and 36 breves, respectively) are 2:3 in relation to each other, whatever their sign or their relation to the other sections may be.

When the non-tenor voices are in ⊙, Busnoys writes the tenor in ⊙ except in Kyrie 2, where O is combined with ℭ. In these combinations, a minim of the tenor equals a semibreve of the other voices, so that the ternary groups of minims in the tenor match the ternary groups of semibreves in O. On the level of *tempus* and prolation, these combinations of signs are governed by the same principles as the corresponding combinations in Ockeghem's mass. Minor *modus* (which corresponds to *tempus* in the augmented signs in the tenor) governs the lengths of sections, which always end on a long *initium*, and most of the principal subdivisions of sections as well. The subdivisions are marked by the entry of the cantus firmus, which is preceded by rests in the opening sections of all movements. In the Et in terra, Patrem, and Sanctus, the entry of the cantus firmus not only conforms to the *modus*-units of the mensuration, but creates 1:2 or 1:1 proportions between the subdivisions of the sections. Only in Agnus 1 does the cantus firmus enter one breve "too late," contradicting the *modus*-units and distorting what would otherwise be a 1:2 proportion between its subdivisions.

The long-units are articulated audibly at the beginnings of the sections in O + ⊙ and O + ℭ, then fade to the level of abstract measuring devices at some point. All of the sections in O + ⊙ (the opening sections of the movements) begin with a head motive (Example 9.13) that establishes both the *tempus* and the *modus*. The lower voice states the opening phrase of the cantus firmus, which defines the *tempus* through its rhythm and suggests the *modus* through the ending of the phrase on a perfect long *initium*. The upper voice knits the first two breves together with a hemiola rhythm that immediately calls attention to a level of measurement larger than the breve. Long-units are reinforced by the limitation of cadences to long *initia* for varying amounts of time in different movements, but at some point, cadences on breve-max *initia* undermine the audible primacy of the long-units. In Kyrie 2, where the minor *modus* is imperfect, all cadences fall on long *initia*, but they are too far apart to provide a clear sense of the binary grouping of the perfect breves.

Example 9.13 Busnoys, *Missa L'homme armé*, Kyrie 1, bars 1–4. After Vatican City, Biblioteca Apostolica Vaticana, Ms. Chigi C VIII 234 ("Chigi Codex"), fols. 205^v–206^r.

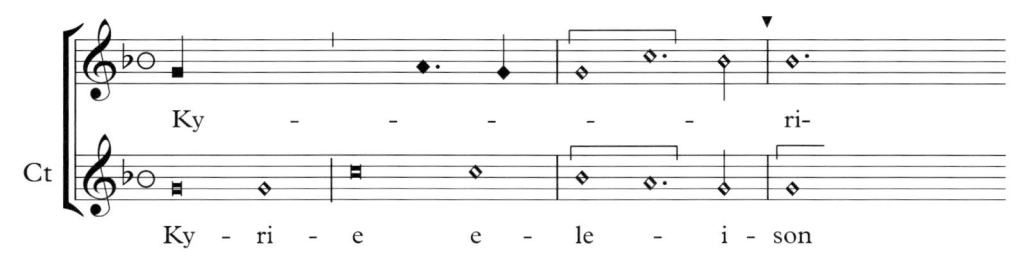

In the sections where the non-tenor voices are in O2, Busnoys writes the tenor in ₵ and sets the tenor minims equal to the breves of the other voices. Unlike Ockeghem, who sometimes positions the tenor in ways that prevent it from implying audible perfect *modus* in the other voices when he combines these two signs, Busnoys always aligns the perfect semibreves of the tenor with the perfect longs of O2, so that the minor *modus* is easily heard when the cantus firmus is present. The theoretical imperfect breve-units of the tenor, which correspond to groups of six breves, or an imperfect maxima, of the other voices, play no role in the audible design, though they may be part of the abstract plan, since all of the sections with these signs except the Et incarnatus end on maxima *initia*. Cadences are predominantly on long *initia*, especially when the cantus firmus is present, but occasionally on breve-max *initia*.

Despite the prominence of the *modus* level, the compositional *tactus* is always the semibreve in O2, and rhythms on the level of the semibreve and its subdivisions are similar to those of O. There are no *fusae*, but semiminims are as common as they are in O and mensural displacements, including syncopation, occur predominantly on the semibreve level. In the Qui tollis and Et incarnatus, the introductory duos feature imitation at the interval of three semibreves, as if the *tempus* were perfect, rather than imperfect (see Example 9.14), in the first four bars. The strategy for articulating the mensuration in these sections is the opposite of that in the opening sections of movements. In the latter, the *modus* units are established at the beginning and then gradually undermined; here even the *tempus* is ambiguous at the beginning and the rhythms are brought into line with the larger levels of the mensuration at later points (see Example 9.15).[23] Rhythms like those in Examples 9.14 and 9.15 require a performance *tactus* that articulates every

---

[23] The bar numbers in my examples correspond to breves. Since Taruskin bars sections in O2 in longs, my numbers differ from those in his edition.

Example 9.14 Busnoys, *Missa L'homme armé*, Gloria (Qui tollis), bars 1–11. After Vatican City, Biblioteca Apostolica Vaticana, Ms. Chigi C VIII 234 ("Chigi Codex"), fols. 207^v–208^r.

Example 9.15 Busnoys, *Missa L'homme armé*, Gloria (Qui tollis), bars 42–51. After Vatican City, Biblioteca Apostolica Vaticana, Ms. Chigi C VIII 234 ("Chigi Codex"), fols. 207^v–208^r.

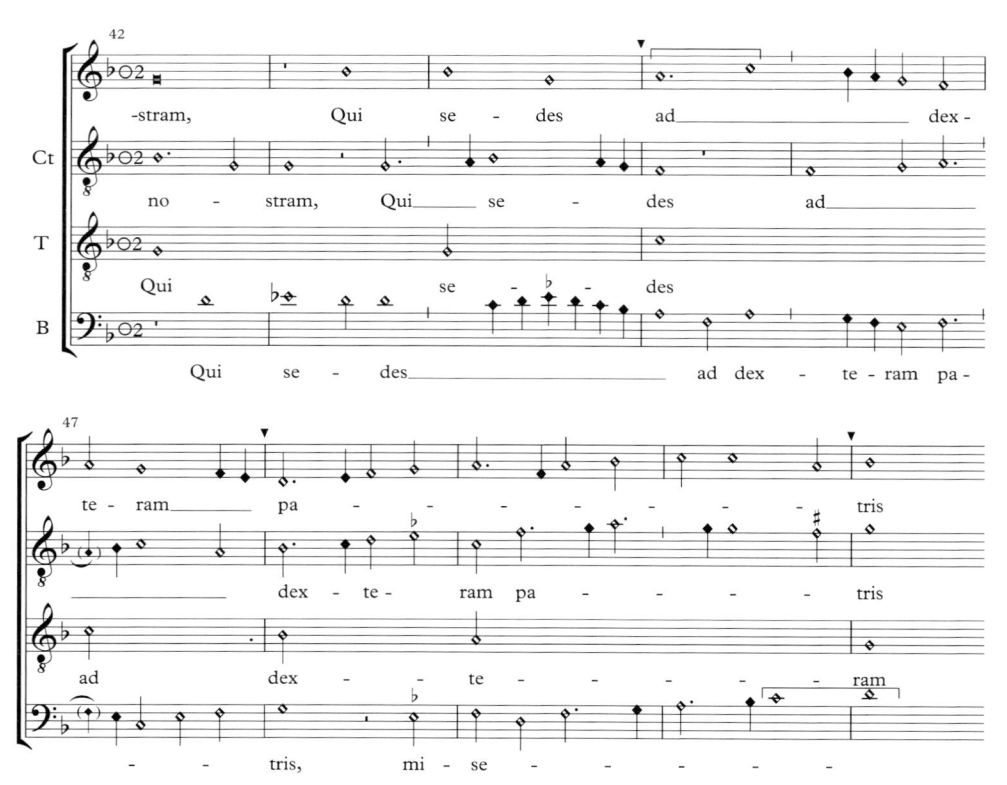

semibreve, but they are more effective with a divided breve *tactus* than with a semibreve *tactus*. Even though the two voices in Example 9.14 are melodically identical in bars 1–4, the mensural displacement of the upper voice gives it a distinctly different feel from the lower voice if it is performed with a breve *tactus*, and that subtle contrast is lost if the performance *tactus* is the semibreve. The difference is difficult to describe in words and must be experienced to be appreciated. It depends on the perception of the grouping of the notes, not on any assumption of dynamic accent on the *tactus*. The reader can perform this experiment by singing both parts with both possible *tactus*, keeping the metronome speed constant. A breve performance *tactus* for the section also has the advantage of making the tenor easier to read and facilitating the grouping of breves on the *modus* level.

Given the many examples in O2 in this work, it ought to be possible to determine whether the intended sign of the Christe and Benedictus was C or O2 on the basis of their rhythmic character. Unfortunately, the matter is not that simple. There is no audible *modus* in either section, but both sections end on what would be a perfect long *initium* if perfect *modus* were part of the structure. The first change of vocal scoring (from one voice pair to another) occurs on a long *initium* in the Christe and on the semibreve following a long *initium* in the Benedictus, but similar changes are not regularly correlated with long-units after those points. The compositional *tactus* is the semibreve, and the rhythms are similar to those of O2 in other sections except that there are three pairs of *fusae* in the Benedictus. All cadences fall on breve *initia*. Since C does not exclude the possibility of perfect *modus*, the difference between C and O2 is slight. If the signs are interpreted in the way most theorists recommend, the performance *tactus* would be the semibreve if the sign were C and the breve if the sign were O2, and the semibreves might be faster in O2 than in C. The rhythms of these sections are compatible with either possibility and do not provide definitive evidence for preferring one sign over the other.

Busnoys creates climactic conclusions to the Gloria and Credo movements by reserving rhythms with ternary divisions of the *tactus* for them. Despite this similarity, the rhythms of the two sections contrast sharply. Like *Il sera par vous/L'homme armé*, the end of the Gloria ("Tu solus") is in C3. Busnoys quotes not only the tenor of the song, but also the fanfare motive from the contratenor, in all voices to give the section a lively character unlike anything else in the mass (see Example 9.16). It goes without saying that the perfect semibreve performance *tactus* that theorists associate with C3 is the only one that does justice to these rhythms. The tempo must surely be quite lively. If it is strictly

Example 9.16 Busnoys, *Missa L'homme armé*, Gloria (Tu solus), bars 5–13. After Vatican City, Biblioteca Apostolica Vaticana, Ms. Chigi C VIII 234 ("Chigi Codex"), fols. 208ᵛ–209ʳ.

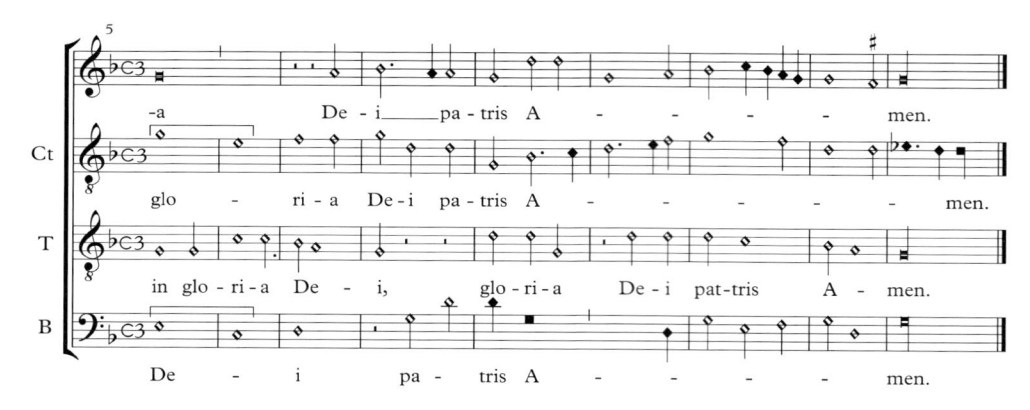

proportional to other tempos in the work (which it need not be on theoretical grounds), it may be preferable to equate the perfect semibreve with the semibreve of the preceding O2, rather than the semibreve of O, if O2 is in fact faster than O in this work. That option would give the section a total length equal to ⅙ of the Et in terra and ¼ of the Qui tollis in Brothers's proportional scheme.

The end of the Credo, in contrast, makes its point not through simple exuberance, but through the most complex mensural relations in the entire mass. Its combination of signs (¢ + ♭) appears to be an attempt to outdo the ¢ (or ℭ?) + ¢ in Ockeghem's Qui tollis. Ockeghem works with a hemiola relation between the two signs: three imperfect breves of ¢ equal two perfect semibreves of ¢, and the performance *tactus* corresponds to two minims, or ⅔ of a perfect semibreve, of ¢ (see Example 9.7). Busnoys instead places three minims of ¢ on the performance *tactus* and sets four minims of ♭ against them in *sesquitertia* proportion (see Example 9.17). The reason for the choice of ♭, rather than the more common ↻, to represent *sesquitertia* is apparently to match the cut sign of the tenor with a cut version of the proportion sign. The choice of performance *tactus* is determined by practical necessity: there is no other way the voices with these two signs can realistically be coordinated. The voices in ♭ sometimes have coloration that brings their rhythms in line with those of ¢. Coloration appears in all voices in the concluding passage, reconciling the energetic conflicts that characterize the section up to that point. There are no theoretical grounds for establishing the tempo of the section, but the complexity of the rhythm surely implies a slower tempo than that of the C3 of Example 9.16.

Example 9.17 Busnoys, *Missa L'homme armé*, Credo (Confiteor), bars 15–23. After Vatican City, Biblioteca Apostolica Vaticana, Ms. Chigi C VIII 234 ("Chigi Codex"), fols. 211ᵛ–212ʳ.

Josquin, *Missa L'homme armé super voces musicales*

If Ockeghem's and Busnoys's *L'homme armé* masses can justly be characterized as dazzlingly complex, Josquin outdoes both of them in his *Missa L'homme armé super voces musicales*, which ranks among the most elaborate mensural constructs ever devised. Its cantus-firmus treatment, modal structure, and canonic devices are equally stunning. The mass takes its name from the appearance of the cantus firmus on each of the six notes of the hexachord (the *voces musicales*) over the course of the work. Table 9.3 shows the cantus-firmus treatment, the mensural structure, and the canons in summary form.

The *Missa L'homme armé super voces musicales* was Josquin's most celebrated mass and one of the most famous works of its period. It survives in eighteen manuscript sources and two prints. Petrucci featured it as the opening number in his first volume of Josquin masses – the first printed collection in history devoted to the works of a single composer; Josquin's other *L'homme*

282   Practice

Table 9.3 Josquin, *Missa L'homme armé super voces musicales*

Section	C.f. segment	C.f. pitch	Mensurations	Canons
Kyrie 1	A	C	O / ⊙	Mensuration canon (S/T)
Christe	B		¢ / C	Mensuration canon (A/T)
Kyrie 2	A′		Φ / ⊙	Mensuration canon (B/T)
Et in terra	Complete[1]	D	O / ⊙	
Qui tollis	Complete (retrograde)		¢ / ⊙	T: "Verte cito" (or "cancrizet")
Patrem	Complete	E	O / ⊙	
Et incarnatus	Complete (retrograde)		¢ / ⊙	T: "Verte cito"
Confiteor	Complete		¢ / ⊙	T: "Reverte citius" (or "equivalet")
Sanctus	A B	F	O / ⊙	
Pleni	———		C	
Osanna	Complete		C3 / ⊙	T: "Gaudet cum gaudentibus"
Benedictus	———		C / ¢	Mensuration canon
Osanna	ut supra			
Agnus 1	A B	G	O / ⊙	
Agnus 2	———		¢3 / ¢ / C	Mensuration canon ("trinitas")
Agnus 3	Complete	A	¢ / ⊙	T: "Clama ne cesses"

1 The cantus firmus is always notated in perfect *tempus* in the A sections and imperfect *tempus* in the B sections. This distinction is not shown from here on.

armé mass concludes the volume. All of the sources agree on the signs in the work, but they differ considerably in the extent to which they transmit Josquin's sometimes cryptic canons and offer resolutions of the canons that they include. Observing the information that is lost in the resolutions sheds

Example 9.18 Josquin, *Missa L'homme armé super voces musicales*, cantus firmus (from Et in terra, tenor, transposed down a step to match the version in the Kyrie). After Vatican City, Biblioteca Apostolica Vaticana, Cappella Sistina, Ms. 197, fol. 2ᵛ.

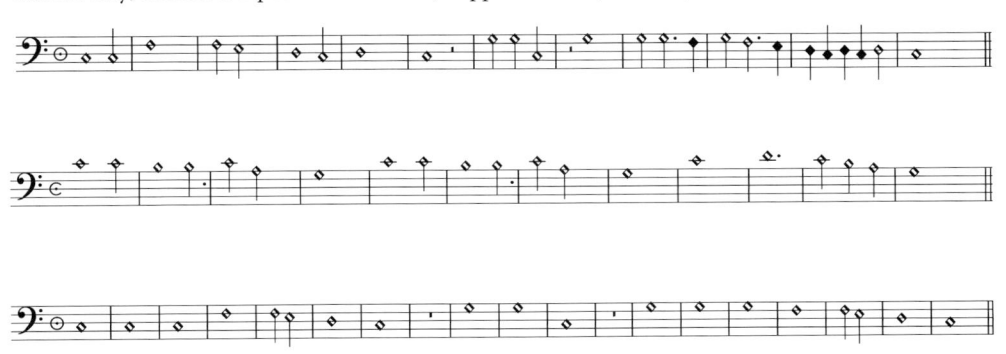

light on the meaning and value of the original notation, which is intrinsic to the compositional concept to a high degree in this work.[24]

The similarity of Josquin's overall mensural design to Ockeghem's and Busnoys's is easily observed.[25] The opening sections of all movements are in O with the tenor in ʘ. Christe, Qui tollis, Et incarnatus, and Agnus 3 combine a sign of diminution (in this case ₵) with C or ʘ. Kyrie 2 is similar to Kyrie 1, but with ⌽ where Ockeghem and Busnoys have O. Pleni, Benedictus, and Agnus 2 have no cantus firmus (and therefore no voice in perfect prolation), though the latter two have more complex mensurations than the corresponding sections in Ockeghem and Busnoys. The Osanna features the C3 mensuration that Ockeghem and Busnoys placed at the end of the Gloria. As in Busnoys, the end of the Credo (Confiteor) has the most complex rhythmic relationships in the mass.

The form of the cantus firmus in this mass is different from that in the song and the two preceding masses. Josquin picked up Ockeghem's technique of preserving the notational appearance of the cantus firmus while changing the notes that are altered and imperfected, though he accomplished this by changing the position of dots, rather than inserting rests. He also changed a few of the written values and added a few pitches. His version of the cantus firmus, in the form beginning on C, is shown in Example 9.18. As in Example 9.3, barlines separate perfect semibreves, semibreves are perfect when there is one in a bar, and the second minim is altered when there are two in a bar. The opening phrase is a kind of musical pun. The rhythm looks like that of the song, but by

---

[24] Blackburn makes this point in "Masses Based on Popular Songs and Solmization Syllables," 57–58.

[25] See Jesse Rodin, *Josquin's Rome: Hearing and Composing in the Sistine Chapel* (Oxford University Press, 2012), 233–69, for a detailed study of the relationship of this mass to these and other earlier works.

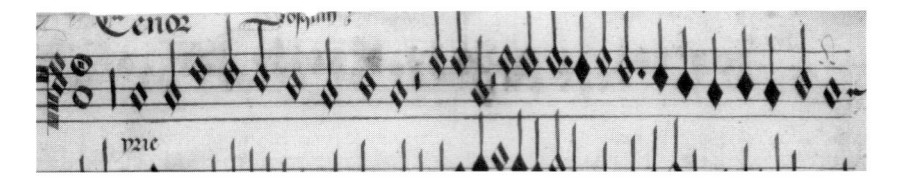

Figure 9.1 Josquin, *Missa L'homme armé super voces musicales*, Kyrie 1, cantus and tenor (beginning). Vatican City, Biblioteca Apostolica Vaticana, Cappella Sistina, Ms. 197, fol. 1ᵛ.

omitting the dot of division between the fourth and fifth notes, Josquin changes the rhythm into something quite different.

The relation between O and ʘ in the opening sections is the same as it is in Ockeghem and Busnoys: the semibreve of O equals the minim of ʘ or ₵. The notated perfect *tempus* of the cantus firmus, which would correspond to perfect minor *modus* in the other voices, is not a factor in the mensural organization, but it affects the values of rests. This function is crucial in the Kyrie, which is structured as a series of mensuration canons in which the initial rests determine the spacing of the voices. The tenor is derived canonically from the superius in Kyrie 1, the alto in the Christe, and the bass in Kyrie 2 by means of double clefs and double mensuration signs.

Josquin's basic rhythmic style in O combined with ʘ or ₵ is similar to Ockeghem's, but Josquin places more emphasis on the semibreve level than Ockeghem does. Both composers use the same range of note values, but semiminims are more common in Josquin, and his cadences sometimes fall on semibreve-max *initia*. In Josquin, suspensions precede cadences by a semibreve, or less often by a minim, but never by two semibreves, as they sometimes do in Ockeghem. Perfect breve-units are often audible as points of reference, while contrasting groupings of both minims and semibreves move in and out of phase with them to create large-scale formal patterns.

In Kyrie 1 (Figure 9.1 and Example 9.19), the superius and tenor form a mensuration canon at the interval of the ninth. The voices contrast both mensurally and tonally. The portion of the superius up to the tenor entry (i.e., the part that will be sung by the tenor) is conceived in perfect prolation. When it is read in augmentation under the sign ʘ in the tenor, the perfect prolation corresponds to the perfect *tempus* of the other voices, but when it is read without augmentation under the sign O in the superius, the minims come in groups of 3+3, conflicting with the 2+2+2 groups implied by the mensuration sign. The rhythms of the superius and tenor differ at some points because the rules of imperfection and alteration apply differently under the two signs. Ironically, the superius matches the original song more closely than the tenor does. Josquin establishes the norms of perfect *tempus* during the two breves

Example 9.19 Josquin, *Missa L'homme armé super voces musicales*, Kyrie 1. After Vatican City, Biblioteca Apostolica Vaticana, Cappella Sistina, Ms. 197, fols. 1ᵛ–2ʳ.

that precede the entry of the superius, then sets the superius in conflict with those norms for the next four breves. The point of strongest conflict is the first half of bar 4, in which a cadence, complete with suspension, falls in a highly irregular position on the fourth minim of the breve-unit, as if the real mensuration were perfect prolation. The force of this irregularity will be stronger if performers highlight the cadence with a C♯.

The entry of the tenor in bar 7 restores mensural order, but challenges the tonal order by beginning on an unexpected C after the first six bars have clearly established D as the modal final. The rhythms conform to the norms of O, with the breve *initia* distinctly marked by strong contrapuntal progressions, for the next seven breves. In bar 14, however, the principal emphasis falls on the second semibreve *initium*, rather than the breve *initium*, because of the tenor entry and the sequential repetition in the bass that begins with a striking octave leap. The emphasis on the second semibreve *initium*, which creates the illusion that the breve *initium* has been shifted, continues for the next two bars and culminates in a strong cadence on the second semibreve *initium* of bar 16. This cadence, to the pitch D, counteracts the tonal pull of the cantus firmus toward C. The real breve *initium* is re-established with the bass arrival on A in bar 17, and the section ends as it began, in conformity with the notated mensuration. A semibreve performance *tactus* (the only feasible one for this section) will make performers aware of the mensural conflicts on the semibreve/minim level, but performers must count semibreves in groups of three in order to appreciate the mensural conflict on the breve/semibreve level in bars 14–16.

A comparison of Petrucci's notation of the tenor of this section with that in the manuscripts that notate the mensuration canon on a single staff shows how much information is lost when Josquin's notation is translated into simpler forms. Since Petrucci published his edition in partbooks, he wrote out the tenor separately from the superius. The canonic relationship between the voices can still be seen by comparing the partbooks, but it could easily be overlooked by singers who were paying attention only to their own parts. Petrucci also includes a resolution of the tenor from ⊙ to O (Figure 9.2). The resolution obscures the relation between the voices still further, since the renotation in perfect *tempus* requires different note values; singers reading only the resolution would not appreciate the fact that their part is derived from the superius by simply changing the mensuration sign. Petrucci added a (technically superfluous) dot after the third note in the resolution, apparently because he did not trust the users of his edition to recognize the need for perfection and alteration when two semibreves come

Figure 9.2 Josquin, *Missa L'homme armé super voces musicales*, Kyrie, tenor. Josquin des Prez, *Liber primus missarum Josquin* (Venice: Ottaviano Petrucci, 1502).

between two breves. When the music is transcribed into modern score notation, the conceptual relation between the tenor and the superius is obscured still further.

In Kyrie 2, ⌽ is combined with ⊙. The proportional relation between the signs is 2:1, as it is in the combination of O and ⊙. The rhythms of ⌽ are similar to those of O, but with fewer complications on the level of the semibreve and its subdivisions. There are no *fusae* or syncopated minims; cadences fall only on breve *initia*, and suspensions always fall a semibreve (never a minim) before cadences. The consensus of theorists of Josquin's time is that ⌽ should have a semibreve *tactus* that is somewhat faster than the semibreve *tactus* of O. The subtle rhythmic distinctions between the two signs suggest that this was Josquin's understanding of the sign in this mass. A faster semibreve in ⌽ of course means that the cantus firmus will be faster in Kyrie 2 than in Kyrie 1 even though it is notated the same way in both sections.[26]

Josquin's combinations of ¢ with ⊙ or ₡ are more complex than his combinations of O with the same signs. The proportional relation between ¢ and perfect prolation is 4:1 in the Christe and Agnus 3, 2:1 in the Qui tollis and Et incarnatus, and 1:1 in Confiteor. The sections with these signs form a large-scale pattern in which the cantus firmus moves increasingly fast with respect to ¢ through the end of the Credo, then returns to its initial four-fold augmentation in Agnus 3. Josquin indicates the different proportional relations not with different signs, but with verbal canons: "verte cito" for the Qui tollis and Et incarnatus and "reverte citius" for the Confiteor. "Verte

---

[26] Rodin, ibid., 259–61, suggests the possibility of an obscure symbolic explanation for the fact that ⌽ is in 2:1 ratio to ₡, while ¢, in which the semibreves probably move at about the same speed, is in 4:1 ratio to the same sign. I would propose a simpler explanation: the standard theoretical and performance *tactus* of ⌽ was the semibreve in Josquin's time, but the theoretical tactus of ¢, which could also function as the performance *tactus* (and seems to be desirable in this Kyrie), was the breve. If performers sing both cut signs with their proper *tactus*, their different proportional relations to ₡ result automatically.

Example 9.20 Josquin, *Missa L'homme armé super voces musicales*, Kyrie (Christe), bars 29–35. After Vatican City, Biblioteca Apostolica Vaticana, Cappella Sistina, Ms. 197, fols. 1ᵛ–2ʳ.

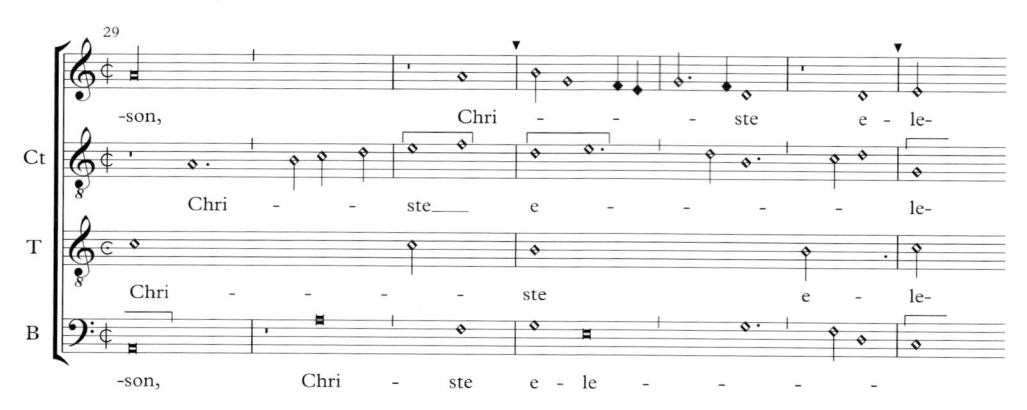

cito" ("turn around fast") means that the cantus firmus is to be sung in retrograde and that it is to be faster than it was in the preceding section. The amount of speeding is probably equivalent to the standard amount of speeding in a change from O to ₵, i.e., exactly or approximately 4:3 on the semibreve level. "Reverte citius" ("turn around again faster") means that the cantus firmus is to be sung forward (after having been sung backward), presumably twice as fast as in the preceding section, since there is no reason for the tempo of ₵ to change from one section to the next.[27]

The changing proportional relations between ₵ and perfect prolation not only cause the cantus firmus to move faster in relation to the other voices, but also generate increasingly complex mensural relationships among the voices. In the Christe and Agnus 3, the perfect semibreves of the cantus firmus correspond to groups of three breves in the other voices, creating regular perfect *modus* (see Example 9.20). In the Qui tollis and Et incarnatus, the perfect semibreves of the cantus firmus correspond to one and a half imperfect breves of the other voices. This relationship creates continuous hemiola between the perfect semibreves of the cantus firmus and the groups of three breves in the other voices (see Example 9.21). This is the same relation that Ockeghem used in his Qui tollis (Example 9.7) with the signs ₵ and ₵, if the stroke in the latter sign is authentic. In the Confiteor, the perfect semibreves of the cantus firmus correspond to ¾ of an imperfect

---

[27] The tempo implications of these instructions are discussed in Richard Sherr, "The Performance of Josquin's *L'homme armé* Masses," *Early Music* 19 (1991), 261–64.

Example 9.21 Josquin, *Missa L'homme armé super voces musicales*, Gloria (Qui tollis), bars 63–69. After Vatican City, Biblioteca Apostolica Vaticana, Cappella Sistina, Ms. 197, fols. 3^v–4^r.

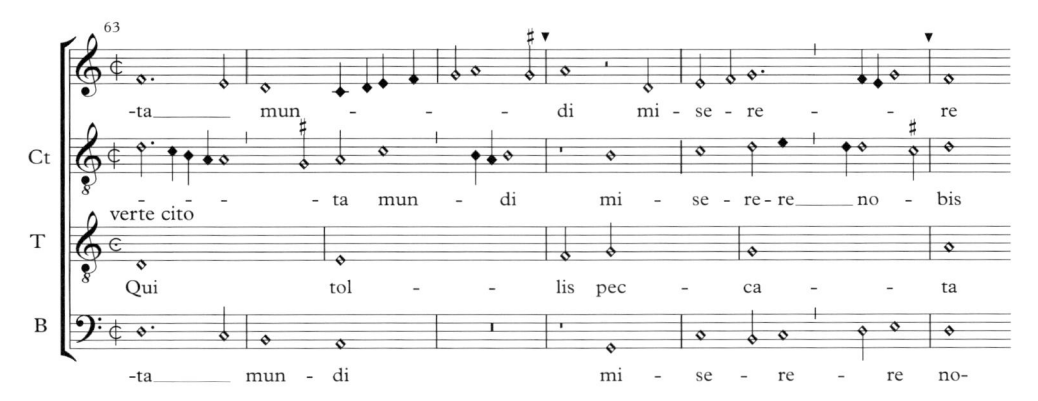

breve of the other voices. This four-against-three relation was probably inspired by Busnoys's Confiteor (Example 9.17), but while Busnoys divided the *tactus* into simultaneous quadruple and triple groups, Josquin sets the minims of the two mensurations equal, so that the conflict applies on a larger mensural level. The two mensurations coincide after groups of three breves of ¢, but the cantus firmus enters on a semibreve-max *initium*, complicating the relation between the voices still further. Although the breve-units of ¢ govern the total length of the section and the majority of the cadences, they are not generally audible, and the meaningful mensural conflict is between the perfect semibreves of the cantus firmus and the imperfect semibreves of the other voices (see Example 9.22).

The contrasting relations of ¢ to the mensuration of the cantus firmus complicate the issue of the performance *tactus* of ¢. Where the proportion is 4:1, a lightly divided breve performance *tactus* seems preferable, since it brings out the simple ternary grouping of breves that is created by the cantus firmus and supported by the other voices. Where the proportion is 2:1, a breve performance *tactus* is still advantageous in that it calls attention to the mensural conflict between the cantus firmus and the other voices, but it must be more distinctly divided than when the proportion is 4:1, since alternate perfect semibreve *initia* of the cantus firmus correspond to the midpoints of the breve-units of the other voices. When the proportion is 1:1, however, the mensural conflict is on the semibreve level, and a breve performance *tactus* would make the cantus firmus very difficult to sing and do nothing to clarify the rhythmic relationships among the voices. Even

Example 9.22 Josquin, *Missa L'homme armé super voces musicales*, Credo (Confiteor), bars 231–36. After Vatican City, Biblioteca Apostolica Vaticana, Cappella Sistina, Ms. 197, fols. 6ᵛ–7ʳ.

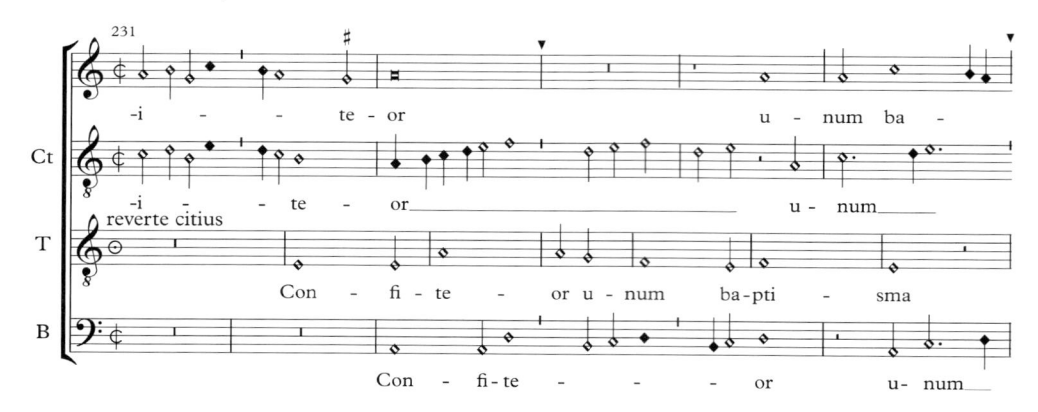

with a semibreve *tactus*, which seems to be the only feasible one in this case, the singers of the cantus firmus must measure groups of three minims against a *tactus* that equals two minims. These distinctions of *tactus* type correspond to significant mensural differences among the sections, but not to differences in the duration of the semibreve, which is probably the same for all sections in ₵.

The only other section with the cantus firmus is the Osanna, which is in C3 combined with ⊙. The mensuration corresponds to that of the end of the Gloria in the masses of Busnoys and Ockeghem; the *tactus* in both the compositional and the performance sense is the perfect semibreve, and there is no regular grouping of semibreves. The verbal canon "gaudet cum gaudentibus" ("it [the cantus firmus] rejoices with those who are rejoicing [the other voices]") indicates that the cantus firmus is to be sung at the same lively tempo and with the same *tactus* as the other voices (see Example 9.23). As in the section of the Busnoys mass with the same mensuration, the tempo is not necessarily specified by the sign.

The Pleni, Benedictus, and Agnus 2 have no cantus firmus. The Pleni is in C, the Benedictus is a two-voice mensuration canon (C + ₵), and Agnus Dei 2 is a three-voice mensuration canon (C + ₵ + ₵3 or 3). In the mensuration canons, ₵ and C are in 2:1 relation, and ₵3 (or 3) is in 3:1 relation to C and 3:2 to ₵. In Agnus Dei 2, the compositional *tactus* corresponds to the semibreve of C, the imperfect breve of ₵, and the perfect breve of ₵3. The only feasible performance *tactus* is the same value. Despite its compositional complexity, the canon is quite easy to read by simply

Example 9.23 Josquin, *Missa L'homme armé super voces musicales*, Sanctus (Osanna), bars 76–81. After Vatican City, Biblioteca Apostolica Vaticana, Cappella Sistina, Ms. 197, fols. 8ᵛ–9ʳ.

Figure 9.3 Josquin, *Missa L'homme armé super voces musicales*, Agnus Dei 2. Vatican City, Biblioteca Apostolica Vaticana, Cappella Sistina, Ms. 197, fol. 9ᵛ.

measuring the values of each voice in relation to the *tactus* (see Figure 9.3 and Example 9.24). The Benedictus works the same way, but with only two simultaneous mensurations (see Example 9.25). The Pleni (Example 9.26) seems to require a semibreve performance *tactus*, in conformity with its sign. Apart from the grouping of semibreves, which is inaudible after the first eight breves, its rhythms resemble those of O, rather than ¢. The rhythms include pairs of *fusae* and syncopated minims; cadences may fall on any semibreve *initium*, and suspensions may fall a minim before final notes of cadences. Rests in the bass that are syncopated with respect to the breve-units support the conclusion that the semibreve is the primary unit of measure in this section. They occur in bars 56–57 and 59–60 of Example 9.26; the former is a two-breve rest in the source that is transcribed as a semibreve + breve rest because the example begins on the second semibreve

Example 9.24 Josquin, *Missa L'homme armé super voces musicales*, Agnus Dei 2, bars 37–42. After Vatican City, Biblioteca Apostolica Vaticana, Cappella Sistina, Ms. 197, fol. 9ᵛ.

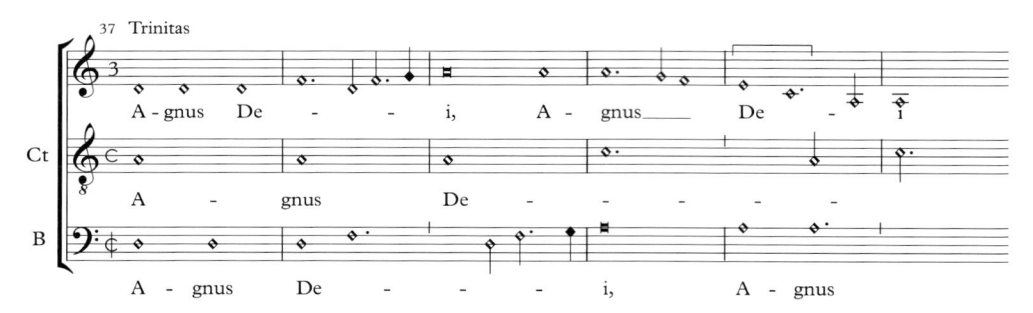

Example 9.25 Josquin, *Missa L'homme armé super voces musicales*, Sanctus (Benedictus), bars 1–9. After Vatican City, Biblioteca Apostolica Vaticana, Cappella Sistina, Ms. 197, fol. 9ʳ.

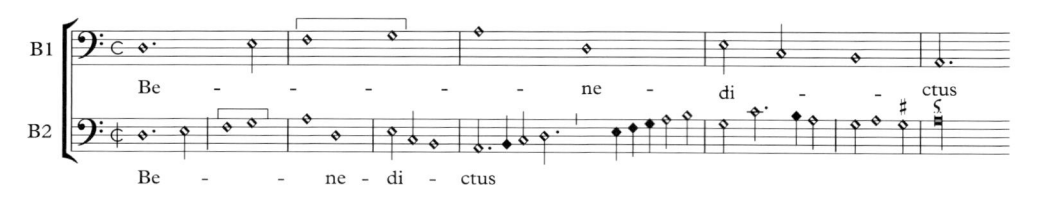

Example 9.26 Josquin, *Missa L'homme armé super voces musicales*, Sanctus (Pleni), bars 56–60. After Vatican City, Biblioteca Apostolica Vaticana, Cappella Sistina, Ms. 197, fols. 7ᵛ–8ʳ.

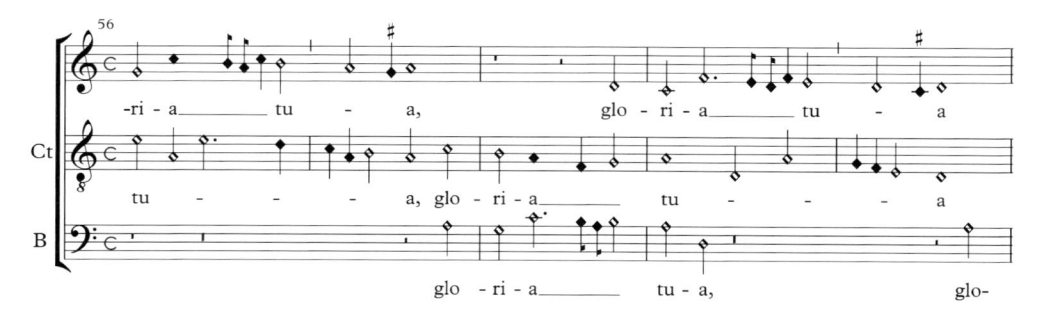

of the rest. A tempo in which the semibreves are equal to those of O would make sense for this section.[28]

Since ¢ and C are in 2:1 proportion in the Benedictus and Agnus Dei 2, but most likely in (exact or approximate) 4:3 proportion elsewhere, it is

[28] The *tactus* and tempo of the Pleni were already controversial in the early sixteenth century. See Chapter 7, p. 200.

impossible for both of the signs in the mensuration canons to have the same tempo that they have in other sections of the mass. There are no theoretical grounds for equating the tempo of either sign with its tempo in other sections. Since the rhythmic styles of the voices in ₵ resemble those of other sections in ₵, it may be that the voices with that sign should determine the tempo of the canons, though a slightly faster tempo would bring out the rhythms of the voices in C more effectively. This decision must be based on musical judgment. Theoretical generalizations were never meant to cover the highly complex and unusual mensural relationships that govern this extraordinary work.

Josquin, *Missa L'homme armé sexti toni*

Josquin's *Missa L'homme armé sexti toni* is a very different work from the *Missa L'homme armé super voces musicales*. The mass takes its name from its mode, which presents an interesting compositional challenge in that the mode of the cantus firmus is authentic and that of the mass is plagal. The cantus firmus is primarily in the tenor, but it is subject to constant variation that at times renders it barely recognizable, and it infiltrates the other voices to a much greater extent than it does in the *Missa L'homme armé super voces musicales*. From a mensural point of view as well, the two works are hardly comparable. The *Missa L'homme armé sexti toni* combines contrasting signs in simultaneous relation only at the end of the Credo and in the Agnus Dei 3, but its overall mensural layout is analogous to that of the preceding *L'homme armé* masses in many respects. The opening section of each movement is in perfect *tempus*, the second principal section is in imperfect *tempus* in diminution, Kyrie 2 returns to perfect *tempus*, and *sesquialtera* sections appear near the end of the Gloria and Credo (see Table 9.4).

Simplicity of mensuration signs does not mean simplicity of rhythmic design. Josquin employs a wide range of mensural structures, from passages in which the largest regular unit is the semibreve to passages with regular minor *modus*, in both O and ₵. He groups the notes in a variety of ways, both in conformity with the prevailing mensural structure and in opposition to it. The shorter sections in O (Kyrie 1, Sanctus, and Agnus Dei 1) operate primarily on the level of the breve and its subdivisions, but imperfect minor *modus* plays a structural role in the Et in terra and Patrem. *Modus*, which is marked primarily by means of long notes in the cantus firmus, is operative throughout the Et in terra, although one phrase of the cantus firmus (bars 36–39) is displaced with respect to the long-units by means of

Table 9.4 Josquin, *Missa L'homme armé sexti toni*

Section	Cantus firmus segment	Mensuration	Canons
Kyrie 1	A	O	
Christe	B	¢	
Kyrie 2	A′	⊙	
Et in terra	A	O	
Qui tollis	Complete	¢→3→¢	
Patrem	A	O	
Et resurrexit	BA′	¢	
Et unam sanctam	Complete	¢3→¢ ↺	
Sanctus	A	O	Tenor/Alto
Pleni	———	¢	
Osanna	A	⊙	Tenor/Bass
Benedictus	———	¢	Superius/Tenor
Osanna	ut supra		
Agnus 1	A	O	
Agnus 2	———	¢	
Agnus 3	BA′	O2 or ¢ O	Superius 1/Superius 2, Alto 1/Alto 2 Tenor/Bass (retrograde)

odd numbers of rests preceding and following it. The Patrem begins similarly, but abandons the *modus* groupings after the first 32 breves.

Kyrie 1 (Example 9.27) illustrates the range of rhythmic groupings found on the level of the breve and its subdivisions in O. In bars 1–8, the principal level of rhythmic organization is the breve, and the rhythms conform clearly and regularly to the norms of the mensuration. The cantus firmus reinforces the mensural clarity by appearing in its familiar form in the tenor in bars 5–8 with only a touch of ornamentation in bar 6. A syncopated imperfect breve in the tenor between bars 8 and 9 introduces a subtle mensural conflict, but the breve *initia* remain clearly audible up to the cadence at the beginning of bar 11, which marks the beginning of phrase A2 of the cantus firmus. The rhythm of the phrase in bars 11–12 is a variant of the version of the melody in perfect prolation, rather than perfect *tempus*, and the other voices in those measures support the regrouping of the minims as 3+3, rather than 2+2+2. A repetition of phrase A2, displaced by a semibreve and drastically out of phase with the

Example 9.27 Josquin, *Missa L'homme armé sexti toni*, Kyrie 1. After Vatican City, Biblioteca Apostolica Vaticana, Ms. Chigi C VIII 234 ("Chigi Codex"), fols. 183ᵛ–184ʳ.

Example 9.28 Josquin, *Missa L'homme armé sexti toni*, Gloria (Et in terra), bars 45–49. After Vatican City, Biblioteca Apostolica Vaticana, Ms. Chigi C VIII 234 ("Chigi Codex"), fols. 185ᵛ–186ʳ.

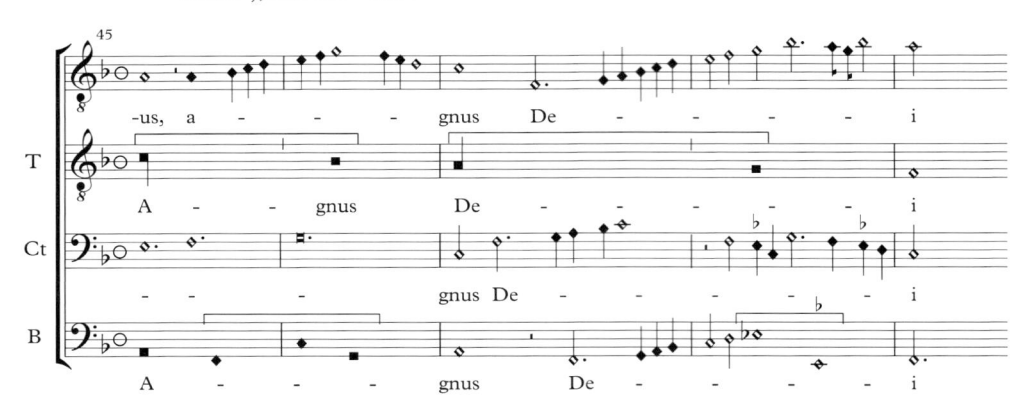

mensural structure of perfect *tempus*, begins on the third semibreve of bar 12. From that point until the final cadence, the largest regular time unit is the semibreve, and the breve *initium* in bar 14 is actively overruled by the continuation of notes from the preceding breve-unit in all voices. Complex syncopations at the minim level in the superius add to the focus on the smallest temporal units at the expense of the breves. Nevertheless, the theoretical *tempus* is not irrelevant during this passage. It has been established firmly enough at the beginning of the section that an attentive listener will remember where the hidden breve *initia* fall and experience the sense of resolution that accompanies the re-emergence of the breve-unit in the final cadence.

The beginning of the last cantus-firmus phrase of the Et in terra illustrates the superposition of mensural complications on the level of groups of minims, semibreves, and breves in O (see Example 9.28). The cantus-firmus rhythm, which is supported by the bass, implies ternary groups of imperfect breves in hemiola relation to the perfect *tempus*, while the contratenor in bar 45 divides the perfect breve into two groups of three minims instead of three groups of two. The fast runs that begin in the superius in bar 45 are imitated by all voices except the tenor at intervals of a minim in bar 47, creating a swirl of activity in which the breve-units play no part. Nevertheless, the interactions of all of the voices leave no doubt about the location of the breve *initia*, and the rhythmic interest of the contrasting patterns in the different voices derives not only from their durational relationships, but from their contrasting relationships to the audible norms of the mensuration.

The rhythms of the sections in Φ (Kyrie 2 and Osanna) are simpler than those in O or ₵. The breve-units are clearly audible, and the rhythms of the

Example 9.29 Josquin, *Missa L'homme armé sexti toni*, Kyrie 2, bars 65–73. After Vatican City, Biblioteca Apostolica Vaticana, Ms. Chigi C VIII 234 ("Chigi Codex"), fols. 184ᵛ–185ʳ.

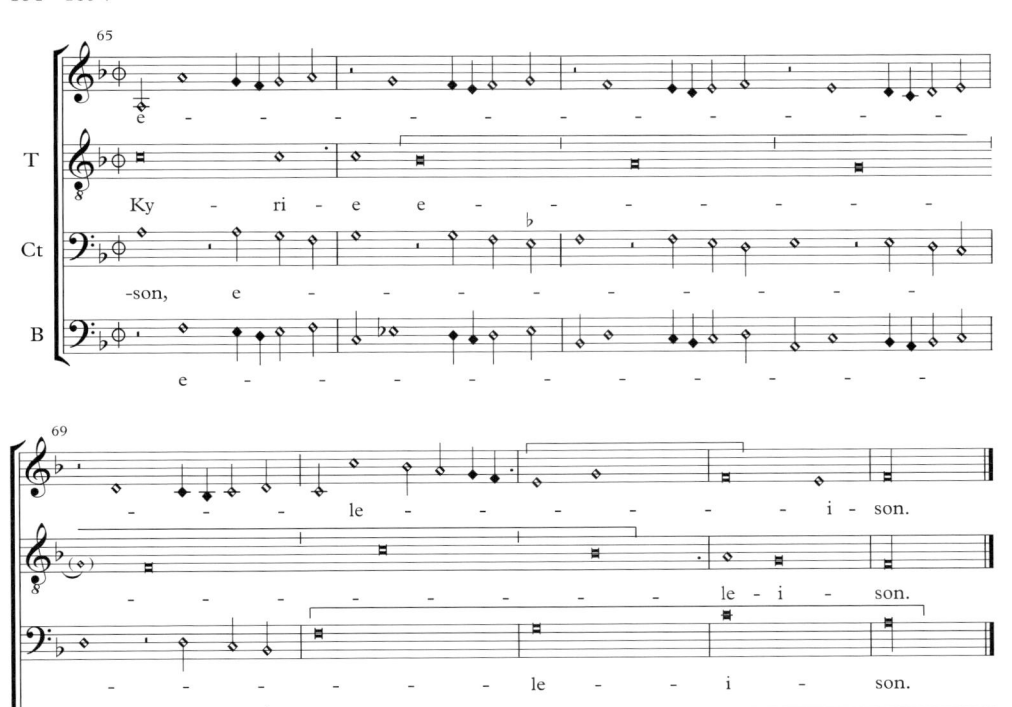

individual voices rarely conflict with them. As in the *Missa L'homme armé super voces musicales*, there are no *fusae* or syncopated minims in ϕ, and cadences fall exclusively on breve *initia*. The rhythms of the Osanna are particularly simple and lively. Tenor and bass have the cantus-firmus melody in canon at the interval of a breve, and the rhythms resemble those of the original song closely enough to capture its dance-like character. This simplicity is highly effective after the complications that characterize the rhythms of most of the preceding sections. Kyrie 2 is more intricate than the Osanna and even includes an extended passage in which the perfect breves of the tenor are syncopated with respect to the breve *initia* (see Example 9.29). Its final cadence, however, is one that is typical of ¢3, where the *tactus* is the perfect breve, not ϕ, where it is the semibreve. The penultimate interval is an imperfect breve, and the suspension lasts for a full semibreve. This cadence aggressively overrides the preceding syncopations and confirms the centrality of the breve-units in ϕ.

The only unusual sign in the mass is ↺, which appears in two of the four voices after a section in ¢3 at the end of the Credo; the other voices return to ¢ at that point (see Example 6.2). The sign represents 4:3 proportion of ¢3 (four semibreves in the time of three) and, by extension, duple proportion of ¢, since ¢3 was already 3:2 proportion of ¢.[29] (In the series ¢ ¢3 ↺, the semibreves are reduced first to ⅔, then to ¾ of ⅔, or ½, of their value in ¢.) This notational complication serves no obvious purpose. It may be a symbolic reference to the ↺ in the concluding section of Busnoys's Credo (Example 9.17), and by extension, an allusion to the mensural complexities of *L'homme armé* masses in general.

The *Missa L'homme armé sexti toni* is for the most part characterized by subtlety, rather than flamboyance, but Josquin makes up for this restraint with one of his most dazzling displays of technical virtuosity in the Agnus Dei 3. The texture is expanded from four voices to six. Tenor and bass perform the B and A′ sections of the cantus firmus in retrograde canon, while the two superius voices and the two alto voices each have canons at the interval of a minim (see Example 9.30). The two lower voices are in O, and the four upper ones are probably meant to be in O2, though Petrucci and some manuscripts have the sign ¢ instead. Both signs are in 2:1 proportion to O; the only

Example 9.30 Josquin, *Missa L'homme armé sexti toni*, Agnus Dei 3, bars 78–84. After Casale Monferrato, Archivio Capitolare, Ms. M(D), fols. 99ᵛ–100ʳ.

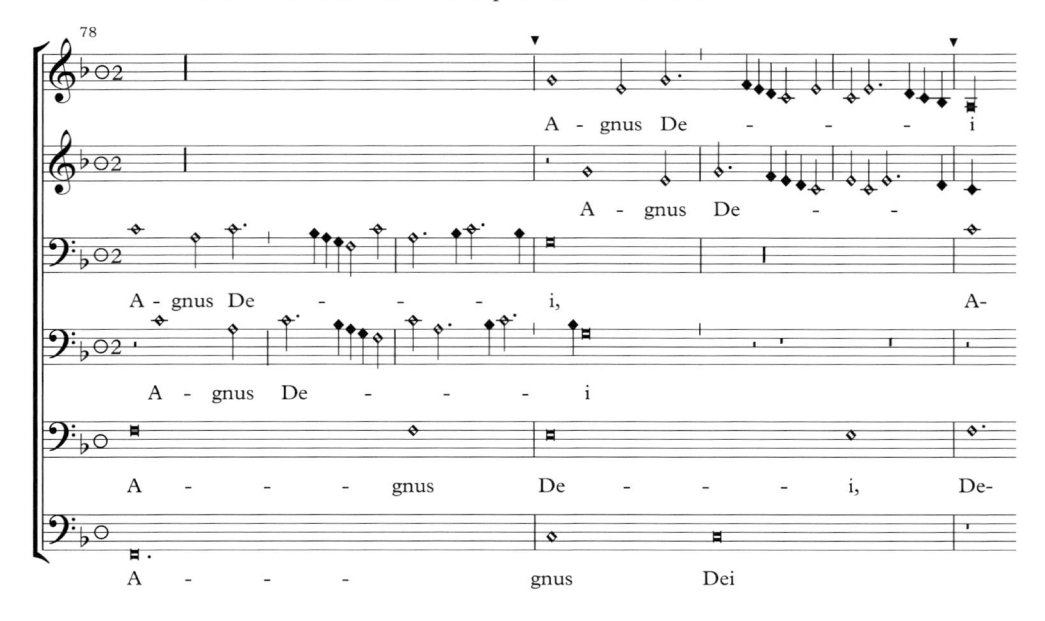

---

[29] Pietro Aaron discusses Josquin's use of ↺ in this passage in his *Libri tres de institutione harmonica*. See Chapter 6, p. 170.

theoretical difference between them is that O2 makes the perfect minor *modus* explicit, while ¢ does not. The *modus* is a consequence of the proportion: each perfect breve of the tenor and bass equals three imperfect breves of the other voices. The strong ternary rhythm of the cantus firmus makes the *modus* unmistakable at all times, even when the lower voices have hemiola rhythms in relation to the perfect *tempus*. The upper voices have mostly stepwise runs and no syncopated minims or other rhythmic complications that might impede their exuberant forward momentum.

As in the mensuration canons in the *Missa L'homme armé super voces musicales*, the performance *tactus* of this section must conform to the theoretical *tactus* of each sign (the semibreve of O and the breve of O2), but the notation does not specify the tempo. The tempo might be based on the equivalence of O with O in other sections, the equivalence of O2 (or ¢) with ¢ in other sections, or something between these extremes. Richard Sherr suggests the first option,[30] but that choice results in wildly fast tempos in O2 and rhythms that are unlike anything Josquin ever wrote in ordinary values in ¢. I believe a tempo in which the upper voices are somewhat faster than ¢, but the lower voices are not quite as fast as O, in other sections of the mass is a reasonable possibility. This solution is in line with the principle that it is the voices without the cantus firmus that determine the tempo relationships in the *L'homme armé* masses discussed previously. The character of the performance *tactus* is at least as important as the tempo. A *tactus* with little or no subdivision will enhance the rhythmic vitality of the lower voices and allow the upper voices to flow – or fly! – freely over the underlying foundation. As long as the tempo and *tactus* allow the listener to feel the rhythmic relationships on all levels, this *tour de force* will provide an awe-inspiring climax to the entire work.

L'homme armé masses like those discussed in this chapter are not typical examples of mensural notation. They are not only displays of exceptional compositional virtuosity, but structures that were inspired by the extreme possibilities of the notational system itself. They could not have been conceived in any other system. Although it is possible to translate the

---

[30] Sherr, "The Performance of Josquin's *L'homme armé* Masses," 264. Sherr cites Zacconi's discussion of the *tactus* when O2 and O are combined in 2:1 ratio (*Prattica di musica*, book 2, ch. 25, fols. 105ʳ–106ʳ) as evidence for his interpretation. Zacconi favors a *tactus* on the breve of O2 and explains that the semibreves of O2 are then "twice as fast" as those of O. He does not, however, advocate a fixed tempo for the *tactus* of any sign, and he often offers a choice of breve or semibreve *tactus* without any implication that the choice affects the speed of the notes. His statement that O2 is twice as fast as O in this proportion therefore does not imply that O2 is twice as fast as O in other contexts. See DeFord, "Zacconi's Theories of *Tactus* and Mensuration," 151–82.

patterns of note durations that their notation represents into modern notation, much of the meaning of the music is lost in that process. The works are fascinating demonstrations of the principle that a notational system can be not only a tool for recording musical ideas, but a source of inspiration for them as well.

10 | The five- and six-voice motets of Josquin

Josquin's motets for five and six voices are among his most celebrated works. They were copied and reprinted for many decades after his death and served as classic models for sixteenth-century composers. Their extraordinary popularity led to confusion between genuine works and imitations even in the years immediately following his death. In the preface to a 1540 print, the Nuremberg publisher Georg Forster famously quipped that Josquin was said to have written more music after he died than he did during his lifetime.[1] The fifteen works listed in Table 10.1 are identified in a recent study by John Milsom as the central core of Josquin's most securely attributed motets for more than four voices.[2] These works are the subject of this chapter.

The mensuration signs in Josquin's motets are much simpler than those in his *Missa L'homme armé super voces musicales*. Although there is some doubt about the original signs of some of the works, since the surviving sources are not always reliable in this respect, ten of the fifteen motets apparently use only the sign ₵, often with subsidiary passages in *sesquialtera*. The original notation of *Ave nobilissima creatura* and *Huc me sydereo* probably included O, C, and ₵2 in simultaneous relation with ₵. *Illibata Dei virgo nutrix* uses O and ₵2 in all voices simultaneously. *Praeter rerum seriem* has one section in O2, and the sole sign in *De profundis* is C. Some motets also have regular perfect or imperfect *modus* that is not represented explicitly in the notation.

The principles governing rhythms on the level of the breve and its subdivisions are similar in all of the works in ₵ and O2. The compositional *tactus* corresponds to the semibreve most of the time, but the breve takes on that function intermittently. The note values range for the most part from the semiminim to the breve. Slow cantus firmi include longs in some pieces,

---

[1] Georg Forster, Preface to *Selectissimarum mutetarum partim quinque partim quatuor vocum, tomus primus* (Nuremberg: Johann Petreius, 1540).

[2] John Milsom, "Motets for Five or More Voices," in *The Josquin Companion*, ed. Richard Sherr (Oxford University Press, 2000), 281–320. Milsom's chapter provides an excellent overview of the works under consideration. Valuable comments on most of these works are also found in David Fallows, *Josquin*, "Épitome musical" (Turnhout: Brepols, 2009).

Table 10.1 Josquin, five- and six-voice motets

Title	No. of voices	Signs (excluding *sesquialtera*)	Cantus firmus	Canon	No. of *partes*	Diminution	Other large-scale mensural features
Absolve	6	₵	Requiem	T/A	1		
Ave nobilissima	6	₵[O C]	Benedicta tu		2	3:2:1	Perfect *modus* in *prima pars*
Benedicta es	6	₵	Benedicta es	T/S (free)	3	6:4:3:2 (free)	
De profundis	5	C		S/A/B	1		
Huc me sydereo	5	O₵₵2	Plangent eum		2	6:2:1	Perfect *modus* in *prima pars*
Illibata	5	O₵₵2	la-mi-la		2	6:3:2:3 (*secunda pars*)	Ternary groupings on all levels in *prima pars*
Inviolata	5	₵	Inviolata	T1/T2	3		3:2:1 spacing of canonic voices
Miserere mei	5	₵	motto		3	2:1:2 (motto only)	6-breve motto
O virgo prudentissima	6	₵	Beata mater	T/A	2	variable	
O virgo virginum	6	₵	O virgo virginum	T/S	2		
Pater noster – Ave Maria	6	₵	Ave Maria (*secunda pars*)	T/A	2		Canon at 3 breves; perfect *modus* in *secunda pars*
Praeter rerum seriem	6	O2 ₵	Praeter rerum seriem	T/S (free)	2	6:3:1 (free)	
Salve Regina	5	₵	motto		3		Regular units of 7+7 breves
Stabat mater	5	₵	Comme femme		2		Perfect major *modus*
Virgo salutiferi	5	₵	Ave Maria	S/T/T	3	3:2:1 (free)	3:2:1 spacing of canonic voices

and *fusae*, which are usually limited to pairs on minim-max *initia*, appear occasionally. The shortest value that may carry a separate syllable is the minim. Breve-units are usually audible, but they may be suspended temporarily to create mensural contrast. Strong cadences end on breve *initia*, and weaker ones may end on semibreve-max *initia*. Penultimate intervals of cadences are usually semibreves, but sometimes breves when the final notes fall on breve *initia*. Dissonances are no longer than minims, and most non-suspension dissonances are semiminims or *fusae*. Both breves and semibreves may be syncopated, but syncopation on the semibreve level is more common and more prominent.

Sesquialtera passages may be notated in perfect breves or perfect semibreves under a variety of signs that may or may not be original. *Sesquialtera* notated in perfect semibreves appears only in simultaneous relation with other signs in which the semibreves are imperfect. With a single exception (in *De profundis*), *sesquialtera* notated in perfect breves appears in all voices in self-contained formal sections that do not overlap with sections governed by other signs. As in other repertoires of the time, the tempo relations between the sections of *sesquialtera* notated in perfect breves and the preceding or following sections in binary mensurations are problematic.

The principles governing mensural organization on levels larger than the breve are variable. Thirteen of the fifteen motets display some form of meaningful temporal organization on levels ranging from regular minor *modus* to large-scale proportional designs governing entire works. No two are alike in this respect. Three motets (*Ave nobilissima creatura*, *Huc me sydereo*, and *Illibata Dei virgo nutrix*) have regular *modus* and strictly proportional designs. Another six (*O virgo prudentissima*, *Virgo salutiferi*, *Inviolata*, *Praeter rerum seriem*, *Benedicta es*, and *Miserere mei, Deus*) employ the principles of diminution and *modus* in a freer sense. Four (*Pater noster – Ave Maria*, *O virgo virginum*, *Salve Regina*, and *Stabat mater*) mark more or less regular units of time above the level of the breve without using diminution. Only two (*Absolve, quaesumus* and *De profundis*) lack any form of mensural regularity above the level of the breve. The diverse mensural structures of these works serve rhetorical, as well as formal, purposes, and the close integration of formal and rhetorical functions is one of their most impressive features.

Theoretical evidence makes it clear that the standard performance *tactus* in Josquin's time was the semibreve in O and C and that either the semibreve or the divided breve could serve that function in ¢ and O2. The divided breve has the advantage of keeping performers aware of the breve-units, which are significant most of the time, and making larger units easier to project. There are some passages, however, in which a breve performance *tactus* must be divided into strictly equal semibreves in order to conform to the musical rhythms. Some motets present special complications with respect to *tactus* that are discussed below.

Motets with strict diminution

The principle of organizing motets on the basis of systematic diminution of a cantus firmus goes back to the thirteenth century. This compositional technique is traditionally called "isorhythm" by modern scholars, but that term has been challenged in recent studies.[3] It was associated with works of exceptionally serious character in the fifteenth century. It often involves perfect *modus*, which creates a sense of gravity through the long time units articulated by the perfect long-units of the mensuration.[4] Josquin's motets with strict diminution, all of which make use of perfect *modus* at least in the *prima pars*, are *Ave nobilissima creatura*, *Huc me sydereo*, and *Illibata Dei virgo nutrix*.

Ave nobilissima creatura and *Huc me sydereo* are closely related and were probably conceived as a pair.[5] Their cantus firmi are nearly identical melodically and their mensural schemes are very similar. In subject matter and affective character, however, they are opposites. *Ave nobilissima creatura* is an Annunciation motet based on the antiphon *Benedicta tu*, and *Huc me sydereo* is a Passion motet based on *Plangent eum*. Both motets present the cantus firmus three times in the tenor voice: once in the *prima pars* and twice in the *secunda pars*.

The original notation of these motets is open to question. *Huc me sydereo* is notated in different ways in different sources. Its original notation probably had the signs O, ₵, and ₵2 in the three statements of the tenor and ₵ throughout in the other voices. In this version, the written values of the tenor are identical in each statement, and the breve of ₵ equals the semibreve of O and the long of ₵2. *Ave nobilissima creatura* is notated in O2 in the first statement and ₵ in the second and third statements in the surviving sources, but the analogy with *Huc me sydereo* suggests that the original signs were O, C, and ₵ in the tenor and ₵ in the other voices, with the semibreve of O and C equal to the breve of ₵.[6] These relationships are shown schematically in Table 10.2. The tenor signs O and C imply regular

---

[3] See Margaret Bent, "Isorhythm," *Oxford Music Online*, www.oxfordmusiconline.com (accessed 24 July 2010).
[4] These principles are discussed in Rolf Dammann, "Spätformen der isorhythmischen Motette im 16. Jahrhundert," *Archiv für Musikwissenschaft* 10 (1953), 16–40, and Thomas Brothers, "Vestiges of the Isorhythmic Tradition in Mass and Motet, ca. 1450–1475," *Journal of the American Musicological Society* 44 (1991), 1–56.
[5] The relation between these motets is discussed in Milsom, "Motets for Five or More Voices," 286–88.
[6] See Willem Elders, "Zusammenhänge zwischen den Motetten *Ave nobilissima creatura* und *Huc me sydereo* von Josquin des Prez," *Tijdschrift van de Vereniging voor Nederlandse Muziekgeschiedenis* 22 (1971), 67–73.

Table 10.2 Mensural equivalencies in Josquin's *Ave nobilissima creatura* and *Huc me sydereo* (with signs reconstructed hypothetically for *Ave nobilissima creatura*)

Ave nobilissima creatura		Huc me sydereo	
Prima pars	Secunda pars	Prima pars	Secunda pars
¢ 𝄽 𝄽 𝄽 ¢ 𝄽 𝄽 ¢ 𝄽		¢ 𝄽 𝄽 𝄽 ¢ 𝄽 𝄽 ¢ 𝄽	
O ◊ ◊ ◊ C ◊ ◊ ¢ 𝄽		O ◊ ◊ ◊ ¢ 𝄽 𝄽 ¢2 𝄽	

Example 10.1 Josquin, *Ave nobilissima creatura*, tenor. After *Motetti de la corona*, *libro tertio* (Fossombrone: Petrucci, 1519), with the notation reconstructed as explained in the text. Petrucci notates the *prima pars* in O2 and the *secunda* and *tertia partes* in ¢.

modus in the simultaneous voices in ¢, because the perfect breve of O equals three breves of ¢ and the imperfect breve of C equals two.

The sequence of signs in the tenor creates mensural transformation, as well as systematic diminution, in these motets, because the breves are perfect (unless imperfected) in O and imperfect in the other tenor signs. The tenor of *Ave nobilissima creatura* is shown in Example 10.1 with the notation reconstructed as suggested above. The proportional ratios among the three statements are in principle 3:2:1, but they are not exact in the phrases that include semibreves. The second phrase, for example, has twelve semibreve-units in O, but ten in C. Only the perfect breves (the first and last notes) are reduced to ⅔ of their value in C; the imperfected breve (the second note) and the semibreves have the same value in both O and C. In the sections in C and ¢, exactly half of the forty-six breve-units are occupied by rests and half by notes in the tenor.

The systematic diminution of the cantus firmus is mirrored on a smaller scale by the decreasing length of the notes from one phrase to the next within the cantus firmus itself. The first phrase consists only of breves; the second mixes breves, semibreves, and a dotted figure; the third introduces a rhythm that weakens the breve-units with a dotted semibreve that crosses a breve *initium* in O (because the dotted semibreve imperfects the preceding breve and the value added by the dot falls in the next breve-unit); and the fourth consists only of semibreves and a dotted figure until the last two notes. As the breve-units in the tenor decrease in prominence, the listener's attention shifts from larger to smaller units of time. In the last three phrases of the third cantus-firmus statement, where the tenor reaches its fastest point (bars 245–68), the non-tenor voices join the tenor in referring to Jesus, as well as Mary, for the first time. This brilliant stroke brings the elements of music and text together at the point of culmination toward which both have been aiming throughout the work.[7]

The opening section of the *prima pars* of *Ave nobilissima creatura* (the 48 non-tenor breves preceding the entry of the cantus firmus) is divided by changes of scoring, thematic material, and text into two sections of 24 breves each. There is audible imperfect *modus* (not perfect *modus*, as would be expected from the mensuration of the silent tenor) in the first 24 breve-units. The last ten bars of this section (bars 38–48) quote the words "Ave Maria, gratia plena, Dominus tecum," which lead directly into the words of the cantus firmus ("Benedicta tu . . . ") in bar 49. These words are highlighted by a striking shift to homophonic texture, with all non-tenor voices present for the first time, and by a slowing of the rhythmic motion from semibreves and minims to breves and semibreves (see Example 10.2).

Huc me sydereo follows the pattern of *Ave nobilissima creatura* closely in some respects, but departs from it in others. The cantus firmi of the two motets are identical in the *prima pars* except that the first phrase is one note (and one breve) shorter in *Huc me sydereo* and the last group of rests (following phrase 3) has two breves instead of three. The adjustment in the number of rests maintains the equality of the number of semibreve-units with and without tenor notes in the statements in imperfect *tempus*.[8] The cantus-firmus statements in the *secunda pars* are only half as long as they are in *Ave nobilissima creatura*, however, and the overall proportional ratios are therefore in principle 6:2:1, rather than 3:2:1, with slight irregularities resulting from the different interpretations of perfect and imperfect *tempus*. The *secunda pars* is correspondingly shorter and less weighty, perhaps because the text does not lead toward a climax like that in *Ave nobilissima creatura*. The opening of the *prima pars*, in contrast, is heavier, in conformity with the affect of the text. The opening words are "Huc me sydereo descendere jussit Olympo" ("Hither from starry Olympus [love]

---

[7] See Milsom, "Motets for Five or More Voices," 286.
[8] Milsom, ibid., 287, suggests that *Huc me sydereo* was probably modeled on *Ave nobilissima creatura*, rather than the other way around. Regardless of the order of composition, the difference in the lengths of the rests in the two works supports the hypothesis that the identity in the total number of breve-units with and without notes in the second and third *partes* was an intentional element of their design.

Example 10.2 Josquin, *Ave nobilissima creatura*, bars 36–42. After *Motetti de la corona, libro tertio* (Fossombrone: Petrucci, 1519), with the tenor reconstructed as in Example 10.1.

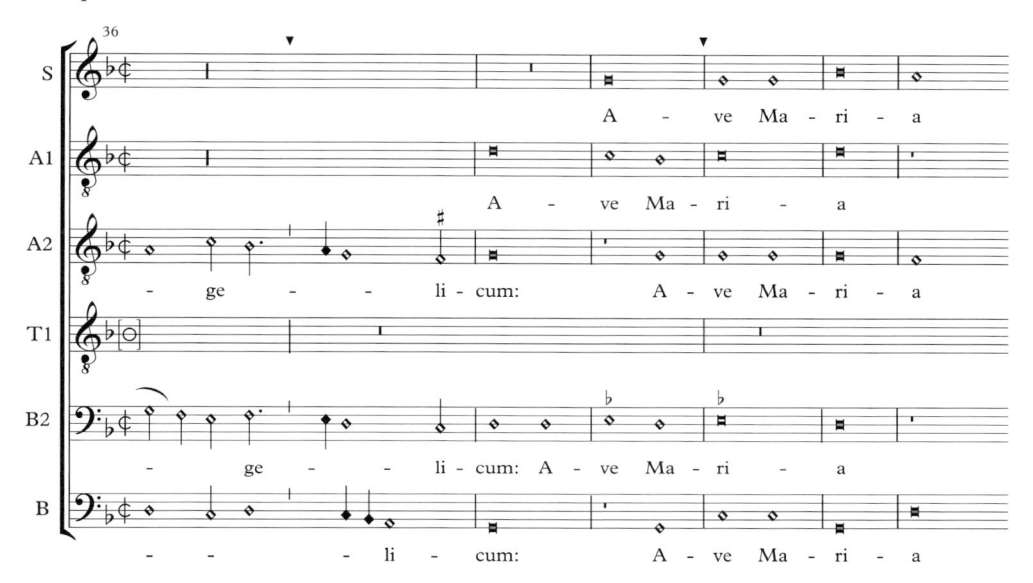

commanded me to descend"). The music for the first three words is organized in audible perfect long-units (corresponding to the notated perfect breve-units of the silent tenor) by means of voice entries, phrase ends, and long notes. Perfect *modus* portrays the grandeur of "starry Olympus," and its disappearance from the audible musical structure at "descendere" marks the transition from heaven to earth. The point is underscored by a striking descending scale on the phrase beginning with the word "descendere"(see Example 10.3).

The non-tenor voices of *Ave nobilissima creatura* and *Huc me sydereo* are in rhythmic styles similar to Josquin's other works in ₵. A breve performance *tactus* is especially desirable in them, because it allows the tenor to be measured in semibreves in O and C. Given that interpretation, O and C are integral and ₵ is diminished with respect to the performance *tactus*, but with respect to the compositional *tactus*, which corresponds mostly to the semibreve in ₵ and the minim in O and C, ₵ is integral and the uncut signs are in subduple (1:2) proportion. The tempos of the tenor signs must be derived from that of the standard ₵ of the other voices.

Illibata Dei virgo nutrix is a setting of an anonymous poem in praise of the Virgin that features an acrostic of Josquin's name in the text of the *prima pars*. It is based on a pattern of systematic diminution that leads to a

Example 10.3 Josquin, *Huc me sydereo*, bars 13–30. After Vatican City, Biblioteca Apostolica Vaticana, Cappella Sistina, Ms. 45, fols. 181^v–187^r. The sixth voice in that source may not be authentic. It is not included in the example.

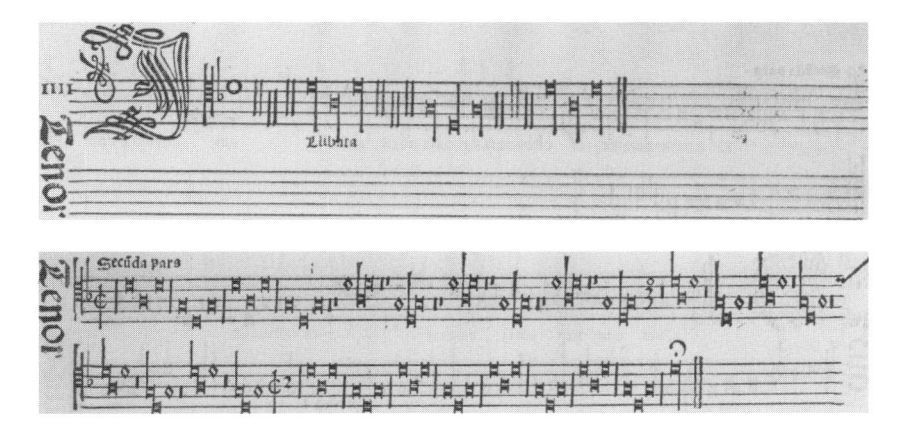

Figure 10.1 Josquin, *Illibata Dei virgo nutrix*, tenor. *Motetti a cinque, libro primo* (Venice: Ottaviano Petrucci, 1508).

textual and musical climax similar to that in *Ave nobilissima creatura*. The cantus firmus is a three-note figure, which appears alternately on D and G, corresponding to the solmization syllables la-mi-la, a *soggetto cavato dalle vocali* representing the name "Maria." The *prima pars* praises her in general terms, while the *secuna pars* addresses her directly and culminates in the prayer "Consola la-mi-la canentes in tua laude" ("Comfort those singing la-mi-la in your honor"). The work may have been composed for the papal choir, whose members would have appreciated both the compositional sophistication of the work and the spirit of collective prayer that it embodies.[9]

Figure 10.1 shows the tenor of the motet as it appears in Petrucci's 1508 print, and Figure 10.2 shows the overall mensural design in schematic form. It is enlightening to contrast the clarity with which the design emerges from the facsimile with the difficulty of extracting it from a modern edition in score. The *prima pars* is in perfect *tempus* with perfect minor and major *modus*, although both of the surviving sources group the perfect long rests in pairs, rather than in groups of three. The major *modus*-units (groups of three perfect longs) are themselves organized in groups of three, with the first two groups in each set corresponding to rests and the third to statements of the cantus firmus. There are three such groups in the *prima pars*: a total of 81 perfect breves subdivided and

---

[9] Richard Sherr, "*Illibata Dei virgo nutrix* and Josquin's Roman Style," *Journal of the American Musicological Society* 41 (1988), 434–64, discusses this motet in detail and argues for its composition during Josquin's Roman years, in part on grounds of this interpretation of the text.

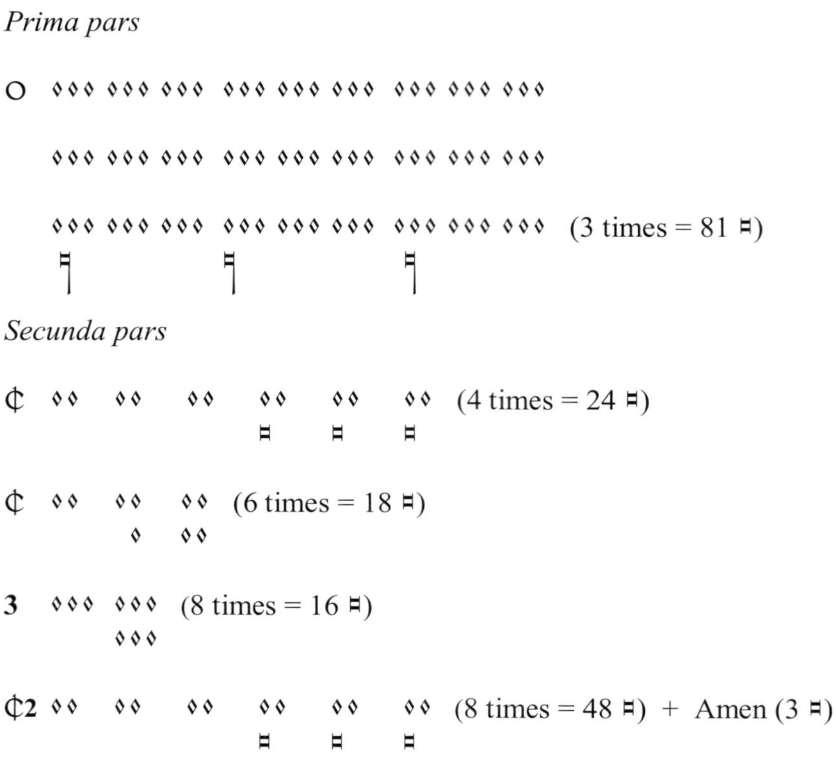

Prima pars

◯ ◊◊◊ ◊◊◊ ◊◊◊   ◊◊◊ ◊◊◊ ◊◊◊   ◊◊◊ ◊◊◊ ◊◊◊

◊◊◊ ◊◊◊ ◊◊◊   ◊◊◊ ◊◊◊ ◊◊◊   ◊◊◊ ◊◊◊ ◊◊◊

◊◊◊ ◊◊◊ ◊◊◊   ◊◊◊ ◊◊◊ ◊◊◊   ◊◊◊ ◊◊◊ ◊◊◊   (3 times = 81 ▯)

▯   ▯   ▯

Secunda pars

₵ ◊◊   ◊◊   ◊◊   ◊◊   ◊◊   ◊◊   (4 times = 24 ▯)
            ▯   ▯   ▯

₵ ◊◊   ◊◊   ◊◊   (6 times = 18 ▯)
      ◊   ◊◊

3 ◊◊◊ ◊◊◊   (8 times = 16 ▯)
   ◊◊◊

₵2 ◊◊   ◊◊   ◊◊   ◊◊   ◊◊   ◊◊   (8 times = 48 ▯) + Amen (3 ▯)
            ▯   ▯   ▯

Figure 10.2 Josquin, *Illibata Dei virgo nutrix*: mensural structure. The upper lines show the structure of the non-tenor voices; the lower lines show the durations of the notes of the tenor where it is present. The tenor has rests where no notes are shown for it.

grouped in threes on every level from the semibreve to the complete *pars*. In the *secunda pars*, statements of the cantus firmus occupy three breves of ₵, then three semibreves of ₵, then three semibreves of *sesquialtera*, and finally three breves of ₵2. Each cantus-firmus statement is preceded by an equivalent number of rests. The non-tenor voices have the same signs as the tenor.

In the *prima pars*, Josquin varies the grouping of breves in the non-tenor voices to create a sense of surface acceleration over the solid, unvarying cantus firmus. The section corresponding to the first eighteen breves of tenor rest (bars 1–18) is divided into three phrases of six breves, each scored for a different pair of voices and ending with a strong cadence. The voice entries are spaced at intervals of a breve in the first two phrases, and the prevailing rate of surface motion is the minim (see Example 10.4).

Example 10.4 Josquin, *Illibata Dei virgo nutrix*, bars 1–6. After *Motetti a cinque, libro primo* (Venice: Petrucci, 1508).

Example 10.5 Josquin, *Illibata Dei virgo nutrix*, bars 28–33. After *Motetti a cinque, libro primo* (Venice: Petrucci, 1508).

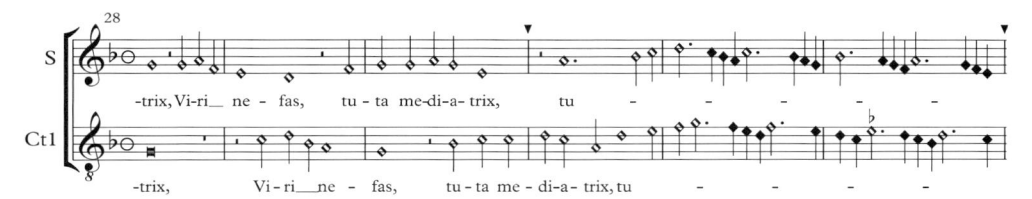

These phrases establish the mensural units on the breve level and suggest the ternary grouping of breves through the six-breve phrase lengths; the grouping of the perfect long-units, however, is in pairs, rather than threes.

The section corresponding to the second 18 breves of tenor rest (bars 28–45) is divided into two phrases of nine breves that conform to the ternary grouping of longs, but the surface rhythms call attention away from the larger time units by setting up mensural conflicts on the level of the breve and semibreve (see Example 10.5). The opening imitation is at the interval of two semibreves, so that the rhythms of the lower voice are displaced with respect to the breve-units. The sequential repetitions beginning in bar 32 occur at intervals of three minims and are imitated at the interval of one minim, effectively eliminating the listener's awareness of larger time units. Similar mensural disruptions occur within the second nine-breve phrase, in which a cadence after five breves (bar 42) undermines the abstract ternary grouping of breves.

The section corresponding to the third 18 breves of tenor rest (bars 55–72; see Example 10.6) is not divided into regular ternary units even on paper. Individual breve-units are marked at first by the alternation of pairs of voices and by cadences on breve *initia*, but the cadences soon move to the second semibreve *initium* of each breve (bar 60) and finally appear on every

Example 10.6 Josquin, *Illibata Dei virgo nutrix*: (a) bars 57–61; (b) bars 66–69. After *Motetti a cinque, libro primo* (Venice: Petrucci, 1508), with the second contratenor (missing in the only extant copy of Petrucci) after Vatican City, Biblioteca Apostolica Vaticana, Cappella Sistina, Ms. 15, fols. 242ᵛ–246ʳ.

other semibreve (bars 66–69), directly contradicting the perfect breve-units of the mensuration. The shift from melismatic to syllabic declamation in this section increases the emphasis on the shorter time units. Order is re-established with the final entry of the cantus firmus at the end of the section (bar 73), but the cadences that mark breve *initia* from there to the end do not coincide with the long *initia* of the cantus firmus. This dramatic progression from the articulation of very long to very short mensural units is accomplished with no change in the rhythmic character of the individual voices. It can be appreciated only if the listener is aware of the constantly shifting balance among the different mensural levels that govern the abstract design of the work.

Example 10.7 Josquin, *Illibata Dei virgo nutrix*, bars 83–89. After *Motetti a cinque, libro primo* (Venice: Petrucci, 1508), with the second contratenor (missing in the only extant copy of Petrucci) after Vatican City, Biblioteca Apostolica Vaticana, Cappella Sistina, Ms. 15, fols. 242^v–246^r.

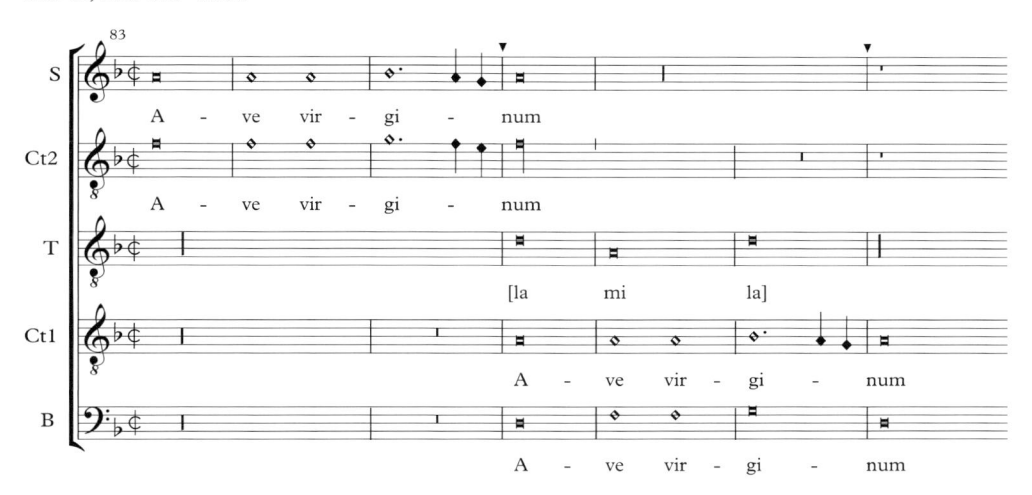

In the *secunda pars*, an analogous sense of acceleration is built into the structure of the cantus firmus itself and supported by the rhythms of the other voices. Perfect minor *modus* applies to all sections except the *sesquialtera*. In the first section (bars 83–106), perfect long-units are marked by changes of scoring that at first coincide with the tenor rests and cantus-firmus statements (see Example 10.7), but after the first fifteen breves, the phrases overlap in ways that shift attention to shorter mensural units. In the second section (bars 107–24), the ternary groups of semibreves in the tenor conflict with the binary groups in the other voices. Most of the cadences fall on semibreve *initia* that coincide with neither the imperfect breve *initia* of the mensuration nor the implied perfect breve *initia* of the tenor (see Example 10.8). After the first four breves (bars 107–10), the semibreve is the exclusive compositional *tactus* and the largest audible mensural unit. The breve rest in contratenor 1, bars 110–11, is notated incorrectly in both surviving sources of the piece; since it crosses from one breve-unit to another, it should have been written as two semibreve rests. This suggests that a copyist at some point in the transmission of the work, or perhaps the composer himself, was aware that the breve-units were not musically meaningful at this point. The *sesquialtera* section (bars 125–40) resolves the preceding complications into a simple triple meter with a perfect breve compositional *tactus*. It appears at the climactic point in the text where the

Example 10.8 Josquin, *Illibata Dei virgo nutrix*, bars 107–112. After *Motetti a cinque, libro primo* (Venice: Petrucci, 1508), with the second contratenor (missing in the only extant copy of Petrucci) after Vatican City, Biblioteca Apostolica Vaticana, Cappella Sistina, Ms. 15, fols. 242^v–246^r.

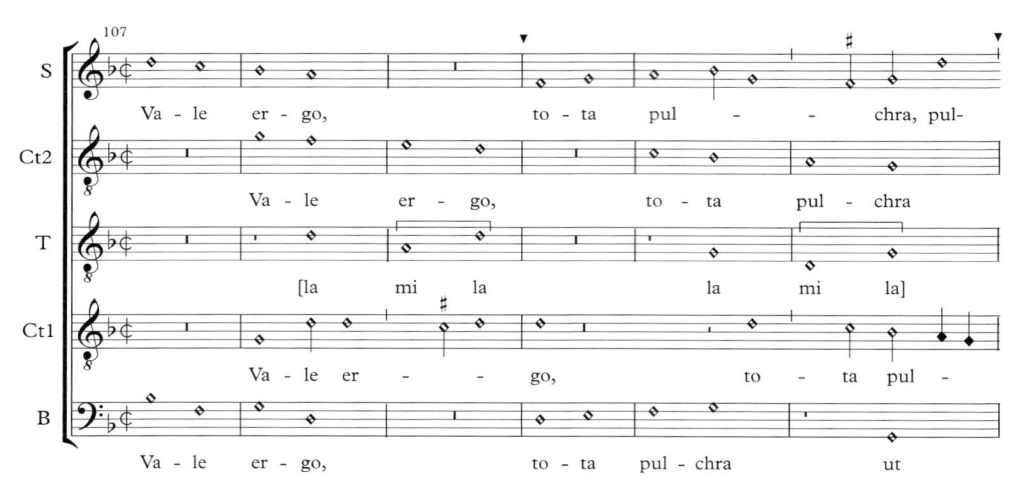

singers refer to themselves as those singing "la-mi-la." For the first and only time in the piece, the cantus firmus ceases to be a contrasting element, and its rhythms and melody permeate all of the voices (see Example 10.9). The concluding section (bars 141–92) consists of a four-fold repetition of a simple, direct petition, with twelve breves in each statement. Its opening motive (Example 10.10) resembles the beginning of the *secunda pars* (Example 10.7), but notated under the sign ¢2, rather than ¢. The compositional *tactus* of this section is the undivided breve. The contrapuntal rhythm moves exclusively in breves, declamation is on semibreves, syncopations are limited to breves, penultimate intervals of cadences are breves, and suspensions are semibreves. The cantus firmus creates regular ternary groups of breves that make the perfect *modus*-units easily audible.

O and ¢2 function differently here than they do in simultaneous relation with ¢ in the two preceding motets. The compositional *tactus* of O is the semibreve, and its performance *tactus* must be a semibreve that is only a little slower than the semibreve of ¢. ¢ itself corresponds to two distinct rhythmic styles that suggest different performance tactus. In the first section of the *secunda pars*, ¢ works well with a lightly divided breve performance *tactus*, but in the second section, a distinctly divided breve or semibreve performance *tactus* fits the rhythms better. The *sesquialtera* section requires a perfect breve performance tactus corresponding to its compositional

Example 10.9 Josquin, *Illibata Dei virgo nutrix*, bars 130–35. After *Motetti a cinque, libro primo* (Venice: Petrucci, 1508), with the second contratenor (missing in the only extant copy of Petrucci) after Vatican City, Biblioteca Apostolica Vaticana, Cappella Sistina, Ms. 15, fols. 242^v–246^r.

Example 10.10 Josquin, *Illibata Dei virgo nutrix*, bars 141–46. After *Motetti a cinque, libro primo* (Venice: Petrucci, 1508), with the second contratenor (missing in the only extant copy of Petrucci) after Vatican City, Biblioteca Apostolica Vaticana, Cappella Sistina, Ms. 15, fols. 242^v–246^r.

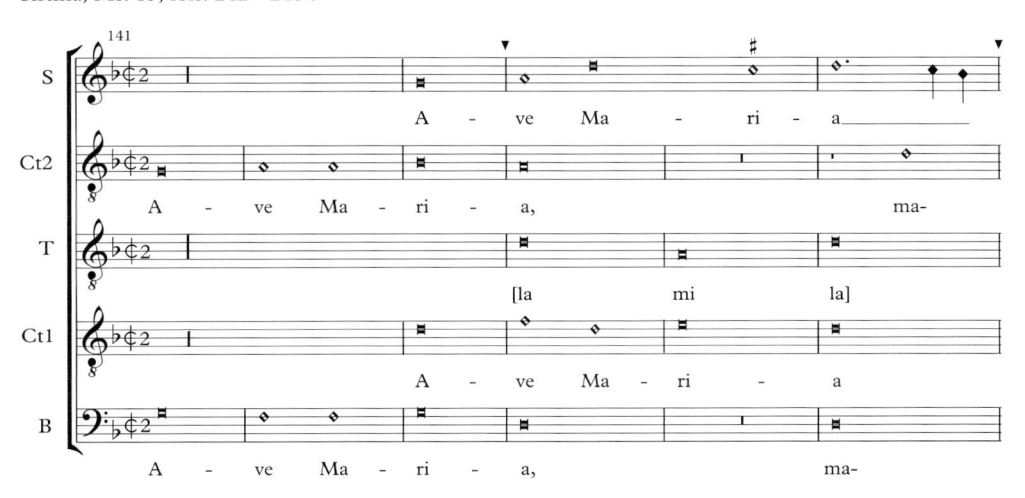

tactus. If its tempo is interpreted literally, as it probably should be given the overall design of the work, it will sound slower than the preceding ¢ even though the cantus firmus moves faster, because the compositional *tactus* is twice as long and the surface motion is slower. The following ¢2 should probably be in 4:3 proportion to the *sesquialtera* on the semibreve level, such that ₵2 is equivalent to ↺, the more common sign of 4:3 proportion following *sesquialtera*; this interpretation makes it twice as fast as the opening ₵. Its performance *tactus* should theoretically be the imperfect long, as in *Huc me sydereo*, but that *tactus* contradicts the perfect *modus* and causes every phrase, including the final one, to end in the middle of a *tactus*. An undivided breve performance tactus makes more musical sense.

Motets with free forms of diminution

Six of Josquin's motets use the principle of diminution in a variety of ways that do not depend on strict repetition. *O virgo prudentissima* and *Virgo salutiferi* have cantus firmi that are independent of the main text and stated once in each *pars*; each subsequent statement is a free diminution of the preceding one. *Praeter rerum seriem*, *Inviolata*, and *Benedicta es* have chants associated with their main texts as cantus firmi; these cantus firmi are not repeated, but they are rhythmically compressed in other ways as the works progress. *Miserere mei, Deus* is based on a short motto that is diminished strictly in the *secunda pars*, but surrounded by free material between its appearances. The first five of these motets treat the cantus firmus in strict or free canon between two voices and involve some mensural groupings on the level of *modus*, but strict *modus* is found only in *Praeter rerum seriem*.

O virgo prudentissima is a setting of a poem by Angelo Poliziano with the cantus firmus *Beata mater*. It builds energy over the course of the work by compressing the mensural units both within each *pars* and from one *pars* to the next. Each *pars* is divided by the tenor cantus firmus into four sections with carefully calculated, but not formulaic, proportional lengths (see Table 10.3).[10] As in *Ave nobilissima creatura* and *Huc me sydereo*, the large-scale compression is mirrored by a move to shorter values in consecutive phrases of the cantus firmus itself. In the *prima pars*, it begins in breves, then moves to a mix of semibreves and minims; in the *secunda pars*, it is stated mostly in semibreves with a few minims until the last phrase before the final "Alleluia," which ends with a segment entirely in minims and semiminims except for the penultimate note (see Example 10.11). The interval between the canonic voices (tenor and alto) remains fixed at two breves, creating a foundation of regularity beneath the pattern of surface acceleration.

---

[10] The final longs of the tenor of both *partes*, over which the other voices continue for an additional three breves, are excluded from these counts.

Table 10.3 Proportional relations in Josquin's *O virgo prudentissima*

Tenor		*Prima pars*	*Secunda pars*
I	Rests	32 breves (1–32)	32 breves (109–40)
II	Four cantus-firmus phrases	32 breves (33–64)	24 breves (141–64)
III	Rests	16 breves (*sesquialtera*; 65–80)	8 breves (165–72)
IV	Two cantus-firmus phrases	24 breves (81–104)	7 breves (173–79)
	Coda ("Alleluia")		7 breves (180–86)

Example 10.11 Josquin, *O virgo prudentissima*, tenor: (a) *prima pars*; (b) *secunda pars*. After Vatican City, Biblioteca Apostolica Vaticana, Cappella Sistina, Ms. 24, fols. 18ᵛ–23ʳ.

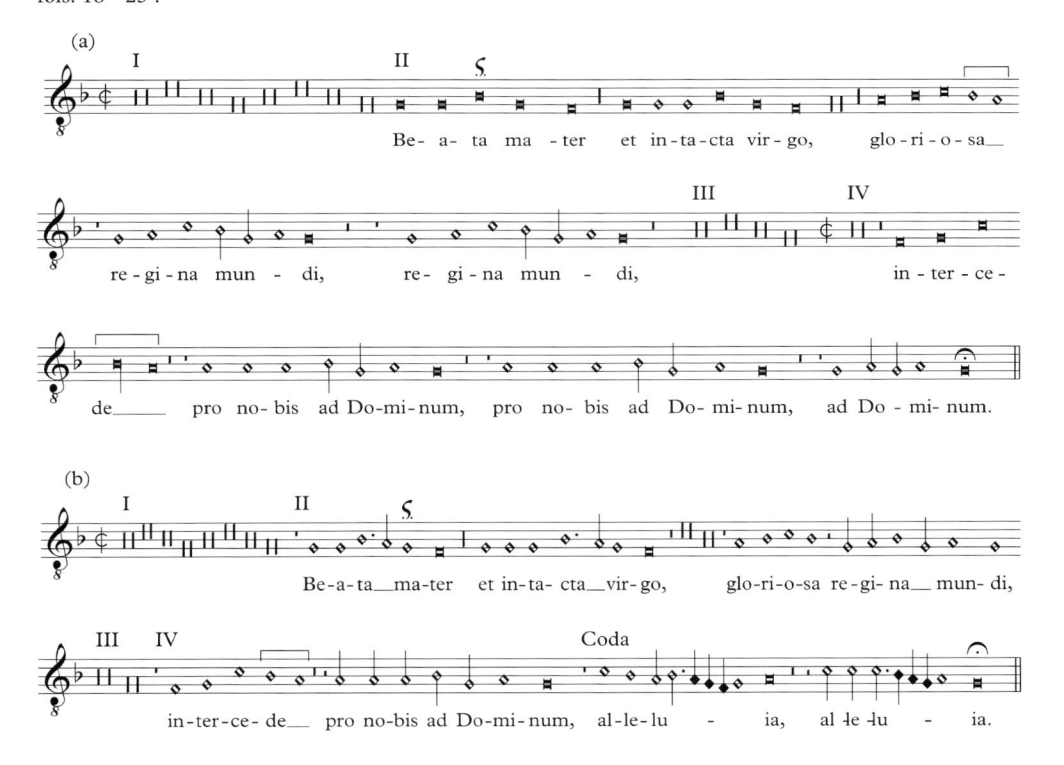

The other voices support the tenor pattern by articulating time units that progress from larger to smaller over the course of the work. In the *prima pars*, the first section is divided into four eight-bar segments, suggesting regular mensural organization on the levels of imperfect minor and major *modus*, as well as *tempus*. In the *secunda pars*, the opening thirty-two breves are divided into 16+16, but asymmetrical phrasing within the sections

Example 10.12 Josquin, *Virgo salutiferi*, *prima pars*, tenor. After Florence, Biblioteca Medicea-Laurenziana, Ms. 666 ("Medici Codex"), fols. 112ᵛ–116ʳ.

A -ve Ma-ri - a, gra-ti-a ple-na, Do-mi-nus te-cum, Do-mi-nus te- cum.

obscures the larger-scale symmetry. The point of maximum rhythmic and mensural compression coincides with the place where the non-canonic voices drop their text and take up the prayer of the cantus firmus: "Gloriosa regina mundi, intercede pro nobis ad Dominum, Alleluia" ("Glorious queen of the world, intercede for us with the Lord, Alleluia").

Virgo salutiferi, a setting of a poem by Ercole Strozzi with the cantus firmus *Ave Maria*, makes use of similar principles, but with less regular temporal organization above the level of the breve. The interval between the canonic voices (tenor and superius) is three breves in the *prima pars*, two breves in the *secunda pars*, and one breve in the *tertia pars*. The rhythms of the cantus firmus are correspondingly diminished in a roughly 3:2:1 ratio, but they are different in each statement and the diminution is far from exact. The relative lengths of the three *partes* (108, 59, and 41 breves)[11] and their internal subdivisions are likewise related through principles of informal, rather than strictly numerical, balance.

As in the preceding motets, the time units articulated by the music decrease in length over the course of the work. There is no regular grouping of breves in the section of the *prima pars* preceding the entry of the cantus firmus (bars 1–40), but the section with the cantus firmus (bars 41–109) is organized on the basis of large-scale time units defined by the phrases and rests in the cantus firmus. The first cantus-firmus phrase consists of nine breves divided into three groups of three, conforming to the three-breve interval between the canonic voices. The remaining phrases consist of four breves with binary subdivisions that conflict with the interval between the voices. The rests last for twelve breves after the first phrase, ten after the second, and six after the third (see Example 10.12). In the *secunda pars*, there is little regular grouping of breves except in the first phrase of the cantus firmus. In the *tertia pars*, even the pairing of semibreves is weak except in the first phrase of the cantus firmus. As in *O virgo prudentissima*, this mensural compression makes a rhetorical, as well as a

---

[11] The music ends at different points in different voices in each of the *partes*. My counts end just before the final note in the *comes* of the canon. The point about the informal relations among the lengths of the sections remains regardless of where one chooses to end the counts.

Example 10.13 Josquin, *Virgo salutiferi*, bars 194–99. After Florence, Biblioteca Medicea-Laurenziana, Ms. 666 ("Medici Codex"), fols. 112ᵛ–116ʳ.

musical, point. The last phrase of the cantus firmus, which completes the text and music of the antiphon ("Benedicta tu in mulieribus, alleluia"), appears for the first time at this point (see Example 10.13). After this dramatic climax, a repeated three-breve phrase plus a three-breve *supplementum* (bars 206–14) brings back the larger time units that lead the work to a satisfying conclusion.

Inviolata resembles *Virgo salutiferi* in that it makes use of a cantus firmus in canon at the interval of three breves in the *prima pars*, two breves in the *secunda pars*, and one breve in the *tertia pars*, but in other respects time units larger than the breve play a very different role in the work. The cantus firmus is stated mostly in semibreves, so that its rhythms blend seamlessly with those of the other voices. At the beginning (bars 1–15), the voices enter at intervals of three breves, anticipating the interval between the canonic voices. This pattern suggests perfect *modus*, which lends an aura of dignity to the work, though *modus*-level rhythms play no further role in the *prima pars*. The scribes of two sources picked up on the *modus* implications of the opening and notated the rests as perfect longs (see Figure 10.3).[12] This notation cannot be correct, because it implies perfect *modus* throughout the canonic voices and would require alteration of the breve in bar 20 (the second syllable of "Maria") and perfection of the following long, but it confirms the significance of the musical allusion to perfect *modus* in the

---

[12] Florence, Biblioteca Medicea-Laurenziana, Ms. 666 ("Medici Codex") and Vatican City, Biblioteca Apostolica Vaticana, Cappella Sistina, Ms. 15.

Figure 10.3 Josquin, *Inviolata*, tenor. Florence, Biblioteca Medicea-Laurenziana, Ms. 666 ("Medici Codex"), fol. 89ᵛ.

minds of some sensitive copyists. The beginning of the *secunda pars* establishes imperfect *modus* (corresponding to the time interval of the canon) through the spacing of initial voice entries and the limitation of cadences to imperfect long *initia*. The *modus* is weakened by the entry of a cantus-firmus phrase on a breve-max *initium* in bar 86, however, and the *pars* ends on a breve-max *initium*.

The *tertia pars* begins with a three-fold repetition of a five-breve phrase that sets three parallel invocations ("O benigna, O regina, O Maria"). The superius is set off from the other voices through syncopation and an expressive melisma on the final syllable. Both the asymmetry of the phrase and the syncopation contribute to the speech-like quality of these invocations, which lends a powerful sense of urgency to the words. The effect contrasts strongly with the more formal mensural character of the rest of the work (see Example 10.14). Ternary groups of breves, recalling those at the beginning of the *prima pars*, re-emerge in the last nine breves preceding the final long of the tenor (Example 10.15). The formal cadence that would be expected on the last note of the tenor cantus firmus (bar 138) is denied, because the ternary groups of breves in the *comes* voice of the canon are displaced by a breve with respect to those of the tenor. The cadence is therefore all the more satisfying when it finally arrives six breves later (bar 144). The bass concludes with a tag that ends part-way through the next implied perfect long-unit of the preceding passage, adding grace to the cadence and hinting at an imagined continuation of the music beyond the end of the work.

Example 10.14 Josquin, *Inviolata*, bars 108–12. After Florence, Biblioteca Medicea-Laurenziana, Ms. 666 ("Medici Codex"), fols. 89ᵛ–92ʳ.

Praeter rerum seriem resembles *Ave nobilissima creatura* and *Huc me sydereo* in its use of imperfect *tempus* with strict perfect *modus* in the *prima pars*, but the role of the *modus* in the rhythmic structure of the piece and its relation to the process of diminution is quite different. The cantus firmus is a Sequence with the form AA'BB'CC' (sections with the same letter have the same music, but different words, in the chant). The A sections correspond to the *prima pars*, which is in imperfect *tempus* with perfect *modus* (O2), and the B and C sections to the *secunda pars*, which is in imperfect *tempus* (¢) followed by *sesquialtera* signed 3. The cantus firmus appears mostly in the tenor and superius in free canon with little overlap between the voices. Some of its phrases move to other voices, and the tenor and superius have some free material as well as the cantus firmus.

The text has a strong and regular trochaic meter with lines of 7+7+4 syllables in each section:

Praeter rerum seriem	parit Deum hominem	virgo mater,
Nec vir tangit virginem,	nec prolis originem	novit pater.
(etc.)		

Josquin projects the text rhythm with regular musical rhythms in the cantus firmus. In all sections except B', accented syllables are set to notes twice as long as unaccented syllables in the first two phrases of each section, while the third phrase usually has notes of equal value. The notes in the cantus firmus are longs and breves in A, breves and semibreves in A' and B,

Example 10.15 Josquin, *Inviolata*, bars 135–46. After Florence, Biblioteca Medicea-Laurenziana, Ms. 666 ("Medici Codex"), fols. 89ᵛ–92ʳ.

and breves and semibreves of *sesquialtera* in C and C′ until the last phrase. Example 10.16 shows the first phrase of each section of the cantus firmus in its simplest rhythmic form, as it appears in the tenor. The mensural *initia* (longs, breves, and semibreves in A and A′; breves and semibreves in the other sections) are shown above the staff.

The ternary rhythm of the cantus firmus relates to the mensuration and rhythms of the other voices in a different way in each section. In the A section, it is supported with faster rhythms that do not challenge the dominance of the perfect *modus*. In the A′ section, the ternary groups of semibreves in the cantus firmus conflict with the imperfect *tempus* of the

Example 10.16 Josquin, *Praeter rerum seriem*, tenor, bars 1–4, 20–21, 40–44, 65–69, 86–89, and 107–10. After Vatican City, Biblioteca Apostolica Vaticana, Cappella Sistina, Ms. 16, fols. 160^v–164^r.

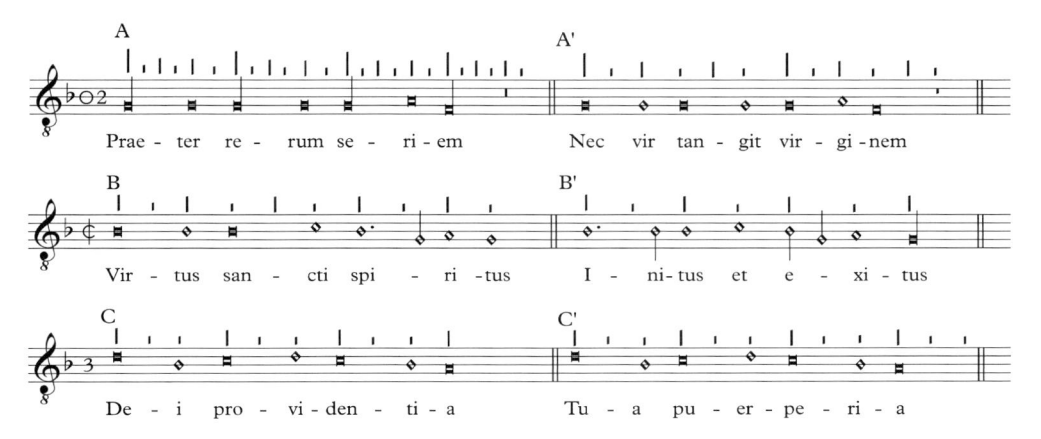

Example 10.17 Josquin, *Praeter rerum seriem*, bars 20–21 (long-units), tenor, bass 1, and bass 2. After Vatican City, Biblioteca Apostolica Vaticana, Cappella Sistina, Ms. 16, fols. 160^v–164^r.

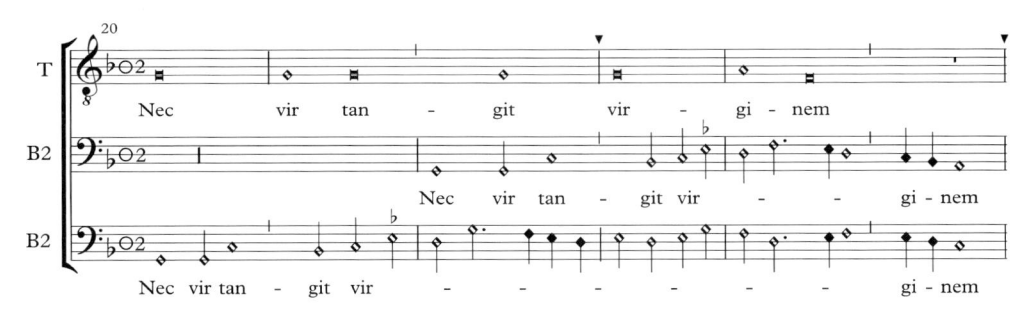

mensuration. The other voices articulate groups of three minims that are out of phase with the *tempus* and with each other at the beginning of the section. These conflicting groups are reconciled only at the end of the first phrase, which corresponds to the end of two perfect long-units (see Example 10.17). The conflicts are still more intense at the beginning of the B section (Example 10.18). In the first phrase, the lowest voice (the tenor) marks the imperfect breve-units with agogic accents, a repeated motive, and a phrase end on a breve *initium*. The middle voice (contratenor 2) displaces the tenor's motive by a minim, while the cantus firmus articulates groups of three semibreves. The mensural norms underlying these conflicting rhythms are not irrelevant abstractions, but forces of rhythmic attraction that

Example 10.18 Josquin, *Praeter rerum seriem*, bars 31–35. After Vatican City, Biblioteca Apostolica Vaticana, Cappella Sistina, Ms. 16, fols. 160^v–164^r.

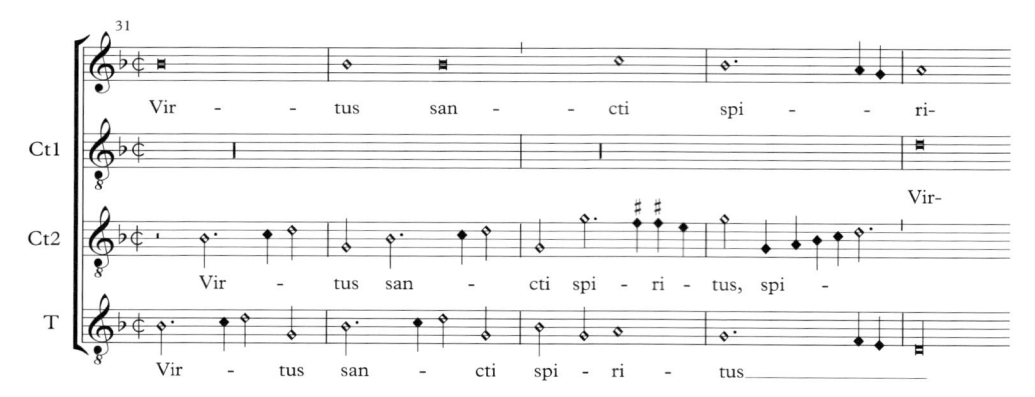

Example 10.19 Josquin, *Praeter rerum seriem*, bars 83–86. After Vatican City, Biblioteca Apostolica Vaticana, Cappella Sistina, Ms. 16, fols. 160^v–164^r.

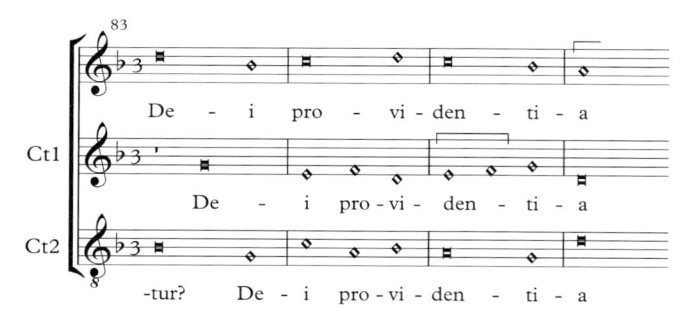

generate tension and resolution as the rhythms move out of and into alignment with the mensuration. A performance *tactus* on the imperfect breve in the A, A′, B, and B′ sections, subdivided as needed to measure the shorter values, brings out these conflicts more effectively than a semibreve *tactus*, because many of the conflicts are on the breve/semibreve level.

The simple, exuberant rhythms of the C and C′ sections draw their power from their contrast with the preceding sections and from the accommodation of the ternary rhythms of the cantus firmus to a compositional and performance *tactus* with ternary subdivision (see Example 10.19). If the C and C′ sections are interpreted as *sesquialtera* proportion, their cantus-firmus phrases are the same length as those of B′, but if they are interpreted as triple proportion (with the perfect breve equal to the semibreve of the preceding sections), they are half as long. The latter seems preferable from a musical point of view, not only because it makes the concluding section

Example 10.20 Josquin, *Benedicta es*, cantus firmus, bars 1–4 (superius), 38–41 (superius), 74–76 (tenor), 87–88 (superius), 138–41 (superius). After Vatican City, Biblioteca Apostolica Vaticana, Cappella Sistina, Ms. 16, fols. 155ᵛ–159ʳ.

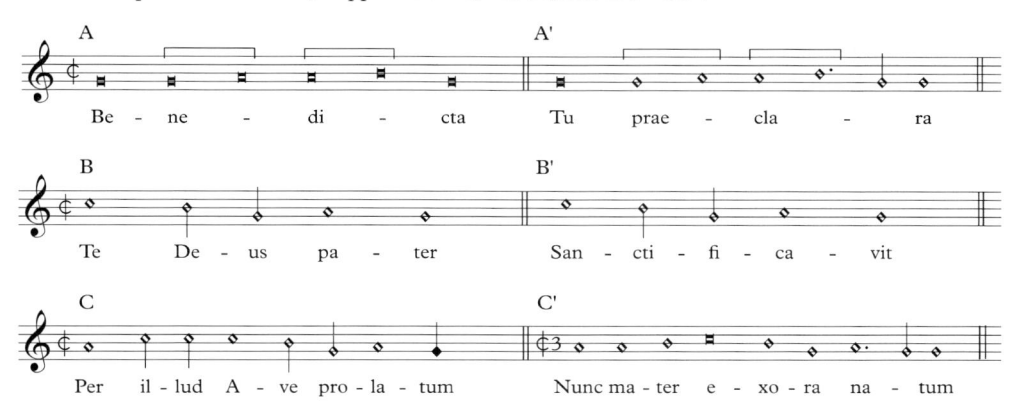

more climactic, but also because the written values are much larger in the C and C′ sections than in the preceding sections. A perfect breve *tactus* somewhat slower than the semibreve of the preceding sections is also possible and might create an even more climactic feel than a strict triple proportion.

Benedicta es is similar in structure to *Praeter rerum seriem*, but quite different in effect, since it has no perfect *modus* and implies regular imperfect *modus* only in its opening section. The text and cantus firmus are drawn from a Sequence of the same form as *Praeter rerum seriem* (AA′BB′CC′), but one without regular meter or phrase lengths in the text. The A, A′, B, and B′ sections correspond to the *prima pars*, the C section to the *secunda pars*, and the C′ section to the *tertia pars*. The mensuration is ¢ with a semibreve compositional *tactus* in the *prima* and *secunda partes* and ¢3 with a perfect breve compositional *tactus* in the *tertia pars*.

The cantus firmus is treated in free canon between superius and tenor. The lengths of the opening phrases of the cantus firmus in the A, A′, C, and C′ sections are 12, 8, 6, and 4 compositional *tactus*, respectively (see Example 10.20). This creates the feel of a series of diminutions in a very free 6:4:3:2 relation over the course of the work. The opening phrases of the B and B′ sections are shorter, because they have fewer notes, but their rhythms are like those of C. The tempo relation of ¢3 to ¢ presents the same problem that it does in other works, but the increase in the number of cantus-firmus notes on each compositional *tactus* creates a sense of mensural compression no matter what tempo is chosen for ¢3.

Although regular groupings of breves play little role in this work, large-scale time units are carefully controlled through the different rhythmic treatments of the cantus firmus and by other means. The opening section (Example 10.21), for example, consists of twenty breves corresponding to the first two phrases of the cantus firmus (a single phrase of the chant, broken into two phrases because of its very slow motion). Each phrase takes

Example 10.21 Josquin, *Benedicta es*, bars 1–16. After Vatican City, Biblioteca Apostolica Vaticana, Cappella Sistina, Ms. 16, fols. 155^v–159^r.

Example 10.21 (cont.)

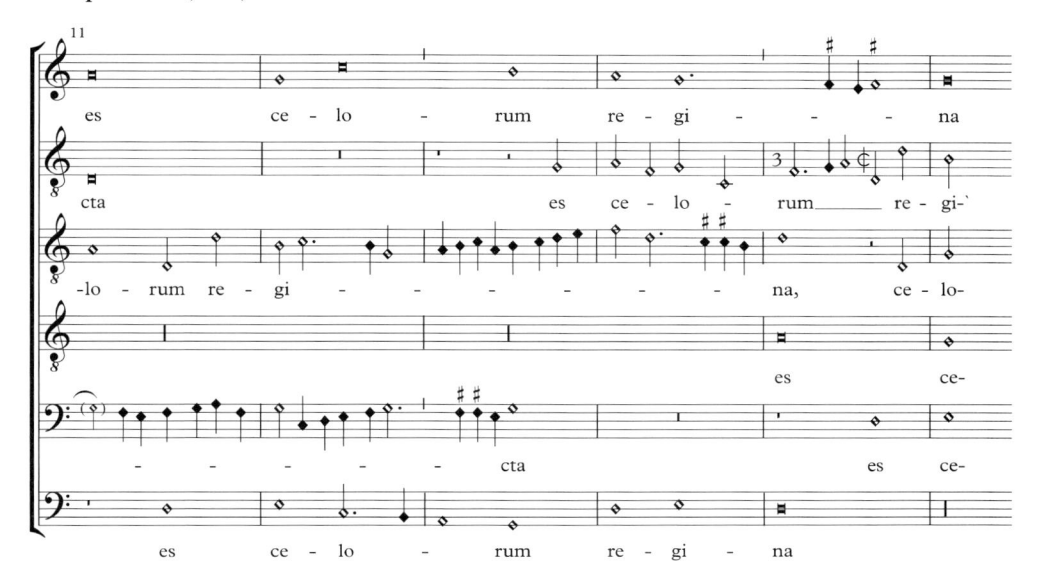

six breves, and the phrases are separated by four breves of rest. The canonic entries are spaced at a distance of four breves, so that units of four and six breves are overlapped. Elements of symmetry and asymmetry compete throughout the section. The latter gradually gain the upper hand, as cadences are spaced at increasingly shorter and less regular intervals (after 4, 4, 3, 1½, 1½, and 1 breves, in bars 5, 9, 12, 13 [beat 2], 15, and 16), but the definitive cadence in bars 15–16, which has a breve penultimate highlighted by a suspension, asserts the continuing importance of the symmetrical design as well. Breve-units play a role in the mensural organization throughout the A and A′ sections except in the short codetta that ends the A′ section (Example 10.22), which features repeated figures lasting for (or imitated after) three semibreves in contratenor 2 and the two basses. The compression of the largest audible unit to the semibreve in this section enhances the excitement generated by the fast surface rhythms.

In the B and B′ sections, the largest audible unit is the semibreve until the final phrase, which sets off the angelic salutation ("Ave plena gratia") with a sudden shift to motion in steady breves enlivened only by the syncopations in the tenor (see Example 10.23).

The C section (the *secunda pars*) is a duo featuring close imitation at the interval of a semibreve. The imitation equalizes the semibreves from a mensural point of view, but the breve-units are nevertheless made audible by the limitation of cadences to breve *initia*. In the C′ section (the *tertia*

328   Practice

Example 10.22 Josquin, *Benedicta es*, bars 68–73. After Vatican City, Biblioteca Apostolica Vaticana, Cappella Sistina, Ms. 16, fols. 155^v–159^r.

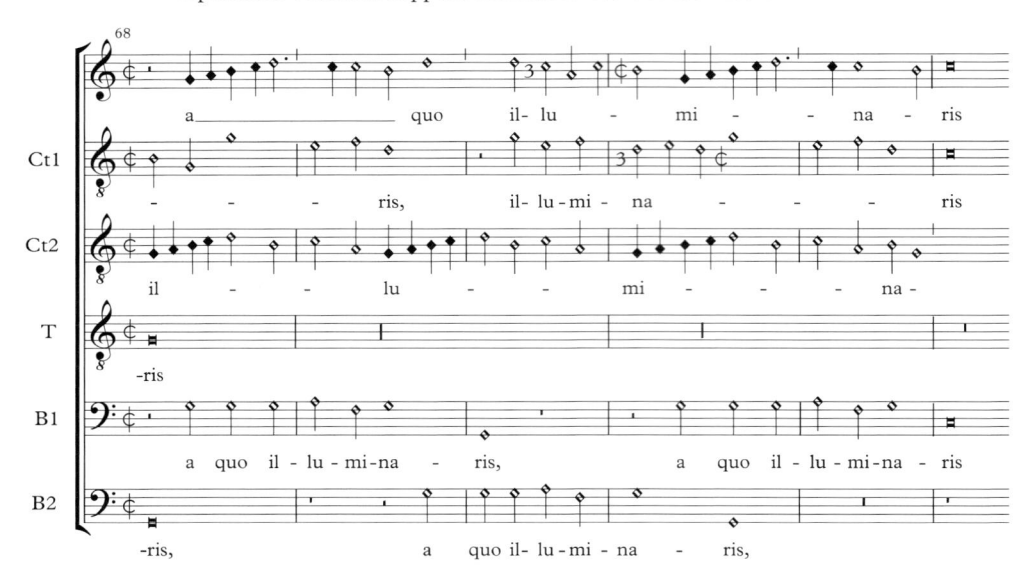

Example 10.23 Josquin, *Benedicta es*, bars 99–107. After Vatican City, Biblioteca Apostolica Vaticana, Cappella Sistina, Ms. 16, fols. 155^v–159^r.

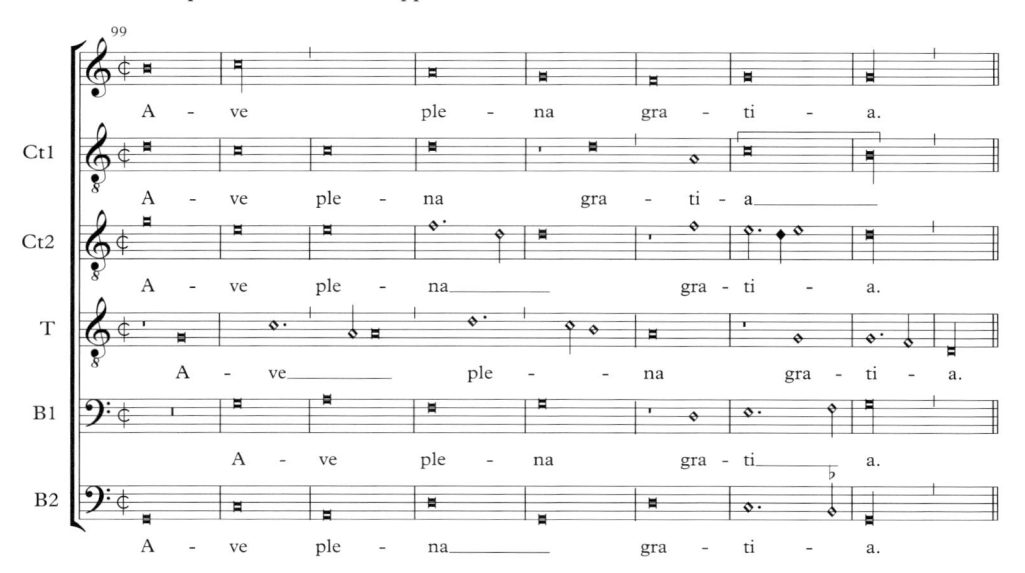

Example 10.24 Josquin, *Miserere mei, Deus*, motto. After Florence, Biblioteca Medicea-Laurenziana, Ms. 666 ("Medici Codex"), fols. 103ᵛ–112ʳ.

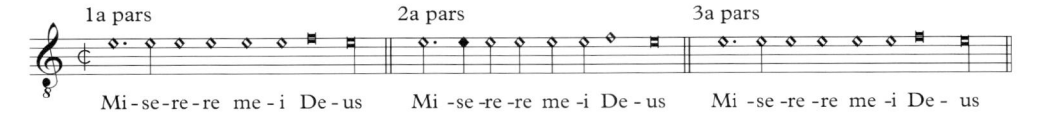

pars), the ternary division of the *tactus* overshadows any larger groupings until the "Amen," which returns to ₵ and expands upon the theme of the codetta that concludes the A′ section. It concludes with a cadence in which the penultimate notes last for four breves in three of the voices, tying the end to the beginning and dissipating the rhythmic energy that has been built up throughout the work.

Miserere mei, Deus employs diminution in a different way from the preceding motets. It is a monumental setting of Psalm 50 with the verses punctuated by a motto set to the opening words. The motto appears on consecutive steps of a scale that descends from e to E in the *prima pars*, ascends from E to e in the *secuna pars*, and descends again from e to a in the *tertia pars*. It occupies six breves in the first and third *partes* and three breves in the second, where it is reduced to half values (see Example 10.24). The power of the mensural design lies in the contrast between variable lengths and flexible rhythms of the verses and the invariable length and fixed rhythm of the motto that separates them. In the outer *partes*, the motto creates groups of three breves through the agogic, tonic, and textual accent on the first syllable of "Deus," the only point where it departs from monotone recitation. In the *secuna pars*, the corresponding groups are of three semibreves. The conflict between these groups and the imperfect breve-units of the mensuration, which are subtly audible, enhances the urgency of the shortened version of the motto. Unlike the preceding motets, *Miserere mei, Deus* does not end with the shortest version of its cantus firmus, but returns to the opening mensural structure in the *tertia pars*, creating a pattern of large-scale symmetry, rather than a build-up toward an end-oriented climax.

Motets without diminution

The six motets that do not use diminution have little else in common. Each of them has a distinct affective character and a mensural structure that supports its affect. Two motets (*Salve Regina* and *Stabat mater*) articulate time units larger than the breve regularly, two (*Pater noster – Ave Maria* and *O virgo virginum*) employ large time units less systematically, and two (*Absolve, quaesumus, Domine* and *De profundis*) are organized principally on the level of the breve and its subdivisions. Some maintain a consistent mensural profile throughout, and others use mensural contrasts of various kinds to support their formal and expressive designs.

Pater noster – Ave Maria is the most similar to the works discussed in the preceding sections in that it makes use of mensural contrasts to create a sense of large-scale form and dramatic build-up over the course of the work. The two *partes* may have originated as separate compositions (*Ave Maria* enjoyed widespread circulation independently of *Pater noster*), but they make an ideal pair in any case.[13] Both are based on canons between tenor and alto. The canon is freely composed in *Pater noster* and based on a chant melody in *Ave Maria*. The time interval between the canonic voices is three breves in both *partes*, though the pitch interval is the fifth in *Pater noster* and the unison in *Ave Maria*.

The overall mensural progression of the work is from complexity and artfulness to simplicity and directness. The three-breve interval between the canonic voices implies that perfect *modus* might be an organizing feature of the work, but in the *prima pars*, implicit *modus* plays a role only in the opening bars. In the first fifteen breves (Example 10.25), the phrase structure of the canon marks regular groups of three breves. This allusion to the principle of perfect *modus* lends dignity and gravity to the opening, but it is no more than a brief suggestion, since the cantus-firmus phrases are independent of *modus* units after that point. While the *modus* units last, Josquin takes advantage of them to create conflicting rhythmic groupings that generate the usual sense of acceleration in the opening section. The opening motive, on the words "Pater noster," consists of two groups of three semibreves that conflict with the imperfect *tempus*. This motive appears in each of the first five groups of three breve-units. In the first three statements, two voices share the same rhythm while a third imitates the motive two semibreves later, creating displaced groups of three semibreves and at the same time marking the *initium* of the true, imperfect, breve of the mensuration. In the fourth statement, three voices share the same rhythm, but in the fifth statement, the words "qui es in celis" are set against "Pater noster" to firmly binary rhythms that emphasize every semibreve and counteract the ternary groups of both breves and semibreves suggested by the opening

---

[13] Milsom, "Motets for Five or More Voices," 305.

Example 10.25 Josquin, *Pater noster*, bars 1–15. After Vatican City, Biblioteca Apostolica Vaticana, Cappella Sistina, Ms. 55, fols. 118ᵛ–123ʳ.

rhythms (see Example 10.25).[14] The mensural groupings in the remainder of the *prima pars* are on the level of the breve and its subdivisions. A very unusual cadence near the end of the *prima pars* (bars 100–01) has a breve penultimate that is out of phase with the breve *initium*. This mensural displacement of a cadence is unique in the works considered in this chapter.

[14] In this example and the following, I have made some emendations to the text underlay to make the words fit the music better.

Ordinarily, cadences that resolve on semibreve-max *initia* have semibreve penultimates; those that resolve on breve *initia* may have either breve or semibreve penultimates.

The perfect *modus* suggested by the interval of the canonic imitation is much more prominent in *Ave Maria* than in *Pater noster*. Groups of three breves are articulated audibly by means of texture changes, cadence placement, and repeated motives throughout most of the work, but with one curious anomaly: an extra breve-unit in bar 178 shifts the ternary groups of breves with respect to their previous position for the rest of the work. This section consists of four pairs of statements of a motive that sets the words "Sancta Maria, regina caeli, dulcis et pia, o mater Dei" ("Holy Mary, queen of heaven, gentle and faithful, O mother of God"). The motive is four semibreves long, but since the last note of each statement is elided with the first note of the following one, each statement takes three semibreves and each pair of statements takes three breves. The binary grouping of semibreves implied by the mensuration plays no role in the rhythm at this point. The scribe of the source of Example 10.26 wrote some of the rests, such as the one in the superius in bars 174–75, in syncopated positions, evidently assuming that the singers would be measuring in semibreves at this point. The elision is omitted in bar 178 to set off another series of three-breve units, likewise created through elisions of phrases, on the concluding words: "ora pro nobis peccatoribus, ut cum electis te videamus" ("pray for us sinners, so that with the blessed we may see you"). Example 10.26 shows the point where the elision is omitted (bar 178) along with the preceding and following six breves. The *initia* of the implicit (but not notated) perfect *modus*-units that have governed the mensuration throughout the *pars* are shown by wedges above the staff; the shifted *initia*, which are audible until the end and govern the final cadence, are shown by wedges in brackets. The stark simplicity of the rhythm in this section contrasts strikingly with the complexity and sophistication of the opening of the work (Example 10.25). The contrast underlines the rhetorical progression from formal prayer to God the Father in the *prima pars* to abstract praise of the more accessible Virgin Mary at the beginning of the *secunda pars* and finally to direct, urgent supplication to her at the end of the piece. Appeal to the intellect gives way to straightforward expression that speaks directly to the heart.

In *O virgo virginum*, the cantus firmus is treated as a free canon between tenor and superius. It moves mostly in longs and breves, but speeds up in the concluding section of each of the two *partes*. The long notes of the cantus firmus create regular imperfect *modus* for about the first half of the

Example 10.26 Josquin, *Ave Maria* (*secunda pars* of *Pater noster*), bars 172–85. After Vatican City, Biblioteca Apostolica Vaticana, Cappella Sistina, Ms. 55, fols. 118ᵛ–123ʳ.

prima pars (bars 1–58) and a bit less than half of the *secunda pars* (bars 101–34). *Modus* plays no further role in either *pars*, and the longs of the cantus firmus are out of phase with the initial *modus* in bars 68–76 of the *prima pars*. The work is structured as a series of episodes of approximately equal length, each corresponding to one phrase of the cantus firmus. Mensural contrast is created by the presence or absence of regular *modus*, the faster motion of the cantus firmus in the concluding section of the *prima pars*, and the use of *sesquialtera* in the final episode, but these contrasts do not lead to

Example 10.27 Josquin, *Salve Regina*: motto (tenor). After Vatican City, Biblioteca Apostolica Vaticana, Cappella Sistina, Ms. 24, fols. 79ᵛ–83ʳ.

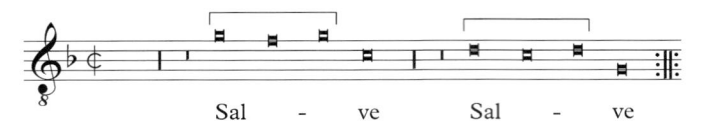

Sal - ve   Sal - ve

the kinds of large-scale formal and rhetorical patterns observed in the works discussed previously.

Salve Regina resembles *Illibata Dei virgo nutrix* in that it is based on a short motto that appears alternately on two different pitch levels in the tenor throughout the work. The motto is a four-note figure corresponding to the first four notes of the chant. Each of its notes lasts for a breve, and each statement is preceded by three breves of rest. This pattern creates regular groups of seven breves that are paired by the changes of pitch level to make groups of fourteen breves (see Example 10.27). There are twenty-four statements of the motto in the work: twelve in the *prima pars*, four in the *secuna pars*, and eight in the *tertia pars*. Notes are added to the tenor at the end of each *pars* (one each in the first two *partes* and two in the third) to facilitate the final cadences, which require a descending step in the tenor or the voice that performs its contrapuntal function. A paraphrase of the complete chant appears in the superius (with a few phrases moved to other voices), while the remaining voices have free material that sometimes includes imitation of the chant motives.

The mensural design of the work serves both expressive and symbolic purposes. The obsessive, unchanging repetitions of the motto lend urgency to the prayer that it embodies. The asymmetrical divisions of the seven-breve units keep the listener slightly off balance in spite of their predictability and thereby enhance the expressive intensity of the work. Josquin's decision to organize the work in units of seven breves may also have been prompted by the traditional symbolic association of the number seven with the Virgin. The twelve pairs of statements of the motto within the work may represent the twelve stars in the crown of the apocalyptic woman with whom she was identified. The total number of notes in the tenor, including the four notes that are added to the motto at the ends of the three *partes*, is one hundred; this number has been interpreted as a symbol of Christ.[15]

The temporal structure of the work depends not only on the time units articulated by the repetitions of the motto, but also on the units defined

---

[15] Willem Elders, "Symbolism in the Sacred Music of Josquin," in *The Josquin Companion*, ed. Richard Sherr (Oxford University Press, 2000), 545.

by the text, musical phrases, and cadences in the non-tenor voices. Phrases that correspond to meaningful units of text are separated by cadences that vary in strength depending on the strength of the textual articulation. The points at which they begin and end rarely coincide with the beginnings or ends of the motto statements. In the *prima pars*, for example, the principal formal units in the non-tenor voices end in bars 22, 38, 56, and 86. None of them coincides with the beginning of the motto, and only one (bar 56) coincides with its last note. Even the ends of the *partes* require extensions of the tenor to bring the motto into line with the other voices. The lack of correspondence between the motto and the phrases in the other voices counteracts the tendency of the motto to break the music into short units and maintains the tension that propels the music to its conclusion.

Stabat mater is a lament of the Virgin at the Crucifixion. The cantus firmus is the tenor of Binchois's rondeau *Comme femme desconfortée*, a lament of an ordinary woman that relates symbolically to the lament of the Virgin. Each note of the tenor is augmented four-fold, so that a minim becomes a breve, a semibreve becomes a long, and a breve becomes a maxima in the motet. This procedure transforms the perfect *tempus* of the rondeau into the equivalent of perfect major *modus* with imperfect minor *modus* in the motet. The *modus* is not represented explicitly in the notation, however; notes that function as perfect maximas in perfect major *modus* are notated as dotted maximas in ₵. Listeners may or may not recognize the major *modus* consciously, but the large-scale temporal regularity contributes to the weighty character of the work. Unlike most of the motets discussed previously, *Stabat mater* eschews mensural contrast and makes its effect through extreme uniformity. The cantus firmus enters on the first note of the piece and has no rests from beginning to end. Other voices move in and out, but the continuity of the cantus firmus makes the grief that it expresses feel inescapable. The only mensural contrast in the piece appears in the section just before the end (bars 160–74), where the text turns to a prayer for salvation. The crucial words are emphasized by means of *sesquialtera* rhythms that are sometimes set directly against duple divisions of the semibreve-units (see Example 10.28). All voices return to duple divisions for the concluding words, "Paradisi gloria."

Absolve, quaesumus, Domine and *De profundis* are the only motets in this group in which regular mensural organization is consistently limited to the level of the breve and its subdivisions. It is probably no coincidence that they are also the only ones that consist of a single *pars*. Temporal units larger than the breve play important roles in structuring multipartite motets, but

Example 10.28 Josquin, *Stabat mater*, bars 171–75. After Vatican City, Biblioteca Apostolica Vaticana, Ms. Chigi C VIII 234 ("Chigi Codex"), fols. 233^v–237^r.

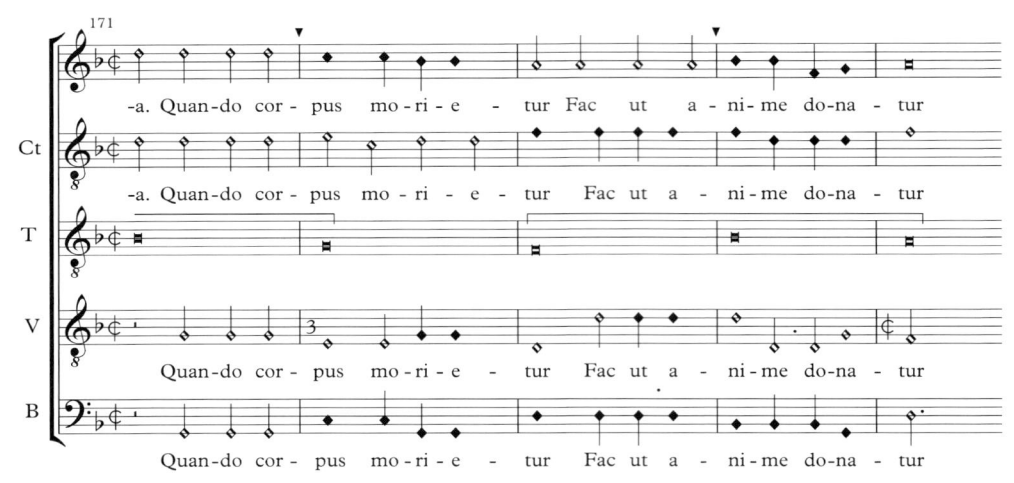

they are less useful, and might even seem out of proportion, in shorter works. *Absolve, quaesumus, Domine* displays no unusual mensural features, but *De profundis*, a setting of the penitential Psalm 129 with a series of acclamations alluding to death, lies at the opposite extreme from the other works discussed here. It is based on a three-voice, freely composed canon at the interval of two breves. Although the canonic structure might suggest regular imperfect *modus*, even the *tempus* is hardly audible, because the work renounces most of the features that create audible mensural structures. The rhythms are extremely uniform, consisting mostly of semibreves and minims (the latter mostly repeated notes) that are varied only occasionally by dotted rhythms and touches of syncopation. The text setting is obsessively syllabic. Most phrases end without contrapuntal cadences, and there are no suspensions and few other dissonances to distinguish one mensural position from another. The effect is one of heavy, inexorably plodding semibreves that convey the profound grief of the words. Breve-units are articulated only weakly and intermittently. When the final notes of phrases are breves, they always fall on breve *initia*, but many phrases end on semibreve-max *initia*, and phrases ending with breves are too infrequent to mark the breve-units with any regularity. An unusual passage of breve *sesquialtera* simultaneous with the imperfect *tempus* (unique among the works discussed here) is found on the words "quia apud Dominum misericordia" ("for with the Lord there is mercy"; bars 76–84), perhaps to lend subtle emphasis to the message. It is aligned with the breve *initia* and marks the breve-units in the passage in which it occurs.

Example 10.29 Josquin, *De profundis*, bars 29–35. After Vatican City, Biblioteca Apostolica Vaticana, Cappella Sistina, Ms. 38, fols. 106^v–110^r.

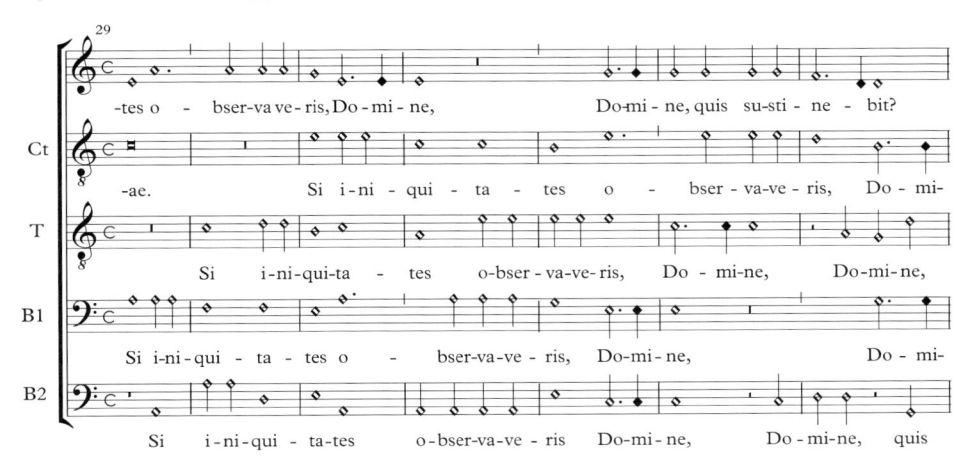

De profundis is the only motet in this group to use the sign C, which was quite unusual by Josquin's time in a non-proportional context (see Example 10.29).[16] It probably means that the semibreves are slower and more weakly paired than the semibreves of ₵ and that the performance *tactus* should be the semibreve. The notation of breve rests in syncopated positions in Example 10.29 implies that the scribe of its source understood the work to be measured in semibreves. An equal emphasis on every semibreve, which would be encouraged by a semibreve performance *tactus*, may be more vital to the character of the work than the tempo. The work will sound slow even if the semibreves have the same duration as those typical of ₵. Notes shorter than minims are rare, and the large number of repeated notes makes the contrapuntal rhythm slower than the surface rhythms. A tempo much slower than that typical of ₵ would interfere with the effect of speech-like declamation, which is also essential to the expressive character of the work. As in *Stabat mater*, mensural uniformity makes time seem to stand still and immerses the listener in deep sorrow that achieves no resolution.

As the examples discussed in this chapter demonstrate, Josquin followed no regular formula in his uses of mensuration and rhythm for formal and expressive purposes in his motets. He was, however, keenly aware of the

---

[16] The motet has the sign C in both of its manuscript sources (Vatican City, Biblioteca Apostolica Vaticana, Cappella Sistina, Ms. 38, and Kassel, Murhard'sche und Landesbibliothek, Ms. Mus. 24). The sign is ₵ in Antico's *Motetti, libro secondo* (Venice, 1521), probably because C was so rare that Antico thought it might confuse buyers of the print. Because C is unusual, it is unlikely to be an error in the manuscripts.

power of temporal organization on all levels, from the smallest to the largest, to shape his works in ways that allowed the music to conform to the structure and meaning of the words. Although the larger levels are rarely represented explicitly in the notation, analysis of the music reveals that Josquin devoted careful attention to them. The balance and integration of temporal structures on multiple levels is one of the most impressive features of these works.

11 | The *Choralis Constantinus* of Isaac

Heinrich Isaac (*c.* 1450–1517) was one of Josquin's most illustrious contemporaries. He is noted especially for his polyphonic settings of chants of the Mass Proper. Most of his works in that category are found in a monumental collection entitled *Choralis Constantinus*, which was published in three volumes in Nuremberg more than thirty years after his death. Volume I appeared in 1550 and volumes II and III in 1555. Volume II contains music for the highest feasts of the liturgical year, along with music for the feasts of three saints (Geberhard, Pelagius, and Conrad) of special importance to the city of Constance. Volume I contains music for lesser feasts, and volume III contains music for the Common and Propers of saints and five Mass Ordinaries. The three volumes, which comprise over 1,700 pages in the published partbooks, include nearly 400 liturgical items for 99 different masses. The selection of items varies from one mass to another, but usually includes Introit, Alleluia, and Communion. Sequences and Tracts are also common, and there are two settings of Graduals as well.

The history of the work is extremely complex and only partially understood. Isaac composed the music over a period of about twenty years, from the time he was first employed by Maximilian I in 1496 to his death. He received a commission for music for high feasts from the cathedral chapter of Constance in 1508 and fulfilled that assignment within the following year. The title of the collection refers to that commission, although the content includes works for both the Imperial court and the Constance cathedral. Most scholars agree that the music for Constance coincides with volume II, plus the Trinity Sunday mass from volume I and perhaps the *Missa paschalis* from volume III, although the issue is still open to debate.[1] The music was collected and assembled into its published form by the Nuremberg publisher Johannes Ott, who announced the forthcoming publication in 1537. Numerous complications, including Ott's death in 1546, delayed the

---

[1] See David J. Burn, "What Did Isaac Write for Constance?" *The Journal of Musicology* 20 (2003), 45–72. Burn includes a good overview of the extensive literature on this topic. See also Manfred Schuler, "Zur Überlieferung des *Choralis Constantinus* von Heinrich Isaac," *Archiv für Musikwissenschaft* 36 (1979), 68–76, 146–54.

completion of the publication for over a decade, but manuscript copies of the printer's exemplar (which is no longer extant) make it clear that, by the late 1530s, the work was in a form very close to that in which it finally appeared.[2]

Choralis Constantinus occupies a special place in the history of mensural notation, because it contains the most complex examples of proportional notation in the entire repertoire. Despite their notoriety, these proportions are rare and not at all typical of Isaac's notation. Over 90 percent of the pieces in the collection are in imperfect *tempus*, usually signed ¢, but occasionally C, C2, or O2. Most of the rest are in perfect *tempus*, signed O or ϕ. *Sesquialtera* proportions, normally represented by the sign ¢3, 3, or coloration, appear frequently within sections and sometimes throughout short verses. Other proportions and unusual signs constitute striking exceptions to the norm.[3]

All of the compositions in *Choralis Constantinus* consist of short, independent sections corresponding to the sections of the chants on which they are based. The cantus firmus is normally in the top voice (labeled "discantus" in the print) in volumes I and II and the bass in volume III. Introits are in two sections (antiphon and verse), each of which begins with a chant incipit. Alleluias are likewise in two sections (Alleluia and verse); the beginning of the Alleluia and the verse are set in polyphony, and the *jubilus* is monophonic. Communions consist of a single polyphonic section. Sequences and Tracts alternate polyphonic verses with verses sung in chant or performed on the organ. (Only the polyphonic verses appear in the print.) The Ordinary movements follow a similar *alternatim* structure.

The individual sections of each liturgical number, which I shall call "verses" even though that term is not always strictly appropriate, are quite short. Most are about ten to fifty breves long, and some are even shorter. There are more than 1,000 such verses in the three volumes of the collection. The aesthetic principle governing the relations among them is one of variety. Each verse functions like an independent composition that is joined to the complete liturgical number only through the cantus firmus. Large-scale formal considerations like those that govern the masses and motets discussed in the

---

[2] David J. Burn, "The Mass-Proper Cycles of Henricus Isaac: Genesis, Transmission, and Authenticity," 2 vols. (Ph.D. diss., Oxford University, 2002), I: 110–12.

[3] Philip Gossett, "The Mensural System and the 'Choralis Constantinus'," in *Studies in Renaissance and Baroque Music in Honor of Arthur Mendel*, ed. Robert L. Marshall (Kassel: Bärenreiter, 1974), 97–107, catalogs all of the instances in which two or more signs appear simultaneously or successively in the same verse in *Choralis Constantinus*. See also Ruth I. DeFord, "Who Devised the Proportional Notation in Isaac's *Choralis Constantinus*?" in *Heinrich Isaac and Polyphony for the Proper of the Mass in the Late Middle Ages and Renaissance*, ed. David J. Burn and Stefan Gasch, "Épitome musical" (Turnhout: Brepols, 2011), 167–213.

preceding chapters play no role in these works. Isaac varies the treatment of the cantus firmus, the number of voices, the relationships among the voices, and the rhythmic character from one verse to the next to keep the music interesting. Contrasting mensurations create one form of rhythmic variety, but there are also significant rhythmic contrasts among verses in the same mensuration. Isaac experiments with unusual and highly inventive rhythmic groupings in some verses, yet the notated mensuration forms a subtle frame of reference for even the most irregular surface rhythms.

The modern editions of *Choralis Constantinus* do not provide the information necessary for a study of mensural practices in the work.[4] Signs are reported inconsistently or not at all, proportional relations are sometimes misinterpreted, and the scale of reduction of note values is not always consistent. There is a published facsimile of the work that is indispensable for basic information about the original notation.[5] Variant signs in other sources of the music, which are also of great importance, are catalogued in several places, but that information is not easily accessible and it is organized in ways that make the sources difficult to compare.[6] A new modern edition of the work is urgently needed.

In the following discussion, verses are identified by the volume of *Choralis Constantinus* (CC), the number and name of the mass, the liturgical function and opening words of the complete piece, and the number and opening words of the verse. For pieces with chant incipits, the opening words of the incipit are separated from the opening words of the polyphony with a slash. Although this method of identification is cumbersome, it

---

[4] Heinrich Isaac, *Choralis Constantinus*, 3 vols. (Nuremberg: Formschneider, 1550–55). Modern edition of vol. I, ed. Emil Bezecny and Walter Rabl, Denkmäler der Tonkunst in Österreich 10, Jg. 5/i (Vienna: Artaria, 1898, repr. 1959). Modern edition of vol. II, ed. Anton von Webern, Denkmäler der Tonkunst in Österreich 32, Jg. 16/i (Vienna: Artaria, 1909; repr. 1959). Modern edition of vol. III (Mass Propers), ed. Louise Cuyler (Ann Arbor: University of Michigan Press, 1950). Modern edition of vol. III (Mass Ordinaries), ed. Louise Cuyler (Ann Arbor: University of Michigan Press, [1956]).

[5] Heinrich Isaac, *Choralis Constantinus*, 3 vols. (Nuremberg: Formschneider, 1550–55). Facsimile, ed. Edward R. Lerner, 3 vols., Facsimile Series for Scholars and Musicians (Peer, Belgium: Alamire, 1990–94).

[6] Gerhard-Rudolf Pätzig, "Liturgische Grundlagen und handschriftliche Überlieferung von Heinrich Isaacs 'Choralis Constantinus'" (Ph.D. diss., Universität Tübingen, 1956), vol. II, lists many variants among the sources. Pätzig includes corrections to Cuyler's edition of vol. III and lists some of the variants between the print and the manuscript sources of that volume in "Das Chorbuch Mus. ms. 40024 der Deutschen Staatsbibliothek Berlin: Eine wichtige Quelle zum Schaffen Isaacs aus der Hand Leonhard Pämingers," in *Festschrift Walter Gerstenberg*, ed. Georg von Dadelsen and Andreas Holschneider (Wolfenbüttel: Möseler, [c1964]), 122–42. The most complete list of variants involving mensuration and proportion signs in the sources of all three volumes is found in Gossett, "The Mensural System and the 'Choralis Constantinus'," 97–107.

facilitates unambiguous identification of sections in both the facsimile and the modern editions.

Imperfect *tempus*

The signs in *Choralis Constantinus* that designate imperfect *tempus* outside of proportional contexts are ₵, C2, O2, and C. ₵ and C2 are synonymous. The latter is rare; as a non-proportional sign, it appears in only two verses.[7] O2 is equivalent to ₵ with perfect minor *modus*. C is uncommon and probably represents a slower tempo than the other signs. Verses in imperfect *tempus* often have no signs in the print. The standard sign ₵ may be assumed in those cases.

The basic principles governing rhythms in ₵ are the same as those in the music of Josquin. The compositional *tactus* is the semibreve. Note values range for the most part from semiminims to breves; longs, maximas, and pairs of *fusae* on the second halves of minim-units are found occasionally. At least one voice normally moves on every minim-unit except at beginnings of sections. Suspensions are minims, and non-suspension dissonances are semiminims or *fusae*. Cadences may fall on any semibreve *initium*, and penultimate intervals of cadences are normally semibreves. Semibreve-units are often, but not always, paired consistently or intermittently within sections. In a few cases, they are grouped in regular units of three, five, or seven that are independent of the binary groups suggested by the sign ₵. The total length of sections in ₵ is almost always a whole number of imperfect breve-units, however. The few exceptions to this principle are probably a result of inadvertence, but they prove that the breve-unit was not always a significant organizing factor for rhythms in ₵; if it were, the composer could hardly lose track of the count of breves within a verse.

The opening verse in CC II/1 (*Natalis Domini*), Introit (*Puer natus est/et filius*; Example 11.1), provides a good illustration of Isaac's most common rhythms under the sign ₵. Both the breve *initium* and the semibreve *initium* are established at the outset by means of a subject that moves in semibreves and enters at intervals of a breve in imitation. The first cadence (bar 7), which coincides with a point in the text that is not a grammatical articulation, falls on a semibreve-max *initium*, and the second (bar 12), which

---

[7] It appears in all voices of CC III/6 (*De virginibus*), Sequence (*Exultent filiae Syon*), v. 6 ("Insidias") and in the alto (with C in the other voices) in the concluding section (bb. 29–35) of CC III/7 (*De annunciatione*), Sequence (*Fortem expediat*), v. 6 ("Qui nobis").

Example 11.1 Heinrich Isaac, *Choralis Constantinus* (Nuremberg: Formschneider, 1550–55), II/1 (*Natalis Domini*), Introit (*Puer natus est/et filius*), bars 1–23.

marks the end of the first logical unit of the text, falls on a breve *initium*. This distinction makes the second cadence audibly stronger than the first. All but one of the remaining cadences fall on breve *initia*, and the exception (bar 20), like the cadence in bar 7, falls in the middle of a grammatical unit.

Several of the cadences on breve *initia*, including those in bars 17 and 23, have breves in one or two voices on their final chords, reinforcing the audible identity of the breve-units, but those units are not noticeably marked between cadences. Either a semibreve or a divided breve performance *tactus* would be suitable for the music. The latter has the advantage of calling the performers' attention to the subtle compositional role of the breve-units.

In some verses, Isaac cultivates a declamatory style that creates a sense of even pulse with little or no regular grouping of semibreves. This style is often associated with Introit verses, which have predominantly monotone cantus firmi. In these pieces, the chant-like effect of the rhythm reinforces the recitational melodic character of the cantus firmus. A striking case is CC II/17 (*De Sancto Pelagio*), Introit (*Letabitur/in Domino*), verse ("Exaudi/a timore"; Example 11.2), in which all four voices are mostly monotone until a few bars before the final cadence.

Example 11.2 Heinrich Isaac, *Choralis Constantinus* II/17 (*De Sancto Pelagio*), Introit (*Letabitur/in Domino*), verse ("Exaudi/a timore").

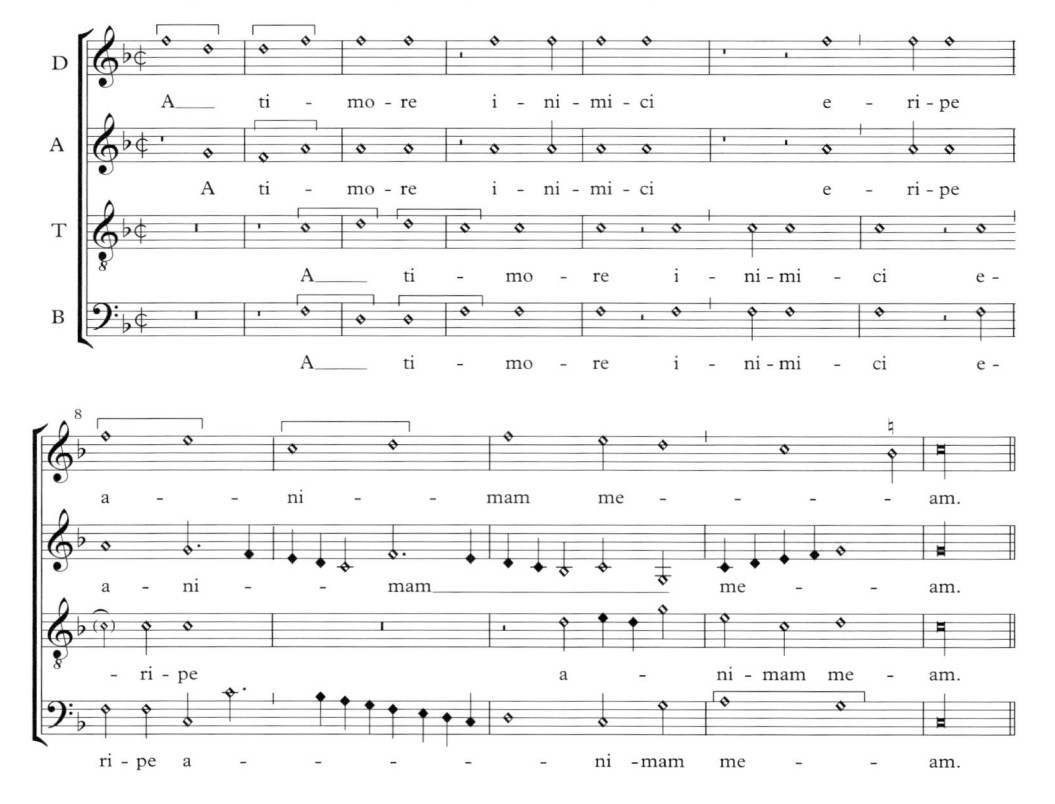

Example 11.3 Heinrich Isaac, *Choralis Constantinus* II/14 (*Marie Magdalene*), Introit (*Gaudeamus/omnes*): (a) bars 1–6; (b) bars 19–21.

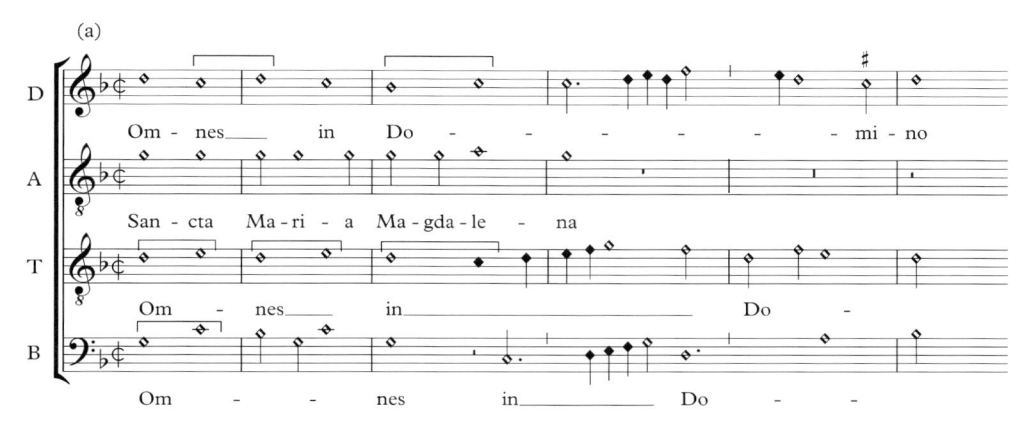

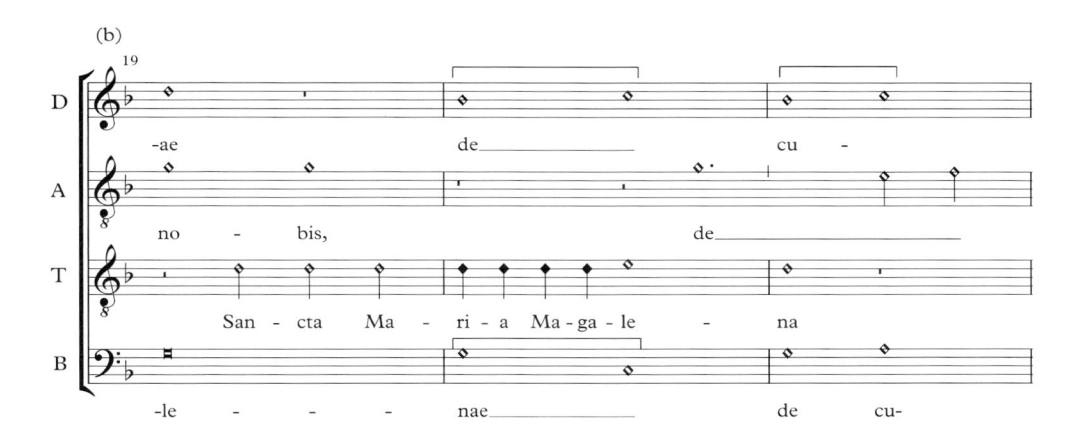

Isaac combines declamatory rhythm with his usual ₵ style to good effect in CC II/14 (*Marie Magdalene*), Introit (*Gaudeamus/omnes*; Example 11.3). In the opening phrase, the discant, tenor, and bass are in a style similar to that of Example 11.1, while the alto declaims a contrasting litany text in a style like that of Example 11.2. The points that are emphasized by textual, agogic, and tonic accents ("Maria Magdalena") in the first phrase of the alto (Example 11.3a) fall on minim-max or semibreve-max *initia* in relation to the other voices; the independence of the voice from the breve-units gives the litany a flexible, speech-like quality. The litany motive reappears several times in the verse (in various voices) with its rhythm accommodated to the prevailing mensuration, such that the syllables that were mensurally

Example 11.4 Heinrich Isaac, *Choralis Constantinus* II/11 (*Johannis et Pauli*), Sequence (*Quam velut*), v. 6 ("Vos Christi"), bars 1–6.

displaced in the first statement fall on semibreve *initia* (Example 11.3b). The declamation on semiminims that leads to the alignment of text accents with mensural *initia* is very unusual and adds intensity to the repetitions of the prayer.

In some verses, the cantus firmus moves in equal notes (usually semibreves or breves) that mark the corresponding unit of the mensuration aurally. In rare cases, the cantus firmus is stated in still longer values, creating regular mensural groupings on the level of *modus*, as well as *tempus*. CC II/11 (*Johannis et Pauli*), Sequence (*Quam velut*), v. 6 ("Vos Christi"; Example 11.4) has a cantus firmus in equal longs preceded by a maxima. The cantus firmus creates audible imperfect *modus*, which is supported by imitation at the interval of two breves in the lower voices, yet the verse ends by dissipating the *modus* groupings and coming to a halt on a breve-max *initium* in the voices that are still moving at that point. (The end of the verse is not shown in the example.)

Isaac's most inventive rhythms in ¢ involve extended groups of semibreves that contradict the mensural binary grouping on the *tempus* level. Some of these groups are ternary, but they are never regular in such a way that they could have been notated in perfect *tempus*. Others involve quintuple or septuple groups of semibreves. A relatively simple example of ternary groups is found in CC II/9 (*De Corpore Christi*), Introit (*Cibavit/ex adipe*), verse ("Exultate Deo/jubilate"; Example 11.5). The discant has a swinging ternary rhythm alternating imperfect breves and semibreves throughout, but it begins on the second semibreve of the breve-unit and is therefore out of phase with the place it would be if the *tempus* were perfect. The accompanying voices also mark groups of three

Example 11.5 Heinrich Isaac, *Choralis Constantinus* II/9 (*De Corpore Christi*), Introit (*Cibavit/ex adipe*), verse ("Exultate Deo/jubilate").

semibreves by means of imitation at the interval of three semibreves in the opening bars, but their groups are out of phase with those of the discant. The only internal cadence (bar 4) coincides with the beginning of a ternary group in the discant, but not with a breve *initium* in the notated mensuration. Imperfect breve-units have no audible role in the mensural structure, but the total length of the verse is a whole number of imperfect, and not perfect, breve *tempora*. The verse ends on what sounds like a perfect breve *initium*, but would not be if the *tempus* were perfect, because the ternary groups of semibreves in the cantus firmus begin in the second semibreve-unit.

CC II/8 (*De Sancto Spiritu*), *Alleluia Veni Sancte Spiritus* (Example 11.6) is similar, but more complex. The discant proceeds in regular dotted breves until the two penultimate bars. The bass rhythms agree with the discant; the tenor has groups of three minims in hemiola with the discant and bass, and the alto imitates the bass at a distance of one semibreve, creating groups of

Example 11.6 Heinrich Isaac, *Choralis Constantinus* II/8 (*De Sancto Spiritu*), *Alleluia Veni Sancte Spiritus*.

three semibreves that are displaced with respect to the other voices. All voices switch to binary groups of semibreves in conformity with the mensuration two bars before the end.

CC II/16 (*De S. Geberhardo*), Sequence (*Quae sanctos*), v. 9 ("Hic hominem"; Example 11.7) opens with regular groups of four minims in the alto, then juxtaposes them with dotted semibreves in the lower voices, thereby threatening the integrity of the semibreve, as well as the breve, units of the mensuration. As in Example 11.6, order is restored by a mensurally regular cadence (not shown in the example) at the end.

Extended groups of five or seven semibreves or minims work against the norms of imperfect *tempus* in much the same way as the ternary groups in the preceding examples. Verse 2 of the Sequence in Example 11.7 ("Meritis quorum"; Example 11.8) has a bass cantus firmus in equal notes of seven minims set against regular rhythms in the other voices until the last two bars, in which all voices conform to the norms of the notated mensuration.

Example 11.7 Heinrich Isaac, *Choralis Constantinus* II/16 (*De S. Geberhardo*), Sequence (*Quae sanctos*), v. 9 ("Hic hominem"), bars 1–6.

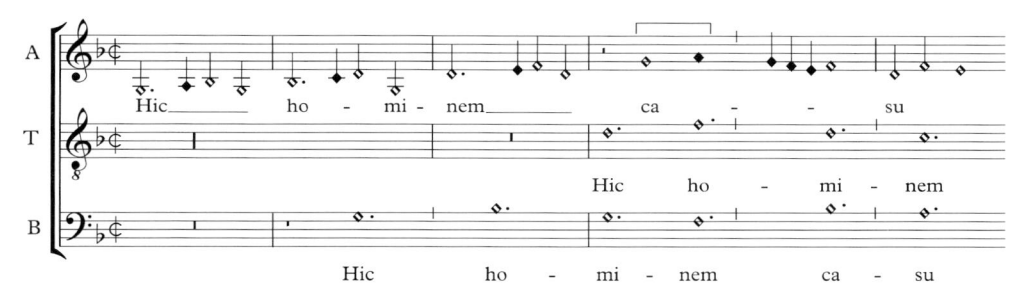

Example 11.8 Heinrich Isaac, *Choralis Constantinus* II/16 (*De S. Geberhardo*), Sequence (*Quae sanctos*), v. 2 ("Meritis quorum"), bars 1–8.

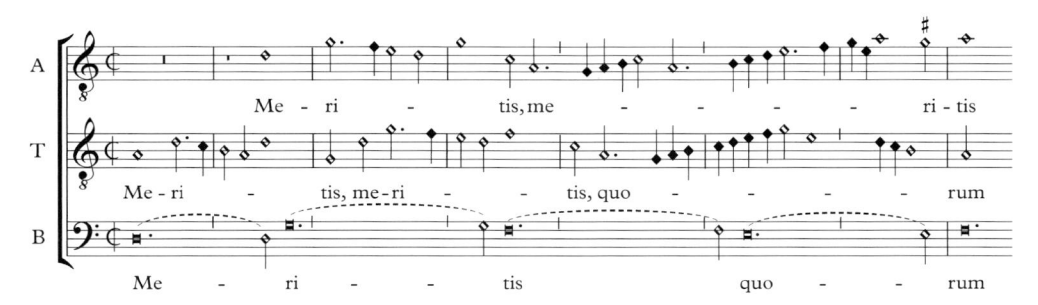

Since there is no way to notate a value of seven minims in imperfect *tempus*, each bass pitch is written as two notes (a dotted breve plus a minim) that are presumably meant to be tied. Isaac takes the opportunity to put an internal cadence at the one place where a change of pitch in the bass coincides with a breve *initium* of the mensuration (bar 8). Despite the irregularity of the rhythm, he seems not to have been indifferent to the theoretical mensural framework that provides the background for the unconventional durations in the piece.

The concluding section of CC II/15 (*Assumptio Marie*), Sequence (*Quae sine virili*), v. 8 ("Ut sibi auxilium"; Example 11.9) marks rhythmic groups of five semibreves, then five minims, not with long notes, but with a repeated, quasi-*ostinato* figure. The pattern is most regular in the bass. The other voices imitate it starting at various points in a pattern of escalating complexity. In bars 9–13, all entries of the figure fall on semibreve *initia*. In bars 14–17, some voices begin the pattern on minim-max *initia*, then in bar 20, the figure itself is reduced to half-values and imitated at the interval of a minim. Even at this point, however, the semibreve

Example 11.9 Heinrich Isaac, *Choralis Constantinus* II/15 (*Assumptio Marie*), Sequence (*Quae sine virili*), v. 8 ("Ut sibi auxilium"), bars 9–26.

initium is audible as a point of reference, since it has just been confirmed by a cadence in bar 19. As usual, the rhythms realign with the breve *initium* in the concluding bars.

The above examples (except for Example 11.1) represent exceptional, not typical, rhythmic structures. They illustrate the limits of the kinds of temporal organization that could be accommodated under the sign ¢ in Isaac's work. The semibreve-unit is always audible even when the rhythms of some voices work against it, but the breve-unit sometimes has little or no meaningful role except to provide an abstract reference to which the music must return in order to conclude properly. In such cases, a breve performance *tactus* would have to be divided into strictly equal halves and would have little or no practical advantage over a semibreve performance *tactus*. The exceptional verses in ₵ with odd numbers of semibreves call even more clearly for a performance *tactus* on the semibreve.

The sign C appears in non-proportional contexts much less often than the sign ₵. It is not used at all in *Choralis Constantinus* I. Taking account of the most probable corrections of errors (including differences between the print and its manuscript sources and cases in which ₵ and C appear simultaneously without a proportional relation between them), there are four sections in *Choralis Constantinus* II and thirteen in *Choralis Constantinus* III in which C is the exclusive sign in a verse.[8] The notated rhythms under C are indistinguishable from those under ₵, but the signs need not be synonymous for that reason. C normally appears at or near the beginnings of liturgical numbers, either in the opening section or in the second section after an opening section in O; it is not usually found after sections with cut signs of either imperfect or perfect *tempus* (₵ or ⏀), though there are a few exceptions. Given this context, it is logical to conclude that C represents a slower tempo than ₵, presumably with a semibreve performance *tactus*, as many theorists affirm. How much difference there should be between the two signs is not clear.

The sign O2 is equivalent to ₵ with perfect minor *modus*. It appears as the sole sign in two sections in *Choralis Constantinus* II and ten in *Choralis Constantinus* III, and it is found simultaneously with ₵ in another section of *Choralis Constantinus* III.[9] All sections signed O2 have whole numbers of perfect long-units, but the extent to which the perfect long-unit is audible as an organizing factor varies. The theoretical *modus* is often inaudible, and it is unclear why the sign is O2 rather than ₵. The clearest example of audible perfect *modus* is found in CC III/5 (*De confessoribus*), Sequence 2 (*Ad laudes salvatoris*), v. 2 ("Sentiant hunc"; Example 11.10). The bass cantus firmus, which proceeds in a strongly ternary rhythm alternating imperfect longs and breves, is preceded by anticipatory imitation in diminution. The

---

[8] The ones in the Propers are listed (along with other non-simultaneous signatures) in Gossett, "The Mensural System and the 'Choralis Constantinus'," 105–07. My count excludes the verses in which C appears simultaneously with O (with semibreve equivalence between the signs) and those in which it is mistakenly combined with ₵ without a 2:1 proportion between the signs.

[9] Gossett, "The Mensural System and the 'Choralis Constantinus'," 99–101, 105–07.

Example 11.10 Heinrich Isaac, *Choralis Constantinus* III/5 (*De confessoribus*), Sequence 2 (*Ad laudes salvatoris*), v. 2 ("Sentiant hunc"), bars 1–18.

effect is like perfect *tempus* that is superseded by perfect *modus* at the point where the cantus firmus enters. Despite the ternary grouping of semibreves in the opening bars, an imperfect breve performance *tactus*, which will be in hemiola relation to these groups, is more effective than a semibreve *tactus* for bringing out the *modus*-level rhythms in this verse.

Perfect *tempus*

The signs that designate perfect *tempus* in *Choralis Constantinus* are O and ɸ. The rhythms that Isaac writes under the two signs are indistinguishable, but O is generally associated with opening sections of liturgical numbers and probably represents a slower tempo than ɸ, which may appear either in opening sections or in later ones. Both signs have a semibreve compositional *tactus*, and both evidently require a semibreve performance *tactus* in non-proportional contexts as well. There is no regular pairing of breves in ɸ that might suggest an imperfect breve performance *tactus*, and sections with that sign often have odd numbers of breve-units, so that they would end on upbeats if they were measured with an imperfect breve *tactus*.

The breve-unit is more consistently audible in perfect *tempus* than in imperfect *tempus*, though the degree of emphasis on it varies from one verse to another. Some verses in perfect *tempus* have a distinctly ternary character, with cadences exclusively or predominantly on perfect breve *initia*, while others have extended passages in which the breve-unit is not noticeably marked. Rhythmic complications and irregular groupings are possible in perfect, as well as imperfect, *tempus*.

CC II/10 *(Johannis Baptistae)*, Sequence (*Solemnia celebrantes*), v. 1 (Example 11.11), and CC II/1 (*Natalis Domini*), Communion (*Viderunt/omnes*; Example 11.12), illustrate the range of emphasis that may accrue to the breve-units in perfect *tempus*. In Example 11.11 the breve-units are brought out strongly and consistently by the musical rhythms, while in Example 11.12 a canon between the lower voices at the semibreve interval obscures the ternary grouping of semibreves throughout most of the piece. In the latter example, the mensural framework is nevertheless established at the beginning and reaffirmed at the end. The opening bars create ternary groups of semibreves by means of cadences on the second and third breve *initia*. This grouping is difficult to hear in most of the rest of the verse, but the rhythms realign with the *tempus* through cadences on breve *initia* and a sequential pattern in the discant in bars 13–15.

The most common rhythmic groupings that counteract the ternary groups of semibreves in perfect *tempus* are hemiola patterns: groups of three minims, which divide the breve into 3+3, rather than 2+2+2, minims, and groups of three imperfect breves in coloration, which divide a long into three imperfect, rather than two perfect, breves. CC II/8 (*De Sancto Spiritu*), Sequence (*Quae corda*), v. 2 ("Spiritus alme"; Example 11.13),

Example 11.11 Heinrich Isaac, *Choralis Constantinus* II/10 *(Johannis Baptistae)*, Sequence *(Solemnia celebrantes)*, v. 1.

features a discant cantus firmus that is consistently in dotted semibreves (= three-minim groups) in Φ until the penultimate breve. The bass and alto bring out the perfect breves, while the tenor agrees with the discant until the concluding passage.

Perfect mensurations occasionally serve as vehicles for quintuple rhythms. The simplest way to notate such groups is with alternating white and black notes. This pattern appears in verse 9 ("Tu divisum"; Example 11.14) of the Sequence shown in Example 11.13. The tenor alternates white and black breves (the former equal to three and the latter to two semibreves) throughout the section until the penultimate bar. The other voices feature subjects in imitation that begin on every semibreve *initium* and often repeat at overlapping intervals of five semibreves in individual voices, obliterating any sense of the perfect breve-units. Nevertheless, the opening rhythm of the discant, the mensural position of the second note of the tenor, and the bass entry orient the listener to the mensuration at the beginning and all

Example 11.12 Heinrich Isaac, *Choralis Constantinus* II/1 (*Natalis Domini*), Communion (*Viderunt/omnes*): (a) bars 1–4; (b) bars 11–15.

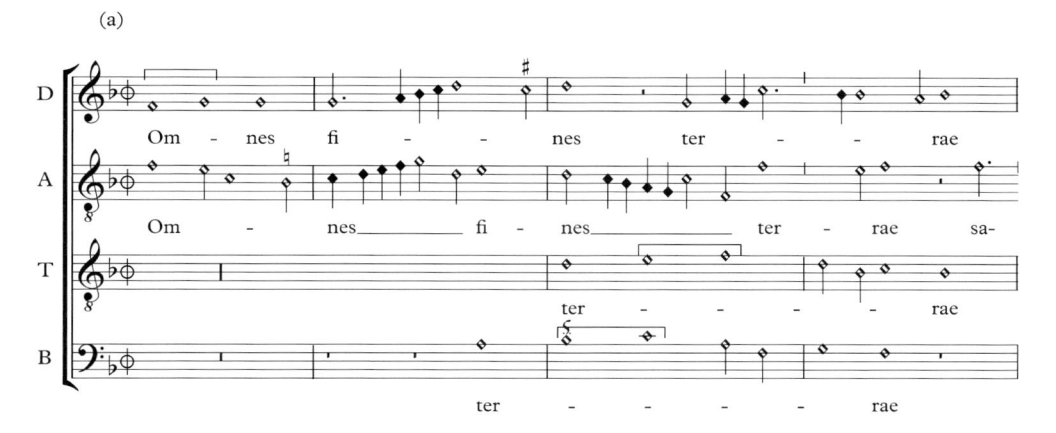

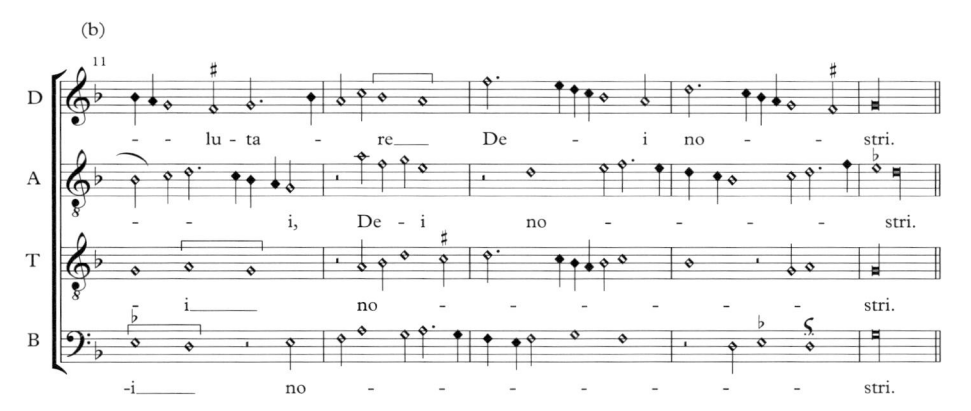

voices reaffirm it in the penultimate bar (not shown in the example). The fact that the count of semibreves turns out right in the end may not be perceptible, but it must have been an element of the composer's concept of the mensural structure.

Isaac's understanding of the relationship between imperfect and perfect *tempus* may be elucidated by the two verses in which both mensurations appear successively, under the signs Φ and ₵, in a single verse: CC III/8 (*De Beata Virgine post nativitatem Christi*), Sequence (*Regem regum*), v. 3 ("Sicut sydus"; Example 11.15) and CC III/17 (*Visitationis Marie*), Sequence (*Veni praecelsa Domina*), v. 4 ("Veni deposite"). The series of signs in both examples is Φ, ₵3, ₵. The ternary grouping of semibreves in the opening section and the binary grouping in the concluding section are clear in both. These examples suggest that despite the liberties that may be taken

Example 11.13 Heinrich Isaac, *Choralis Constantinus* II/8 (*De Sancto Spiritu*), Sequence (*Quae corda*), v. 2 ("Spiritus alme").

in the grouping of semibreves in both perfect and imperfect *tempus*, Isaac regarded the theoretical structures of the mensurations as meaningful compositional considerations.

Sesquialtera proportions

Passages of *sesquialtera* are common in *Choralis Constantinus*. There are also a few complete verses in *sesquialtera*. Issac's usual signs for the proportion are ₵3 at beginnings of sections and 3 or coloration (sometimes both) within sections. The signs are sometimes interchanged, and they appear simultaneously often enough to prove that their meanings are synonymous, except that breves are always perfect under ₵3, while semibreves are occasionally perfect under 3. The value that comes in ternary groups in coloration is usually the semibreve, but occasionally the minim.

Example 11.14 Heinrich Isaac, *Choralis Constantinus* II/8 (*De Sancto Spiritu*), Sequence (*Quae corda*), v. 9 ("Tu divisum"), bars 1–5.

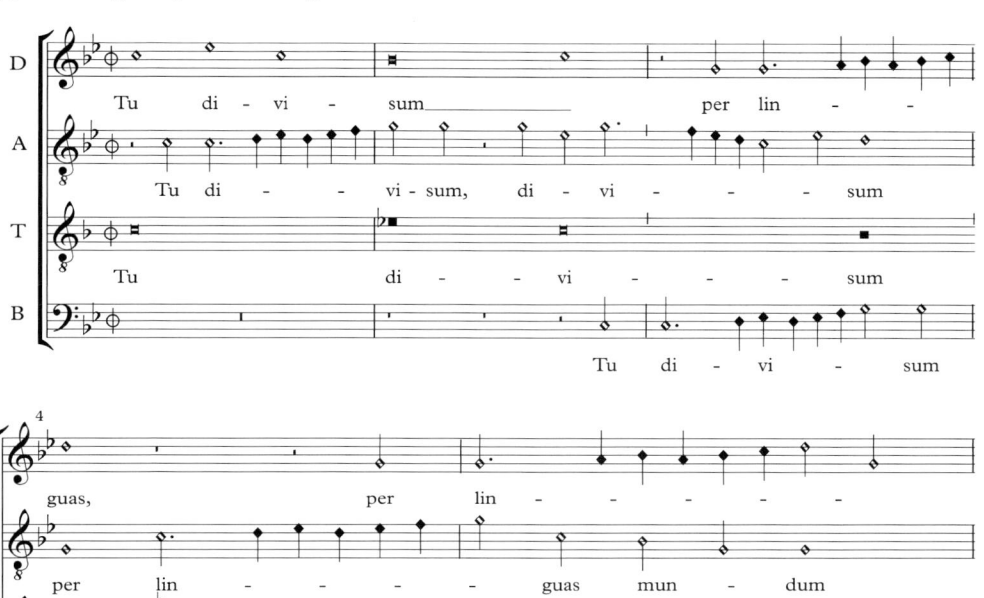

Many additional *sesquialtera* signs appear only once or twice in the collection, mostly in *Choralis Constantinus* III. They include $^O_3$, $^C_3$, $^{O2}_3$, ℭ3, ϕ3, and Ↄ with coloration. In one case coloration appears under the sign 6, where notation in half-values under the sign 3 would have been normal. The rhythms associated with these signs are the same as those associated with the more common *sesquialtera* signs.

Sesquialtera notated with perfect breves or groups of three black semibreves differs fundamentally from perfect *tempus*. Both the compositional *tactus* and the performance *tactus* correspond to the perfect breve or a group of three black semibreves. Note values normally range from the minim to the perfect breve, though seminimims appear occasionally in stepwise melismas. The semibreve is the shortest value that may receive separate syllables. Cadences fall only on breve *initia*, and the penultimate intervals of cadences normally last for two semibreves. Suspensions are semibreves, and non-suspension dissonances are minims. The ternary

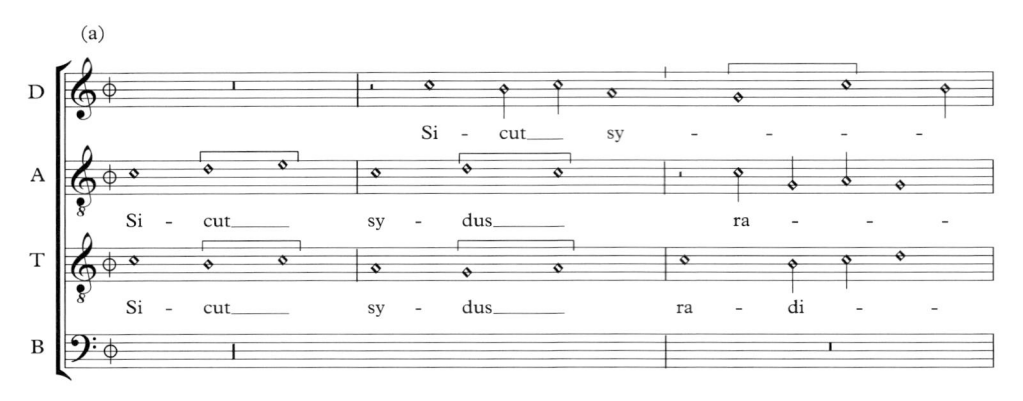

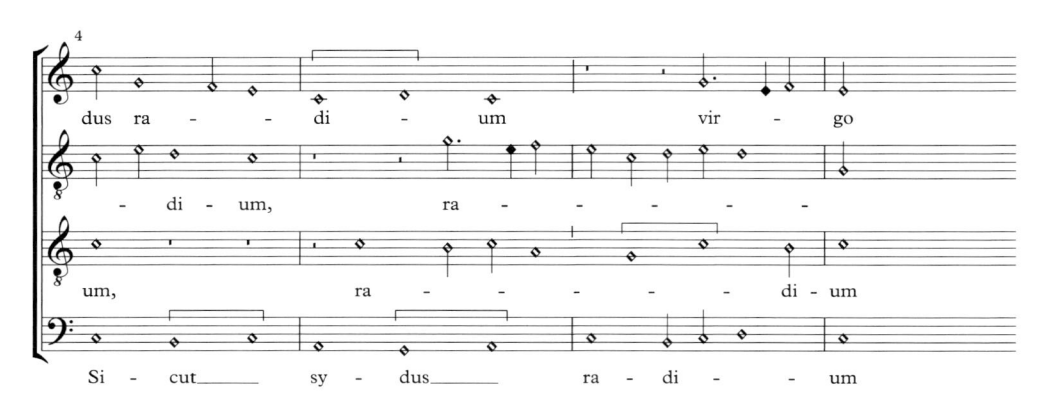

Example 11.15 Heinrich Isaac, *Choralis Constantinus* III/8 (*De Beata Virgine post nativitatem Christi*), Sequence (*Regem regum*), v. 3 ("Sicut sydus"): (a) bars 1–7; (b) bars 17–20.

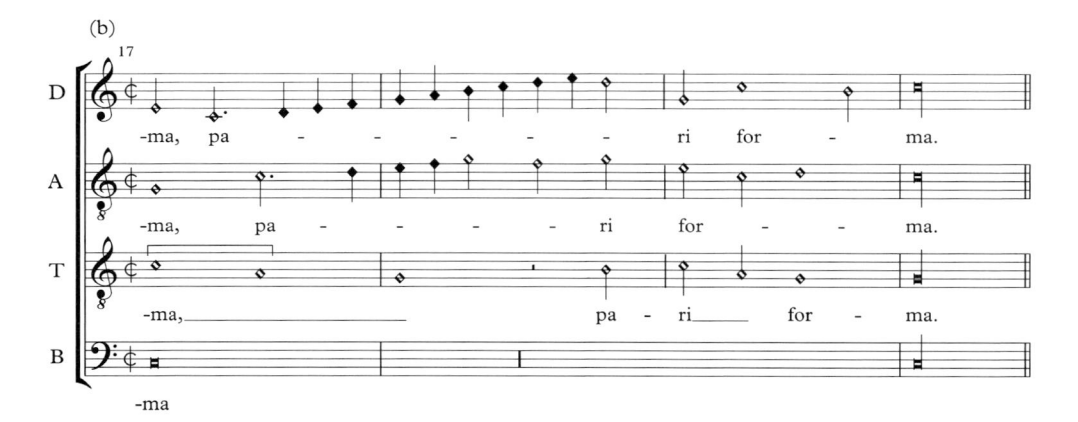

Example 11.16 Heinrich Isaac, *Choralis Constantinus* II/8 (*De Sancto Spiritu*), *Alleluia Veni Sancte Spiritus*, verse, bars 1–5.

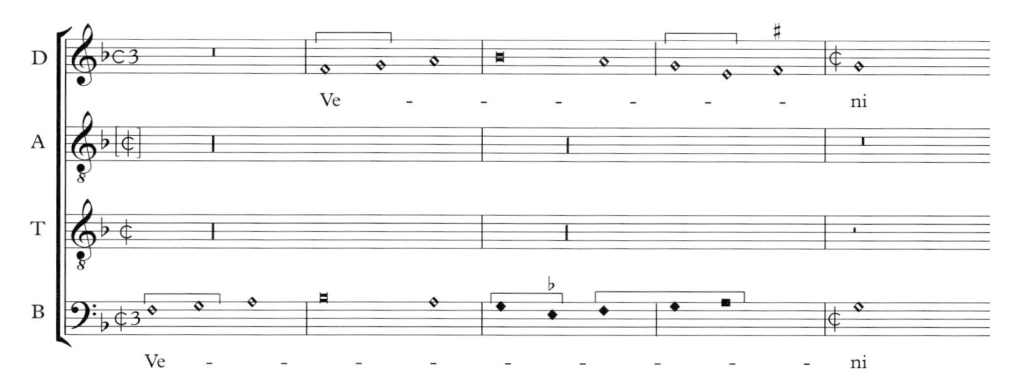

Example 11.17 Heinrich Isaac, *Choralis Constantinus* II/17 (*De Sancto Pelagio*), Sequence (*In mensa Domini*), v. 9 ("Pro nobis"), bars 1–6.

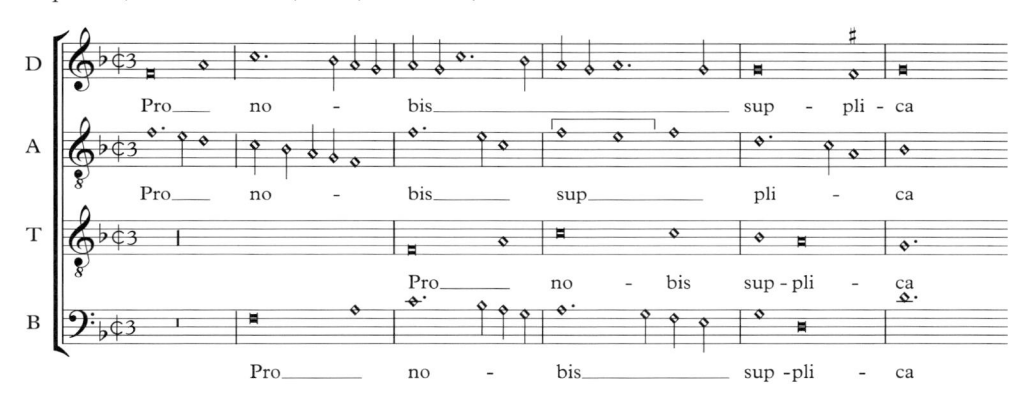

character of the rhythms is always clear. The verse of the *Alleluia Veni Sancte Spiritus* from CC II/8 (*De Sancto Spiritu*; Example 11.16) is a simple but interesting example. It follows Example 11.6 (above) and opens with the same pitches in the discant, prompting the listener to hear the sections in relation to each other. Example 11.6 features complex ternary rhythms in relation to ¢, and Example 11.16 resolves the tension with a lilting, dance-like setting of the same melody. (The absence of the stroke through the mensuration sign in the discant is an error in the print.)

A more complex example of *sesquialtera* with perfect breves appears in CC II/17 (*De Sancto Pelagio*), Sequence (*In mensa Domini*), v. 9 ("Pro nobis"; Example 11.17). Here the rhythms are more varied than in Example 11.16, but the feel of the ternary subdivision of the *tactus* is still clear.

The opening verse of CC II/14 (*Marie Magdalene*), Sequence (*Coeli, terrae, maris*), v. 10 ("Qualis sit") is the only example of *sesquialtera* that does not conform to the above principles. It is signed ₵3, but its musical style is like Φ. The consistency of the distinction that Isaac normally makes between Φ and ₵3 suggests that the sign in this verse should have been Φ.

Sesquialtera notated in perfect semibreves (or groups of three black minims) is like the simpler examples of *sesquialtera* notated in perfect breves (or groups of three black semibreves) notated in half-values. The compositional *tactus* is the perfect semibreve or a group of three black minims. The written values are predominantly semibreves and minims; semiminims (analogous to minims of ₵3) appear only in isolation following dotted minims. This type of *sesquialtera* is generally limited to passages no longer than two or three breves.

In the great majority of cases, *sesquialtera* signs appear simultaneously in all voices. When they do not, the voices in *sesquialtera* often appear against rests (as in Example 11.16) or sustained notes in the other voices. Rhythms that juxtapose simultaneous duple and triple divisions of the *tactus* are rare. The general problem of the tempo relationship between *sesquialtera* and other signs therefore applies to most instances of *sesquialtera* in *Choralis Constantinus*. *Sesquialtera* notated with perfect breves (or groups of three black semibreves) is probably slower than *sesquialtera* notated with perfect semibreves (or groups of three black minims), since it often entails more complex subdivisions of the *tactus*. The latter can be performed comfortably with three minims in the time of two of ₵ or C, but interpreting the former as a literal *sesquialtera* proportion, with three semibreves in the time of two of ₵, makes the compositional *tactus* of ₵3 twice as slow as that of ₵ and results in extremely slow tempos under that sign. It seems likely, therefore, that the perfect breve *tactus* of *sesquialtera* should normally be faster than the divided imperfect breve *tactus* (or two semibreve *tactus*) of ₵ despite the evidence of passages such as Example 11.16 in which the two signs overlap.[10]

Other proportions and unusual signs

Although verses with proportional notation make up only a tiny percentage of *Choralis Constantinus*, it is largely to them that the collection owes its reputation in the history of music. Theorists began publishing examples of

---

[10] See Chapter 7, pp. 200–06.

this notation even before the collection itself was published, and the same examples have been featured prominently in studies of mensural notation ever since. Sebald Heyden included two of the most complex verses in the 1537 edition of his *De arte canendi* and added a third in the 1540 edition.[11] Later sixteenth-century theorists copied these examples from him, and modern historians of mensural notation have assigned them an importance that is far out of proportion to their number. Philip Gossett concluded a study of the notation of *Choralis Constantinus* with the claim that the work "probably represents the most extensive and unified single source we have for information about the practical workings of the mensural system."[12] The widespread myth that mensural notation is often unnecessarily cryptic is based almost entirely on the small handful of *Choralis* verses to which that characterization legitimately applies.

I have proposed in a recent study that the most complex notation in *Choralis Constantinus* is not Isaac's at all, but that it was revised (sometimes quite drastically) by Heyden for didactic purposes.[13] This hypothesis cannot be proved, because the earliest surviving sources of the verses with questionable notation date from the mid 1530s (two decades after Isaac's death), but the following considerations make it likely: (1) The notation in question differs drastically from that in Isaac's other works and the works of his contemporaries. It makes use of signs that are rare or non-existent in other practical sources, and the unusual signs serve no evident musical purpose. (2) The same signs are featured prominently in Heyden's treatise. Some of them have different meanings from those that were acknowledged by theorists of Isaac's time. (3) Heyden is known to have changed the notation of many of his examples for purposes of pedagogical demonstration. The two *Choralis* examples in the 1537 edition appear in prominent positions toward the end of the treatise, where they serve to sum up and "prove" Heyden's conclusions. At least one other example with the same function was altered in a way that makes it look very much like the *Choralis* example that follows it in the treatise, although its notation in sources close to the composer is entirely normal. (4) One of the verses with complex proportional notation appears in an independent source without

---

[11] Sebald Heyden, *Musicae, id est artis canendi libri duo* (Nuremberg: Johann Petreius, 1537), and Sebald Heyden, *De arte canendi* (Nuremberg: Johann Petreius, 1540; repr. New York: Broude, 1969). On Heyden's use of examples, see Cristle Collins Judd, *Reading Renaissance Music Theory: Hearing with the Eyes*, Cambridge Studies in Music Theory and Analysis 14 (Cambridge University Press, 2000), 94–114.

[12] Gossett, "The Mensural System and the 'Choralis Constantinus'," 96.

[13] See DeFord, "Who Devised the Proportional Notation in Isaac's *Choralis Constantinus*?" for a detailed discussion of the points in this paragraph.

the proportions. (5) The placement of the verses with problematic notation in the *Choralis* print suggests a didactic function. The verses appear in order of increasing complexity in volumes II and III, and two of them appear prominently in the opening and closing masses of volume II. Since the order of the masses is liturgical, this systematic plan is likely to have been imposed on the work through later alterations of its notation. (6) Heyden was developing his theory and writing his treatise in Nuremberg at exactly the same time that Ott was preparing the publication of *Choralis Constantinus*. The two of them must have been in close contact and shared manuscript copies of the work. Heyden may have envisioned the print as an authoritative didactic anthology that would lend support to his controversial theory. His great reputation as a scholar could have induced Ott to concur with such a plan. (7) The *Choralis* print was not a functional liturgical manuscript like the sources that originally contained Isaac's music, but an imposing monument to a dead composer who had achieved canonical status in sixteenth-century Germany. Ott may well have felt that a touch of impressive notation would enhance the cultural status of the work, as well as increase its value for didactic purposes. He presumably accepted Heyden's claim that revised notation did not alter the substance of the music.

Not all of the proportions in *Choralis Constantinus* are of questionable authenticity. Some of them conform to Isaac's usual practice, and a few are confirmed by independent sources. Proportions that are not typical of Isaac range from slightly to highly dubious, with no sharp distinction between these categories. If my hypothesis about Heyden's intervention in the notation is correct, the theorist may in some cases have built upon existing proportions by enhancing their complexity, rather than inventing them from scratch. Although authentic and inauthentic proportions cannot be distinguished with certainty, it is possible to distinguish proportions that are in line with the practices of Isaac's time from those that are not. The historical significance of the unusual proportions must be evaluated in light of this distinction, regardless of who devised them and what their intended purpose may have been.

The most striking feature of the unusual proportions in *Choralis Constantinus* is the mismatch between the complexity of their appearance and the simplicity of the rhythms that they denote. The same rhythms could have been notated equally correctly and much more simply without them. Unlike the proportions in the masses and motets discussed in the preceding chapters, which are essential to the compositional structures of the works in which they appear, most of the proportions in *Choralis Constantinus* are purely visual devices that often do more to conceal than to reveal the sense of the rhythms that they represent.

For present purposes, I shall define all mensurations in which the compositional *tactus* is a value other than the imperfect semibreve as "proportions," in line with the informal sense of the term in the fifteenth and sixteenth centuries. By this definition, proportions other than *sesquialtera* (but including duple proportion of *sesquialtera*) appear in thirty verses in *Choralis Constantinus*.[14] With the exception of cases that are almost certainly errors, the relations among simultaneous signs with binary *tactus* follow a consistent pattern that conforms to Heyden's theory: a dot in the middle of a sign doubles the values; a stroke through the sign, a figure 2 following it, or a reversal of the semicircle cuts the values in half; and two such devices in combination cut them to a quarter.

Combinations of ¢ with C and ¢2 are found in other works of Isaac and are likely to be authentic. ¢ is the basic sign in them, and the contrasting sign is limited to a single voice or two voices in canon. ¢ has the same rhythmic style that it has in non-proportional contexts. From the point of view of the compositional *tactus*, therefore, C may be understood as subduple (1:2) proportion of ¢, rather than ¢ as duple proportion of C. The function of the proportion sign is to highlight one or two voices, often those with the cantus firmus, visually. Example 11.18 uses ¢2 to set off a retrograde canon between discant and tenor in CC II/10 (*Johannis Baptistae*), Sequence (*Solemnia celebrantes*), v. 6 ("Et agni vellere"). The voice is written only in the discant; the tenor has the instruction "in Discanto cancrisat."

The combination of ɸ2 with ɸ is more complex than the combination of ¢2 with ¢, because doubling the speed of the notated perfect breves creates hemiola against the perfect breves of ɸ in the other voices. ɸ2 is an unusual sign that Isaac does not use outside of *Choralis Constantinus*, and even there it appears only once, in CC III/2 (*De apostolis*), Sequence (*Clare sanctorum*), v. 4b ("Ethiopes horridos"; Example 11.19).[15] It represents duple proportion of perfect *tempus*, not perfect *modus*. The sign might be authentic, since the context in which it appears involves a hemiola relationship that is integral to the musical structure, though Isaac often wrote the same type of rhythm without a proportion, as in Example 11.13 above.

Short passages of duple proportion, usually represented by the figure 2 and limited to individual voices within verses in ¢, C, or O, appear

---

[14] For a complete list of them, see ibid., pp. 172–74.
[15] The text of this verse is problematic, since it is identical to that of the preceding verse.

Example 11.18 Heinrich Isaac, *Choralis Constantinus* II/10 (*Johannis Baptistae*), Sequence (*Solemnia celebrantes*), v. 6 ("Et agni vellere").

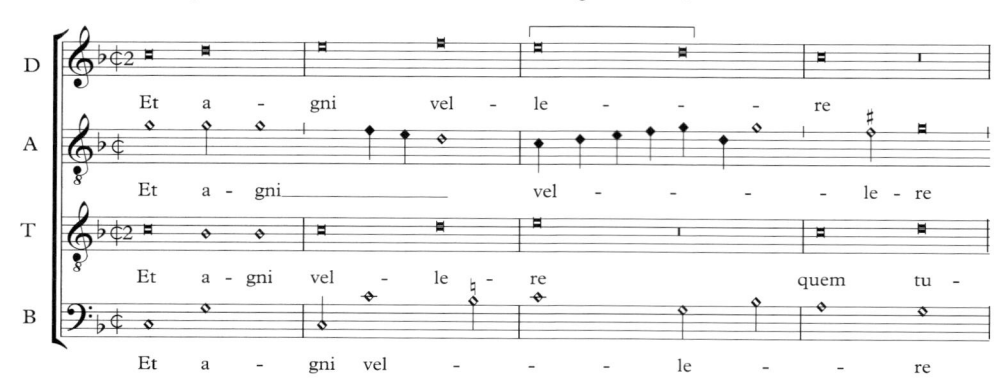

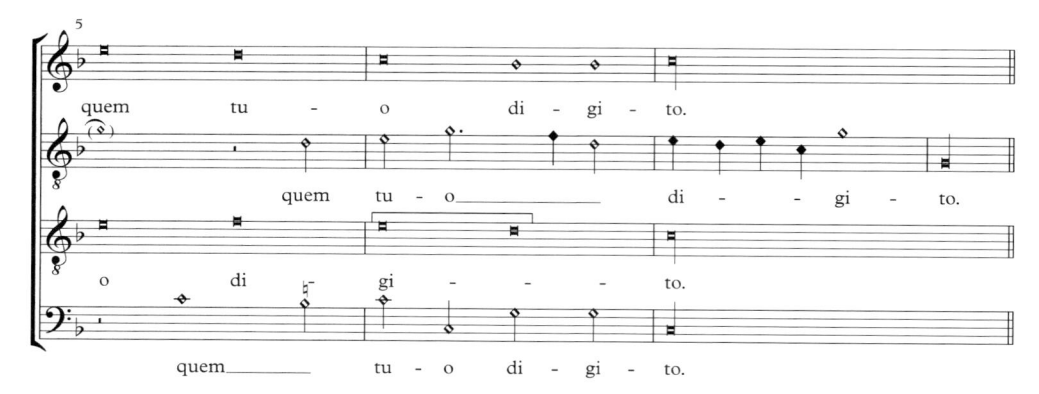

Example 11.19 Heinrich Isaac, *Choralis Constantinus* III/2 (*De apostolis*), Sequence (*Clare sanctorum*), v. 4b ("Ethiopes horridos"), bars 1–5.

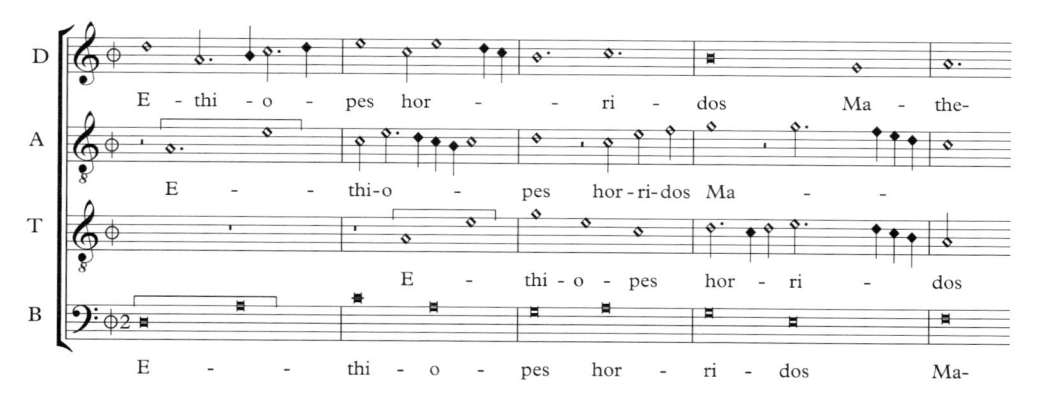

Example 11.20 Heinrich Isaac, *Choralis Constantinus* II/25 (*Conceptionis Marie*), *Alleluia Conceptio* ("Alleluia"), bass.

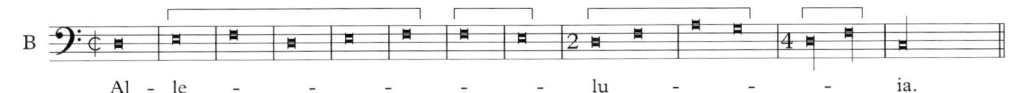

occasionally. The proportion is sometimes set off with black notation that has no mensural meaning. Duple proportions of this type, which often serve no apparent musical or textual purpose, appear in other works of Isaac and are therefore likely to be authentic. Even the black notation may be genuine, since Ornithoparchus cites a now-lost work of Isaac as an example of the use of black notation to represent duple proportion.[16] In CC II/25 (*Conceptionis Marie*), *Alleluia Conceptio* (Example 11.20), a quadruple proportion of questionable authenticity follows a duple proportion of this type. The duple proportion marks the point where the values in the bass double their speed, but the quadruple proportion is a pointless visual complication. Quadruple proportion is found nowhere else in the works of Isaac and is extremely rare outside of theoretical treatises. The example appears in the concluding mass of volume II, where it is particularly noticeable. If it is Heyden's enhancement of Isaac's notation, as I suspect, this would be a logical place for it to be featured.

Perfect prolation appears both in simultaneous combination with O, C, O2, or Φ and in all voices of a passage or verse in *Choralis Constantinus*. In combination with another mensuration, it is limited to a single voice. The meanings of the signs of the other voices are the same as they are in non-proportional contexts. ʘ and ₵ function as subduple proportion in relation to O and C and as subquadruple proportion in relation to O2; ₵ and ꝺ function as subduple proportion in relation to Φ. These relationships are like those in the *L'homme armé* masses discussed in Chapter 9 except that subduple proportion of Φ is notated as ₵ or ꝺ, in conformity with Heyden's theory. The combination of O and ʘ in CC II/9 (*De Corpore Christi*), Sequence *Quantum potes*, v. 1, must be authentic, because it involves a mensuration canon.[17] The motive for the notation may have been the word "maior" (suggesting major prolation) in the text of the verse.

---

[16] Andreas Ornithoparchus, *Musice active micrologus* (Leipzig: Valentin Schumann, 1517), book 2, ch. 11 ("De imperfectione"), fol. Giii^v; trans. John Dowland (London: T. Adams, 1609), 57.

[17] The notation appears in Stuttgart, Württembergische Landesbibliothek, Ms. I 40, which was copied before 1550 from a source independent of the printer's exemplar. See Schuler, "Zur Überlieferung," 147–48.

Example 11.21 Heinrich Isaac, *Choralis Constantinus* II/13 (*Visitationis Marie*), Sequence (*Piae vocis laudes canta*), v. 1, bars 1–11.

Perfect prolation in all voices simultaneously is more problematic. CC II/13 (*Visitationis Marie*), Sequence *Piae vocis laudes canta*, v. 1 (Example 11.21) is probably authentic, because it involves another notational pun on the word "maior." The passage with perfect prolation in all voices is limited to a single breve on the word "maior" itself. Isaac highlights the special word with the bass entry and distinct cadences following each of its syllables.[18] Where perfect prolation applies to all voices at the beginning of a verse or throughout a verse, however, the notation is highly suspect. In these cases, ₵ has a minim compositional *tactus* and a rhythmic style like that of O or ⌽ written in half-values. It must therefore be understood to imply augmentation even though no simultaneous sign confirms this interpretation. There is nothing in the text or musical style to justify the unconventional notation. My guess is that the original sign in these

---

[18] The first and third notes of the altus are mistakenly printed in black in the source. The error is corrected in the example.

Example 11.22 Heinrich Isaac, *Choralis Constantinus* III/4 (*De uno martyre*), Sequence 1 (*Morte Christum imitatus*), v. 4 ("Caeci claudi"), bars 23–28.

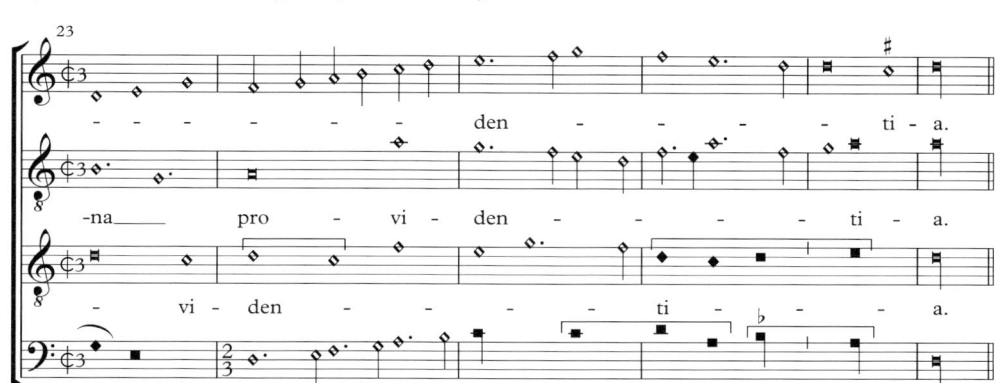

verses was Φ and the notated values in the sections in ₵ were twice as large in Isaac's original notation.

Duple proportion of *sesquialtera*, notated with very unusual signs, is found in a few verses. In CC III/4 (*De uno martyre*), Sequence 1 (*Morte Christum imitatus*), v. 4 ("Caeci claudi"; Example 11.22), it is represented by $\frac{2}{3}$ toward the end of a section in ₵3. The longs under $\frac{2}{3}$ are perfect. The proportion is found only in the last few bars of the bass, which could have been written in values half as large with no proportion sign, like the nearly identical rhythms in the tenor.

In CC III/5 (*De confessoribus*), Sequence 2 (*Ad laudes salvatoris*), v. 5 ("Qui cuique"; Example 11.23) the perfect values under ₵$\frac{2}{3}$ are breves, rather than longs. The verse in which this sign appears has the most complex rhythms (though not the most complex notation) of any verse in *Choralis Constantinus*, and the proportional notation is integral to its structure. The bass has quintuple groups of semibreves, notated as alternating white and black breves as in Example 11.14, under the signs Φ, O$\frac{2}{3}$, and ₵$\frac{2}{3}$. Because these proportion signs are the basis of the structural design of the verse, they must be authentic, though their original forms were probably the ones that were more common in Isaac's time: 3 for *sesquialtera* and 2 for the following duple proportion. The signs are in 3:2:1 ratio: O$\frac{2}{3}$ is *sesquialtera* of Φ, and ₵$\frac{2}{3}$ is duple proportion of the *sesquialtera*. The upper voices have O, in 1:2 ratio (subduple proportion) with the bass in the opening section and $\frac{O}{3}$ or 3 (triple proportion of O) in the second and third sections. The tenor is in ₵ throughout and employs *sesquialtera* notated with coloration in the second

Example 11.23 Heinrich Isaac, *Choralis Constantinus* III/5 (*De confessoribus*), Sequence 2 (*Ad laudes salvatoris*), v. 5 ("Qui cuique").

Example 11.23 (cont.)

and third sections. The rationale for these signs is unclear.[19] There is no obvious reason why the upper voices should have different signs or why the *sesquialtera* should be notated differently in different voices.[20] All of the upper voices may originally have been in Φ, like the bass. Alternatively, they may have been ₵, to alert the singers to the role of the imperfect breve as a standard of reference for the later proportions. The grouping of semibreves

---

[19] The signs in the two manuscripts that were evidently copied from the printer's exemplar differ from those in the print and from each other in this verse. See DeFord, "Who Devised the Proportional Notation in Isaac's *Choralis Constantinus*?," 176.

[20] Gossett, "The Mensural System and the 'Choralis Constantinus'," 82, proposes a symbolic interpretation for the mensural complexity of this verse. He offers the following translation of the obscure text: "This man who gives his measure of wheat to each man; who, by herding the little sheep into the folds of faith has forestalled the ambush of the wolf." He then suggests tentatively that the multiple mensurations at the beginning might represent the ambush of the wolf (which might trap the unwary singers) and the similarity of the notation of the bass to that of the other voices at the end might represent escape from that ambush. This interpretation does not seem convincing to me. The notation is not consistent with Isaac's usual practice and seems to me to represent the kind of intervention by Heyden that I propose for other verses of *Choralis Constantinus*.

implied by the signs O (shown by wedges in Example 11.23), and ¢ (shown by barlines) are not audible; both are overshadowed by the quintuple grouping of semibreves in the bass. It is hard to avoid the suspicion that Heyden enhanced the complexity of the original notation of this verse by using a variety of signs and proportions in the upper voices in order to make them look as complex as the bass.

The time unit that ties all of these signs together is the semibreve of O, which equals the imperfect breve of ¢ and ɸ. It is the only practical performance *tactus* for the verse if the *tactus* remains the same throughout. It must be distinctly divided into two parts in the opening section (bars 1–12), because the compositional *tactus* is half of its value (a semibreve of ¢ and a minim of O) and the bass notes are alternately worth three and two half-*tactus*. In the second section (bars 13–24, where the bass has O_3^2), all voices subdivide the same *tactus* into three parts (three semibreves of *sesquialtera*), and the bass notes alternate between three-thirds and two-thirds of the *tactus*. In the third section (bars 25–30) the compositional *tactus* switches from the perfect breve to the semibreve of the *sesquialtera*. The bass counts twice as fast (six subdivisions per *tactus*) with its notes alternating between three-sixths and two-sixths (or half and a third) of the *tactus*. The rhythms are so complex that it might be necessary to use a *tactus* on the semibreve of the *sesquialtera* in the second and third sections; a divided form of that *tactus* would facilitate the performance of the bass in the third section.

The verses with the most complex notation are the most famous examples in *Choralis Constantinus*, and also the most bizarre. Most of the signs in them probably stem from Heyden, rather than the composer. CC II/1 (*Natalis Domini*), Sequence (*Per quem fit machina*), v. 4 ("Nec gregum"), in which the bass goes through a systematic series of proportions that have no relation to the rhythm or the text, survives in an earlier, independent source with the bass in ¢ throughout. This source provides compelling evidence that the unconventional proportions were not part of Isaac's original notation, at least in this case.

The notational complications of CC II/25 (*Conceptionis Marie*), Sequence (*De radice Jesse*), v. 1 are the most extreme in the entire repertoire of mensural music. Twenty-seven signs, including the unique composite sign ¢ Ɔ (which is synonymous with ¢2), are found in the space of a mere eighteen breves. This verse functions as the final "proof" of Heyden's *tactus* theory in *De arte canendi* (see Figure 11.1). Its look is something only a theorist could love, but its sound is sweet and innocent, as may be seen in a transcription of it into ordinary values

Figure 11.1 Isaac, *De radice Jesse*. Sebald Heyden, *De arte canendi* (Nuremberg: Johann Petreius, 1540), 114–15.

(Example 11.24). The signs in the print are the same as those in the treatise. Like Example 11.15, *De radice Jesse* begins with ternary groups of semibreves and switches to binary groups around the middle. Its original signs were probably O in the first section, C in the second section, and 3 for the *sesquialtera*. Heyden "resolved" the whole verse into ¢ in his treatise, evidently doubling the original values in the process, since the compositional *tactus* of his resolution is the breve, while the compositional *tactus* of Isaac's ¢ is always the semibreve, even in proportional contexts (see Figure 11.2). This was Heyden's standard procedure for transcribing O to ¢. It is based on the untenable theoretical view that the breve *tactus* of ¢ is equivalent in form, duration, and compositional function to the semibreve *tactus* of O – a principle that does not conform to the practice of any period.

Apart from the few instances of unusual proportions, the notation of *Choralis Constantinus* conforms to the practices of Isaac's contemporaries and the prescriptions of the theorists of his time. All of the usual signs (C, ¢, C2, O2, O, and Φ) have a semibreve compositional *tactus* in non-proportional contexts. C and O are apparently slower than the other signs by an unspecified, but not very large, amount. The grouping of semibreves agrees broadly with the implications of the signs (binary in C, ¢, C2, and O2; ternary in O and Φ), especially at the beginnings and ends of verses, but

Example 11.24 Heinrich Isaac, *Choralis Constantinus* II/25 (*Conceptionis Marie*), Sequence (*De radice Jesse*), v. 1: transcription in ordinary values with ordinary signs.

Example 11.24 (cont.)

Figure 11.2 Isaac, *De radice Jesse*, with the notation "resolved" into ₵. Sebald Heyden, *De arte canendi* (Nuremberg: Johann Petreius, 1540), 116–17.

allows for considerable flexibility within them. A semibreve performance *tactus* is always possible, and it is musically preferable where the rhythms are independent of the theoretical grouping of semibreves for extended passages. In many verses, however, a divided breve *tactus* has the advantage of making performers aware of subtle compositional distinctions between semibreve and breve *initia*. *Sesquialtera* passages have a compositional *tactus* on the perfect breve or perfect semibreve or a group of three black semibreves or minims. Their tempo relations to passages with binary *tactus* are ambiguous in the usual ways.

The compositional treatment of signs in proportional contexts differs from that in non-proportional contexts. In proportions, the compositional *tactus* is the semibreve of cut signs and the minim of uncut signs, so that uncut signs function as subduple (1:2) proportions of cut signs. Heyden's theory of "uniform *tactus*" erases this distinction by applying the same performance *tactus* to all pieces. This view not only contradicts the views of Isaac's contemporaries, but also creates mismatches between compositional and performance *tactus* that make no musical sense even apart from the extreme contrasts of tempo that it entails.

The consistency of the relationships among signs in proportional relations in *Choralis Constantinus* has been used as an argument for applying the same principles to non-proportional relationships among signs.[21] If, as I suspect, the unusual proportion signs were devised by Heyden for the express purpose of supporting his theory, they obviously cannot provide evidence for Isaac's understanding of signs, but in any case, they are so rare and out of the ordinary that it makes no sense to draw general conclusions about the principles of mensural notation from them. They are fascinating documents of the sixteenth-century reception of Isaac's music and the notation of his time, but the view that they are extreme examples of normal mensural practice, which has held sway for nearly five hundred years, cannot withstand critical scrutiny.

---

[21] Gossett, "The Mensural System and the 'Choralis Constantinus'," 92–95.

12 | The masses of Palestrina

Palestrina's 104 masses have had a greater impact on later concepts of Renaissance style than any other repertoire of fifteenth- or sixteenth-century music. They were elevated to the status of ideal models of sacred music shortly after the composer's death and have been regarded as such ever since. They have also played a prominent role in music pedagogy from the seventeenth century to the present, because they embody the principles of counterpoint taught by Zarlino in exceptionally pure form. All aspects of Palestrina's compositional practice, including rhythm, have been subjected to detailed analysis and codified as rules for the teaching of strict counterpoint.[1] The general claims that scholars have made about the nature of "Renaissance rhythm" are often tacitly based on Palestrina's sacred style, as if it were the standard model for all of the music of its time.

The most obvious difference in mensural character between the sacred music of Palestrina and that of Josquin and his contemporaries is that Palestrina's principal mensuration is almost always ₵. Sections notated as *sesquialtera* with perfect breves, usually signed Φ_2^3, provide occasional contrast. In many respects, the sign ₵ means the same thing to Palestrina that it does to Josquin. The compositional *tactus* is principally the semibreve, but it may shift occasionally to the breve. The prevailing note values range from breves to minims, with *fusae* and longs appearing occasionally. The shortest note that may be syncopated is the semibreve, and the shortest note that may receive separate syllables of text is the minim. (A dotted minim and semiminim may substitute for a semibreve or a pair of minims from these points of view.) Cadences may fall on any semibreve *initium*, and cadential penultimates are predominantly semibreves, but occasionally breves. Dissonances are no longer than minims, and non-suspension dissonances are mostly semiminims and *fusae*.

The principal difference between Palestrina's and Josquin's treatment of ₵ is that Palestrina's rhythms are heavily dependent on the text rhythm and

---

[1] The classic study of the subject is Knud Jeppesen, *The Style of Palestrina and the Dissonance*, 2nd edn., trans. Margaret Hamerik (Copenhagen: E. Munksgaard, 1946; repr. New York: Dover, 1970, and Mineola, NY: Dover, 2005).

function mostly on the level of the semibreve and its subdivisions. Palestrina brings out the accented syllables of his texts by means of either agogic or mensural accent. Accented syllables are usually set to longer notes than unaccented syllables, which may or may not be aligned with stronger mensural positions than the shorter notes that follow them. In a series of equal minims, however, accented syllables fall on semibreve *initia* and unaccented syllables on minim-max *initia* about 80–90 percent of the time. Agogic accents that are independent of the semibreve *initia* lead to irregular and constantly shifting groups of minims within phrases. Semibreve *initia* are always audible, however, and final notes of phrases fall on semibreve *initia* whether or not they are supported by cadences.

Given the rhythmic focus on shifting groupings of minims within phrases, it is not surprising that regular mensural groupings on levels larger than the semibreve play a much smaller role in Palestrina than they do in Josquin. Palestrina is exquisitely sensitive to the balance among phrases and sections of pieces, but he prefers flexible and variable relationships to numerical regularity on these levels. *Modus*, which plays a vital role in many of Josquin's masses and motets, is usually non-existent in Palestrina. Even the pairing of semibreves implied by the sign ₵ is weak. Breve-units move into and out of audibility in both Josquin and Palestrina, but for Josquin, audibility is the norm and inaudibility the exception, whereas for Palestrina, the reverse is true. Nevertheless, Palestrina rarely loses track of the breve-units altogether. His works in ₵ almost always end on breve *initia*, and cadences on breve *initia* outnumber cadences on semibreve-max *initia* by a factor of about three or four to one.[2] When Palestrina moves the rhythmic activity to the breve level to emphasize an important phrase or cadence, he aligns the rhythms correctly with the breve-units. Breve *initia* correlate with points of rhythmic and textual emphasis, and cadences with breve penultimates are never syncopated with respect to the breve-units.

Theoretical evidence demonstrates that by Palestrina's time, the performance *tactus* of ₵ was almost always the semibreve, even though the theoretical *tactus* was still the breve. A semibreve performance *tactus* makes sense for music in which the preponderance of rhythmic interest is on the

---

[2] Raffaele Casimiri, *La polifonia vocale del sec. xvi e la sua trascrizione in figurazione musicale moderna* (Rome: Psalterium, 1942), 43–45, n. 94, lists all of Palestrina's works in ₵ that have odd numbers of semibreves. The list is long enough to prove that Palestrina did not always pay close attention to breve-units in that mensuration, but short enough to demonstrate that he normally followed the rule that pieces in ₵ should have whole numbers of breve-units, whether or not those units played a significant role in the internal mensural organization.

semibreve level. It is possible that the semibreves should be somewhat slower in Palestrina than in Josquin because of the greater emphasis on small-scale time units at the expense of larger ones, but the difference between them cannot be great, since the range and functions of note values in the music of the two composers is similar.

The three masses of Palestrina considered in this chapter offer points of direct comparison with works of Josquin that highlight the similarities and differences between the rhythmic styles of the two composers. Their dates of composition are unknown. The *Missa Benedicta es* is Palestrina's only mass based on a Josquin motet. It was not published during his lifetime and is generally regarded as an early work. The five-voice *Missa L'homme armé* is a self-consciously historicist work that was published in 1570, but probably composed during Palestrina's tenure in the Sistine choir in 1555. The four-voice *Missa L'homme armé* was published in 1582, but could have been composed much earlier. It was entitled "Missa quarta" in the print, probably because of the widespread opposition to the use of secular songs as mass cantus firmi in the wake of the Council of Trent.[3] Since the four-voice *Missa L'homme armé* has the fewest constraints imposed by the pre-existent material, it will be discussed first.

Missa L'homme armé a 4

Palestrina's four-voice *Missa L'homme armé* resembles Josquin's *Missa L'homme armé sexti toni* in that it treats the cantus firmus quite freely. Palestrina's version of the traditional tune differs from the original in that it consists of only the A and B sections. It appears most often in imitation between two voices, but it sometimes remains in a single voice for extended passages and is occasionally taken up by all of the voices in imitation. One section of the Gloria (from "Gratias agimus tibi" through "filius Patris") and much of the Credo make little or no reference to it.

Unlike Josquin, for whom interactions between the ternary rhythm of the cantus firmus and the various mensurations in which it appears are central to the mensural character of *L'homme armé* masses, Palestrina ignores the ternary implications of the cantus firmus altogether throughout most of this mass. Although the melody is not at all disguised, the transformation of its rhythm rendered it unrecognizable to no less a scholar than Franz Xaver

---

[3] James Haar, "Palestrina as Historicist: The Two *L'homme armé* Masses," *Journal of the Royal Musical Association* 121 (1996), 191–205.

Haberl, who mistook it for a chant in his critical edition of the work for the Palestrina *Werke*.[4] The only sections of Palestrina's mass in which the cantus firmus retains something of its ternary character are the beginnings of the Christe and Et in terra, where the rhythms are in groups of three minims, the beginning of Agnus Dei 2, where they are in groups of three semibreves with the ternary character weakened by the omission of note repetitions, and the Osanna, which displays the melody triumphantly in Φ_2^3 in the original rhythm with a perfect breve *tactus*. Even where the rhythms of the cantus firmus are ternary, they sound like the kinds of temporary irregular groupings that are ubiquitous in Palestrina's ¢, rather than cross-rhythms that conflict actively with the other voices. The cantus firmus is stated in equal breves that mark the breve-units of the mensuration in Kyrie 2 and Benedictus. Elsewhere it is integrated seamlessly with the rhythms of the other voices and articulates mensurally equal semibreves. Example 12.1 shows a selection of the rhythmic forms of the cantus firmus from different sections of the mass. (See Example 9.1 for the original form of the tune with the phrase labels used in the following discussion.)

Comparisons of parallel passages in Josquin's *Missa L'homme armé sexti toni* and Palestrina's four-voice *Missa L'homme armé* illustrate the

Example 12.1 Palestrina, *Missa L'homme armé a 4*, cantus firmus (selections): (a) Kyrie 1, cantus, bars 1–4; (b) Kyrie (Christe), bass, bars 18–21; (c) Kyrie 2, altus, bars 32–40; (d) Gloria (Et in terra), cantus, bars 2–5; (e) Gloria (Qui tollis), tenor, bars 44–48; (f) Gloria (Cum Sancto Spiritu), bass, bars 78–79; (g) Credo (Patrem), cantus, bars 1–4; (h) Benedictus (Osanna), bass, bars 26–29; (i) Agnus Dei 2, tenor, bars 1–6. After Palestrina, *Missarum . . . liber quartus* (Venice: Gardano, 1582).

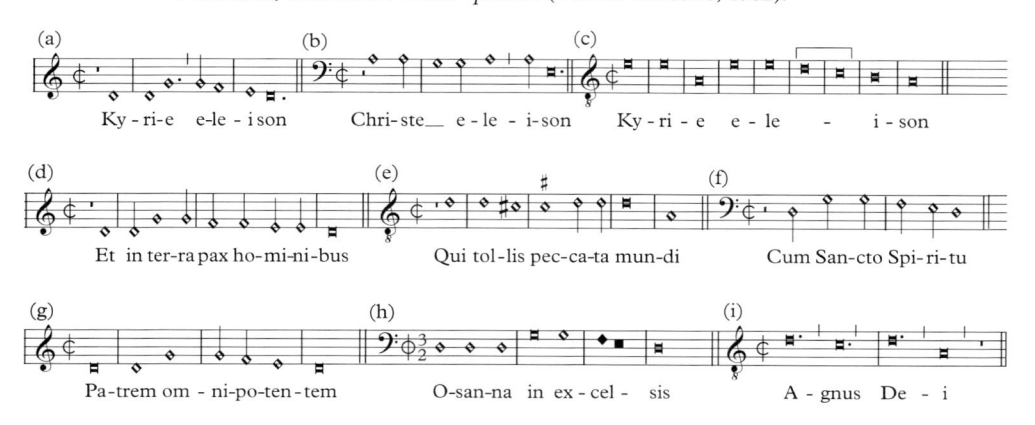

---

[4] Franz Xaver Haberl, preface to Giovanni Pierluigi da Palestrina, *Werke*, ed. Franz Xaver Haberl et al., 33 vols. (Leipzig: Breitkopf & Härtel, [1862–1907]), XIII: vii.

Example 12.2 (a) Josquin, *Missa L'homme armé sexti toni*, Gloria (Qui tollis), bars 54–61. After Vatican City, Biblioteca Apostolica Vaticana, Ms. Chigi C VIII 234 ("Chigi Codex"), fols. clxxxvi[v]–clxxxvii[r]. (b) Palestrina, *Missa L'homme armé a 4*, Gloria (Qui tollis), bars 44–48. After Palestrina, *Missarum . . . liber quartus* (Venice: Gardano, 1582).

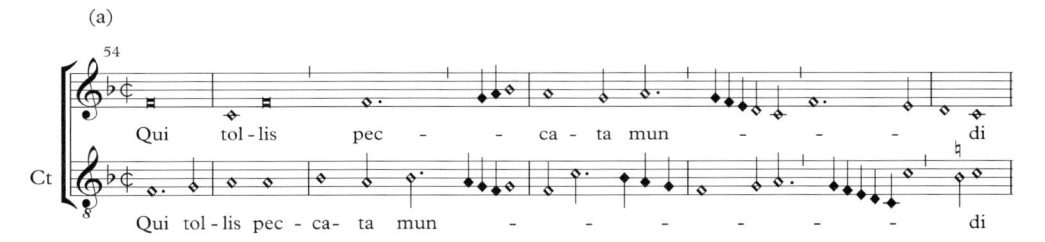

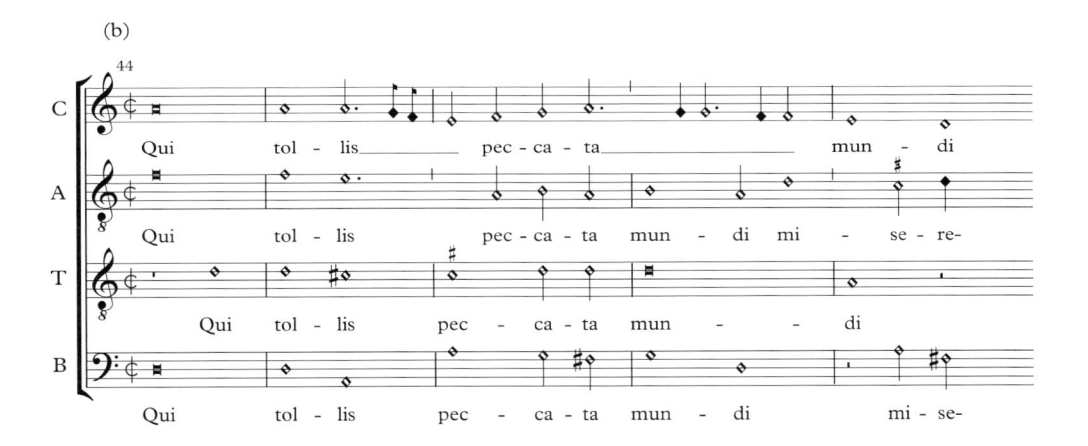

differences between the rhythmic styles of the two composers. In the first phrase of the Qui tollis (Example 12.2), both composers begin by laying out the primary mensural units with a syllabic setting of the opening words to a breve followed by two semibreves. Thereafter Josquin spins out an extended melismatic motive (in duo texture at this point) that has little relation to the words, while Palestrina picks up the declamatory pace, setting each syllable to a minim in bar 46. At the beginning of the Christe, the text setting is melismatic in both works (see Example 12.3). Josquin places the B-1 phrase of the cantus firmus in the bass and the B-3 phrase in the tenor. Both of these voices move in very slow binary rhythms that suggest a pairing of breves that is supported by the other voices. Semibreves are rhythmically undivided (except with ornamental notes) until the end of the phrase. Palestrina likewise places the B-1 phrase in the bass, but he employs ternary groups of minims derived from the original form of the cantus firmus. He begins the cantus firmus with a syncopated semibreve, so that the last note

Example 12.3 (a) Josquin, *Missa L'homme armé sexti toni*, Kyrie (Christe), bars 1–9. After Vatican City, Biblioteca Apostolica Vaticana, Ms. Chigi C VIII 234 ("Chigi Codex"), fols. clxxxiii^v–clxxxiiii^r. The longs in the top voice in bar 1 and the contratenor in bar 5 are half-black. (b) Palestrina, *Missa L'homme armé a 4*, Kyrie (Christe), bars 1–5. After Palestrina, *Missarum . . . liber quartus* (Venice: Gardano, 1582).

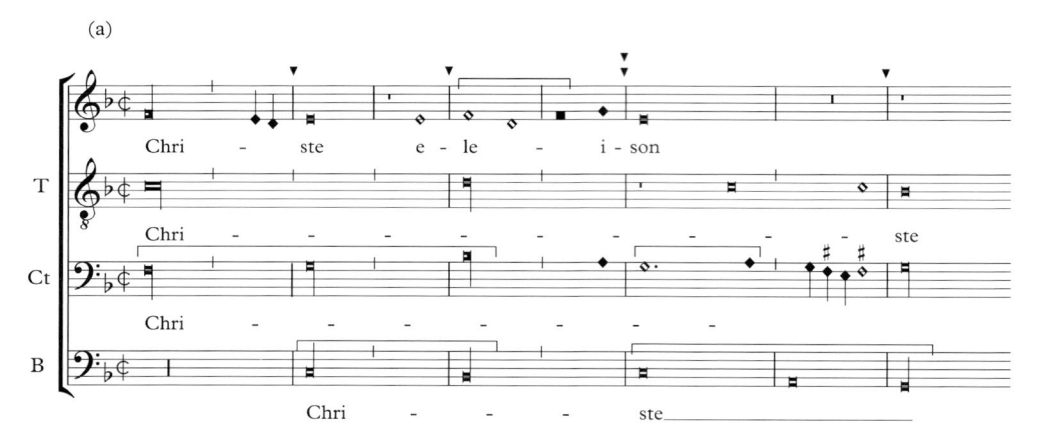

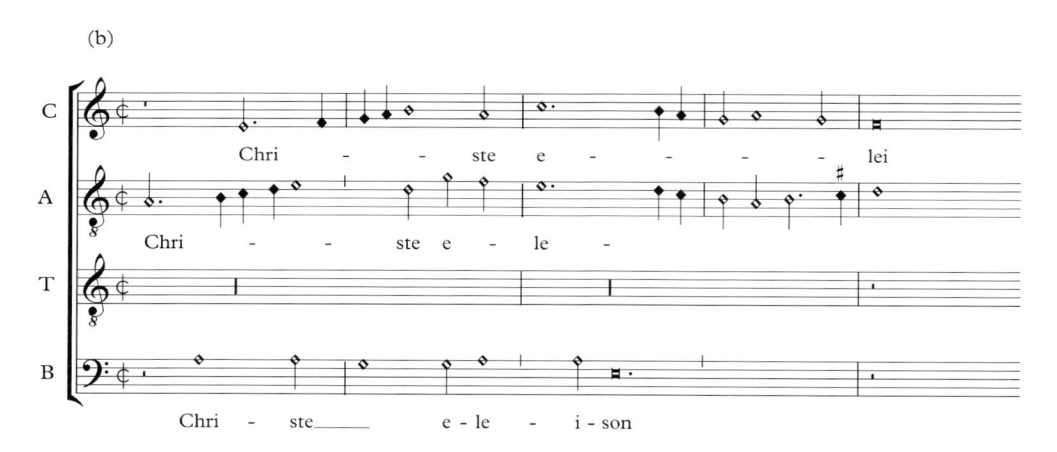

of the phrase will fall on a semibreve *initium*. Syncopated semibreves in all voices are offset in such a way that one voice has a syncopation over every semibreve *initium* until the end of the cantus-firmus phrase. In context, therefore, the ternary rhythms of the bass do not stand out as a foreign element against the binary mensuration, but blend into the larger pattern of fluctuating groups of minims that are resolved through realignment with the mensuration at the cadence.

Palestrina occasionally shifts the rhythmic activity from the semibreve/minim level to the breve/semibreve level to emphasize words of particular

Example 12.4 (a) Josquin, *Missa L'homme armé sexti toni*, Gloria (Qui tollis), bars 114–21. After Vatican City, Biblioteca Apostolica Vaticana, Ms. Chigi C VIII 234 ("Chigi Codex"), fols. clxxxvi^v–clxxxvii^r. (b) Palestrina, *Missa L'homme armé a 4*, Gloria (Qui tollis), bars 75–78. After Palestrina, *Missarum . . . liber quartus* (Venice: Gardano, 1582).

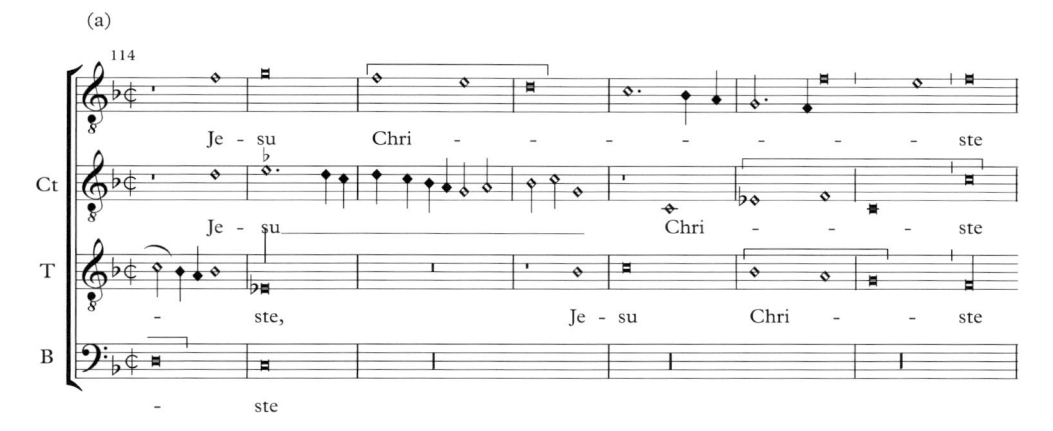

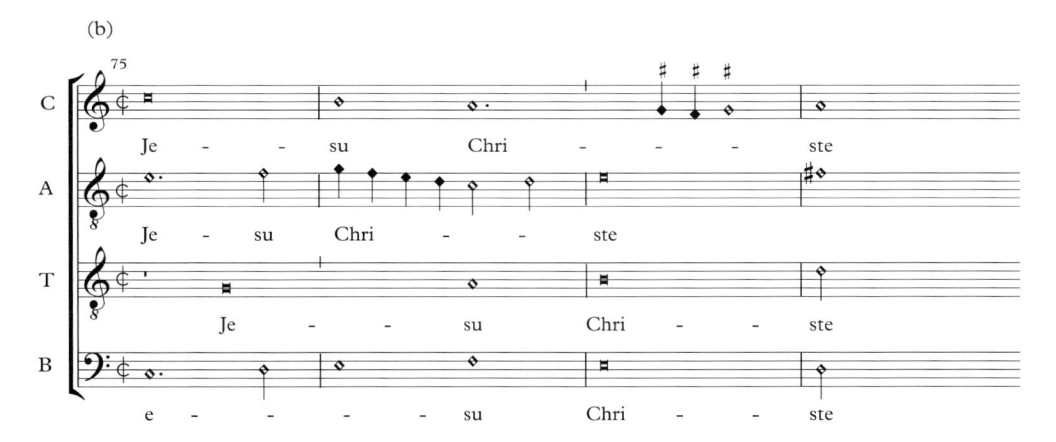

importance. His rhythmic style comes closest to Josquin's in these passages. The setting of the words "Jesu Christe" in the Qui tollis sections of the two masses (Example 12.4) provides an example. Both composers set the text at the rate of approximately one syllable per breve, though Josquin extends the phrase with melismas. The contrapuntal rhythm moves in breves and semibreves. The cadential penultimate is a breve in both works, but Josquin's suspension lasts for a full semibreve, while Palestrina limits the length of the dissonance to a minim by ornamenting the resolution. Palestrina's compositional *tactus* is effectively the breve at this point, even though dissonances do not exceed the length of a minim. Palestrina

Example 12.5 (a) Josquin, *Missa L'homme armé sexti toni*, Credo (Et unam sanctam), bars 189–94. After Vatican City, Biblioteca Apostolica Vaticana, Ms. Chigi C VIII 234 ("Chigi Codex"), fols. clxxxx^v–clxxxxi^r. (b) Palestrina, *Missa L'homme armé a 4*, Benedictus (Osanna), bars 26–29. After Palestrina, *Missarum . . . liber quartus* (Venice: Gardano, 1582).

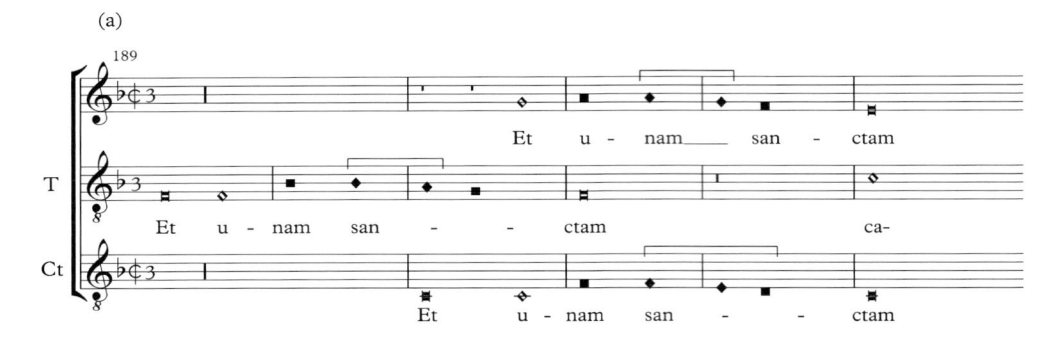

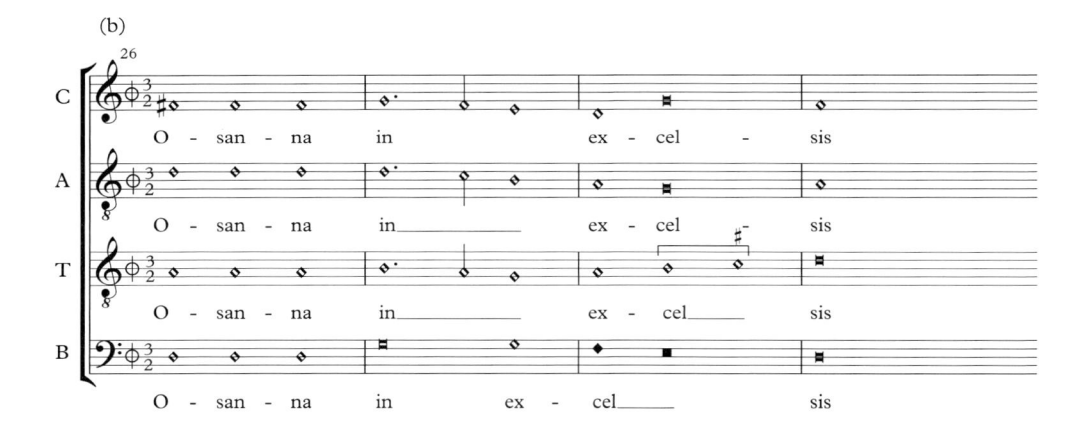

matches the rhythms more closely to the natural declamation of the words than Josquin does, but from the point of view of mensural character, the two passages are similar.

The rhythmic styles of *sesquialtera* sections changed little from Josquin's time to the end of the sixteenth century, probably because the number of rhythms that work effectively in relation to a beat with ternary subdivision is limited. Josquin uses this mensuration for the Et unam sanctam section of his mass, and Palestrina uses it for the Osanna (see Example 12.5). The two are quite similar, even though Josquin's texture (which includes only three voices in this excerpt) is imitative and Palestrina's is homophonic. Josquin's signs are ₵3 and 3 (in different voices), and Palestrina's is ₵$^3_2$, but all of these signs have the same meaning.

Example 12.6 Palestrina, *Missa L'homme armé a 4*, Agnus Dei 2, bars 1–10. After Palestrina, *Missarum . . . liber quartus* (Venice: Gardano, 1582).

Like Josquin, Palestrina expands the texture of his mass (in this case to five voices) in the final Agnus Dei. In the opening bars of that section, he states the cantus firmus in relatively long values and surrounds it with exuberant semiminim runs. Both features recall Josquin's treatment of the corresponding passage, although Josquin gives each note of the cantus firmus twice as much time as Palestrina does (see Examples 9.30 and 12.6). Josquin maintains this distinctive rhythm and texture throughout the section, so that the perfect *modus* of the cantus-firmus voices provides a grand underpinning to the fast runs in the other voices from beginning to end, but Palestrina abandons the texture after eight breves, reduces the tenor notes to semibreves, and uses only a few semiminims in the other voices. The cadence on a semibreve-max *initium* in bar 10 cancels the initial ternary grouping of semibreves in the tenor and moves the mensural focus to the level of the semibreve, where it remains to the end of the section. Even the cadences marking the last note of the cantus firmus and the end of the coda fall on semibreve-max *initia*, so that the total length of the section is, exceptionally, an odd number of semibreve-units.

Missa Benedicta es

Palestrina's *Missa Benedicta es* is modeled on Josquin's motet of the same name. Among Josquin's works, *Benedicta es* has an exceptionally high percentage of passages in which the rhythms operate primarily on the semibreve level. These passages lend themselves more readily to Palestrina's style than passages with more prominent breve-units. Palestrina takes over some of the larger mensural groupings from his model, but his transformations of the borrowed material often involve shortening, weakening, or undoing Josquin's larger-scale mensural structures.

Palestrina draws on the themes from his model in ways that lend formal clarity to the mass as a whole. The Kyrie, Gloria, and Credo are based exclusively on themes from the *prima pars* of the motet, except that the Credo ends with the "Amen" theme from the end of the motet. The theme from Josquin's *secunda pars* appears only in the Pleni, and the lively *sesquialtera* theme from his *tertia pars* is found in the Osanna (immediately following the theme from the *secunda pars*, as in the motet) and Agnus Dei 2. Josquin's opening theme (bars 1–16; Example 10.21) appears only at the beginnings of movements and subsidiary sections (Qui tollis, Crucifixus, Et in Spiritum, Benedictus, and perhaps Et incarnatus) of the mass. Josquin's "Amen" theme (bars 166–75) serves analogous coda-like functions at the ends of the Credo and Agnus Dei. The related theme from the codetta of his A section (Example 10.22) serves as the opening theme of the Christe, where its placement is an incidental result of the use of the themes from the A section of the motet in their original order in the Kyrie. The striking theme in equal breves that highlights the angelic salutation at the end of Josquin's *prima pars* (Example 10.23) appears in modified form at several crucial points in the mass.[5]

---

[5] The sole source of this mass (Vatican City, Biblioteca Apostolica Vaticana, Cappella Sistina, Ms. 22) is badly damaged. I have depended on the modern editions for the readings of some of my examples, but the mensuration signs are legible in a copy of the source that I have seen.

Palestrina does not make use of systematic mensural compression in the way that Josquin does, but he integrates Josquin's themes increasingly into his own style in successive movements. This procedure leads to a decrease in the mensural articulation of breves and larger units at the openings of the movements over the course of the work. Palestrina follows Josquin most closely in the opening of the Kyrie. The initial six-breve phrase of the cantus firmus, stated in breves, is imitated by another voice at the interval of four breves in both works. Josquin lays out these units with maximum clarity by bringing in pairs of voices every four breves and leaving the pairs exposed, with no additional material competing for attention, for the first eight breves (see Example 10.21). Palestrina, in contrast, draws attention away from the four- and six-breve units by bringing in a third voice in the fourth breve-unit and keeping five or six voices active during the second statement of the phrase (see Example 12.7). In the second cantus-firmus phrase (Example 12.8), he reduces Josquin's note values by half, ends the phrase on a semibreve-max *initium*, and repeats it in a position that is displaced by a semibreve with respect to the breve-units of the mensuration.

The opening theme from the motet articulates decreasing numbers of breve-units in subsequent movements of Palestrina's mass (see Example 12.9). Units larger than the breve play no role in the mass after Kyrie 1. The Gloria begins with imitation of the opening phrase in breves, but the first statement is preceded by a breve of rest and extended to a length of seven breves, undermining the larger-scale symmetries of Josquin's version. In the Credo, the first phrase is reduced to five breves and likewise preceded by a breve of rest. Some of the breves are broken into semibreves by means of repeated notes. In the Sanctus, the theme appears in breves without imitation in another voice. In the Agnus Dei 1, it is reduced to semibreves and stated in all voices in imitation.

Several rhythms found in this mass are not typical of Palestrina. Groups of four *fusae* subdivide several minim-units in bars 37–43 of the Credo, and syncopated minims appear in cadential ornaments at several points, such as bars 19 and 73 of the Gloria. Simultaneous two-against-three rhythms, modeled on bars 23 and 27 of Josquin, appear in bar 66 of the Credo (see Example 12.10). Given that Palestrina uses this rhythm in the mass, it is surprising that he translated a similar *sesquialtera* figure from Josquin's motet into an atypical rhythm of two semiminims followed by a minim within a semibreve-unit in bars 41–42 (see Example 12.11) and 45–46 of the Christe. Rhythms of this type are usually limited to stepwise patterns in Palestrina's music. Most of them are preceded by one or more minims, and those that are not are nearly always followed by syncopations that

Example 12.7 Palestrina, *Missa Benedicta es*, Kyrie 1, bars 1–10. After Vatican City, Biblioteca Apostolica Vaticana, Cappella Sistina, Ms. 22, fols. xlii^v–xliii^r.

lead directly to cadential suspensions. These features allow them to blend smoothly into the larger rhythmic trajectory of a phrase. The pair of semi-minims in the second semibreve-unit (bar 40) of Example 12.11 conforms to these norms, but the pair in bar 41 does not. It involves melodic skips and is preceded and followed by minims. The effect is blunt and out of character with Palestrina's graceful and elegant rhythmic style. By the mid sixteenth

Example 12.8 (a) Josquin, *Benedicta es*, cantus, bars 11–16. After Vatican City, Biblioteca Apostolica Vaticana, Cappella Sistina, Ms. 16, fol. clv^v. (b) Palestrina, *Missa Benedicta es*, Kyrie 1, cantus, bars 14–21. After Vatican City, Biblioteca Apostolica Vaticana, Cappella Sistina, Ms. 22, fol. xlii^v.

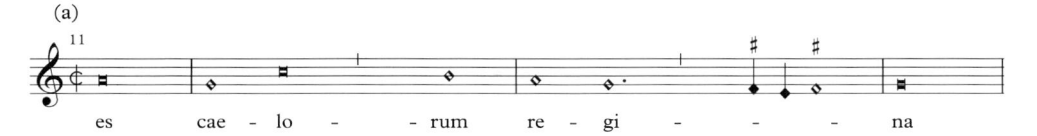

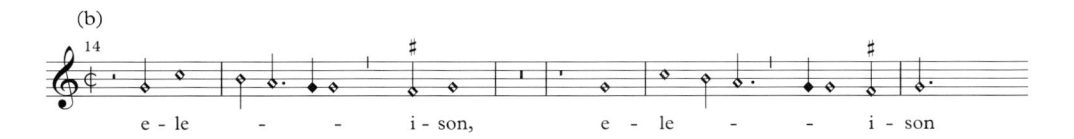

Example 12.9 Palestrina, *Missa Benedicta es*, cantus: (a) Gloria, bars 2–8; (b) Credo, bars 2–6; (c) Sanctus, bars 2–7; (d) Agnus Dei 1, bars 4–6. After Vatican City, Biblioteca Apostolica Vaticana, Cappella Sistina, Ms. 22, fols. xlv^v, li^v, lx^v, lxv^v.

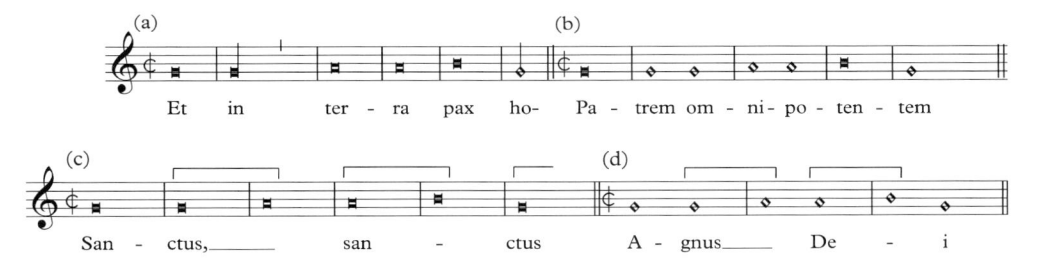

century it was becoming increasingly common for performers to "square off" ternary rhythms in simultaneous relation to binary ones in this manner, and some singers may have interpreted the groups of three minims in *sesquialtera* in Example 12.10 as pairs of semiminims followed by minims, but the fact that Palestrina notates the two passages differently suggests that he intended both of them to be read literally. Why he retained Josquin's *sesquialtera* rhythm in Example 12.10, but altered it in Example 12.11, is unclear.

Missa L'homme armé a 5

Palestrina's five-voice *Missa L'homme armé*, which was first published in his third book of masses of 1570, belongs to the century-old tradition of

388 Practice

Example 12.10 (a) Josquin, *Benedicta es*, bars 27–28. After Vatican City, Biblioteca Apostolica Vaticana, Cappella Sistina, Ms. 16, fols. clv^v–clvi^r. (b) Palestrina, *Missa Benedicta es*, Credo (Patrem), bars 66–67. After Vatican City, Biblioteca Apostolica Vaticana, Cappella Sistina, Ms. 22, fols. liii^v–liv^r.

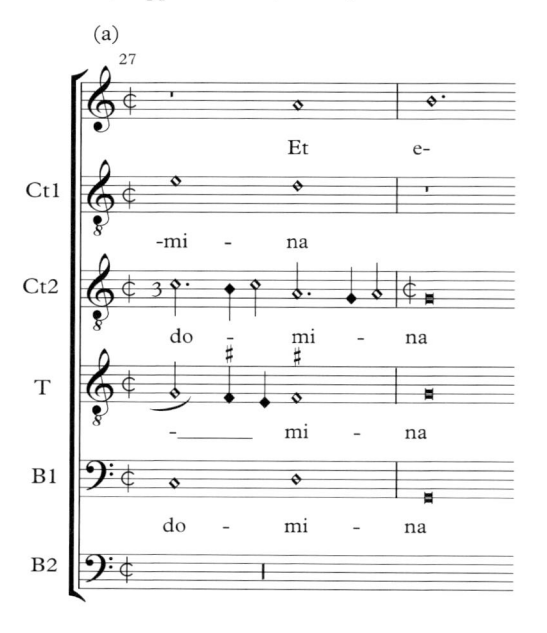

Example 12.11 Palestrina, *Missa Benedicta es*, Kyrie (Christe), bars 40–41 (altus 2). After Vatican City, Biblioteca Apostolica Vaticana, Cappella Sistina, Ms. 22, fol. xliv[r].

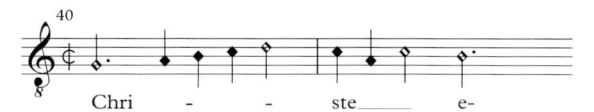

Chri - - ste___ e-

L'homme armé masses, but relates to that tradition in a very different way than its predecessors do. By the time Palestrina undertook his composition, *L'homme armé* masses and the compositional complexities with which they were associated had become historical objects that were no longer generally understood, either musically or theologically. James Haar has argued persuasively that Palestrina's mass was probably composed, or at least conceived, while the composer was a member of the Sistine chapel choir in 1555.[6] The chapel library owned a large collection of *L'homme armé* masses and continued to perform at least some of them, and its members prided themselves on their knowledge of the notational complications that those works embody.[7] We do not know which earlier *L'homme armé* masses Palestrina studied, but the ones that seem most likely to have served as models for his work are Josquin's *Missa L'homme armé super voces musicales*, the *Missa L'homme armé* of Marbriano de Orto, and the two *L'homme armé* masses of Morales.[8]

Apart from the choice of cantus firmus, the aspect of Palestrina's mass that ties it to the earlier *L'homme armé* tradition is the use of complex mensuration signs, which were entirely obsolete by his time. Palestrina's interpretations of these signs demonstrate vividly the gulf between fifteenth- and sixteenth-century concepts of mensuration. Table 12.1 shows the signs and proportional relationships in Palestrina's mass. As in many earlier *L'homme armé* masses, the tenor is notated in ℃ or ⊙, which represents augmentation in combination with signs of perfect and imperfect *tempus*, throughout much of the work. The relation between the cantus firmus and the other voices, however, is nothing like it is in the masses discussed in Chapter 9. Rather than serving as the foundation of the musical structure, the cantus firmus is simply superimposed upon the other voices, which are composed in Palestrina's usual style. Haar characterizes it aptly as "[sounding] like – as indeed it is – a visitor from another

---

[6] Haar, "Palestrina as Historicist," 203–05.
[7] Evidence of this interest is found in the setting of a section of words omitted from the Credo of Josquin's *Missa L'homme armé super voces musicales* by a papal singer of the mid sixteenth century. See Jesse Rodin, "Finishing Josquin's 'Unfinished' Mass: A Case of Stylistic Imitation in the *Cappella Sistina*," *The Journal of Musicology* 22 (2005), 412–53.
[8] Haar, "Palestrina as Historicist," 191–200.

390   Practice

Table 12.1 Palestrina, *Missa L'homme armé a 5*

Section	C.f. segment	Signs	Compositional *tactus*	Performance *tactus* (Zacconi)
Kyrie 1	A-1	O ◊◊◊ / ⊙ ♩♩♩	◊ ↓ ◊	◊ ↓ ◊
Christe	A-1a A-2	¢ ◊◊◊ / ₵ ♩♩♩	◊ ↓ ◊	◊ ↓ ◊
Kyrie 2	B	O ◊◊◊ / Φ₂³ ♩♩♩	◊ ↓ ♩ (perfect)	◊ ↓ ♩ (perfect)
Et in terra	A	¢ ♩♩♩ → ¢ ◊◊◊ / ₵ ♩♩♩ → Ↄ ♩♩♩	◊ → ◊ ↓ ↓ ♦ → ◊	♩ → ♩ (imperfect) ◊ → ◊
Qui tollis	B	¢ ♩♩ → ¢ ♩♩ / C ◊◊ → ¢ ♩♩	◊ ↓ ◊	[♩] [◊]
Patrem	A B	O ◊◊◊ / ⊙ ♩♩♩	◊ ↓ ◊	◊ ↓ ◊
Crucifixus	——	¢ ♩ ♩ ♩ / ¢ ♩ → Φ₂³ ♩♩ → ¢ ♩	◊→♩ (perfect)→◊	
Et in Spiritum	A B	Φ₂³ ♩♩♩ → ¢ ♩ / O ◊◊◊ → ¢ ♩	♩ (perfect) ◊	♩ (perfect) ◊
Sanctus	A	C ◊◊◊ / ₵ ♩♩♩	◊ ↓ ◊	◊ ↓ ◊
Pleni	B	C ◊◊◊ / ₵ ♩♩♩	◊ ↓ ◊	◊ ↓ ◊
Osanna	A B	O3 ◊◊◊ / ₵3 ♩♩♩	♩ (perfect) ◊ (perfect)	♩ (perfect) ◊ (perfect)
Benedictus	A-1	¢ ♩♩♩ → ¢ ♩♩ → ¢ ♩ / ₵ ♩♩♩ → C ◊◊ → ¢ ♩	◊ → ◊ → ◊ ↓ ↓ ↓ ♦ → ◊ → ◊	♩ → ♩ → ♩ ↓ ◊ → ◊ → ♩
Osanna	ut supra			
Agnus Dei 1	A B	C ◊◊◊ / ₵ ♩♩♩	◊ ↓ ◊	◊ ↓ ◊
Agnus Dei 2	A	¢ ♩♩♩ / ₵ ♩♩♩	◊ ↓ ◊	♩ ↓ ◊ (imperfect)

century."[9] The cantus firmus imposes constraints on the other voices with regard to dissonance treatment, but is otherwise quite independent of them.

The voices without the cantus firmus are notated in O, C, ¢, Φ₂³, and O3. The rhythms of O, C, and ¢ are identical to each other and indistinguishable from the rhythms that Palestrina normally writes in ¢. The compositional *tactus* is the semibreve, and the grouping of semibreves is quite free. The intermittent, subtle pairing of breves that characterizes Palestrina's usual ¢ is largely absent, in part because the grouping of semibreves suggested by

[9] Ibid., 195.

the cantus firmus often conflicts with the mensuration of the other voices. The only sections in which semibreves fall into regular, audible groups from beginning to end are Kyrie 1 (perfect *tempus*) and Agnus Dei 2 (imperfect *tempus*, perfect *modus*). It is unclear whether or not Palestrina intended to prescribe a difference of tempo between uncut and cut signs in this work.

The cantus firmus is notated in seven different mensurations (☉, ℭ, ↄ, C, O, ¢₂³, and ℭ3) and has a different rhythm in every section. The ternary rhythms of the original melody are notated mostly in groups of three (perfect or imperfect) semibreves in the Kyrie, Gloria, and Credo and in groups of three minims in the Sanctus and Agnus Dei, but the B section of Agnus Dei 1 switches to groups of three semiminims. Palestrina's rhythms often conflict with both the ternary groupings of the original melody and the groupings implied by the mensuration sign. Example 12.12 shows all of the versions of the cantus firmus except those in *tripla* or *sesquialtera* (¢₂³ and ℭ3). Barlines (notated as short lines at the top of the staff when notes cross them) separate notated breves, and wedges above the staff mark the beginnings of logical rhythmic groupings, some of which may be open to debate.

The notated mensuration of the cantus firmus sometimes corresponds to the rhythmic grouping and sometimes contradicts it. When the *tempus* is perfect, the ternary rhythmic groups of the cantus firmus correspond consistently to the perfect breves of the mensuration only in Kyrie 1. They are displaced with respect to the notated mensuration in parts of the Patrem (bars 7–10 and 16–19) and Et in spiritum (bars 13–16). When the *tempus* is imperfect and the cantus firmus is notated in breves and semibreves, there is a built-in conflict between the notated mensuration and the rhythm of the melody. This conflict appears in its simplest form in the Christe. In the Et in terra and Qui tollis, there are changes of mensuration that double the speed of the notes, adding yet another layer of complication. These sections could have been written more simply in perfect *tempus* (☉ or O). Palestrina apparently chose imperfect *tempus* so that the *tempus* of the cantus firmus would match that of the other voices, even though the mensural groupings do not match the rhythms because of the augmentation of the tenor.

In the Sanctus and Agnus Dei, the initial mensuration of the cantus firmus is always ℭ, but the relation between mensuration and rhythm is quite variable. It is most straightforward in the Sanctus. The Pleni adds a touch of hemiola coloration before the final cadence. The Benedictus presents three statements of the cantus firmus (written once, with three superimposed mensuration signs) in a pattern of 3:2:1 diminution. Palestrina indulges in a bit of old-fashioned mensural transformation here: the last three notes of the cantus firmus are perfect semibreves in the first statement and imperfect semibreves in the second two statements, so that the first statement differs in rhythm from

Example 12.12 Palestrina, *Missa L'homme armé a 5*, cantus firmus (tenor): (a) Kyrie 1; (b) Christe; (c) Et in terra; (d) Qui tollis; (e) Patrem; (f) Et in Spiritum (g) Sanctus; (h) Pleni; (i) Benedictus; (j) Osanna; (k) Agnus Dei 1; (l) Agnus Dei 2. After Palestrina, *Missarum liber tertius* (Rome: Dorico, 1570). Barring in these examples differs from that in the published editions.

Example 12.12 (cont.)

(i) Benedictus

(j) Osanna

(k) Agnus Dei 1

(l) Agnus Dei 2

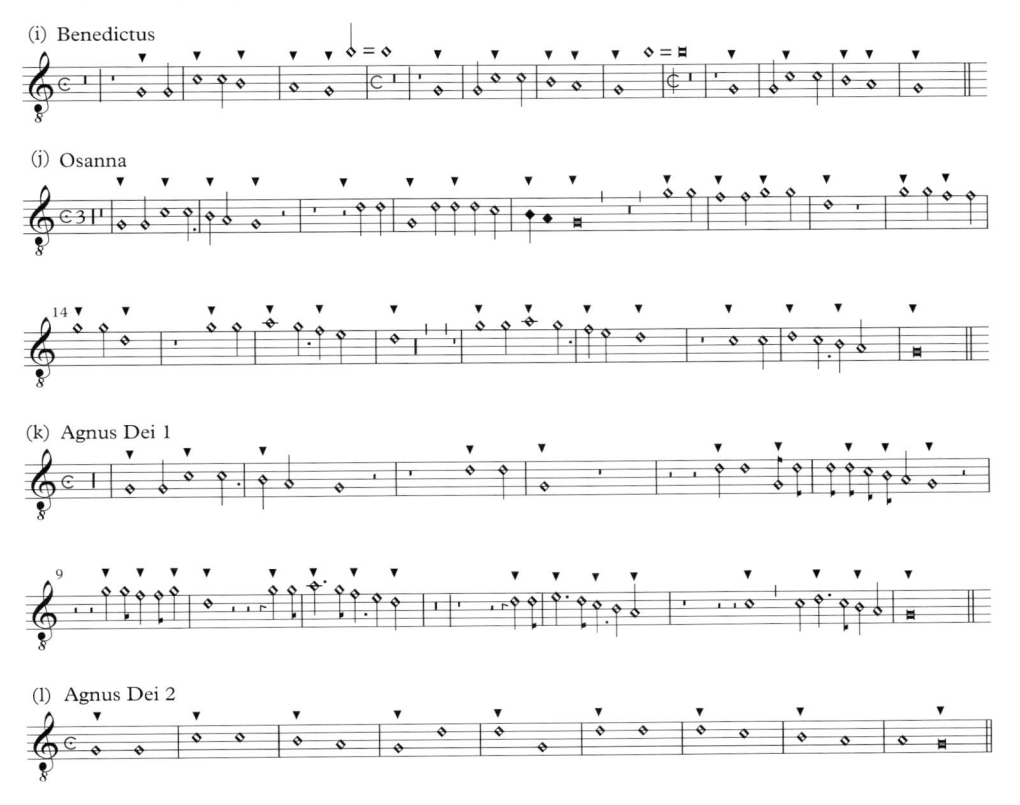

Example 12.13 Palestrina, *Missa L'homme armé a 5*: Agnus Dei 1, bars 7–17 of Example 12.12 notated in ¢.

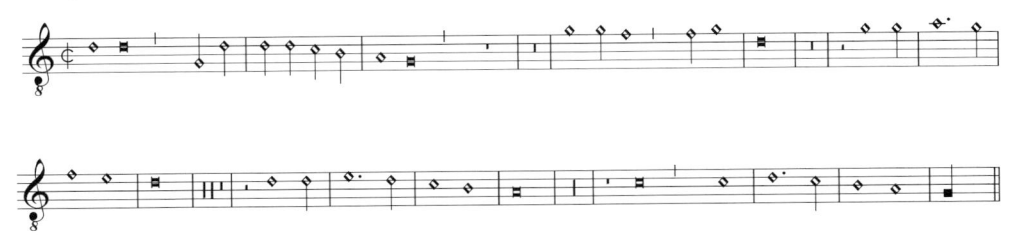

the other two even though it has the same written note values. Agnus Dei 1 begins simply, but switches in bar 7 to rhythmic patterns on the minim/semiminim level that have no relation to the notated mensuration and are extremely difficult to read. They seem to have been conceived in ¢, in which they look quite normal, then transcribed into C to demonstrate the composer's erudition and challenge the singers' wits. The frequent, but irregular, ternary groups of minims (notated as semiminims in augmentation) are not unusual in

Example 12.14 Palestrina, *Missa L'homme armé a 5*: Kyrie 1, bars 1–10. After Palestrina, *Missarum liber tertius* (Rome: Dorico, 1570).

Palestrina's normal ₵ style. Example 12.13 shows the conclusion of Agnus Dei 1 in ₵. After this climactic passage, in which the cantus firmus loses its separate identity and merges into the web of the other voices, Agnus Dei 2 reverts to the simplest possible version of the cantus firmus in steady semibreves.

The relations among simultaneous contrasting signs in this mass are governed by standard conventions. Perfect prolation represents 1:2 augmentation in relation to uncut signs; ↺ cancels the augmentation; and cut signs represent 2:1 diminution in relation to uncut signs or 4:1 in relation to perfect prolation. When C is combined with ₵, it functions as subduple proportion with a minim compositional *tactus*. When the cantus firmus is in augmentation, its rhythmic groups appear to imply large-scale temporal patterns that might extend to all of the voices, but those groupings are seldom audible. Only in Kyrie 1 (Example 12.14) do the surface rhythms, voice entries, and cadences work together to bring out the mensuration of the cantus firmus and allow it to determine the overall audible mensural structure of the section. In the Benedictus, the cantus firmus is placed in the highest voice, so that its systematic pattern of diminution is readily audible, and in Agnus Dei 2, the steady perfect semibreves of the cantus firmus (corresponding to groups of three breves in the other voices) create a sense of slow, regular motion that lends an air of gravity to the section.

In the other sections, the placement of the cantus firmus in the middle of the texture minimizes its aural prominence, and the other voices do little or nothing to bring out its structure. The Patrem (Example 12.15) is typical in these respects. Although the *tempus* of the non-cantus-firmus voices is perfect, the surface rhythm and the placement of voice entries and cadences create unambiguously binary, not ternary, groups of semibreves in bars 1–4. The cadence in bar 5 falls on a semibreve-max *initium* with respect to both binary and ternary groups of semibreves, undermining any regular grouping of semibreves at that point. The cantus firmus enters unobtrusively under a suspension that creates the expectation of a cadence (bar 7), and when the cadence finally materializes (bar 9), it is not at the point where the cantus firmus moves to its second pitch (a breve *initium* in all voices), but one semibreve earlier. The cadence and the prominent entry of the bass make the subsequent breve *initium* sound like an afterbeat, rather than a prominent moment in the mensural structure. In light of similar mismatches between the cantus-firmus structure and the points of articulation in the other voices throughout the mass, it appears that the function of the rhythmic irregularities in the cantus firmus is not to explore interesting variants of a simple rhythm, but rather to support the flexible, prose-like quality of Palestrina's rhythms by avoiding any possible sense of mensural regularity or predictability. The contrast of Palestrina's attitude toward complex mensural structures with that of his predecessors could not be more extreme.

Tripla or *sesquialtera* rhythms appear in four sections of this mass, each time in a different context (see Example 12.16). In Kyrie 2, the tenor is in ϕ_2^3, which functions as triple proportion of O in the other voices. In Et in Spiritum, these relations are reversed: the tenor is in O while the other voices are in ϕ_2^3. The Crucifixus (*a 4*, without cantus firmus) has a passage in ϕ_2^3 in two voices against rests in ₵ in the other voices at the words "Et resurrexit." The Osanna is in O3, with the tenor in ₵3; perfect breves of the former correspond to perfect semibreves of the latter.

Example 12.15 Palestrina, *Missa L'homme armé a 5*: Credo (Patrem), bars 1–10. After Palestrina, *Missarum liber tertius* (Rome: Dorico, 1570).

Example 12.16 Palestrina, *Missa L'homme armé a 5*: (a) Kyrie 2, bars 5–7; (b) Credo (Et in Spiritum), bars 1–6; (c) Credo (Crucifixus), bars 18–25; (d) Sanctus (Osanna), bars 7–10. After Palestrina, *Missarum liber tertius* (Rome: Dorico, 1570).

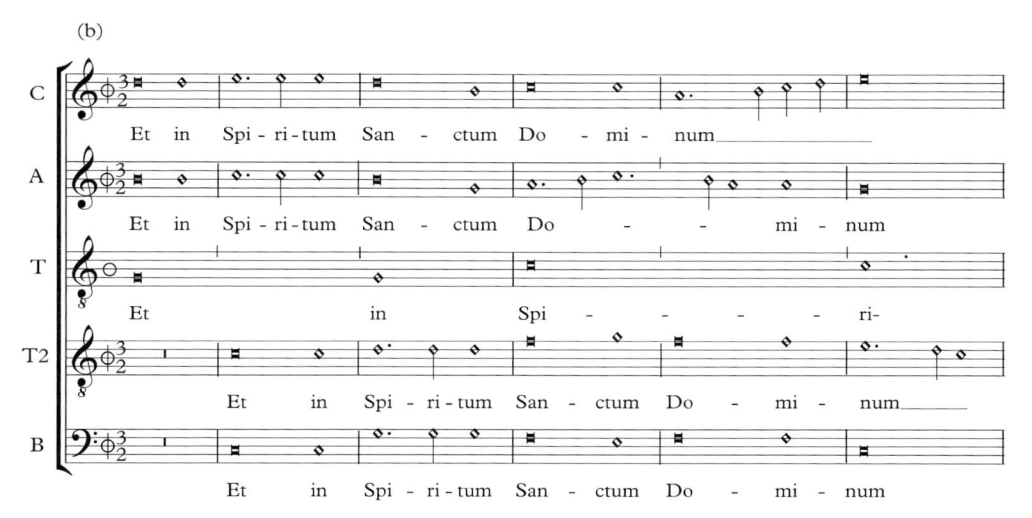

Several of Palestrina's contemporaries and immediate successors attempted to explain the mensural structure of this mass or translate its complex notation into simpler forms. The first to do so was Ludovico Zacconi, who devoted a long chapter of his *Prattica di musica* (1592) to an explanation of the notation of the work and advertised that chapter as a special attraction of his book on the

Example 12.16 (cont.)

title page.[10] Zacconi explains how all of the proportional mensurations can be realized by placing the performance *tactus* on the theoretical *tactus* of each sign: the imperfect breve of ₵, the imperfect semibreve of O, C, and Ɔ, the minim of ⊙ and ℭ, the perfect breve of Φ_2^3 and O3, and the perfect semibreve of ℭ3. His rationale for this recommendation, which calls for interpreting ₵ with a breve performance *tactus*, rather than the semibreve performance *tactus* that had become

---

[10] Ludovico Zacconi, *Prattica di musica*, book 1, ch. 38 ("Come si prova esser il vero che nelle Prolationi si possino cantare una Minima per tatto, se di sopra sempre n'habbiamo veduto andarcene tre"), fols. 115ʳ–122ʳ.

standard by his time, is purely pragmatic: he believes it is easier to sing ¢ with a breve *tactus* than perfect prolation with a semiminim *tactus*, which would be necessary if ¢ were measured in semibreves:

... perche chi volesse particularmente cantar questa Gloria al tatto della Semib. la parte che ha la Prolatione seria obligata à fare doppia consideratione, et haver riguardo al valor già per la detta Prolatione multiplicato, et poi di novo à multiplicarlo per causa della simplicità del tatto: et sappiamo bene che uno intento à piu cose, è forza che in uno manchi.[11]	... because if one wanted to sing this Gloria to a semibreve *tactus*, the part that has the [perfect] prolation would be obliged to do two things: both to pay attention to the value of the previously explained augmented prolation, and then to augment it again because of the simplicity of the *tactus* [i.e., the *tactus* on the semiminim]; and we know well that someone who is intent on more than one thing will necessarily err in one of them.

Since the compositional tactus of ¢ is the semibreve and semibreves do not come in regular mensural groups in this mass, the breve performance *tactus* that measures ¢ must be distinctly divided into equally articulated semibreve-units.

Zacconi transcribes sample passages of the tenor in various mensurations with perfect prolation into O, C, and ¢ to illustrate how to read those signs. His choice of cut or uncut versions of the signs in the transcriptions depends on the signs in the other voices; for example, ¢ in the Christe is transcribed to C, but the same mensuration in the Gloria is transcribed to ¢ (in values twice as large), so that the sign in the transcription matches the sign in the other voices. His transcriptions obscure any hints of mensural grouping or displacement that may be present in the original notation. Figure 12.1 shows the original versions and Zacconi's transcriptions of the tenor of the Christe and Et in terra (cf. Examples 12.12b and c above). Zacconi does not comment on the difference (if any) between cut and uncut signs in the non-cantus-firmus voices, and he makes it clear elsewhere that he regards C and ¢ as virtually synonymous.[12] If he believed that notes under cut signs should move faster than notes under uncut signs in this work, he does not say so. The implication is that the breve *tactus* is twice as slow as the semibreve *tactus* in this case.

---

[11] Ibid., fol. 119ᵛ.   [12] See DeFord, "Zacconi's Theories of *Tactus* and Mensuration," 154–60.

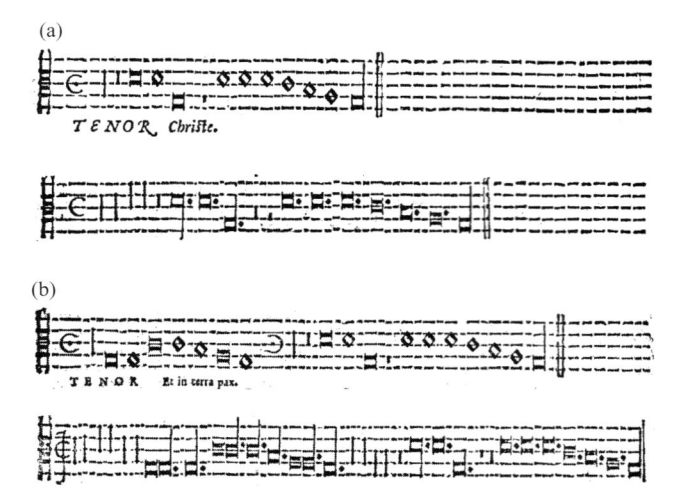

Figure 12.1 Palestrina, *Missa L'homme armé a 5*, (a) Christe and (b) Et in terra, tenor, in original notation and transcribed into C and ₵. Ludovico Zacconi, *Prattica di musica* (Venice: Girolamo Polo, 1592), fols. 116ᵛ, 117ʳ, 119ʳ, and 119ᵛ.

Pietro Cerone likewise devoted a lengthy section of his *El melopeo y maestro* (1613) to Palestrina's *Missa L'homme armé a 5*.[13] His discussion is modeled on Zacconi's, but he allows singers to use a semibreve *tactus* in ₵ and double the values of the voice in augmentation if they find the breve *tactus* too difficult:

Y no aviendo Cantores habiles para cantar *perdimidium*, entonces (por no la dexar del todo) podrase cantar à Compasillo, passando una Semibreve al Compas.[14]	And if you do not have singers able to sing *per medium*, then (so as not to abandon it [the work] entirely), it [₵] can be sung to the *compasillo*, with one semibreve per *compas*.

Both Zacconi and Cerone devote special attention to the *tactus* of the triple and *sesquialtera* proportions. Zacconi says that three semibreves of ₵³₂ combined with O should be measured with an equally divided *tactus* in Kyrie 2 (Example 12.16a) because of the mensuration of the other voices, but he makes it clear elsewhere that this method of measuring does not imply modifying the rhythms to adapt them to the binary *tactus*.[15] Cerone says that ₵³₂ in this section should be measured with an unequal *tactus* while the other voices measure simultaneously with an equal *tactus*. For practice, he allows singers to measure ₵³₂ with an equal *tactus* and adjust the rhythms

---

[13] Cerone, *El melopeo y maestro*, book 20, 1028–36. [14] Ibid., 1031.
[15] See DeFord, "Zacconi's Theories of *Tactus* and Mensuration," 165–66.

accordingly until they develop the skill to sing the three-against-two rhythms (see Figure 12.2).[16] Zacconi and Cerone agree that the same combination of signs (O and ϕ_2^3) calls for an unequal *tactus* in the Et in Spiritum (Example 12.16b), where four voices have ϕ_2^3 and the tenor has O, presumably because there are no duple subdivisions of the *tactus* in this section. The Osanna (Example 12.16d) likewise calls for an unequal *tactus*, which measures a perfect semibreve in the tenor and a perfect breve in the other voices. Zacconi does not mention the brief passage of ϕ_2^3 in the Crucifixus (Example 12.16c), but Cerone points out that the four breves of ϕ_2^3 in the lower voices are measured with four unequal *tactus*, and that singers who have been counting in semibreves must reduce the number of rests by half, such that four breve rests get four *tactus*, rather than eight, in this passage. He recommends adding the sign ϕ_2^3 to the voices with the rests for clarification.[17] The implication is that the perfect breve *tactus* of ϕ_2^3 is equal in length to the semibreve *tactus* of ¢, and that singers who use a breve *tactus* in ¢ will have to double the speed of the *tactus*, as well as change its subdivision, when the other voices have the proportion.

Angelo Gardano published an edition of the complete mass in ¢, with the *tripla* and *sesquialtera* passages in ϕ_2^3, in 1599. He left the note values in the voices without the cantus firmus unchanged, thereby obliterating not only the original mensurations, but also the notational distinction between cut and uncut signs, although he could have transcribed O into C and left C unchanged without creating difficulties for the readers. His choice of ¢ for Palestrina's O and C reflects the fact that the rhythms of O and C in this mass resemble those typical of ¢, not C, which applied to madrigals in a very different rhythmic style in his day. If he believed that cut and uncut signs implied different tempos in Palestrina's original notation, he must have regarded that information as dispensable. He also adjusted the notation in other ways to make the music easier to read. To avoid the excessively long notes that a literal transcription of some of the tenor parts would require, he divided long notes into shorter ones, and he anticipated Cerone's later advice by applying the sign ϕ_2^3 to all of the voices at "Et resurrexit." His version of the tenor of the Et in terra is shown in Figure 12.3 (cf. Example 12.12c and Figure 12.1). Because ¢ was almost invariably sung with a

---

[16] Cerone, *El melopeo y maestro*, book 20, 1030. Agostino Pisa, *Battuta della musica*, 87, advocates only the "squared-off" versions, not only for these rhythms, but also for the ternary rhythms in the Osanna, which appear in all voices. His treatise is speculative in nature, however, and not in line with common practice, as his complaints about the practices of musicians make abundantly clear.

[17] Cerone, *El melopeo y maestro*, book 20, 1032.

semibreve *tactus* in the late sixteenth century, the users of Gardano's edition would have assumed that the intended *tactus* was the semibreve in all parts of the work except the ternary proportions, in which it was the perfect breve.

Scholars of the first half of the twentieth century engaged in lengthy and heated debates over how to edit this mass. Franz Xaver Haberl and Raffaele Casimiri included the piece in their complete editions of Palestrina's works.[18] Both of them based their editions on Gardano, rather than the first edition. Haberl mentions the mensural complexities briefly in his preface, but does not explain them in detail or even report the original signs in his edition. Casimiri reports most, but not all, of the original signs, in one case (Et in Spiritum) inaccurately. Haberl retains the note values from Gardano's edition; Casimiri reduces the values in 2:1 ratio in ₵ and 4:1 in *tripla* and *sesquialtera*. Both editors bar ₵ in units corresponding to imperfect breves of the original, even where ₵ is a substitute for O with the same written values. They bar ternary proportions in units corresponding to perfect breves except in Kyrie 2, where they put two perfect breves in a bar because the perfect breves correspond to semibreves of ₵ (see Figures 12.4 and 12.5; cf. Example 12.16a). Haberl interprets ternary rhythms against binary rhythms in the "squared-off" manner illustrated by Cerone (Figure 12.2); Casimiri faults him vociferously for this, pointing out among other things that this interpretation creates rhythms in which a semiminim followed by a dotted minim occupies a semibreve-unit – a rhythm found nowhere else in Palestrina's music.[19]

Casimiri's edition provoked impassioned objections from Antoine Auda, who believed that the *tactus* was the fundamental unit of measure in mensural music and that it should also be the unit in which modern editions are barred.[20] Auda would therefore bar all uncut signs (including the O in the above Kyrie 2) in semibreves and ₵ in imperfect breves. This method yields a score with so many barlines in O and C that the continuity of the music is nearly impossible to perceive. Furthermore, Auda's view takes no account of the comments of Cerone and the edition of Gardano that allow

---

[18] Palestrina, *Werke*, ed. Haberl, vol. XII. Giovanni Pierluigi da Palestrina, *Le opere complete*, ed. Raffaele Casimiri et al., 35 vols. (Rome: Fratelli Scalera, 1939–99), vol. XI.

[19] Raffaele Casimiri, "Il 'Kyrie' della Messa 'L'homme armé' di Giov. Pierluigi di Palestrina e una trascrizione errata," *Note d'archivio per la storia musicale* 10 (1933), 101–08.

[20] Antoine Auda, "La mesure dans la Messe 'L'homme armé' de Palestrina," *Acta musicologica* 13 (1941), 39–59, and "Le 'tactus' dans la Messe 'L'homme armé' de Palestrina," *Acta musicologica* 14 (1942), 27–43. Casimiri's responses appeared in *La polifonia vocale*, 36–39, and "Un dibattito musicologico a proposito della Missa *L'homme armé* del Palestrina," *Note d'archivio per la storia musicale* 20 (1943), 18–42.

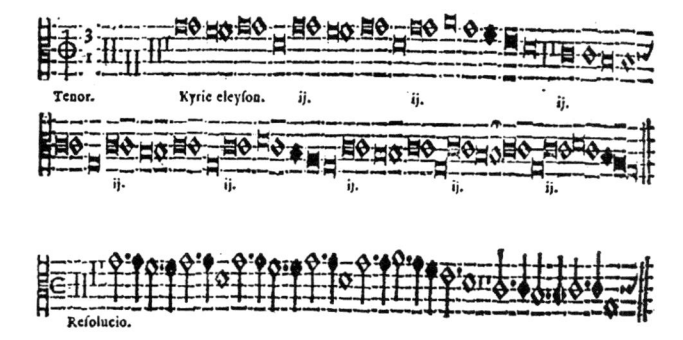

Figure 12.2 Palestrina, *Missa L'homme armé a 5*, Kyrie 2, tenor, in original notation and "resolution" in C. Pietro Cerone, *El melopeo y maestro* (Naples: Juan Bautista Gargano & Lucrecio Nucci, 1613), 1030.

Figure 12.3 Palestrina, *Missa L'homme armé a 5*, Et in terra, tenor (called "quintus"). Palestrina, *Missarum liber tertius* (Venice: Angelo Gardano, 1599).

for a semibreve *tactus* in ¢, nor does it acknowledge the identity of rhythmic character among O, C, and ¢ in this work.

A 1979 edition by Anna Maria Monterosso Vacchelli[21] does more justice to the original notation of the work than any earlier edition. It includes complete facsimiles of both the original and the 1599 editions. Sections in O and C in the non-tenor voices are barred in units corresponding to the original (perfect or imperfect) breves with the values reduced by 2:1; sections originally in ¢ are barred in units of two breves with the values reduced 4:1. Vacchelli justifies this procedure on grounds of Zarlino's claim that pieces in ¢ ought to be

---

[21] Anna Maria Monterosso Vacchelli, *La Messa L'homme armé di Palestrina: Studio paleografico ed edizione critica* (Cremona: Fondazione Claudio Monteverdi, 1979).

Figure 12.4 Palestrina, *Missa L'homme armé a 5*, Kyrie 2. Palestrina, *Werke*, vol. XII, ed. Franz Xaver Haberl (Leipzig: Breitkopf & Härtel, [1881]).

composed in units of two breves.[22] She does not recommend the same tempo for the *tactus* under all signs, but suggests that the original semibreve should be around MM 72 in O and C, MM 104 in ¢, and MM 60 where one or more voices have ternary proportions.[23] Her version of the end of the passage in Examples 12.16a and Figures 12.4 and 12.5 is shown in Figure 12.6.

Vacchelli's editorial procedures make sense for O and C, though the original notation, which is crucial to the concept of the work, would be easier to grasp in unreduced values. I see no justification for using a different scale of reduction and a different principle of barring in ¢, however. Even though Zacconi recommends a breve performance *tactus* in ¢ for the benefit of the singers reading the tenor in augmentation, he clearly understands that the compositional *tactus* of that sign is the semibreve, as Cerone and Gardano confirm. The different scale of reduction obscures the essential similarity between the rhythms of uncut and cut signs in this mass. Zarlino's claim that ¢ ought to observe imperfect long-units is purely speculative; the

[22] Ibid., 36–37.   [23] Ibid., 40.

Figure 12.5 Palestrina, *Missa L'homme armé a 5*, Kyrie 2. Palestrina, *Le opere complete*, vol. VI, ed. Raffaele Casimiri (Rome: Fratelli Scalera, [1939]).

sign was never interpreted that way in practice, even in his own compositions. In this mass of Palestrina, even the imperfect breve-units are not regularly observed in ¢, and barring the music in original long-units creates an appearance of radical syncopations where none exist.

Figure 12.6 Palestrina, *Missa L'homme armé a 5*, Kyrie 2. Anna Maria Monterosso Vacchelli, *La Messa L'homme armé di Palestrina: Studio paleografico ed edizione critica* (Cremona: Fondazione Claudio Monteverdi, 1979), 85.

It is of course easier to find fault with existing editions than to propose a better system for editing a work like this. Regular barlines are needed to coordinate the voices in a score, but the frequent mismatches between mensuration and rhythm create a situation in which no form of regular barring can conform to the real rhythmic groupings in the piece. Sixteenth-century scores were typically barred in imperfect breves, often with some irregularities, without necessarily implying that those units had any rhythmic significance in the music. The principles of barring in the editions of Haberl and Casimiri could be justified with respect to that historical practice. Unlike most music of the late sixteenth century, however, this work places the display of obsolete signs at the core of its conceptual foundation. Barring in conformity with the original signs (which often leads to different barring in different voices) does not always align the barlines with the rhythmic groups in the music, but it calls attention to the mismatches between mensuration and rhythm that lie at the root of Palestrina's conception.

Palestrina's five-voice *Missa L'homme armé* appears to provide ample evidence for the proposition that mensuration and rhythm are unrelated. It would not be fair, however, to generalize that conclusion from this example. What the work demonstrates is the extent of the contrast between fifteenth- and sixteenth-century rhythmic styles and concepts of mensuration. Palestrina understood fifteenth-century mensural principles, as he demonstrates in Kyrie 1, which could just as well have been by Josquin from the point of view of mensural structure. In the rest of the mass, however, he repudiates those principles and demonstrates how he can reconcile obsolete notation, and even the principle of a slow cantus firmus in augmentation, with his own concept of rhythm and mensuration. Palestrina preserved historical tradition not by freezing it in place, but by renewing it through cross-breeding with the very different musical culture of his own day.

13 | The madrigals of Rore

Cipriano de Rore (1515/16–65) was one of the greatest and most influential madrigal composers in the sixteenth century. He began as a follower of Adrian Willaert, stretching only slightly the norms of the reserved, classic style of the early decades of the century, and developed into a radical innovator, famously hailed by Monteverdi as the father of the *seconda prattica*.[1] Seven numbered madrigal books (five for five voices and two for four) appeared in print with his name on the title page, but only the first *a 5* and the first *a 4* are devoted exclusively to his works. The others were evidently assembled by publishers without the involvement of the composer. Other madrigals appeared in anthologies. The problematic publication history of Rore's madrigals raises questions about the authenticity of some works attributed to him in the prints. Modern scholars accept the attribution of approximately one hundred madrigals to him.[2]

Rore was one of the pioneers of a new type of madrigal, called *madrigali a note nere* (madrigals with black notes) or *a misura (di) breve* (in the short measure), that began to appear in print around 1540.[3] The roughly synonymous term *madrigali cromatici* ("chromatic," or "colored," madrigals) appeared on the title page of the 1544 edition of Rore's Book I *a 5;* the book was first published in 1542 without a label calling attention to this novel feature. *Note nere* madrigals are a new mensural type that originated as a self-conscious revival of the obsolete sign C with a meaning quite different from what it had in the fifteenth century. By 1540, the sign ¢ had come to be associated with a breve theoretical *tactus* and a semibreve compositional *tactus*, as in the masses of Palestrina. The composers who created the *note nere* style evidently reasoned by analogy that C must require a semibreve theoretical *tactus* and a minim compositional *tactus*. In that sense, it could be, and sometimes was, simply a graphic variant of ¢ in which

---

[1] Claudio and Giulio Cesare Monteverdi, "Dichiaratione della lettera stampata nel quinto libro de' suoi madregali," in Claudio Monteverdi, *Scherzi musicali a tre voci* (Venice: Amadino, 1607).

[2] Jessie Ann Owens, "Rore, Cipriano de," in *Oxford Music Online*, www.oxfordmusiconline.com (accessed 1 August 2010).

[3] The most important study of the *note nere* madrigal is James Haar, "The *Note Nere* Madrigal," *Journal of the American Musicological Society* 18 (1965), 22–41.

all note values were half as large and the mensuration sign called for a doubling of the values. Some theorists might explain this relationship in the opposite way: since ¢ was still theoretically a sign of diminution with a breve *tactus* even though its *tactus* in the compositional and performance sense was the semibreve, the new C could be conceived as a restoration of *integer valor* notation with a theoretical semibreve *tactus*. Since the *note nere* style arose at a time when most Italian theorists had lost interest in the fine points of mensural notation, however, there are no detailed discussions of it in theoretical writings.

The significance of the *note nere* style lies not in its graphic form or theoretical classification, but in the opportunities that it created for combining the mensural properties of ¢ and C in a single piece under either sign. A madrigal that makes use of the properties of both signs may have a compositional *tactus* that shifts freely between the minim and the semibreve; in ¢ the compositional *tactus* may even rise occasionally to the level of the breve, in conformity with the theoretical definition of the sign. The compositional *tactus* may be subdivided and grouped in many ways, and it may also vary within a piece. This flexibility gives the composer a rich palette of rhythmic devices to support the affective demands of the poetic text.

Mixing the properties of both mensural types in a single piece naturally leads to ambiguities in the meanings of the signs. Most composers observed some distinction between the signs to the end of the sixteenth century, but the differences are often subtle, and different composers used different criteria to distinguish them. Michael Praetorius, looking at the late sixteenth century from the vantage point of the early seventeenth, despaired of finding consistent meanings for the signs, but clarified their differences as well as he could at that time:

| Und wenn ich jetztiger zeit der Italorum Compositiones, so in gar wenig Jahren gantz uff eine andere sonderbahre newe Art gerichtet worden / ansehe / so befinde ich in praefixione Signorum Tactus aequalis & Inaequalis sehr grosse discrepantias und Varieteten. Denn Iohann Gabriel hat alle seine Concerten, Symphonien, Canzonen und Sonaten mit und ohne Text / mit dem ¢ durch und durch bezeichnet / also / daß noch biß an | And if I now examine the compositions of the Italians that have been composed in [the past] few years in another altogether special and new way, I find in the prescription of signs of equal and unequal *tactus* very great discrepancies and variety. Giovanni Gabrieli signed all of his concertos, symphonies, canzoni, and sonatas, with and without text, exclusively with ¢, so that until now I have never found the sign C in any of his works. Some, however, and |

jetzo in allen seinen Operibus das Signum C ich niemals befunden. Etliche aber / und die meisten behalten das C durch und durch gantz allein. Claudius de Monte Verde praeponirt das ¢ in denen / so er uff Motetten Art gesetzet / und ad Tactum alla Breve musicirt werden können: In den andern allen aber / dorinnen mehr schwartze / als weisse Noten / praeponiret er das C. Lud. Viadana gebraucht sich das ¢ in allen seinen Sachen cum Textu: In den Symphoniis aber sine Textu, hat er das C behalten. Etliche vermengen es durch einander / bald in diesem ¢, im andern das C. unnd kan man gleichwol an den Noten / oder gantzem Gesange keinen unterscheid erkennen.[4]

indeed most, use exclusively C. Claudio Monteverdi prescribes ¢ in those works that are composed in motet style and can be performed with a *tactus alla breve*. In all others, however, in which there are more black notes than white, he prescribes C. Ludovico Viadana uses ¢ in all of his works with text, but in the symphonies without text he uses C. Some mix things up, using ¢ in one piece and C in another, in such a way that one cannot discover any difference between them in the notes, or even in the whole song.

Rore did make a distinction between the signs, but the complexity and variety of his rhythms are such that the differences are not always easy to define.

Rore's rhythms display an exceptional degree of independence from the mensural units that underlie them on all levels. This irregularity is a consequence of the variety of techniques that he uses to bring out the subtleties of poetic rhythms in music. The Italian poetry on which his madrigals are based is composed of lines of seven and eleven syllables. Textual accents are obligatory on the penultimate syllables of lines, and eleven-syllable lines also have a secondary accent on either the fourth or the sixth syllable that subdivides the line into unequal segments of 5+7 or 7+5 syllables.[5] Because these regular accents fall on even-numbered syllables, there is a tendency for the poetic rhythm to fall into an underlying iambic pattern in which even-numbered syllables are accented. This tendency is frequently overridden by the placement

---

[4] Praetorius, *Syntagma musicum*, vol. III, ch. 7 ("De tactu, seu notarum mensura; (italis battuta) & signis"), 51.

[5] The principles of Italian versification are such that the syllable following the first secondary accent in an eleven-syllable line counts as part of both hemistichs. Segments of 7+5 or 5+7 syllables therefore combine to make a line of 11 syllables.

of word accents, but it contributes a subtle background regularity that interacts in complex ways with the varied foreground rhythms in the poetry. Rore uses combinations of agogic accent (emphasis associated with note length), tonic accent (emphasis associated with high pitch or melodic leap), and mensural accent (emphasis associated with mensural *initia*) to mirror the rhythms of his poetic texts. Conflicts between agogic accents and mensural accents are the principal source of rhythmic groupings that do not align with the mensural units in his madrigals.

Some rhythmic patterns that are common at the beginnings and ends of phrases of madrigals are inherently ambiguous with respect to accent. Rore exploits this ambiguity to adapt his musical rhythms to a variety of textual rhythms. An initial long note that falls on a mensural *initium* may be heard either as an accented note by virtue of its length and position or as an extended, unaccented upbeat. Initial long notes are often shortened, turning them into true upbeats, when phrases are imitated or repeated. A similar ambiguity applies to the accentual implications of cadences. Unless a cadence is unexpectedly compressed for purposes of textual expression, both the penultimate interval (the one supporting the suspension, if any) and the final interval of a cadential progression fall on *initia* of the compositional *tactus*-units. If the *tactus*-units are regularly paired, the final sonority is usually, but not always, on a higher-level *initium* than the penultimate. For example, if the mensural structure consists of paired semibreves, the penultimate interval of most cadences will fall on a semibreve-max *initium* and the final interval will fall on a breve *initium*. Despite the accentual implications of this mensural structure, final sonorities of cadences are invariably associated with unaccented syllables of text, because the final syllables of poetic verses are unaccented. This paradox can be resolved by interpreting the *initium* on which a cadence concludes as a marker of the point of completion of the preceding time unit, rather than a point of mensural accent. It may function simultaneously as an accent in voices that are not involved in the cadence.

The editorial policy adopted in Bernhard Meier's complete edition of Rore's music obscures important features of the composer's mensural practices and makes them unnecessarily difficult to study.[6] Meier retains the original note values in C and reduces the values by half in ¢, implying that C is the same as ¢ notated in half-values. That principle applies in some of Rore's earliest madrigals, but not in the later ones. The visual impression conveyed by Meier's editions of the later madrigals is therefore seriously misleading.

---

[6] Cipriano de Rore, *Opera Omnia*, ed. Bernhard Meier, 8 vols., Corpus mensurabilis musicae 14 ([Rome]: American Institute of Musicology, 1959–77).

C and ₵ in the early madrigals

Rore's first and second books of madrigals *a* 5 use the signs C and ₵ in consistent ways that may serve as a standard of comparison for his more complex uses of the signs in later works. Book I *a* 5 (1542) contains eighteen madrigals in C and two in ₵; the 1544 reprint, which adds the words "madregali cromatici" on the title page, includes one additional piece in C. Book II *a* 5 (1544), which is labeled "a misura comune" ("in the common measure") in explicit contrast to "madregali cromatici," contains eight madrigals in ₵ by Rore along with nineteen by other composers. Although Rore was probably not involved in the preparation of the 1544 prints, the contrast between "black note" pieces in C and "white note" pieces in ₵ that is highlighted on their title pages is clearly present in the compositions.

The pieces in C in Book I *a* 5 are organized mensurally on levels from the *semifusa* to the breve. The compositional *tactus* is almost always the minim. The theoretical pairing of minims is audible only occasionally, but the semibreve-units are acknowledged through the placement of a clear majority of the final sonorities of cadences (about 70–80 percent) on semibreve *initia* and by the consistent notation of rests in conformity with the semibreve-units. The breve-units are purely theoretical. Rore evidently intended to respect them by including a whole number of breve-units in each *parte* of every piece, but the breve level was sufficiently abstract that he either miscounted breve-units in six of the thirty-five individual *parti* or cared little enough about the issue that this anomaly did not concern him.[7] He sometimes notated rests in conformity with the breve-units, but did not apply that principle consistently. Note values shorter than the minim function as subdivisions of the compositional *tactus*. Minims, semiminims, and their dotted variants (dotted minim + semiminim and dotted semiminim + *fusa*) are the principal bearers of text syllables. With a single exception (in *Per mezz'i boschi*), consecutive *fusae* are found only in melismas, and *semifusae* appear only in pairs on mensurally weak *fusae*.

---

[7] In his sacred music in ₵, where the breve is analogous to the semibreve in his early madrigals in C, Rore was concerned about the integrity of the breve-units, but they were at times subtle enough that he could lose track of them while composing. Jessie Ann Owens, "The Milan Partbooks: Evidence of Cipriano de Rore's Compositional Process," *Journal of the American Musicological Society* 37 (1984), 271–76, reports a fascinating discovery that confirms this point. Rore lost track of the breve-units at one point during the composition of his motet *Miserere mei*. When he discovered the error, he went back and revised the music to correct it. He may have had a similar attitude toward the semibreves of C in his early madrigals.

Example 13.1 Rore, *Hor che'l ciel e la terra*, bars 30–33, bass. After Rore, *I madrigali a cinque voci* (Venice: Scotto, 1542).

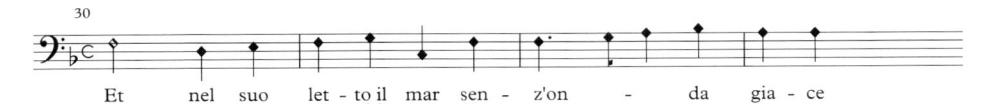

Several techniques make the minim-units consistently clear even when the rhythms temporarily work against them. The contrapuntal rhythm moves in minims and semiminims. Progressions to semiminim-max *initia* are weaker than progressions to minim *initia* in that they normally include sustained or repeated pitches in at least one voice. Suspensions fall on minim-max *initia* and are no longer than a semiminim except in the rare instances in which the compositional *tactus* shifts briefly to the semibreve; other dissonances are limited to *fusae* and *semifusae* and do not appear on minim *initia*. The penultimate and final sonorities of cadences fall on minim *initia*. Most syncopations involve mensurally displaced minims; syncopated semibreves are uncommon, and they are musically meaningful only when the regular pairing of minims is audible. The interval of imitation between voices is usually a minim. When a segment of text with accents on alternate syllables is set to a series of semiminims, the accented syllables fall on the minim *initia* and the unaccented syllables on the semiminim-max *initia*, as in Example 13.1.

The opening bars of *Per mezz'i boschi*, a setting of a Petrarch sonnet, illustrate some of Rore's techniques for establishing the norms of the C mensuration at the beginning of a piece and for using rhythm to project the declamation and meaning of a line of text with consistent iambic rhythm (see Example 13.2).[8] The text of the passage is "Per mezz'i boschi inhospiti e selvaggi" ("Through the midst of the inhospitable and savage woods"). All of the voices declaim the text to the same rhythm, though their pitches vary. The opening note is the longest one in the phrase, but the neutrality of the word associated with it ensures that it will be heard as an extended upbeat, not an agogic accent; it is shortened to a semiminim when the phrase is repeated in the upper voices. The accented syllables of the three crucial words, "boschi" ("woods"), "inhospiti" ("inhospitable"), and "selvaggi" ("savage"), are brought out with agogic accents. The dotted rhythm on "inhospiti" has a rough quality that captures its affect, as well as its

---

[8] Martha Feldman, *City Culture and the Madrigal at Venice* (Berkeley: University of California Press, 1995), 267–84, analyzes the relationships between music and text in this madrigal in detail.

Example 13.2 Rore, *Per mezz'i boschi*, bars 1–9. After Rore, *I madrigali a cinque voci* (Venice: Scotto, 1542).

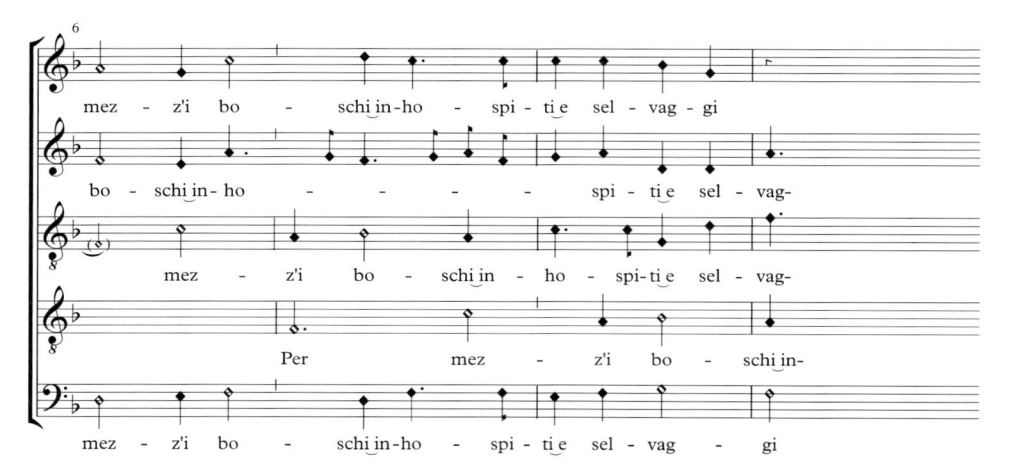

pronunciation. All of the longer notes in the phrase except the one on "boschi" align with the minim *initia*. This pattern leaves no doubt as to where the minim *initia* are located, but avoids monotony by creating groups of three semiminims that work against the mensuration on the words "mezz'i boschi." The semibreve-units are articulated by the entries of the first member of each pair of voices, but the imitation at the minim level between the members of the pair and the irregular grouping of semiminims near the beginning of the phrase focus the listener's attention on the minim/semiminim level and away from the larger units.

Bars 25–35 of the same piece (Example 13.3) illustrate some of Rore's techniques for dealing with more complex patterns of accents within a

Example 13.3 Rore, *Per mezz'i boschi*, bars 25–35. After Rore, *I madrigali a cinque voci* (Venice: Scotto, 1542).

poetic line. The words are "Altri che'l sol c'ha d'amor vivo i raggi" ("Anything but the sun, which has rays of living love"). Here the textual accents fall on syllables 1, 4, 7, 8 and 10. The first syllable of "Altri" is brought out by higher pitch than the second syllable in the three voices (canto, quinto, and bass) in which it falls on a weak semiminim. The placement of the accent on the second syllable of "amor" in a metrically unexpected position in the poem, immediately before another accented syllable, highlights the word and calls attention to the disruptive power of love. Consecutive textual accents are a challenge to a composer, because musical accents fall naturally in alternate mensural positions. Rore solves the problem in several different ways in this passage. One technique (quinto, bars 27–28; bass, bars 29–30; tenor, bars 30–31 and 33; canto, bars 32–33) is to place the accented syllable of "amor" on a weak semiminim, but emphasize it through a tonic accent. This approach has the advantage of respecting the underlying poetic meter, as well as the text accents, since the metrically accented first syllable of "amor" falls on a stronger mensural *initium* than the verbally accented second syllable. It also allows the accented syllable of "vivo" to fall on a minim *initium*. A second technique (alto, bars 30 and 33–34) is to place the accented syllables of both "amor" and "vivo" on minim *initia*. A third (canto, bar 29) is to place the accented syllable of "amor" on a minim *initium* and stress the first syllable of "vivo" with an agogic accent and syncopation. A fourth (quinto, bars 30–31) is to highlight the second syllable of "amor" with an agogic accent and arrange the rhythm so that the first syllable of "vivo" falls on a minim *initium*.

Rore's musical responses to this line are typical of his approach to the poetic texts in this book. The variety and subtlety of his techniques for dealing with poetic declamation are inexhaustible. They create a rich counterpoint of accents in which the voices interact in constantly changing ways.

Since the theoretical *tactus* of Rore's C is the semibreve, even though the compositional *tactus* is normally the minim, the sign C allows for the possibility of shifting the compositional *tactus* temporarily to the semibreve for expressive effect. This technique, which is usually associated with the expression of extreme despair, is surprisingly rare in Rore's early madrigals in C. One striking example occurs in *Hor che 'l ciel e la terra*, a setting of another Petrarch sonnet (see Example 13.4). The first quatrain, which Rore

Example 13.4 Rore, *Hor che'l ciel e la terra*, bars 37–44. After Rore, *I madrigali a cinque voci* (Venice: Scotto, 1542).

sets in a rhythmic style similar to that of the preceding examples, paints a picture of the pure stillness of nature at night. The second quatrain juxtaposes this calm with the poet's agitation, which is depicted initially by a series of disconnected verbs that contrast starkly with the long sentences in the first quatrain: "Veggio, penso, ardo, piango" ("I wake, I think, I burn, I weep"). Rore responds to these words with a series of equally disconnected musical gestures that disrupt the former rhythmic norms. At "Veggio," the compositional *tactus* is shifted suddenly to the semibreve by means of slow motion and a semibreve syncopation. It returns to the minim as the note values are cut in half for "penso, ardo," and the tension is increased at that point through simultaneous syncopation in all voices. It moves back to the semibreve for "piango," but now the syncopations produce suspensions that last for a full minim in bars 42 and 44. The effect of these dissonances is quite radical in relation to the minim compositional *tactus* that has governed the piece in the first quatrain. Suspensions raise the expectation of cadences, especially when they are followed by raised leading tones, but Rore leaves the leading tones unresolved here, just as the distress of the speaker is unresolved in the poem.

Temporary shifts of *tactus*-like features to a smaller level are even more exceptional than shifts to a larger level in Book I *a* 5. The only piece that includes a passage with consecutive texted *fusae*, along with some other features (such as imitation at the interval of a semiminim) suggestive of a semiminim compositional *tactus*, is *Per mezz'i boschi*. The device is straightforward text painting illustrating the words "fuggir per l'herba verde" ("flee through the green grass"). Its effect is striking, but too brief to undermine the role of the minim as the governing compositional *tactus* of the passage in which it occurs.

The ten pieces in ¢ in Books I and II *a* 5 are mirror images of the pieces in C notated in double values. All of the general statements about the pieces in C apply to the next larger value in ¢. There is no apparent difference between the texts of the pieces in different mensurations; serious poems, mostly sonnets (especially those of Petrarch), predominate in both groups. It is difficult to see any purpose to the use of *note nere* in Book I other than notational novelty. The opening of *Da quei bei lumi* (Example 13.5), one of the Book I pieces in ¢, illustrates the parallels between the two mensurations. The compositional *tactus* is the semibreve, and the theoretical pairing of semibreves is weakly articulated. Declamation is mostly in semibreves and minims. Syncopation is on the level of the semibreve; it creates irregular groups of minims that provide contrast against, but do not obscure, the mensural pairing of minims. Suspensions are minims, and other

Example 13.5 Rore, *Da quei bei lumi*, bars 1–9. After Rore, *I madrigali a cinque voci* (Venice: Scotto, 1542).

dissonances are semiminims or *fusae*. The opening words are "Da quei bei lumi ond'io sempre sospiro" ("From those beautiful lights for which I always sigh"). Rore brings out the metric accents of the poem with a mix of agogic and mensural accents. In this case he seems unconcerned about the mismatch between metric accent and word accent on "sempre," perhaps because the word is relatively unimportant; in all but one instance, he allows the musical emphasis (often in more than one form) to fall on the second syllable of that word.

The pieces in ¢ deviate from their mensural norms even less frequently than the pieces in C. Despite the theoretical breve *tactus*, the compositional *tactus* rarely rises above the level of the semibreve, and semibreves are never dissonant. Only one piece in ₵ (*Cantiamo lieti*) includes a short passage with texted semiminims, which, like the texted *fusae* in *Per mezz'i boschi*, do not challenge the primacy of the established *tactus*. It appears on the words "s'allegra il ciel" ("heaven rejoices") and expresses the affect of happiness.

The theoretical and compositional *tactus* of all of these madrigals are easily determined, but the performance *tactus* and tempos are less clear. By the 1540s the standard performance *tactus* of ₵ was the semibreve, although a few theorists still insisted that it ought to be the breve.[9] If a breve performance *tactus* were chosen for this group of madrigals in ₵, it would have to be distinctly subdivided to articulate the semibreve compositional *tactus*. It would have little advantage over a semibreve performance *tactus*, because the breve does not play a significant role in the musical structure. The performance *tactus* of C is more problematic. By analogy with ₵ it ought to be the minim, but since there was no tradition of a minim performance *tactus*, singers may have preferred a semibreve performance *tactus* with distinct subdivisions. The semibreve *tactus* would be advantageous in the exceptional passages like Example 13.4 in which the compositional *tactus* rises temporarily to the level of the semibreve. Since the rhythmic values under the two signs are in 2:1 ratio, it seems reasonable to assume that their metronome speeds should be in the same ratio, such that the minim of C equals the semibreve of ₵. This makes the tempo, in the sense of perceived rate of motion, identical under the two signs. A value for the compositional *tactus* that falls within the "moderate" range recommended by theorists makes musical sense for these works.

₵ in the later madrigals

Rore adopted ₵ as the usual sign for his madrigals after 1544; it appears in 65 of the 78 madrigals securely attributed to him after that date. With few exceptions, these madrigals use the style associated with ₵ in Books I and II *a 5* only as an underlying norm and vary it with features borrowed from the earlier C-style. Because the traditional ₵-style serves as a standard of reference, semibreve-units are musically significant and usually audible throughout a piece. Passages in C-style therefore have a different effect than they do in Book I *a 5*, because they function in relation to audible semibreve-units. In some pieces, breve-units are also articulated more regularly than they are in

---

[9] See Chapter 6, pp. 156–59.

Books I and II *a* 5. The result is a broad range of rhythmic possibilities that Rore exploits in an endless variety of ways to mold the music to the declamation, meaning, form, and affect of his poetic texts.

Alla dolce ombra, a setting of a Petrarch *sestina* that opens Book I *a 4* (1550), provides a good example of this new interpretation of ¢. The complete *prima parte* is shown in Example 13.6. Its text is as follows:

1 Alla dolce ombra de le belle frondi	In the soft shade of the beautiful leafy branches
2 Corsi fuggendo un dispietato lume,	A pitiless light ran fleetingly
3 Che 'n fin qua giù m'ardea dal terzo cielo,	That burned me down here from the third heaven,
4 E disgombrava già di neve in poggi	And the snow on the hilltops was melted
5 L'aura amorosa che rinova il tempo,	By the amorous breeze that renews the weather,
6 E fiorian per le piagge l'herbe e i rami.	And through the meadows the grasses and branches blossomed.

The breve-units play a significant role in the large-scale design of the piece, though they are audibly marked only at strategic points. They are established in the opening bars by the accented syllable of "ombra" in the lower voices and the entry of the alto on the second breve *initium*, then quickly obscured by the canto entry and subsequent rhythmic activity on lower levels. All of the structurally important cadences (bars 9–10, 13–15, 19–20, 22–23, and 36–37) conclude on breve *initia*. (The last of these is not a cadence from the contrapuntal point of view, but it is the end of the *parte* and has the rhythmic form of a cadence.) They are differentiated by the lengths of their penultimate sonorities. Cadential penultimates, which support suspensions in most cases, normally fall a semibreve before their notes of resolution, but the suspension in bar 22 appears a minim before the resolution to increase the continuity of the last two lines of the poem. The strongest cadences (bars 14–15 and 36–37), which mark the midpoint and end of the text, are supported by breves in the bass even though the suspension in the former falls only a semibreve before the resolution. The cadence in bars 14–15 is further strengthened by another cadence (a fifth higher) in the preceding bar. The breve-units thus anchor the mensural structure and support the large-scale trajectory of the music from one

Example 13.6 Rore, *Alla dolce ombra, prima parte*. After Rore, *Il primo libro de madregali a quatro voci* (Venice: Gardano, 1557; first edition published 1550).

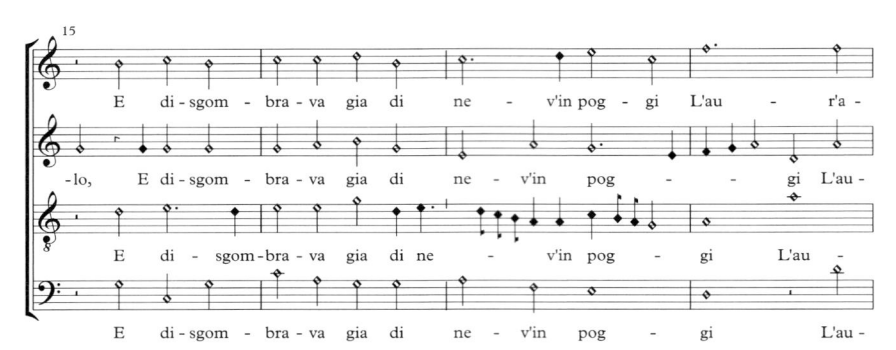

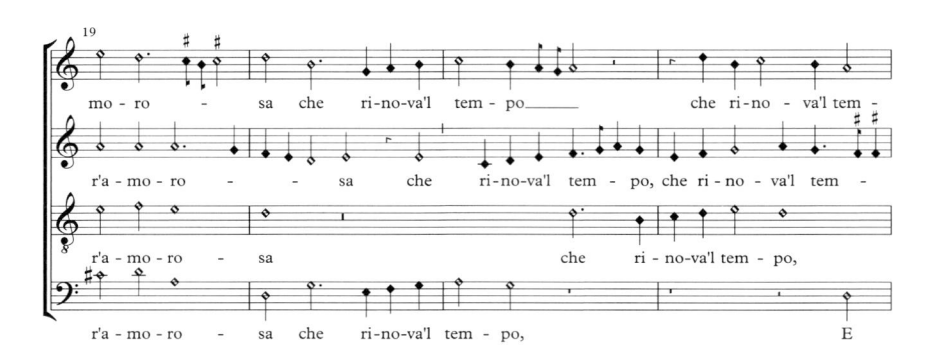

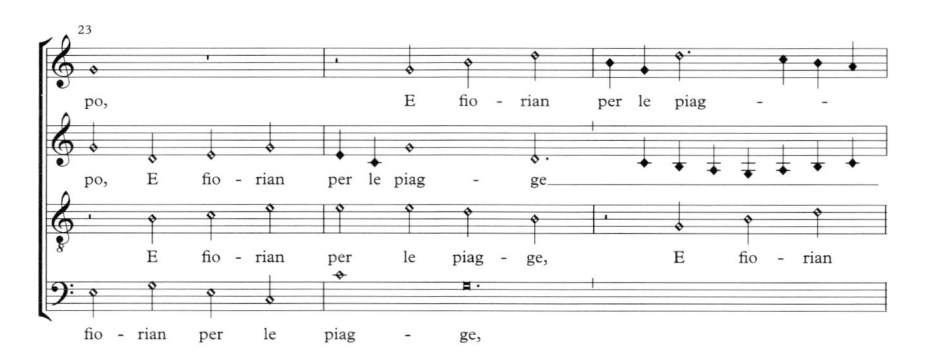

Example 13.6 (cont.)

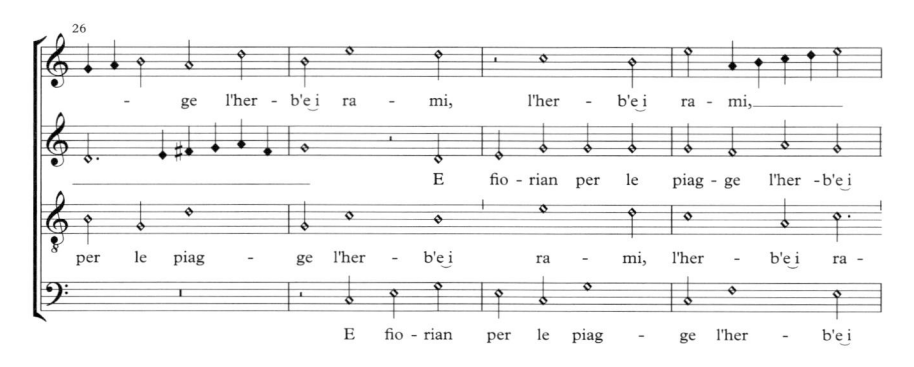

Example 13.6 (cont.)

principal cadence to the next, while leaving the rhythm free to operate on smaller levels between these points. Rore uses other techniques, such as the disappearance of all but one of the voices on the final sonority of the cadence in bar 15 and the weak contrapuntal progression in bars 36–37, to avoid a sense of finality, even at the end of the piece (since it is only the first of six *parti*), but the strong rhythmic profiles of these cadences nevertheless play a crucial role in establishing the breve-units as essential components of the mensural structure.

The semibreve is the compositional *tactus* throughout most of the piece. The semibreve-units are challenged at times, but never overshadowed, by rhythmic activity on the level of the minim. The setting of the first line proceeds sedately in paired minims until bar 4, where the doubling of the rate of declamation in the canto (foreshadowed by the same technique in the tenor in bars 2–3) shifts the compositional *tactus* to the minim. The setting of the penultimate syllable of the line to a minim, where a semibreve would have been expected on the basis of the opening rhythm, reinforces the grammatical continuity of the first two lines. The minim *tactus*, articulated by texted semiminims and minim-level imitation, remains in effect in bars 5–8 to capture the sense of the words "corsi fuggendo" ("ran fleetingly"), but the pairing of minims established in the opening bars remains audible as a background norm. The placement of the principal accents of "corsi fuggendo" on minim-max *initia* (in the canto in the first statement and all voices in the second) therefore has a disruptive effect, just as the pitiless sunlight disrupts the peace of the shade in the poem. The minim compositional *tactus* allows Rore to conclude the first statement of line 2 (bar 7) with a cadential progression of two minims ending on a minim-max *initium*, giving it a nervous, chopped-off quality and avoiding any break in continuity between the two statements of the line. The semibreve compositional *tactus* returns in bars 9–10, giving strong closure to the opening pair of lines, and continues through bar 20. In bars 20–22, the minim compositional *tactus* returns in a new guise to create graceful ternary groups of minims (out of phase in the different voices) that lighten the feel of the rhythm and capture the affective quality of the spring weather described by the text.

Bars 23–37 display what appears to be a simple rhythm consisting mostly of minims with semibreves for some of the accented syllables, but is in fact quite complex because of the irregular relation between the textual and musical accents. The word "fiorian" ("blossomed") is highlighted in the poem by a metrically irregular accent on the third syllable of the line. Rore brings out this textual accent with a tonic accent, but places it on a mensurally weak minim *initium*, mirroring the conflict between meter and rhythm in the poem with an analogous conflict in the music. Many of the other accented syllables likewise fall on mensurally weak minim *initia*; tonic, and usually also agogic, accents compensate for the lack of mensural emphasis on these syllables in the music. The complex rhythmic groupings in the individual voices do not conceal the semibreve-units of the mensuration, which are marked by long notes in the bass (bars 24–25 and 30–31) and cadential progressions (bars 26–27 and 36–37), but work against the mensural norms to create the expressive effect. Bars 30–37 are a literal repeat of bars 24–30 (with slight adjustment to allow for the overlap between the two statements) except that the penultimate note of the final cadence is lengthened from a semibreve to a breve to make the second cadence stronger than the first and to restore the alignment of the music with the breve-units of the mensuration.

In bars 17–18, Rore exploits the accentual ambiguity of cadences to create both a point of articulation and an elision between lines 4 and 5 of the poem, which are joined by an enjambment that highlights the words "l'aura amorosa" ("the amorous breeze"). The descending step in consecutive semibreves in the bass implies a cadence at the end of line 4. The tenor and alto support this cadential motion rhythmically, but not contrapuntally, since there is no leading tone to create a contrapuntal cadence, while the canto cuts the end of the line short with a rhythm of two minims and places the first syllable of "L'aura" on a note with strong textual, mensural, agogic, and tonic accent on the breve *initium* in bar 18. This accent counteracts the strong-weak interpretation of the would-be cadence in the other voices and joins the lines forcibly in the music, just as they are joined by the enjambment in the poem.

Rore's *Anchor che col partire* (also from Book I *a* 4), one of the most popular madrigals of the century, mixes the standard features of C and ¢ to an exceptionally high degree. Rhythms based on a minim compositional *tactus* are more frequent and more drastic than in *Alla dolce ombra*, and breve-units play no significant role in the piece, although the cadences that set off the principal formal sections (bars 18, 30, and 41) fall on breve *initia*. The greater emphasis on smaller mensural levels and the corresponding inattention to the largest regular level may relate to the playful tone of the poem, which toys with the theme of death and parting as sexual metaphors. The text is as follows:

1 Anchor che col partire	Although in parting
2 Io mi senta morire,	I feel myself dying,
3 Partir vorrei ogn'hor, ogni momento,	I would like to part every hour, every moment,
4 Tant'è 'l piacer ch'io sento	So great is the pleasure that I feel
5 De la vita ch'acquisto nel ritorno.	From the life that I gain in returning.
6 E così mille mille volt'il giorno	And thus a thousand thousand times a day
7 Partir da voi vorrei,	I would like to part from you,
8 Tanto son dolci gli ritorni miei.	So sweet are my returns.

The opening phrase (Example 13.7) establishes the mensural units on the semibreve and minim levels, but not the breve level. Semibreve-units govern the textual and agogic accents in three of the four voice entries (alto, tenor, and bass), and the suspension on a semibreve *initium* in bar 3 confirms them. The canto, however, imitates the opening motive at the interval of a minim, so that its textual and agogic accents are out of phase with the semibreve units. This device prepares the listener for the important role that the minim-units will play in the rest of the piece.

Irregular groupings of minims, which relate in a variety of ways to the local semibreve or minim compositional *tactus*, play a prominent role in many of the subsequent phrases. In bars 4–7 of Example 13.7, the minims fall into out-of-phase groups of 3+4+4 (or 3 in the *canto*). The mensural pairing of minims is made audible by the alignment of the last two notes of the alto and bass (bars 6–7) with semibreve *initia*. This allows for the witty portrayal of the word "morire" ("die") with suspension figures in the canto and tenor that are heard as strong-weak motions – an effect that would be lost if the minims were perceived as mensurally equal. In other passages, such as those in Example 13.8, irregular groups of minims that are imitated at the interval of a minim temporarily obscure all sense of the semibreve-units.

Example 13.7 Rore, *Anchor che col partire*, bars 1–7. After Rore, *Il primo libro de madregali a quatro voci* (Venice: Gardano, 1557; first edition published 1550).

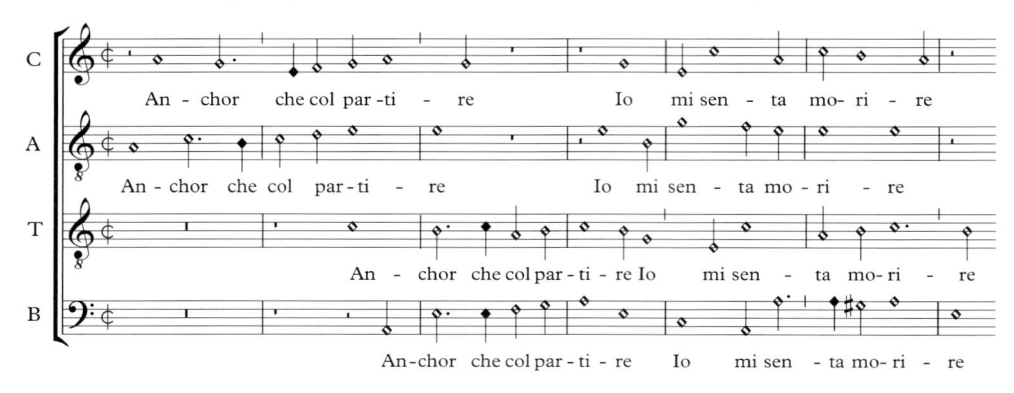

Example 13.8 Rore, *Anchor che col partire*, bars 10–12. After Rore, *Il primo libro de madregali a quatro voci* (Venice: Gardano, 1557; first edition published 1550).

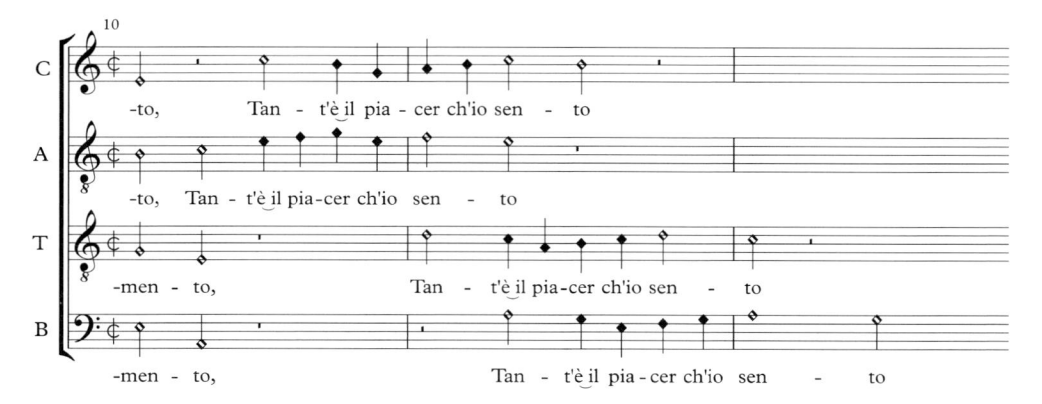

Example 13.9 Rore, *Anchor che col partire*, bars 22–30. After Rore, *Il primo libro de madregali a quatro voci* (Venice: Gardano, 1557; first edition published 1550).

Despite the constant flirtation with irregular groups of minims in this piece, the integrity of the semibreve-units is essential to the mensural design and the musical interpretation of the poem. Rore associates the idea of "parting" with irregular groups of minims and "returning" with regular groups that align with the semibreve-units of the mensuration. In Example 13.9, he contrasts the rational certainty of line 7 (bars 23–25), in which the rhythms conform clearly to the semibreve-units, with the irrational sweetness of the beginning of line 8 (bars 25–27), where the motive on "tanto son dolci" ("so sweet are") is imitated at the interval of three minims. At the words "gli ritorni miei" ("my returns"; bars 28–30), the rhythms return to their proper alignment with the semibreve-units.

The tone of Rore's madrigals becomes more radically expressive in the books published in and after 1557. The textures are more homophonic than they are in the earlier madrigals. Homophony enhances the effect of mensural irregularities, since there are no contrasting voices to counterbalance the mensural irregularities in individual voices. Contrasts between homophonic and polyphonic passages within a piece may enhance contrasts generated by rhythm and other means. The later madrigals in ₵ make less use of features borrowed from C than the ones from *c.* 1550, but when they do employ them, the effect is powerful.

The *prima parte* of Rore's setting of Petrarch's sestina *Mia benigna fortuna* employs radical shifts of mensural level to represent a radical reversal of fortune. The first four lines of the text describe the poet's former happiness. Line 5 interrupts these pleasant thoughts with the revelation of the sudden transformation of sweetness into pain and weeping, caused (as the following stanza reveals) by the death of his beloved:

1 Mia benigna fortuna e 'l viver lieto,	My benevolent fortune and happy life,
2 I chiari giorni e le tranquille notti	The bright days and tranquil nights
3 E i soavi sospiri e 'l dolce stile	And the gentle sighs and the sweet style
4 Che solea resonar in versi e 'n rime,	That used to resound in verses and rhymes,
5 Volti subitamente in doglia e'n pianto,	Turned suddenly to pain and weeping,
6 Odiar vita mi fanno e bramar morte.	Make me hate life and long for death.

The rhythm of the poem captures the affect of line 5 dramatically. Lines 1–4 begin gently, with unstressed syllables. In line 5, the accent on the first syllable of the word "volti" ("turned" or "transformed") transforms the poetic rhythm jarringly. It is followed by four unaccented syllables that propel the text rapidly through the word "subitamente" ("suddenly"). The heavy accents on "doglia" ("pain") and "pianto" ("weeping") slow the declamation to a pace appropriate to the affect of the words. Rore's musical rhythms build on and enhance these features of the poetic rhythm (see Example 13.10). Line 4 (bars 20–23) provides a background of calm regularity: the motion is mostly in even minims, and the verbal and musical accents conform to the relative strengths of the mensural *initia* on both the semibreve and the breve level. Line 5 begins shockingly, a minim earlier than expected, with a displaced accent on a minim-max *initium* in the bass

Example 13.10 Rore, *Mia benigna fortuna*, bars 20–29. After Rore, *Il secondo libro de madregali a quatro voci* (Venice: Gardano, 1557).

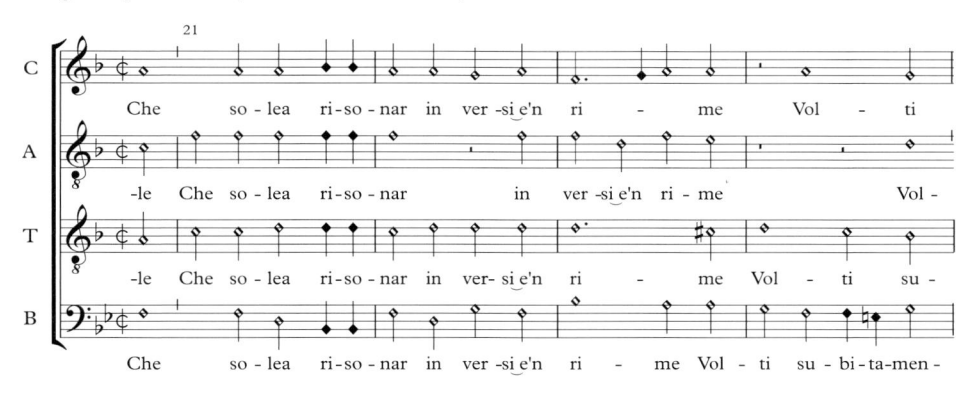

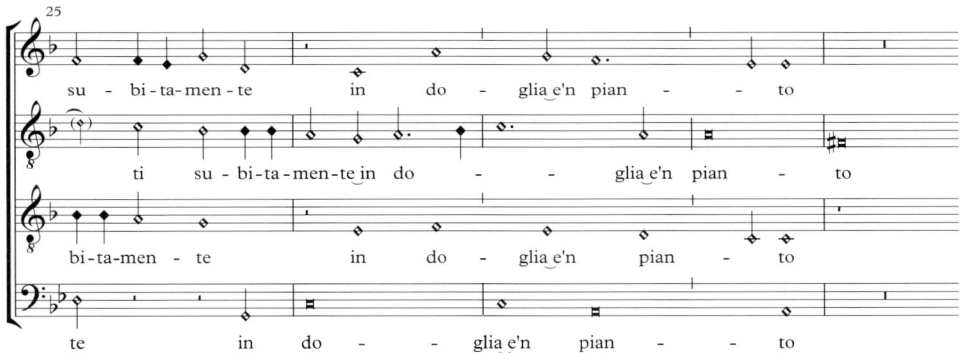

(bar 23). The tenor completes the wrenching transformation by imitating the bass at the interval of a minim; the canto and alto follow the bass in placing the word "volti" at points where its accent is out of phase with the mensural *initia*. Rore captures the rapid-fire declamation of "subitamente" with texted semiminims, then shifts the compositional *tactus* directly from the minim to the undivided semibreve by means of contrapuntal progressions in semibreves and suspensions over consecutive semibreve *initia* in bars 27 and 28. A more vivid musical counterpart to the emotional turmoil of the poetry is hard to imagine.

In *Datemi pace*, a setting of a Petrarch sonnet from Book II *a 4*, Rore uses contrasts between ternary and binary groups of semibreves and minims to bring out the affective contrasts in the text. The poem expresses an ardent wish for peace through freedom from painful thoughts. Its first three lines are as follows:

1 Datemi pace, o duri miei pensieri.	Give me peace, O my harsh thoughts.
2 Non basta ben ch'Amor, fortuna e morte	Is it not enough that Love, fortune, and death
3 Mi fanno guerra intorno e'n su le porte	Make war on me all around and at my doors

Rather than focusing exclusively on thoughts of pain, which dominate in the poem, Rore depicts the contrast between longed-for peace and present pain by associating the former with ternary rhythms and the latter with binary rhythms and moving from the former to the latter within each of the first three phrases (see Example 13.11). In line 1 (bars 1–10), the ternary rhythms are groups of semibreves; the rhythm therefore consists of ternary groups of compositional *tactus*, which are replaced by binary groups at the word "duri" ("harsh"; bar 7). The ternary rhythms in lines 2 and 3 (bars 10–19) differ from those of line 1 in that they work against the *tactus*, rather than simply grouping the *tactus* in sets of three. This tension contributes at least as much to the enhanced urgency of these lines as does the increased speed of the notes. The shift to binary groups at the word "morte" ("death"; bar 14) makes its effect not only through the change of grouping, but also through the duration of the note on the first syllable of the word, which lasts a minim longer than the preceding pattern leads the listener to expect. At a later point in the piece, Rore introduces *sesquialtera* rhythms to capture the sense of the word "leggieri" ("light"; see Example 13.12). Because of their different relationship to the compositional *tactus*, these ternary groups produce an entirely different effect from the ternary groups of *tactus* and half-*tactus* in Example 13.11.

In *O sonno*, a setting of a sonnet by Giovanni della Casa from Book II *a 4*, Rore experiments with a very unusual rhythmic style. The text has a prose-like quality resulting from the extreme use of enjambment to override the symmetries of the poetic form. It represents an emotional state that is too intense to be constrained by ordinary poetic regularities:

1 O sonno! O della quet'humid' ombrosa	O sleep! O of quiet, humid, shadowy
2 Notte placido figlio, o de' mortali	Night placid son, O of ailing
3 Egri conforto, oblio dolce de' mali	Mortals comfort, sweet forgetfulness of evils
4 Sì grave, ond'è la vita aspra e noiosa,	So great, which make life bitter and painful,

The madrigals of Rore 431

Example 13.11 Rore, *Datemi pace*, bars 1–19. After Rore, *Il secondo libro de madregali a quatro voci* (Venice: Gardano, 1557).

Rore mimics the rhythmic qualities of the poem with musical rhythms that move mostly in semibreves that are constantly shifted in relation to the mensuration by means of freely placed minims and breves in an almost purely homophonic texture (see Example 13.13). Since the semibreves are mensurally equal, the effect is one of declamatory freedom unconstrained by regular

Example 13.12 Rore, *Datemi pace*, bars 42–43. After Rore, *Il secondo libro de madregali a quatro voci* (Venice: Gardano, 1557).

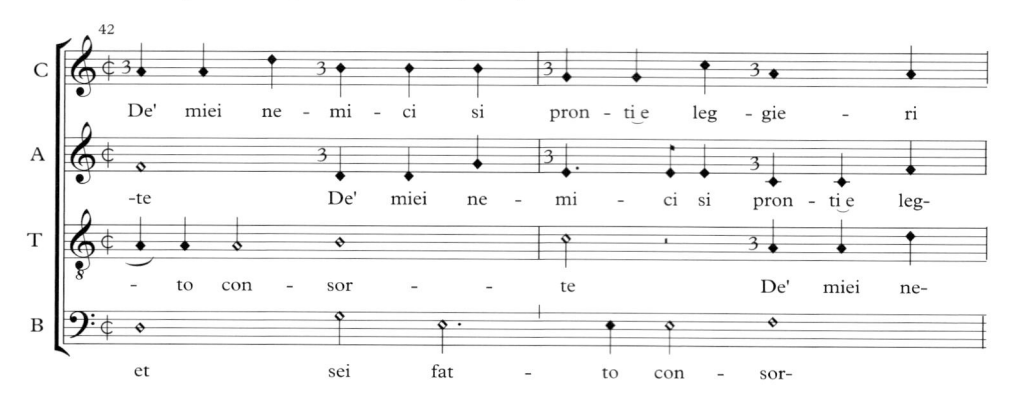

Example 13.13 Rore, *O sonno* (II/4), bars 1–11. After Rore, *Il secondo libro de madregali a quatro voci* (Venice: Gardano, 1557).

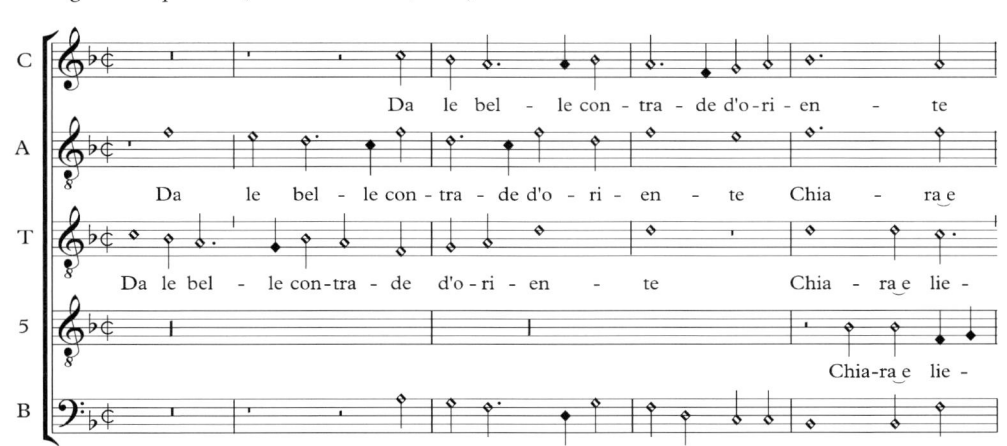

Example 13.14 Rore, *Da le belle contrade*, bars 1–5. After Rore, *Il quinto libro di madrigali a cinque voci* (Venice: Gardano, 1566).

mensural grouping of any kind. The semibreve pulse holds the rhythm together, and the mensural groupings on both the semibreve and the breve level emerge at the occasional spots where suspensions mark cadences or enhance the expression of pain in the text (e.g., bars 69–72 and 80–86), but the overall effect is one of almost unmeasured, prose-like declamation.

Da le belle contrade, from Rore's posthumously published Book V *a* 5 (1566), illustrates the extreme limits of the mensural possibilities of ¢ in Rore's late madrigals. The text, an anonymous sonnet, is a narration of a passionate love scene from the perspective of the man; an extended quotation of the woman's words in the central section adds vividness and immediacy to the emotions that it expresses. The opening section describes an idyllic scene that sets the background for the lovers' encounter. Rore characterizes it rhythmically with flexible groups of minims in relation to a placid semibreve compositional *tactus*. The first phrase, with the words "Da le belle contrade d'oriente" ("From the beautiful countries of the east"), establishes the tone (see Example 13.14).

The stormy emotions that follow tear the compositional *tactus* from one extreme to the other. The first section of the woman's emotional outburst culminates in a phrase with the words "Che sarà qui di me scura e dolente?" ("What will become of me, dark and sad?") that not only moves in semibreves and breves, but includes a suspension lasting for a full semibreve on the word "dolente" ("sad"; see Example 13.15). Phrases with rhythms that imply a breve compositional *tactus* are not uncommon in Rore's madrigals

Example 13.15 Rore, *Da le belle contrade*, bars 36–40. After Rore, *Il quinto libro di madrigali a cinque voci* (Venice: Gardano, 1566).

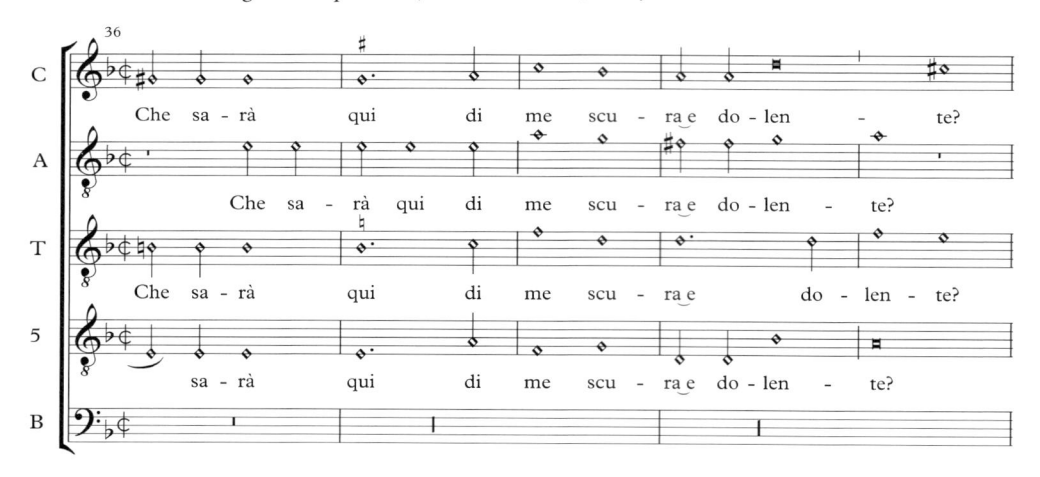

Example 13.16 Rore, *Da le belle contrade*, bars 59–63. After Rore, *Il quinto libro di madrigali a cinque voci* (Venice: Gardano, 1566).

in ¢, but dissonances lasting for half of that *tactus* are extremely rare. At the opposite extreme, Rore compresses the compositional *tactus* to the minim and avoids any larger mensural grouping for the words "cinseme forte, iterando gl'amplessi" ("she embraced me tightly, repeating her embraces"; see Example 13.16). The motive on the words "cinseme forte" features a pronounced, regular alternation of accented and unaccented notes on the

Example 13.17 Rore, *Da le belle contrade*, bars 66–74. After Rore, *Il quinto libro di madrigali a cinque voci* (Venice: Gardano, 1566).

minim level that might be taken to represent the systole and diastole of a rapidly beating heart. Imitation of this motive on alternate minims obliterates the mensural pairing of minims in the composite rhythm and enhances the intensity of the effect.

To resolve the tension generated by this compression of the *tactus*, Rore gradually expands the length of the rhythmic groups and brings them into line with the breve-units of the mensuration (see Example 13.17; the most prominent rhythmic groupings are shown with wedges above the top staff). The melisma on the word "nodi" ("knots"), the last word of the penultimate line, begins the process by drawing out that word (while illustrating it pictorially), but the cadence that concludes the line (bar 67) still has a breathless quality, since its penultimate is only a minim. The beginning of the last line, "Che giamai ne fer più l'Edra o l'Acanto" ("That never ivy nor acanthus made more"), expands the rhythmic groups to three minims through the placement of the textual accents of "giamai" and "più" at intervals of three minims. On the word "l'Edra" ("ivy") – the melodic high point in the top voice – the rhythmic groups expand to four minims, or a full breve, and align at last with the breve-units of the mensuration. The following two breves (bars 72–73) form a single rhythmic unit of double length because of the syncopation in the bass, slowing the structural motion still further (despite the ornamental runs in the canto) in preparation for the cadence. After a brief extension, the last phrase is repeated to bring the madrigal to a close.

What might this extreme variety of rhythms imply about the performance *tactus* and tempo of ¢ in Rore's later madrigals? The ideal performance *tactus* for pieces that include passages with a breve compositional *tactus* might be a divided breve, but theoretical evidence shows that singers of the time preferred a semibreve performance *tactus*. The semibreve *tactus* works well as long as its subdivisions are not strongly marked, even in passages where minims are irregularly grouped or the compositional *tactus* shifts to the minim, because the expressive effect of those irregularities depends on their non-conformity with the semibreve-units. A strongly divided semibreve *tactus* would make some of these complex rhythms easier to perform, but it would flatten their effect by equalizing all of the minim-units. The *tactus* should surely be kept in the background when the rhythms conflict with it, but its subtle presence is essential to both the sense of freedom of the irregular rhythms and the effect of resolution when the rhythms realign with the time units of the mensuration.

The tempo of pieces that include c-style passages must be slower than that of the early madrigals in ¢ to prevent the faster sections from sounding rushed, but not so slow that the semibreve *tactus* drags. Pieces without c-style passages might be somewhat faster, and *O sonno*, which moves predominantly in semibreves, might be even faster. Flexibility of tempo within pieces is also possible, and probably desirable. When Vicentino recommended varying the tempo for expressive effect in the performance of madrigals in 1555,[10] he was employed by Cardinal Ippolito d'Este, the brother of

---

[10] Vicentino, *L'antica musica ridotta alla moderna prattica*, book 4, ch. 42 ("Regola da concertare cantando ogni sorte di compositione"), fol. 88ᵛ.

Rore's employer, Duke Ercole II of Ferrara. The recent madrigals of Rore are among the works most likely to have inspired this recommendation.

C in the later madrigals

Despite the enormous range of rhythms that were possible in ₵, Rore never abandoned the sign C altogether. The relation between the two signs in his later madrigals is not a categorical opposition, as it is in Books I and II *a 5*, but a subtle difference in the degree of emphasis on different levels of the mensuration. Two of the later madrigals in C (*Se voi poteste*, from Book III *a 5*, and *Quel foco che tant'anni*, from Book I *a 4*) resemble the C pieces of Book I *a 5* in rhythmic character, but in the others, the typical features of the older C and ₵ are combined, as they are in the madrigals in ₵.

Quando, signor, lasciaste, from Book IV *a 5* (1557), offers a unique opportunity for direct comparison of the signs, because its *prima parte* is in C and its *seconda parte* is in ₵. The use of different signs for different *parti* of a madrigal is extremely unusual.[11] In this piece the two signs represent opposite affects: C is associated with sadness and ₵ with happiness. The text is a sonnet by Giovanni Battista Giraldi Cinzio celebrating the return to the court of Ferrara of Prince Alfonso d'Este, who had fled to France without his father's permission. It is as follows:

1 Quando, signor, lasciaste entro a le rive	When, lord, you left sad between its banks
2 Mesto il fiume più bel ch'Italia bagne,	The most beautiful river that bathes Italy,
3 Restar gl'arbori tutti e le campagne	All of the trees and the fields remained
4 Di fior, di frond' e di vaghezza prive.	Without flowers, leaves, and beauty.
5 La figlia di Latona e le compagne	The daughter of Latona and her companions
6 Dire s'udiro, d'ogni gioia schive,	Were heard to say, deprived of all joy,
7 "Perche da noi, signor, hor ti scompagne?	"Why, lord, do you absent yourself from us?

---

[11] The only other example that I know of is Giovanni Maria Nanino's *Le strane voci*, in which the affective connotations of the two signs are the opposite of what they are in this madrigal of Rore. I thank Anthony Newcomb for calling my attention to this piece.

8 Perche del maggior ben nostro ne prive?"	Why do you deprive us of our greatest good?"
9 Ma poi che vostr'altezza a noi ritorna,	But now that your highness has returned to us,
10 Ripiglian l'honor suo gl'arbor, le valli,	The trees and the valleys regain their honor,
11 E festa fan tutte le Nimphe insieme.	And all of the Nymphs celebrate together.
12 Alza dal molle suo letto le corna	The Po raises his horns from his watery bed,
13 Il Po, e ripieno di leggiadra speme	And full of pleasing hope
14 Si gode a pien tra i suoi puri cristalli.	He enjoys himself fully among his pure crystals.

Both of the signs in this piece include the same range of note values, from the *fusa* to the semibreve. The semibreve is the penultimate value in cadences under both signs (except in the final cadence of the *seconda parte*), but the preparations of the cadential suspensions are semiminims in C (except in the final cadence of the *prima parte*) and minims in ₡. The minim is the most common text-bearing value under both signs, but in C, the declamation proceeds in a mix of minims and semiminims, while in ₡ it proceeds in minims and semibreves with only occasional pairs of texted semiminims. The predominant level of syncopation is the minim in C and the semibreve in ₡; there are a few syncopated semibreves in C, but no syncopated minims in ₡. The semibreve is the largest regular unit of measure in C; cadences may conclude on any semibreve *initium*, and the complete *parte* has an odd number of semibreves preceding the final long. Breve-units govern the large-scale form and occasionally play a role within phrases in ₡; all cadences with suspensions conclude on breve *initia*, and the complete *parte* has a whole number of breve-units. Examples 13.18 and 13.19 show the opening bars and one later phrase of each *parte* of this madrigal. The semibreve is the principal unit articulated in both openings, but it is divided by declamation on minims and a pair of semiminims in C and relatively undivided in ₡.

The essential difference between C and ₡ in this piece is that the principal pulse, or compositional *tactus*, is the semibreve in ₡ and the minim in C. Both signs, however, require a semibreve performance *tactus* to articulate the role of the semibreve in the mensural structure, especially at cadences. If the semibreve performance *tactus* reflects the character of the musical

Example 13.18 Rore, *Quando, signor, lasciaste*: (a) bars 1–6; (b) bars 27–41. After Rore, *Il quarto libro d'i madrigali a cinque voci* (Venice: Gardano, 1557).

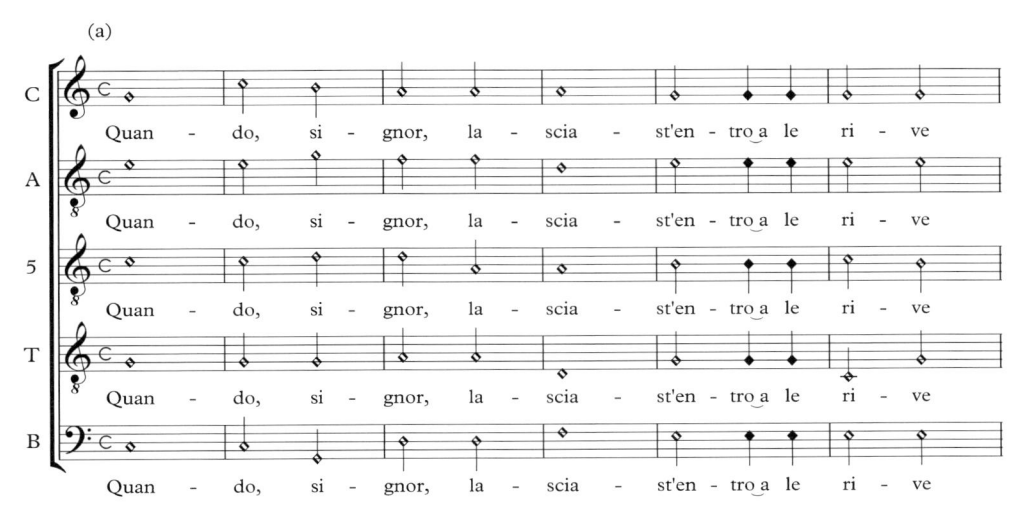

[Musical notation: five voices (C, A, 5, T, B) setting the text "Quan-do, si-gnor, la-scia-st'en-tro a le ri-ve"]

rhythms, it will be without marked subdivision in ¢ and clearly subdivided in C. The tempo relation between the signs is a matter of judgment. Given the similarities between the signs, the 2:1 relation implied by Meier's edition, in which the values are reduced by half in ¢, is surely excessive. Any lesser increase in the speed of the written values in ¢ is possible as long as it is sufficient to bring out the contrasting affects of the two *parti*.

L'inconstantia che seco han (Book I *a 4*) contrasts the styles normally associated with C and ¢ in a different way. The text (a madrigal by Giraldi Cinzio) is a reflection on the inconstancy of human fortune:

1 L'inconstantia che seco han le mortali	The inconstancy that mortal affairs have
2 Cose cagion è sola	Is the sole reason
3 Che chi è lieto e felice	That he who is cheerful and happy
4 Misero anche divenga, e chi infelice	Will yet become sad, and he who is sad
5 Trovi fin a suoi mali,	Will find an end to his troubles,
6 Tal che quel che n'invola	Such that the thing that takes away
7 Il bene anche ce 'l rende,	The good also returns it to us,
8 E quel stesso ne giova che n'offende.	And the same thing that helps also hurts.
9 Onde chi 'l ver comprende	Therefore he who understands the truth

Example 13.18 (cont.)

(b)

Example 13.19 Rore, *Quando, signor, lasciaste*: (a) bars 59–64; (b) bars 69–74. After Rore, *Il quarto libro d'i madrigali a cinque voci* (Venice: Gardano, 1557).

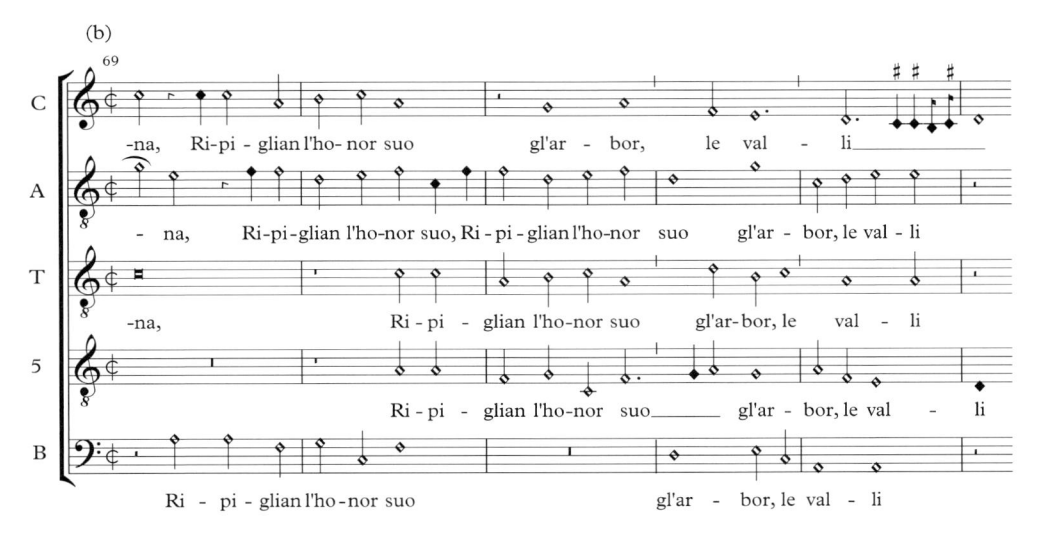

10 Non giudicherà tali
11 Le doglie nostre, che chi piagn'e geme
12 Non poss'haver d'uscir d'affanno speme.

Will not judge
Our sorrows to be such that he who weeps and moans
May not have hope of escaping from misery.

The sign for the work is C. Rhythms in C-style are associated with happiness and rhythms in ¢-style with sorrow (see Example 13.20). Rore may have

Example 13.20 Rore, *L'inconstantia che seco han*, bars 58–75. After Rore, *Il primo libro de madregali a quatro voci* (Venice: Gardano, 1557; first edition published 1550).

chosen C as the sign for the whole piece because the overall point is optimistic. The sad/happy associations of the signs in this piece are the opposite of those in *Quando, signor, lasciaste*, because when both styles appear under a single sign at a (more or less) constant tempo, the phrases in ¢-style will be slower than the phrases in C-style. Separate pieces or *parti* with different signs allow for a contrast of metronome speed that may compensate for the effect of the larger written values of ¢. Later in the century, ¢ came to be regularly associated with pathos and C with cheerfulness.

Alfred Einstein calls attention to the mixture of the rhythmic styles of C and ¢ in his discussion of Rore's *Anchor che col partire* and concludes that the combination of features of both mensurations within the piece renders the sign irrelevant.[12] I cannot agree with this conclusion. Except in *L'inconstantia che seco han*, in which the sign might have gone either way, Rore seems always to have chosen his signs in such a way that they reveal something about the roles of the various temporal levels in the mensural structure, and therefore the presence or absence of marked subdivisions and groupings of the *tactus*. Similar or identical rhythms may appear under both signs, but their character differs depending on their relation to the underlying mensural structure. Tempo may also be a factor, but it is much more elusive and variable than the relationships of the rhythms to the *tactus*. These points are subtle, and individual instances may be subject to more than one interpretation, but the care with which Rore controls the constantly shifting relations of his rhythms to the mensural structure implies that the issue is crucial to his highly sensitive musical interpretations of his poetic texts.

Sesquialtera proportion

Sesquialtera proportion appears in three different forms in Rore's madrigals: groups of three minims in ¢, groups of three semibreves in ¢, and groups of three minims in C. The first type, which may be seen in Example 13.12, is the simplest. It is always notated in coloration, sometimes with a number 3 before each ternary group of minims to avoid possible confusion between colored minims and semiminims. Rhythms in this mensuration, which function simply as triplets in relation to the semibreve compositional *tactus*, always have distinctly ternary character. They often appear in only some of the voices, while other voices remain in ¢. There is no doubt, therefore, that their proportional relation to ¢ is to be interpreted literally.

Sesquialtera in groups of three semibreves is quite different. It appears only in all voices simultaneously, although it occasionally overlaps with a

---

[12] Alfred Einstein, *The Italian Madrigal*, 3 vols. (Princeton University Press, 1949; repr. 1971), I: 404.

long note or group of rests in ¢ in one voice. Rore's signs for this mensuration are Φ3, 3, and coloration, all of which have the same meaning except that notes in coloration are notationally imperfect. The rhythms that Rore writes in this mensuration, unlike those of most of his contemporaries, have no ternary character. This suggests that for him the proportion represents only a relative tempo, not a meaningful mensural structure, and that it should also be interpreted literally. The function of the proportion is usually to emphasize the words on which it occurs, rather than to represent their meanings in a specific way. Phrases or sections of madrigals in ¢ are sometimes repeated in *sesquialtera* with identical rhythms notated in the next larger values; this procedure makes the second statement slower than the first by a factor of 4:3 (since the written values are doubled, then reduced to ⅔). Rore uses this procedure with clever symbolic effect in the final line of the *terza parte* of *Alla dolce ombra*, where the words are "Che non cangiasser qualitade a tempo" ('Which do not change quality with time").

Another example is found in *Felice sei, Trevigi*, a madrigal from the posthumous *Le vive fiamme* (1565) honoring Giovan Francesco Libertà, prior of the Augustinian monastery of Santa Margarita in Treviso.[13] To convey the celebratory character of the concluding words, "Viva sempre lo spirto pellegrino, Giovan Francesco Libertà divino" ("Long live that rare spirit, the divine Giovan Francesco Libertà"), Rore sets the final section (Example 13.21) in an almost march-like style, with the regular semibreve *initia* distinctly accented in all voices. He repeats the section in *sesquialtera* with the notated values twice as large to slow the tempo the second time, but the rhythms remain emphatically binary except at one point (bar 80), where a semibreve is added to make the length of the *sesquialtera* section add up to a whole number of perfect breves. The added beat, which causes the suspension in bar 81 to fall on a weak beat in relation to the binary rhythm (but not in relation to the notated mensuration) of the preceding bars, is puzzling, and the conclusion of the deceptive cadence in bar 81 on the third semibreve of a perfect breve, following a suspension two semibreves earlier, is highly irregular.

It is unclear how *sesquialtera* of this type would have been measured in performance. Theorists unanimously recommend a performance *tactus* of three semibreves for this form of *sesquialtera*, but that *tactus* fits Rore's rhythms quite awkwardly. The passage is not one in which the expressive character would benefit from tension between the rhythm and the *tactus*. A

[13] Jane A. Bernstein, *Music Printing in Renaissance Venice: The Scotto Press, 1539–1572* (New York: Oxford University Press, 1998), 674.

Example 13.21 Rore, *Felice sei, Trevigi*, bars 57–83. After Rore, *Le vive fiamme de' vaghi e dilettevoli madrigali a quattro et cinque voci* (Venice: Scotto, 1565).

semibreve *tactus* is the only one that accommodates the added beat and suspension in bars 80–81. The semibreve *tactus* would be ⅔ as long as the *tactus* of ₵ (since the written semibreves are reduced to ⅔ of their length by the proportion), but it would measure half as many notes, because the notated values are twice as large. An alternative that fits the music better would be to measure the *sesquialtera* in imperfect breves (corresponding to the semibreves of the preceding section), then switch to a semibreve *tactus* where the added beat occurs. This option would encourage a sense of *ritardando* at the end of the section by emphasizing shorter time units, even if the tempo does not slow down.

The complex relation between C and ₵ in Rore's later madrigals and the subtlety of the difference in mensural structure and performance *tactus* that the signs imply are typical of the madrigal for the rest of the century. Both signs allow for a compositional *tactus* that fluctuates between the semibreve and the minim and may even rise occasionally to the breve in ₵, but the semibreve predominates in ₵ and the minim in C. The meaning of ₵ in contemporaneous sacred music, such as the masses of Palestrina, is quite different, because the compositional *tactus* never falls to the level of the minim in that style.

The different styles associated with C and ₵ in different repertoires imply different interpretations of the semibreve performance *tactus* with respect to subdivision and tempo. Sacred music in ₵ calls for an undivided semibreve *tactus* and a moderate tempo that is fast enough to bring out groups of semibreves where they are musically significant. Madrigals in ₵ must have a slower semibreve *tactus* to accommodate passages in which the compositional *tactus* shifts to the minim. Madrigals in C may require an even slower semibreve *tactus* than madrigals in ₵, but the tempo relation between the signs must depend on the style and affect of the pieces to which they apply. In passages where the compositional *tactus* falls primarily on the minim in either ₵ or C, the semibreve *tactus* may need to be divided in performance in order to conform to the rhythms. The semibreve performance *tactus* is not a single entity associated with a single form and tempo, but a flexible performance measure that can be adapted to any of the diverse styles of serious music of the sixteenth century. Its interpretation in a given piece must be determined by the nature of the music, and not by theoretical formulas.

14 | Popular songs and dances

The repertoire of sixteenth-century music includes many genres of a more popular character than those considered in the preceding chapters. They are often quite different in rhythmic character from their highbrow counterparts. Their relatively homophonic textures preclude complex rhythmic interplay among voices and encourage a pronounced sense of beat. They employ the same mensuration signs as the more serious genres, but sometimes with different meanings. This chapter considers three types of music with distinctive rhythmic styles that stretch or alter the traditional meanings of mensuration signs – the villanesca and villanella, the canzonetta, and the galliard – along with songs employing galliard-like rhythms.

The villanesca and villanella

The villanesca is a strophic song in Neapolitan style. It first appeared in print in 1537. In its original form, it is characterized by rustic texts that often include touches of Neapolitan dialect, three-voice texture with the principal melody in the top voice, stanza forms with sectional repeats (usually AABCC or AABB), and in some cases parallel fifths between the outer voices. The composers of three-voice villanescas were Neapolitans; composers in northern Italy often arranged these songs for four voices. Adrian Willaert and his Venetian colleagues were the most important composers of villanesca arrangements. Around 1560 composers from northern Italy began composing three-voice songs in a style resembling the villanesca, but with a less pronounced regional character. Their works are generally called "villanellas" or simply "canzoni alla napolitana" in the prints. Villanellas were arranged for four, five, and six voices, and pieces in villanella style were composed for 4–6 voices without three-voice models.

    The standard mensuration sign for the villanesca and villanella is C. In this context, the sign represents a compositional *tactus* on the minim and a theoretical *tactus* on the semibreve, as in Rore's first book of madrigals *a 5*. The theoretical *tactus*, however, plays a much less prominent role in these genres than it does in the madrigal, often to the point of having no role at all in the compositional structure. Repeated sections may be displaced by a minim with respect to the semibreve-units of the mensuration, and rhythmic groups within sections are often unrelated to the theoretical semibreve *tactus*, though the minim compositional *tactus* is always significant. The limitation of mensural regularity to the shortest possible time unit is one of the features that gives these works their low-style character.

Sectional repeats are shown with repeat signs in most villanescas and villanellas for three voices and some for four voices, but not in those for more than four voices. This notational detail, which also reflects subtle distinctions of stylistic level, influences the mensural character of the works, because repeat signs can obscure the semibreve-units of the mensuration and encourage compositional structures that take no account of the theoretical *tactus*. When repeats are written out, composers normally respect the theoretical *tactus* at least in the notation of rests and the total lengths of pieces, although their rhythms may be otherwise independent of the semibreve-units. When repeats are indicated with repeat signs, however, even the total lengths of pieces need not be a whole number of semibreves.

When a phrase that includes semibreves appears in a section that is repeated with minim displacement, composers who write out repeats sometimes make minor adjustments to avoid syncopating semibreves with respect to the theoretical semibreve-units, even though there is no way a listener could be aware of those units. In Giovanni Ferretti's *Dolce mi saria* (Example 14.1), the displaced repeat would place the final notes of the cadence in bars 23–24 in syncopated positions in the canto and quinto in bars 31–32 if it were literal. To avoid this, Ferretti reduces the length of the problematic notes to minims in the repeat. Details like this demonstrate that composers were sometimes aware of the theoretical *tactus*-units even when those units have no audible role in the rhythm of a piece.

The villanesca and villanella differ only slightly in basic mensural norms from Rore's earliest madrigals in C, but their rhythmic character is worlds apart from Rore's complex and subtle madrigal style.[1] Gasparo Fiorino's *Ancor che col partir* (Example 14.2), a parody of Rore's famous madrigal, illustrates these differences. Fiorino transforms Rore's flexible rhythmic shapes into a square form with a pronounced accent on every minim. In the opening phrase (bars 1–2), he reduces the note values to half and arranges the imitation in a way that avoids both the conflict between agogic

---

[1] The use of the sign C for pieces with a minim compositional *tactus* appeared around the same time (the late 1530s) in both the madrigal and the villanesca, but it is unclear whether or not there was any historical connection between the two. Haar, "The *Note Nere* Madrigal," 29–30, suggests that the rhythms associated with "black notes" in the two genres are so different that there may not be any relation between them.

Example 14.1 Giovanni Ferretti, *Dolce mi saria*: (a) bars 21–24; (b) bars 29–32. After Ferretti, *Il secondo libro delle canzoni alla napolitana a cinque voci* (Venice: Scotto, 1569).

and mensural accents and the conflicting accents in different voices in Rore's madrigal (cf. Example 13.7). In bars 9–13, the absence of regular semibreve-units in the villanella eliminates the possibility of the shifting relations between agogic and mensural accents that give Rore's theme its expressive character (cf. Example 13.9). In bars 14–17, Fiorino begins the motive with the words "gli ritorni miei" in the same way that Rore does, but continues with a simple series of minims imitated in syncopation, rather than expanding some of the notes into longer values and mixing syncopated and non-syncopated notes in individual voices (cf. Example 13.9).

The rhythms of villanescas and villanellas are composed predominantly of minims, semiminims, and dotted semiminims with *fusae*. Short groups of *fusae* appear occasionally in melismas, and in rare cases with separate

Example 14.2 Gasparo Fiorino, *Ancor che col partir*. After Fiorino, *La nobilità di Roma* (Venice: Scotto, 1571). The repeat signs indicate the repeat of the preceding section only, even though the double dots appear on both sides of the double bar. The repeated concluding section begins at the long vertical bar through each staff, which is not in exactly the same place in every voice.

syllables of text. The penultimate notes of cadences are normally minims (with semiminim suspensions, if any); final notes of cadences may fall on any minim *initium*. The principal source of rhythmic variety is the constantly shifting grouping of minims. These shifts have a different effect from irregular groups of minims in madrigals, because they are not anchored by any tension against audible semibreve-units, but free-floating and unpredictable. Modern editors normally bar villanescas and villanellas in irregular units, as they must do in order to make sense of the music. The barring in my examples is in regular semibreves; it is meant to illustrate the contrast between mensuration and rhythmic grouping, not to suggest that the mensural units necessarily have any relation to the rhythm on levels higher than the minim. In some examples, wedges above the staves mark logical rhythmic groups.

Willaert's *O bene mio* (Example 14.3) provides a simple example in which the grouping shifts from an obvious ternary pattern to an equally obvious binary one. The transition is effected through a semibreve that is syncopated with respect to both groupings (bar 26). As shown by the wedges above the staff in Example 14.3, I believe the syncopation is meant to be heard as such. In her edition of the piece, Donna Cardamone places a barline before that semibreve, rather than in the middle of it, implying a change of grouping, rather than a syncopation.[2] There are no theoretical criteria for distinguishing between her interpretation and mine, but the choice makes a difference in the way the rhythm would be performed and perceived. The mensuration sign in this piece is ₵, but the rhythmic style is the same as that of pieces signed C in the same book.

Semiminims, as well as minims, may be grouped irregularly in villanescas and villanellas. Since the mensural pairing of semiminims is always audible, however, these irregular groups pull against the minim compositional *tactus* and create a very different effect from irregular groups of minims. They appear most often in the form of 3+3 semiminims in place of 2+2+2. This rhythmic cliché is common before cadences, where the rhythm leading to the cadence may be either 3+3+2 or 3+3+2+2 semiminims, but it may also appear elsewhere within phrases. The anonymous *O faccia che rallegra* (Example 14.4) places ternary groups of semiminims at the beginnings of the A and B sections and follows them with ternary groups of minims, creating hemiola against the three-semiminim groups. The beginning of the

---

[2] Adrian Willaert and His Circle, *Canzone villanesche alla napolitana and villotte*, ed. Donna G. Cardamone, Recent Researches in the Music of the Renaissance 30 (Madison, WI: A-R Editions, c1978), 22. The bar numbers in Cardamone's edition are different from those in my example.

Example 14.3 Adrian Willaert, *O bene mio*, bars 20–33. After Willaert, *Canzone villanesche a quatro voci* (Venice: Gardane, 1545).

C section alternates binary and ternary groups of minims; the three-semiminim groups return in the passage immediately before the final cadence. It is difficult to bar this piece in semibreve-units even for purposes of illustration, since the second statements of both sections, which are notated with repeat signs, would be displaced with respect to the mensural semibreve-units if they were written out, but I have made the attempt in order to show just how irrelevant the semibreve-units can be to the rhythmic organization of a villanella.

Passages in which the compositional *tactus* rises briefly to the level of the semibreve are uncommon in villanescas and villanellas (especially those for three voices), but they are found occasionally. Nola's *O dolce vita mia* (Example 14.5) includes an amusing example, complete with a minim suspension (bar 19) to confirm the semibreve compositional *tactus*.

Example 14.4 Anonymous, *O faccia che rallegra*. After *Il terzo libro delle villotte alla napolitana . . . a tre voci* (Venice: Gardano, 1560). The notation of the repeats is the same as in Example 14.2.

[Musical score for three voices: C (Cantus), T (Tenor), B (Bassus), setting the text "O faccia che rallegra il paradiso, O occhi ch'illustrate la mia vita, Porgetimi di gratia qual ch'a i ta."]

Given the freedom in the grouping of minims and the superficial or nonexistent role of the semibreve-units in villanesca and villanella rhythms, one may question whether the conventional sign C has any meaning at all in these genres. At the very least, the sign indicates that all notes are to be read as imperfect and implies that the mensural groupings are not exclusively ternary. Beyond that, its significance may be understood as an extension of the new meaning assigned to it in the *note nere* madrigal, where it designates a semibreve theoretical *tactus* and a minim compositional *tactus*. The minim compositional *tactus* applies to the villanesca and villanella in the

Example 14.5 Gian Domenico del Giovane da Nola, *O dolce vita mia*, bars 13–20. After Nola, *Canzone villanesche a tre voci novamente ristampate, libro secundo* (Venice: Gardane, 1545).

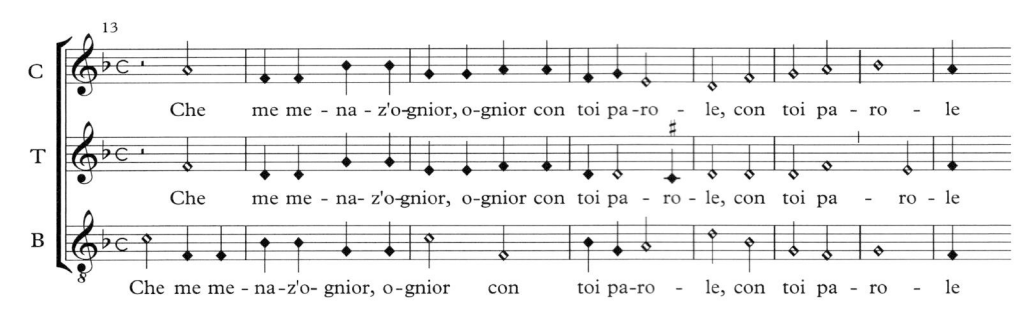

same way that it does to the *note nere* madrigal, but the semibreve theoretical *tactus* is reduced to an inaudible formality that may be jettisoned altogether when repeats are notated schematically with repeat signs. The fact that composers took the trouble to make their music conform to the semibreve theoretical *tactus* at all when they wrote out repeats is testimony to the importance that they placed on theoretical mensural structures.

As the largest time unit that has any meaningful role in the music, the minim must function as the performance *tactus* in these pieces. Considering the simplicity and low status of the villanesca and villanella, it is not surprising that theorists almost never bothered to mention the existence of this *tactus*. The character of the works suggests a lively tempo, surely faster than that of contemporaneous madrigals in C that feature more somber texts and more complex polyphony. If the mensuration sign were primarily an indicator of tempo, ¢ would be more appropriate to the villanesca and villanella than C, but ¢ implies a principal compositional *tactus* on the semibreve (except where it appears erroneously or arbitrarily) and would therefore be inappropriate for pieces like these.

The canzonetta

The term "canzonetta" appears for the first time as a genre designation in Orazio Vecchi's first book of *Canzonette a 4*, which was published shortly before 1580.[3] The genre is associated with a distinctive musical style that

---

[3] The first edition is lost. The second edition appeared in 1580, and the first was probably not much earlier.

resembles the villanella in its light-hearted character, strophic form, and internal stanza forms, but borrows techniques from the madrigal to match the music closely to the declamation, syntax, and meaning of the words of the first stanza. The classic scoring of the canzonetta is four voices, usually with three of them in high tessituras, but the canzonetta style was also applied to pieces for three, five, and six voices. Pieces in canzonetta style for three voices are often called "villanellas," and those for five or six voices are sometimes called "canzoni." Other genre terms are also applied to this repertoire.

The minim is the primary compositional *tactus* in the canzonetta style, but the semibreve plays a more important role than it does in the villanesca and villanella. Although entire sections of canzonettas are sometimes displaced by a minim when they are repeated, passages in which the compositional *tactus* rises to the level of the semibreve for expressive purposes are not unusual, and the semibreve-units of the mensuration are often audible even where the compositional *tactus* is the minim. Rests conform to the semibreve-units, and complete pieces have whole numbers of semibreve-units.

The most important innovation in the rhythm of the canzonetta is that groups of two or four *fusae* often carry separate syllables of text. Rhythmic patterns such as a semiminim followed by two *fusae*, or a semiminim upbeat followed by four *fusae*, all with separate syllables of text, contribute to the lively and strongly accentual character of canzonetta rhythms. The articulation of two levels of subdivision of the minim increases the emphasis on the minim *initia*. Perhaps for this reason, irregular groups of minims and semiminims are less common in the canzonetta than they are in the villanesca and villanella.[4]

The standard mensuration sign for canzonettas is C, which has the same mensural meaning that it does in the madrigal: a theoretical semibreve *tactus* and minim compositional *tactus* that may rise at times to the level of the semibreve. By the late sixteenth century, however, the distinction between C and ¢ in the madrigal had become sufficiently subtle that the signs were sometimes applied haphazardly in both madrigals and canzonettas. Sixteen of Vecchi's ninety four-voice canzonettas are signed ¢ in their first editions, although there is no difference between the rhythms of those pieces and the ones that are signed C except in one piece (*Fa una Canzone senza note nere*). Three pieces have the sign C in some voices and ¢ in others (but no duple proportion between them), and one has ¢ at the beginning, then C canceling a *sesquialtera* sign later on.

---

[4] On the role of texted *fusae* in the transformation of rhythmic style around 1580, see Ruth I. DeFord, "The Evolution of Rhythmic Style in Italian Secular Music of the Late Sixteenth Century," *Studi musicali* 10 (1981), 43–74.

Example 14.6 illustrates the typical rhythms of the canzonetta style. Its first stanza is as follows:

Mentre io campai contento	While I lived content
Correvano li giorni piu che 'l vento,	The days ran faster than the wind,
Et mò ch'io vivo in pene,	*And now that I live in pain,*
Dura mill'anni il giorno amaro mene.	*A day lasts a thousand years, poor me.*

The semibreve-units are established at the beginning (a common, but not obligatory, feature), but the principal rate of contrapuntal motion shifts to the minim by the third bar. Semibreve-units are made audible in the concluding section by the imitation at the semibreve interval in bars 11–14, the semibreve in the canto in bar 13, and the placement of the accented syllable of "giorno" on semibreve *initia* when the word is set to two minims, but they function as a background to the more prominent activity on the minim level. The rhythms with texted *fusae*, including the group of four in bar 5 and the pairs that follow semiminims in bars 8–14, place distinct accents on the minim *initia*. Rhythm not only contributes to the generally bright mood of the piece (making it clear that the pains in the text are not to be taken seriously), but also depicts the literal meaning of the second line of the poem in the spirit of the madrigal. The word "correvano" ("ran") is set to fast notes, and the idea of running away faster than the wind is portrayed by the chopped-off phrase ending on a semiminim-max *initium* in bar 6. This example and the following one are pieces in which one of the voices has the sign ¢ for no reason other than carelessness or indifference.

Semibreve-units are sometimes articulated in canzonettas in ways that create a larger context for the minim compositional *tactus*, but do not shift the *tactus* to the semibreve. The most common technique for accomplishing this is to combine motion in minims or semibreves in one voice with short, fast motives in the other voices. In Example 14.7, a bass line in semibreves undergirds rapid-fire imitation of a motive with texted *fusae* at the interval of a minim. The compositional *tactus* moves to the semibreve only in the penultimate bar, where the suspension lasts for a minim. In passages like this, the clear, hierarchical articulation of values from the *fusa* to the semibreve generates energy through strong and predictable accents and eliminates irregular elements entirely.

Vecchi sometimes uses unusual rhythms to capture distinctive ideas in the texts of his canzonettas. He was probably the author of most of his

Example 14.6 Orazio Vecchi, *Mentre io campai contento*. After Vecchi, *Canzonette . . . libro primo a quattro voci* (Venice: Gardano, 1580). The repeats are written out in the source. Repeat signs are used in the example to save space.

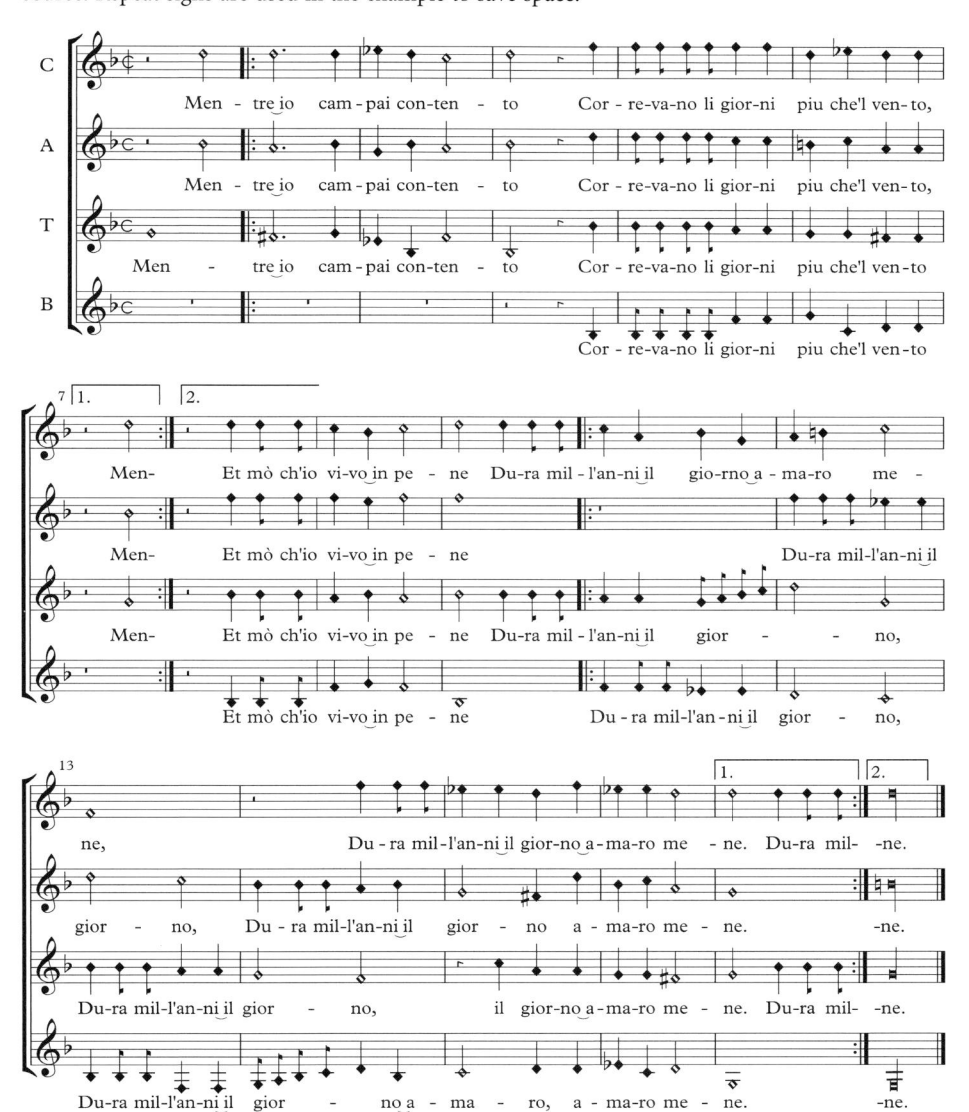

canzonetta texts.[5] It is hard to imagine that anyone other than the composer could have invented the texts that function primarily as vehicles for clever,

---

[5] This hypothesis is discussed in the introduction to Orazio Vecchi, *The Four-Voice Canzonettas*, ed. Ruth I. DeFord, 2 vols., Recent Researches in the Music of the Renaissance 92–93 (Madison, WI: A-R Editions, c1993), I: 3.

Example 14.7 Orazio Vecchi, *Se da le treccie mie*, bars 13–19. After Vecchi, *Canzonette ... libro quarto a quattro voci* (Venice: Gardano, 1590).

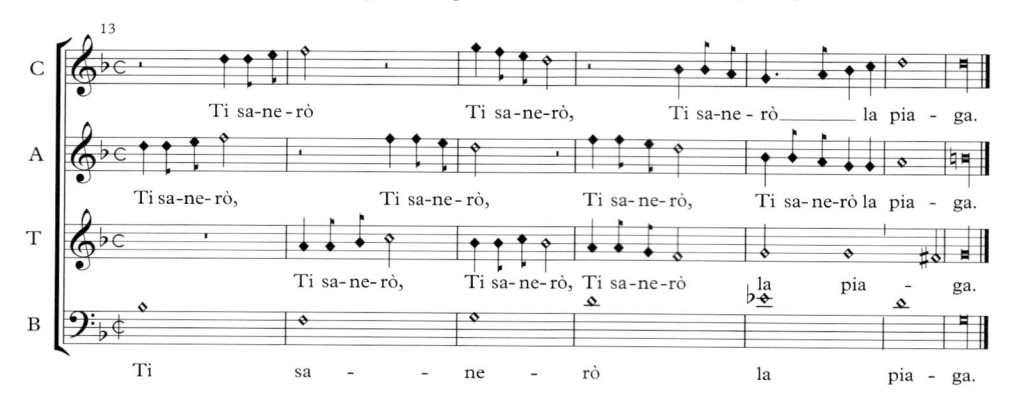

self-referential compositional ideas like those in these pieces. One such text is *Fa una Canzone senza note nere* (Example 14.8), which pokes fun at some of the serious rhythmic ideas discussed in this book and then proceeds to illustrate its points in the music. The text is as follows:

Fa una Canzone senza note nere	Make a song without black notes
Se mai bramasti la mia gratia havere.	If you ever wished to have my favor.
Falla d'un tuono ch'invita al dormire,	*Make it in a mode that invites one to sleep,*
Dolcemente facendola finire.	*Finishing it softly.*
Per entro non vi spargere durezze,	Don't put dissonances into it,
Che le mie orecchie non vi sono avezze.	Because my ears are not used to them.
Falla ...	*Make it ...*
Ne vi far cifra ò segno contra segno;	Don't put in numbers or signs against signs;
Sopra ogni cosa quest'è 'l mio disegno.	Above all, this is my intention.
Falla ...	*Make it ...*
Con questo stile il fortunato Orfeo	With this style fortunate Orpheus
Proserpina la giù placar poteo;	Was able to placate Proserpina in the depths.

Questo è lo stile che quetar già feo *This is the style that quieted*
Con dolcezza à Saul lo spirto reo. *Sweetly the evil spirit in Saul.*

The "black notes" in the opening line are the semiminims and *fusae* of the *note nere* madrigal. The "numbers" in stanza 3 are proportion signs, and "signs against signs" are combinations of simultaneous, contrasting mensurations. Both were symbols of learnedness in serious music, and both had the potential to be abused as a means of showing off without adding anything of substance to a piece. (The bizarre signs in some of the verses of Isaac's *Choralis Constantinus*, for which the composer was probably not responsible, are the ultimate examples of this.) Vecchi avoids black notes entirely in this piece. He works with lively, irregular groups of minims, dividing the eight minims in the second and third bars into 3+3+2 in each of the first two phrases. The first phrase is shown in Example 14.8a. The same grouping recurs just before the final cadence (Example 14.8b).

The sign ¢ in this piece is to be taken seriously. The primary compositional *tactus* is the semibreve, and the contrapuntal motion is often in breves. The tempo must be very quick. An undivided breve *tactus* brings out the rhythms effectively. The 3+3 groupings pull against it in a way that resembles hemiola rhythms in perfect mensurations. That *tactus* runs into a problem at the end of the B section, however, because regular measurement in breves causes the last note (a semibreve) to fall on a breve *initium* and leads to a semibreve displacement of the music with respect to the breve *tactus* in the repeat. Given

Example 14.8 Orazio Vecchi, *Fa una Canzone senza note nere*: (a) bars 1–4; (b) bars 13–19. After Vecchi, *Canzonette . . . libro secondo a quattro voci* (Venice: Gardano, 1581).

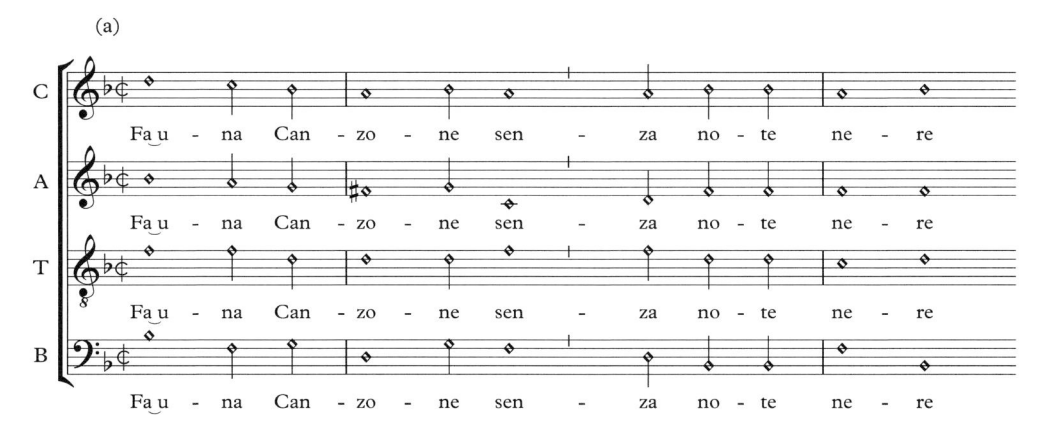

Example 14.8 (cont.)

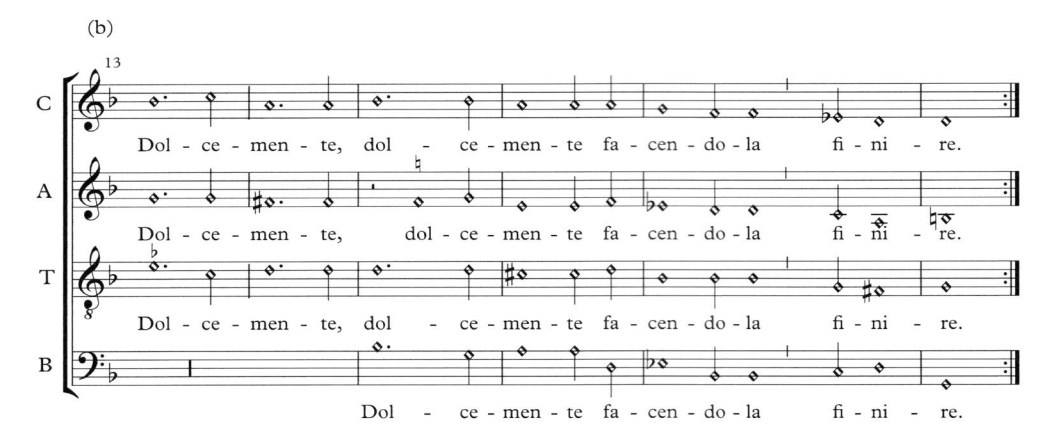

(b) [musical score with four voices C, A, T, B, measure 13, text: "Dol-ce-men-te, dol-ce-men-te fa-cen-do-la fi-ni-re."]

the prominent role of the breve-units in the music, such a displacement is musically impossible. The performance *tactus* must be reduced to the semibreve on the final note, or perhaps the last three semibreve-units of the section, to avoid the displacement. The latter option adds to the liveliness of the conclusion and avoids a chopped-off effect on the last note.

Vecchi uses rhythm to play with the sense of his text in a different way in *Fammi una Canzonetta capriciosa* (Example 14.9). The first stanza is as follows:

Fammi una Canzonetta capriciosa	Make me a capricious Canzonetta
Che nullo o pochi la sappian cantare,	That none or few know how to sing,
E al tuon di quella si possi ballare.	And to its sound one can dance.

The composer trips up the singers in the second line (Example 14.9a) by shifting the compositional *tactus* to the semiminim – something that happens nowhere else in his compositions – in order to make the song literally one that none or few know how to sing. The texted *fusae* are not simply subdivisions of semiminims set to repeated notes or stepwise figures, as in his other canzonettas, but essential melody notes that often move by skip. Rather than being limited to groups of four within a minim-unit or pairs on the second half of a minim-unit, they are placed freely in relation to the semiminim-units. Semiminims are syncopated in the way that minims normally are in the canzonetta style. The rhythms are nearly impossible to perform without articulating semiminims, probably as distinct subdivisions

Example 14.9 Orazio Vecchi, *Fammi una Canzonetta capriciosa*: (a) bars 9–13; (b) bars 14–17. After Vecchi, *Canzonette . . . libro secondo a quattro voci* (Venice: Gardano, 1581).

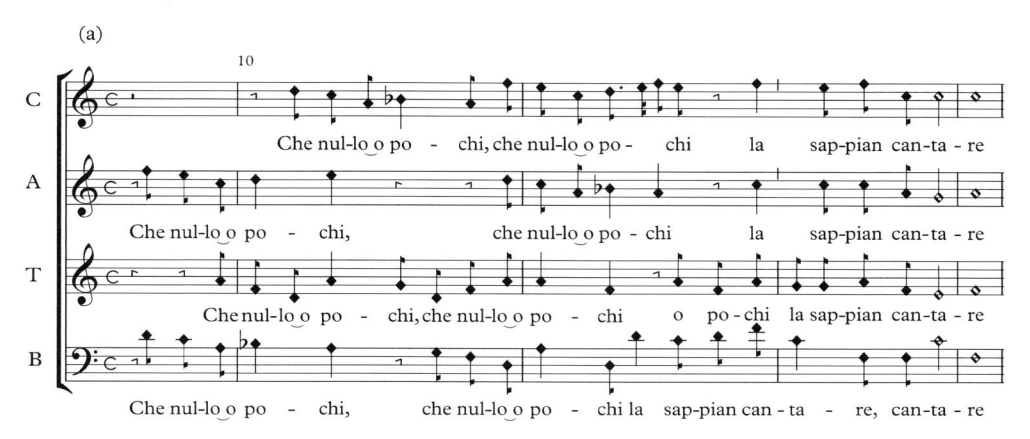

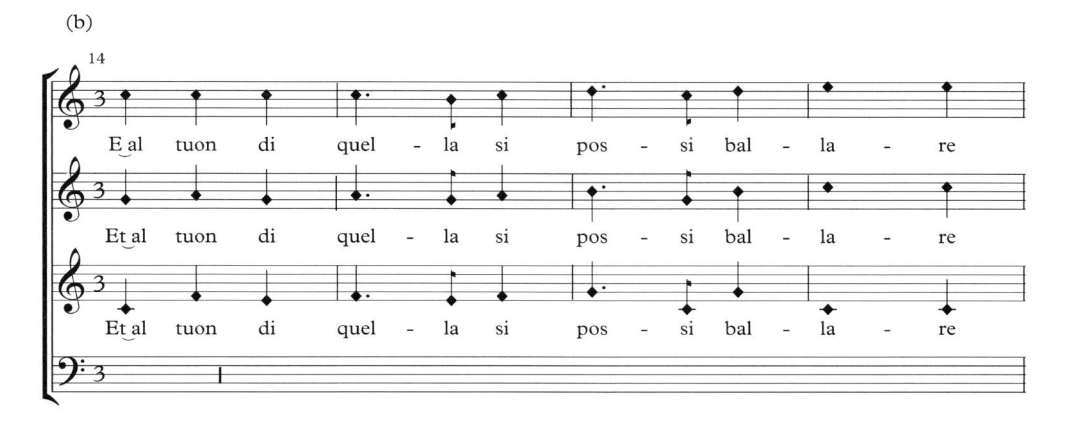

of a minim performance *tactus*. These rhythms are amusing in relation to the words of the other stanzas as well. In stanza 2, the tricky syncopations interpret "Che questo è meglio che tu possi fare" ("For this is the best you can do") [probably not very well], and in stanza 3, the awkwardly fast motion interprets "E affretta il corso col bel solfeggiare" ("And speed up the step with the beautiful sol-fa"). The strange rhythms of line 2 take on a further ironic twist in relation to the refrain ("And to its sound one can dance"; Example 14.9b), which is set to a simple, lilting *sesquialtera*. One could indeed dance to the refrain, but not to the preceding music, although the words claim that the whole piece is a dance song.

The galliard and songs with galliard-like rhythms

Instrumental dances such as the galliard, the most popular triple-meter dance from *c.* 1530 to the end of the century, and some instrumentally accompanied songs in dance-like styles sometimes observe notational conventions that are quite different from those of vocal music. Notational practices in these repertoires were much less standardized than those in the genres that were transmitted as all-vocal polyphony, even though all genres could be performed as accompanied vocal solos or instrumental arrangements.

The rhythm of galliards is organized in groups of six beats, sometimes preceded by upbeats. The primary grouping is 3+3, but 2+2+2 hemiola rhythms are common. The associated dance steps follow a six-beat pattern consisting of four short steps and a leap on the fifth beat. Because of the dance function, the rhythms are strongly articulated in the music. The beats of the galliard are most often represented as minims, but they appear occasionally as semibreves or semiminims. The mensuration signs may be C3 or 3, as in contemporaneous vocal music with rhythms in groups of three minims, or it may be C or ₵, or there may be no sign at all, although mensuration signs were regularly used in vocal music of the time. In lute and keyboard tablatures, vertical lines resembling modern barlines in appearance are often used to align the parts visually. Sometimes these lines, which Daniel Heartz calls "division lines,"[6] divide groups of three minims that coincide with the rhythms of the music, but sometimes they divide three-minim groups that begin with upbeats (and therefore fail to coincide with the groups defined by the rhythm and cadences), groups of four minims that have nothing to do with the rhythm of the music, or irregular time units that are likewise unrelated to the rhythm. A complete survey of these practices is beyond the scope of this book, but a few examples will give some sense of the range of possibilities.

Pierre Attaingnant published three collections containing galliards in 1530 and 1531: *Six gaillardes et six pavanes avec treze chansons musicales* (1529/1530) for ensemble, *Dixhuit basses dances garnies de recoupes et tordions* ... (1530) for lute, and *Quatorze gaillardes neuf pavannes sept branles et deux basses dances* (1531) for keyboard. The galliards in *Six gaillardes* and *Dixhuit basses dances* are notated in groups of three minims

---

[6] This term is used in the introduction to *Keyboard Dances from the Earlier Sixteenth Century*, ed. Daniel Heartz, Corpus of Early Keyboard Music 8 ([Rome]: American Institute of Musicology, 1965), xiii.

or three semibreves. Those in *Six gaillardes* have no division lines, since the publication is in partbooks. Those in *Dixhuit basses dances* usually have lines marking groups of three minims in conformity with the rhythm, though some of them have no lines. Breves are perfect in *Six gaillardes*. It is impossible to tell whether or not semibreves are perfect in the lute galliards, because the tablature notation shows only the shortest rhythmic values, and there are no notes as long as a perfect semibreve in all voices. (The transcription is a reconstruction of the polyphony; it cannot be derived directly from the tablature, which shows the point of attack, but not the duration, of each note.)

Some of the lute galliards in *Dixhuit basses dances* are arrangements of ensemble galliards from *Six gaillardes*. In those pieces, the principal melody, labeled *subjectum*, is written out separately following the tablature. The *subjecta* are signed ₵3 or 3 and written in groups of three semibreves, so that their notated values are twice as large as those of the lute arrangements to which they correspond. Breves in the *subjecta* are perfect unless imperfected. Example 14.10 is an anonymous ensemble galliard, and Example 14.11 is a lute arrangement of it by P[ierre] B[londeau] that illustrates these principles.[7]

Example 14.10 Anonymous, Gaillard no. 4, bars 1–9. After *Six gaillardes et six pavanes* ... (Paris: Attaingnant, 1529/1530). The use of coloration is inconsistent in the source. All of the notes in bars 3 and 7 should be black, and all of the rest should be white.

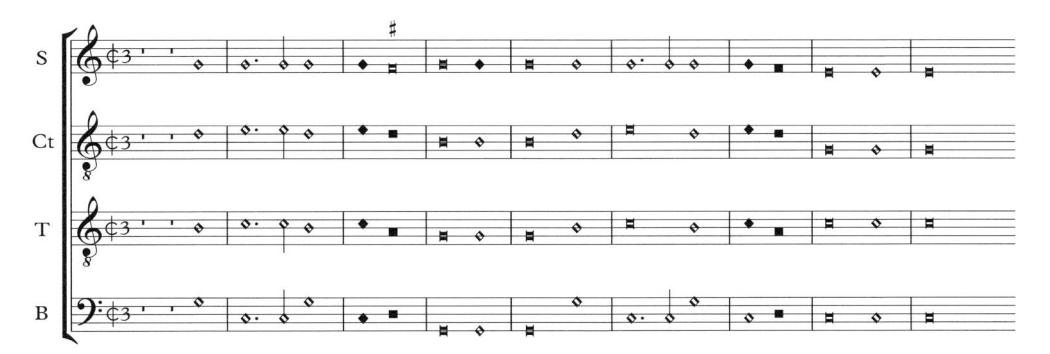

---

[7] On the identity of Pierre Blondeau, see the introduction to *Preludes, Chansons and Dances for Lute, Published by Pierre Attaingnant, Paris (1529–30)*, ed. Daniel Heartz (Neuilly-sur-Seine, France: Société de Musique d'Autrefois, 1964), lv–lxii. Example 14.11 is modeled on the edition of the piece ibid., 107.

Example 14.11 P[ierre] B[londeau], Gaillard, bars 1–9. After *Dixhuit basses dances* ... (Paris: Attaingnant, 1529), fols. xxxiii^v–xxxiiii^r.

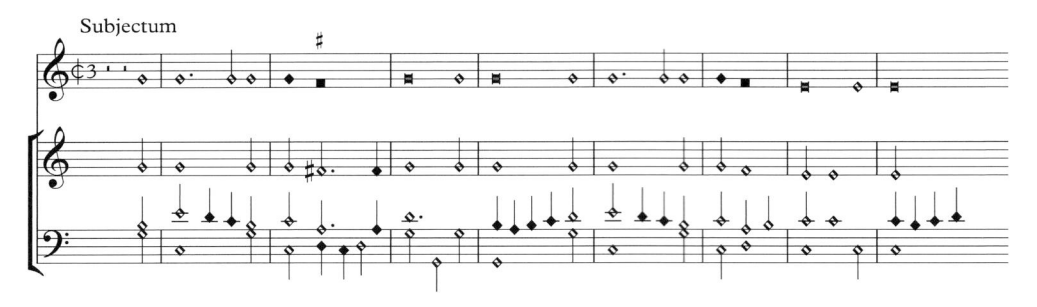

Example 14.12 Anonymous, Gaillard, bars 1–4. After Attaingnant, *Quatorze gaillardes* (Paris: Attaingnant, 1531), fol. 32^v.

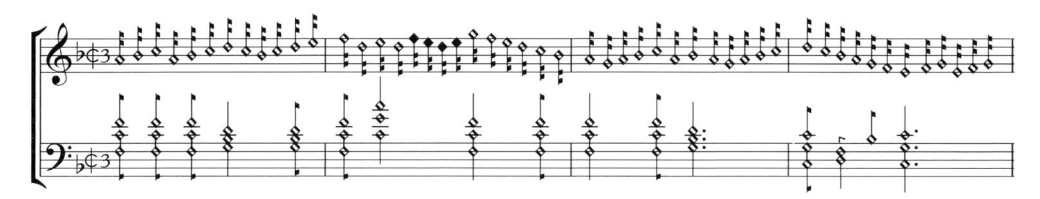

Attaingnant's *Quatorze gaillardes* for keyboard illustrate yet another approach to the notation of galliard rhythms. The pieces have signatures of ¢3 or 3, but the beat corresponds to the semiminim. Division lines divide groups of six semiminims. Despite the mensuration signs and ternary rhythms, there are no perfect notes (as there almost always are in vocal pieces with the same mensuration signs), because minims cannot be perfect. Notes lasting for three semiminim beats are notated as dotted minims, as in modern $\frac{3}{4}$ time. Values range from the dotted minim to the *demisemifusa* (not shown in the example), a note not even acknowledged in contemporaneous theory. Semiminims and *fusae* are written in white flagged forms, and smaller values are black (see Example 14.12). In one piece, the division lines are out of phase with the ternary rhythmic groups from the point of a counting error to the end of the piece.[8]

Galliards for keyboard are also found in the *Intabolatura nova di varie sorte de balli ... libro primo* published by Antonio Gardane in 1551. In those pieces, the rhythms consist of ternary groups of minims, but the mensuration sign is ¢ and the division lines group sets of four minims, as if the sign

---

[8] *Keyboard Dances from the Earlier Sixteenth Century*, no. 25, p. 30.

Example 14.13 Anonymous, *Cathacchio Gagliarda*, bars 1–6. After *Intabolatura nova di varie sorte de balli da sonare* (Venice: Gardane, 1551), fol. 4ʳ.

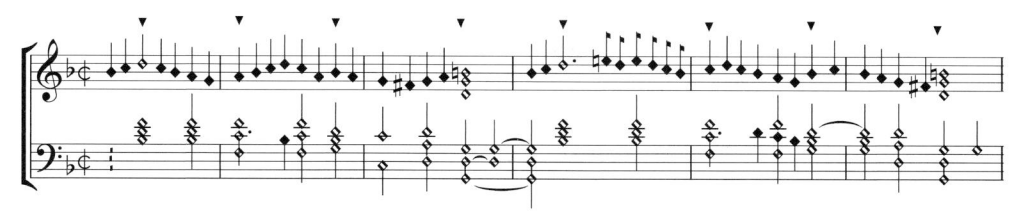

had the same meaning that it usually does in vocal music (see Example 14.13). This practice forces many notes that conform regularly to the rhythm to be written with ties. A reader of the notation would be able to make sense of it only by ignoring the division lines – a challenge that is not overly difficult given the simplicity and regularity of the rhythms. The sign ₵ represents binary mensuration in the sense that no notes are perfect and notes worth three minims must be written as dotted semibreves or semibreves tied to minims (depending on where they appear in relation to the division lines), but it indicates nothing about *tactus* or rhythmic grouping. It may have been chosen to avoid the need for coloration, which would sometimes be required in hemiola, but was not a standard feature of tablature notation.

The issue of *tactus* in both the compositional and the performance sense is less clear in galliards than it is in most vocal music. The harmonic rhythm moves in three-beat groups with hemiolas against pairs of those groups, suggesting a compositional *tactus*, and perhaps a performance *tactus*, on the three-beat group, however it is notated. The dance steps, however, articulate each of the three beats, and the leap on the fifth beat of a group of six suggests a consistent hemiola relation to the three-beat groups of the music.[9] A performance *tactus* on each note of the three-beat group is therefore also a possibility. The principles of dissonance treatment are different from what they are in vocal music, because ornamentation patterns use dissonance quite freely, but dissonances do not normally last as long as a third of a ternary unit (however it is notated), as they often do in vocal music with the *tactus* on a perfect note.

Songs of popular character that feature prominent, and occasionally exclusive, ternary rhythmic organization are sometimes likewise notated

---

[9] The complex issue of matching the dance steps to the music in extant choreographies from the sixteenth century is discussed in Yvonne Kendall, "Rhythm, Meter, and *Tactus* in 16th-Century Italian Court Dance: Reconstruction from a Theoretical Base," *Dance Research* 8 (1990), 3–27.

in C or ₵. Where the ternary groups are not consistent throughout a piece, the reason for the choice of sign is clear. In sixteenth-century practice, the only way to notate shifting rhythmic groups in which the minim remains constant is to write all of them under a single sign. Signs of binary mensuration were standard in such cases, because ternary signs implied consistent ternary rhythms.

In Example 14.14, a frottola by Marco Cara arranged for voice and lute by Francesco Bossinensis, the mensuration is ₵. As in Example 14.13, division lines mark groups of four minims in the lute part even though those groups have nothing to do with the rhythm of the piece. The primary rhythmic groups consist of three semibreves, with groups of three minims set against them at the beginnings of phrases (Example 14.14a), but the grouping of semibreves in the concluding section (Example 14.14b) is irregular. There are eleven semibreves from the final cadence of the main body of the song (bar 18, beat 1) to the last note of the melody (bar 23, beat 2), then six more semibreves preceding the final note of the *supplementum* that extends the final cadence (bars 23–26). If the piece were notated in perfect *tempus*, the mensuration would not conform to the rhythmic groupings in the concluding section, and both the last note of the melody and the last note of the *supplementum* would fall on the second semibreve *initium* of a perfect breve-unit. Those points also correspond to the second semibreve *initia* of the artificial binary groups of semibreves marked by the division lines in the lute part. The sign ₵ in this case means simply that the compositional *tactus* is the semibreve and implies nothing about how the semibreves are grouped rhythmically, even in the abstract.

Example 14.14 Marco Cara, *Io non compro piu speranza*, arranged by Francesco Bossinensis: (a) bars 1–6; (b) bars 18–26. After Bossinensis, *Tenori e contrabassi intabulati col sopran in canto figurato ... libro primo* ([Venice: Petrucci, 1509]), fols. xxxiiii[r]–xxxiiii[v].

Example 14.14 (cont.)

(b)

[musical notation with text: -ti - a, Che gli-è fal - sa mer - can - ci - - - - - - - - a.]

Dances and songs in which partially or consistently ternary rhythms are notated in binary mensurations have played a significant role in promoting the myth that mensuration in general has nothing to do with rhythmic organization in fifteenth- and sixteenth-century music. These pieces, however, belong to distinct traditions with rhythmic styles and notational conventions that differ from those of the more polyphonic vocal genres of their time. Although the relation between mensuration and rhythm in vocal music is often complex, pieces like some of the examples in this chapter are the only ones in the repertoires discussed in this book in which the notated mensuration is in some cases truly irrelevant to the rhythmic structure of the music.

Conclusion

The theoretical views, rhythmic styles, and notational conventions discussed in this book are extraordinarily diverse. Nevertheless, some general principles apply to them as a group. They are summarized below.

Tactus

(1) The term "tactus" has three primary meanings: (i) the physical motion that measures time in performance, or the unit of time corresponding to that motion (performance *tactus*); (ii) the unit of time that governs the contrapuntal structure of a piece (compositional *tactus*); (iii) the unit of time associated with a mensuration sign in music theory (theoretical *tactus*). These definitions do not always apply to the same value in a particular piece. Some of the apparent contradictions among *tactus* theories, as well as seemingly contradictory statements about the subject in a single source, result from uses of the term in different senses.

(2) Most pieces have a primary compositional *tactus* that can be identified through analysis of the music. That value may shift temporarily to adjacent larger or smaller values within a piece. Two adjacent values occasionally share the function of compositional *tactus* equally.

(3) The compositional *tactus* is always audible. When two values share that function, both are audible. Rhythms are regularly syncopated against the compositional *tactus*, but they do not obscure it. When the compositional *tactus* shifts to a smaller level, however, the larger level to which it applied previously may become inaudible.

(4) The audibility of the compositional *tactus* does not depend on dynamic accent or other forms of emphasis in performance. The beginnings of the *tactus*-units carry an implicit accent because of the compositional principles that apply to them. This accent may vary from pronounced to subtle, but it is always a factor in the rhythmic design of compositions.

(5) The performance *tactus* may be either a unitary measure or one that is divided into two parts that are equal or unequal in length. The degree of emphasis on the subdivision (if any) may vary.

(6) The performance *tactus* normally corresponds to the compositional *tactus*, but an equally divided performance *tactus* may correspond to two compositional *tactus*. A divided performance *tactus* is especially appropriate when the compositional *tactus* is ambiguous or changes within a piece.

(7) There is sometimes a choice of which value to use as the performance *tactus*. In such cases, the choice may have a subtle effect on the way the rhythm is projected in performance. Placing the *tactus* on a smaller value will tend to emphasize rhythms on a smaller scale, and placing it on a larger value will encourage the projection of larger units of time. This choice is a matter of aesthetic judgment, not correct or incorrect interpretation.

(8) Groupings of *tactus* are flexible. When they are regular, they range from consistently audible to abstract and inaudible. Their audibility often varies within a piece.

(9) The theoretical concept of *tactus* changed over time. In the fifteenth century, it was equivalent to the primary compositional *tactus*; in the sixteenth, it was often equivalent to two compositional *tactus*. It is roughly equivalent to the modern concept of "beat" in the former sense and "bar" in the latter sense. This change allowed the theoretical *tactus* to maintain its association with the same value when changes in rhythmic style shifted the compositional *tactus* to the next shorter value under the most common signs.

(10) The duration of the *tactus* (i.e., the tempo) is not fixed. When the *tactus* changes within a piece, the relative durations of the two *tactus* are often ambiguous. There is no evidence for the view (once commonly held) that the *tactus* was associated with a single, fixed duration.

(11) Mensuration signs provide clues about the level of the compositional and/or performance *tactus* and the duration of the *tactus*, but they do not prescribe them reliably or unambiguously. Judgments about these matters must depend on analysis of the rhythm and character of particular pieces, not on theoretical formulas.

Mensuration

(1) Notated mensurations almost always correspond to real rhythmic structures. The only exceptions in the repertoires considered in this book are some triple-meter dances and songs in dance-like styles.

(2) Different levels of mensuration have different roles in the musical structure. The most prominent one is the one corresponding to the compositional *tactus*. Rhythmic groups may contradict the mensuration temporarily, but in the examples in this book, they never do so throughout an entire piece. Even in the exceptional cases where the rhythms under a binary sign are predominantly ternary, they entail some complications that are not typical of ternary mensurations.

(3) Mensural groupings are normally regular on levels up to the breve except in augmentation, where the semibreve may be the largest regular level, but the audibility of time units larger than the compositional *tactus* is variable. In the sixteenth century, the sign C came to signify a mensuration in which the semibreve was the largest regular unit.

(4) Levels of mensuration larger than those prescribed in the notation may play a role in the musical structure. They may be regular or irregular. Since they are not notated, they can be identified only through analysis of the music.

(5) Levels of mensuration above the compositional *tactus* often move in and out of audibility. When they are explicitly prescribed by the mensuration, they remain in phase with it when they are audible even if they have been inaudible for long enough that the listener may no longer be conscious of them. Shifts of larger mensural units between the foreground and the background of the rhythm are often an important part of the design of a composition.

Rhythm

(1) Like the rhythms of later periods, rhythms in the fifteenth and sixteenth century derive their musical interest and expressive power from the interaction between regular and irregular elements. Conflicts between them create tension that requires resolution.

(2) The regular time units that play meaningful roles in music cannot be determined solely by mensuration signs, but must be identified through analysis of all compositional factors that contribute to the perception of rhythm. Perceptible mensural regularities are created not by notation, but by compositional regularities that make them audible. Such regularities raise the expectation that deviations will be followed by a return to the established norms.

(3) The rhythms of fifteenth- and sixteenth-century music are as fascinating and as expressive as those of any other period. Past scholarship has too

often been preoccupied with the issues of tempo and the level of the *tactus* at the expense of deeper and more important aspects of rhythm. It is my hope that the analyses in this book will inspire similar studies of other repertoires. Such studies will broaden our understanding of the possibilities of rhythm and mensuration in the period and lead to a more complete picture of the information that mensural notation can provide.

Implications for editing

The conclusions of this study have implications for the editing and performance of the music under consideration, but they do not lead to simple formulas for making decisions about these issues. Editing involves decisions about such matters as the frequency and style of barlines, the level of reduction (if any) of note values, and principles of beaming. Judgments about these matters should depend on the nature of the music and the intended function of the edition. There are no ideal or universally valid ways of handling them.

Barlines are a practical necessity for aligning parts in a score. They should ideally separate regular mensural units that have a meaningful role in the music, but that ideal is not always feasible in practice. When a group of two or three compositional *tactus* is a meaningful unit of rhythm, it makes sense to use it as the basis for barring. This principle enables users of an edition to see where the rhythms conform to the mensuration and where they do not. When there are mensural regularities on larger levels, it is helpful to mark them editorially as well. When the compositional *tactus* is also the largest regular time unit in a piece, bars corresponding to it may be too short to make sense in a modern score. In that case, editors must choose between regular barring by pairs of *tactus* and irregular barring based on the rhythmic groups in the music. Neither is ideal, because the former is arbitrary and the latter may be subject to more than one reasonable interpretation.

Barlines through the staff necessitate numerous ties in a modern score. They are undesirable in that they place more visual emphasis on the regular mensural units and less on the irregular surface rhythms than the original notation does. Editors sometimes avoid ties by using *Mensurstriche* (lines between, rather than through, the staves) in place of barlines. Since *Mensurstriche* do not cut the staff, notes may extend past them without being written with ties. The main drawback of *Mensurstriche* is that they preclude the possibility of barring different voices independently, as is sometimes desirable when contrasting mensurations are combined. Another possibility is to separate bars with short line segments at the top and bottom of each staff. This approach solves the problems of both barlines and *Mensurstriche*, but it may be difficult to read and visually unpleasant.

Editors often reduce note values in order to make them easier for modern readers to grasp. This practice is helpful to many modern users, but it has several disadvantages. The original notation conveys information that goes beyond the literal representation of note durations, and people familiar with it can grasp that information more easily if the values are unreduced. A useful analogy is transposing the pitch level of a piece. Although the written notes do not have the same meaning that they do now with respect to absolute pitch, transposing a piece obscures the significance of the original pitches and accidentals, which have connotations that go beyond the representation of intervals.

Reduced values also create complications from the point of view of barring and beaming. If, for example, the largest regular time unit in a piece is the breve, it is no problem to bar a modern edition in breves if the values are unchanged, or perhaps even if they are reduced in 2:1 ratio (such that the breve becomes a modern whole note), but if they are reduced in 4:1 ratio, barring in modern half notes will make the bars in the edition look too short, while barring in modern whole notes gives the appearance of mensural regularity on a level where it does not exist. The beaming of eighth notes and smaller values creates similar problems. It requires the editor to choose between the mensural units and the rhythmic groups as a basis for beaming. The former principle emphasizes the beats more than the original notation does, while the latter obscures them in a way that the original notation does not. Readers of the original notation can group the notes visually in conformity with both the mensuration and the rhythmic groups, but a modern edition with beams forces a choice of one at the expense of the other. The greater the scale of reduction, the more notes require beams in a modern edition. This problem can be avoided almost entirely by retaining the original values in modern editions.

Proportions in which different notes are equated in different voices pose special problems for editors. They convey various meanings that are lost if editors reduce them to a common standard in an edition. It should not be impossible for modern users to grasp the point that, for example, a whole note in one voice equals a half note in another voice when the parts are aligned in score. An edition that preserves relationships of this type can call the user's attention to the significance of the proportional notation, whatever it may be in a particular case.

Although there are no one-size-fits-all rules for editing mensural notation, informed users of modern editions can profit from the observance of a few general principles. First, editions should always show the user what the original signs and note values were, whether or not they are retained in the edition. If there are changes of sign within a piece, that information should be provided in the score itself, not relegated to the critical notes. Second, original values should be preferred over reduced values if they do not reduce the clarity of the rhythms for the intended users. If values are reduced, the smallest practical scale of reduction should be preferred. Third, if note values are reduced, the scale of reduction should be consistent throughout an edition. Editors should not impose their views of the relative meanings of different signs by using different scales of reduction for different signs. Fourth, given the uncertainty surrounding tempo relationships among signs, editors should either avoid prescribing them or put them in brackets except in cases where the context leaves no room for doubt. Fifth, when it is feasible to bar the music in conformity with a unit of the mensuration that has a meaningful role in the rhythmic structure, that option should be preferred to barring in irregular units. When that option is not feasible or seems undesirable for some reason, editors must use judgment based on the nature of the music and the purpose of the edition.

Implications for performance

The conclusions of this study suggest considerations for performance interpretations, but do not prescribe fixed rules for them. Performers should understand the rhythmic features of individual works and not base their interpretations on general notions about the nature of "mensural music" or theoretical definitions of mensuration signs. They should be aware of the regular units of measure on all levels to which they apply and the ways in which rhythms both reinforce these units and work against them. They should aim for good balance in the projection of regular and irregular elements of rhythm in performance, but the nature of that balance in particular cases is a matter of aesthetic judgment.

The level and form of the performance *tactus* and the tempo should be chosen with the above principles in mind. Different values for the performance *tactus*, and different degrees of emphasis on its subdivision (if any), may encourage emphasis on different levels of the mensuration. Tempo may also influence the relative prominence of different mensural levels. Faster tempos may make the larger levels easier to perceive. In some cases, they may actually make the music sound slower (and heavier) by increasing the prominence of the longer time units.

None of these judgments can be reduced to formulas. Mensuration signs and theoretical advice can be useful inputs in performance decisions, but rhythm is too complex to reduce to a set of rules. Interpreting it will always be an art, not a science.

Bibliography

Early writings

Anonymous, *The Berkeley Manuscript: University of California Music Library, Ms. 744 (olim Phillipps 4450)*, ed. and trans. Oliver B. Ellsworth, Greek and Latin Music Theory (Lincoln: University of Nebraska Press, c1984).

Anonymous, [*Compendium breve artis musicae*], in Bernhold Schmid, "Ein Mensuralkompendium aus der Handschrift Clm 24809," in *Quellen und Studien zur Musiktheorie des Mittelalters*, ed. Michael Bernhard, Veröffentlichungen der musikhistorischen Kommission 8 (Munich: Bayerische Akademie der Wissenschaften; C. H. Beck, 1990), 71–75.

Anonymous, [*Compendium secundum famosiores musicos*], in Jill Palmer, "A Late Fifteenth-Century Anonymous Mensuration Treatise: (Ssp) Salzburg, Erzabtei St. Peter, a VI 44, 1490; cod pap. 206 × 149 mm. 75ff," *Musica disciplina* 39 (1985), 89–103.

Anonymous, *De vera et compendiosa seu regulari constructione contrapuncti*, in *Anonymi Tractatus de cantu figurativo et de contrapuncto (c. 1430–1520)*, ed. Christian Meyer, Corpus scriptorum de musica 41 (n.p.: American Institute of Musicology; Hänssler-Verlag, 1997), 58–65.

Anonymous, *Exposition of the Proportions, According to the Teaching of "Mestre Joan Violant" [Vaillant], the Teacher of Paris* (Florence, Biblioteca Nazionale, Magl. III,70), in Israel Adler, *Hebrew Writings Concerning Music*, RISM B IX 2 (Munich and Duisberg: G. Henle, 1975), 55–77.

Anonymous, *Institutio in musicen mensuralem* (Erfurt: Johann Knapp, 1513).

Anonymous, *The Pathway to Musicke* (London: [by J. Danter] for William Barley, 1596).

Anonymous, *Sequuntur alie regule cantus figurati sive mensurati* (Florence, Biblioteca Medicea Laurentiana, Plut. 29.48, fols. 113^v–120^v).

Anonymous, *Sequuntur proportiones* (Innsbruck, Universitätsbibliothek, Cod. 962, fols. 142^r–144^r), facsimile and ed. in Renate Federhofer-Königs, "Ein Beitrag zur Proportionenlehre in der zweiten Hälfte des 15. Jahrhunderts," in *Bence Szabolcsi Septuagenario*, ed. Dénes Bartha, Studia musicologica Academiae Scientiarum Hungaricae 11 (Budapest: Akadémiai Kiadó, 1969), 148–57.

Anonymous, *Tractatulus de cantu mensurali seu figurativo musice artis*, ed. F. Alberto Gallo, Corpus scriptorum de musica 16 ([Dallas, Texas]: American Institute of Musicology, 1971).

Anonymous, *Tractatulum prolationum cum tabulis*, in Ars cantus figurati, Antonius de Luca; Capitulum de quattuor mensuris, anonymus; Tractatulus mensurationum, anonymus; Compendium breve de proportionibus, anonymus; Tractatulus prolationum cum tabulis, anonymus, ed. Heinz Ristory, Corpus scriptorum de musica 38 (Neuhausen-Stuttgart: American Institute of Musicology; Hänssler-Verlag, 1997), 84–92.

Anonymous (attr. B. G. Frank), *Ein tütsche musica,* ed. Arnold Geering, 2 vols., Schriften der literarischen Gesellschaft Bern 9 (Bern: Herbert Lang, 1964).

Anonymous 5, *Ars cantus mensurabilis mensurata per modos iuris*, ed. and trans. C. Matthew Balensuela, Greek and Latin Music Theory 10 (Lincoln: University of Nebraska Press, 1994).

Anonymous 10, *De minimis notulis*, ed. Edmond de Coussemaker, *Scriptorum de musica medii aevi*, 4 vols. (Paris: Durand, 1864–76; repr. Hildesheim: Olms, 1963), III: 413–15.

Anonymous 11, [*Tractatus de musica plana et mensurabili*], in Richard J. Wingell, "Anonymous XI (CS III): An Edition, Translation, and Commentary," 3 vols. (Ph.D. diss., University of Southern California, 1973), I: 1–173.

Anonymous 12, *Tractatus et compendium cantus figurati*, ed. Jill M. Palmer, Corpus scriptorum de musica 35 (Neuhausen-Stuttgart: American Institute of Musicology; Hänssler-Verlag, 1990).

Aaron, Pietro, *Libri tres de institutione harmonica* (Bologna: Benedetto di Ettore, 1516; repr. New York: Broude Bros., 1978).

Lucidario in musica di alcune oppenioni antiche, et moderne con le loro oppositioni, et resolutioni (Venice: Girolamo Scotto, 1545; repr. New York: Broude, 1978).

Thoscanello de la musica (Venice: Bernardino & Matheo de Vitali, 1523; repr. [of 2nd edn., *Toscanello in musica*] Bologna: Forni, 1999).

Adam von Fulda, *Musica*, ed. Martin Gerbert, *Scriptores ecclesiastici de musica sacra potissimum*, 3 vols. (St. Blaise: Typis San-Blasianis, 1784; repr. Hildesheim: Olms, 1963), III: 359–66.

Agricola, Martin, *Musica figuralis deudsch* (Wittenberg: Georg Rhau, 1532; repr. Hildesheim and New York: Georg Olms, 1969).

Scholia in musicam planam Venceslai Philomatis (n.p., 1538).

Anselmi, Giorgio, *De musica*, ed. Giuseppe Massera, Historia musicae cultores, Bibliotheca 14 (Florence: Leo S. Olschki, 1961).

Antonius de Luca, *Ars cantus figurati*, in *Ars cantus figurati, Antonius de Luca; Capitulum de quattuor mensuris, anonymus; Tractatulus mensurationum, anonymus; Compendium breve de proportionibus, anonymus; Tractatulus prolationum cum tabulis, anonymus*, ed. Heinz Ristory, Corpus scriptorum de musica 38 (Neuhausen-Stuttgart: American Institute of Musicology; Hänssler-Verlag, 1997), 24–59.

Aranda, Matheo de, *Tractado de canto mensurable* (Lisbon: German Galharde, 1535).
Artusi, Giovanni Maria, *L'arte del contraponto* (Venice: Giacomo Vincenzi & Ricciardo Amadino, 1586; repr. Bologna: Forni, 1980).
Balbi, Marco Antonio, *Regula brevis musice practicabilis* (n.p., n.d.).
Banchieri, Adriano, *Cartella musicale nel canto figurato, fermo, et contrapunto*, 3rd edn. (Venice: Giacomo Vincenti, 1614; repr. Bologna: Forni, 1968).
Bathe, William, *A Briefe Introduction to the Skill of Song* (London: Thomas East, [1596?]; repr. Kilkenny, Ireland: Boethius Press, c1982).
  A Brief Introduction to the True Art of Music, ed. Cecil Hill, Critical Texts 10 (Colorado Springs: Colorado College Music Press, 1979).
Bermudo, Juan, *Declaración de instrumentos musicales* (Osuna: Juan de Leon, 1555; repr. Kassel: Bärenreiter, 1957).
Beurhaus, Friedrich, *Musicae erotematum libri duo* (Dortmund: Albert Sartorius, 1573; repr. Cologne: Arno Volk-Verlag, 1961).
Blahoslav, Jan, *Musica: to gest knjžka zpěwákům náležité zpráwy v sobě zavírající*, 2nd edn. (Ivančice, 1569), in Thomas Paul Sovik, "Music Theorists of the Bohemian Reformation: Translation and Critique of the Treatises of Jan Blahoslav and Jan Josquin" (Ph.D. diss., Ohio State University, 1985), 129–99.
Bogentantz, Bernhard, *Collectanea utriusque cantus* (Cologne, 1515).
Bourgeois, Loys, *Le droict chemin de musique* (Geneva: [Jean Gérard], 1550; repr. in *Renaissance française*, ed. Olivier Trachier [Courlay, France: J. M. Fuzeau, 2005], I: 49–112).
Buchner, Hans, *Fundamentbuch*, in Hans Buchner, *Sämtliche Orgelwerke*, vol. I, ed. Jost Harro Schmidt, Das Erbe deutscher Musik 54, Abteilung Orgel/Klavier/Laute 5 (Frankfurt: Henry Litolff's Verlag, 1974).
Burmeister, Joachim, *Musica autoschediastike* (Rostock: Christoph Reusner, 1601).
Burzio, Nicolo, *Musices opusculum* [= *Florum libellus*] (Bologna: Ugo Ruggeri, 1487; repr. Bologna: Forni, 1969).
Calvisius, Seth, *Exercitationes musicae duae* (Leipzig: Franz Schnellboltz, 1600).
Caza, Francesco, *Tractato vulgare de canto figurato* (Milan: G. P. de Lomazzo, 1492; repr. Berlin: M. Breslauer, 1922).
Cerone, Pietro, *El melopeo y maestro* (Naples: Juan Bautista Gargano & Lucrecio Nucci, 1613; repr. Bologna: Forni, 1969).
Cochlaeus, Johannes, *Compendium in praxim atque exercitium cantus figurabilis* ([Cologne: Johann Landen, 1507]).
  Musica, 3rd edn. (Cologne: Johann Landen, 1507).
  Tetrachordum musices (Nuremberg: Johann Weyssenburger, 1511; repr. Hildesheim: Olms, 1971).
Coclico, Adrian Petit, *Compendium musices* (Nuremberg: Johann Berg and Ulrich Neuber, 1552; repr. Kassel: Bärenreiter, 1954).
Dressler, Gallus, *Musicae practicae elementa* (Magdeburg: Wolfgang Kirchner, 1571).

Durán, Domingo Marcos, *Sumula de canto órgano, contrapunto y composicion* (Salamanca: [Giesser?], [*c.* 1504]; repr. Madrid: Joyas Bibliográficas, 1976).

Dygon, John, *Proportiones practicabiles secundum Gaffurium*, ed. and trans. Theodor Dumitrescu (Urbana and Chicago: University of Illinois Press, c2006).

Faber, Gregor, *Musices practicae erotematum libri II* (Basel: Heinrich Petri, 1553).

Faber, Heinrich, *Ad musicam practicam introductio* (Nuremberg: Johann Berg and Ulrich Neuber, 1550).

   Compendiolum musicae pro incipientibus ([Brunswick, 1548]; repr. [of 1594 edn.] Bologna: Forni, 1980).

Finck, Hermann, *Practica musica* (Wittenberg: Georg Rhaus Erben, 1556; repr. Bologna: Forni, 1969).

Florentius de Faxolis, *Liber musices* (= *Book on Music*), ed. and trans. Bonnie J. Blackburn and Leofranc Holford-Strevens (Cambridge, MA, and London: The I Tatti Renaissance Library/Harvard University Press, 2010).

Forster, Georg, Preface to *Selectissimarum mutetarum partim quinque partim quatuor vocum, tomus primus* (Nuremberg: Johann Petreius, 1540).

Franco of Cologne, *Ars cantus mensurabilis*, ed. Gilbert Reaney and André Gilles, Corpus scriptorum de musica 18 ([Rome]: American Institute of Musicology, 1974).

Freig, Johann Thomas, *Paedagogus* (Basel: Sebastian Heinrich Petri, 1582).

Frescobaldi, Girolamo, Preface to *Toccate e partite d'intavolatura di cimbalo ... libro primo*, 2nd edn. (Rome: Nicolò Borboni, 1616).

Frosch, Johann, *Rerum musicarum* (Strassburg: Peter Schöffer & Mathias Apiarius, 1535; repr. New York: Broude, 1967).

Gaffurio, Franchino, *Angelicum ac divinum opus musice* (Milan: Gotardus de Ponte, 1508; repr. Bologna: Antiquae musicae italicae studiosi, 1971).

   Musices practicabilis libellum (Harvard University, Houghton Library, Ms. Mus 142).

   Practica musice (Milan: Ioannes Petrus de Lomatio, 1496; repr. New York: Broude Bros., 1979).

Gerle, Hans, *Musica teusch auf die Instrument* (Nuremberg: Jeronimus Formschneider, 1532).

Glarean, Heinrich, *Dodecachordon* (Basel: Heinrich Petri, 1547; repr. New York: Broude Bros., 1967).

   Musicae epitome, sive Compendium ex Glareani Dodecachordo (Basel: [Heinrich Petri, 1557]).

Guilielmus Monachus, *De preceptis artis musice*, ed. Albert Seay, Corpus scriptorum de musica 11 ([Rome]: American Institute of Musicology, 1965).

Guilliaud, Maximilian, *Rudiments de musique practique* (Paris: Nicolas Du Chemin, 1554; repr. in *Renaissance française*, ed. Olivier Trachier [Courlay, France: J. M. Fuzeau, 2005], II: 229–44).

Heyden, Sebald, *De arte canendi* (Nuremberg: Johann Petreius, 1540; repr. New York: Broude, 1969).

    Musica stoicheiosis (Nuremberg: Friedrich Peypus, 1532).
    Musicae, id est artis canendi libri duo (Nuremberg: Johann Petreius, 1537).
Hofmann, Eucharius, *Musicae practicae praecepta* (Wittenberg: Johann Schwertel, 1572).
Hothby, John, *Opera omnia de musica mensurabili*, ed. Gilbert Reaney, Corpus scriptorum de musica 31 (Neuhausen-Stuttgart: American Institute of Musicology; Hänssler-Verlag, 1983).
Jambe de Fer, Philibert, *Epitome musical* (Lyon: Michel du Bois, 1556; repr. in *Renaissance française*, ed. Olivier Trachier [Courlay, France: J. M. Fuzeau, 2005], III: 197–236).
Koswick, Michael, *Compendiaria musice artis aeditio* (Leipzig: Wolffgang Stöckel, 1516).
Lampadius, Auctor, *Compendium musices* (Bern: Mathias Apiarius, 1537).
Lanfranco, Giovanni Maria, *Scintille di musica* (Brescia: Lodovico Britannico, 1533; repr. Bologna: Forni, 1988).
Listenius, Nicolaus, *Musica* (Wittenberg: Georg Rhau, 1537; repr. [of 1549 edn.] Berlin: M. Breslauer, 1927).
Lossius, Lucas, *Erotemata musicae practicae* (Nuremberg: Johann Berg and Ulrich Neuber, 1563; repr. Bologna: Forni, 1980).
Luscinius (Nachtigall), Othmar, *Musurgia seu praxis musicae* (Strassburg: Johann Schott, 1536).
Lusitano, Vicente, *Introdutione facilissima, et novissima di canto fermo, figurato, contraponto semplice, et inconcerto* (Rome: Antonio Blado, 1553; repr. [of 1561 edn.] Lucca: Libreria Musicale Italiana Editrice, 1988).
Martin, Claude, *Elementorum musices practicae pars prior* (Paris: Nicolas Du Chemin, 1550; repr. in *Renaissance française*, ed. Olivier Trachier [Courlay, France: J. M. Fuzeau, 2005], II: 113–40).
    Institution musicale (Paris: Nicolas Du Chemin, 1556; repr. in *Renaissance française*, ed. Olivier Trachier [Courlay, France: J. M. Fuzeau, 2005], III: 237–44).
Fra Mauro da Firenze, *Utriusque musices epitome*, ed. Frank A. D'Accone, Corpus scriptorum de musica 32 (Neuhausen-Stuttgart: Hänssler, 1984).
Molins de Podio (Despuig), Guillermo, *Ars musicorum* (Valencia: Peter Hagenbach & Leonhard Hutz, 1495; repr. [Bologna]: Forni, 1975).
Monetarius, Stephan, *Epitoma utriusque musices practice* (Cracow: Florian Ungler, 1515; repr. Cracow: Polskie Wydawnictwo Muzyczne, 1975).
Monteverdi, Claudio and Giulio Cesare, "Dichiaratione della lettera stampata nel quinto libro de' suoi madregali," in Claudio Monteverdi, *Scherzi musicali a tre voci* (Venice: Amadino, 1607).
Montfort, Corneille de (*dit* Blockland), *Instruction fort facile pour apprendre la musique practique* (Lyon: Jean de Tournes, 1573; repr. in *Renaissance française*, ed. Olivier Trachier [Courlay, France: J. M. Fuzeau, 2005], IV: 251–310).

Morley, Thomas, *A Plaine and Easie Introduction to Practicall Musicke* (London: Peter Short, 1597; repr. Westmead, Farnborough, Hants, England: Gregg International, 1971).

Muris, Johannes de, *Ars practica mensurabilis cantus secundum Iohannem de Muris: Die Recensio maior des sogenannten Libellus practice cantus mensurabilis*, ed. Christian Berktold, Veröffentlichungen der Musikhistorischen Kommission 14 (Munich: Bayerische Akademie der Wissenschaften, 1999).

Notitia artis musicae, ed. Ulrich Michels, Corpus scriptorum de musica 17 ([Rome]: American Institute of Musicology, 1972).

Neusidler, Hans, *Ein newgeordent künstlich Lautenbuch* (Nuremberg: J. Petreius, 1536; repr. Stuttgart: Cornetto, c2004).

Oridryus, Johannes, *Practicae musicae utriusque praecepta brevia* (Düsseldorf: Jacob Baethen, 1557), ed. in Renate Federhofer-Königs, *Johannes Oridryus und sein Musiktraktat* (Cologne: Arno Volk, 1957), 65–157.

Ornithoparchus, Andreas, *Musice active micrologus* (Leipzig: Valentin Schumann, 1517); trans. John Dowland (London: T. Adams, 1609); repr. of both in *A Compendium of Musical Practice*, ed. Gustave Reese and Steven Ledbetter (New York: Dover, [1973]).

Philomathes, Venceslaus, *Musicorum libri quattuor* (Vienna: Hieronymus Vietor & Johannes Singrenius, 1512).

Picitono, Angelo da, *Fior angelico di musica* (Venice: Agostino Bindoni, 1547).

Piovesana, Francesco, *Misure harmoniche regolate* (Venice: Gardano, 1627).

Pisa, Agostino, *Battuta della musica* (Rome: Bartolomeo Zannetti, 1611; repr. Bologna: Forni, 1969).

Breve dichiaratione della battuta musicale (Rome: Bartolomeo Zannetti, 1611; repr. Lucca: Libreria Musicale Italiana, c1996).

Praetorius, Christoph, *Erotemata musices* (Wittenberg: Johann Schwertel, 1574).

Praetorius, Michael, *Syntagma musicum*, vol. III (Wolfenbüttel: Elias Holwein, 1618–19; repr. Kassel: Bärenreiter, 1958–59).

Prosdocimo de' Beldomandi, *Brevis summula proportionum quantum ad musicam pertinet*, ed. and trans. Jan Herlinger, Greek and Latin Music Theory 4 (Lincoln: University of Nebraska Press, 1987).

Expositiones tractatus practice cantus mensurabilis magistri Johannis de Muris, in Prosdocimi de Beldemandis, *Opera*, ed. F. Alberto Gallo, vol. I, Antiquae Musicae Italicae Scriptores 3 (Bologna: Università degli Studi di Bologna, Istituto di Studi Musicali e Teatrali, 1966).

Tractatus practice cantus mensurabilis ad modum ytalicorum, ed. Claudio Sartori, in *La notazione italiana del Trecento in una redazione inedita del "Tractatus practice cantus mensurabilis ad modum ytalicorum" di Prosdocimo de Beldemandis* (Florence: Leo S. Olschki, 1938), 35–71.

Tractatus practice de musica mensurabili, ed. Edmond de Coussemaker, *Scriptorum de musica medii aevi*, 4 vols. (Paris: Durand, 1864–76; repr. Hildesheim: Olms, 1963), III: 200–28.

Puerto, Diego del, *Portus musice* (Salamanca: [J. de Porras], 1504; repr. Madrid: Joyas Bibliográficas, 1976).
Quercu, Simon de, *Opusculum musices* (Vienna: Johann Winterburg, 1509).
Ramis de Pareja, Bartolomeo, *Musica practica* (Bologna: [Enrico de Colonia?], 1482; repr. Bologna: Forni, 1969).
Raselius, Andreas, *Hexachordum* (Nuremberg: Gerlach, 1589).
Reisch, Gregor, *Margarita philosophica* (Basel: Michael Futerius, 1517; repr. Düsseldorf: Stern-Verlag Janssen & Co., [1973]).
Rhau, Georg, *Enchiridion utriusque musicae practicae*, 3rd edn. (Leipzig: Valentin Schumann, 1520).
Sancta Maria, Tomás de, *Libro llamado arte de tañer fantasia* (Valladolid: Francisco Fernandez de Cordova, 1565; repr. Geneva: Minkoff, 1973).
Schneegass, Cyriacus, *Isagoges musicae* (Erfurt: Georg Baumann, 1591).
Schornburg, Heinrich, *Elementa musica* (Cologne: Nicolaus Grapheus, 1582; repr. Cologne: Arno Volk-Verlag, 1966).
Sebastian of Felsztyn, *Opusculum musicae mensuralis* (Cracow: J. Haller, [*c.* 1518]; repr. Cracow: Polskie Wydawnictwo Muzyczne, 1979).
Spataro, Giovanni, *Dilucide et probatissime demonstratione . . . contra certe frivole et vane excusatione de Franchino Gafurio* (Bologna: Hieronymus de Benedictis, 1521; repr. Berlin: M. Breslauer, 1925).
  Tractato di musica . . . nel quale si tracta de la perfectione da la sesqualtera producta in la musica mensurata exercitate (Venice: Bernardino de Vitali, 1531; repr. Bologna: Forni, [1970]).
Tigrini, Orazio, *Il compendio della musica* (Venice: Ricciardo Amadino, 1588; repr. New York: Broude, 1966).
Tinctoris, Johannes, *Complete Theoretical Works*, in progress at http://earlymusictheory.org/Tinctoris/#.
  Liber de arte contrapuncti, in Johannes Tinctoris, *Opera theoretica*, ed. Albert Seay, 3 vols. in 2, Corpus scriptorum de musica 22 ([Rome]: American Institute of Musicology, 1975–78), II: 11–157.
  Proportionale musices, in Johannes Tinctoris, *Opera theoretica*, ed. Albert Seay, 3 vols. in 2, Corpus scriptorum de musica 22 ([Rome]: American Institute of Musicology, 1975–78), IIa: 9–60.
  Terminorum musicae diffinitorium ([Treviso, *c.* 1495]; repr. New York: Broude Bros., 1966).
  Tractatus de regolari valore notarum, in Johannes Tinctoris, *Opera theoretica*, ed. Albert Seay, 3 vols. in 2, Corpus scriptorum de musica 22 ([Rome]: American Institute of Musicology, 1975–78), I: 125–38.
Tovar, Francisco, *Libro de musica practica* (Barcelona: Johann Rosenbach, 1510; repr. Madrid: Joyas Bibliográficas, 1976).
Ugolino of Orvieto, *Declaratio musicae disciplinae*, ed. Albert Seay, 3 vols., Corpus scriptorum de musica 7 ([Rome]: American Institute of Musicology, 1959–62).

Vanneo, Stephano, *Recanetum de musica aurea* (Rome: Valerio Dorico, 1533; repr. Bologna: Forni, 1969).

Vicentino, Nicola, *L'antica musica ridotta alla moderna prattica* (Rome: Antonio Barre, 1555; repr. Kassel: Bärenreiter, 1959).

Vitry, Philippe de, *Ars nova*, ed. Gilbert Reaney, André Gilles, and Jean Maillard, Corpus scriptorum de musica 8 ([Rome]: American Institute of Musicology, 1964).

Volckmar, Joannes, *Collectanea quedam musice discipline* (Frankfurt an der Oder, 1513).

Wilphlingseder, Ambrosius, *Erotemata musices practicae* (Nuremberg: Heussler, 1563).

Wollick, Nicolaus, *Enchiridion musices* (Paris: Jehan Petit et François Regnault, 1509; repr. in *Renaissance française*, ed. Olivier Trachier [Courlay, France: J. M. Fuzeau, 2005], I: 125–38).

and Melchior Schanppecher, *Opus aureum* (Cologne: Heinrich Quentell, 1501).

Yssandon, Jean, *Traité de la musique pratique* (Paris: Adrian Le Roy & Robert Ballard, 1582; repr. in *Renaissance française*, ed. Olivier Trachier [Courlay, France: J. M. Fuzeau, 2005], IV: 169–212).

Zacconi, Ludovico, *Prattica di musica* (Venice: Girolamo Polo, 1592; repr. Hildesheim: Olms, 1982).

Prattica di musica, seconda parte (Venice: Alessandro Vincenti, 1622; repr. Hildesheim: Olms, 1982).

Zanger, Johann, *Practicae musicae praecepta* (Leipzig: Georg Hantzsch, 1554).

Zarlino, Gioseffo, *Le istitutioni harmoniche* (Venice, 1558; repr. New York: Broude Bros., 1965).

Secondary literature

Apel, Willi, *The Notation of Polyphonic Music, 900–1600*, 5th edn. (Cambridge, MA: The Mediaeval Academy of America, 1953).

Auda, Antoine, "La mesure dans la Messe 'L'homme armé' de Palestrina," *Acta musicologica* 13 (1941), 39–59.

"Le 'tactus' dans la Messe 'L'homme armé' de Palestrina," *Acta musicologica* 14 (1942), 27–73.

Bank, J[oannes] A[ntonius], *Tactus, Tempo and Notation in Mensural Music from the 13th to the 17th Century* (Amsterdam: Annie Bank, 1972).

Bellermann, Heinrich, *Die Mensuralnoten und Taktzeichen des XV. und XVI. Jahrhunderts* (Berlin: G. Reimer, 1858; 4th expanded edn., ed. Heinrich Husmann, Berlin: W. de Gruyter, 1963).

Bent, Margaret., "The Early Use of the Sign ¢," *Early Music* 24 (1996), 199–225.

ed., *Fifteenth-Century Liturgical Music II: Four Anonymous Masses*, Early English Church Music 22 (London: Stainer and Bell, 1979).

"Isorhythm," *Oxford Music Online*, www.oxfordmusiconline.com (accessed 24 July 2010).

"On the Interpretation of ⏁ in the Fifteenth Century: A Response to Rob Wegman," *Journal of the American Musicological Society* 53 (2000), 597–612.

"The Use of Cut Signatures in Sacred Music by Binchois," in *Binchois Studies*, ed. Andrew Kirkman and Dennis Slavin (Oxford University Press, 2000), 277–312.

"The Use of Cut Signatures in Sacred Music by Ockeghem and His Contemporaries," in *Johannes Ockeghem: Actes du XLe Colloque international d'études humanistes, Tours, 3–8 février 1997*, ed. Philippe Vendrix, "Épitome musical" 1 (Paris: Klincksieck, 1998), 641–80.

Berger, Anna Maria Busse, "Cut Signs in Fifteenth-Century Musical Practice," in *Music in Renaissance Cities and Courts: Studies in Honor of Lewis Lockwood*, ed. Jessie Ann Owens and Anthony M. Cummings, Detroit Monographs in Musicology/Studies in Music 18 (Warren, MI: Harmonie Park Press, 1997), 101–12.

Mensuration and Proportion Signs: Origins and Evolution (Oxford: Clarendon Press, 1993).

"The Myth of *diminutio per tertiam partem*," *The Journal of Musicology* 8 (1990), 398–426.

"The Origin and Early History of Proportion Signs," *Journal of the American Musicological Society* 41 (1988), 403–33.

"The Relationship of Perfect and Imperfect Time in Italian Theory of the Renaissance," *Early Music History* 5 (1985), 1–28.

Bernstein, Jane A., *Music Printing in Renaissance Venice: The Scotto Press, 1539–1572* (New York: Oxford University Press, 1998).

Besseler, Heinrich, *Bourdon und Fauxbourdon: Studien zum Ursprung der niederländischen Musik*, rev. edn., ed. Peter Gülke (Leipzig: Breitkopf & Härtel, 1974).

Blachly, Alexander, "*Mensura* versus *Tactus*," in *Quellen und Studien zur Musiktheorie des Mittelalters* 3, ed. Michael Bernhard, Veröffentlichungen der Musikhistorischen Kommission 15 (Munich: Bayerische Akademie der Wissenschaften, 2001), 425–67.

"Mensuration and Tempo in Fifteenth-Century Music: Cut Signatures in Theory and Practice" (Ph.D. diss., Columbia University, 1995).

"Reading Tinctoris for Guidance on Tempo," in *Antoine Busnoys: Method, Meaning, and Context in Late Medieval Music*, ed. Paula Higgins (New York: Oxford University Press, 1999), 399–427.

Blackburn, Bonnie J., "Did Ockeghem Listen to Tinctoris?" in *Johannes Ockeghem: Actes du XLe Colloque international d'études humanistes, Tours, 3–8 février 1997*, ed. Philippe Vendrix, "Épitome musical" 1 (Paris: Klincksieck, 1998), 597–640.

"Leonardo and Gaffurio on Harmony and the Pulse of Music," in *Essays on Music and Culture in Honor of Herbert Kellman*, ed. Barbara Haggh, "Épitome musical" 8 (Paris: Minerve, 2001), 128–49.

"Masses Based on Popular Songs and Solmization Syllables," in *The Josquin Companion*, ed. Richard Sherr (Oxford University Press, 2000), 51–87.

"The Sign of Petrucci's Editor," in *Venice 1501: Petrucci e la stampa musicale*, ed. Giulio Cattin and Patrizia dalla Vecchia (Venice: Fondazione Ugo e Olga Levi, 2005), 415–29.

Bonge, Dale, "Gaffurius on Pulse and Tempo: A Reinterpretation," *Musica disciplina* 36 (1982), 167–74.

Boone, Graeme M., "Dufay's Early Chansons: Style and Chronology in the Manuscript Oxford, Bodleian Library, Canonici misc. 213" (Ph.D. diss., Harvard University, 1987).

"Marking Mensural Time," *Music Theory Spectrum* 22 (2000), 1–43.

Patterns in Play: A Model for Text Setting in the Early French Songs of Guillaume Dufay (Lincoln: University of Nebraska Press, 1999).

Brothers, Thomas, "Vestiges of the Isorhythmic Tradition in Mass and Motet, ca. 1450–1475," *Journal of the American Musicological Society* 44 (1991), 1–56.

Brown, Howard Mayer, and Claus Bockmaier, "Tactus," *Oxford Music Online*, www.oxfordmusiconline.com (accessed 7 December 2013).

Burn, David J., "The Mass-Proper Cycles of Henricus Isaac: Genesis, Transmission, and Authenticity," 2 vols. (Ph.D. diss., Oxford University, 2002).

"'Nam erit haec quoque laus eorum': Imitation, Competition and the *L'homme armé* Tradition," *Revue de musicologie* 87 (2001), 249–87.

"What Did Isaac Write for Constance?" *The Journal of Musicology* 20 (2003), 45–72.

Carl, Beate, "Metrum und Rhythmus in einigen Rondeaux von Guillaume Dufay: Anmerkungen zur Auffassung von Rhythmus und Metrum im 15. Jahrhundert," *Musiktheorie* 12 (1997), 147–164.

Casimiri, Raffaele, "Un dibattito musicologico a proposito della Missa *L'homme armé* del Palestrina," *Note d'archivio per la storia musicale* 20 (1943), 18–42.

"Il 'Kyrie' della Messa 'L'homme armé' di Giov. Pierluigi di Palestrina e una trascrizione errata," *Note d'archivio per la storia musicale* 10 (1933), 101–08.

La polifonia vocale del sec. xvi e la sua trascrizione in figurazione musicale moderna (Rome: Psalterium, 1942).

Collins, Michael, "The Performance of Sesquialtera and Hemiolia in the Sixteenth Century," *Journal of the American Musicological Society* 17 (1964), 5–28.

Cooper, Barry, and Wilhelm Seidel, *Entstehung nationaler Traditionen: Frankreich, England*, Geschichte der Musiktheorie 9 (Darmstadt: Wissenschaftliche Buchgesellschaft, 1986).

A Correspondence of Renaissance Musicians, ed. Bonnie J. Blackburn, Edward E. Lowinsky, and Clement A. Miller (Oxford: Clarendon Press, 1991).

Cumming, Julie E., *The Motet in the Age of Du Fay* (Cambridge University Press, 1999).

Dahlhaus, Carl, "Die Tactus- und Proportionenlehre des 15. bis 17. Jahrhunderts," in *Hören, Messen, und Rechnen in der frühen Neuzeit*, Geschichte der Musiktheorie 6 (Darmstadt: Wissenschaftliche Buchgesellschaft, 1987), 333–61.

"Zur Theorie des Tactus im 16. Jahrhundert," *Archiv für Musikwissenschaft* 17 (1960), 22–39.

Dammann, Rolf, "Spätformen der isorhythmischen Motette im 16. Jahrhundert," *Archiv für Musikwissenschaft* 10 (1953), 16–40.
DeFord, Ruth I., "The Evolution of Rhythmic Style in Italian Secular Music of the Late Sixteenth Century," *Studi musicali* 10 (1981), 43–74.
  "The *Mensura* of Φ in the Works of Du Fay," *Early Music* 34 (2006), 111–36.
  "On Diminution and Proportion in Fifteenth-Century Music Theory," *Journal of the American Musicological Society* 58 (2005), 1–67.
  "Sebald Heyden (1499–1561): The First Historical Musicologist?" in *Music's Intellectual History*, ed. Zdravko Blažeković and Barbara Dobbs Mackenzie (New York: Répertoire International de la Littérature Musicale, 2009), 3–15.
  "Tempo Relationships between Duple and Triple Time in the Sixteenth Century," *Early Music History* 14 (1995), 1–51.
  "Who Devised the Proportional Notation in Isaac's *Choralis Constantinus*?" in *Heinrich Isaac and Polyphony for the Proper of the Mass in the Late Middle Ages and Renaissance*, ed. David J. Burn and Stefan Gasch, "Épitome musical" (Turnhout: Brepols, 2011), 167–213.
  "Zacconi's Theories of *Tactus* and Mensuration," *The Journal of Musicology* 14 (1996), 151–82.
Dürr, Walther, *Zwei neue Belege für die sogenannte 'spielmännische' Reduktion*, Biblioteca di Quadrivium, Estratti (Bologna: Arti Frafiche Tamari, 1958).
Einstein, Alfred, *The Italian Madrigal*, 3 vols. (Princeton University Press, 1949; repr. 1971).
Elders, Willem, "Symbolism in the Sacred Music of Josquin," in *The Josquin Companion*, ed. Richard Sherr (Oxford University Press, 2000), 531–68.
  "Zusammenhänge zwischen den Motetten *Ave nobilissima creatura* und *Huc me sydereo* von Josquin des Prez," *Tijdschrift van de Vereniging voor Nederlandse Muziekgeschiedenis* 22 (1971), 67–73.
Fallows, David, *Dufay*, rev. edn., Master Musicians (New York: Vintage Books, 1988).
  Josquin, "Épitome musical" (Turnhout: Brepols, 2009).
  The Songs of Guillaume Dufay: Critical Commentary to the Revision of Corpus mensurabilis musicae, ser. I, vol. VI, Musicological Studies and Documents 47 (Neuhausen-Stuttgart: American Institute of Musicology, 1995).
Federhofer-Königs, Renate, "Ein Beitrag zur Proportionenlehre in der zweiten Hälfte des 15. Jahrhunterts," in *Bence Szabolcsi Septuagenario*, ed. Dénes Bartha, Studia musicologica Academiae Scientiarum Hungaricae 11 (Budapest: Akademiai Kiado, 1969), 145–57.
Feldman, Martha, *City Culture and the Madrigal at Venice* (Berkeley: University of California Press, 1995).
Fitch, Fabrice, *Johannes Ockeghem: Masses and Models*, Ricercar 2 (Paris: H. Champion, 1997).
Frobenius, Wolf, "Tactus," in *Handwörterbuch der musikalischen Terminologie*, ed. Hans Heinrich Eggebrecht (Wiesbaden: F. Steiner, [1972–]).

Galkin, Elliott W., *A History of Orchestral Conducting: In Theory and Practice* (Stuyvesant, New York: Pendragon Press, 1988).
Gallagher, Sean, *Johannes Regis*, "Épitome musical" (Turnhout: Brepols, 2010).
  "Seigneur Leon's Papal Sword: Ferrara, Du Fay, and His Songs of the 1440s," *Tijdschrift van de Koninklijke Vereniging voor Nederlandse Muziekgeschiedenis* 57 (2007), 3–28.
Gallo, F. Alberto, "Die Notationslehre im 14. und 15. Jahrhundert," in *Die mittelalterliche Lehre von der Mehrstimmigkeit*, ed. Hans Heinrich Eggebrecht, Geschichte der Musiktheorie 5 (Darmstadt: Wissenschaftliche Buchgesellschaft, 1984), 257–356.
  La teoria della notazione in Italia dalla fine del XIII all'inizio del XV secolo, Antiquae musicae italicae subsidia theorica (Bologna: Tamari Editori, 1966).
Gásser, Luis, *Luis Milán on Sixteenth-Century Performance Practice* (Bloomington: Indiana University Press, 1996).
Gossett, Philip, "The Mensural System and the 'Choralis Constantinus'," in *Studies in Renaissance and Baroque Music in Honor of Arthur Mendel*, ed. Robert L. Marshall (Kassel: Bärenreiter, 1974), 71–107.
Günther, Ursula, "Polymetric *rondeaux* from Machaut to Dufay: Some Style-Analytical Observations," in *Studies in Musical Sources and Styles: Essays in Honor of Jan LaRue*, ed. Eugene K. Wolf and Edward H. Roesner (Madison, WI: A-R Editions, 1990), 75–108.
Haar, James, "Lessons in Theory from a Sixteenth-Century Composer," in *Essays on Italian Music in the Cinquecento*, ed. Richard Charteris, Altro Polo (Sydney: Frederick May Foundation for Italian Studies, 1990), 51–81.
  "The *Note Nere* Madrigal," *Journal of the American Musicological Society* 18 (1965), 22–41.
  "Palestrina as Historicist: The Two *L'homme armé* Masses," *Journal of the Royal Musical Association* 121 (1996), 191–205.
Ham, Martin, "A Sense of Proportion: The Performance of Sesquialtera ca. 1515–ca. 1565," *Musica disciplina* 56 (2011), 79–274.
Hamm, Charles, *A Chronology of the Works of Guillaume Dufay Based on a Study of Mensural Practice*, Princeton Studies in Music 1 (Princeton University Press, 1964; repr. New York: Da Capo, 1986).
Hatter, Jane, "*Col tempo*: Musical Time, Aging and Sexuality in 16th-Century Venetian Paintings," *Early Music* 39 (2011), 3–14.
Herissone, Rebecca, *Music Theory in Seventeenth-Century England* (Oxford University Press, 2000).
Herlinger, Jan W., "A Fifteenth-Century Italian Compilation of Music Theory," *Acta musicologica* 53 (1981), 90–105.
Houghton, Edward, "Rhythm and Meter in 15th-Century Polyphony," *Journal of Music Theory* 18 (1974), 190–212.

Jacobs, Charles, *Tempo Notation in Renaissance Spain*, Wissenschaftliche Abhandlungen 8 (Brooklyn: Institute of Medieval Music, [c1964]).

Jeppesen, Knud, *The Style of Palestrina and the Dissonance*, 2nd edn., trans. Margaret Hamerik (Copenhagen: E. Munksgaard, 1946; repr. New York: Dover, 1970, and Mineola, NY: Dover, 2005).

Judd, Cristle Collins, *Reading Renaissance Music Theory: Hearing with the Eyes*, Cambridge Studies in Music Theory and Analysis 14 (Cambridge University Press, 2000).

Kendall, Yvonne, "Rhythm, Meter, and *Tactus* in 16th-Century Italian Court Dance: Reconstruction from a Theoretical Base," *Dance Research* 8 (1990), 3–27.

Kümmel, Werner Friedrich, "Zum Tempo in der italienischen Mensuralmusik des 15. Jahrhunderts," *Acta musicologica* 42 (1970), 150–63.

León Tello, Francisco José, *Estudios de historia de la teoría musical*, 2nd edn. (Madrid: Consejo Superior de Investigaciones Científicas, 1991).

Lowinsky, Edward E., "Early Scores in Manuscript," *Journal of the American Musicological Society* 13 (1960), 126–73.

Machatius, Franz-Jochen, "Über mensurale und spielmännische Reduktion," *Die Musikforschung* 8 (1955), 139–51.

Mendel, Arthur, "Some Ambiguities of the Mensural System," in *Studies in Music History: Essays for Oliver Strunk*, ed. Harold S. Powers (Princeton University Press, 1968), 137–60.

Milsom, John, "Motets for Five or More Voices," in *The Josquin Companion*, ed. Richard Sherr (Oxford University Press, 2000), 281–320.

Moser, Hans Joachim, "Johannes Zanger's *Praecepta*," *Musica disciplina* 5 (1951), 195–201.

Neumann, Frederick, "Conflicting Binary and Ternary Rhythms: From the Theory of Mensural Notation to the Music of J. S. Bach," *Music Forum* 6 (1987), 93–127.

Niemöller, Klaus Wolfgang, "Deutsche Musiktheorie im 16. Jahrhundert: Geistes- und institutionsgeschichtliche Grundlagen," in *Deutsche Musiktheorie des 15. bis 17. Jahrhunderts* I: *Von Paumann bis Calvisius*, Geschichte der Musiktheorie 8/1 (Darmstadt: Wissenschaftliche Buchgesellschaft, 2003), 69–98.

Untersuchungen zur Musikpflege und Musikunterricht an den deutschen Lateinschulen vom ausgehenden Mittelalter bis um 1600, Kölner Beiträge zur Musikforschung 54 (Regensburg: Gustav Bosse, 1969).

Owens, Jessie Ann, "The Milan Partbooks: Evidence of Cipriano de Rore's Compositional Process," *Journal of the American Musicological Society* 37 (1984), 270–98.

"Rore, Cipriano de," *Oxford Music Online*, www.oxfordmusiconline.com (accessed 1 August 2010).

Palmer, Jill, "A Late Fifteenth-Century Anonymous Mensuration Treatise: (Ssp) Salzburg, Erzabtei St. Peter, a VI 44, 1490; cod pap. 206 × 149 mm. 75ff," *Musica disciplina* 39 (1985), 87–106.

Pätzig, Gerhard-Rudolf, "Das Chorbuch Mus. ms. 40024 der Deutschen Staatsbibliothek Berlin: Eine wichtige Quelle zum Schaffen Isaacs aus der Hand Leonhard Pämingers," in *Festschrift Walter Gerstenberg*, ed. Georg von Dadelsen and Andreas Holschneider (Wolfenbüttel: Möseler, [c1964]), 122–42.

"Liturgische Grundlagen und handschriftliche Überlieferung von Heinrich Isaacs 'Choralis Constantinus'" (Ph.D. diss., Universität Tübingen, 1956).

Planchart, Alejandro Enrique, "Guillaume Du Fay's Benefices and His Relationship to the Court of Burgundy," *Early Music History* 8 (1988), 117–71.

"The Origins and Early History of *L'homme armé*," *The Journal of Musicology* 20 (2003), 305–57.

"The Relative Speed of *Tempora* in the of Period of Dufay," *Royal Musical Association Research Chronicle* 17 (1981), 33–51.

"Two Fifteenth-Century Songs and Their Texts in a Close Reading," *Basler Jahrbuch für historische Musikpraxis* 14 (1990), 13–36.

Powers, Harold S., "Music as Text and Text as Music," in *Musik als Text: Bericht über den Internationalen Kongress der Gesellschaft für Musikforschung Freiburg im Breisgau 1993*, ed. Hermann Danuser and Tobias Plebuch, 2 vols. (Kassel: Bärenreiter, 1998), I: 16–36.

Prizer, William F., "Music and Ceremonial in the Low Countries: Philip the Fair and the Order of the Golden Fleece," *Early Music History* 5 (1985), 113–53.

Rastall, Richard, *The Notation of Western Music: An Introduction*, 2nd edn. (Leeds University Press, 1998).

Reynolds, Robert Davis, Jr., "Evolution of Notational Practices in Manuscripts between 1400–1450" (Ph.D. diss., Ohio State University, 1974).

Rodin, Jesse, "Finishing Josquin's 'Unfinished' Mass: A Case of Stylistic Imitation in the *Cappella Sistina*," *The Journal of Musicology* 22 (2005), 412–53.

Josquin's Rome: Hearing and Composing in the Sistine Chapel (Oxford University Press, 2012).

"'When in Rome . . . ': What Josquin Learned in the Sistine Chapel," *Journal of the American Musicological Society* 61 (2008), 307–72.

Sachs, Curt, *Rhythm and Tempo: A Study in Music History* (New York: Norton, 1953; repr. New York: Columbia University Press, 1988).

Schmid, Manfred Hermann, "Die Darstellung der Musica im spätmittelalterlichen Bildprogram der 'Margarita philosophica' von Gregor Reisch 1503," *Hamburger Jahrbuch für Musikwissenschaft* 12 (1994), 247–61.

Schroeder, Eunice, "Dissonance Placement and Stylistic Change in the Fifteenth Century: Tinctoris's Rules and Dufay's Practice," *The Journal of Musicology* 7 (1989), 366–89.

"*Mensura* According to Tinctoris, in the Context of Musical Writings of the Fifteenth and Early Sixteenth Centuries" (Ph.D. diss., Stanford University, 1985).

"The Stroke Comes Full Circle: ϕ and $\cent$ in Writings on Music, ca. 1450–1540," *Musica disciplina* 36 (1982), 119–66.

Schuler, Manfred, "Zur Überlieferung des *Choralis Constantinus* von Heinrich Isaac," *Archiv für Musikwissenschaft* 36 (1979), 68–76, 146–54.

Schünemann, Georg, *Geschichte des Dirigierens*, Kleine Handbücher der Musikgeschichte nach Gattungen 10 (Leipzig: Breitkopf & Härtel, 1913; repr. Hildesheim: Olms, 1965).

"Zur Frage des Taktschlagens und der Textbehandlung in der Mensuralmusik," *Sammelbände der Internationalen Musikgesellschaft* 10 (1908–09), 73–114.

Segerman, Ephraim, "A Re-examination of the Evidence on Absolute Tempo before 1700 – I," *Early Music* 24 (1996), 227–48.

Sherr, Richard, "*Illibata Dei virgo nutrix* and Josquin's Roman Style," *Journal of the American Musicological Society* 41 (1988), 434–64.

"The Performance of Josquin's *L'homme armé* Masses," *Early Music* 19 (1991), 261–68.

"Tempo to 1500," in *Companion to Medieval and Renaissance Music*, ed. Tess Knighton and David Fallows (New York: Schirmer Books, 1992), 327–36.

Siraisi, Nancy C., "The Music of Pulse in the Writings of Italian Academic Physicians (Fourteenth and Fifteenth Centuries)," *Speculum* 50 (1975), 689–710.

Smits van Waesberghe, Joseph, "Singen und Dirigieren der mehrstimmigen Musik im Mittelalter: Was Miniaturen uns hierüber lehren," in *Mélanges offerts à René Crozet*, ed. Pierre Gallais and Yves-Jean Rion (Poitiers: Société d'études médiévales, 1966), 1345–54.

Taruskin, Richard, "Antoine Busnoys and the *L'Homme armé* Tradition," *Journal of the American Musicological Society* 39 (1986), 255–93.

Letter to the editor, *Journal of the American Musicological Society* 42 (1989), 443–52.

Vacchelli, Anna Maria Monterosso, *La Messa L'homme armé di Palestrina: Studio paleografico ed edizione critica* (Cremona: Fondazione Claudio Monteverdi, 1979).

Wegman, Rob C., "Concerning Tempo in the English Polyphonic Mass, *c.* 1420–70," *Acta musicologica* 61 (1989), 40–65.

"Different Strokes for Different Folks? On Tempo and Diminution in Fifteenth-Century Music," *Journal of the American Musicological Society* 53 (2000), 461–505.

Letter to the editor, *Journal of the American Musicological Society* 42 (1989), 437–43.

"What Is 'acceleratio mensurae'?" *Music and Letters* 73 (1992), 515–24.

Wingell, Richard J., "Anonymous XI (CS III): An Edition, Translation, and Commentary," 3 vols. (Ph.D. diss., University of Southern California, 1973).

Wolf, Johannes, *Geschichte der Mensural-Notation* (Leipzig: Breitkopf & Härtel, 1904; repr. Hildesheim: Olms, 1965).

Woodley, Ronald, "Minor Coloration Revisited: Okeghem's *Ma bouche rit* and Beyond," in *Théorie et analyse musicales (1450–1650)*, ed. Bonnie J. Blackburn and Anne-Emmanuelle Ceulemans (Louvain-la-Neuve, Belgium: Université Catholique de Louvain, 2001), 39–63.

Wright, Craig, *The Maze and the Warrior: Symbols in Architecture, Theology, and Music* (Cambridge, MA: Harvard University Press, 2001).

Sources of music

Manuscripts

Aosta, Seminario Maggiore, Ms. 15 (formerly A1 D19).
Berlin, Deutsche Staatsbibliothek, Mus. Ms. 40024.
Bologna, Civico Museo Bibliografico Musicale, Ms. Q15. Introduction and facsimile, Margaret Bent, *Bologna Q15: The Making and Remaking of a Musical Manuscript*, 2 vols. (Lucca: Libreria Musicale Italiana, c2008).
Casale Monferrato, Archivio Capitolare, Ms. M(D).
Dijon, Bibliothèque Publique, Ms. 517. Facsimile, ed. Dragan Plamenac, Publications of Medieval Music Manuscripts 12 (Brooklyn: Institute of Mediaeval Music, n.d).
Florence, Biblioteca Medicea-Laurenziana, Ms. 666 ("Medici Codex"). Introduction, facsimile, and modern edition, ed. Edward E. Lowinsky, *The Medici Codex of 1518: A Choirbook of Motets Dedicated to Lorenzo de' Medici, Duke of Urbino*, 3 vols., Monuments of Renaissance Music 3–5 (Chicago and London: University of Chicago Press, 1968).
Florence, Biblioteca Nazionale Centrale, Ms. Mag. xix.176.
Kassel, Murhard'sche und Landesbibliothek, Ms. Mus. 24.
Naples, Biblioteca Nazionale, Ms. VI E 40.
New Haven, Yale University Library, Beinecke Rare Book and Manuscript Library, Ms. 91 ("Mellon Chansonnier"). Introduction, facsimile, and modern edition, ed. Leeman L. Perkins and Howard Garey, 2 vols. (New Haven: Yale University Press, 1979).
Oxford, Bodleian Library, Ms. Canon. Misc. 213. Introduction and facsimile, ed. David Fallows, Late Medieval and Early Renaissance Music in Facsimile 1 (Chicago and London: University of Chicago Press, 1995).
Porto, Biblioteca Pública Municipal, Ms. 714. Introduction and facsimile, ed. Manuel Pedro Ferreira, *Porto 714: un manuscritto precioso*, Campo da música 5 (Porto: Campo das Letras, 2001).
Stuttgart, Württembergische Landesbibliothek, Ms. I 40.
Trent, Castello del Buonconsiglio, Monumenti e Collezioni Provinciale, 1374 (formerly 87). Facsimile: *Codex Tridentinus 87–[93]*, 7 vols. ([Rome: Bibliopola, 1969–70]).
Vatican City, Biblioteca Apostolica Vaticana
  Cappella Sistina, Ms. 15.
  Cappella Sistina, Ms. 16.
  Cappella Sistina, Ms. 22.
  Cappella Sistina, Ms. 24.

Cappella Sistina, Ms. 35.
Cappella Sistina, Ms. 38.
Cappella Sistina, Ms. 45.
Cappella Sistina, Ms. 55.
Cappella Sistina, Ms. 197.
Ms. Chigi C VIII 234 ("Chigi Codex"). Facsimile, ed. Herbert Kellman, Renaissance Music in Facsimile 22 (New York: Garland, 1987).

Prints

Bossinensis, Francesco, *Tenori e contrabassi intabulati col sopran in canto figurato per cantar e sonar col lauto, libro primo* ([Venice: Petrucci, 1509]; repr. Geneva: Minkoff Reprints, 1977).

Cimello, Giovanthomaso, *Libro primo de canti a quatro voci* (Venice: Gardano, 1548). Modern edition: Giovanthomaso Cimello, *The Collected Secular Works*, ed. Donna G. Cardamone and James Haar, Recent Researches in the Music of the Renaissance 126 (Middleton, WI: A-R Editions, c2001).

Dixhuit basses dances garnies de recoupes et tordions . . . (Paris: Attaingnant, 1529).

Ferretti, Giovanni, *Il secondo libro delle canzoni alla napolitana a cinque voci* (Venice: Scotto, 1569).

Fiorino, Gasparo, *La nobilità di Roma* (Venice: Scotto, 1571).

Intabolatura nova di varie sorte de balli da sonare (Venice: Gardane, 1551).

Isaac, Heinrich, *Choralis Constantinus*, 3 vols. (Nuremberg: Formschneider, 1550–55). Facsimile, ed. Edward R. Lerner, 3 vols., Facsimile Series for Scholars and Musicians (Peer, Belgium: Alamire, 1990–94). Modern edition of vol. I, ed. Emil Bezecny and Walter Rabl, Denkmäler der Tonkunst in Österreich 10, Jg. 5/i (Vienna: Artaria, 1898, repr. 1959). Modern edition of vol. II, ed. Anton von Webern, Denkmäler der Tonkunst in Österreich 32, Jg. 16/i (Vienna: Artaria, 1909; repr. 1959). Modern edition of vol. III (Mass Propers), ed. Louise Cuyler (Ann Arbor: University of Michigan Press, 1950). Modern edition of vol. III (Mass Ordinaries), ed. Louise Cuyler (Ann Arbor: University of Michigan Press, [1956]).

Josquin des Prez, *Liber primus missarum Josquin* (Venice: Ottaviano Petrucci, 1502).

Marenzio, Luca, *Il primo libro de madrigali a cinque voci* (Venice: Gardano, 1580).

Il primo libro delle villanelle, a tre voci (Venice: Vincenti & Amadino, 1584). Modern edition, ed. Marco Giuliani (Trent: Edizioni Nova Schuola Musicale, 1995).

Milán, Luis, *Libro de música de vihuela de mano intitulado El maestro* (Valencia: Francisco Díaz Romano, 1536; repr. Geneva, Minkoff Reprint, 1975).

Motetti a cinque, libro primo (Venice: Petrucci, 1508).

Motetti de la corona, libro tertio (Fossombrone: Petrucci, 1519).

Motetti, libro secondo (Venice: Antico, 1521).

Monteverdi, Claudio, *Scherzi musicali a tre voci* (Venice: Amadino, 1607).

Nola, Gian Domenico del Giovane da, *Canzone villanesche a tre voci novamente ristampate, libro secundo* (Venice: Gardane, 1545).

Officiorum (ut vocant) de Nativitate, Circumcisione . . . Tomus primus (Wittenberg: Rhau, 1545; repr. Stuttgart: Cornetto-Verlag, c1997).

Palestrina, Giovanni Pierluigi da, *Missarum . . . liber quartus* (Venice: Angelo Gardano, 1582).

Missarum liber tertius (Rome: Dorico, 1570; new edn., Venice: Gardano, 1599). Facsimiles of both editions of the *Missa L'homme armé* in Anna Maria Monterosso Vacchelli, *La Messa L'homme armé di Palestrina: Studio paleografico ed edizione critica* (Cremona: Fondazione Claudio Monteverdi, 1979).

Primavera, Giovan Leonardo, *Il primo libro de canzone napolitane a tre voci* (Venice: Scotto, 1565).

Quatorze gaillardes neuf pavannes sept branles et deux basses dances (Paris: Attaingnant, [1531]).

Rore, Cipriano de, *I madrigali a cinque voci* (Venice: Scotto, 1542); repr. of 1593 edition: *Il primo libro de madrigali cromatici, a cinque voci*, ed. Greta Haenen (Peer, Belgium: Facsimile Musica Alamire, 1986).

Il primo libro de madregali a quatro voci (Venice: Gardano, 1557; repr. Faksimile-Edition Schermer-Bibliothek Ulm 30 [Stuttgart: Cornetto Verlag, 1997]).

Il quarto libro d'i madrigali a cinque voci (Venice: Gardano, 1557).

Il quinto libro di madrigali a cinque voci (Venice: Gardano, 1566).

Il secondo libro de madregali a quatro voci (Venice: Gardano, 1557; repr. Faksimile-Edition Schermer-Bibliothek Ulm 30 [Stuttgart: Cornetto Verlag, 1997]).

Six gaillardes et six pavanes avec treze chansons musicales a quatre parties (Paris: Attaingnant, 1529/1530).

Il terzo libro delle villotte alla napolitana . . . a tre voci (Venice: A. Gardano, 1560).

Vecchi, Orazio, *Canzonette . . . libro primo a quattro voci* (Venice: Gardano, 1580).

Canzonette . . . libro quarto a quattro voci (Venice: Gardano, 1590).

Canzonette . . . libro secondo a quattro voci (Venice: Gardano, 1580).

Madrigali a cinque voci . . . libro primo (Venice: Gardano, 1589).

Le vive fiamme de' vaghi e dilettevoli madrigali a quattro et cinque voci (Venice: Scotto, 1565).

Willaert, Adrian, *Canzone villanesche a quatro voci* (Venice: Gardane, 1545).

Modern editions not corresponding to the above sources

Busnoys, Antoine, *Collected Works*, parts 2–3, ed. Richard Taruskin, Masters and Monuments of the Renaissance 5 (New York: Broude Trust, 1990).

Dufay, Guillaume, *Opera omnia*, ed. Heinrich Besseler, 6 vols., Corpus mensurabilis musicae 1 (Rome: American Institute of Musicology, 1951–66); rev. edn. of vol. VI, ed. David Fallows (n.p.: American Institute of Musicology, 2006).

Ferretti, Giovanni, *Il secondo libro delle canzoni a sei voci (1575)*, ed. Ruth I. DeFord, Recent Researches in the Music of the Renaissance 57–58 (Madison, WI: A-R Editions, c1983).

Josquin des Prez, *New Josquin Edition* (Utrecht: Koningklijke Vereniging voor Nederlandse Musiekgeschiedenis, 1987–).

Keyboard Dances from the Earlier Sixteenth Century, ed. Daniel Heartz, Corpus of Early Keyboard Music 8 ([Rome]: American Institute of Musicology, 1965).

Ockeghem, Johannes, *Collected Works*, ed. Dragan Plamenac, 2nd edn., 2 vols. ([Philadelphia]: American Musicological Society, 1959–66).

Masses and Mass Sections, ed. Jaap van Benthem (Utrecht: Koninklijke Vereniging voor Nederlandse Musiekgeschiedenis, c1994–).

Palestrina, Giovanni Pierluigi da, *Le opere complete*, ed. Raffaele Casimiri et al., 35 vols. (Rome: Fratelli Scalera, 1939–99).

Werke, ed. Franz Xaver Haberl et al., 33 vols. (Leipzig: Breitkopf & Härtel, [1862–1907]).

Preludes, Chansons and Dances for Lute, Published by Pierre Attaingnant, Paris (1529–30), ed. Daniel Heartz (Neuilly-sur-Seine, France: Société de Musique d'Autrefois, 1964).

Rore, Cipriano de, *Opera omnia*, ed. Bernhard Meier, 8 vols., Corpus mensurabilis musicae 14 ([Rome]: American Institute of Musicology, 1959–77).

Vecchi, Orazio, *The Four-Voice Canzonettas*, ed. Ruth I. DeFord, 2 vols., Recent Researches in the Music of the Renaissance 92–93 (Madison, WI: A-R Editions, c1993).

Willaert, Adrian, et al., *Canzone villanesche alla napolitana and villotte*, ed. Donna G. Cardamone, Recent Researches in the Music of the Renaissance 30 (Madison, WI: A-R Editions, c1978).

Index of signs

☉ 37, 49, 92, 97, 116, 121, 122, 124, 126, 133, 136, 137, 139, 149, 153, 180n2, 181–82, 185, 188n26, 189n28, 189, 190, 197–98, 198n50, 201, 210, 218–19, 220, 223, 224, 225, 232–44, 233n17, 244n27, 245–46, 250, 254, 255–56, 262, 263, 264, 268, 269, 271, 272, 273, 274, 275, 276, 277, 280, 282, 283, 284, 286, 288, 291, 292, 293, 294, 296, 298, 299n30, 299, 301, 302, 303, 304–05, 307, 314, 340, 351n8, 353, 363, 365, 366, 367, 370, 371, 390, 391, 395, 398, 399, 400, 401–04

☾ 37, 49, 92n11, 97, 116, 121, 122, 124, 126, 127, 135, 136, 137, 139, 144, 145–66, 169, 170, 171, 177, 178, 181–82, 185, 186, 190, 191, 197, 198n50, 198, 199, 200, 201, 205, 208, 211, 220, 223, 225, 239, 250, 255–56, 262, 263, 268, 269, 271, 272, 273, 274, 275, 279, 282, 290, 292, 293, 301, 302, 303, 304–05, 307, 337n16, 337, 340, 342, 351n8, 351, 360, 363, 365, 371, 390, 391, 394, 398, 399, 401–04, 408–10, 411–17, 412n7, 418, 419, 425, 428, 436, 437–43, 446, 447, 448n1, 448, 451, 453, 454, 455, 462, 466, 470

⊙ 37, 49, 121–22, 124, 136, 137, 149, 153, 166–67, 181–82, 185, 220, 223, 244, 262, 263, 264, 273, 274, 276, 282, 283, 284, 286, 290, 365, 389, 390, 391, 398

☾ 37, 49, 92, 121n8, 121–22, 124, 125, 135, 136, 137, 149, 153, 166–67, 181–82, 185, 209, 218, 220, 223, 224, 225–31, 233, 235, 236–37, 244, 245, 255, 262, 263, 264, 265, 266, 269, 271n13, 271, 272, 273, 274, 275, 276, 277, 280, 282, 283, 284, 287n26, 287, 365, 366, 367, 389, 390, 391, 393, 398, 399

ϕ 92n11, 92, 116, 122n15, 122, 124, 125, 126, 127, 132–34, 139, 140, 145–66, 163n54, 172, 188n26, 188n28, 189n28, 189, 194, 197, 198, 199n55, 200n55, 218–19, 224, 225, 233n17, 244n27, 244, 245–46, 247, 248, 254, 282, 283, 287n26, 287, 294, 296, 297, 340, 351, 353, 354, 355, 360, 363, 365, 366, 367, 369, 370, 371

¢ 52, 97, 107, 108, 109, 116, 122, 124, 125, 126–27, 129, 132–34, 136, 139, 144, 145–66, 147n7, 168n75, 168, 169, 170, 171, 172, 176, 178, 188n28, 190, 191, 197–98, 198n50, 199, 201, 202, 205, 206, 211, 220, 239, 250, 254n29, 254, 262, 263, 265, 266, 267, 268, 271, 272, 274, 280, 282, 283, 287n26, 287, 288, 289, 290, 291, 292, 293, 294, 296, 298, 299, 301, 302, 303, 304–05, 307, 310, 314, 315, 316, 321, 325, 329, 335, 337n16, 337, 340, 342n7, 342–51, 351n8, 355, 359, 360, 363, 367, 369, 370, 371, 375, 376n2, 376, 378, 390, 393, 394, 395, 398, 399, 400, 401–04, 405, 408–10, 411–12, 412n7, 417–44, 446, 451, 454, 455, 456, 459, 464, 465, 466

ϕ 122, 124, 153, 166–67, 220, 223, 244n27, 244

¢ 122, 124, 153, 166–67, 262, 263, 266, 267, 272, 273, 274, 275, 280, 288, 365

☽ 135, 170–71, 171n80, 198n50, 280, 294, 298n29, 298, 316

☾ 135, 171, 171n80, 357, 365, 390, 391, 394, 398

☽ 135, 171, 273, 274, 280, 298

☽ 171

¢☽ 171, 370

☉2 37, 122, 124, 136, 137, 138, 147n7, 147, 149, 151, 153, 155, 168n75, 168, 176, 180n2, 185, 189n28, 272, 273, 274, 275, 276, 277n23, 277, 279, 280, 294, 298, 299n30, 299, 301, 302, 303, 304, 321, 340, 342, 351–52, 365, 371

☾2 37, 97, 122, 124, 129, 136, 137, 138, 141, 145, 149, 151, 153, 155, 165, 168n75, 168, 185, 186, 192, 220, 250, 274, 340, 342, 371

⊙2 122, 151, 152, 153, 167, 168

☾2 167

☉3 37, 136, 137, 138, 139, 140, 150, 153, 168–69, 172, 185, 201, 203, 390, 395, 398

☾3 37, 136, 137, 138, 140, 153, 155, 168–69, 172n84, 172, 185, 203, 261, 273, 274, 275, 279, 280, 282, 283, 290, 462

⊙3 153, 167, 172

☾3 167, 172, 357, 390, 391, 395, 398

Index of signs 495

ɸ2 167, 363
¢2 167, 301, 302, 304, 305, 310, 314, 315, 316, 363, 370
ɸ2 167
¢2 167

ɸ3 138, 140, 141, 167, 172, 357, 444
¢3 138, 140, 167, 170, 172n84, 172, 282, 290, 294, 297, 298, 325, 340, 355, 356, 360, 367, 382, 463, 464
ɸ3 167, 172
¢3 167, 172

ɸ$_2^3$ 375, 378, 382, 390, 391, 395, 398, 400, 401–02

O$_3$ 172, 357, 367
C$_3$ 357

O$_3^2$ 357, 367, 370
¢$_3^2$ 367

2 134, 140, 363, 367
3 134, 138, 141, 220, 248, 260, 261, 262, 267, 290, 294, 321, 340, 356, 357, 367, 371, 382, 444, 462, 463, 464
4 134
6 357

$_1^2$ 134
$_1^3$ 172
$_2^3$ 134, 172, 174
$_3^2$ 367

General index

Aaron, Pietro, 28, 46, 161, 163, 164, 166, 170, 185, 186, 198, 269, 271, 298n29
   Libri tres de institutione harmonica, 11, 27, 28
   Lucidario in musica, 12, 27, 197, 198, 201–02
   Thoscanello de la musica. See *Toscanello in musica*
   Toscanello in musica, 11, 27
acceleratio mensurae. See diminution
accent
   agogic, 94–95, 228-31, 376, 410–11, 413–16, 424–25
   mensural, 228–31, 376, 410–11, 413–16, 424–25, 428–29
   tonic, 228–31, 410–11, 413–16, 424–25
   verbal, 105–06, 228–31, 376, 410–11, 413–16, 424–25, 428–29
Adam von Fulda, 16, 21, 22, 59, 65, 73, 82, 122, 126, 137, 145, 147, 151, 167n69
   Musica, 10, 17, 56–58, 134n37
Agricola, Martin, 22, 24, 167, 174, 175, 176, 192
   Musica figuralis deudsch, 11, 65, 67–68, 155–56, 205
alteration, 39–41
   definition, 39
   notation, 40, 45
Anonymous, *Capitulum de quattuor mensuris*, 10
Anonymous, *Compendium breve artis musicae*, 10, 16, 55
Anonymous, *Compendium breve de proportionibus*, 10
Anonymous, *Compendium secundum famosiores musicos*, 11, 17
Anonymous, *De vera et compendiosa seu regulari constructione contrapuncti*, 87n4
Anonymous, *Exposition of the Proportions, According to the Teaching of "Mestre Joan Violant" [Vaillant]*, 10, 19–20
Anonymous, *L'homme armé*, 258, 259–60, 262
Anonymous, *Institutio in musicen mensuralem*, 11, 22, 152
Anonymous, *O faccia che rallegra*, 451–52, 453

Anonymous, *The Pathway to Musicke*, 13, 32
Anonymous, *Sequuntur proportiones*, 10, 20
Anonymous, *Tractatulus de cantu mensurali seu figurativo musice artis*, 123n15
Anonymous, *Tractatulus mensurationum*, 10
Anonymous, *Tractatulus prolationum cum tabulis*, 10
Anonymous, *Ein tütsche musica*, 11, 17, 126, 189
"Anonymous 5," 15, 16
   Ars cantus mensurabilis mensurata per modos iuris, 10
"Anonymous 10," 15
   De minimis notulis, 10
"Anonymous 11," 121n8, 124
   Tractatus de musica plana et mensurabili, 10, 16, 123–24, 124n17
"Anonymous 12," 16, 21, 22, 23, 97, 145, 146, 147, 149, 150, 189, 192, 271
   Tractatus et compendium cantus figurati, 10, 17–18, 124n17, 125–26, 126n20
Anselmi, Giorgio, 183, 184, 207
   De musica, 10, 15, 54–55
Antonius de Luca, 15
   Ars cantus figurati, 10
Apel, Willi, 26, 180, 188
Aranda, Matheo de, 161, 207
   Tractado de canto mensurable, 11, 31, 163–64
Aristotle, 73
   Physics, 57–58
Artusi, Giovanni Maria, 29, 162
   L'arte del contraponto, 13
Attaingnant, Pierre, 462, 464
Auda, Antoine, 402
augmentation, 48, 118, 121, 122, 135, 136, 156–57, 166, 169, 261, 272, 284, 287, 389, 391, 393, 394

Balbi, Marco Antonio, 97
Banchieri, Adriano, 173
   Cartella musicale, 98
barlines, 40, 232, 246, 402, 407, 451, 452, 462, 471–72

Bathe, William
　A Brief Introduction to the True Art of Music, 32
　A Briefe Introduction to the Skill of Song, 13, 32
baton, 59–60, 76
Bellermann, Heinrich, 26
Berkeley Manuscript, 14
Bermudo, Juan, 60, 76, 161, 162
　Declaración de instrumentos musicales, 12, 30
Besseler, Heinrich, 217, 218, 224, 232, 233, 237, 245, 246, 248, 250
Beurhaus, Friedrich, 27
　Musicae erotematum libri duo, 13
Blahoslav, Jan, 59
Blockland, Corneille de. *See* Montfort (Blockland), Corneille de
Blondeau, Pierre, 463
　Gaillard, 464
Bogentantz, Bernhard, 21, 148
　Collectanea utriusque cantus, 11, 21, 193
Boone, Graeme, 218, 224, 225, 233, 234, 237, 239
Bossinensis, Francesco, 466
Bourgeois, Loys, 31, 160, 167n69, 173n90, 175
　Le droict chemin de musique, 12, 31
Brack, Georg, 23
Breu, Jörg, the Elder
　choir scene, 60, 61
breve equivalence. *See under* tempo
Brothers, Thomas, 275, 280
Bruck, Arnold von, 200
Buchner, Hans, 209
Burmeister, Joachim, 178, 204
　Musica autoschediastike, 75–76, 159–60, 211
Burzio, Nicolo, 142
Busnoys, Antoine, 258
　Missa L'homme armé, 272–81, 283, 284, 289, 290, 298

cadence, 101–05
　definition, 101–02
　relation to *tactus*, 87, 88, 102–03, 104–05
　types
　　evaded, 102
　　maggiore, 103
　　minima, 103
　　minore, 103
Calvisius, Seth, 27
　Exercitationes musicae duae, 13
canon, 228, 231, 281, 282, 297, 298, 302, 316, 319, 321, 325, 330, 332, 336, 353, 363
　definition, 48

mensuration canon, 49, 253, 255, 258, 284, 286, 290, 293, 299, 365
canzonetta, 447, 454–61
Cara, Marco
　Io non compro piu speranza, 466
Cardamone, Donna, 451
Casimiri, Raffaele, 402, 405, 407
Castellanus, Petrus, 172n82
Caza, Francesco, 19
　Tractato vulgare de canto figurato, 11
Cerone, Pietro, 402, 404
　El melopeo y maestro, 13, 30, 400–01
Cimello, Giovanthomaso, 12, 29, 177–78
clocks, striking of, 77, 180, 210
Cochlaeus, Johannes, 21, 23, 24, 146, 148, 150, 152, 154, 166, 168, 193, 207
　Compendium in praxim atque exercitium cantus figurabilis, 21n38, 150
　Musica, 11, 21, 150–51
　Tetrachordum musices, 11, 21, 151, 192–93
Coclico, Adrian Petit, 25, 178
　Compendium musices, 12
Cologne school, 21–22, 25, 148, 151, 154, 155, 189, 192
coloration, 45–47, 134, 203
　definition, 45
　as dotted rhythm, 46, 47
　hemiola coloration, 45, 202
　incomplete coloration, 45
　as internal indicator of mensuration, 48
　triplet coloration, 46
contra battuta. *See* syncopation
contra tatto. *See* syncopation
contrapuntal rhythm
　definition, 84
　relation to *tactus*, 84–85
contrapuntal structure. *See* counterpoint
counterpoint
　relation to *tactus*, 83–93
cut signs. *See under* mensuration signs
cut-circle motet, 235n22

Dahlhaus, Carl, 26
de Domarto, Petrus
　Missa Spiritus almus, 128
de Orto, Marbriano, 258n2
　Missa L'homme armé, 389
del Lago, Giovanni, 28, 144n1
del Puerto, Diego. *See* Puerto, Diego del
des Prez, Josquin. *See* Josquin des Prez
Despuig, Guillermo. *See* Molins de Podio (Despuig), Guillermo

diminution, 48, 137, 147, 148, 149, 150, 152, 154, 168, 232–44, 250, 302, 304–29, 391, 395, 409
   acceleratio mensurae, 48, 115, 116, 118, 125–27, 129–32, 154
   by canon, 128
   by proportion, 128–29, 168n75
   by stroke, 129, 130, 131, 154, 168n75
   definitions, 115, 128
   mensural, 115, 116, 117–18, 123–25, 154
   per medium, 118, 133, 134, 171n80
   per semi, 118
   proportional, 115, 116–17
   semiditas, 118, 125, 126, 147, 148, 150, 151, 154, 169, 193, 194
   signs, 122–34, 136–38, 145–66, 167–69
dissonance
   relation to *tactus*, 83, 85–87, 88, 89, 90, 91–92, 93
division lines, 462, 463, 464, 465, 466
dots, 41–42
   of addition, 41, 42, 47–48
   of division, 41–42, 47–48
   as internal indicators of mensuration, 47–48
Dowland, John, 23, 59
Dressler, Gallus, 27, 202
   Musicae practicae elementa, 13
Du Fay, Guillaume, 136, 182, 217–57, 258, 265
   Adieu ces bons vins, 218, 239, 240, 245
   Adieu m'amour, 220, 251–53
   Adyeu quitte, 219
   Belle plaisant, 218
   Belle, que vous ay je, 220, 253, 255
   Belle, vueillés moy retenir, 220, 244, 245
   Belle, vueillés moy vengier, 220, 248, 249
   Belle, vueillés vostre mercy, 219, 237
   Bien veignés vous, 217, 220, 253–54
   Bon jour, bon mois, 219, 237
   Ce jour de l'an, 218
   Ce jour le doibt, 218, 237
   Ce moys de may, 218, 228
   C'est bien raison, 218, 235, 237
   Craindre vous vueil, 102, 219, 242–43
   De ma haulte et bonne aventure, 218, 246
   Dieu gard la bone, 220, 248
   Dona gentile, 218
   Dona, i ardenti ray, 220, 250
   Donnés l'assault, 44, 99, 100, 219
   Du tout m'estoie, 220
   En triumphant, 219, 246, 247
   Entre les plus plaines, 219, 233n17
   Entre vous, 220, 250
   Estrinés moy, 219, 237
   Franc cuer gentil, 219, 246
   Gloria de quaremiaux, 239–40
   Hé compaignons, 219, 237
   Helas, et quant vous veray, 219, 238, 239, 243
   Helas, ma dame, 218
   Helas mon dueil, 220
   Iste sunt due olive, 91–93
   J'atendray tant, 218
   J'ay grant dolour, 219
   J'ay mis mon cuer, 218
   Je donne a tous, 219, 237
   Je me complains, 218, 227
   Je n'ay doubté, 219
   Je ne puis plus, 220, 253
   Je ne suy plus, 218, 227
   Je prens congié, 219, 237
   Je requier, 219, 237
   Je veuil chanter, 218, 228
   L'alta belleza tua, 218, 228
   La belle se siet, 227
   La dolce vista, 218, 227
   La plus mignonne, 220
   Las, que feray, 219, 237
   Le serviteur, 219
   Les douleurs, 220, 253, 255–56
   Ma belle dame, je vous pri, 220, 244, 245
   Ma belle dame souveraine, 218
   Malheureulx cuer, 220, 246, 251
   Mille bonjours, 219
   Mon bien, m'amour, 219, 246
   Mon chier amy, 220, 227, 235, 237
   Mon cuer me fait, 219, 237
   Navré je sui, 219, 240–41
   Ne je ne dors, 220, 251
   Or pleust a Dieu, 219, 242
   Par droit je puis bien, 218, 228–31
   Par le regard, 219
   Passato è il tempo, 218, 238, 243
   Pour ce que veoir, 218, 226
   Pour l'amour de ma doulce amye, 219, 237
   Pouray je avoir, 219, 237
   Puisque celle, 219, 233n17
   Puisque vous estez, 220
   Quel fronte signorille, 46, 218, 242–43
   Qu'est devenue leauté, 219, 233n17
   Resvelliés vous, 220, 227, 235, 237
   Resvelons nous, 218, 239, 240
   Se la face ay pale, 218, 238, 243
   Se ma dame je puis veir, 219, 237
   Seigneur Leon, 219
   Va t'en, mon cuer, 219
   Vergene bella, 218, 235n22, 235–37, 238, 243
   Vostre bruit, 220

General index

Du Fay, Guillaume(?)
   Il sera par vous/L'homme armé, 260–61, 279
Durán, Domingo Marcos, 67
   Sumula de canto órgano, 11, 30, 65–66, 163
Dygon, John, 31
   Proportiones practicabiles secundum Gaffurium, 12

editing, 471–73
Einstein, Alfred, 443

Faber, Gregor, 25, 158, 167n69
   Musices practicae erotematum libri II, 12
Faber, Heinrich, 25, 158
   Ad musicam practicam introductio, 12
   Compendiolum musicae pro incipientibus, 12, 26, 159
Fallows, David, 217, 218, 224, 254
Felsztyn, Sebastian of. *See* Sebastian of Felsztyn
Ferretti, Giovanni
   Dolce mi saria, 448, 449
figures, 34
   notation, 33
Finck, Hermann, 25, 77, 158
   Practica musica, 12, 172n82, 202, 209
Fiorino, Gasparo
   Ancor che col partir, 448–50
Florentius de Faxolis, 47
Forster, Georg, 301
Franco of Cologne, 14
   Ars cantus mensurabilis, 57
Frescobaldi, Girolamo, 212
Frosch, Johann
   Rerum musicarum, 12, 24
frottola, 466
Fulda, Adam von. *See* Adam von Fulda

Gabrieli, Giovanni, 409
Gaffurio, Franchino, 16, 18–19, 22, 23, 25, 28, 31, 65, 79, 101, 104, 148, 150, 151, 167, 170, 174, 179, 180n3, 181n3, 182, 185, 186, 189, 192, 193, 194, 207–08, 208n80
   Angelicum ac divinum opus musice, 11, 19, 23, 27, 28, 58–59, 63–64, 78, 132–34, 146, 147, 153, 160, 163, 208
   Musices practicabilis libellum, 10, 18, 19
   Practica musice, 11, 18, 19, 21, 23, 28, 31, 53, 55, 63, 64, 78, 127–32, 140–41, 145, 147, 148, 150, 153, 154, 160, 168n75, 182–83, 191–92, 208
Gallagher, Sean, 218, 224, 235
galliard, 462–65, 447, 465

Gardane, Antonio, 464
Gardano, Angelo, 401–02, 403, 404
Gerle, Hans, 77, 209
Glarean, Heinrich, 25, 144, 173, 178, 189
   Dodecachordon, 12, 22, 131–32, 146, 172n82, 204
   Musicae epitome, 12, 146
Gossett, Philip, 361
Guilielmus Monachus, 16, 137, 146, 170
   De preceptis artis musice, 10, 17, 121n8, 133, 134n37, 171n80
Guilliaud, Maximilian, 160, 198
   Rudiments de musique practique, 12, 31

Haar, James, 389
Haberl, Franz Xaver, 378, 402, 404, 407
Hamm, Charles, 218, 224
Heartz, Daniel, 462
hemiola, 45, 100–01, 173, 204, 227, 228, 231, 235, 237, 238, 248, 249, 254, 256, 267, 276, 280, 296, 299, 347, 352, 353, 363, 391, 451, 459, 462, 465
   relation to syncopation, 46, 100–01
   relation to *tactus*, 100, 101
Heyden, Sebald, 24–26, 31, 68, 146, 147, 156, 157, 158, 159, 160, 166–67, 168, 171, 172, 174, 198, 207, 210, 211, 362, 363, 365, 369n20, 370, 374
   De arte canendi, 12, 24, 25, 98, 156, 172n82, 188, 194–97, 361–62, 370–71, 373
   Musica stoicheiosis, 11, 24, 156, 157
   Musicae, id est artis canendi libri duo, 12, 24, 156
Hofmann, Eucharius, 25, 27, 173
   Musicae practicae praecepta, 13, 204
Hothby, John, 10, 16–17, 18, 37, 136, 137, 168

ictus
   as accent, 72–74
   as synonym for *tactus*, 51
imperfection, 39–41
   a parte ante, 39–40
   a parte post, 39–40
   ad partem, 40–41
   ad partes, 40–41
   definition, 39
   notation, 39–40, 45
initium
   definition, 38–39
integral measurement. *See ut iacet* measurement
Isaac, Heinrich, 339–74
   Choralis Constantinus, 339–74, 459

Isaac, Heinrich (cont.)
- *Alleluia Conceptio*, 365
- *Alleluia Veni Sancte Spiritus*, 347–48, 359
- *Caeci claudi*, 367
- *De radice Jesse*, 171n81, 370–71, 372, 373
- *Et agni vellere*, 363, 364
- *Ethiopes horridos*, 363, 364
- *Exaudi/a timore*, 344
- *Exultate Deo/jubilate*, 346–47
- *Gaudeamus/omnes*, 345–46
- *Hic hominem*, 348, 349
- *Insidias*, 342n7
- *Meritis quorum*, 348–49
- *Nec gregum*, 370
- *Piae vocis laudes canta*, 366
- *Pro nobis*, 359
- *Puer natus est/et filius*, 342–44
- *Qualis sit*, 360
- *Quantum potes*, 365
- *Qui cuique*, 367–70
- *Qui nobis*, 342n7
- *Sentiant hunc*, 351–52
- *Sicut sydus*, 355–56, 358
- *Solemnia celebrantes*, 353, 354
- *Spiritus alme*, 353–54, 356
- *Tu divisum*, 354–55, 357
- *Ut sibi auxilium*, 349–50
- *Veni deposite*, 355–56
- *Viderunt/omnes*, 353, 355
- *Vos Christi*, 346

isorhythm, 304

Jambe de Fer, Philibert, 160, 169, 199, 206
- *Epitome musical*, 12, 31

Johannes de Muris. *See* Muris, Johannes de

Josquin des Prez, 200, 258, 339, 342, 375–77, 407
- *Absolve, quaesumus, Domine*, 302, 303, 330, 335, 336
- *Ave nobilissima creatura*, 301, 302, 303, 304–06, 307, 309, 316, 321
- *Benedicta es*, 302, 303, 316, 325–29, 384–87, 388
- *De profundis*, 301, 302, 303, 330, 335–37
- *Huc me sydereo*, 301, 302, 303, 304–05, 306–07, 308, 316, 321
- *Illibata Dei virgo nutrix*, 301, 302, 303, 304, 307–16, 334
- *Inviolata*, 302, 303, 316, 319–20, 321, 322
- *Miserere mei, Deus*, 302, 303, 316, 329
- *Missa L'homme armé sexti toni*, 52, 170, 282, 293–99, 377–84
- *Missa L'homme armé super voces musicales*, 200, 281–93, 297, 299, 301, 389n7, 389
- *Missa Pange lingua*, 108–13
- motets, 301–38
- *O virgo prudentissima*, 302, 303, 316–18
- *O virgo virginum*, 302, 303, 330, 332–34
- *Pater noster – Ave Maria*, 302, 303, 330–32
- *Praeter rerum seriem*, 301, 302, 303, 316, 321–25
- *Salve Regina*, 302, 303, 329, 334–35
- *Stabat mater*, 302, 303, 329, 335, 337
- *Virgo salutiferi*, 302, 303, 316, 318–19

Koswick, Michael, 22, 152
- *Compendiaria musice artis aeditio*, 11

Lampadius, Auctor
- *Compendium musices*, 12, 24, 108

Lanfranco, Giovanni Maria, 28, 161, 164, 165, 186
- *Scintille di musica*, 11, 28, 165

Lapicida, Erasmus, 200

Leonardo da Vinci, 210

levels of measurement, 35–36, *See also modus*, major; *modus*, minor; prolation; *tempus*
- imperfect, 35
- perfect, 35

ligatures, 34–35

Listenius, Nicolaus, 25
- *Musica*, 12, 24, 67n34

Lossius, Lucas
- *Erotemata musicae practicae*, 32n123

Luca della Robbia
- *Cantoria*, 53, 54

Luscinius, Othmar, 22, 77
- *Musurgia seu praxis musicae*, 12, 147n7, 190

Lusitano, Vicente, 161
- *Introdutione facilissima, et novissima di canto fermo, figurato, contraponto semplice, et inconcerto*, 12, 29

madrigal, 144, 191, 210, 212, 401, 408–46, 447, 448, 449, 451, 454, 455, 456
- *a misura (di) breve*. See *a note nere*
- *a misura comune*, 412
- *a note nere*, 197, 408–09, 412, 417, 453, 454, 459
- *madrigali cromatici*. See *a note nere*

Mahu, Stephan, 200

Marenzio, Luca
- *Dolorosi martir*, 203
- *Perch'io non ho speranza*, 203

Martin, Claude, 31, 77, 160, 198
   Elementorum musices practicae, 12, 31
mass, 108, 258–300, 375–407, 446
Mauro da Firenze, Fra, 208
maximodus, 36n2, *See also modus*, major
Meier, Bernhard, 411, 439
mensura. See *tactus*
mensural structure, 38, 39
   definition, 37–39
   relation to notated mensuration, 50
mensural transformation, 305, 391
mensuration signs, 36–37
   cut signs, 122–34, 145–66
   mode-rest signs, 37
   modus cum tempore signs, 37, 122, 136–38, 152, 167–69, 172n82, 185, 189, 208, 275
   prolation signs, 36–37
   relation to performance practice, 141–42
   tempus signs, 36–37
Mensurstriche. See barlines
Milán, Luys
   El maestro, 210
Milsom, John, 301
minim equivalence. See *under* tempo
mode-rest signs. See *under* mensuration signs
modus cum tempore signs. See *under* mensuration signs
modus, major
   definition, 35
   signs. See mensuration signs, mode-rest signs
modus, minor
   definition, 35
   signs. See mensuration signs, mode rest-signs
Molins de Podio, Guillermo
   Ars musicorum, 30
Monetarius, Stephan, 22, 189
   Epitoma utriusque musices practice, 11, 131
Monteverdi, Claudio, 408, 410
Montfort (Blockland), Corneille de
   Instruction fort facile pour apprendre la musique practique, 13, 31
Morales, Cristóbal de
   Missa L'homme armé, 389
Morley, Thomas, 32
   A Plaine and Easie Introduction to Practicall Musicke, 13, 32
motet, 191, 210, 274, 301–38, 410
Muris, Johannes de, 117, 118, 123, 128, 189, 233
   Ars practica mensurabilis cantus, 10, 14–15, 42, 116–17
   Libellus cantus mensurabilis. See *Ars practica mensurabilis cantus*

Nanino, Giovanni Maria
   Le strane voci, 437n10
Neusidler, Hans, 209
Nola, Gian Domenico da
   O dolce vita mia, 452, 454
notes. See figures

Ockeghem, Johannes, 53, 140, 141, 258
   L'autre d'antan, 139, 141, 201
   Missa L'homme armé, 261–71, 272, 273, 276, 277, 280, 281, 283, 284, 288, 290
   Missa prolationum, 49, 135n39
Oridryus, Johannes, 25, 158, 167n69
   Practicae musicae utriusque praecepta brevia, 12
Ornithoparchus, Andreas, 24, 25, 28, 59, 65, 147, 152–54, 155, 157, 162, 168, 170, 171, 192, 207, 365
   Musice active micrologus, 11, 22, 23, 59, 67, 152–54, 193–94
Orto, Marbriano de. See de Orto, Marbriano
Ott, Johannes, 339, 362
Ovid
   Metamorphoses, 57, 58

Palestrina, Giovanni Pierluigi da, 375–407, 408, 446
   Missa Benedicta es, 377, 384–87, 388, 389
   Missa L'homme armé a 4, 377–84
   Missa L'homme armé a 5, 377, 387–407
per medium. See *under* diminution
per semi. See *under* diminution
Petrucci, Ottaviano, 281, 286, 298, 309
Philippe de Vitry. See Vitry, Philippe de
Philomathes, Venceslaus, 22
   Musicorum libri quattuor, 11, 22, 76, 147, 167n69
Picitono, Angelo da, 161
   Fior angelico di musica, 12, 28
Pisa, Agostino, 29
   Battuta della musica, 13, 67, 401n16
   Breve dichiaratione della battuta musicale, 13
poetic feet, 79
Praetorius, Christoph, 27
   Erotemata musices, 13, 159
Praetorius, Michael, 179, 204
   Syntagma musicum, 13, 27, 146, 190–91, 211, 409–10
prolation
   definition, 35
   signs. See mensuration signs
proportions, 19–20, 48, 119–21, 169–79, 472
   categories, 119

proportions (cont.)
  duple, 119, 126, 127, 129, 130, 134, 140, 169, 170–71, 188, 191–92, 193, 197–98, 206, 254, 363–65, 367–70
  quadruple, 134, 169, 170, 171, 365
  sesquialtera, 119, 134, 138–41, 144, 169, 171–77, 172n84, 182, 200–6, 248, 303, 310, 314–15, 321, 322, 324–25, 333, 335, 336, 340, 367, 370, 374, 375, 382, 384, 385, 387, 395, 400–01, 430, 443–46, 461
  sesquitertia, 119, 121n8, 135, 169, 170
  subduple, 177–78, 307, 363, 365, 367, 374, 394
  subquadruple, 365
  triple, 119, 134, 135, 138–41, 144, 169, 171–77, 172n84, 200–06, 227, 248, 367, 395, 400–01
  unequal, 174–75
  definitions, 119, 120–21
  of equality, 139, 140, 173, 187
  of inequality, 139, 173
  relation to diminution and augmentation, 119–21, 194–97
  signs, 134–36, 138–41, 169–79
  ternary
    binary interpretation, 175–77, 385–87, 402
    mensuration, 174
    signs, 171–73
    tactus, 174–75
    terminology, 173–74
Prosdocimo de' Beldomandi, 134, 135
  Brevis summula proportionum quantum ad musicam pertinet, 19
  Expositiones tractatus practice cantus mensurabilis magistri Johannis de Muris, 10, 15, 117
  Tractatus practice cantus mensurabilis ad modum ytalicorum, 10, 15
  Tractatus practice de musica mensurabili, 10, 15, 19, 118, 119–20
Puerto, Diego del, 133
  Portus musice, 11, 30
pulse, 63–65, 77–79, 192, 207–09
pulse framework. *See* mensural structure

quaternaria, 208, 209
Quercu, Simon de, 22
  Opusculum musices, 11, 147n7

Ramis de Pareja, Bartolomeo, 16, 28, 122, 138, 184, 185, 207–08
  Musica practica, 10, 17, 55–56, 77–78, 137–38, 183, 208n80

Raselius, Andreas, 27
  Hexachordum, 13
Recueil de chants royaux, 53, 54
Reisch, Gregor
  Margarita philosophica, 60, 62
rests, 34, 41
  as internal indicators of mensuration, 47
  notation, 33, 41, 291–92, 309, 313, 332, 337, 412
Rhau, Georg, 22, 23–24, 25, 59, 155, 168n75, 171
  Enchiridion utriusque musicae practicae, 11, 23, 59, 154, 189–90
Rore, Cipriano de, 408–46, 447
  Alla dolce ombra, 420–25, 444
  Anchor che col partire, 425–27, 443, 450
  Cantiamo lieti, 419
  Da le belle contrade, 433–36
  Da quei bei lumi, 417–18
  Datemi pace, 429–30, 431, 432
  Felice sei, Trevigi, 444–46
  Hor che'l ciel e la terra, 413, 416–17
  L'inconstantia che seco han, 439–43
  Mia benigna fortuna, 428–29
  Miserere mei, 412n7
  O sonno, 430–33
  Per mezz'i boschi, 412, 413–16, 417, 419
  Quando, signor, lasciaste, 437–39, 441, 442
  Quel foco che tant'anni, 437
  Se voi poteste, 437

Sachs, Curt, 26
Sancta Maria, Tomás de
  Arte de tañer fantasia, 13, 30, 68–69, 73–74
Savonarola, Michaele, 208–09, 210
Schanppecher, Melchior, 21, 31, 150, 151, 152
  Opus aureum, 11, 21, 148–49
Schneegass, Cyriacus, 27
  Isagoges musicae, 13, 212
Schroeder, Eunice, 218, 224, 225, 233, 234
Schumann, Valentin, 23
Sebastian of Felsztyn, 22
  Opusculum musicae mensuralis, 11
semibreve equivalence. *See under* tempo
semiditas. *See under* diminution
senaria imperfecta, 209
Sherr, Richard, 299
Spataro, Giovanni, 17, 28, 107, 163, 164, 174, 183, 185–86, 197, 198, 208n80
  Tractato di musica, 11, 183–85
suspensions, 101–02
  relation to *tactus*, 87, 89, 91, 104, 105

syncopation, 42–44, 46
  definition, 42–43
  effects of, 96, 97–100
  levels, 96–97
  nested, 43–44
  relation to *tactus*, 83, 95–100
  of rests, 44
  as synonym for diminution, 125–26

tactus
  categories
    compasejo, 65, 66, 67, 163
    compaset, 162, 163
    compasillo, 400
    equal, 159, 161, 162, 174–75, 400
    generalis, 151, 152
    half, 68–69, 152, 155, 205
    imperfect, 158
    major, 150, 152, 153, 155, 156, 158, 159, 207
    minor, 150, 152, 155, 156, 207
    perfect, 158
    as physical motion, 53–61
    proportionate, 67–68, 150, 152, 167, 174, 196, 204, 205
    specialis, 151, 152
    unequal, 159, 161, 162, 174, 400
    whole, 65–66, 67, 155, 157, 167, 196, 205
  definitions
    compositional *tactus*, 51, 52, 82–83, 84, 89, 91, 95
    duration of *tactus*, 52
    performance *tactus*, 51, 52, 53–61, 83
    tactus-unit, 51, 52
    theoretical *tactus*, 51, 52
    value of *tactus*, 52
  groupings, 62, 82, 106
  quality, 72–81
  subdivisions, 61–72, 82
  synonyms, 51
Taruskin, Richard, 273, 274, 275
tempo, 48, 210, 419, 436–37, 439, 446, 454, See also diminution; proportion
  absolute, 207–12
  breve equivalence, 181–82, 183–84, 185–86
  diminution, 187–200
  minim equivalence, 181–83, 186–87
  relations among integral mensurations, 181–87
  semibreve equivalence, 182
  ternary proportions, 200–6
tempus
  definition, 35

  signs. *See* mensuration signs
  as synonym for breve-unit, 38
  as synonym for *tactus*, 57
text setting, 35, 105–06, 225
  relation to *tactus*, 105–06
text-setting model, 225, 227, 229, 239, 243, 246, 247, 251, 256
Tigrini, Orazio, 29, 162
  Il compendio della musica, 13
time unit
  breve-unit, 37–38
  definition, 37–38
  long-unit, 37–38
  minim-unit, 37–38
  semibreve-unit, 37–38
Tinctoris, Johannes, 16, 18, 19, 37, 46, 84, 85, 86, 87–88, 90, 91, 103, 104, 112, 121, 131, 135, 145, 167, 169, 170, 173, 174, 182, 186, 187, 189, 192, 194, 201, 203, 234, 261, 269
  Liber de arte contrapuncti, 10, 18, 82
  Proportionale musices, 10, 18, 126–27, 128, 139–40, 173n86, 194
  Terminorum musicae diffinitorium, 10, 18, 42, 48, 56
Tovar, Francisco, 161, 162, 189
  Libro de musica practica, 11, 30, 162–63

Ugolino of Orvieto, 134
  Declaratio musicae disciplinae, 10, 15
ut iacet measurement, 114, 116

Vacchelli, Anna Maria Monterosso, 403–05, 406
Vanneo, Stephano, 161
  Recanetum de musica aurea, 11, 28, 60–61, 73, 201
Vecchi, Orazio, 454
  Fa una Canzone senza note nere, 455, 458–60
  Fammi una Canzonetta capriciosa, 460–61
  Il bianco e dolce cigno, 70–71
  Mentre io campai contento, 456, 457
  Se da le treccie mie, 456, 458
Vetulus de Anagnia, Johannes
  Liber de musica, 210
Viadana, Ludovico, 410
Vicentino, Nicola, 161, 173, 178, 436
  L'antica musica ridotta alla moderna prattica, 12, 29, 212
villanella, 447–54, 455
villanesca. *See* villanella
Vitry, Philippe de, 14

Volckmar, Joannes, 22, 151, 152
   Collectanea quedam musice discipline, 11

Willaert, Adrian, 408, 447
   O bene mio, 451, 452
Wilphlingseder, Ambrosius
   Erotemata musices practicae, 13, 25
Wolf, Johannes, 26
Wollick, Nicolaus, 21, 23, 148, 150, 151, 152
   Enchiridion musices, 11, 31, 67n34, 150
Wollick, Nicolaus, and Melchior Schanppecher
   Opus aureum. *See* Schanppecher, Melchior, *Opus aureum*

Yssandon, Jean, 160
   Traité de la musique pratique, 13, 31

Zacconi, Ludovico, 67, 96, 97, 100, 107, 164, 165, 172, 173, 176, 177n103, 180n2, 204, 211, 400, 404
   Prattica di musica, 13, 29, 69, 74–75, 79–81, 95, 173n89, 175, 299n30, 397–99, 400–01
Zanger, Johann, 25, 159
   Practicae musicae praecepta, 12, 200
Zarlino, Gioseffo, 28–29, 79, 89, 96, 103, 112, 161, 165, 167, 375, 404
   Le istitutioni harmoniche, 13, 28, 43, 44, 64, 78–79, 88–89, 95–96, 160, 161